THE SPORT AMERICANA®

TEAM
Baseball Card
CHECKLIST

NO. 3

By
JEFF FRITSCH
AND
DENNIS W. ECKES

ISBN 0-937424-34-X

REPRINTS OF THOSE FABULOUS CARDS OF THE 1930'S

All cards of these reprint sets are on thick, high-quality stock and are clearly marked "reprint"

1934 GOUDEY
$ 10.00 plus postage & handling

This set of 96 cards contains two cards of Lou Gehrig, both are among the most popular of the Gehrig cards. Jimmy Foxx, Dizzy Dean, Lefty Grove and eleven other Hall of Famers are included. The originals of this set are currently worth about $ 2000.00.

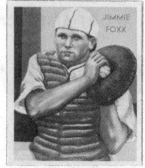

1934 – 1936 DIAMOND STARS
$ 10.00 plus postage & handling

The entire set of 108 cards, including the difficult-to-obtain high numbers, are reproduced superbly in this reprint edition. More than 25 Hall of Famers — Foxx, Grove, Greenberg, Hornsby, and most of the greats of the period — are contained within this set.

1935 GOUDEY
$ 5.00 plus postage & handling

This 36-card set, commonly called the Goudey 4-in-1 or Goudey Puzzle set, features four players per card with red or blue borders separating the players. Ruth, Dean, Foxx, Klein and many other Hall of Famers are included. The originals are worth well over $ 500.00.

1935 NATIONAL CHICLE FOOTBALL CARD SET
$ 5.00 plus postage & handling

"The" classic football card set of all time features the two most valuable football cards in existence — Knute Rockne and Bronco Nagurski. The 36-card set features the National Chicle art-deco style which has contributed to the lasting popularity of the set.

POSTAGE & HANDLING SCHEDULE
$ .01 to $ 20.00 add $ 2.00
$ 20.01 to $ 29.99 add $ 2.50
$ 30.00 to $ 49.99 add $ 3.00
$ 50.00 or more add $ 4.00

MARYLAND RESIDENTS ADD 5% SALES TAX
CANADIAN ORDERS — BOOKS ONLY
Canadian orders, orders outside the contiguous
United States, APO and FPO add 25% additional
U.S. FUNDS ONLY

DEN'S COLLECTORS DEN
HOME OF SPORT AMERICANA
Dept. TC
P.O. BOX 606, LAUREL, MD 20707

JOE DI MAGGIO, Yankees

1938 GOUDEY HEADS UP
$ 7.00 plus postage & handling

This unusual, and extremely popular, 48-card set features the first gum cards of Joe DiMaggio and Bob Feller. Of the 48 cards, 14 feature Hall of Famers. The originals of this set are worth well over $ 2000.00. This set ended the great 1930's Goudey issues.

SEND ONLY $ 1.00 for DEN'S BIG CATALOGUE
CATALOGUE sent FREE with each ORDER

1933 SPORT KINGS REPRINTS
$ 7.00 plus postage & handling

This set of 48 full-color cards contains the best assortment of sport stars ever made. Included are baseball greats Babe Ruth, Ty Cobb and Carl Hubbell, plus Red Grange, Jim Thorpe, Knute Rockne, Jack Dempsey, Johnny Weissmuller, Eddie Shore, Bobby Jones, Bill Tilden, Willie Hoppe, Babe Didrickson and many more. A set such as this is a joy to all sport fans. The cards are all marked "Reprint".

"1937 DIAMOND STARS"
Produced in 1981 by Sport Americana
$ 3.00 plus postage & handling

This set was produced from unissued artwork, traced to 193_x_ of what appears to be an addition to the National Chicle Diamond Stars set. This 12-card set is not a reprint but a new issue from older, non-released artwork. Hornsby, Gomez, Goslin and Bottomley are among those included.

SPORT AMERICANA BASEBALL
TEAM CHECKLIST
TABLE OF CONTENTS

HOW TO USE THE TEAM CHECKLIST

While the text of this book is straight forward and easy to follow, several conventions and clarifying abbreviations are used in the text to attain consistency. These abbreviations and conventions are explained below.

ABBREVIATIONS

(B)   BACK ONLY—appears when the team name of a player is different on the back from that on the front.

(C)   COACH—appears when the card is of a coach of that particular team.

(F))   FRONT ONLY—appears when the team name of a player is different on the front from that on the back.

(FS)   FUTURE STAR—more than one player per card listed as Future Stars.

(HC)   HEAD COACH—appears only on the cards of Bob Kennedy of 1964 and 1965 when he is listed as Head Coach of the Cubs.

(M)   MANAGER—appears when the card is a manager of that particular team.

(P)   PROSPECT— more than one player per card; listed as Prospect in 1979 Topps and Major League Prospect in 1985-1987 Fleer.

(R)   ROOKIE—more than one player per card listed as Rookie Stars.

CONVENTIONS

For Bowman, Goudey and Play Ball issues, the team on the front of the card is determined by the uniform worn. The team on the back of the card is determined by the team name actually printed on the back. For all Topps, Fleer, and Donruss issues (except the 1951 Topps Red and Blue Backs which have no writing on the back), the team name is determined by the team name printed on the front and back respectively. When a difference in the team name printed on the front and back exists; e.g., 1979 Topps Bump Wills exist with both the Rangers (correct) and Blue Jays (error) printed on the front, and the 1969 Topps Donn Clendenon exists with both Houston (correct) and Expos (error) printed on the front; the correct version only is used in the text.

Individuals sharing the same name are noted by the inclusion of middle initials or names. This situation occurs only when the Major League careers of the players sharing the same name overlap. Such is the case of Hal R. Smith and Hal W. Smith. Contrastly, Ron Jackson whose card appears in the late 1950's and early 1960's is not distinguished from the Ron Jackson whose card appears in the late 1970's. Kindly refer to the Encyclopedia of Baseball, Baseball Register, etc., for correct identifications. In the case of Bob Sadowski, pitcher, certain publications list him as having the middle initial "F". Through research, this information has been found to be in error; in fact, he has neither a middle initial nor a middle name. To differentiate him from Bob Sadowski, infielder, he is listed herein as merely "Bob Sadowski," while the infielder is listed as "Bob Frank Sadowski". Frank Baker whose card appears in 1970 and 1971 has no middle name or initial; he is listed as Frank Baker. Frank Baker whose card appears in 1971, 1972, and 1974 is referred to as Frank W. Baker. There are several cards in many of the sets that have been omitted from the checklists within because the players are not committed to any current team; e.g., old timers from the 1940 Play Ball set, 1976 Topps All-Time Greats, 1933 Goudey Lajoie, etc. Likewise, special cards have been omitted, e.g., All-Star Cards, multiplayer cards, league leader cards, Donruss Diamond Kings, boyhood picture cards, etc. All sets are in color unless noted as being in black and white.

Several of the card sets included in this book contain special instruction to the sets because of an indiginous peculiarity of the set itself. The 1934-36 Diamond Stars and the Sportflics are preceded by clarifying narratives. Please read these narratives before attempting to use the team checklist for these sets.

1948 BOWMAN (48)
2 1/16" X 2 1/2"
BLACK & WHITE

BOSTON BRAVES

- ☐ 1. BOB ELLIOTT
- ☐ 12. JOHNNY SAIN
- ☐ 18. WARREN SPAHN

BOSTON RED SOX

NO CARDS ISSUED

BROOKLYN DODGERS

- ☐ 7. PETE REISER
- ☐ 41. REX BARNEY
- ☐ 43. BRUCE EDWARDS

CHICAGO CUBS

NO CARDS ISSUED

CHICAGO WHITE SOX

NO CARDS ISSUED

CINCINATTI REDS

- ☐ 2. EWELL BLACKWELL
- ☐ 39. AUGIE GALAN
- ☐ 44. JOHNNY WYROSTEK
- ☐ 45. HANK SAUER
- ☐ 46. HERMAN WEHMEIER

CLEVELAND INDIANS

- ☐ 5. BOB FELLER

DETROIT TIGERS

NO CARDS ISSUED

NEW YORK GIANTS

- ☐ 4. JOHNNY MIZE
- ☐ 9. WALKER COOPER
- ☐ 13. WILLARD MARSHALL
- ☐ 16. JACK LOHRKE
- ☐ 20. BUDDY KERR
- ☐ 23. LARRY JANSEN
- ☐ 27. SID GORDON
- ☐ 30. WHITEY LOCKMAN
- ☐ 32. BILL RIGNEY
- ☐ 34. SHELDON JONES
- ☐ 37. CLINT HARTUNG
- ☐ 42. RAY POAT
- ☐ 47. BOBBY THOMSON
- ☐ 48. DAVE KOSLO

NEW YORK YANKEES

- ☐ 6. YOGI BERRA
- ☐ 8. PHIL RIZZUTO
- ☐ 11. JOHNNY LINDELL
- ☐ 14. ALLIE REYNOLDS
- ☐ 19. TOMMY HENRICH
- ☐ 22. BILL BEVENS
- ☐ 26. FRANK SHEA
- ☐ 29. JOE PAGE
- ☐ 33. BILLY JOHNSON
- ☐ 35. GEORGE STIRNWEISS

PHILADELPHIA ATHLETICS

- ☐ 10. BUDDY ROSAR
- ☐ 15. EDDIE JOOST
- ☐ 21. FERRIS FAIN
- ☐ 25. BARNEY MCCOSKEY
- ☐ 31. BILL MCCAHAN

PHILADELPHIA PHILLIES

- ☐ 24. DUTCH LEONARD
- ☐ 28. EMIL VERBAN

PITTSBURGH PIRATES

- ☐ 3. RALPH KINER

ST. LOUIS BROWNS

NO CARDS ISSUED

ST. LOUIS CARDINALS

- ☐ 17. ENOS SLAUGHTER
- ☐ 36. STAN MUSIAL
- ☐ 38. RED SCHOENDIENST
- ☐ 40. MARTY MARION

WASHINGTON SENATORS

NO CARDS ISSUED

1949 BOWMAN (240)
2 1/16" X 2 1/2"

BOSTON BRAVES

- ☐ 1. VERN BICKFORD
- ☐ 17. EARL TORGESON
- ☐ 33. WARREN SPAHN
- ☐ 47. JOHNNY SAIN
- ☐ 58. BOB ELLIOTT
- ☐ 67. ALVIN DARK
- ☐ 72. TOMMY HOLMES
- ☐ 88. BILL SALKELD
- ☐ 104. ED STANKY

- ☐ 153. PHIL MASI
- ☐ 169. JEFF HEATH
- ☐ 185. PETE REISER
- ☐ 201. SIBBY SISTI
- ☐ 213. CHARLES BARRETT
- ☐ 235. JIM RUSSELL
- ☐ 239. FRANK MCCORMICK

BOSTON RED SOX

- ☐ 7. JOE DOBSON
- ☐ 23. BOBBY DOERR
- ☐ 39. BILL GOODMAN
- ☐ 53. JACK KRAMER
- ☐ 64. DOM DIMAGGIO
- ☐ 71. VERN STEPHENS
- ☐ 86. JOHNNY PESKY
- ☐ 102. STAN SPENCE
- ☐ 118. SAM MELE
- ☐ 151. MICKEY HARRIS
- ☐ 167. BORIS MARTIN
- ☐ 183. LOU STRINGER
- ☐ 199. TEX HUGHSON
- ☐ 211. DAVE FERRISS
- ☐ 231. EARL JOHNSON

BROOKLYN DODGERS

- ☐ 20. GENE HERMANSKI
- ☐ 36. PEE WEE REESE
- ☐ 50. JACKIE ROBINSON
- ☐ 61. REX BARNEY
- ☐ 70. CARL FURILLO
- ☐ 73. BILLY COX
- ☐ 84. ROY CAMPANELLA
- ☐ 100. GIL HODGES
- ☐ 116. JOE HATTEN
- ☐ 146. MIKE MCCORMICK
- ☐ 162. PREACHER ROE
- ☐ 178. TOMMY BROWN
- ☐ 179. HUGH CASEY(F)
- ☐ 194. RALPH BRANCA
- ☐ 206. BRUCE EDWARDS
- ☐ 226. DUKE SNIDER

CHICAGO CUBS

- ☐ 6. PHIL CAVARRETTA
- ☐ 22. PEANUTS LOWREY
- ☐ 38. EMIL VERBAN
- ☐ 52. JOHNNY SCHMITZ
- ☐ 63. ANDY PAFKO
- ☐ 76. BILL NICHOLSON(F)
- ☐ 83. BOB SCHEFFING
- ☐ 99. FRANK GUSTINE(B)
- ☐ 115. DUTCH LEONARD(B)
- ☐ 130. HARRY WALKER(B)
- ☐ 134. HANK BOROWY(F)
- ☐ 142. EDDIE WAITKUS(F)
- ☐ 152. CLARENCE MADDERN
- ☐ 168. DOYLE LADE
- ☐ 184. BOB CHIPMAN
- ☐ 200. JESS DOBERNIC
- ☐ 212. RALPH HAMNER

CHICAGO WHITE SOX

- ☐ 12. CASS MICHAELS
- ☐ 28. DON KOLLOWAY
- ☐ 44. DAVE PHILLEY
- ☐ 87. RANDY GUMPERT(B)
- ☐ 96. TAFT WRIGHT(F)
- ☐ 103. JOE TIPTON(B)
- ☐ 119. FLOYD BAKER
- ☐ 133. AARON ROBINSON(F)
- ☐ 141. TONY LUPIEN(F)
- ☐ 159. GLEN MOULDER

1

☐ 175. LUKE APPLING
☐ 191. JOE HAYNES
☐ 217. MARINO PIERETTI

CINCINNATI REDS

☐ 5. HANK SAUER
☐ 21. FRANK BAUMHOLTZ
☐ 37. JOHN WYROSTEK
☐ 51. HERMAN WEHMEIER
☐ 62. GRADY HATTON
☐ 81. VIRGIL STALLCUP
☐ 97. DANNY LITWHILER
☐ 113. RAY LAMANNO
☐ 128. JOHNNY VANDER MEER
☐ 160. JIM BLACKBURN
☐ 176. KEN RAFFENSBERGER
☐ 192. HARRY GUMBERT

KEN KELTNER

CLEVELAND INDIANS

☐ 11. LOU BOUDREAU(M)
☐ 27. BOB FELLER
☐ 43. DALE MITCHELL
☐ 57. GENE BEARDEN
☐ 78. SAM ZOLDAK
☐ 94. MICKEY VERNON(B)
☐ 103. JOE TIPTON(F)
☐ 110. EARLY WYNN(B)
☐ 125. KEN KELTNER
☐ 136. HANK EDWARDS
☐ 150. ALLIE CLARK
☐ 166. MIKE TRESH
☐ 182. HAL PECK
☐ 198. STEVE GROMEK
☐ 210. JOE GORDON
☐ 224. SATCHELL PAIGE
☐ 233. LARRY DOBY
☐ 238. BOB LEMON

DETROIT TIGERS

☐ 10. TED GRAY
☐ 26. GEORGE KELL
☐ 42. HOOT EVERS
☐ 56. PAT MULLIN
☐ 75. EDDIE MAYO
☐ 91. DICK WAKEFIELD
☐ 107. EDDIE LAKE
☐ 122. GEORGE VICO
☐ 133. AARON ROBINSON(B)
☐ 141. TONY LUPIEN(B)
☐ 148. BOB SWIFT
☐ 164. VIC WERTZ
☐ 180. CONNIE BERRY
☐ 196. FRED HUTCHINSON
☐ 208. DIZZY TROUT
☐ 219. VIRGIL TRUCKS

NEW YORK GIANTS

☐ 2. WHITEY LOCKMAN
☐ 18. BOBBY THOMSON
☐ 34. DAVE KOSLO
☐ 48. WILLARD MARSHALL
☐ 59. JACK LOHRKE
☐ 68. SHELDON JONES
☐ 85. JOHNNY MIZE
☐ 101. SID GORDON
☐ 117. WALKER COOPER
☐ 154. CLINT HARTUNG
☐ 170. BILL RIGNEY
☐ 186. BUDDY KERR
☐ 202. LARRY JANSEN
☐ 220. JOHNNY MCCARTHY
☐ 221. BOB MUNCRIEF(F)

☐ 223. BOB HOFMAN
☐ 230. AUGIE GALAN
☐ 237. MONTE KENNEDY

NEW YORK YANKEES

☐ 3. BOB PORTERFIELD
☐ 19. BOBBY BROWN
☐ 35. VIC RASCHI
☐ 49. FRANK SHEA
☐ 60. YOGI BERRA
☐ 69. TOMMY HENRICH
☐ 82. JOE PAGE
☐ 87. RANDY GUMPERT(F)
☐ 98. PHIL RIZZUTO
☐ 114. ALLIE REYNOLDS
☐ 129. BILL JOHNSON
☐ 149. ROY PARTEE
☐ 165. GEORGE STIRNWEISS
☐ 181. GUS NIARHOS
☐ 197. JOHNNY LINDELL
☐ 209. CHARLIE KELLER
☐ 218. DICK KRYHOSKI
☐ 225. GERRY COLEMAN
☐ 229. ED LOPAT
☐ 232. GEORGE MCQUINN
☐ 236. FRED SANFORD
☐ 240. NORMAN YOUNG

PHILDELPHIA ATHLETICS

☐ 9. FERRIS FAIN
☐ 25. CARL SHEIB
☐ 41. LOU BRISSIE
☐ 55. EDDIE JOOST
☐ 66. ELMER VALO
☐ 80. BILL MCCAHAN
☐ 96. TAFT WRIGHT(B)
☐ 112. SAM CHAPMAN
☐ 127. HENRY MAJESKI
☐ 138. BUDDY ROSAR
☐ 155. MIKE GUERRA
☐ 171. DICK FOWLER
☐ 187. PHIL MARCHILDON
☐ 203. BARNEY MCCOSKY
☐ 222. ALEX KELLNER

PHILADELPHIA PHILLIES

☐ 14. CURT SIMMONS
☐ 30. ANDY SEMINICK
☐ 46. ROBIN ROBERTS
☐ 76. BILL NICHOLSON(B)
☐ 92. WILLIE JONES
☐ 108. KEN HEINTZELMAN
☐ 115. DUTCH LEONARD(F)
☐ 123. JOHNNY BLATNIK
☐ 130. HARRY WALKER(F)
☐ 134. HANK BOROWY(B)
☐ 142. EDDIE WAITKUS(B)
☐ 145. BLIX DONNELLY
☐ 161. JOCKO THOMPSON
☐ 177. STAN LOPATA
☐ 193. KEN TRINKLE
☐ 205. DICK SISLER
☐ 214. RICHIE ASHBURN
☐ 216. SCHOOLBOY ROWE
☐ 228. JACKIE MAYO

PITTSBURGH PIRATES

☐ 8. MURRY DICKSON
☐ 13. BOB CHESNES
☐ 29. RALPH KINER
☐ 45. WALLY WESTLAKE
☐ 77. ERNIE BONHAM
☐ 93. ED STEVENS
☐ 99. FRANK GUSTINE(F)
☐ 109. ED FITZGERALD
☐ 124. DANNY MURTAUGH
☐ 135. STAN ROJEK
☐ 147. BERT SINGLETON
☐ 163. CLYDE MCCULLOUGH
☐ 179. HUGH CASEY(B)
☐ 195. EDDIE BOCKMAN
☐ 207. JOHNNY HOPP
☐ 215. KIRBY HIGBE
☐ 221. BOB MUNCRIEF(B)
☐ 227. FRITZ OSTERMUELLER
☐ 234. RIP SEWELL

ST. LOUIS BROWNS

☐ 4. JERRY PRIDDY
☐ 15. NED GARVER
☐ 31. DICK KOKOS
☐ 89. MIZELL PLATT
☐ 105. BILL KENNEDY
☐ 120. CLIFF FANNIN
☐ 131. PAUL LEHNER
☐ 139. HANK ARFT
☐ 143. BOB DILLINGER
☐ 156. AL ZARILLA
☐ 172. EDDIE PELLAGRINI
☐ 188. KARL DREWS
☐ 204. BOB SAVAGE

ST. LOUIS CARDINALS

☐ 24. STAN MUSIAL
☐ 40. RED MUNGER
☐ 54. MARTY MARION
☐ 65. ENOS SLAUGHTER
☐ 79. RON NORTHEY
☐ 95. HOWIE POLLET
☐ 111. RED SCHOENDIENST
☐ 126. AL BRAZLE
☐ 137. TED WILKS
☐ 158. HARRY BRECHEEN
☐ 174. TERRY MOORE(C)
☐ 190. JIM HEARN

WASHINGTON SENATORS

☐ 16. AL KOZAR
☐ 32. EDDIE YOST
☐ 74. TOM MCBRIDE
☐ 90. GIL COAN
☐ 94. MICKEY VERNON(F)
☐ 106. JAKE EARLY
☐ 110. EARLY WYNN(F)
☐ 121. MARK CHRISTMAN
☐ 132. AL EVANS
☐ 140. RAY SCARBOROUGH
☐ 144. MICKEY HAEFNER
☐ 157. WALT MASTERSON
☐ 173. EDDIE STEWART
☐ 189. EARL WOOTEN

1950 BOWMAN (252)
2 1/16" X 2 1/2"

BOSTON BRAVES

☐ 19. WARREN SPAHN
☐ 20. BOB ELLIOTT
☐ 55. BUDDY KERR
☐ 56. DEL CRANDALL
☐ 57. VERN BICKFORD
☐ 73. WILLARD MARSHALL
☐ 74. JOHNNY ANTONELLI
☐ 109. SID GORDON
☐ 110. TOMMY HOLMES
☐ 111 WALKER COOPER
☐ 163. EARL TORGESON
☐ 164. SIBBY SISTI
☐ 192. BOB CHIPMAN
☐ 193. PETE REISER
☐ 248. SAM JETHROE

1950 Bowman

BOSTON RED SOX

- 1. MEL PARNELL
- 2. VERN STEPHENS
- 3. DOM DIMAGGIO
- 43. BOBBY DOERR
- 44. JOE DOBSON
- 45. AL ZARILLA
- 97. MICKEY MCDERMOTT
- 98. TED WILLIAMS
- 99. BILLY GOODMAN
- 136. WARREN ROSAR
- 137. JOHNNY PESKY
- 152. ELLIS KINDER
- 153. WALT MASTERSON
- 186. KEN KELTNER
- 187. LOU STRINGER
- 188. EARL JOHNSON
- 245. AL PAPAI
- 246. WALT DROPO

BROOKLYN DODGERS

- 21. PEE WEE REESE
- 22. JACKIE ROBINSON
- 23. DON NEWCOMBE
- 58. CARL FURILLO
- 59. RALPH BRANCA
- 75. ROY CAMPANELLA
- 76. REX BARNEY
- 77. DUKE SNIDER
- 112. GIL HODGES
- 113. GENE HERMANSKI
- 165. BRUCE EDWARDS
- 166. JOE HATTEN
- 167. PREACHER ROE
- 194. BILLY COX
- 222. BOBBY MORGAN
- 223. JIMMY RUSSELL
- 224. JACK BANTA

CHICAGO CUBS

- 24. JOHNNY SCHMITZ
- 25. HANK SAUER
- 60. ANDY PAFKO
- 61. BOB RUSH
- 78. MICKEY OWEN
- 79. JOHNNY VANDER MEER
- 114. WAYNE TERWILLIGER
- 115. ROY SMALLEY
- 169. HANK EDWARDS
- 170. EMIL LEONARD
- 195. PHIL CAVARRETTA
- 196. DOYLE LADE
- 229. FRANK FRISCH(M)
- 230. BILL SERENA
- 231. PRESTON WARD

CHICAGO WHITE SOX

- 4. GUS ZERNIAL
- 5. BOB KUZAVA
- 37. LUKE APPLING
- 38. BILL WIGHT
- 91. CASS MICHAELS
- 92. HANK MAJESKI
- 127. DAVE PHILLEY
- 128. PHIL MASI
- 146. FLOYD BAKER
- 183. MICKEY HAEFNER
- 184. RANDY GUMPERT
- 185. HOWIE JUDSON
- 236. BOB CAIN
- 237. BILL SALKELD

CINCINNATI REDS

- 26. GRADY HATTON
- 27. HERMAN WEHMEIER
- 62. TED KLUSZEWSKI
- 63. EWELL BLACKWELL
- 80. HOWARD FOX
- 81. RON NORTHEY
- 116. VIRGIL STALLCUP
- 168. BOB SCHEFFING
- 172. PEANUTS LOWREY
- 173. LLOYD MERRIMAN
- 197. JOHNNY WYROSTEK
- 198. DANNY LITWHILER

CLEVELAND INDIANS

- 6. BOB FELLER
- 7. JIM HEGAN
- 39. LARRY DOBY
- 40. BOB LEMON
- 93. GENE BEARDEN
- 94. LOU BOUDREAU(M)
- 129. JOE GORDON
- 130. DALE MITCHELL
- 131. STEVE GROMEK
- 132. MICKEY VERNON
- 147. MIKE GARCIA
- 148. EARLY WYNN
- 181. MARINO PIERETTI
- 182. SAM ZOLDAK
- 232. AL ROSEN
- 233. ALLIE CLARK

DETROIT TIGERS

- 8. GEORGE KELL
- 9. VIC WERTZ
- 41. HOOT EVERS
- 42. ART HOUTTEMAN
- 95. AARON ROBINSON
- 96. VIRGIL TRUCKS
- 133. DON KOLLOWAY
- 134. DIZZY TROUT
- 135. PAT MULLIN
- 149. BOB SWIFT
- 150. GEORGE VICO
- 151. FRED HUTCHINSON
- 210. TED GRAY
- 211. CHARLIE KELLER
- 212. GERRY PRIDDY
- 240. EDDIE LAKE
- 241. NEIL BERRY
- 242. DICK KRYHOSKI
- 243. JOHNNY GROTH

NEW YORK GIANTS

- 28. BOBBY THOMSON
- 29. ED STANKY
- 64. AL DARK
- 65. DAVE KOSLO
- 66. LARRY JANSEN
- 82. WHITEY LOCKMAN
- 83. SHELDON JONES
- 117. BILL RIGNEY
- 118. CLINT HARTUNG
- 174. HANK THOMPSON
- 175. MONTE KENNEDY
- 199. JACK KRAMER
- 200. KIRBY HIGBE
- 220. LEO DUROCHER(M)
- 221. DON MUELLER
- 235. TOOKIE GILBERT

NEW YORK YANKEES

- 10. TOMMY HENRICH
- 11. PHIL RIZZUTO
- 12. JOE PAGE
- 46. YOGI BERRA
- 47. JERRY COLEMAN
- 100. VIC RASCHI
- 101. BOBBY BROWN
- 102. BILLY JOHNSON
- 138. ALLIE REYNOLDS
- 139. JOHNNY MIZE
- 154. GUS NIARHOS
- 155. FRANK SHEA
- 156. FRED SANFORD
- 215. ED LOPAT
- 216. BOB PORTERFIELD
- 217. CASEY STENGEL(M)
- 218. CLIFF MAPES
- 219. HANK BAUER

PHILADELPHIA ATHLETICS

- 13. FERRIS FAIN
- 14. ALEX KELLNER
- 48. LOU BRISSIE
- 49. ELMER VALO
- 103. EDDIE JOOST
- 104. SAM CHAPMAN
- 105. BOB DILLINGER

- 140. PETE SUDER
- 141. JOE COLEMAN
- 157. MIKE GUERRA
- 158. PAUL LEHNER
- 159. JOE TIPTON
- 213. CARL SCHEIB
- 214. DICK FOWLER
- 234. BOBBY SHANTZ

PHILADELPHIA PHILLIES

- 30. EDDIE WAITKUS
- 31. DEL ENNIS
- 32. ROBIN ROBERTS
- 67. WILLIE JONES
- 68. CURT SIMMONS
- 84. RICHIE ASHBURN
- 85. KEN HEINTZELMAN
- 119. DICK SISLER
- 120. JOHN THOMPSON
- 121. ANDY SEMINICK
- 176. BLIX DONNELLY
- 177. HANK BOROWY
- 204. GRANNY HAMNER
- 205. MIKE GOLIAT
- 206. STAN LOPATA
- 225. EDDIE SAWYER(M)
- 226. JIM KONSTANTY
- 227. BOB J. MILLER
- 228. BILL NICHOLSON

PITTSBURGH PIRATES

- 33. RALPH KINER
- 34. MURRY DICKSON
- 69. WALLY WESTLAKE
- 70. BOB CHESNES
- 86. STAN ROJEK
- 87. BILL WERLE
- 122. JOHNNY HOPP
- 123. DINO RESTELLI
- 124. CLYDE MCCULLOUGH
- 171. HARRY GUMBERT
- 178. ED FITZGERALD
- 201. PETE CASTIGLIONE
- 202. CLIFF CHAMBERS
- 203. DANNY MURTAUGH
- 244. DALE COOGAN

ST. LOUIS BROWNS

- 16. ROY SIEVERS
- 50. DICK KOKOS
- 51. NED GARVER
- 106. CLIFF FANNIN
- 142. SHERMAN LOLLAR
- 145. JACK GRAHAM
- 189. OWEN FRIEND
- 190. KEN WOOD
- 191. DICK STARR
- 249. GEORGE STIRNWEISS
- 250. RAY COLEMAN
- 251. LES MOSS
- 252. BILLY DEMARS

ST. LOUIS CARDINALS

- 35. ENOS SLAUGHTER
- 36. EDDIE KAZAK
- 71. RED SCHOENDIENST
- 72. HOWIE POLLET
- 88. MARTY MARION
- 89. RED MUNGER
- 90. HARRY BRECHEEN
- 125. DEL RICE

☐ 126. AL BRAZLE
☐ 179. CHUCK DIERING
☐ 180. HARRY WALKER
☐ 207. MAX LANIER
☐ 208. JIM HEARN
☐ 209. JOHNNY LINDELL
☐ 238. NIPPY JONES
☐ 239. BILL HOWERTON

WASHINGTON SENATORS

☐ 15. AL KOZAR
☐ 17. SID HUDSON
☐ 18. EDDIE ROBINSON
☐ 52. SAM MELE
☐ 53. CLYDE VOLLMER
☐ 54. GIL COAN
☐ 107. SAM DENTE
☐ 108. RAY SCARBOROUGH
☐ 143. EDDIE STEWART
☐ 144. AL EVANS
☐ 160. MICKEY HARRIS
☐ 161. SHERRY ROBERTSON
☐ 162. EDDIE YOST
☐ 247. IRV NOREN

1951 BOWMAN (324)
2 1/16″ X 3 1/8″

RAY SCARBOROUGH

BOSTON BRAVES

☐ 19. SID GORDON
☐ 20. DEL CRANDALL
☐ 42. VERN BICKFORD
☐ 66. BOB ELLIOTT
☐ 98. WILLARD MARSHALL
☐ 99. EARL TORGESON
☐ 134. WARREN SPAHN
☐ 135. WALKER COOPER
☐ 170. SIBBY SISTI
☐ 171. BUDDY KERR
☐ 207. BILLY SOUTHWORTH(M)
☐ 208. BLIX DONNELLY
☐ 242. SAM JETHROE
☐ 243. JOHNNY ANTONELLI
☐ 277. ROY HARTSFIELD
☐ 278. NORMAN ROY
☐ 312. GENE MAUCH
☐ 313. RAY MUELLER
☐ 314. JOHNNY SAIN

BOSTON RED SOX

☐ 15. JOHNNY PESKY
☐ 16. MICKEY McDERMOTT
☐ 38. AL EVANS
☐ 39. RAY SCARBOROUGH
☐ 62. LOU BOUDREAU
☐ 91. CLYDE VOLLMER
☐ 92. VERN STEPHENS
☐ 128. ELLIS KINDER
☐ 129. MATT BATTS
☐ 164. BILL WIGHT
☐ 165. TED WILLIAMS
☐ 201. STEVE O'NEIL(M)
☐ 202. MIKE GUERRA(F)
☐ 210. LES MOSS(B)
☐ 236. WARREN ROSAR
☐ 237. BILLY GOODMAN
☐ 270. WILLARD NIXON
☐ 271. TOMMY WRIGHT
☐ 306. JIM PIERSALL
☐ 307. WALT MASTERSON

BROOKLYN DODGERS

☐ 6. DON NEWCOMBE
☐ 7. GIL HODGES
☐ 31. ROY CAMPANELLA
☐ 32. DUKE SNIDER
☐ 55. GENE HERMANSKI
☐ 56. RALPH BRANCA
☐ 80. PEE WEE REESE
☐ 81. CARL FURILLO
☐ 116. BRUCE EDWARDS
☐ 117. EDDIE MIKSIS
☐ 118. PREACHER ROE
☐ 152. CAL ABRAMS
☐ 153. REX BARNEY
☐ 189. ERV PALICA
☐ 190. JOE HATTEN
☐ 224. BILLY COX
☐ 225. DAN BANKHEAD
☐ 259. CHARLIE DRESSEN(M)
☐ 260. CARL ERSKINE
☐ 299. CLYDE KING

CHICAGO CUBS

☐ 22. HANK SAUER
☐ 44. ROY SMALLEY
☐ 69. JOHNNY SCHMITZ
☐ 70. RON NORTHEY
☐ 102. DUTCH LEONARD
☐ 103. ANDY PAFKO
☐ 138. PHIL CAVARRETTA
☐ 139. DOYLE LADE
☐ 174. MICKEY OWEN
☐ 175. WAYNE TERWILLIGER
☐ 211. HAL JEFFCOAT
☐ 212. BOB RUSH
☐ 246. BILL SERENA
☐ 247. BOB RAMAZZOTTI
☐ 248. JOHNNY KLIPPSTEIN
☐ 282. FRANK FRISCH(M)
☐ 283. WALT DUBIEL
☐ 317. SMOKY BURGESS
☐ 318. WARREN HACKER

CHICAGO WHITE SOX

☐ 12. HANK MAJESKI
☐ 35. AL ZARILLA
☐ 36. JOE DOBSON
☐ 59. RANDY GUMPERT
☐ 60. CHICO CARRASQUEL
☐ 87. FLOYD BAKER
☐ 88. EDDIE ROBINSON
☐ 123. HOWIE JUDSON
☐ 124. GUS NIARHOS
☐ 159. EDDIE STEWART
☐ 160. PHIL MASI
☐ 195. PAUL RICHARDS(M)
☐ 196. BILLY PIERCE
☐ 197. BOB CAIN(F)
☐ 231. LUIS ALOMA
☐ 232. NELSON FOX
☐ 266. HARRY DORISH
☐ 267. KEN HOLCOMBE
☐ 302. JIM BUSBY
☐ 303. MARV ROTBLATT

CINCINNATI REDS

☐ 24. EWELL BLACKWELL
☐ 47. GRADY HATTON
☐ 48. KEN RAFFENSBERGER
☐ 72. LLOYD MERRIMAN
☐ 107. JOHNNY WYROSTEK
☐ 108. VIRGIL STALLCUP
☐ 143. TED KLUSZEWSKI
☐ 144. HERMAN WEHMEIER
☐ 179. DANNY LITWHILER
☐ 180. HOWIE FOX
☐ 215. KEN PETERSON
☐ 216. CONNIE RYAN
☐ 251. WILLARD RAMSDELL
☐ 252. DIXIE HOWELL
☐ 286. BOB USHER
☐ 287. JIM BLACKBURN
☐ 288. BOBBY ADAMS
☐ 322. LUKE SEWELL(M)
☐ 323. JOE ADCOCK
☐ 324. JOHNNY PRAMESA

CLEVELAND INDIANS

☐ 5. DALE MITCHELL
☐ 21. GEORGE STIRNWEISS(B)
☐ 29. ALLIE CLARK
☐ 30. BOB FELLER
☐ 53. BOB LEMON
☐ 54. RAY BOONE
☐ 78. EARLY WYNN
☐ 79. JIM HEGAN
☐ 114. SAM ZOLDAK(F)
☐ 115. STEVE GROMEK
☐ 150. MIKE GARCIA
☐ 151. LARRY DOBY
☐ 155. LOU BRISSIE(B)
☐ 187. AL ROSEN
☐ 188. BOBBY AVILA
☐ 222. THURMAN TUCKER
☐ 223. JOHNNY VANDER MEER
☐ 257. BIRDIE TEBBETTS
☐ 258. LUKE EASTER
☐ 295. AL LOPEZ(M)
☐ 296. BOB KENNEDY

VIRGIL "FIRE" TRUCKS

DETROIT TIGERS

☐ 23. HOOT EVERS
☐ 45. ART HOUTTEMAN
☐ 46. GEORGE KELL
☐ 71. JERRY PRIDDY
☐ 104. VIRGIL TRUCKS
☐ 105. DON KOLLOWAY
☐ 106. PAT MULLIN
☐ 140. EDDIE LAKE
☐ 141. FRED HUTCHINSON
☐ 142. AARON ROBINSON
☐ 176. VIC WERTZ
☐ 177. CHARLIE KELLER
☐ 178. TED GRAY
☐ 197. BOB CAIN(B)
☐ 213. NEIL BERRY
☐ 214. BOB SWIFT
☐ 249. JOHNNY GROTH
☐ 250. HANK BOROWY
☐ 284. GENE BEARDEN
☐ 285. JOHNNY LIPON
☐ 319. RED ROLFE(M)
☐ 320. HAL WHITE
☐ 321. EARL JOHNSON

1951 Bowman

NEW YORK GIANTS

- 13. ED STANKY
- 14. AL DARK
- 37. WHITEY LOCKMAN
- 61. JIM HEARN
- 89. HENRY THOMPSON
- 90. DAVE KOSLO
- 125. BILL RIGNEY
- 126. BOBBY THOMSON
- 127. SAL MAGLIE
- 161. WES WESTRUM
- 162. LARRY JANSEN
- 163. MONTE KENNEDY
- 198. MONTE IRVIN
- 199. SHELDON JONES
- 200. JACK KRAMER(F)
- 233. LEO DUROCHER(M)
- 234. CLINT HARTUNG
- 235. JACK LOHRKE
- 268. DON MUELLER
- 269. RAY NOBLE
- 304. ALLEN GETTEL
- 305. WILLIE MAYS

NEW YORK YANKEES

- 1. WHITEY FORD
- 2. YOGI BERRA
- 25. VIC RASCHI
- 26. PHIL RIZZUTO
- 49. JERRY COLEMAN
- 50. JOHNNY MIZE
- 73. TOMMY BYRNE
- 74. BILLY JOHNSON
- 109. ALLIE REYNOLDS
- 110. BOBBY BROWN
- 145. FRED SANFORD
- 146. JOHNNY HOPP
- 181. CASEY STENGEL(M)
- 182. TOM FERRICK
- 183. HANK BAUER
- 200. JACK KRAMER(B)
- 217. JOE PAGE
- 218. ED LOPAT
- 219. GENE WOODLING
- 253. MICKEY MANTLE
- 254. JACKIE JENSEN
- 280. FRANK OVERMIRE(B)
- 289. CLIFF MAPES
- 290. BILL DICKEY(C)
- 291. TOMMY HENRICH(C)

PHILADELPHIA ATHLETICS

- 8. PAUL LEHNER
- 9. SAM CHAPMAN
- 33. BOB HOOPER
- 57. ALEX KELLNER
- 82. JOE TIPTON
- 83. CARL SCHEIB
- 84. BARNEY MCCOSKY
- 114. SAM ZOLDAK(B)
- 119. EDDIE JOOST
- 120. JOE COLEMAN
- 154. PETE SUDER
- 155. LOU BRISSIE(F)
- 191. BILLY HITCHCOCK
- 192. HANK WYSE(F)
- 226. JIMMY DYKES(M)
- 227. BOBBY SHANTZ
- 261. WALLY MOSES
- 262. GUS ZERNIAL
- 297. DAVE PHILLEY
- 298. JOE ASTROTH

PHILADELPHIA PHILLIES

- 3. ROBIN ROBERTS
- 4. DEL ENNIS
- 27. JIM KONSTANTY
- 28. EDDIE WAITKUS
- 51. ANDY SEMINICK
- 52. DICK SISLER
- 75. RUSS MEYER
- 76. STAN LOPATA
- 77. MIKE GOLIAT
- 111. CURT SIMMONS
- 112. WILLIE JONES
- 113. BILL NICHOLSON
- 147. KEN HEINTZELMAN
- 148. GRANNY HAMNER
- 149. BUBBA CHURCH
- 184. EDDIE SAWYER(M)
- 185. JIMMY BLOODWORTH
- 186. RICHIE ASHBURN
- 220. BOB J. MILLER
- 221. DICK WHITMAN
- 255. MILO CANDINI
- 256. KEN SILVESTRI
- 292. EDDIE PELLAGRINI
- 293. KEN JOHNSON
- 294. JOCKO THOMPSON

PITTSBURGH PIRATES

- 17. PETE CASTIGLIONE
- 40. GUS BELL
- 63. BOB DILLINGER
- 64. BILL WERLE
- 93. DANNY O'CONNELL
- 94. CLYDE MCCULLOUGH
- 130. TOM SAFFELL
- 131. CLIFF CHAMBERS
- 166. STAN ROJEK(F)
- 167. MURRY DICKSON
- 203. VERNON LAW
- 204. VIC LOMBARDI
- 229. BILL HOWERTON(B)
- 238. PETE REISER
- 239. BILL MACDONALD
- 263. HOWIE POLLET(B)
- 272. BILLY MEYER(M)
- 273. DANNY MURTAUGH
- 274. GEORGE METKOVICH
- 308. TED BEARD
- 309. MEL QUEEN
- 310. ERV DUSAK

ST. LOUIS BROWNS

- 21. GEORGE STIRNWEISS(F)
- 43. BILLY DEMARS
- 67. ROY SIEVERS
- 68. DICK KOKOS
- 100. SHERM LOLLAR
- 101. OWEN FRIEND
- 136. RAY COLEMAN
- 137. DICK STARR
- 172. NED GARVER
- 173. HANK ARFT
- 209. KEN WOOD
- 210. LES MOSS(F)
- 244. CLIFF FANNIN
- 245. JOHN BERARDINO
- 279. JIM DELSING
- 280. FRANK OVERMIRE(F)
- 281. AL WIDMAR
- 315. ZACK TAYLOR(M)
- 316. DUANE PILLETTE

ST. LOUIS CARDINALS

- 10. RED SCHOENDIENST
- 11. RED MUNGER
- 34. MARTY MARION(M)
- 58. ENOS SLAUGHTER
- 85. EDDIE KAZAK
- 86. HARRY BRECHEEN
- 121. GERRY STALEY
- 122. JOE GARAGIOLA
- 156. DEL RICE
- 157. AL BRAZLE
- 158. CHUCK DIERING
- 166. STAN ROJEK(B)
- 193. TED WILKS
- 194. HARRY LOWREY
- 228. CLOYD BOYER
- 229. BILL HOWERTON(F)
- 230. MAX LANIER
- 263. HOWIE POLLET(F)
- 264. DON RICHMOND
- 265. STEVE BILKO
- 300. HAL RICE
- 301. TOMMY GLAVIANO

WASHINGTON SENATORS

- 18. GIL COAN
- 41. EDDIE YOST
- 65. MICKEY VERNON
- 95. SHERRY ROBERTSON
- 96. SANDY CONSUEGRA
- 97. BOB KUZAVA
- 132. CASS MICHAELS
- 133. SAM DENTE
- 168. SAM MELE
- 169. SID HUDSON
- 192. HANK WYSE(B)
- 202. MIKE GUERRA(B)
- 205. MICKEY GRASSO
- 206. CONRADO MARRERO
- 240. JOE HAYNES
- 241. IRV NOREN
- 275. BUCKY HARRIS(M)
- 276. FRANK QUINN
- 311. MICKEY HARRIS

1952 BOWMAN (252)
2 1/16" X 3 1/8"

BOSTON BRAVES

- 12. MAX SURKONT
- 28. ROY HARTSFIELD
- 48. VERN BICKFORD
- 60. SID GORDON
- 72. EARL TORGESON
- 84. SAM JETHROE
- 97. WILLARD MARSHALL
- 100. SIBBY SISTI
- 120. CHET NICHOLS
- 132. DAVE COLE
- 156. WARREN SPAHN
- 172. EBBA ST. CLAIRE
- 192. JOHN CUSICK
- 208. WALKER COOPER
- 215. SHELDON JONES
- 228. BOB CHIPMAN
- 244. LEW BURDETTE

BOSTON RED SOX

- 9. VERN STEPHENS
- 25. MICKEY MCDERMOTT
- 45. JOHNNY PESKY
- 57. CLYDE VOLLMER

1952 Bowman

☐ 81. BILLY GOODMAN
☐ 106. RANDY GUMPERT
☐ 117. BILL WIGHT
☐ 129. GUS NIARHOS
☐ 140. RAY SCARBOROUGH
☐ 153. FRED HATFIELD
☐ 169. WALT DROPO
☐ 189. JIM PIERSALL
☐ 205. WALT MASTERSON
☐ 225. DEL WILBER
☐ 241. MEL PARNESS
☐ 250. IVAN DELOCK

BROOKLYN DODGERS

☐ 8. PEE WEE REESE
☐ 24. CARL FURILLO
☐ 44. ROY CAMPANELLA
☐ 56. CLYDE KING
☐ 70. CARL ERSKINE
☐ 80. GIL HODGES
☐ 86. CAL ABRAMS
☐ 96. RALPH BRANCA
☐ 116. DUKE SNIDER
☐ 128. DON NEWCOMBE
☐ 152. BILLY COX
☐ 168. PREACHER ROE
☐ 188. CHARLIE DRESSEN(M)
☐ 204. ANDY PAFKO
☐ 224. JOHNNY SCHMITZ
☐ 240. BILLY LOES

CHICAGO CUBS

☐ 16. TURK LOWN
☐ 22. WILLARD RAMSDELL
☐ 32. EDDIE MIKSIS
☐ 64. ROY SMALLEY
☐ 88. BRUCE EDWARDS
☐ 104. HAL JEFFCOAT
☐ 126. PHIL CAVARRETTA(M)
☐ 136. GENE HERMANSKI
☐ 144. JOE HATTEN
☐ 159. DUTCH LEONARD
☐ 175. RANSOM JACKSON
☐ 195. FRANK BAUMHOLTZ
☐ 211. PAUL MINNER
☐ 231. DEE FONDY
☐ 236. TOMMY BROWN(B)
☐ 247. JOHN PRAMESA

CHICAGO WHITE SOX

☐ 5. MINNIE MINOSO
☐ 21. NELSON FOX
☐ 41. CHICO CARRASQUEL
☐ 54. BILLY PIERCE
☐ 68. JIM BUSBY
☐ 77. EDDIE ROBINSON
☐ 93. PAUL RICHARDS(M)
☐ 113. AL ZARILLA
☐ 149. HOWIE JUDSON
☐ 165. SAUL ROGOVIN
☐ 185. EDDIE STEWART
☐ 201. RAY COLEMAN
☐ 221. LOU KRETLOW
☐ 237. SHERMAN LOLLAR

CINCINNATI REDS

☐ 6. VIRGIL STALLCUP
☐ 42. JOHNNY WYROSTEK
☐ 55. KEN RAFFENSBERGER
☐ 69. JOE ADCOCK
☐ 78. LLOYD MERRIMAN
☐ 94. LUKE SEWELL(M)
☐ 114. FRANK HILLER
☐ 127. DICK SISLER
☐ 141. HANK EDWARDS
☐ 150. HERMAN WEHMEIER
☐ 166. BOBBY ADAMS
☐ 186. FRANK SMITH
☐ 202. HARRY PERKOWSKI
☐ 222. DIXIE HOWELL
☐ 238. ROY MCMILLAN

CLEVELAND INDIANS

☐ 7. MIKE GARCIA
☐ 23. BOB LEMON
☐ 43. BOB FELLER

☐ 79. LOU BRISSIE
☐ 95. LUKE EASTER
☐ 115. LARRY DOBY
☐ 124. BIRDIE TEBBETTS
☐ 142. EARLY WYNN
☐ 151. AL ROSEN
☐ 167. BOB AVILA
☐ 187. JIM HEGAN
☐ 203. STEVE GROMEK
☐ 214. RAY BOONE
☐ 223. HARRY SIMPSON
☐ 239. DALE MITCHELL

DETROIT TIGERS

☐ 3. FRED HUTCHINSON
☐ 13. CLIFF MAPES
☐ 39. VIC WERTZ
☐ 67. JOHNNY GROTH
☐ 75. GEORGE KELL
☐ 91. DON KOLLOWAY
☐ 111. HOOT EVERS
☐ 131. BOB SWIFT
☐ 139. JERRY PRIDDY
☐ 147. MARLIN STUART
☐ 163. JOHNNY LIPON
☐ 183. PAT MULLIN
☐ 199. TED GRAY
☐ 209. DICK LITTLEFIELD
☐ 216. MATT BATTS
☐ 219. NEIL BERRY
☐ 235. STEVE SOUCHOCK

NEW YORK GIANTS

☐ 2. BOBBY THOMSON
☐ 18. DON MUELLER
☐ 34. AL DARK
☐ 38. WHITEY LOCKMAN
☐ 49. JIM HEARN
☐ 66. SAL MAGLIE
☐ 74. WES WESTRUM
☐ 90. LARRY JANSEN
☐ 110. MAX LANIER
☐ 121. AL CORWIN
☐ 146. LEO DUROCHER(M)
☐ 162. MONTE IRWIN
☐ 178. DAVE WILLIAMS
☐ 182. DAVE KOSLO
☐ 198. CHUCK DIERING
☐ 213. MONTE KENNEDY
☐ 218. WILLIE MAYS
☐ 234. FRED FITZSIMMONS(C)
☐ 249. HANK THOMPSON

NEW YORK YANKEES

☐ 1. YOGI BERRA
☐ 17. ED LOPAT
☐ 33. GIL MCDOUGALD
☐ 37. VIC RASCHI
☐ 52. PHIL RIZZUTO
☐ 65. HANK BAUER
☐ 73. JERRY COLEMAN
☐ 101. MICKEY MANTLE
☐ 105. BOBBY BROWN
☐ 109. TOM MORGAN
☐ 145. JOHNNY MIZE
☐ 161. JACKIE JENSEN(F)
☐ 177. GENE WOODLING
☐ 181. JOE COLLINS
☐ 197. CHARLIE SILVERA
☐ 217. CASEY STENGEL(M)
☐ 233. BOB KUZAVA
☐ 252. FRANK CROSETTI(C)

PHILADELPHIA ATHLETICS

☐ 10. BOB HOOPER
☐ 26. EDDIE JOOST
☐ 46. CARL SCHEIB
☐ 58. HANK MAJESKI
☐ 82. GUS ZERNIAL
☐ 89. BILLY HITCHCOCK
☐ 98. JIMMY DYKES(M)
☐ 118. RAY MURRAY
☐ 130. ALLIE CLARK
☐ 154. FERRIS FAIN
☐ 170. JOE ASTROTH
☐ 179. PETE SUDER
☐ 190. DICK FOWLER
☐ 206. ELMER VALO
☐ 226. ALEX KELLNER
☐ 242. EVERETT KELL

PHILADELPHIA PHILLIES

☐ 4. ROBIN ROBERTS
☐ 20. WILLIE JONES
☐ 35. GRANNY HAMNER
☐ 40. BUBBA CHURCH
☐ 53. RICHIE ASHBURN
☐ 76. DEL ENNIS
☐ 92. EDDIE WAITKUS
☐ 112. SMOKEY BURGESS
☐ 125. HOWIE FOX
☐ 148. KEN HEINTZELMAN
☐ 164. CONNIE RYAN
☐ 184. CURT SIMMONS
☐ 200. KEN SILVESTRI
☐ 220. RUSS MEYER
☐ 236. TOMMY BROWN(F)
☐ 251. JACK LOHRKE

PITTSBURGH PIRATES

☐ 11. RALPH KINER
☐ 27. JOE GARAGIOLA
☐ 47. PETE CASTIGLIONE
☐ 59. MURRAY DICKSON
☐ 71. VERNON LAW
☐ 83. HOWIE POLLET
☐ 99. CLYDE MCCULLOUGH
☐ 108. GEORGE METKOVICH
☐ 119. BILL HOWERTON
☐ 138. TED WILKS
☐ 155. BILL MEYER(M)
☐ 171. MEL QUEEN
☐ 180. ED FITZ GERALD
☐ 191. BOB FRIEND
☐ 207. GEORGE STRICKLAND
☐ 227. CLYDE SUKEFORTH(C)
☐ 243. RED MUNGER

ST. LOUIS BROWNS

- ☐ 19. BOB CAIN
- ☐ 29. NED GARVER
- ☐ 61. TOMMY BYRNE
- ☐ 85. MARTY MARION(C)
- ☐ 133. DICK KRYHOSKI
- ☐ 137. STAN ROJEK
- ☐ 157. JIM DELSING
- ☐ 173. GENE BEARDEN
- ☐ 193. BOBBY YOUNG
- ☐ 229. HANK ARFT
- ☐ 245. GEORGE SCHMEES

ST. LOUIS CARDINALS

- ☐ 14. CLIFF CHAMBERS
- ☐ 30. RED SCHOENDIENST
- ☐ 50. GERRY STALEY
- ☐ 62. JOE PRESKO
- ☐ 102. PEANUTS LOWREY
- ☐ 107. DEL RICE
- ☐ 122. BILLY JOHNSON
- ☐ 134. AL BRAZLE
- ☐ 160. EDDIE STANKY(M)
- ☐ 176. HARRY BRECHEEN
- ☐ 196. STAN MUSIAL
- ☐ 212. SOLLY HEMUS
- ☐ 232. ENOS SLAUGHTER
- ☐ 248. BILL WERLE

WASHINGTON SENATORS

- ☐ 15. SAM MELE
- ☐ 31. EDDIE YOST
- ☐ 36. CASS MICHAELS
- ☐ 51. GIL COAN
- ☐ 63. IRV NOREN
- ☐ 87. MICKEY VERNON
- ☐ 103. JOE HAYNES
- ☐ 123. SID HUDSON
- ☐ 135. MICKEY HARRIS
- ☐ 143. SANDY CONSUEGRA
- ☐ 158. BUCKY HARRIS(M)
- ☐ 161. JACKIE JENSEN(B)
- ☐ 174. MICKEY GRASSO
- ☐ 194. BOB PORTERFIELD
- ☐ 210. ARCHIE WILSON
- ☐ 230. FRANK SHEA
- ☐ 246. JERRY SNYDER

1953 BOWMAN (160)
2 1/2" X 3 3/4"
COLOR

BOSTON RED SOX

- ☐ 25. HOOT EVERS
- ☐ 35. MICKEY MCDERMOTT
- ☐ 41. SAMMY WHITE
- ☐ 57. LOU BOUDREAU(M)
- ☐ 61. GEORGE KELL
- ☐ 66. MEL PARNELL
- ☐ 123. JOHNNY LIPON
- ☐ 148. BILLY GOODMAN

BROOKLYN DODGERS

- ☐ 12. CARL ERSKINE
- ☐ 14. BILLY LOES
- ☐ 33. PEE WEE REESE
- ☐ 46. ROY CAMPANELLA
- ☐ 78. CARL FURILLO
- ☐ 92. GIL HODGES
- ☐ 117. DUKE SNIDER
- ☐ 124. CHARLIE DRESSEN(M)
- ☐ 129. RUSS MEYER
- ☐ 135. BOBBY MORGAN
- ☐ 145. GEORGE SHUBA

CHICAGO CUBS

- ☐ 7. HARRY CHITI
- ☐ 30. PHIL CAVARRETTA(M)
- ☐ 42. TOMMY BROWN
- ☐ 48. HANK SAUER
- ☐ 71. PAUL MINNER
- ☐ 94. BOB ADDIS
- ☐ 110. BOB RUSH
- ☐ 112. TOBY ATWELL
- ☐ 122. BILL SERENA
- ☐ 144. WARREN HACKER
- ☐ 154. TURK LOWN

CHICAGO WHITE SOX

- ☐ 18. NELSON FOX
- ☐ 36. MINNIE MINOSO
- ☐ 39. PAUL RICHARDS(M)
- ☐ 50. LOU KRETLOW
- ☐ 54. CHICO CARRASQUEL
- ☐ 73. BILLY PIERCE
- ☐ 75. SAUL ROGOVIN
- ☐ 88. JOE DOBSON
- ☐ 98. HECTOR RODRIQUEZ
- ☐ 137. SAM DENTE
- ☐ 157. SHERMAN LOLLAR

CINCINNATI REDS

- ☐ 23. HERMAN WEHMEIER
- ☐ 26. ROY MCMILLAN
- ☐ 58. WILLARD MARSHALL
- ☐ 62. TED KLUSZEWSKI
- ☐ 87. HARRY PERKOWSKI
- ☐ 90. JOE NUXHALL

- ☐ 106. KEN RAFFENSBERGER
- ☐ 108. BOBBY ADAMS
- ☐ 138. BUBBA CHURCH

CLEVELAND INDIANS

- ☐ 8. AL ROSEN
- ☐ 29. BOBBY AVILA
- ☐ 40. LARRY DOBY
- ☐ 43. MIKE GARCIA
- ☐ 79. RAY BOONE
- ☐ 86. HARRY SIMPSON
- ☐ 102. JIM HEGAN
- ☐ 104. LUKE EASTER
- ☐ 114. BOB FELLER
- ☐ 119. DALE MITCHELL
- ☐ 143. AL LOPEZ(M)
- ☐ 146. EARLY WYNN

DETROIT TIGERS

- ☐ 4. ART HOUTTEMAN
- ☐ 6. JOE GINSBERG
- ☐ 45. WALT DROPO
- ☐ 47. NED GARVER
- ☐ 72. TED GRAY
- ☐ 91. STEVE SOUCHOCK
- ☐ 100. BILL WIGHT
- ☐ 125. FRED HATFIELD
- ☐ 132. FRED HUTCHINSON(M)
- ☐ 134. JOHNNY PESKY

MIKWAUKEE BRAVES

- ☐ 3. SAM JETHROE*
- ☐ 5. SID GORDON*
- ☐ 37. JIM WILSON*
- ☐ 69. CHARLIE GRIMM(M)
- ☐ 83. JACK DANIELS
- ☐ 97. EDDIE MATHEWS
- ☐ 99. WARREN SPAHN
- ☐ 151. JOE ADCOCK
- ☐ 156. MAX SURKONT

NEW YORK GIANTS

- ☐ 1. DAVEY WILLIAMS
- ☐ 19. AL DARK
- ☐ 51. MONTE IRVIN
- ☐ 55. LEO DUROCHER(M)
- ☐ 74. DON MUELLER
- ☐ 76. JIM HEARN
- ☐ 96. SAL MAGLIE
- ☐ 126. AL CORWIN
- ☐ 128. WHITEY LOCKMAN
- ☐ 149. AL CORWIN

NEW YORK YANKEES

- ☐ 9. PHIL RIZZUTO
- ☐ 27. VIC RASCHI
- ☐ 59. MICKEY MANTLE
- ☐ 63. GIL MCDOUGALD
- ☐ 68. ALLIE REYNOLDS
- ☐ 84. HANK BAUER
- ☐ 118. BILLY MARTIN
- ☐ 121. YOGI BERRA
- ☐ 136. JIM BRIDEWESER
- ☐ 153. WHITEY FORD

PHILADELPHIA ATHLETICS

- ☐ 11. BOBBY SHANTZ
- ☐ 13. GUS ZERNIAL
- ☐ 31. JIMMY DYKES(M)
- ☐ 38. HARRY BYRD
- ☐ 82. JOE ASTROTH
- ☐ 95. WALLY MOSES(C)
- ☐ 105. EDDIE JOOST
- ☐ 107. ALEX KELLNER
- ☐ 130. CASS MICHAELS
- ☐ 150. CARL SCHEIB
- ☐ 155. ALLIE CLARK

PHILADELPHIA PHILLIES

- ☐ 10. RICHIE ASHBURN
- ☐ 28. SMOKY BURGESS
- ☐ 60. GRANNY HAMNER
- ☐ 64. CURT SIMMONS
- ☐ 65. ROBIN ROBERTS

* Nos. 3, 5, 37 appear with Boston Braves
on the back of the card.

☐ 67. MEL CLARK
☐ 103. DEL ENNIS
☐ 113. KARL DREWS
☐ 131. CONNIE RYAN
☐ 133. WILLIE JONES
☐ 158. HOWARD FOX

PITTSBURGH PIRATES

☐ 16. BOB FRIEND
☐ 21. JOE GARAGIOLA
☐ 80. RALPH KINER
☐ 147. CLEM KOSHOREK
☐ 160. CAL ABRAMS

ST. LOUIS BROWNS

☐ 2. VIC WERTZ
☐ 20. DON LENHARDT
☐ 52. MARTY MARION(M)
☐ 56. BOB CAIN
☐ 70. CLINT COURTNEY
☐ 111. JIM DYCK
☐ 120. MARLIN STUART
☐ 127. DICK KRYHOSKI

ST. LOUIS CARDINALS

☐ 17. GERRY STALEY
☐ 32. STAN MUSIAL
☐ 49. EDDIE STANKY(M)
☐ 53. DEL RICE
☐ 81. ENOS SLAUGHTER
☐ 85. SOLLY HEMUS
☐ 101. RED SCHOENDIENST
☐ 115. CLOYD BOYER
☐ 140. AL BRAZLE
☐ 142. LARRY MIGGINS

WASHINGTON SENATORS

☐ 15. JIM BUSBY
☐ 22. BOB PORTERFIELD
☐ 24. JACKIE JENSEN
☐ 34. GIL COAN
☐ 77. MICKEY GRASSO

☐ 89. SANDY CONSUEGRA
☐ 109. KEN WOOD
☐ 116. EDDIE YOST
☐ 139. PETE RUNNELS
☐ 141. FRANK SHEA
☐ 152. CLYDE VOLLMER
☐ 159. MICKEY VERNON

1953 BOWMAN (64)
2 1/2" X 3 3/4"
BLACK & WHITE

BOSTON RED SOX

☐ 2. WILLARD NIXON
☐ 11. DICK GERNERT
☐ 24. DEL WILBER
☐ 29. SID HUDSON
☐ 36. JIM PIERSALL
☐ 49. FLOYD BAKER

BROOKLYN DODGERS

☐ 26. PREACHER ROE
☐ 52. RALPH BRANCA
☐ 60. BILLY COX

CHICAGO CUBS

☐ 5. DEE FONDY
☐ 12. RANDY JACKSON
☐ 37. HAL JEFFCOAT
☐ 41. BOB RAMAZZOTTI
☐ 50. DUTCH LEONARD
☐ 56. ROY SMALLEY

CHICAGO WHITE SOX

NO CARDS ISSUED

CINCINATTI REDS

☐ 1. GUS BELL
☐ 7. ANDY SEMINICK
☐ 21. BUD PODBIELAN
☐ 32. ROCKY BRIDGES
☐ 42. HOWIE JUDSON

CLEVELAND INDIANS

☐ 13. JOE TIPTON
☐ 27. BOB LEMON
☐ 63. STEVE GROMEK

DETROIT TIGERS

☐ 4. PAT MULLIN
☐ 18. BILLY HOEFT
☐ 22. MATT BATTS
☐ 44. JIM DELSING

MILWAUKEE BRAVES

☐ 30. WALKER COOPER
☐ 34. EBBA ST. CLAIR
☐ 38. DAVE COLE
☐ 51. LOU BURDETTE
☐ 57. ANDY PAFKO

NEW YORK GIANTS

☐ 3. BILL RIGNEY
☐ 28. HOYT WILHELM
☐ 40. LARRY JANSEN

NEW YORK YANKEES

☐ 15. JOHNNY MIZE
☐ 25. JOHN SAIN
☐ 31. GENE WOODLING
☐ 33. BOB KUZAVA
☐ 39. CASEY STENGEL(M)
☐ 45. IRV NOREN
☐ 54. BILL MILLER
☐ 61. TOM GORMAN

PHILADELPHIA ATHLETICS

☐ 6. RAY MURRAY
☐ 8. PETE SUDER
☐ 20. EDDIE ROBINSON
☐ 43. HAL BEVAN
☐ 53. MORRIS MARTIN
☐ 62. KEITH THOMAS

PHILADELPHIA PHILLIES

☐ 14. BILL NICHOLSON
☐ 35. JOHNNY WYROSTEK
☐ 47. JACK LOHRKE
☐ 48. STEVE RIDZIK
☐ 58. JIM KONSTANTY
☐ 64. ANDY HANSEN

PITTSBURGH PIRATES

☐ 19. PAUL LA PALME

ST. LOUIS BROWNS

- ☐ 17. VIRGIL TRUCKS
- ☐ 59. DUANE PILLETTE

ST. LOUIS CARDINALS

- ☐ 10. DICK SISLER
- ☐ 16. STU MILLER
- ☐ 23. WILMER MIZELL

WASHINGTON SENATORS

- ☐ 9. WALT MASTERSON
- ☐ 46. BUCKY HARRIS(M)
- ☐ 55. DON JOHNSON

1954 BOWMAN (224)
2 1/2″ X 3 3/4″

BALTIMORE ORIOLES

- ☐ 5. BILL HUNTER
- ☐ 21. VIC WERTZ
- ☐ 37. DICK KOKOS
- ☐ 53. DON LENHARDT
- ☐ 69. CLINT COURTNEY
- ☐ 85. JIM DYCK
- ☐ 101. DON LARSEN
- ☐ 117. DICK KRYHOSKI
- ☐ 133. DUANE PILLETTE
- ☐ 149. BOB YOUNG
- ☐ 165. JOHNNY GROTH
- ☐ 181. LES MOSS
- ☐ 197. LOU KRETLOW
- ☐ 213. DICK LITTLEFIELD

BOSTON RED SOX

- ☐ 2. JACKIE JENSEN
- ☐ 18. HOOT EVERS
- ☐ 34. SAMMY WHITE
- ☐ 50. GEORGE KELL
- ☐ 66. TED WILLIAMS
- ☐ 66. JIM PIERSALL
- ☐ 82. BILLY GOODMAN
- ☐ 98. ELLIS KINDER
- ☐ 114. WILLARD NIXON
- ☐ 130. MILT BOLLING
- ☐ 146. DICK GERNERT
- ☐ 162. TED LEPCIO
- ☐ 178. DEL WILBER
- ☐ 194. SID HUDSON
- ☐ 210. JIM PIERSALL

BROOKLYN DODGERS

- ☐ 10. CARL ERSKINE
- ☐ 26. BILLY COX
- ☐ 42. BILLY LOES
- ☐ 58. PEE WEE REESE
- ☐ 74. JIM GILLIAM
- ☐ 90. ROY CAMPANELLA
- ☐ 106. CLEM LABINE
- ☐ 122. CARL FURILLO

- ☐ 138. GIL HODGES
- ☐ 154. DON NEWCOMBE
- ☐ 170. DUKE SNIDER
- ☐ 186. RUSS MEYER
- ☐ 202. GEORGE SHUBA
- ☐ 218. PREACHER ROE

CHICAGO CUBS

- ☐ 13. PAUL MINNER
- ☐ 29. JOHNNY KLIPPSTEIN
- ☐ 45. RALPH KINER
- ☐ 61. EDDIE MIKSIS
- ☐ 77. BOB RUSH
- ☐ 93. BILL SERENA
- ☐ 109. ROY SMALLEY
- ☐ 125. WARREN HACKER
- ☐ 141. JOE GARAGIOLA
- ☐ 157. TURK LOWN
- ☐ 173. DEE FONDY
- ☐ 189. RANDY JACKSON
- ☐ 205. HAL JEFFCOAT
- ☐ 221. FRANK BAUMHOLTZ

CHICAGO WHITE SOX

- ☐ 6. NELSON FOX
- ☐ 22. SAM MELE
- ☐ 38. MINNIE MINOSO
- ☐ 54. CHICO CARRASQUEL
- ☐ 70. WILLARD MARSHALL(B)
- ☐ 86. HARRY DORISH
- ☐ 102. BILLY PIERCE
- ☐ 118. BOB BOYD
- ☐ 134. LUIS ALOMA
- ☐ 150. CASS MICHAELS
- ☐ 166. SANDY CONSUEGRA
- ☐ 182. SHERMAN LOLLAR
- ☐ 198. VIRGIL TRUCKS
- ☐ 214. FERRIS FAIN

CINCINNATI REDS

- ☐ 12. ROY MCMILLAN
- ☐ 28. JIM GREENGRASS
- ☐ 44. HARRY PERKOWSKI
- ☐ 60. FRED BACZEWSKI
- ☐ 70. WILLARD MARSHALL(F)
- ☐ 76. JOE NUXHALL
- ☐ 92. KEN RAFFENSBERGER
- ☐ 108. BOBBY ADAMS
- ☐ 124. GUS BELL
- ☐ 140. SAUL ROGOVIN
- ☐ 156. ROCKY BRIDGES
- ☐ 172. ANDY SEMINICK
- ☐ 188. FRANK SMITH
- ☐ 204. JACKIE COLLUM
- ☐ 220. HOBIE LANDRITH

CLEVELAND INDIANS

- ☐ 4. BOB HOOPER
- ☐ 20. ART HOUTTEMAN
- ☐ 36. GEORGE STRICKLAND
- ☐ 52. JOE GINSBERG
- ☐ 68. BOBBY AVILA
- ☐ 84. LARRY DOBY
- ☐ 100. MIKE GARCIA
- ☐ 116. LUKE EASTER
- ☐ 132. BOB FELLER
- ☐ 148. DALE MITCHELL
- ☐ 164. EARLY WYNN
- ☐ 184. MICKEY GRASSO
- ☐ 196. BOB LEMON
- ☐ 212. OWEN FRIEND

DETROIT TIGERS

- ☐ 7. WALT DROPO
- ☐ 23. HARVEY KUENN
- ☐ 39. NED GARVER
- ☐ 55. JIM DELSING
- ☐ 71. TED GRAY
- ☐ 87. DON LUND
- ☐ 103. STEVE SOUCHOCK
- ☐ 119. FRED HATFIELD
- ☐ 135. JOHNNY PESKY
- ☐ 151. PAT MULLIN
- ☐ 167. BILLY HOEFT
- ☐ 183. MATT BATTS
- ☐ 199. STEVE GROMEK
- ☐ 215. JOHNNY BUCHA

MILWAUKEE BRAVES

- ☐ 16. JIM WILSON
- ☐ 32. DEL CRANDALL
- ☐ 48. JACK DITTMER
- ☐ 64. EDDIE MATHEWS
- ☐ 80. JOHNNY LOGAN
- ☐ 96. JOE ADCOCK
- ☐ 112. ANDY PAFKO
- ☐ 144. ERNIE JOHNSON
- ☐ 160. DANNY O'CONNELL
- ☐ 176. VERN BICKFORD
- ☐ 192. LEW BURDETTE
- ☐ 201. BOBBY THOMSON
- ☐ 224. BILL BRUTON

NEW YORK GIANTS

- ☐ 9. DAVE WILLIAMS
- ☐ 25. WES WESTRUM
- ☐ 41. AL DARK
- ☐ 57. HOYT WILHELM
- ☐ 73. DON MUELLER
- ☐ 89. WILLIE MAYS
- ☐ 105. SAL MAGLIE
- ☐ 121. RAY KATT
- ☐ 128. EBBA ST. CLAIRE
- ☐ 137. AL CORWIN
- ☐ 153. WHITEY LOCKMAN
- ☐ 169. LARRY JANSEN
- ☐ 185. DARYL SPENCER
- ☐ 208. JOHNNY ANTONELLI
- ☐ 217. HANK THOMPSON

NEW YORK YANKEES

- ☐ 1. PHIL RIZZUTO
- ☐ 17. TOM GORMAN
- ☐ 33. VIC RASCHI
- ☐ 49. HARRY BYRD
- ☐ 65. MICKEY MANTLE
- ☐ 81. JERRY COLEMAN
- ☐ 97. GIL MCDOUGALD
- ☐ 113. ALLIE REYNOLDS
- ☐ 129. HANK BAUER
- ☐ 145. BILLY MARTIN
- ☐ 161. YOGI BERRA
- ☐ 177. WHITEY FORD
- ☐ 193. EDDIE ROBINSON
- ☐ 209. GENE WOODLING

PHILADELPHIA ATHLETICS

- ☐ 3. MARION FRICANO
- ☐ 19. BOBBY SHANTZ
- ☐ 35. EDDIE JOOST
- ☐ 51. ALEX KELLNER
- ☐ 67. CARL SCHEIB
- ☐ 83. RAY MURRAY
- ☐ 99. PETE SUDER
- ☐ 115. DON BOLLWEG
- ☐ 131. JOE ASTROTH
- ☐ 147. JOE DEMAESTRI
- ☐ 163. DAVE PHILLEY
- ☐ 179. MORRIS MARTIN
- ☐ 195. BOB CAIN
- ☐ 211. AL ROBERTSON

PHILADELPHIA PHILLIES

- [ ] 15. RICHIE ASHBURN
- [ ] 31. SMOKEY BURGESS
- [ ] 47. GRANNY HAMNER
- [ ] 63. EARL TORGESON
- [ ] 79. CURT SIMMONS
- [ ] 95. ROBIN ROBERTS
- [ ] 111. MURRY DICKSON
- [ ] 127. DEL ENNIS
- [ ] 143. WILLIE JONES
- [ ] 159. JOHNNY LINDELL
- [ ] 175. MEL CLARK
- [ ] 191. KARL DREWS
- [ ] 207. STAN LOPATA
- [ ] 223. STEVE RIDZIK

PITTSBURGH PIRATES

- [ ] 11. SID GORDON
- [ ] 27. DICK COLE
- [ ] 43. BOB FRIEND
- [ ] 59. BOB SCHULTZ
- [ ] 75. MAX SURKONT
- [ ] 91. CAL ABRAMS
- [ ] 107. PAUL LA PALME
- [ ] 123. TOBY ATWELL
- [ ] 139. PRESTON WARD
- [ ] 155. FRANK THOMAS
- [ ] 171. CARLOS BERNIER
- [ ] 187. VERN LAW
- [ ] 203. VIC JANOWICZ
- [ ] 219. HAL RICE

ST. LOUIS CARDINALS

- [ ] 14. GERRY STALEY
- [ ] 30. DEL RICE
- [ ] 46. RIP REPULSKI
- [ ] 62. ENOS SLAUGHTER
- [ ] 78. SAL YVARS
- [ ] 94. SOLLY HEMUS
- [ ] 110. RED SCHOENDIENST
- [ ] 126. CLIFF CHAMBERS
- [ ] 142. AL BRAZLE
- [ ] 158. STU MILLER
- [ ] 174. PETE CASTIGLIONE
- [ ] 190. JOE PRESKO
- [ ] 206. STEVE BILKO
- [ ] 222. MEMO LUNA

WASHINGTON SENATORS

- [ ] 8. JIM BUSBY
- [ ] 24. BOB PORTERFIELD
- [ ] 40. GIL COAN
- [ ] 56. MICKEY MCDERMOTT
- [ ] 72. EDDIE YOST
- [ ] 88. TOM UMPHLETT
- [ ] 104. FRANK SHEA
- [ ] 120. MEL HODERLEIN
- [ ] 136. CLYDE VOLLMER
- [ ] 152. MICKEY VERNON
- [ ] 168. ED FITZ GERALD
- [ ] 180. JOE TIPTON
- [ ] 200. CONNIE MARRERO
- [ ] 216. JERRY SNYDER

1955 BOWMAN (320)
2 1/2" X 3 3/4"

BALTIMORE ORIOLES

- [ ] 3. JOE COLEMAN
- [ ] 4. EDDIE WAITKUS
- [ ] 55. CAL ABRAMS
- [ ] 56. BILLY COX
- [ ] 77. JIM MCDONALD
- [ ] 78. GIL COAN
- [ ] 79. WILLIE MIRANDA
- [ ] 101. DON JOHNSON
- [ ] 108. LOU KRETLOW
- [ ] 109. VERN STEPHENS
- [ ] 159. HARRY BYRD
- [ ] 161. MATT BATTS
- [ ] 162. CHARLIE MAXWELL
- [ ] 215. BOB KUZAVA
- [ ] 216. PREACHER ROE
- [ ] 225. PAUL RICHARDS(M)
- [ ] 241. JOHN PESKY
- [ ] 244. DUANE PILLETTE
- [ ] 245. BILL MILLER

BOSTON RED SOX

- [ ] 15. FRANK SULLIVAN
- [ ] 16. JIM PIERSALL
- [ ] 47. SAMMY WHITE
- [ ] 48. MILT BOLLING
- [ ] 126. BILLY GOODMAN
- [ ] 147. SAM MELE
- [ ] 150. BILL KLAUS
- [ ] 177. WILLARD NIXON
- [ ] 178. TOM BREWER
- [ ] 221. HECTOR BROWN
- [ ] 222. RUSS KEMMERER
- [ ] 256. OWEN FRIEND
- [ ] 264. BILL R. HENRY
- [ ] 276. IVAN DELOCK
- [ ] 290. HERSHELL FREEMAN
- [ ] 302. FRANK MALZONE
- [ ] 318. SID HUDSON
- [ ] 319. AL SCHROLL
- [ ] 320. GEORGE SUSCE

BROOKLYN DODGERS

- [ ] 21. DON HOAK
- [ ] 22. ROY CAMPANELLA
- [ ] 37. PEE WEE REESE
- [ ] 39. BOB DARNELL
- [ ] 65. DON ZIMMER
- [ ] 66. GEORGE SHUBA
- [ ] 97. JOHNNY PODRES
- [ ] 98. JIM GILLIAM
- [ ] 143. DON NEWCOMBE
- [ ] 156. JIM HUGHES
- [ ] 158. GIL HODGES
- [ ] 169. CARL FURILLO
- [ ] 170. CARL ERSKINE
- [ ] 195. ERV PALICA
- [ ] 196. RUSS MEYER
- [ ] 240. BILLY LOES
- [ ] 261. WALT MORYN
- [ ] 270. CHICO FERNANDEZ
- [ ] 278. CHARLIE NEAL
- [ ] 310. KEN LEHMAN

CHICAGO CUBS

- [ ] 7. GENE BAKER
- [ ] 8. WARREN HACKER
- [ ] 52. HAL RICE
- [ ] 87. RANDY JACKSON
- [ ] 88. STEVE BILKO
- [ ] 137. BOB TALBOT
- [ ] 181. EDDIE MIKSIS
- [ ] 182. BOB RUSH
- [ ] 223. HAL JEFFCOAT
- [ ] 224. DEE FONDY
- [ ] 227. FRANK BAUMHOLTZ
- [ ] 229. JIM BROSNAN
- [ ] 242. ERNIE BANKS
- [ ] 247. DUTCH LEONARD(C)
- [ ] 273. BUBBA CHURCH
- [ ] 280. CLYDE MCCULLOUGH
- [ ] 304. HARRY CHITI

CHICAGO WHITE SOX

- [ ] 25. MINNIE MINOSO
- [ ] 26. VIRGIL TRUCKS
- [ ] 33. NELSON FOX
- [ ] 34. CLINT COURTNEY
- [ ] 85. CASS MICHAELS
- [ ] 86. TED GRAY
- [ ] 116. SANDY CONSUEGRA
- [ ] 117. JOHNNY GROTH
- [ ] 131. WILLARD MARSHALL
- [ ] 135. LLOYD MERRIMAN
- [ ] 145. BOB NIEMAN
- [ ] 148. BOB CHAKALES
- [ ] 151. JIM BRIDEWESER
- [ ] 173. CHICO CARRASQUEL
- [ ] 174. SHERMAN LOLLAR
- [ ] 213. GEORGE KELL
- [ ] 214. BILLY PIERCE
- [ ] 230. AL BRAZLE
- [ ] 233. BILL SERENA
- [ ] 248. HARRY DORISH
- [ ] 251. STAN JOK
- [ ] 266. MIKE FORNIELES
- [ ] 282. PHIL CAVARRETTA
- [ ] 285. WALT DROPO

CINCINNATI REDS

- [ ] 31. JOHNNY TEMPLE
- [ ] 32. WALLY POST
- [ ] 49. JIM GREENGRASS
- [ ] 50. HOBIE LANDRITH
- [ ] 51. ELVIN TAPPE
- [ ] 93. ANDY SEMINICK
- [ ] 118. BOBBY ADAMS
- [ ] 136. ROCKY BRIDGES
- [ ] 152. JOHNNY KLIPPSTEIN
- [ ] 155. GERRY STALEY
- [ ] 189. JACK COLLUM
- [ ] 190. FRED BACZEWSKI
- [ ] 193. HOWIE JUDSON
- [ ] 194. JOE NUXHALL
- [ ] 232. BIRDIE TEBBETTS(M)
- [ ] 234. DICK BARTELL(C)
- [ ] 243. GUS BELL

CLEVELAND INDIANS

- [ ] 19. BOBBY AVILA
- [ ] 20. AL SMITH
- [ ] 38. EARLY WYNN
- [ ] 40. VIC WERTZ
- [ ] 96. RAY NARLESKI
- [ ] 127. HANK MAJESKI

☐ 128. MIKE GARCIA
☐ 129. HAL NARAGON
☐ 134. BOB FELLER
☐ 142. RUDY REGALADO
☐ 144. ART HOUTTEMAN
☐ 191. BOB LEMON
☐ 192. GEORGE STRICKLAND
☐ 197. RALPH KINER
☐ 198. DAVE POPE
☐ 259. DON MOSSI
☐ 263. EDDIE JOOST
☐ 271. BOB HOOPER
☐ 308. AL LOPEZ(M)
☐ 312. BILL WIGHT
☐ 314. DALE MITCHELL

DETROIT TIGERS

☐ 23. AL KALINE
☐ 24. AL ABER
☐ 35. BILL TUTTLE
☐ 36. WAYNE BELARDI
☐ 91. DICK MARLOWE
☐ 92. GEORGE ZUVERINK
☐ 121. RUFUS CRAWFORD
☐ 132. HARVEY KUENN
☐ 133. CHARLES KING
☐ 154. FRANK LARY
☐ 187. FRED HATFIELD
☐ 188. NED GARVER
☐ 203. STEVE GROMEK
☐ 204. FRANK BOLLING
☐ 228. BUBBA PHILLIPS
☐ 254. BENNETT FLOWERS
☐ 274. JIM DELSING

KANSAS CITY ATHLETICS

☐ 5. JIM ROBERTSON
☐ 6. PETE SUDER
☐ 53. ALEX KELLNER
☐ 54. DON BOLLWEG
☐ 80. LOU LIMMER
☐ 89. LOU BOUDREAU(M)
☐ 90. ART DITMAR
☐ 119. JOE ASTROTH
☐ 120. ED BURTSCHY
☐ 140. BOBBY SHANTZ
☐ 149. CLOYD BOYER
☐ 175. BILLY SHANTZ
☐ 176. JOE DEMAESTRI
☐ 211. SONNY DIXON
☐ 316. MARION FRICANO

MILWAUKEE BRAVES

☐ 11. BILLY BRUTON
☐ 12. ANDY PAFKO
☐ 43. BOB BUHL
☐ 44. DANNY O'CONNELL
☐ 70. LOU BURDETTE
☐ 71. DAVE JOLLY
☐ 72. CHET NICHOLS
☐ 102. BOBBY THOMSON
☐ 103. EDDIE MATHEWS
☐ 157. ERNIE JOHNSON
☐ 179. HANK AARON
☐ 180. JOHNNY LOGAN
☐ 212. JACK DITTMER
☐ 217. DEL CRANDALL
☐ 218. JOE ADCOCK
☐ 252. ROY SMALLEY
☐ 253. JIM WILSON
☐ 298. CHARLIE GRIMM(M)

AARON

NEW YORK GIANTS

☐ 1. HOYT WILHELM
☐ 2. AL DARK
☐ 94. HANK THOMPSON
☐ 95. SAL MAGLIE
☐ 122. AL CORWIN
☐ 123. MARV GRISSOM
☐ 124. JOHNNY ANTONELLI
☐ 125. PAUL GIEL
☐ 138. DAVEY WILLIAMS
☐ 141. WES WESTRUM
☐ 146. DON LIDDLE
☐ 183. RAY KATT
☐ 184. WILLIE MAYS
☐ 219. WHITEY LOCKMAN
☐ 220. JIM HEARN
☐ 249. BILLY GARDNER
☐ 269. JOE AMALFITANO

NEW YORK YANKEES

☐ 9. GIL MCDOUGALD
☐ 10. PHIL RIZZUTO
☐ 59. WHITEY FORD
☐ 60. ENOS SLAUGHTER
☐ 63. IRV NOREN
☐ 67. DON LARSEN
☐ 68. ELSTON HOWARD
☐ 69. BILL HUNTER
☐ 99. JERRY COLEMAN
☐ 100. TOM MORGAN
☐ 153. EDDIE ROBINSON
☐ 160. BILL SKOWRON
☐ 167. BOB GRIM
☐ 168. YOGI BERRA
☐ 201. ALLIE REYNOLDS
☐ 202. MICKEY MANTLE
☐ 231. JIM KONSTANTY
☐ 246. HANK BAUER
☐ 300. TOMMY BYRNE
☐ 306. BOB CERV

PHILADELPHIA PHILLIES

☐ 17. DEL ENNIS
☐ 18. STAN LOPATA
☐ 41. MEL CLARK
☐ 42. BOB GREENWOOD
☐ 64. CURT SIMMONS
☐ 81. BOB MORGAN
☐ 110. BOB J. MILLER
☐ 111. STEVE RIDZIK
☐ 112. GRANNY HAMNER
☐ 130. RICHIE ASHBURN
☐ 171. ROBIN ROBERTS
☐ 172. WILLIE JONES
☐ 209. SMOKY BURGESS
☐ 210. EARL TORGESON
☐ 236. MURRAY DICKSON
☐ 237. JOHNNY WYROSTEK
☐ 287. RON MROZINSKI
☐ 292. MARV BLAYLOCK
☐ 294. WALLY MOSES(C)

PITTSBURGH PIRATES

☐ 27. PRESTON WARD
☐ 28. DICK COLE
☐ 57. BOB FRIEND
☐ 58. FRANK THOMAS
☐ 82. LEE WALLS
☐ 83. MAX SURKONT
☐ 84. GEORGE FREESE
☐ 113. BOB HALL
☐ 114. VIC JANOWICZ
☐ 115. ROGER BOWMAN
☐ 163. SID GORDON
☐ 164. TOBY ATWELL
☐ 199. VERNON LAW
☐ 200. DICK LITTLEFIELD
☐ 288. DICK SMITH

ST. LOUIS CARDINALS

☐ 29. RED SCHOENDIENST
☐ 30. BILL SARNI
☐ 61. PAUL LAPALME
☐ 62. ROYCE LINT
☐ 75. BROOKS LAWRENCE

☐ 76. TOM POHOLSKY
☐ 106. DEL RICE
☐ 107. SOLLY HEMUS
☐ 185. VIC RASCHI
☐ 186. ALEX GRAMMAS
☐ 205. RIP REPULSKI
☐ 206. RALPH BEARD
☐ 238. EDDIE STANKY(M)
☐ 257. TOM ALSTON
☐ 296. BILL VIRDON

WASHINGTON SENATORS

☐ 13. CLYDE VOLLMER
☐ 14. GUS KERIAZAKOS
☐ 45. TOM UMPHLETT
☐ 46. MICKEY VERNON
☐ 73. EDDIE YOST
☐ 74. JERRY SNYDER
☐ 104. BOB PORTERFIELD
☐ 105. JOHNNY SCHMITZ
☐ 165. MICKEY MCDERMOTT
☐ 166. JIM BUSBY
☐ 207. FRANK SHEA
☐ 208. ED FITZ GERALD
☐ 255. PETE RUNNELS
☐ 262. JIM LEMON
☐ 268. ROY HAWES

1934–36 DIAMOND STARS (108)
2 3/8" X 2 7/8"

The National Chicle Diamond Stars baseball cards were released over a period of three years. Some of the players changed teams during that period of time; consequently, some of the cards in the lists below appear with more than one team.

MAX BISHOP

BOSTON BRAVES

☐ 3. WALTER (RABBIT) MARANVILLE
☐ 20. FRANCIS (FRANK) HOGAN
☐ 25. WALTER (WALLY) BERGER
☐ 37. BILL URBANSKI
☐ 49. BAXTER (BUCK) JORDAN
☐ 62. FRED FRANKHOUSE
☐ 82. JOHNNY BABICH
☐ 108. WALTER BERGER

BOSTON RED SOX

☐ 1. LEFTY GROVE
☐ 6. MAX BISHOP
☐ 30. HENRY (HEINIE) MANUSH
☐ 48. RICK FERRELL

1934-36 Diamond Stars

☐ 61. BILLY WERBER
☐ 73. FRED (FRITZ) OSTERMUELLER
☐ 94. WES FERRELL

BROOKLYN DODGERS

☐ 19. VAN MUNGO
☐ 28. AL LOPEZ
☐ 55. TONY CUCCINELLO
☐ 68. SAM LESLIE
☐ 82. JOHNNY BABICH
☐ 89. JOE STRIPP
☐ 97. AL LOPEZ
☐ 102. VAN MUNGO

CHICAGO CUBS

☐ 31. HAZEN (KIKI) CUYLER
☐ 34. STANLEY HACK
☐ 52. GEORGE STAINBACK
☐ 107. STANLEY HACK

CHICAGO WHITE SOX

☐ 2. AL SIMMONS
☐ 7. LEW FONSECA
☐ 42. JIMMY DYKES
☐ 43. TED LYONS
☐ 51. JOHN WHITEHEAD
☐ 65. HENRY (ZEKE) BONURA
☐ 72. ANTHONY (TONY) PIET
☐ 95. LUKE APPLING

CINCINNATI REDS

☐ 18. CHARLES (CHICK) HAFEY
☐ 24. EARL (SPARKY) ADAMS
☐ 31. KIKI CUYLER
☐ 36. ERNEST (ERNIE) LOMBARDI
☐ 46. CHARLES (RED) LUCAS
☐ 59. JIMMY BOTTOMLEY
☐ 84. SAM BYRD
☐ 96. LEW RIGGS
☐ 105. ERNEST (ERNIE) LOMBARDI
☐ 106. CHARLES (RED) LUCAS

CLEVELAND INDIANS

☐ 2. JOE VOSMIK
☐ 13. GEORGE BLAEHOLDER
☐ 32. EDGAR (SAM) RICE
☐ 35. EARL AVERILL
☐ 58. GLENN MYATT
☐ 70. HAROLD (HAL) TROSKY
☐ 79. WILLIS HUDLIN
☐ 87. STEVE O'NEIL
☐ 100. EARL AVERILL

DETROIT TIGERS

☐ 2. AL SIMMONS
☐ 5. TOM BRIDGES
☐ 9. GORDON (MICKEY) COCHRANE
☐ 33. LYNWOOD (SCHOOLBOY) ROWE
☐ 45. JOYNER (JO-JO) WHITE
☐ 54. HANK GREENBERG
☐ 67. MARVIN OWEN
☐ 76. BILL ROGELL
☐ 77. CHARLEY GEHRINGER
☐ 90. RAY HAYWORTH
☐ 93. ALVIN CROWDER
☐ 98. LYNWOOD (SCHOOLBOY) ROWE

NEW YORK GIANTS

☐ 14. BILL TERRY
☐ 15. DICK BARTELL
☐ 21. JOHNNY VERGES
☐ 39. CARL HUBBELL
☐ 50. MEL OTT
☐ 63. TRAVIS JACKSON
☐ 101. DICK BARTELL

NEW YORK YANKEES

☐ 11. BILL DICKEY
☐ 12. FRED (DIXIE) WALKER
☐ 29. ROBERT (RED) ROLFE
☐ 38. WILLIAM (BEN) CHAPMAN
☐ 60. CHARLES (RED) RUFFING
☐ 74. ANTHONY (TONY) LAZZERI
☐ 86. FRANK CROSETTI
☐ 88. GEORGE SELKIRK
☐ 103. BILL DICKEY
☐ 104. ROBERT (RED) ROLFE

PHILADELPHIA ATHLETICS

☐ 10. ROY MAHAFFEY
☐ 64. JIMMIE ("Y") FOXX

PHILADELPHIA PHILLIES

☐ 15. DICK BARTELL
☐ 21. JOHNNY VERGES
☐ 22. JIMMIE WILSON
☐ 40. JOHN (BLONDY) RYAN
☐ 41. HARVEY HENDRICK
☐ 80. LOU CHIOZZA
☐ 92. ETHAN ALLEN

PITTSBURGH PIRATES

☐ 16. LLOYD WANER
☐ 27. HAROLD (PIE) TRAYNOR
☐ 56. AUGUST (GUS) SUHR
☐ 57. DARRELL (CY) BLANTON
☐ 69. EARL GRACE

☐ 83. PAUL WANER
☐ 99. HAROLD (PIE) TRAYNOR

ST. LOUIS BROWNS

☐ 10. ROY MAHAFFEY
☐ 13. GEORGE BLAEHOLDER
☐ 44. ROGERS HORNSBY
☐ 53. OSCAR MELILLO
☐ 75. IRVING (JACK) BURNS
☐ 85. JULIUS SOLTERS

ROGERS HORNSBY

ST. LOUIS CARDINALS

☐ 17. FRANK FRISCH
☐ 23. BILL HALLAHAN
☐ 26. JOHN (PEPPER) MARTIN
☐ 66. JOSEPH (DUCKY) MEDWICK
☐ 81. BILL DELANCEY

WASHINGTON SENATORS

☐ 4. CHARLES (BUDDY) MEYER
☐ 30. HENRY (HEINIE) MANUSH
☐ 47. CLIFF BOLTON
☐ 71. OSWALD (OSSIE) BLUEGE
☐ 78. JOE KUHEL
☐ 91. BUCKY HARRIS

1981 DONRUSS (605)
2 1/2″ X 3 1/2″

FLOYD BANNISTER PITCHER

ATLANTA BRAVES

- ☐ 66. JEFF BURROUGHS
- ☐ 77. GENE GARBER
- ☐ 88. LUIS GOMEZ
- ☐ 99. BOB HORNER
- ☐ 186. BRIAN ASSELSTINE
- ☐ 197. RICK CAMP
- ☐ 208. BRUCE BENEDICT
- ☐ 219. CHRIS CHAMBLISS
- ☐ 306. GARY MATTHEWS
- ☐ 317. RICK MATULA
- ☐ 328. PHIL NIEKRO
- ☐ 339. JERRY ROYSTER
- ☐ 426. BOBBY COX(M)
- ☐ 437. DALE MURPHY
- ☐ 448. DOYLE ALEXANDER
- ☐ 459. GLENN HUBBARD
- ☐ 523. PRESTON HANNA
- ☐ 550. AL HRABOSKY
- ☐ 584. LARRY BRADFORD
- ☐ 597. TOMMY BOGGS

BALTIMORE ORIOLES

- ☐ 112. EDDIE MURRAY
- ☐ 113. RICK DEMPSEY
- ☐ 114. SCOTT MCGREGOR
- ☐ 115. KEN SINGLETON
- ☐ 116. GARY ROENICKE
- ☐ 232. RICH DAUER
- ☐ 233. DAN GRAHAM
- ☐ 234. MIKE FLANAGAN
- ☐ 235. JOHN LOWENSTEIN
- ☐ 236. BENNY AYALA
- ☐ 352. DOUG DECINCES
- ☐ 353. JIM PALMER
- ☐ 354. TIPPY MARTINEZ
- ☐ 355. AL BUMBRY
- ☐ 356. EARL WEAVER(M)
- ☐ 472. MARK BELANDER
- ☐ 473. JIM PALMER
- ☐ 474. SAMMY STEWART
- ☐ 475. TIM STODDARD
- ☐ 476. STEVE STONE
- ☐ 499. LENN SAKATA
- ☐ 507. TERRY CROWLEY
- ☐ 514. KIKO GARCIA
- ☐ 533. DENNIS MARTINEZ
- ☐ 552. DAVE FORD
- ☐ 600. H. PAT KELLY

BOSTON RED SOX

- ☐ 94. CARL YASTRZEMSKI
- ☐ 95. GLENN HOFFMAN
- ☐ 96. DENNIS ECKERSLEY
- ☐ 97. TOM BURGMEIER
- ☐ 98. WIN REMMERSWAAL
- ☐ 214. CARL YASTRZEMSKI
- ☐ 215. JERRY REMY
- ☐ 216. MIKE TORREZ
- ☐ 217. SKIP LOCKWOOD
- ☐ 218. FRED LYNN

- ☐ 334. TONY PEREZ
- ☐ 335. CARLTON FISK
- ☐ 336. DICK DRAGO
- ☐ 337. STEVE RENKO
- ☐ 338. JIM RICE
- ☐ 454. RICK BURLESON
- ☐ 455. GARY ALLENSON
- ☐ 456. BOB STANLEY
- ☐ 457. JOHN TUDOR
- ☐ 458. DWIGHT EVANS
- ☐ 512. DAVE RADER
- ☐ 544. DAVE STAPLETON
- ☐ 577. JIM DWYER

CALIFORNIA ANGELS

- ☐ 49. ROD CAREW
- ☐ 50. BERT CAMPANERIS
- ☐ 51. TOM DONOHUE
- ☐ 52. DAVE FROST
- ☐ 53. ED HALICKI
- ☐ 54. DAN FORD
- ☐ 169. ROD CAREW
- ☐ 170. FRED PATEK
- ☐ 171. FRANK TANANA
- ☐ 172. ALFREDO MARTINEZ
- ☐ 173. CHRIS KNAPP
- ☐ 174. JOE RUDI
- ☐ 289. BOBBY GRICH
- ☐ 290. DICKIE THON
- ☐ 291. MARK CLEAR
- ☐ 292. DAVE LEMANCZYK
- ☐ 293. JASON THOMPSON
- ☐ 294. RICK MILLER
- ☐ 409. CARNEY LANSFORD
- ☐ 410. BRIAN DOWNING
- ☐ 411. DON AASE
- ☐ 412. JIM BARR
- ☐ 413. DON BAYLOR
- ☐ 414. JIM FREGOSI(M)
- ☐ 532. GEOFF ZAHN
- ☐ 542. BUTCH HOBSON
- ☐ 572. BOBBY CLARK
- ☐ 581. ANDY HASSLER

CHICAGO CUBS

- ☐ 482. BILL BUCKNER
- ☐ 483. IVAN DEJESUS
- ☐ 485. LENNY RANDLE
- ☐ 501. STEVE DILLAR
- ☐ 513. MICK KELLEHER
- ☐ 515. LARRY BIITTNER
- ☐ 519. SCOT THOMPSON
- ☐ 520. JIM TRACY
- ☐ 521. CARLOS LEZCANO
- ☐ 522. JOE AMALFITANO(M)
- ☐ 535. STEVE MACKO
- ☐ 551. DICK TIDROW
- ☐ 553. DAVE KINGMAN
- ☐ 558. BARRY FOOTE
- ☐ 559. TIM BLACKWELL
- ☐ 561. RICK REUSCHEL
- ☐ 562. LYNN MCGLOTHEN
- ☐ 573. DENNIS LAMP
- ☐ 586. BILL CAUDILL
- ☐ 587. DOUG CAPILLA
- ☐ 588. GEORGE RILEY
- ☐ 589. WILLIE HERNANDEZ

CHICAGO WHITE SOX

- ☐ 38. LAMAR JOHNSON
- ☐ 39. KEVIN BELL
- ☐ 40. ED FARMER
- ☐ 41. ROSS BAUMGARTEN
- ☐ 42. LEO SUTHERLAND
- ☐ 158. JIM MORRISON
- ☐ 159. GLENN BORGMANN
- ☐ 160. LAMARR HOYT
- ☐ 161. RICH WORTHAM
- ☐ 162. THAD BOSLEY
- ☐ 278. GREG PRYOR
- ☐ 279. BRITT BURNS
- ☐ 280. RICH DOTSON
- ☐ 281. CHET LEMON
- ☐ 282. RUSTY KUNTZ
- ☐ 398. MIKE SQUIRES
- ☐ 399. MARVIS FOLEY
- ☐ 400. STEVE TROUT

- ☐ 401. WAYNE NORDHAGEN
- ☐ 402. TONY LARUSSA(M)
- ☐ 503. JIM ESSIAN
- ☐ 576. RON LEFLORE
- ☐ 596. MIKE PROLY

CINCINNATI REDS

- ☐ 61. RAY KNIGHT
- ☐ 62. JOHNNY BENCH
- ☐ 63. MARIO SOTO
- ☐ 64. DOUG BAIR
- ☐ 65. GEORGE FOSTER
- ☐ 181. DAVE CONCEPCION
- ☐ 182. JOHNNY BENCH
- ☐ 183. MIKE LACOSS
- ☐ 184. KEN GRIFFEY
- ☐ 185. DAVE COLLINS
- ☐ 301. DAN DRIESSEN
- ☐ 302. JOE NOLAN
- ☐ 303. PAUL HOUSEHOLDER
- ☐ 304. HARRY SPILMAN
- ☐ 305. CESAR GERONIMO
- ☐ 421. CHARLIE LEIBRANDT
- ☐ 422. TOM SEAVER
- ☐ 423. RON OESTER
- ☐ 424. JUNIOR KENNEDY
- ☐ 425. TOM SEAVER
- ☐ 554. MIKE VAIL

CLEVELAND INDIANS

- ☐ 78. MIKE HARGROVE
- ☐ 79. DAVE ROSELLO
- ☐ 80. RON HASSEY
- ☐ 81. SID MONGE
- ☐ 82. JOE CHARBONEAU
- ☐ 198. ANDRE THORNTON
- ☐ 199. TOM VERYZER
- ☐ 200. GARY ALEXANDER
- ☐ 201. RICK WAITS
- ☐ 202. RICK MANNING
- ☐ 318. TOBY HARRAH
- ☐ 319. DUANE KUIPER
- ☐ 320. LEN BARKER
- ☐ 321. VICTOR CRUZ
- ☐ 322. DELL ALSTON
- ☐ 438. JERRY DYBZINSKI
- ☐ 439. JORGE ORTA
- ☐ 440. WAYNE GARLAND
- ☐ 441. MIGUEL DILONE
- ☐ 442. DAVE GARCIA(M)
- ☐ 517. BO DIAZ

DETROIT TIGERS

- ☐ 5. ALAN TRAMMELL
- ☐ 6. TOM BROOKENS
- ☐ 7. DUFFY DYER
- ☐ 8. MARK FIDRYCH
- ☐ 9. DAVE ROZEMA
- ☐ 10. RICKY PETERS
- ☐ 125. RICHIE HEBNER
- ☐ 126. MARK WAGNER
- ☐ 127. JACK MORRIS
- ☐ 128. DAN PETRY
- ☐ 129. BRUCE ROBBINS
- ☐ 130. CHAMP SUMMERS
- ☐ 245. JOHN WOCKENFUSS
- ☐ 246. STAN PAPI
- ☐ 247. MILT WILCOX
- ☐ 248. DAN SCHATZEDER
- ☐ 249. STEVE KEMP
- ☐ 250. JIM LENTINE
- ☐ 365. LOU WHITAKER
- ☐ 366. LANCE PARRISH
- ☐ 367. TIM CORCORAN
- ☐ 368. PAT UNDERWOOD
- ☐ 369. AL COWENS
- ☐ 370. SPARKY ANDERSON(M)

HOUSTON ASTROS

- ☐ 18. JOE MORGAN
- ☐ 19. RAFAEL LANDESTOY
- ☐ 20. BRUCE BOCHY
- ☐ 21. JOE SAMBITO
- ☐ 23. DAVE SMITH
- ☐ 24. TERRY PUHL
- ☐ 138. ENOS CABELL

☐ 139. DAVE BERGMAN
☐ 140. J.R. RICHARD
☐ 141. KEN FORSCH
☐ 143. FRANK LACORTE
☐ 144. DENNIS WALLING
☐ 258. ART HOWE
☐ 259. ALAN ASHBY
☐ 260. NOLAN RYAN
☐ 261. VERN RUHLE
☐ 263. CESAR CEDENO
☐ 264. JEFF LEONARD
☐ 378. CRAIG REYNOLDS
☐ 379. LUIS PUJOLS
☐ 380. JOE NIEKRO
☐ 381. JOAQUIN ANDUJAR
☐ 383. JOSE CRUZ
☐ 384. BILL VIRDON(M)
☐ 490. DAVE W. ROBERTS

KANSAS CITY ROYALS

☐ 100. GEORGE BRETT
☐ 101. DAVE CHALK
☐ 102. DENNIS LEONARD
☐ 103. RENIE MARTIN
☐ 104. AMOS OTIS
☐ 220. WILLIE AIKENS
☐ 221. JOHN WATHAN
☐ 222. DAN QUISENBERRY
☐ 223. WILLIE WILSON
☐ 224. CLINT HURDLE
☐ 340. FRANK WHITE
☐ 341. JAMIE QUIRK
☐ 342. PAUL SPLITTORFF
☐ 343. MARTY PATTIN
☐ 344. PETE LACOCK
☐ 460. U.L. WASHINGTON
☐ 461. LARRY GURA
☐ 462. RICH GALE
☐ 463. HAL MCRAE
☐ 464. JIM FREY(M)
☐ 504. RANCE MULLINIKS

STEVE GARVEY FIRST BASE

LOS ANGELES DODGERS

☐ 56. STEVE GARVEY
☐ 57. BILL RUSSELL
☐ 58. DON SUTTON
☐ 59. REGGIE SMITH
☐ 60. RICK MONDAY
☐ 176. STEVE GARVEY
☐ 177. JOE FERGUSON
☐ 178. BOB WELCH
☐ 179. DUSTY BAKER
☐ 180. RUDY LAW
☐ 296. RON CEY
☐ 297. STEVE YEAGER
☐ 298. BOBBY CASTILLO
☐ 299. MANNY MOTA
☐ 300. JAY JOHNSTONE
☐ 416. DAVE LOPES
☐ 417. JERRY REUSS
☐ 418. RICK SUTCLIFFE
☐ 419. DERREL THOMAS
☐ 420. TOM LASORDA(M)
☐ 511. STEVE HOWE
☐ 526. MICKEY HATCHER
☐ 534. GARY THOMASSON
☐ 541. BURT HOOTON
☐ 557. DON STANHOUSE

MILWAUKEE BREWERS

☐ 83. CECIL COOPER
☐ 84. SAL BANDO
☐ 85. MOOSE HAAS
☐ 86. MIKE CALDWELL
☐ 87. LARRY HISLE
☐ 203. PAUL MOLITOR
☐ 204. JIM GANTNER
☐ 205. PAUL MITCHELL
☐ 206. REGGIE CLEVELAND
☐ 207. SIXTO LEZCANO
☐ 323. ROBIN YOUNT
☐ 324. CHARLIE MOORE
☐ 325. LARY SORENSEN
☐ 326. GORMAN THOMAS
☐ 327. BOB RODGERS(M)
☐ 443. DON MONEY
☐ 444. BUCK MARTINEZ
☐ 445. JERRY AUGUSTINE
☐ 446. BEN OGLIVIE
☐ 447. JIM SLATON
☐ 508. BILL TRAVERS
☐ 510. BOB MCCLURE
☐ 528. DICK DAVIS
☐ 578. BILL CASTRO

MINNESOTA TWINS

☐ 487. ROY SMALLEY
☐ 488. JOHN CASTINO
☐ 489. RON JACKSON
☐ 492. MIKE CUBBAGE
☐ 493. ROB WILFONG
☐ 494. DANNY GOODWIN
☐ 495. JOSE MORALES
☐ 527. JOHN GORYL(M)
☐ 529. BUTCH WYNEGAR
☐ 530. SAL BUTERA
☐ 531. JERRY KOOSMAN
☐ 546. DOUG CORBETT
☐ 547. DARRELL JACKSON
☐ 548. PETE REDFERN
☐ 549. ROGER ERICKSON
☐ 564. JOHN VERHOEVEN
☐ 565. KEN LANDREAUX
☐ 566. GLENN ADAMS
☐ 567. HOSKEN POWELL
☐ 592. RICK SOFIELD
☐ 593. BOMBO RIVERA
☐ 594. GARY WARD

MONTREAL EXPOS

☐ 89. LARRY PARRISH
☐ 90. GARY CARTER
☐ 91. BILL GULLICKSON
☐ 92. FRED NORMAN
☐ 93. TOMMY HUTTON
☐ 209. RODNEY SCOTT
☐ 210. JOHN TAMARGO
☐ 211. BILL LEE
☐ 212. ANDRE DAWSON
☐ 213. ROWLAND OFFICE
☐ 329. CHRIS SPEIER
☐ 330. STEVE ROGERS
☐ 331. WOODIE FRYMAN
☐ 332. WARREN CROMARTIE
☐ 333. JERRY WHITE
☐ 449. TONY BERNAZARD
☐ 450. SCOTT SANDERSON
☐ 451. DAVE PALMER
☐ 452. STAN BAHNSEN
☐ 453. DICK WILLIAMS(M)
☐ 538. TIM RAINES
☐ 540. KEN MACHA
☐ 545. BOB PATE
☐ 599. ELIAS SOSA

NEW YORK METS

☐ 34. LEE MAZZILLI
☐ 35. JOHN STEARNS
☐ 36. ROY JACKSON
☐ 37. MIKE SCOTT
☐ 154. FRANK TAVERAS
☐ 155. CRAIG SWAN
☐ 156. JEFF REARDON
☐ 157. STEVE HENDERSON
☐ 274. MIKE JORGENSEN
☐ 275. PAT ZACHRY

☐ 276. NEIL ALLEN
☐ 277. JOEL YOUNGBLOOD
☐ 394. DOUG FLYNN
☐ 395. PETE FALCONE
☐ 396. TOM HAUSMAN
☐ 397. ELLIOTT MADDOX
☐ 506. JOE TORRE(M)
☐ 524. RAY BURRIS
☐ 575. MOOKIE WILSON

NEW YORK YANKEES

☐ 105. GRAIG NETTLES
☐ 106. ERIC SODERHOLM
☐ 107. TOMMY JOHN
☐ 108. TOM UNDERWOOD
☐ 109. LOU PINIELLA
☐ 111. BOBBY MURCER
☐ 225. BOB WATSON
☐ 226. JIM SPENCER
☐ 227. RON GUIDRY
☐ 228. REGGIE JACKSON
☐ 229. OSCAR GAMBLE
☐ 231. LUIS TIANT
☐ 345. WILLIE RANDOLPH
☐ 346. RICK CERONE
☐ 347. RICH GOSSAGE
☐ 348. REGGIE JACKSON
☐ 349. RUPPERT JONES
☐ 351. YOGI BERRA(C)
☐ 465. BUCKY DENT
☐ 466. DENNIS WERTH
☐ 467. RON DAVIS
☐ 468. REGGIE JACKSON
☐ 469. BOBBY BROWN
☐ 471. GAYLORD PERRY
☐ 486. LARRY MILBOURNE
☐ 500. GENE MICHAEL(M)
☐ 571. JOE LEFEBVRE

OAKLAND A'S

☐ 110. MICKEY KLUTTS
☐ 117. DAVE REVERING
☐ 118. MIKE NORRIS
☐ 119. RICKEY HENDERSON
☐ 120. MIKE HEATH
☐ 230. JEFF COX
☐ 237. WAYNE GROSS
☐ 238. RICK LANGFORD
☐ 239. TONY ARMAS
☐ 240. BOB LACEY
☐ 350. DAVE MCKAY
☐ 357. ROB PICCIOLO
☐ 358. MATT KEOUGH
☐ 359. DWAYNE MURPHY
☐ 360. BRIAN KINGMAN
☐ 470. MIKE DAVIS
☐ 477. JEFF NEWMAN
☐ 478. STEVE MCCATTY
☐ 479. BILLY MARTIN(M)
☐ 480. MITCHELL PAGE
☐ 484. CLIFF JOHNSON
☐ 497. MIKE EDWARDS
☐ 585. FRED STANLEY

PHILADELPHIA PHILLIES

☐ 11. MIKE SCHMIDT
☐ 22. MANNY TRILLO
☐ 33. STEVE CARLTON
☐ 44. RON REED
☐ 55. GARRY MADDOX
☐ 131. PETE ROSE
☐ 142. LARRY BOWA
☐ 153. DICK RUTHVEN
☐ 164. DEL UNSER
☐ 175. GREG LUZINSKI
☐ 251. PETE ROSE
☐ 262. BOB BOONE
☐ 273. TUG MCGRAW
☐ 284. SPARKY LYLE
☐ 295. LONNIE SMITH
☐ 371. PETE ROSE
☐ 382. KEITH MORELAND
☐ 393. BOB WALK
☐ 404. BAKE MCBRIDE
☐ 415. DALLAS GREEN(M)
☐ 568. DICK NOLES
☐ 574. RANDY LERCH
☐ 598. GREG GROSS

PITTSBURGH PIRATES

- ☐ 12. WILLIE STARGELL
- ☐ 13. TIM FOLI
- ☐ 14. MANNY SANGUILLEN
- ☐ 15. GRANT JACKSON
- ☐ 16. EDDIE SOLOMON
- ☐ 17. OMAR MORENO
- ☐ 132. WILLIE STARGELL
- ☐ 133. ED OTT
- ☐ 134. JIM BIBBY
- ☐ 135. BERT BLYLEVEN
- ☐ 136. DAVE PARKER
- ☐ 137. BILL ROBINSON
- ☐ 252. BILL MADLOCK
- ☐ 253. DALE BERRA
- ☐ 254. KENT TEKULVE
- ☐ 255. ENRIQUE ROMO
- ☐ 256. MIKE EASLER
- ☐ 257. CHUCK TANNER(M)
- ☐ 372. PHIL GARNER
- ☐ 373. STEVE NICOSIA
- ☐ 374. JOHN CANDELARIA
- ☐ 375. DON ROBINSON
- ☐ 376. LEE LACY
- ☐ 377. JOHN MILNER
- ☐ 563. BOB OWCHINKO

ST. LOUIS CARDINALS

- ☐ 67. KEITH HERNANDEZ
- ☐ 68. TOM HERR
- ☐ 69. BOB FORSCH
- ☐ 70. JOHN FULGHAM
- ☐ 71. BOBBY BONDS
- ☐ 187. GARRY TEMPLETON
- ☐ 188. MIKE PHILLIPS
- ☐ 189. PETE VUCKOVICH
- ☐ 190. JOHN URREA
- ☐ 191. TONY SCOTT
- ☐ 307. KEN REITZ
- ☐ 308. TED SIMMONS
- ☐ 309. JOHN LITTLEFIELD
- ☐ 310. GEORGE FRAZIER
- ☐ 311. DANE IORG
- ☐ 427. LEON DURHAM
- ☐ 428. TERRY KENNEDY
- ☐ 429. SILVIO MARTINEZ
- ☐ 430. GEORGE HENDRICK
- ☐ 431. RED SCHOENDIENST(C)
- ☐ 505. DARRELL PORTER
- ☐ 536. JIM KAAT
- ☐ 539. KEITH SMITH
- ☐ 560. BRUCE SUTTER
- ☐ 580. MARK LITTELL
- ☐ 583. KEN OBERKFELL

SAN DIEGO PADRES

- ☐ 1. OZZIE SMITH
- ☐ 2. ROLLIE FINGERS
- ☐ 3. RICK WISE
- ☐ 4. GENE RICHARDS
- ☐ 121. DAVE CASH
- ☐ 122. RANDY JONES
- ☐ 123. ERIC RASMUSSEN
- ☐ 124. JERRY MUMPHREY
- ☐ 241. GENE TENACE
- ☐ 242. BOB SHIRLEY
- ☐ 243. GARY LUCAS
- ☐ 244. JERRY TURNER
- ☐ 361. BILL FAHEY
- ☐ 362. STEVE MURA
- ☐ 363. DENNIS KINNEY
- ☐ 364. DAVE WINFIELD
- ☐ 525. BRODERICK PERKINS
- ☐ 595. DAVE EDWARDS

SAN FRANCISCO GIANTS

- ☐ 72. RENNIE STENNETT
- ☐ 73. JOE STRAIN
- ☐ 74. ED WHITSON
- ☐ 75. TOM GRIFFIN
- ☐ 76. BILL NORTH
- ☐ 192. DARRELL EVANS
- ☐ 193. MILT MAY
- ☐ 194. BOB KNEPPER
- ☐ 195. RANDY MOFFITT
- ☐ 196. LARRY HERNDON

- ☐ 312. MIKE IVIE
- ☐ 313. DENNIS LITTLEJOHN
- ☐ 314. GARY LAVELLE
- ☐ 315. JACK CLARK
- ☐ 316. JIM WOHLFORD
- ☐ 432. JOHN LEMASTER
- ☐ 433. VIDA BLUE
- ☐ 434. JOHN MONTEFUSCO
- ☐ 435. TERRY WHITFIELD
- ☐ 436. DAVE BRISTOL(M)
- ☐ 498. MIKE SADEK
- ☐ 555. JERRY MARTIN
- ☐ 556. JESUS FIGUEROA
- ☐ 579. GREG MINTON

SEATTLE MARINERS

- ☐ 43. DAN MEYER
- ☐ 45. MARIO MENDOZA
- ☐ 46. RICK HONEYCUTT
- ☐ 47. GLENN ABBOTT
- ☐ 48. LEON ROBERTS
- ☐ 163. JULIO CRUZ
- ☐ 165. JIM ANDERSON
- ☐ 166. JIM BEATTIE
- ☐ 167. SHANE RAWLEY
- ☐ 168. JOE SIMPSON
- ☐ 283. TED COX
- ☐ 285. LARRY COX
- ☐ 286. FLOYD BANNISTER
- ☐ 287. BYRON MCLAUGHLIN
- ☐ 288. RODNEY CRAIG
- ☐ 403. BRUCE BOCHTE
- ☐ 405. JERRY NARRON
- ☐ 406. ROB DRESSLER
- ☐ 407. DAVE HEAVERLO
- ☐ 408. TOM PACIOREK
- ☐ 501. DAVE A. ROBERTS
- ☐ 516. WILLIE NORWOOD
- ☐ 518. JUAN BENIQUEZ
- ☐ 543. BILL STEIN

TEXAS RANGERS

- ☐ 25. BUMP WILLS
- ☐ 26. JOHN ELLIS
- ☐ 27. JIM KERN
- ☐ 28. RICHIE ZISK
- ☐ 145. BUDDY BELL
- ☐ 146. FERGUSON JENKINS
- ☐ 147. DANNY DARWIN
- ☐ 148. JOHN GRUBB
- ☐ 265. PAT PUTNAM
- ☐ 266. JON MATLACK
- ☐ 267. DAVE RAJSICH
- ☐ 268. BILLY SAMPLE
- ☐ 385. JIM SUNDBERG
- ☐ 386. DOC MEDICH
- ☐ 387. AL OLIVER
- ☐ 388. JIM NORRIS
- ☐ 496. MICKEY RIVERS
- ☐ 509. NELSON NORMAN

Blue Jays
ALFREDO GRIFFIN SHORTSTOP

TORONTO BLUE JAYS

- ☐ 29. JOHN MAYBERRY
- ☐ 30. BOB DAVIS
- ☐ 31. JACKSON TODD
- ☐ 32. AL WOODS

- ☐ 149. ALFREDO GRIFFIN
- ☐ 150. JERRY GARVIN
- ☐ 151. PAUL MIRABELLA
- ☐ 152. RICK BOSETTI
- ☐ 269. DAMASO GARCIA
- ☐ 270. TOM BUSKEY
- ☐ 271. JOEY MCLAUGHLIN
- ☐ 272. BARRY BONNELL
- ☐ 389. BOB BAILOR
- ☐ 390. ERNIE WHITT
- ☐ 391. OTTO VELEZ
- ☐ 392. ROY HOWELL
- ☐ 569. DANNY AINGE
- ☐ 570. BOBBY MATTICK(M)
- ☐ 582. DAVE STIEB

1982 DONRUSS (660)
2 1/2" X 3 1/2"

ATLANTA BRAVES

- ☐ 47. CHRIS CHAMBLISS
- ☐ 58. CLAUDELL WASHINGTON
- ☐ 97. AL HRABOSKY
- ☐ 123. GENE GARBER
- ☐ 149. MATT SINATRO
- ☐ 173. BOB HORNER
- ☐ 184. BRIAN ASSELSTINE
- ☐ 223. RICK CAMP
- ☐ 249. TOMMY BOGGS
- ☐ 275. BRETT BUTLER
- ☐ 299. DALE MURPHY
- ☐ 310. RUFINO LINARES
- ☐ 349. MICKEY MAHLER
- ☐ 375. BRUCE BENEDICT
- ☐ 401. STEVE BEDROSIAN
- ☐ 425. EDDIE MILLER
- ☐ 436. GLENN HUBBARD
- ☐ 475. PHIL NIEKRO
- ☐ 501. KEN DAYLEY
- ☐ 527. LARRY MCWILLIAMS
- ☐ 543. GAYLORD PERRY
- ☐ 546. RAFAEL RAMIREZ
- ☐ 553. LARRY BRADFORD
- ☐ 555. JERRY ROYSTER

BALTIMORE ORIOLES

- ☐ 27. EARL WEAVER(M)
- ☐ 77. RICK DEMPSEY
- ☐ 79. DENNIS MARTINEZ
- ☐ 105. KEN SINGLETON
- ☐ 131. TIM STODDARD
- ☐ 153. AL BUMBRY
- ☐ 203. JOSE MORALES
- ☐ 205. TIPPY MARTINEZ
- ☐ 231. JIM PALMER
- ☐ 257. RICH DAUER
- ☐ 279. DOUG DECINCES
- ☐ 329. MIKE FLANAGAN
- ☐ 331. SCOTT MCGREGOR
- ☐ 357. STEVE STONE
- ☐ 383. TERRY CROWLEY
- ☐ 405. CAL RIPKEN
- ☐ 455. DAN GRAHAM
- ☐ 457. SAMMY STEWART
- ☐ 483. EDDIE MURRAY

1982 Donruss

☐ 509. GARY ROENICKE
☐ 579. CAL RIPKEN, SR.(C)
☐ 581. BENNY AYALA
☐ 597. DAVE FORD
☐ 599. JOHN LOWENSTEIN
☐ 610. BOB BONNER
☐ 611. JIM DWYER
☐ 644. LENN SAKATA

BOSTON RED SOX

☐ 30. DENNIS ECKERSLEY
☐ 74. CARL YASTRZEMSKI
☐ 82. CARNEY LANSFORD
☐ 109. DWIGHT EVANS
☐ 134. BOB STANLEY
☐ 156. JERRY REMY
☐ 200. JIM RICE
☐ 208. DAVE STAPLETON
☐ 235. MIKE TORREZ
☐ 260. JOHN TUDOR
☐ 282. RALPH HOUK(M)
☐ 326. FRANK TANANA
☐ 334. RICK MILLER
☐ 361. TOM BURGMEIER
☐ 386. GARY ALLENSON
☐ 408. TONY PEREZ
☐ 452. MARK CLEAR
☐ 460. GLENN HOFFMAN
☐ 487. BILL CAMPBELL
☐ 512. RICH GEDMAN
☐ 540. BOB OJEDA
☐ 560. JULIO VALDEZ
☐ 564. STEVE CRAWFORD
☐ 586. JOE RUDI
☐ 608. GARRY HANCOCK
☐ 632. REID NICHOLS

CALIFORNIA ANGELS

☐ 38. STEVE RENKO
☐ 66. BRUCE KISON
☐ 90. BOBBY GRICH
☐ 115. BRIAN DOWNING
☐ 141. GENE MAUCH(M)
☐ 164. GEOFF ZAHN
☐ 192. ED OTT
☐ 216. ROD CAREW
☐ 241. FRED PATEK
☐ 267. DON AASE
☐ 290. DAVE FROST
☐ 318. BOB CLARK
☐ 342. RICK BURLESON
☐ 367. FRED LYNN
☐ 393. KEN FORSCH
☐ 416. MIKE WITT
☐ 444. JOHN HARRIS
☐ 468. DAN FORD
☐ 493. DON BAYLOR
☐ 519. ANDY HASSLER
☐ 577. BUTCH HOBSON
☐ 587. JUAN BENIQUEZ
☐ 593. BERT CAMPANERIS

CHICAGO CUBS

☐ 48. IVAN DEJESUS
☐ 57. HECTOR CRUZ
☐ 99. TIM BLACKWELL
☐ 126. RANDY MARTZ
☐ 151. LEON DURHAM
☐ 174. STEVE DILLARD
☐ 183. STEVE HENDERSON
☐ 225. JODY DAVIS
☐ 252. LEE SMITH
☐ 277. KEN REITZ
☐ 300. MIKE LUM
☐ 309. JERRY MORALES
☐ 351. MIKE KRUKOW
☐ 378. KEN KRAVEC
☐ 403. BILL BUCKNER
☐ 426. BILL CAUDILL
☐ 435. MIKE TYSON
☐ 477. DICK TIDROW
☐ 504. DOUG BIRD
☐ 529. PAT TABLER
☐ 533. MIKE GRIFFIN
☐ 554. SCOTT FLETCHER
☐ 633. DAVE GEISEL

CHICAGO WHITE SOX

☐ 39. MIKE SQUIRES
☐ 67. WAYNE NORDHAGEN
☐ 104. ROSS BAUMGARTEN
☐ 117. LAMARR HOYT
☐ 143. TONY BERNAZARD
☐ 165. RON LEFLORE
☐ 193. GREG LUZINSKI
☐ 230. BRITT BURNS
☐ 243. STEVE TROUT
☐ 269. LAMAR JOHNSON
☐ 291. CHET LEMON
☐ 319. TONY LARUSSA(M)
☐ 356. RICHARD DOTSON
☐ 369. JIM ESSIAN
☐ 395. JIM MORRISON
☐ 417. BOB MOLINARO
☐ 445. VADA PINSON(C)
☐ 482. ED FARMER
☐ 495. CARLTON FISK
☐ 521. GREG PRYOR
☐ 568. HAROLD BAINES
☐ 603. JERRY KOOSMAN
☐ 609. JERRY TURNER
☐ 619. DENNIS LAMP
☐ 631. KEVIN HICKEY
☐ 637. BILL ALMON

CINCINNATI REDS

☐ 43. LARRY BIITTNER
☐ 62. JOE NOLAN
☐ 103. MARIO SOTO
☐ 122. FRANK PASTORE
☐ 148. TOM SEAVER
☐ 169. DAVE COLLINS
☐ 188. JUNIOR KENNEDY
☐ 229. TOM HUME
☐ 248. DAN DRIESSEN
☐ 274. GEORGE FOSTER
☐ 295. SAM MEJIAS
☐ 314. PAUL HOUSEHOLDER
☐ 355. PAUL MOSKAU
☐ 374. RAY KNIGHT
☐ 400. JOHNNY BENCH
☐ 421. DAVE CONCEPCION
☐ 440. MIKE LACOSS
☐ 481. JOE PRICE
☐ 500. RON OESTER
☐ 526. JOHN MCNAMARA(M)
☐ 538. MIKE O'BERRY
☐ 634. KEN GRIFFEY

CLEVELAND INDIANS

☐ 33. RICK WAITS
☐ 72. TOBY HARRAH
☐ 85. RICK MANNING
☐ 111. BERT BLYLEVEN
☐ 137. LEN BARKER
☐ 159. ALAN BANNISTER
☐ 198. DUANE KUIPER
☐ 211. JORGE ORTA
☐ 237. VON HAYES
☐ 263. BO DIAZ
☐ 285. MIKE STANTON
☐ 324. ANDRE THORNTON
☐ 337. DAVE GARCIA(M)
☐ 363. JOE CHARBONEAU
☐ 389. MIKE HARGROVE
☐ 411. DAN SPILLNER
☐ 450. TOM VERYZER
☐ 463. RON HASSEY
☐ 489. WAYNE GARLAND
☐ 515. MIGUEL DILONE
☐ 551. CHRIS BANDO
☐ 572. JOHN DENNY
☐ 617. DAVE ROSELLO
☐ 620. SID MONGE
☐ 647. JERRY DYBZINSKI

DETROIT TIGERS

☐ 29. SPARKY ANDERSON(M)
☐ 76. ALAN TRAMMELL
☐ 81. CHAMP SUMMERS
☐ 107. JACK MORRIS
☐ 133. DAN PETRY
☐ 155. RICK PETERS
☐ 202. TOM BROOKENS

☐ 207. AL COWENS
☐ 233. MILT WILCOX
☐ 259. DAVE ROZEMA
☐ 281. LANCE PARRISH
☐ 328. RICHIE HEBNER
☐ 333. STAN PAPI
☐ 359. AURELIO LOPEZ
☐ 385. DAN SCHATZEDER
☐ 407. KIRK GIBSON
☐ 454. LOU WHITAKER
☐ 459. JOHN WOCKENFUSS
☐ 485. KEVIN SAUCIER
☐ 511. DAVE TOBIK
☐ 542. LYNN JONES
☐ 583. RICK LEACH
☐ 594. STEVE KEMP
☐ 601. MICK KELLEHER
☐ 602. RON JACKSON

HOUSTON ASTROS

☐ 41. BOB KNEPPER
☐ 65. JOE SAMBITO
☐ 92. ART HOWE
☐ 118. CESAR CEDENO
☐ 144. BILL VIRDON(M)
☐ 167. JOE NIEKRO
☐ 191. DAVE SMITH
☐ 218. JOE PITTMAN
☐ 244. JOSE CRUZ
☐ 270. FRANK LACORTE
☐ 293. VERN RUHLE
☐ 317. ALAN ASHBY
☐ 344. CRAIG REYNOLDS
☐ 370. TERRY PUHL
☐ 396. MIKE IVIE
☐ 419. NOLAN RYAN
☐ 443. DON SUTTON
☐ 470. KIKO GARCIA
☐ 496. DENNY WALLING
☐ 522. TONY SCOTT
☐ 544. PHIL GARNER
☐ 576. LUIS PUJOLS
☐ 625. DAVE W. ROBERTS

KANSAS CITY ROYALS

☐ 34. GEORGE BRETT
☐ 70. AMOS OTIS
☐ 86. JOHN WATHAN
☐ 112. DAN QUISENBERRY
☐ 138. RICH GALE
☐ 160. U.L. WASHINGTON
☐ 196. HAL MCRAE
☐ 212. JAMIE QUIRK
☐ 238. RENIE MARTIN
☐ 264. DENNIS LEONARD
☐ 286. FRANK WHITE
☐ 322. CESAR GERONIMO
☐ 338. LARRY GURA
☐ 364. KEN BRETT
☐ 390. DARRYL MOTLEY
☐ 412. WILLIE AIKENS
☐ 448. WILLIE WILSON
☐ 464. PAUL SPLITTORFF
☐ 490. JIM L. WRIGHT
☐ 516. CLINT HURDLE
☐ 570. LEE MAY
☐ 590. DAVE CHALK
☐ 630. RANCE MULLINIKS

LOS ANGELES DODGERS

☐ 32. BURT HOOTON
☐ 75. BOB WELCH
☐ 84. STEVE GARVEY
☐ 110. TOM LASORDA(M)
☐ 136. PEDRO GUERRERO
☐ 158. STEVE HOWE
☐ 201. STEVE YEAGER
☐ 210. RON CEY
☐ 236. BOBBY CASTILLO
☐ 262. JAY JOHNSTONE
☐ 284. JERRY REUSS
☐ 327. DAVEY LOPES
☐ 336. DUSTY BAKER
☐ 362. TERRY FORSTER
☐ 388. KEN LANDREAUX
☐ 410. DAVE STEWART
☐ 453. BILL RUSSELL

☐ 462. FERNANDO VALENZUELA
☐ 488. REGGIE SMITH
☐ 514. RICK MONDAY
☐ 537. DERREL THOMAS
☐ 562. MIKE MARSHALL
☐ 598. MIKE SCIOSCIA
☐ 604. DAVE GOLTZ
☐ 624. STEVE SAX

MILWAUKEE BREWERS

☐ 28. ROLLIE FINGERS
☐ 78. PAUL MOLITOR
☐ 80. JIM SLATON
☐ 106. TED SIMMONS
☐ 132. GORMAN THOMAS
☐ 154. MARK BROUHARD
☐ 204. ROY HOWELL
☐ 206. MOOSE HAAS
☐ 232. BOB RODGERS(M)
☐ 258. CECIL COOPER
☐ 280. CHARLIE MOORE
☐ 330. MIKE CALDWELL
☐ 332. JERRY AUGUSTINE
☐ 358. LARRY HISLE
☐ 384. DON MONEY
☐ 406. JIM GANTNER
☐ 456. REGGIE CLEVELAND
☐ 458. PETE VUCKOVICH
☐ 484. BEN OGLIVIE
☐ 510. ROBIN YOUNT
☐ 536. EDDIE ROMERO
☐ 578. HARVEY KUENN(C)
☐ 592. SAL BANDO
☐ 595. RANDY LERCH
☐ 618. RICKEY KEETON
☐ 623. JAMIE EASTERLY

MINNESOTA TWINS

☐ 51. PETE REDFERN
☐ 53. DOUG CORBETT
☐ 102. DAVE ENGLE
☐ 130. ROB WILFONG
☐ 177. FERNANDO ARROYO
☐ 179. DARRELL JACKSON
☐ 228. HOSKEN POWELL
☐ 256. JOHN CASTINO
☐ 303. ROGER ERICKSON
☐ 305. DANNY GOODWIN
☐ 354. PETE MACKANIN
☐ 382. BRAD HAVENS
☐ 429. AL WILLIAMS
☐ 431. GLENN ADAMS
☐ 480. MICKEY HATCHER
☐ 508. BUTCH WYNEGAR
☐ 532. SAL BUTERA
☐ 539. JACK O'CONNOR
☐ 549. TIM LAUDNER
☐ 557. KENT HRBEK
☐ 566. JOHNNY PODRES(C)
☐ 571. GARY WARD
☐ 573. ROY SMALLEY
☐ 591. BILLY GARDNER(M)

MONTREAL EXPOS

☐ 36. STEVE ROGERS
☐ 68. WOODIE FRYMAN
☐ 88. ANDRE DAWSON
☐ 114. GARY CARTER
☐ 140. TIM WALLACH
☐ 162. BILL GULLICKSON
☐ 194. BILL LEE
☐ 214. TIM RAINES
☐ 240. RODNEY SCOTT
☐ 266. JOHN MILNER
☐ 288. SCOTT SANDERSON
☐ 320. CHARLIE LEA
☐ 340. WARREN CROMARTIE
☐ 366. CHRIS SPEIER
☐ 392. STAN BAHNSEN
☐ 414. RAY BURRIS
☐ 446. ELIAS SOSA
☐ 466. LARRY PARRISH
☐ 492. JIM FANNING(M)
☐ 518. GRANT JACKSON
☐ 547. JEFF REARDON
☐ 621. JERRY WHITE
☐ 627. TERRY FRANCONA
☐ 650. FELIPE ALOU(C)

NEW YORK METS

☐ 49. LEE MAZZILLI
☐ 56. RUSTY STAUB
☐ 98. FRANK TAVERAS
☐ 128. MIKE SCOTT
☐ 175. MOOKIE WILSON
☐ 182. DAVE KINGMAN
☐ 224. MIKE JORGENSEN
☐ 254. PAT ZACHRY
☐ 301. TOM HAUSMAN
☐ 308. BOB BAILOR
☐ 350. ALEX TREVINO
☐ 380. PETE FALCONE
☐ 427. DOUG FLYNN
☐ 434. JOHN STEARNS
☐ 476. HUBIE BROOKS
☐ 506. NEIL ALLEN
☐ 589. CRAIG SWAN
☐ 605. ELLIS VALENTINE
☐ 613. JOEL YOUNGBLOOD
☐ 641. ED LYNCH
☐ 646. JESSE OROSCO
☐ 649. RON GARDENHIRE

NEW YORK YANKEES

☐ 31. DAVE WINFIELD
☐ 73. DAVE RIGHETTI
☐ 83. BARRY FOOTE
☐ 108. BOB WATSON
☐ 135. LOU PINIELLA
☐ 157. RICK REUSCHEL
☐ 199. RICK CERONE
☐ 209. BUCKY DENT
☐ 234. DAVE REVERING
☐ 261. JERRY MUMPHREY
☐ 283. RICH GOSSAGE
☐ 325. RUDY MAY
☐ 335. GRAIG NETTLES
☐ 360. OSCAR GAMBLE
☐ 387. YOGI BERRA(C)
☐ 409. TOMMY JOHN
☐ 451. RON DAVIS
☐ 461. WILLIE RANDOLPH
☐ 486. BOBBY MURCER
☐ 513. GENE NELSON
☐ 535. REGGIE JACKSON
☐ 548. RON GUIDRY
☐ 552. BOBBY BROWN
☐ 569. DAVE LAROCHE
☐ 584. GEORGE FRAZIER
☐ 614. LARRY MILBOURNE
☐ 635. BOB LEMON(M)

OAKLAND A'S

☐ 35. STEVE MCCATTY
☐ 71. MATT KEOUGH
☐ 87. BRIAN KINGMAN
☐ 113. RICKEY HENDERSON
☐ 139. WAYNE GROSS
☐ 161. RICK LANGFORD
☐ 197. MIKE NORRIS
☐ 213. JEFF JONES
☐ 239. DWAYNE MURPHY
☐ 265. JIM SPENCER
☐ 287. BOB OWCHINKO
☐ 323. TOM UNDERWOOD
☐ 339. CLIFF JOHNSON

☐ 365. TONY ARMAS
☐ 391. DAVE MCKAY
☐ 413. MIKE HEATH
☐ 449. FRED STANLEY
☐ 465. ROB PICCIOLO
☐ 491. BILLY MARTIN(M)
☐ 517. JEFF NEWMAN
☐ 534. KELVIN MOORE
☐ 556. SHOOTY BABITT
☐ 616. KEITH DRUMRIGHT
☐ 626. RICK BOSETTI

PHILADELPHIA PHILLIES

☐ 42. STEVE CARLTON
☐ 63. LARRY BOWA
☐ 93. MARTY BYSTROM
☐ 119. KEITH MORELAND
☐ 147. DICK DAVIS
☐ 168. PETE ROSE
☐ 189. SPARKY LYLE
☐ 219. LARRY CHRISTENSON
☐ 245. MANNY TRILLO
☐ 273. DEL UNSER
☐ 294. MIKE SCHMIDT
☐ 315. GARRY MADDOX
☐ 345. MIKE PROLY
☐ 371. GREG GROSS
☐ 399. RON REED
☐ 420. TUG MCGRAW
☐ 441. GARY MATTHEWS
☐ 471. BOB BOONE
☐ 497. BAKE MCBRIDE
☐ 525. DICK RUTHVEN
☐ 606. LONNIE SMITH
☐ 622. LUIS AGUAYO

PITTSBURGH PIRATES

☐ 45. STEVE NICOSIA
☐ 59. ENRIQUE ROMO
☐ 95. DAVE PARKER
☐ 124. TONY PENA
☐ 150. CHUCK TANNER(M)
☐ 171. JIM BIBBY
☐ 185. ROD SCURRY
☐ 221. MIKE EASLER
☐ 250. DALE BERRA
☐ 276. LEE LACY
☐ 297. JOHN CANDELARIA
☐ 311. KENT TEKULVE
☐ 347. OMAR MORENO
☐ 376. TIM FOLI
☐ 402. BILL ROBINSON
☐ 423. RICK RHODEN
☐ 437. EDDIE SOLOMON
☐ 473. RANDY NIEMANN
☐ 502. JASON THOMPSON
☐ 528. JOHNNY RAY
☐ 582. VANCE LAW
☐ 639. WILLIE STARGELL
☐ 651. HARVEY HADDIX(C)
☐ 653. BILL MADLOCK

ST. LOUIS CARDINALS

☐ 40. GEORGE HENDRICK
☐ 64. SIXTO LEZCANO
☐ 91. BOB FORSCH
☐ 120. BOB SHIRLEY
☐ 152. GENE TENACE
☐ 166. DANE IORG
☐ 190. WHITEY HERZOG(M)
☐ 217. JIM KAAT
☐ 246. LARY SORENSEN
☐ 278. KEITH HERNANDEZ
☐ 292. TITO LANDRUM
☐ 316. MIKE RAMSEY
☐ 343. JOHN MARTIN
☐ 372. BRUCE SUTTER
☐ 404. KEN OBERKFELL
☐ 418. STEVE BRAUN
☐ 442. MARK LITTELL
☐ 469. SILVIO MARTINEZ
☐ 498. DARRELL PORTER
☐ 530. TOM HERR
☐ 545. GARRY TEMPLETON
☐ 588. LUIS DELEON
☐ 607. JOAQUIN ANDUJAR
☐ 615. GENE ROOF

☐ 636. ORLANDO SANCHEZ
☐ 640. BOB SYKES
☐ 645. JULIO GONZALEZ

SAN DIEGO PADRES

☐ 44. CHRIS WELSH
☐ 61. TIM FLANNERY
☐ 94. OZZIE SMITH
☐ 121. TERRY KENNEDY
☐ 145. JOHN LITTLEFIELD
☐ 170. RICK WISE
☐ 187. DANNY BOONE
☐ 220. JUAN BONILLA
☐ 247. DAVE EDWARDS
☐ 271. BARRY EVANS
☐ 296. GARY LUCAS
☐ 313. JOHN URREA
☐ 346. RUPPERT JONES
☐ 373. JOE LEFEBVRE
☐ 397. BRODERICK PERKINS
☐ 422. JUAN EICHELBERGER
☐ 439. RANDY BASS
☐ 472. LUIS SALAZAR
☐ 499. GENE RICHARDS
☐ 523. STEVE MURA

SAN FRANCISCO GIANTS

☐ 46. JACK CLARK
☐ 60. GARY LAVELLE
☐ 96. DOYLE ALEXANDER
☐ 125. ALLEN RIPLEY
☐ 146. DAVE BERGMAN
☐ 172. LARRY HERNDON
☐ 186. FRED BREINING
☐ 222. VIDA BLUE
☐ 251. EDDIE WHITSON
☐ 272. ENOS CABELL
☐ 298. JERRY MARTIN
☐ 312. JOE MORGAN
☐ 348. GREG MINTON
☐ 377. AL HOLLAND
☐ 398. DARRELL EVANS
☐ 424. FRANK ROBINSON(M)
☐ 438. JEFF LEONARD
☐ 474. TOM GRIFFIN
☐ 503. MILT MAY
☐ 524. JOHNNIE LEMASTER
☐ 563. RENNIE STENNETT
☐ 574. BOB BRENLY

SEATTLE MARINERS

☐ 50. JULIO CRUZ
☐ 55. JOE SIMPSON
☐ 100. FLOYD BANNISTER
☐ 127. RICHIE ZISK
☐ 176. DAN MEYER
☐ 181. JIM ANDERSON
☐ 226. MIKE PARROTT
☐ 253. TOM PACIOREK
☐ 302. GLENN ABBOTT
☐ 307. LENNY RANDLE
☐ 352. SHANE RAWLEY
☐ 379. JEFF BURROUGHS
☐ 428. LARRY ANDERSEN
☐ 433. JERRY NARRON
☐ 478. JIM BEATTIE
☐ 505. BRUCE BOCHTE
☐ 567. PAUL SERNA
☐ 596. BRYAN CLARK
☐ 600. RENE LACHEMANN(M)
☐ 612. TERRY BULLING
☐ 648. TOMMY DAVIS(C)

TEXAS RANGERS

☐ 37. BILL STEIN
☐ 69. BILLY SAMPLE
☐ 89. JIM KERN
☐ 116. AL OLIVER
☐ 142. GEORGE MEDICH
☐ 163. MARK WAGNER
☐ 195. DON ZIMMER(M)
☐ 215. JON MATLACK
☐ 242. MICKEY RIVERS
☐ 268. JIM SUNDBERG
☐ 289. BUMP WILLS
☐ 321. DANNY DARWIN

☐ 341. STEVE COMER
☐ 368. BUDDY BELL
☐ 394. MARIO MENDOZA
☐ 415. LEON ROBERTS
☐ 447. CHARLIE HOUGH
☐ 467. JOHN GRUBB
☐ 494. RICK HONEYCUTT
☐ 520. PAT PUTNAM
☐ 550. JOHN HENRY JOHNSON
☐ 565. BOB BABCOCK
☐ 642. JOHN ELLIS
☐ 643. FERGIE JENKINS

TORONTO BLUE JAYS

☐ 52. DAVE STIEB
☐ 54. JORGE BELL
☐ 101. ALFREDO GRIFFIN
☐ 129. LLOYD MOSEBY
☐ 178. JACKSON TODD
☐ 180. AL WOODS
☐ 227. JIM CLANCY
☐ 255. LUIS LEAL
☐ 304. OTTO VELEZ
☐ 306. JOHN MAYBERRY
☐ 353. GARTH IORG
☐ 381. ERNIE WHITT
☐ 430. JERRY GARVIN
☐ 432. BARRY BONNELL
☐ 479. DAMASO GARCIA
☐ 507. JOEY MCLAUGHLIN
☐ 541. ROY LEE JACKSON
☐ 559. MARK BOMBACK
☐ 561. BUCK MARTINEZ
☐ 580. JUAN BERENGUER
☐ 629. PAUL MIRABELLA
☐ 638. DANNY AINGE
☐ 652. WILLIE UPSHAW

1983 DONRUSS (660)
2 1/2" X 3 1/2"

ATLANTA BRAVES

☐ 47. DALE MURPHY
☐ 58. BOB HORNER
☐ 97. PHIL NIEKRO
☐ 123. CHRIS CHAMBLISS

☐ 149. RICK CAMP
☐ 173. STEVE BEDROSIAN
☐ 184. GLENN HUBBARD
☐ 223. GENE GARBER
☐ 249. CLAUDELL WASHINGTON
☐ 275. RUFINO LINARES
☐ 299. BRUCE BENEDICT
☐ 310. RAFAEL RAMIREZ
☐ 349. TOMMY BOGGS
☐ 375. KEN DAYLEY
☐ 401. BOB WALK
☐ 425. JERRY ROYSTER
☐ 436. BIFF POCOROBA
☐ 475. AL HRABOSKY
☐ 501. LARRY WHISENTON
☐ 527. RICK MAHLER
☐ 551. BOB WATSON
☐ 557. PASCUAL PEREZ
☐ 562. CARLOS DIAZ
☐ 607. TERRY HARPER
☐ 622. MATT SINATRO
☐ 628. JOE TORRE(M)
☐ 636. BRETT BUTLER

BALTIMORE ORIOLES

☐ 27. GARY ROENICKE
☐ 77. JIM PALMER
☐ 79. JOE NOLAN
☐ 105. MIKE FLANAGAN
☐ 131. GLENN GULLIVER
☐ 153. JOHN LOWENSTEIN
☐ 203. SAMMY STEWART
☐ 205. LENN SAKATA
☐ 231. DENNIS MARTINEZ
☐ 257. KEN SINGLETON
☐ 279. CAL RIPKEN
☐ 329. RICK DEMPSEY
☐ 331. BENNY AYALA
☐ 357. TIPPY MARTINEZ
☐ 383. AL BUMBRY
☐ 405. EDDIE MURRAY
☐ 455. RICH DAUER
☐ 457. TERRY CROWLEY
☐ 483. SCOTT MCGREGOR
☐ 509. DAN FORD
☐ 581. TIM STODDARD
☐ 583. JIM DWYER
☐ 619. STORM DAVIS

BOSTON RED SOX

☐ 30. GARY ALLENSON
☐ 74. JERRY REMY
☐ 82. RICK MILLER
☐ 109. LUIS APONTE
☐ 134. BRUCE HURST
☐ 156. RICH GEDMAN
☐ 200. DAVE STAPLETON
☐ 208. JIM RICE
☐ 235. TOM BURGMEIER
☐ 260. BOB OJEDA
☐ 282. GLENN HOFFMAN
☐ 326. CARL YASTRZEMSKI
☐ 334. CHUCK RAINEY
☐ 361. MARK CLEAR
☐ 386. BOB STANLEY
☐ 408. CARNEY LANSFORD
☐ 452. DWIGHT EVANS

☐ 460. REID NICHOLS
☐ 487. DENNIS ECKERSLEY
☐ 512. MIKE TORREZ
☐ 534. ROGER LAFRANCOIS
☐ 563. JOHN TUDOR
☐ 578. TONY PEREZ
☐ 586. WADE BOGGS

CALIFORNIA ANGELS

☐　38. DON AASE
☐　66. GEOFF ZAHN
☐　90. ROD CAREW
☐ 115. REGGIE JACKSON
☐ 141. DARYL SCONIERS
☐ 164. KEN FORSCH
☐ 192. BOB BOONE
☐ 216. DOUG DECINCES
☐ 241. FRED LYNN
☐ 267. BRUCE KISON
☐ 290. ANDY HASSLER
☐ 318. RICK BURLESON
☐ 342. TIM FOLI
☐ 367. BRIAN DOWNING
☐ 393. STEVE RENKO
☐ 416. MIKE WITT
☐ 444. BOBBY CLARK
☐ 468. BOBBY GRICH
☐ 493. DON BAYLOR
☐ 519. LUIS SANCHEZ
☐ 542. LUIS TIANT
☐ 570. TOMMY JOHN
☐ 604. JOE FERGUSON
☐ 612. ROB WILFONG
☐ 639. RON JACKSON
☐ 640. JUAN BENIQUEZ

CHICAGO CUBS

☐　48. DOUG BIRD
☐　57. ALLEN RIPLEY
☐　99. BILL BUCKNER
☐ 126. MEL HALL
☐ 151. RANDY MARTZ
☐ 174. WILLIE HERNANDEZ
☐ 183. JODY DAVIS
☐ 225. MIKE PROLY
☐ 252. STEVE HENDERSON
☐ 277. RYNE SANDBERG
☐ 300. FERGIE JENKINS
☐ 309. KEITH MORELAND
☐ 351. BUMP WILLS
☐ 378. SCOT THOMPSON
☐ 403. LEE SMITH
☐ 426. DICKIE NOLES
☐ 435. LARRY BOWA
☐ 477. LEON DURHAM
☐ 504. BILL CAMPBELL
☐ 529. JUNIOR KENNEDY
☐ 552. PAT TABLER
☐ 561. JAY JOHNSTONE
☐ 596. BOBBY MOLINARO
☐ 614. LEE ELIA(M)
☐ 631. GARY WOODS

CHICAGO WHITE SOX

☐　39. JERRY KOOSMAN
☐　67. SALOME BAROJAS
☐ 104. CARLTON FISK
☐ 117. VANCE LAW
☐ 143. HAROLD BAINES
☐ 165. DENNIS LAMP
☐ 193. BRITT BURNS
☐ 230. MARC HILL
☐ 243. TOM PACIOREK
☐ 269. STEVE KEMP
☐ 291. ERNESTO ESCARREGA
☐ 319. RICHARD DOTSON
☐ 356. BILL ALMON
☐ 369. AURELIO RODRIGUEZ
☐ 395. GREG LUZINSKI
☐ 417. STEVE TROUT
☐ 445. KEVIN HICKEY
☐ 482. TONY BERNAZARD
☐ 495. MIKE SQUIRES
☐ 521. RUDY LAW
☐ 543. RON LEFLORE
☐ 571. TONY LARUSSA(M)
☐ 616. JERRY HAIRSTON
☐ 632. LAMARR HOYT
☐ 652. MARVIS FOLEY

CINCINNATI REDS

☐　43. CESAR CEDENO
☐　62. FRANK PASTORE
☐ 103. BRUCE BERENYI
☐ 122. TOM SEAVER
☐ 148. DAVE CONCEPCION
☐ 169. EDDIE MILNER
☐ 188. DAVE VANGORDER
☐ 229. TOM HUME
☐ 248. MARIO SOTO
☐ 274. DAN DRIESSEN
☐ 295. GREG HARRIS
☐ 314. WAYNE KRENCHICKI
☐ 355. JIM KERN
☐ 374. ALEX TREVINO
☐ 400. TOM LAWLESS
☐ 421. CHARLIE LIEBRANDT
☐ 440. LARRY BIITTNER
☐ 481. JOE PRICE
☐ 500. JOHNNY BENCH
☐ 526. RON OESTER
☐ 547. BRAD LESLEY
☐ 566. PAUL HOUSEHOLDER
☐ 597. MIKE VAIL
☐ 624. DUANE WALKER

CLEVELAND INDIANS

☐　33. CHRIS BANDO
☐　72. RICK SUTCLIFFE
☐　85. MIGUEL DILONE
☐ 111. LEN BARKER
☐ 137. DAN SPILLNER
☐ 159. RON HASSEY
☐ 198. RICK MANNING
☐ 211. ANDRE THORNTON
☐ 237. JOHN DENNY
☐ 263. RICK WAITS
☐ 285. ALAN BANNISTER
☐ 324. VON HAYES
☐ 337. TOBY HARRAH
☐ 363. LARY SORENSEN
☐ 389. ED WHITSON
☐ 411. LARRY MILBOURNE
☐ 450. MIKE HARGROVE
☐ 463. JACK PERCONTE
☐ 489. MIKE FISCHLIN
☐ 515. RODNEY CRAIG
☐ 537. ED GLYNN
☐ 576. JERRY DYBZINSKI
☐ 589. BERT BLYLEVEN

DETROIT TIGERS

☐　29. PAT UNDERWOOD
☐　76. JOHN WOCKENFUSS
☐　81. RICK LEACH
☐ 107. JACK MORRIS
☐ 133. DAVE ROZEMA
☐ 155. MILT WILCOX
☐ 202. ENOS CABELL
☐ 207. ALAN TRAMMELL
☐ 233. LARRY PASHNICK
☐ 259. ELIAS SOSA
☐ 281. BILL FAHEY
☐ 328. HOWARD JOHNSON
☐ 333. LOU WHITAKER
☐ 359. DAN PETRY
☐ 385. DAVE TOBIK
☐ 407. LANCE PARRISH
☐ 454. TOM BROOKENS
☐ 459. KIRK GIBSON
☐ 485. MIKE IVIE
☐ 511. CHET LEMON
☐ 533. SPARKY ANDERSON(M)
☐ 580. GLEN WILSON
☐ 585. LARRY HERNDON
☐ 600. JERRY UJDUR
☐ 641. DAVE RUCKER

HOUSTON ASTROS

☐　41. JOSE CRUZ
☐　65. HARRY SPILMAN
☐　92. BOB KNEPPER
☐ 118. NOLAN RYAN
☐ 144. ALAN ASHBY
☐ 167. TERRY PUHL
☐ 191. DICKIE THON
☐ 218. FRANK LACORTE

☐ 244. JOE SAMBITO
☐ 270. PHIL GARNER
☐ 293. TONY SCOTT
☐ 317. CRAIG REYNOLDS
☐ 344. MIKE LACOSS
☐ 370. DAVE SMITH
☐ 396. ART HOWE
☐ 419. DENNY WALLING
☐ 443. DANNY HEEP
☐ 470. JOE NIEKRO
☐ 496. BERT ROBERGE
☐ 522. RAY KNIGHT
☐ 545. RANDY MOFFITT
☐ 569. KIKO GARCIA
☐ 620. ALAN KNICELY
☐ 627. VERN RUHLE
☐ 642. LUIS PUJOLS

KANSAS CITY ROYALS

☐　34. VIDA BLUE
☐　70. DAN QUISENBERRY
☐　86. JOHN WATHAN
☐ 112. WILLIE WILSON
☐ 138. JERRY MARTIN
☐ 160. LARRY GURA
☐ 196. DON SLAUGHT
☐ 212. WILLIE AIKENS
☐ 238. HAL MCRAE
☐ 264. GREG PRYOR
☐ 286. PAUL SPLITTORFF
☐ 322. BUD BLACK
☐ 338. GEORGE BRETT
☐ 364. AMOS OTIS
☐ 390. DON HOOD
☐ 412. DENNIS LEONARD
☐ 448. CESAR GERONIMO
☐ 464. FRANK WHITE
☐ 490. U.L. WASHINGTON
☐ 516. ONIX CONCEPCION
☐ 538. LEE MAY
☐ 574. KEITH CREEL
☐ 590. DICK HOWSER(M)

LOS ANGELES DODGERS

☐　32. BURT HOOTON
☐　75. MIKE SCIOSCIA
☐　84. RON CEY
☐ 110. PEDRO GUERRERO
☐ 136. TOM LASORDA(M)
☐ 158. JERRY REUSS
☐ 201. STEVE YEAGER
☐ 210. BILL RUSSELL
☐ 236. KEN LANDREAUX
☐ 262. CANDY MALDONADO
☐ 284. FERNANDO VALENZUELA
☐ 327. RON ROENICKE
☐ 336. STEVE SAX
☐ 362. MIKE MARSHALL
☐ 388. JORGE ORTA
☐ 410. BOB WELCH
☐ 453. TERRY FORSTER
☐ 462. DUSTY BAKER
☐ 488. STEVE GARVEY
☐ 514. MARK BELANGER
☐ 536. TOM NIEDENFUER
☐ 579. GREG BROCK
☐ 588. DAVE STEWART
☐ 630. STEVE HOWE
☐ 643. RICK MONDAY

MILWAUKEE BREWERS

☐　28. DWIGHT BERNARD
☐　78. ROLLIE FINGERS
☐　80. PETE VUCKOVICH
☐ 106. CECIL COOPER
☐ 132. DON MONEY
☐ 154. MIKE CALDWELL
☐ 204. MOOSE HAAS
☐ 206. CHARLIE MOORE
☐ 232. JIM GANTNER
☐ 258. ROBIN YOUNT
☐ 280. JAMIE EASTERLY
☐ 330. JIM SLATON
☐ 332. TED SIMMONS
☐ 358. ROY HOWELL
☐ 384. BEN OGLIVIE
☐ 406. MARSHALL EDWARDS
☐ 456. ROB PICCIOLO

☐ 458. NED YOST
☐ 484. PAUL MOLITOR
☐ 510. GORMAN THOMAS
☐ 531. DON SUTTON
☐ 532. MARK BROUHARD
☐ 582. BOB MCCLURE
☐ 584. ED ROMERO
☐ 608. HARVEY KUENN(M)

MINNESOTA TWINS

☐ 51. JACK O'CONNOR
☐ 53. GARY GAETTI
☐ 102. BOBBY CASTILLO
☐ 130. JOHN PACELLA
☐ 177. TIM LAUDNER
☐ 179. KENT HRBEK
☐ 228. RON DAVIS
☐ 256. PETE REDFERN
☐ 303. JOHN CASTINO
☐ 305. RANDY JOHNSON
☐ 354. TERRY FELTON
☐ 382. FRANK VIOLA
☐ 429. GARY WARD
☐ 431. RON WASHINGTON
☐ 480. BRAD HAVENS
☐ 508. AL WILLIAMS
☐ 555. TOM BRUNANSKY
☐ 615. MICKEY HATCHER
☐ 646. DAVE ENGLE
☐ 650. JESUS VEGA

MONTREAL EXPOS

☐ 36. RAY BURRIS
☐ 68. DAVID PALMER
☐ 88. BYRN SMITH
☐ 114. MIKE GATES
☐ 140. AL OLIVER
☐ 162. WOODIE FRYMAN
☐ 194. JEFF REARDON
☐ 214. TIM BLACKWELL
☐ 240. DOUG FLYNN
☐ 266. CHRIS SPEIER
☐ 288. BILL GULLICKSON
☐ 320. STEVE ROGERS
☐ 340. GARY CARTER
☐ 366. BRAD MILLS
☐ 392. TIM WALLACH
☐ 414. CHARLIE LEA
☐ 446. SCOTT SANDERSON
☐ 466. WARREN CROMARTIE
☐ 492. ROY JOHNSON
☐ 518. ANDRE DAWSON
☐ 540. TIM RAINES
☐ 572. JOEL YOUNGBLOOD
☐ 592. TERRY FRANCONA
☐ 602. JERRY WHITE

JOHN STEARNS

NEW YORK METS

☐ 49. HUBIE BROOKS
☐ 56. MOOKIE WILSON
☐ 98. NEIL ALLEN
☐ 128. CHARLIE PULEO
☐ 175. RON GARDENHIRE
☐ 182. PETE FALCONE
☐ 224. SCOTT HOLMAN
☐ 254. CRAIG SWAN

☐ 301. DAVE KINGMAN
☐ 308. ED LYNCH
☐ 350. RUSTY STAUB
☐ 380. JOHN STEARNS
☐ 427. GEORGE FOSTER
☐ 434. JESSE OROSCO
☐ 476. RON HODGES
☐ 506. BOB BAILOR
☐ 553. BRENT GAFF
☐ 560. PAT ZACHRY
☐ 599. GARY RAJSICH
☐ 618. WALLY BACKMAN
☐ 634. TERRY LEACH

NEW YORK YANKEES

☐ 31. RON GUIDRY
☐ 73. STEVE BALBONI
☐ 83. GRAIG NETTLES
☐ 108. MIKE MORGAN
☐ 135. RUDY MAY
☐ 157. RICH GOSSAGE
☐ 199. DAVE RIGHETTI
☐ 209. ROY SMALLEY
☐ 234. DAVE COLLINS
☐ 261. BOBBY MURCER
☐ 283. WILLIE RANDOLPH
☐ 325. BUTCH WYNEGAR
☐ 335. LOU PINIELLA
☐ 360. JERRY MUMPHREY
☐ 387. ANDRE ROBERTSON
☐ 409. DAVE WINFIELD
☐ 451. DOYLE ALEXANDER
☐ 461. OSCAR GAMBLE
☐ 486. KEN GRIFFEY
☐ 513. SHANE RAWLEY
☐ 535. GEORGE FRAZIER
☐ 577. RICK CERONE
☐ 587. JAY HOWELL
☐ 638. LEE MAZZILLI

OAKLAND A'S

☐ 35. RICKEY HENDERSON
☐ 71. TONY ARMAS
☐ 87. KELVIN MOORE
☐ 113. DAVE BEARD
☐ 139. MIKE NORRIS
☐ 161. DWAYNE MURPHY
☐ 197. FRED STANLEY
☐ 213. DAVE MCKAY
☐ 239. MATT KEOUGH
☐ 265. BOB OWCHINKO
☐ 287. JOE RUDI
☐ 323. JEFF BURROUGHS
☐ 339. DAVEY LOPES
☐ 365. RICK LANGFORD
☐ 391. TOM UNDERWOOD
☐ 413. DAN MEYER
☐ 449. JIMMY SEXTON
☐ 465. MICKEY KLUTTS
☐ 491. STEVE MCCATTY
☐ 517. MIKE HEATH
☐ 539. BOB KEARNEY
☐ 575. BILLY MARTIN(M)
☐ 591. WAYNE GROSS
☐ 601. CLIFF JOHNSON
☐ 635. JEFF NEWMAN
☐ 651. JEFF JONES

PHILADELPHIA PHILLIES

☐ 42. PETE ROSE
☐ 63. GARRY MADDOX
☐ 93. MARTY BYSTROM
☐ 119. MIKE KRUKOW
☐ 147. BO DIAZ
☐ 168. MIKE SCHMIDT
☐ 189. BOB DERNIER
☐ 219. STEVE CARLTON
☐ 245. SID MONGE
☐ 273. DAVE W. ROBERTS
☐ 294. MANNY TRILLO
☐ 315. GEORGE VUKOVICH
☐ 345. LARRY CHRISTENSON
☐ 371. TUG MCGRAW
☐ 399. IVAN DEJESUS
☐ 420. GARY MATTHEWS
☐ 441. GREG GROSS
☐ 471. ED FARMER

☐ 497. DICK RUTHVEN
☐ 525. JULIO FRANCO
☐ 546. LUIS AGUAYO
☐ 567. RON REED
☐ 606. OZZIE VIRGIL
☐ 626. PAT CORRALES(M)

PITTSBURGH PIRATES

☐ 45. LARRY MCWILLIAMS
☐ 59. TONY PENA
☐ 95. JASON THOMPSON
☐ 124. CHUCK TANNER(M)
☐ 150. JIM MORRISON
☐ 171. DON ROBINSON
☐ 185. DALE BERRA
☐ 221. MIKE EASLER
☐ 250. RICK RHODEN
☐ 276. LEE LACY
☐ 297. KENT TEKULVE
☐ 311. BILL MADLOCK
☐ 347. OMAR MORENO
☐ 376. ROD SCURRY
☐ 402. JIMMY SMITH
☐ 423. MATT GUANTE
☐ 437. JOHNNY RAY
☐ 473. DAVE PARKER
☐ 502. MANNY SARMIENTO
☐ 528. STEVE NICOSIA
☐ 549. JOHN CANDELARIA
☐ 610. WILLIE STARGELL
☐ 647. DICK DAVIS

ST. LOUIS CARDINALS

☐ 40. BRUCE SUTTER
☐ 64. BOB FORSCH
☐ 91. LONNIE SMITH
☐ 120. OZZIE SMITH
☐ 152. KEITH HERNANDEZ
☐ 166. DAVID GREEN
☐ 190. WILLIE MCGEE
☐ 217. TOM HERR
☐ 246. KEN OBERKFELL
☐ 278. DARRELL PORTER
☐ 292. STEVE MURA
☐ 316. JOAQUIN ANDUJAR
☐ 343. JIM KAAT
☐ 372. DOUG BAIR
☐ 404. GEORGE HENDRICK
☐ 418. GLENN BRUMMER
☐ 442. GENE TENACE
☐ 469. DANE IORG
☐ 498. TITO LANDRUM
☐ 530. WHITEY HERZOG(M)
☐ 544. DAVE LAPOINT
☐ 568. MIKE RAMSEY
☐ 617. JOHN MARTIN
☐ 621. JOHN STUPER

SAN DIEGO PADRES

☐ 44. FLOYD CHIFFER
☐ 61. TIM LOLLAR
☐ 94. CHRIS WELSH
☐ 121. BRODERICK PERKINS
☐ 145. GARRY TEMPLETON
☐ 170. JOHN CURTIS
☐ 187. GARY LUCAS
☐ 220. TERRY KENNEDY
☐ 247. JOE PITTMAN
☐ 271. GENE RICHARDS
☐ 296. LUIS DELEON
☐ 313. JOHN MONTEFUSCO
☐ 346. JUAN BONILLA
☐ 373. RUPPERT JONES
☐ 397. ALAN WIGGINS
☐ 422. JUAN EICHELBERGER
☐ 439. ERIC SHOW
☐ 472. TIM FLANNERY
☐ 499. SIXTO LEZCANO
☐ 523. JOE LEFEBVRE
☐ 548. LUIS SALAZAR
☐ 565. DAVE EDWARDS
☐ 598. TONY GWYNN
☐ 625. DICK WILLIAMS(M)
☐ 633. STEVE SWISHER

SAN FRANCISCO GIANTS

- ☐ 46. ALAN FOWLKES
- ☐ 60. GARY LAVELLE
- ☐ 96. TOM O'MALLEY
- ☐ 125. JOHNNIE LEMASTER
- ☐ 146. AL HOLLAND
- ☐ 172. RICH GALE
- ☐ 186. GREG MINTON
- ☐ 222. JACK CLARK
- ☐ 251. DARRELL EVANS
- ☐ 272. RENIE MARTIN
- ☐ 298. ATLEE HAMMAKER
- ☐ 312. MILT MAY
- ☐ 348. CHARLES DAVIS
- ☐ 377. BOB BRENLY
- ☐ 398. JIM BARR
- ☐ 424. BILL LASKEY
- ☐ 438. JOE MORGAN
- ☐ 474. JEFF LEONARD
- ☐ 503. FRED BREINING
- ☐ 524. JIM WOHLFORD
- ☐ 550. DAVE BERGMAN
- ☐ 564. FRANK ROBINSON(M)
- ☐ 605. GUY SULARZ
- ☐ 611. REGGIE SMITH

SEATTLE MARINERS

- ☐ 50. FLOYD BANNISTER
- ☐ 55. GENE NELSON
- ☐ 100. ED VANDEBERG
- ☐ 127. BRUCE BOCHTE
- ☐ 176. JIM BEATTIE
- ☐ 181. LARRY ANDERSEN
- ☐ 226. TERRY BULLING
- ☐ 253. MANNY CASTILLO
- ☐ 302. BILL CAUDILL
- ☐ 307. GAYLORD PERRY
- ☐ 352. RICK SWEET
- ☐ 379. JULIO CRUZ
- ☐ 428. MIKE MOORE
- ☐ 433. MIKE STANTON
- ☐ 478. JIM ESSIAN
- ☐ 505. TODD CRUZ
- ☐ 554. AL COWENS
- ☐ 559. RICHIE ZISK
- ☐ 603. BRYAN CLARK
- ☐ 637. GARY GRAY
- ☐ 649. AL CHAMBERS

TEXAS RANGERS

- ☐ 37. JOHN BUTCHER
- ☐ 69. CHARLIE HOUGH
- ☐ 89. DAVE HOSTETLER
- ☐ 116. GEORGE WRIGHT
- ☐ 142. LAMAR JOHNSON
- ☐ 163. STEVE COMER
- ☐ 195. JON MATLACK
- ☐ 215. BUDDY BELL
- ☐ 242. BILLY SAMPLE
- ☐ 268. MARK WAGNER
- ☐ 289. DANNY DARWIN
- ☐ 321. DAVE J. SCHMIDT
- ☐ 341. JOHN GRUBB
- ☐ 368. MIKE RICHARDT
- ☐ 394. MICKEY RIVERS
- ☐ 415. RICK HONEYCUTT
- ☐ 447. FRANK TANANA
- ☐ 467. LARRY PARRISH
- ☐ 494. BOBBY JOHNSON
- ☐ 520. TERRY BOGENER
- ☐ 541. PAUL MIRABELLA
- ☐ 573. WAYNE TOLLESON
- ☐ 593. DON WERNER
- ☐ 594. BILL STEIN
- ☐ 609. JIM SUNDBERG

TORONTO BLUE JAYS

- ☐ 52. STEVE SENTENEY
- ☐ 54. DAMASO GARCIA
- ☐ 101. JIM CLANCY
- ☐ 129. LUIS LEAL
- ☐ 178. BUCK MARTINEZ
- ☐ 180. ALFREDO GRIFFIN
- ☐ 227. JERRY GARVIN
- ☐ 255. JOEY MCLAUGHLIN
- ☐ 304. ERNIE WHITT
- ☐ 306. GARTH IORG
- ☐ 353. JIM GOTT
- ☐ 381. DALE MURRAY
- ☐ 430. BARRY BONNELL
- ☐ 432. RANCE MULLINIKS
- ☐ 479. ROY LEE JACKSON
- ☐ 507. DAVE STIEB
- ☐ 556. LLOYD MOSEBY
- ☐ 558. WILLIE UPSHAW
- ☐ 595. JESSE BARFIELD
- ☐ 623. GENE PETRALLI
- ☐ 629. ANTHONY JOHNSON
- ☐ 644. HOSKEN POWELL

1984 DONRUSS (660)
2 1/2" X 3 1/2"

RUDY LAW OF

ATLANTA BRAVES

- ☐ 36. BRAD KOMMINSK
- ☐ 66. DALE MURPHY
- ☐ 77. BIFF POCOROBA
- ☐ 141. BRETT BUTLER
- ☐ 165. RICK CAMP
- ☐ 188. PHIL NIEKRO
- ☐ 199. KEN DAYLEY
- ☐ 263. GERALD PERRY
- ☐ 287. GENE GARBER
- ☐ 310. CLAUDELL WASHINGTON
- ☐ 321. RANDY JOHNSON
- ☐ 385. PETE FALCONE
- ☐ 409. BRUCE BENEDICT
- ☐ 432. GLENN HUBBARD
- ☐ 443. LEN BARKER
- ☐ 507. PASCUAL PEREZ
- ☐ 531. JERRY ROYSTER
- ☐ 535. BOB HORNER
- ☐ 537. CHRIS CHAMBLISS
- ☐ 565. STEVE BEDROSIAN
- ☐ 589. RAFAEL RAMIREZ*
- ☐ 599. CRAIG MCMURTRY

*RAMIREZ IS SHOWN ON THIS CARD
WITH THE A'S. HOWEVER HE WAS
NEVER WITH THE A'S ORGANIZA-
TION DURING THIS TIME PERIOD.
THEREFORE IT IS THE FEELING OF
THE AUTHORS THAT THIS CARD IS
AN ERROR AND BELONGS IN THE
ATLANTA BRAVES TEAM SET.

BALTIMORE ORIOLES

- ☐ 47. EDDIE MURRAY
- ☐ 88. JOE ALTOBELLI(M)
- ☐ 106. CAL RIPKEN
- ☐ 123. MIKE BODDICKER
- ☐ 148. TODD CRUZ
- ☐ 169. MIKE FLANAGAN
- ☐ 210. AL BUMBRY
- ☐ 228. JOHN LOWENSTEIN
- ☐ 245. TIM STODDARD
- ☐ 270. BENNY AYALA
- ☐ 291. JOHN SHELBY
- ☐ 332. ALLAN RAMIREZ
- ☐ 350. RICH DAUER
- ☐ 367. DAN FORD
- ☐ 392. GARY ROENICKE
- ☐ 413. RICK DEMPSEY
- ☐ 454. JIM DWYER
- ☐ 472. TIPPY MARTINEZ
- ☐ 489. JOE NOLAN
- ☐ 514. SAMMY STEWART
- ☐ 576. JIM PALMER
- ☐ 585. STORM DAVIS
- ☐ 594. SCOTT MCGREGOR
- ☐ 610. KEN SINGLETON
- ☐ 620. LENN SAKATA
- ☐ 621. MIKE YOUNG
- ☐ 622. JOHN STEFERO
- ☐ 633. DENNIS MARTINEZ

BOSTON RED SOX

- ☐ 50. JIM RICE
- ☐ 91. JOHN HENRY JOHNSON
- ☐ 127. ED JURAK
- ☐ 151. WADE BOGGS
- ☐ 172. JERRY REMY
- ☐ 213. BRUCE HURST
- ☐ 249. JEFF NEWMAN
- ☐ 273. DAVE STAPLETON
- ☐ 294. TONY ARMAS
- ☐ 335. GARY ALLENSON
- ☐ 371. LUIS APONTE
- ☐ 395. DWIGHT EVANS
- ☐ 416. JOHN TUDOR
- ☐ 457. DENNIS BOYD
- ☐ 493. RICK MILLER
- ☐ 517. MIKE BROWN
- ☐ 538. BOB OJEDA
- ☐ 579. RICH GEDMAN
- ☐ 606. GLENN HOFFMAN
- ☐ 611. MARK CLEAR
- ☐ 614. REID NICHOLS
- ☐ 639. DENNIS ECKERSLEY
- ☐ 644. BOB STANLEY

CALIFORNIA ANGELS

- ☐ 35. DICK SCHOFIELD
- ☐ 42. MIKE BROWN
- ☐ 57. REGGIE JACKSON
- ☐ 85. RICK ADAMS
- ☐ 108. FRED LYNN
- ☐ 133. RON JACKSON
- ☐ 158. BOB BOONE
- ☐ 179. BOBBY GRICH
- ☐ 207. JUAN BENIQUEZ
- ☐ 230. DOUG DECINCES
- ☐ 255. ANDY HASSLER
- ☐ 280. KEN FORSCH
- ☐ 301. TOMMY JOHN
- ☐ 329. ROB WILFONG
- ☐ 352. ROD CAREW
- ☐ 377. STEVE LUBRATICH
- ☐ 402. GEOFF ZAHN
- ☐ 423. BRIAN DOWNING
- ☐ 451. DARYL SCONIERS
- ☐ 474. TIM FOLI
- ☐ 499. BRUCE KISON
- ☐ 524. BOBBY CLARK
- ☐ 597. LUIS SANCHEZ
- ☐ 647. GARY PETTIS

CHICAGO CUBS

- ☐ 41. JOE CARTER
- ☐ 67. LEON DURHAM
- ☐ 76. CHUCK RAINEY
- ☐ 117. BILL BUCKNER
- ☐ 144. GARY WOODS
- ☐ 167. SCOT THOMPSON
- ☐ 189. FERGUSON JENKINS
- ☐ 198. STEVE LAKE
- ☐ 239. LARRY BOWA
- ☐ 266. DICKIE NOLES
- ☐ 289. LEE SMITH
- ☐ 311. RYNE SANDBERG
- ☐ 320. MIKE PROLY
- ☐ 361. RON CEY
- ☐ 388. CRAIG LEFFERTS
- ☐ 411. MEL HALL
- ☐ 433. JODY DAVIS
- ☐ 442. WARREN BRUSSTAR
- ☐ 483. KEITH MORELAND
- ☐ 510. DICK RUTHVEN
- ☐ 533. STEVE TROUT
- ☐ 540. JAY JOHNSTONE
- ☐ 555. BILL CAMPBELL
- ☐ 623. CARMELO MARTINEZ

CHICAGO WHITE SOX

- ☐ 27. JOEL SKINNER
- ☐ 58. HAROLD BAINES
- ☐ 86. JERRY HAIRSTON
- ☐ 122. GREG LUZINSKI
- ☐ 135. KEVIN HICKEY
- ☐ 160. JERRY DYBZINSKI
- ☐ 180. RICHARD DOTSON
- ☐ 208. JUAN AGOSTO
- ☐ 244. RON KITTLE
- ☐ 257. RUDY LAW
- ☐ 282. TOM PACIOREK
- ☐ 302. CARLTON FISK
- ☐ 330. MARC HILL
- ☐ 366. FLOYD BANNISTER
- ☐ 379. JULIO CRUZ
- ☐ 404. MIKE SQUIRES
- ☐ 424. BRITT BURNS
- ☐ 452. SCOTT FLETCHER
- ☐ 488. LAMARR HOYT
- ☐ 501. JERRY KOOSMAN
- ☐ 526. DENNIS LAMP
- ☐ 546. VANCE LAW
- ☐ 570. SALOME BAROJAS
- ☐ 609. GREG WALKER

CINCINNATI REDS

- ☐ 62. RON OESTER
- ☐ 81. TOM FOLEY
- ☐ 121. DAVE CONCEPCION
- ☐ 140. RICH GALE
- ☐ 164. FRANK PASTORE
- ☐ 184. GARY REDUS
- ☐ 203. BILL SCHERRER
- ☐ 243. DAN DRIESSEN
- ☐ 262. JEFF JONES
- ☐ 286. ALEX TREVINO
- ☐ 306. CESAR CEDENO
- ☐ 325. DUAN WALKER
- ☐ 365. EDDIE MILNER
- ☐ 384. KELLY PARIS
- ☐ 408. DANN BILARDELLO
- ☐ 428. MARIO SOTO
- ☐ 447. TED POWER
- ☐ 487. BRUCE BERENYI
- ☐ 506. JOE PRICE
- ☐ 530. CHARLIE PULEO
- ☐ 550. TOM HUME
- ☐ 569. JEFF RUSSELL
- ☐ 602. NICK ESASKY

CLEVELAND INDIANS

- ☐ 43. MIKE JEFFCOAT
- ☐ 94. ANDRE THORNTON
- ☐ 102. TOM BRENNAN
- ☐ 129. BERT BLYLEVEN
- ☐ 154. ALAN BANNISTER
- ☐ 216. JULIO FRANCO
- ☐ 224. CHRIS BANDO
- ☐ 251. TOBY HARRAH
- ☐ 276. BRODERICK PERKINS
- ☐ 338. RICH SUTCLIFFE
- ☐ 346. RICK BEHENNA
- ☐ 373. NEAL HEATON
- ☐ 398. JUAN EICHELBERGER
- ☐ 460. RON HASSEY
- ☐ 468. GEORGE VUKOVICH
- ☐ 495. MIKE HARGROVE
- ☐ 520. GERRY WILLARD
- ☐ 536. PAT TABLER
- ☐ 542. BROOK JACOBY
- ☐ 574. GORMAN THOMAS
- ☐ 582. DAN SPILLNER
- ☐ 590. BUD ANDERSON
- ☐ 608. RICHARD BARNES
- ☐ 629. JIM ESSIAN
- ☐ 635. LARY SORENSEN

DETROIT TIGERS

- ☐ 49. LANCE PARRISH
- ☐ 90. JOHN GRUBB
- ☐ 105. DAN PETRY
- ☐ 125. JUAN BERENGUER
- ☐ 150. JOHN WOCKENFUSS
- ☐ 171. CHET LEMON
- ☐ 212. HOWARD BAILEY

- ☐ 227. LOU WHITAKER
- ☐ 247. MARTY CASTILLO
- ☐ 272. DAVE ROZEMA
- ☐ 293. ALAN TRAMMELL
- ☐ 334. WAYNE KRENCHICKI
- ☐ 349. LARRY HERNDON
- ☐ 369. DOUG BAIR
- ☐ 394. LARRY PASHNICK
- ☐ 415. JACK MORRIS
- ☐ 456. ENOS CABELL
- ☐ 471. MILT WILCOX
- ☐ 491. MIKE LAGA
- ☐ 516. AURELIO LOPEZ
- ☐ 578. TOM BROOKENS
- ☐ 593. KIRK GIBSON
- ☐ 618. GLENN WILSON

HOUSTON ASTROS

- ☐ 60. NOLAN RYAN
- ☐ 84. BOB LILLIS(M)
- ☐ 110. JOE NIEKRO
- ☐ 136. MIKE SCOTT
- ☐ 161. MIKE MADDEN
- ☐ 182. JOSE CRUZ
- ☐ 206. MIKE LACOSS
- ☐ 232. RAY KNIGHT
- ☐ 258. HARRY SPILMAN
- ☐ 283. FRANK LACORTE
- ☐ 304. DICKIE THON
- ☐ 328. BILL DAWLEY
- ☐ 354. PHIL GARNER
- ☐ 380. JOHN MIZEROCK
- ☐ 405. CRAIG REYNOLDS
- ☐ 426. JERRY MUMPHREY
- ☐ 450. KEVIN BASS
- ☐ 476. TERRY PUHL
- ☐ 502. FRANK DIPINO
- ☐ 527. TONY SCOTT
- ☐ 539. ALAN ASHBY
- ☐ 548. DAVE SMITH
- ☐ 564. VERN RUHLE
- ☐ 572. BOB KNEPPER
- ☐ 580. BILL DORAN
- ☐ 641. DENNY WALLING

KANSAS CITY ROYALS

- ☐ 53. GEORGE BRETT
- ☐ 95. ONIX CONCEPCION
- ☐ 100. LARRY GURA
- ☐ 130. BUD BLACK
- ☐ 155. WILLIE AIKENS
- ☐ 175. WILLIE WILSON
- ☐ 217. MIKE ARMSTRONG
- ☐ 222. FRANK WHITE
- ☐ 252. CESAR GERONIMO
- ☐ 277. BUTCH DAVIS
- ☐ 297. HAL MCRAE
- ☐ 339. MARK HUISMANN
- ☐ 344. DARRYL MOTLEY
- ☐ 374. GREG PRYOR
- ☐ 399. LEON ROBERTS
- ☐ 419. DON SLAUGHT
- ☐ 461. DANNY JACKSON
- ☐ 466. JOHN WATHAN
- ☐ 496. JOE SIMPSON
- ☐ 521. PAUL SPLITTORFF
- ☐ 543. U.L. WASHINGTON
- ☐ 583. DAN QUISENBERRY
- ☐ 588. PAT SHERIDAN

LOS ANGELES DODGERS

- ☐ 44. SID FERNANDEZ
- ☐ 52. FERNANDO VALENZUELA
- ☐ 93. CANDY MALDONADO
- ☐ 104. STEVE SAX
- ☐ 128. TOM NIENDENFUER
- ☐ 153. BOB WELCH
- ☐ 174. PEDRO GUERRERO
- ☐ 215. PAT ZACHRY
- ☐ 226. DUSTY BAKER
- ☐ 250. ALEJANDRO PENA
- ☐ 275. JOSE MORALES
- ☐ 296. GREG BROCK
- ☐ 337. JOE BECKWITH
- ☐ 348. MIKE MARSHALL
- ☐ 372. JACK FIMPLE
- ☐ 397. DERREL THOMAS

- ☐ 418. JERRY REUSS
- ☐ 459. BURT HOOTON
- ☐ 470. KEN LANDREAUX
- ☐ 494. RICK HONEYCUTT
- ☐ 519. DAVE SAX
- ☐ 581. STEVE YEAGER
- ☐ 587. BILL RUSSELL
- ☐ 642. DAVE ANDERSON

MILWAUKEE BREWERS

- ☐ 31. DION JAMES
- ☐ 48. ROBIN YOUNT
- ☐ 89. ED ROMERO
- ☐ 107. PAUL MOLITOR
- ☐ 115. JIM GANTNER
- ☐ 124. PETE LADD
- ☐ 149. TOM TELLMANN
- ☐ 170. RICK MANNING
- ☐ 211. MARK BROUHARD
- ☐ 229. BEN OGLIVIE
- ☐ 237. MIKE CALDWELL
- ☐ 246. BOB GIBSON
- ☐ 271. NED YOST
- ☐ 292. CHARLIE MOORE
- ☐ 333. CHUCK PORTER
- ☐ 351. CECIL COOPER
- ☐ 359. BOB MCCLURE
- ☐ 368. MOOSE HAAS
- ☐ 393. TOM CANDIOTTI
- ☐ 414. DON SUTTON
- ☐ 455. ROB PICCIOLO
- ☐ 473. TED SIMMONS
- ☐ 481. JIM SLATON
- ☐ 490. MARSHALL EDWARDS
- ☐ 515. BILL SCHROEDER

RON DAVIS P

MINNESOTA TWINS

- ☐ 37. TIM TEUFEL
- ☐ 39. GREG GAGNE
- ☐ 70. KENT HRBEK
- ☐ 72. KEN SCHROM
- ☐ 120. JOHN CASTINO
- ☐ 147. MICKEY HATCHER
- ☐ 192. GARY WARD
- ☐ 194. PETE FILSON
- ☐ 242. TOM BRUNANSKY
- ☐ 269. RON DAVIS
- ☐ 314. GARY GAETTI
- ☐ 316. AL WILLIAMS
- ☐ 364. FRANK VIOLA
- ☐ 391. RON WASHINGTON
- ☐ 436. BOBBY CASTILLO
- ☐ 438. SCOTT ULLGER
- ☐ 486. BRYAN OELKERS
- ☐ 513. RANDY BUSH
- ☐ 558. LEN WHITEHOUSE
- ☐ 560. RICK LYSANDER
- ☐ 598. DAVE ENGLE

MONTREAL EXPOS

- ☐ 29. MIKE STENHOUSE
- ☐ 33. ANGEL SALAZAR
- ☐ 40. MIKE FUENTES
- ☐ 55. GARY CARTER
- ☐ 87. BOB JAMES
- ☐ 97. ANDRE DAWSON
- ☐ 132. DAN SCHATZEDER

1984 Donruss

☐ 157. BRYAN LITTLE
☐ 177. AL OLIVER
☐ 209. BOBBY RAMOS
☐ 219. STEVE ROGERS
☐ 254. DOUG FLYNN
☐ 279. JEFF REARDON
☐ 299. TIM RAINES
☐ 331. RAY BURRIS
☐ 341. SCOTT SANDERSON
☐ 376. CHARLIE LEA
☐ 401. BILL GULLICKSON
☐ 421. TIM WALLACH
☐ 453. BRYN SMITH
☐ 463. TERRY FRANCONA
☐ 498. CHRIS WELSH
☐ 523. CHRIS SPEIER
☐ 575. MANNY TRILLO

NEW YORK METS

☐ 30. RON DARLING
☐ 68. DARRYL STRAWBERRY
☐ 75. ED LYNCH
☐ 116. TOM SEAVER
☐ 190. MOOKIE WILSON
☐ 197. JESSE OROSCO
☐ 238. KEITH HERNANDEZ
☐ 312. GEORGE FOSTER
☐ 319. JUNIOR ORTIZ
☐ 360. DAVE KINGMAN
☐ 434. DANNY HEEP
☐ 441. CRAIG SWAN
☐ 482. MIKE FITZGERALD
☐ 554. RUSTY STAUB
☐ 556. MIKE TORREZ
☐ 563. BRIAN GILES
☐ 595. BOB BAILOR
☐ 600. CARLOS DIAZ
☐ 603. RON HODGES
☐ 607. HUBIE BROOKS
☐ 615. DOUG SISK
☐ 640. WALT TERRELL
☐ 643. JOSE OQUENDO

NEW YORK YANKEES

☐ 45. BRIAN DAYETT
☐ 51. DAVE WINFIELD
☐ 92. JUAN ESPINO
☐ 103. DAVE RIGHETTI
☐ 126. JOHN MONTEFUSCO
☐ 152. DON BAYLOR
☐ 173. RON GUIDRY
☐ 214. BOB SHIRLEY
☐ 225. ROY SMALLEY
☐ 248. DON MATTINGLY
☐ 274. LOU PINIELLA
☐ 295. SHANE RAWLEY
☐ 336. BOB MEACHAM
☐ 347. ANDRE ROBERTSON
☐ 370. RAY FONTENOT
☐ 396. RICH GOSSAGE
☐ 417. WILLIE RANDOLPH
☐ 458. BUTCH WYNEGAR
☐ 469. STEVE KEMP
☐ 492. RICK CERONE
☐ 518. GRAIG NETTLES
☐ 577. DALE MURRAY
☐ 591. GEORGE FRAZIER
☐ 613. KEN GRIFFEY
☐ 626. RUDY MAY
☐ 627. MATT KEOUGH
☐ 637. OMAR MORENO

OAKLAND A'S

☐ 54. RICKEY HENDERSON
☐ 96. DON HILL
☐ 101. DWAYNE MURPHY
☐ 131. GORMAN HEIMUELLER
☐ 156. JEFF BURROUGHS
☐ 176. CARNEY LANSFORD
☐ 218. DAVE BEARD
☐ 223. MIKE HEATH
☐ 253. TOM UNDERWOOD
☐ 278. TONY PHILLIPS
☐ 298. MIKE DAVIS
☐ 340. TIM CONROY
☐ 345. CHRIS CODIROLI
☐ 375. WAYNE GROSS
☐ 400. DAVEY LOPES

☐ 420. STEVE MCCATTY
☐ 462. BOB KEARNEY
☐ 467. BILL ALMON
☐ 497. KEITH ATHERTON
☐ 522. TOM BURGMEIER
☐ 631. MIKE WARREN

PHILADELPHIA PHILLIES

☐ 61. PETE ROSE
☐ 82. JOE LEFEBVRE
☐ 111. STEVE CARLTON
☐ 137. BO DIAZ
☐ 163. WILLIE HERNANDEZ
☐ 183. MIKE SCHMIDT
☐ 204. AL HOLLAND
☐ 233. GARY MATTHEWS
☐ 259. MARTY BYSTROM
☐ 285. GREG GROSS
☐ 305. GARRY MADDOX
☐ 326. OZZIE VIRGIL
☐ 355. JOE MORGAN
☐ 381. KEVIN GROSS
☐ 407. JOHN DENNY
☐ 427. IVAN DEJESUS
☐ 448. CHARLIE HUDSON
☐ 477. VON HAYES
☐ 503. TONY PEREZ
☐ 529. RON REED
☐ 541. BOB DERNIER
☐ 545. KIKO GARCIA
☐ 547. TUG MCGRAW
☐ 549. LEN MATUSZEK

PITTSBURGH PIRATES

☐ 38. DOUG FROBEL
☐ 64. JASON THOMPSON
☐ 78. CECILIO GUANTE
☐ 113. BILL MADLOCK
☐ 142. BRIAN HARPER
☐ 166. LEE MAZZILLI
☐ 186. TONY PENA
☐ 200. MANNY SARMIENTO
☐ 235. ROD SCURRY
☐ 264. GENE TENACE
☐ 288. DAVE PARKER
☐ 308. JOHNNY RAY
☐ 322. JIM MORRISON
☐ 357. JOHN CANDELARIA
☐ 386. MILT MAY
☐ 410. KENT TEKULVE
☐ 430. DALE BERRA
☐ 444. MIKE EASLER
☐ 479. LEE LACY
☐ 508. MARVELL WYNNE
☐ 532. DON ROBINSON
☐ 552. RICK RHODEN
☐ 566. LARRY MCWILLIAMS
☐ 592. LEE TUNNELL
☐ 628. JOSE DELEON

ST. LOUIS CARDINALS

☐ 59. OZZIE SMITH
☐ 83. ANDY VAN SLYKE
☐ 109. NEIL ALLEN
☐ 138. GLENN BRUMMER
☐ 168. BOB FORSCH
☐ 181. JOAQUIN ANDUJAR
☐ 205. DAVID VON OHLEN
☐ 231. LONNIE SMITH
☐ 260. DAVE RUCKER
☐ 290. DAVE LAPOINT
☐ 303. DARRELL PORTER
☐ 327. JEFF LAHTI
☐ 353. WILLIE MCGEE
☐ 382. MIKE RAMSEY
☐ 412. JOHN STUPER
☐ 425. DAVID GREEN
☐ 449. DANNY COX
☐ 475. GEORGE HENDRICK
☐ 504. KEN OBERKFELL
☐ 534. BRUCE SUTTER
☐ 571. DANE IORG
☐ 596. TOM HERR

RUPPERT JONES OF

SAN DIEGO PADRES

☐ 34. KEVIN MCREYNOLDS
☐ 63. STEVE GARVEY
☐ 80. KURT BEVACQUA
☐ 112. TERRY KENNEDY
☐ 139. SID MONGE
☐ 162. LUIS DELEON
☐ 185. GARRY TEMPLETON
☐ 202. TIM FLANNERY
☐ 234. JUAN BONILLA
☐ 261. RUPPERT JONES
☐ 284. TIM LOLLAR
☐ 307. GARY LUCAS
☐ 324. TONY GWYNN
☐ 356. LUIS SALAZAR
☐ 383. DOUG GWOSDZ
☐ 406. ERIC SHOW
☐ 429. GENE RICHARDS
☐ 446. DENNIS RASMUSSEN
☐ 478. BOBBY BROWN
☐ 505. MARK THURMOND
☐ 528. ED WHITSON
☐ 551. DAVE DRAVECKY
☐ 568. ALAN WIGGINS

SAN FRANCISCO GIANTS

☐ 46. CHRIS SMITH
☐ 65. JACK CLARK
☐ 79. JIM BARR
☐ 114. CHILI DAVIS
☐ 143. JOHN RABB
☐ 187. GREG MINTON
☐ 201. MARK DAVIS
☐ 236. ATLEE HAMMAKER
☐ 265. BRAD WELLMAN
☐ 309. ANDY MCGAFFIGAN
☐ 323. MAX VENABLE
☐ 358. BILL LASKEY
☐ 387. FRED BREINING
☐ 431. DARRELL EVANS
☐ 445. RENIE MARTIN
☐ 480. JOEL YOUNGBLOOD
☐ 509. MIKE KRUKOW
☐ 553. DUAN KUIPER
☐ 567. JEFF LEONARD
☐ 573. GARY LAVELLE
☐ 601. TOM O'MALLEY
☐ 616. BOB BRENLY
☐ 624. DAVE BERGMAN
☐ 646. SCOTT GARRELTS
☐ 649. JOHNNIE LEMASTER

SEATTLE MARINERS

☐ 69. RICHIE ZISK
☐ 74. JOHN MOSES
☐ 118. BILL CAUDILL
☐ 145. PAT PUTNAM
☐ 191. JIM BEATTIE
☐ 196. RICK SWEET
☐ 240. TONY BERNAZARD
☐ 267. JAMIE ALLEN
☐ 313. SPIKE OWEN
☐ 318. ORLANDO MERCADO
☐ 362. MATT YOUNG
☐ 389. STEVE HENDERSON
☐ 435. EDWIN NÚÑEZ

- ☐ 440. DOMINGO RAMOS
- ☐ 484. RON ROENICKE
- ☐ 511. AL COWENS
- ☐ 557. DAVE HENDERSON
- ☐ 562. BRYAN CLARK
- ☐ 604. ED VANDE BERG
- ☐ 619. BOB STODDARD
- ☐ 630. DARNELL COLES
- ☐ 632. DEL CRANDALL(M)
- ☐ 634. MIKE MOORE
- ☐ 636. RICKY NELSON

TEXAS RANGERS

- ☐ 28. TOM DUNBAR
- ☐ 56. BUDDY BELL
- ☐ 98. FRANK TANANA
- ☐ 99. CURT WILKERSON
- ☐ 134. TOM HENKE
- ☐ 159. DAVE HOSTETLER
- ☐ 178. JIM SUNDBERG
- ☐ 220. JOHN BUTCHER
- ☐ 221. MIKE SMITHSON
- ☐ 256. ODELL JONES
- ☐ 281. PETE O'BRIEN
- ☐ 300. BUCKY DENT
- ☐ 342. LARRY BITTNER
- ☐ 343. DAVE STEWART
- ☐ 378. JON MATLACK
- ☐ 403. BILLY SAMPLE
- ☐ 422. LARRY PARRISH
- ☐ 464. WAYNE TOLLESON
- ☐ 465. MICKEY RIVERS
- ☐ 500. BOB JOHNSON
- ☐ 525. GEORGE WRIGHT
- ☐ 544. DANNY DARWIN
- ☐ 586. DAVE SCHMIDT
- ☐ 638. CHARLIE HOUGH

TORONTO BLUE JAYS

- ☐ 32. TONY FERNANDEZ
- ☐ 71. DAVE STIEB
- ☐ 73. GEORGE BELL
- ☐ 119. JIM CLANCY
- ☐ 146. JIM ACKER
- ☐ 193. JESSE BARFIELD
- ☐ 195. ROY LEE JACKSON
- ☐ 241. DAMASO GARCIA
- ☐ 268. JIM GOTT
- ☐ 315. WILLIE UPSHAW
- ☐ 317. JORGE ORTA
- ☐ 363. LLOYD MOSEBY
- ☐ 390. RANDY MOFFITT
- ☐ 437. ERNIE WHITT
- ☐ 439. DOYLE ALEXANDER
- ☐ 485. LUIS LEAL
- ☐ 512. CLIFF JOHNSON
- ☐ 559. BARRY BONNELL
- ☐ 561. GARTH IORG
- ☐ 584. RANCE MULLINIKS
- ☐ 605. ALFREDO GRIFFIN
- ☐ 612. BUCK MARTINEZ
- ☐ 617. JOEY MCLAUGHLIN
- ☐ 645. DAVE GEISEL
- ☐ 650. DAVE COLLINS

1985 DONRUSS (660)
2 1/2″ X 3 1/2″

ATLANTA BRAVES

- ☐ 66. DALE MURPHY
- ☐ 77. BOB HORNER
- ☐ 141. RAFAEL RAMIREZ
- ☐ 165. LEN BARKER
- ☐ 188. CRAIG MCMURTRY
- ☐ 199. GLENN HUBBARD
- ☐ 263. BRUCE BENEDICT
- ☐ 287. CHRIS CHAMBLISS
- ☐ 310. CLAUDELL WASHINGTON
- ☐ 321. BRAD KOMMINSK
- ☐ 385. RICK MAHLER
- ☐ 409. RICK CAMP
- ☐ 432. KEN OBERKFELL
- ☐ 443. GERALD PERRY
- ☐ 507. PASCUAL PEREZ
- ☐ 531. RANDY JOHNSON
- ☐ 554. JEFF DEDMON
- ☐ 565. ALEX TREVINO
- ☐ 628. STEVE BEDROSIAN
- ☐ 650. DONNIE MOORE

BALTIMORE ORIOLES

- ☐ 36. LARRY SHEETS
- ☐ 45. JIM TRABER
- ☐ 47. EDDIE MURRAY
- ☐ 88. MIKE FLANAGAN
- ☐ 106. RICH DAUER
- ☐ 123. GARY ROENICKE
- ☐ 148. SAMMY STEWART
- ☐ 169. CAL RIPKEN
- ☐ 210. TIPPY MARTINEZ
- ☐ 228. WAYNE GROSS
- ☐ 245. JOHN LOWENSTEIN
- ☐ 270. KEN DIXON
- ☐ 291. MIKE BODDICKER
- ☐ 332. RICK DEMPSEY
- ☐ 350. AL BUMBRY
- ☐ 367. MIKE YOUNG
- ☐ 392. BILL SWAGGERTY
- ☐ 413. SCOTT MCGREGOR
- ☐ 454. STORM DAVIS
- ☐ 472. JOHN SHELBY
- ☐ 489. DAN FORD
- ☐ 514. DENNIS MARTINEZ
- ☐ 535. VIC RODRIGUEZ
- ☐ 576. FLOYD RAYFORD
- ☐ 594. JOE NOLAN

BOSTON RED SOX

- ☐ 29. STEVE LYONS
- ☐ 40. CHARLIE MITCHELL
- ☐ 50. JIM RICE
- ☐ 91. BOB STANLEY
- ☐ 127. MARTY BARRETT
- ☐ 151. DENNIS BOYD
- ☐ 172. WADE BOGGS
- ☐ 213. MIKE EASLER
- ☐ 249. TONY ARMAS
- ☐ 273. ROGER CLEMENS
- ☐ 294. DWIGHT EVANS
- ☐ 335. JACKIE GUTIERREZ
- ☐ 371. BOB OJEDA

- ☐ 395. STEVE CRAWFORD
- ☐ 416. BILL BUCKNER
- ☐ 457. RICH GEDMAN
- ☐ 493. BRUCE HURST
- ☐ 517. RICK MILLER
- ☐ 538. MARK CLEAR
- ☐ 579. ED JURAK
- ☐ 614. AL NIPPER
- ☐ 636. REID NICHOLS

CALIFORNIA ANGELS

- ☐ 57. REGGIE JACKSON
- ☐ 85. ROD CAREW
- ☐ 108. MIKE WITT
- ☐ 133. FRED LYNN
- ☐ 158. BRIAN DOWNING
- ☐ 179. DOUG DECINCES
- ☐ 207. MIKE BROWN
- ☐ 230. BOB BOONE
- ☐ 255. DON AASE
- ☐ 280. BOBBY GRICH
- ☐ 301. GEOFF ZAHN
- ☐ 329. DICK SCHOFIELD
- ☐ 352. LUIS SANCHEZ
- ☐ 377. BRUCE KISON
- ☐ 402. ROB WILFONG
- ☐ 423. TOMMY JOHN
- ☐ 451. RON ROMANICK
- ☐ 474. DOUG CORBETT
- ☐ 499. GARY PETTIS
- ☐ 524. CURT KAUFMAN
- ☐ 545. JIM SLATON
- ☐ 573. JUAN BENIQUEZ
- ☐ 620. DARYL SCONIERS
- ☐ 643. JERRY NARRON
- ☐ 644. DARRELL MILLER

CHICAGO CUBS

- ☐ 39. SHAWON DUNSTON
- ☐ 41. BILLY HATCHER
- ☐ 67. RYNE SANDBERG
- ☐ 76. JODY DAVIS
- ☐ 117. KEITH MORELAND
- ☐ 144. TIM STODDARD
- ☐ 167. GEORGE FRAZIER
- ☐ 189. LEON DURHAM
- ☐ 198. STEVE TROUT
- ☐ 239. GARY MATTHEWS
- ☐ 266. SCOTT SANDERSON
- ☐ 289. RICH BORDI
- ☐ 311. LEE SMITH
- ☐ 320. RON CEY
- ☐ 361. LARRY BOWA
- ☐ 388. THAD BOSLEY
- ☐ 411. HENRY COTTO
- ☐ 433. RICK SUTCLIFFE
- ☐ 442. DENNIS ECKERSLEY
- ☐ 483. DAVE OWEN
- ☐ 510. BOB DERNIER
- ☐ 533. WARREN BRUSSTAR
- ☐ 555. GARY WOODS
- ☐ 564. RICH HEBNER
- ☐ 604. DAVE LOPES

CHICAGO WHITE SOX

- ☐ 33. DARYL BOSTON
- ☐ 58. HAROLD BAINES
- ☐ 86. LAMARR HOYT
- ☐ 122. VANCE LAW
- ☐ 135. JERRY HAIRSTON
- ☐ 160. MARC HILL
- ☐ 180. RON KITTLE
- ☐ 208. CARLTON FISK
- ☐ 244. RUDY LAW
- ☐ 257. BRITT BURNS
- ☐ 282. RON REED
- ☐ 302. RICH DOTSON
- ☐ 330. SCOTT FLETCHER
- ☐ 366. GREG WALKER
- ☐ 379. FLOYD BANNISTER
- ☐ 404. AL JONES
- ☐ 424. TOM SEAVER
- ☐ 452. JULIO CRUZ
- ☐ 488. TOM PACIOREK
- ☐ 501. MIKE SQUIRES
- ☐ 526. JUAN AGOSTO
- ☐ 546. GREG LUZINSKI
- ☐ 574. JOEL SKINNER

☐ 615. GENE NELSON
☐ 622. ROY SMALLEY
☐ 645. TIM HULETT

CINCINNATI REDS

☐ 62. DAVE PARKER
☐ 81. RON OESTER
☐ 121. NICK ESASKY
☐ 140. WAYNE KRENCHICKI
☐ 164. JOHN FRANCO
☐ 184. MARIO SOTO
☐ 203. DAVE CONCEPCION
☐ 243. DANN BILARDELLO
☐ 262. JAY TIBBS
☐ 286. TED POWER
☐ 306. GARY REDUS
☐ 325. ERIC DAVIS
☐ 365. BRAD GULDEN
☐ 384. DAVE VAN GORDER
☐ 408. TOM HUME
☐ 428. EDDIE MILNER
☐ 447. CESAR CEDENO
☐ 487. JEFF RUSSELL
☐ 506. BOB OWCHINKO
☐ 530. SKEETER BARNES
☐ 550. FRANK PASTORE
☐ 569. TOM FOLEY
☐ 608. DUANE WALKER
☐ 627. JOE PRICE
☐ 634. TOM BROWNING
☐ 641. PERE ROSS(M)
☐ 642. WADE ROWDON
☐ 646. ANDY MCGAFFIGAN
☐ 649. RON ROBINSON

CLEVELAND INDIANS

☐ 94. JULIO FRANCO
☐ 102. TONY BERNAZARD
☐ 129. ERNIE CAMACHO
☐ 154. BROOK JACOBY
☐ 216. BRETT BUTLER
☐ 224. BERT BLYLEVEN
☐ 251. MIKE JEFFCOAT
☐ 276. GEORGE VUKOVICH
☐ 338. MEL HALL
☐ 346. JERRY WILLARD
☐ 373. NEAL HEATON
☐ 398. MIKE HARGROVE
☐ 460. PAT TABLER
☐ 468. ANDRE THORNTON
☐ 495. MIKE FISCHLIN
☐ 520. CHRIS BANDO
☐ 582. TOM WADDELL
☐ 590. CARMEN CASTILLO
☐ 611. ROY SMITH
☐ 616. JOE CARTER
☐ 639. DON SCHULZE
☐ 653. STEVE FARR

JULIO FRANCO SS

DETROIT TIGERS

☐ 49. LANCE PARRISH
☐ 90. CHET LEMON
☐ 105. MILT WILCOX
☐ 125. DAVE ROZEMA
☐ 150. LARRY HERNDON
☐ 171. ALAN TRAMMELL
☐ 212. WILLIE HERNANDEZ

☐ 227. DARRELL EVANS
☐ 247. HOWARD JOHNSON
☐ 272. JUAN BERENGUER
☐ 293. LOU WHITAKER
☐ 334. DAN PETRY
☐ 349. AURELIO LOPEZ
☐ 369. DOUG BAIR
☐ 394. MARTY CASTILLO
☐ 415. JACK MORRIS
☐ 456. BARBARO GARBEY
☐ 471. KIRK GIBSON
☐ 491. SCOTTIE EARL
☐ 516. RUSTY KUNTZ
☐ 537. DAVE BERGMAN
☐ 578. JOHN GRUBB
☐ 593. TOM BROOKENS
☐ 612. RUPPERT JONES

HOUSTON ASTROS

☐ 60. NOLAN RYAN
☐ 84. BILL DORAN
☐ 110. ENOS CABELL
☐ 136. KEVIN BASS
☐ 161. PHIL GARNER
☐ 182. JOE NIEKRO
☐ 260. JERRY MUMPHREY
☐ 232. FRANK DIPINO
☐ 258. MIKE SCOTT
☐ 283. ALAN ASHBY
☐ 304. JOSE CRUZ
☐ 328. CRAIG REYNOLDS
☐ 354. BILL DAWLEY
☐ 380. VERN RUHLE
☐ 405. MIKE LACOSS
☐ 426. TERRY PUHL
☐ 450. MARK BAILEY
☐ 476. BOB KNEPPER
☐ 502. JIM PANKOVITZ
☐ 527. DENNY WALLING
☐ 548. DAVE SMITH
☐ 572. JOE SAMBITO

KANSAS CITY ROYALS

☐ 32. JOHN MORRIS
☐ 42. RUSS STEPHANS
☐ 53. GEORGE BRETT
☐ 95. DAN QUISENBERRY
☐ 100. BUD BLACK
☐ 130. JORGE ORTA
☐ 155. ONIX CONCEPCION
☐ 175. FRANK WHITE
☐ 217. LARRY GURA
☐ 222. BRET SABERHAGEN
☐ 252. DANE IORG
☐ 277. GREG PRYOR
☐ 297. WILLIE WILSON
☐ 339. PAT SHERIDAN
☐ 344. MARK GUBICZA
☐ 374. DANNY JACKSON
☐ 399. CHARLIE LEIBRANDT
☐ 419. STEVE BALBONI
☐ 461. DARRYL MOTLEY
☐ 466. JOHN WATHAN
☐ 496. DON SLAUGHT
☐ 521. U.L. WASHINGTON
☐ 541. JOE BECKWITH
☐ 583. MARK HUISMANN
☐ 588. HAL MCRAE
☐ 640. MIKE JONES

LOS ANGELES DODGERS

☐ 31. TONY BREWER
☐ 52. FERNANDO VALENZUELA
☐ 93. BILL RUSSELL
☐ 104. BURT HOOTON
☐ 128. R.J. REYNOLDS
☐ 153. TOM NIEDENFUER
☐ 174. PEDRO GUERRERO
☐ 215. RICK HONEYCUTT
☐ 226. JERRY REUSS
☐ 250. CANDY MALDONADO
☐ 275. DAVE ANDERSON
☐ 296. MIKE MARSHALL
☐ 337. ALEJANDRO PENA
☐ 348. FRANKLIN STUBBS
☐ 372. BOB WELCH
☐ 397. BOB BAILOR

☐ 418. STEVE SAX
☐ 459. MIKE SCIOSCIA
☐ 470. SID BREAM
☐ 494. KEN LANDREAUX
☐ 519. STEVE YEAGER
☐ 540. TERRY WHITFIELD
☐ 581. OREL HERSHISER
☐ 592. KEN HOWELL
☐ 638. GERMAN RIVERA

BILL RUSSELL SS

MILWAUKEE BREWERS

☐ 46. DOUG LOMAN
☐ 48. ROBIN YOUNT
☐ 89. JIM SUNDBERG
☐ 107. DON SUTTON
☐ 115. CHUCK PORTER
☐ 124. BILL SCHROEDER
☐ 149. MARK BROUHARD
☐ 170. CECIL COOPER
☐ 211. DION JAMES
☐ 229. JIM GANTNER
☐ 237. RICK MANNING
☐ 246. TOM TELLMANN
☐ 271. PETE LADD
☐ 292. ROLLIE FINGERS
☐ 333. BEN OGLIVIE
☐ 351. CHARLIE MOORE
☐ 359. PAUL MOLITOR
☐ 368. RICK WAITS
☐ 393. BOB GIBSON
☐ 414. TED SIMMONS
☐ 455. JAIME COCANOWER
☐ 473. MOOSE HAAS
☐ 481. BOBBY CLARK
☐ 490. MIKE CALDWELL
☐ 515. ED ROMERO
☐ 536. BOB MCCLURE
☐ 577. ROY HOWELL
☐ 595. WILLIE LOZADO

MINNESOTA TWINS

☐ 30. JEFF REED
☐ 70. KENT HRBEK
☐ 72. DAVE ENGLE
☐ 120. RON DAVIS
☐ 147. DAVE MEIER
☐ 192. TIM TEUFEL
☐ 194. MICKEY HATCHER
☐ 242. GARY GAETTI
☐ 269. HOUSTON JIMENEZ
☐ 314. JOHN BUTCHER
☐ 316. MIKE SMITHSON
☐ 364. TOM BRUNANSKY
☐ 391. RON WASHINGTON
☐ 436. FRANK VIOLA
☐ 438. KIRBY PUCKETT
☐ 486. KEN SCHROM
☐ 513. LEN WHITEHOUSE
☐ 558. DARRELL BROWN
☐ 560. RICK LYSANDER
☐ 607. PETE FILSON
☐ 633. RANDY BUSH
☐ 652. TIM LAUDNER

MONTREAL EXPOS

☐ 55. GARY CARTER
☐ 87. TIM WALLACH
☐ 97. BILL GULLICKSON

- ☐ 132. TERRY FRANCONA
- ☐ 157. JOE HESKETH
- ☐ 177. CHARLIE LEA
- ☐ 209. BRYN SMITH
- ☐ 219. STEVE ROGERS
- ☐ 254. PETE ROSE
- ☐ 279. BOB JAMES
- ☐ 299. TIM RAINES
- ☐ 331. JEFF REARDON
- ☐ 341. DAVID PALMER
- ☐ 376. MIKE STENHOUSE
- ☐ 401. RAZOR SHINES
- ☐ 421. ANDRE DAWSON
- ☐ 453. MIGUEL DILONE
- ☐ 463. DOUG FLYNN
- ☐ 498. GARY LUCAS
- ☐ 523. ANGEL SALAZAR
- ☐ 543. DAN SCHATZEDER
- ☐ 575. RANDY ST. CLAIRE
- ☐ 585. JIM WOHLFORD
- ☐ 619. DAN DRIESSEN

NEW YORK METS

- ☐ 38. CALVIN SCHIRALDI
- ☐ 68. KEITH HERNANDEZ
- ☐ 75. JESSE OROSCO
- ☐ 116. JOHN GIBBONS
- ☐ 190. DWIGHT GOODEN
- ☐ 197. HUBIE BROOKS
- ☐ 238. MIKE FITZGERALD
- ☐ 312. DARRYL STRAWBERRY
- ☐ 319. WALLY BACKMAN
- ☐ 360. RON GARDENHIRE
- ☐ 434. RON DARLING
- ☐ 441. DOUG SISK
- ☐ 482. MOOKIE WILSON
- ☐ 556. DANNY HEEP
- ☐ 563. SID FERNANDEZ
- ☐ 597. WALT TERRELL
- ☐ 603. GEORGE FOSTER
- ☐ 610. RAFAEL SANTANA
- ☐ 617. RAY KNIGHT
- ☐ 623. ED LYNCH
- ☐ 625. BRUCE BERENYI
- ☐ 626. KELVIN CHAPMAN

NEW YORK YANKEES

- ☐ 37. SCOTT BRADLEY
- ☐ 51. DAVE WINFIELD
- ☐ 92. WILLIE RANDOLPH
- ☐ 103. JAY HOWELL
- ☐ 126. BOBBY MEACHAM
- ☐ 152. BRIAN DAYETT
- ☐ 173. DON BAYLOR
- ☐ 214. RON GUIDRY
- ☐ 225. STEVE KEMP
- ☐ 248. RAY FONTENOT
- ☐ 274. RICK CERONE
- ☐ 295. DON MATTINGLY
- ☐ 336. DAVE RIGHETTI
- ☐ 347. KEN GRIFFEY
- ☐ 370. BOB SHIRLEY
- ☐ 396. CLAY CHRISTIANSEN
- ☐ 417. BUTCH WYNEGAR
- ☐ 458. PHIL NIEKRO
- ☐ 469. REX HUDLER
- ☐ 492. JOSE RIJO
- ☐ 518. DENNIS RASMUSSEN
- ☐ 539. MIKE PAGLIARULO
- ☐ 580. JOHN MONTEFUSCO
- ☐ 591. OMAR MORENO
- ☐ 602. MIKE ARMSTRONG
- ☐ 613. JOE COWLEY
- ☐ 629. VIC MATA
- ☐ 637. DAN PASQUA

OAKLAND A'S

- ☐ 35. STEVE KIEFER
- ☐ 54. DAVE KINGMAN
- ☐ 96. BILL CAUDILL
- ☐ 101. TONY PHILLIPS
- ☐ 131. LARY SORENSEN
- ☐ 156. TIM CONROY
- ☐ 176. RICKEY HENDERSON
- ☐ 218. RAY BURRIS
- ☐ 223. MIKE DAVIS
- ☐ 253. BRUCE BOCHTE
- ☐ 278. MIKE WARREN
- ☐ 298. MIKE HEATH

- ☐ 340. KEITH ATHERTON
- ☐ 345. CARNEY LANSFORD
- ☐ 375. DONNIE HILL
- ☐ 400. TOM BURGMEIER
- ☐ 420. DWAYNE MURPHY
- ☐ 462. CHRIS CODOROLI
- ☐ 467. BILL KRUEGER
- ☐ 497. STEVE MCCATTY
- ☐ 522. CURT YOUNG
- ☐ 542. JEFF BURROUGHS
- ☐ 584. JOE MORGAN
- ☐ 589. BILL ALMON
- ☐ 618. CHUCK RAINEY

PHILADLEPHIA PHILLIES

- ☐ 44. STEVE JELTZ
- ☐ 61. MIKE SCHMIDT
- ☐ 82. OZZIE VIRGIL
- ☐ 111. JOHN DENNY
- ☐ 137. GARRY MADDOX
- ☐ 163. BILL CAMPBELL
- ☐ 183. JUAN SAMUEL
- ☐ 204. IVAN DEJESUS
- ☐ 233. JERRY KOOSMAN
- ☐ 259. LEN MATUSZEK
- ☐ 285. JOE LEFEBVRE
- ☐ 305. STEVE CARLTON
- ☐ 326. VON HAYES
- ☐ 355. CHARLIE HUDSON
- ☐ 381. TIM CORCORAN
- ☐ 407. GREG GROSS
- ☐ 427. AL HOLLAND
- ☐ 448. RICK SCHU
- ☐ 477. KEVIN GROSS
- ☐ 503. LUIS AGUAYO
- ☐ 529. SIXTO LEZCANO
- ☐ 549. JOHN WOCKENFUSS
- ☐ 570. LARRY ANDERSEN
- ☐ 598. AL OLIVER
- ☐ 599. SHANE RAWLEY
- ☐ 609. GLENN WILSON
- ☐ 624. JEFF STONE
- ☐ 648. JOHN RUSSELL

PITTSBURGH PIRATES

- ☐ 28. MIKE BIELECKI
- ☐ 34. ALFONSO PULIDO
- ☐ 64. TONY PENA
- ☐ 78. LARRY MCWILLIAMS
- ☐ 113. MARVELL WYNNE
- ☐ 142. ROD SCURRY
- ☐ 166. BENNY DISTEFANO
- ☐ 186. JOHNNY RAY
- ☐ 200. BILL MADLOCK
- ☐ 235. JOHN TUDOR
- ☐ 264. DON ROBINSON
- ☐ 288. LEE TUNNELL
- ☐ 308. JOSE DELEON
- ☐ 322. JASON THOMPSON
- ☐ 357. CECILIO GUANTE
- ☐ 386. LEE MAZZILLI
- ☐ 410. MILT MAY
- ☐ 430. JOHN CANDELARIA
- ☐ 444. DALE BERRA
- ☐ 479. KENT TEKULVE
- ☐ 508. LEE LACY
- ☐ 532. JIM MORRISON
- ☐ 552. RICK RHODEN
- ☐ 566. BRIAN HARPER
- ☐ 600. DENNY GONZALEZ

ST. LOUIS CARDINALS

- ☐ 59. OZZIE SMITH
- ☐ 83. RICKY HORTON
- ☐ 109. BRUCE SUTTER
- ☐ 138. DAVE LAPOINT
- ☐ 168. TITO LANDRUM
- ☐ 181. GEORGE HENDRICK
- ☐ 205. NEIL ALLEN
- ☐ 231. LONNIE SMITH
- ☐ 260. DAVE RUCKER
- ☐ 290. GLENN BRUMMER
- ☐ 303. DAVID GREEN
- ☐ 327. ANDY VAN SLYKE
- ☐ 353. DARRELL PORTER
- ☐ 382. KURT KEPSHIRE
- ☐ 412. DAVE VON OHLEN
- ☐ 425. TOM HERR

- ☐ 449. JOAQUIN ANDUJAR
- ☐ 475. WILLIE MCGEE
- ☐ 504. RALPH CITARELLA
- ☐ 534. TERRY PENDLETON
- ☐ 547. MARK SALAS
- ☐ 571. DANNY COX
- ☐ 596. TOM NIETO

SAN DIEGO PADRES

- ☐ 63. TONY GWYNN
- ☐ 80. ALAN WIGGINS
- ☐ 112. DAVE DRAVECKY
- ☐ 139. KEVIN MCREYNOLDS
- ☐ 162. JERRY DAVIS
- ☐ 185. RICH GOSSAGE
- ☐ 202. ERIC SHOW
- ☐ 234. GRAIG NETTLES
- ☐ 261. CRAIG LEFFERTS
- ☐ 284. MARK THURMOND
- ☐ 307. STEVE GARVEY
- ☐ 324. TIM LOLLAR
- ☐ 356. GARRY TEMPLETON
- ☐ 383. BOBBY BROWN
- ☐ 406. LUIS DELEON
- ☐ 429. TERRY KENNEDY
- ☐ 446. ED WHITSON
- ☐ 478. CARMELO MARTINEZ
- ☐ 505. BRUCE BOCHY
- ☐ 528. ANDY HAWKINS
- ☐ 551. TIM FLANNERY
- ☐ 568. LUIS SALAZAR
- ☐ 647. KURT BEVACQUA

SAN FRANCISCO GIANTS

- ☐ 43. ALEJANDRO SANCHEZ
- ☐ 65. JACK CLARK
- ☐ 79. JOEL YOUNGBLOOD
- ☐ 114. JOHNNIE LEMASTER
- ☐ 143. GREG MINTO
- ☐ 187. BOB BRENLY
- ☐ 201. JEFF ROBINSON
- ☐ 236. JOHN RABB
- ☐ 265. GARY LAVELLE
- ☐ 309. RANDY LERCH
- ☐ 323. FRANK WILLIAMS
- ☐ 358. JEFF LEONARD
- ☐ 387. BILL LASKEY
- ☐ 431. MANNY TRILLO
- ☐ 445. DUSTY BAKER
- ☐ 480. CHILI DAVIS
- ☐ 509. ATLEE HAMMAKER
- ☐ 553. MARK DAVIS
- ☐ 567. DAN GLADDEN
- ☐ 601. MARK GRANT
- ☐ 630. MIKE KRUKOW

SEATTLE MARINERS

- ☐ 27. DANNY TARTABULL
- ☐ 69. ALVIN DAVIS
- ☐ 74. JACK PERCONTE
- ☐ 118. DARNELL COLES
- ☐ 145. STEVE HENDERSON
- ☐ 191. BARRY BONNELL
- ☐ 196. AL COWENS
- ☐ 240. JIM PRESLEY
- ☐ 267. MATT YOUNG
- ☐ 313. JIM BEATTIE
- ☐ 318. KEN PHELPS
- ☐ 362. BOB KEARNEY
- ☐ 389. AL CHAMBERS
- ☐ 435. SPIKE OWEN
- ☐ 440. MIKE MOORE
- ☐ 484. EDWIN NUNEZ
- ☐ 511. ED VANDE BERG
- ☐ 557. MARK LANGSTON
- ☐ 562. MIKE STANTON
- ☐ 605. SALOME BAROJAS
- ☐ 631. PHIL BRADLEY

TEXAS RANGERS

- ☐ 56. BUDDY BELL
- ☐ 98. DANNY DARWIN
- ☐ 99. CURTIS WILKERSON
- ☐ 134. BOBBY JONES
- ☐ 159. TOMMY DUNBAR
- ☐ 178. PETE O'BRIEN
- ☐ 220. FRANK TANANA

☐ 221. NED YOST
☐ 256. GEORGE WRIGHT
☐ 281. MIKE MASON
☐ 300. LARRY PARRISH
☐ 342. GARY WARD
☐ 343. DAVE STEWART
☐ 378. WAYNE TOLLESON
☐ 403. TOM HENKE
☐ 422. CHARLIE HOUGH
☐ 464. BILLY SAMPLE
☐ 465. MICKEY RIVERS
☐ 500. MARVIS FOLEY
☐ 525. ODELL JONES
☐ 544. DONNIE SCOTT
☐ 586. DAVE SCHMIDT
☐ 587. JEFF KUNKEL
☐ 621. BILL STEIN

TORONTO BLUE JAYS

☐ 71. WILLIE UPSHAW
☐ 73. ALFREDO GRIFFIN
☐ 119. DENNIS LAMP
☐ 146. GEORGE BELL
☐ 193. DAVE STIEB
☐ 195. JESSE BARFIELD
☐ 241. DAVE COLLINS
☐ 268. ERNIE WHITT
☐ 315. DAMASO GARCIA
☐ 317. LUIS LEAL
☐ 363. GARTH IORG
☐ 390. TONY FERNANDEZ
☐ 437. LLOYD MOSEBY
☐ 439. JIM CLANCY
☐ 485. RANCE MULLINIKS
☐ 512. CLIFF JOHNSON
☐ 559. JIMMY KEY
☐ 561. DOYLE ALEXANDER
☐ 606. ROY LEE JACKSON
☐ 632. JIM GOTT

1986 DONRUSS (660)
2 1/2 X 3 1/2

JOHN CANDELARIA P

ATLANTA BRAVES

☐ 36. MARTY CLARY
☐ 66. DALE MURPHY
☐ 77. RICK MAHLER
☐ 141. GLENN HUBBARD
☐ 165. GERALD PERRY
☐ 188. BOB HORNER
☐ 199. STEVE BEDROSIAN
☐ 263. RAFAEL RAMIREZ
☐ 287. CLAUDELL WASHINGTON
☐ 310. RICK CERONE
☐ 321. BRUCE SUTTER
☐ 385. RICK CAMP
☐ 409. LEN BARKER
☐ 432. TERRY FORSTER
☐ 443. JEFF DEDMON
☐ 507. MILT THOMPSON
☐ 531. KEN OBERKFELL
☐ 554. BRUCE BENEDICT
☐ 565. ZANE SMITH
☐ 618. CHRIS CHAMBLISS
☐ 624. JOE JOHNSON
☐ 627. TERRY HARPER

BALTIMORE ORIOLES

☐ 45. JOHN HABYAN
☐ 47. MIKE BODDICKER
☐ 88. EDDIE MURRAY
☐ 106. RICK DEMPSEY
☐ 123. MIKE YOUNG
☐ 148. KEN DIXON
☐ 169. STORM DAVIS
☐ 210. CAL RIPKEN
☐ 228. LEE LACY
☐ 245. FRED LYNN
☐ 270. SAMMY STEWART
☐ 291. SCOTT MCGREGOR
☐ 332. FLOYD RAYFORD
☐ 350. LARRY SHEETS
☐ 367. NATE SNELL
☐ 392. DON AASE
☐ 413. JIM DWYER
☐ 454. DENNIS MARTINEZ
☐ 472. GARY ROENICKE
☐ 489. AL PARDO
☐ 514. TIPPY MARTINEZ
☐ 535. WAYNE GROSS
☐ 576. MIKE FLANAGAN
☐ 594. BILL SWAGGERTY
☐ 599. BRAD HAVENS
☐ 607. ALAN WIGGINS
☐ 643. JOHN SHELBY

BOSTON RED SOX

☐ 50. OIL CAN BOYD
☐ 91. BOB STANLEY
☐ 127. TONY ARMAS
☐ 151. BILL BUCKNER
☐ 172. ROGER CLEMENS
☐ 213. JIM RICE
☐ 249. DWIGHT EVANS
☐ 273. RICH GEDMAN
☐ 294. MARTY BARRETT
☐ 335. JACKIE GUTIERREZ
☐ 371. WADE BOGGS
☐ 395. MIKE EASLER
☐ 416. STEVE CRAWFORD
☐ 457. GLENN HOFFMAN
☐ 493. MARK CLEAR
☐ 517. BRUCE HURST
☐ 538. AL NIPPER
☐ 579. STEVE LYONS
☐ 614. MARC SULLIVAN
☐ 616. BRUCE KISON
☐ 620. TIM LOLLAR
☐ 636. BOB OJEDA

CALIFORNIA ANGELS

☐ 35. MARK MCLEMORE
☐ 57. DOUG DECINCES
☐ 85. RON ROMANICK
☐ 108. BRIAN DOWNING
☐ 133. DICK SCHOFIELD
☐ 158. GARY PETTIS
☐ 179. MIKE WITT
☐ 207. BOBBY GRICH
☐ 230. BOB BOONE
☐ 255. DONNIE MOORE
☐ 280. ROD CAREW
☐ 301. STU CLIBURN
☐ 329. URBANO LUGO
☐ 352. JUAN BENIQUEZ
☐ 377. REGGIE JACKSON
☐ 402. JIM SLATON
☐ 423. RUPPERT JONES
☐ 451. JERRY NARRON
☐ 474. KIRK MCCASKILL
☐ 499. JOHN CANDELARIA
☐ 524. JACK HOWELL
☐ 545. CRAIG GERBER
☐ 573. AL HOLLAND
☐ 611. DON SUTTON

CHICAGO CUBS

☐ 32. JOHNNY ABREGO
☐ 67. RYNE SANDBERG
☐ 76. GARY MATTHEWS
☐ 117. STEVE TROUT
☐ 144. LEE SMITH
☐ 167. KEITH MORELAND
☐ 189. RICK SUTCLIFFE

☐ 198. RON CEY
☐ 239. DENNIS ECKERSLEY
☐ 266. BOB DERNIER
☐ 289. JODY DAVIS
☐ 311. SHAWON DUNSTON
☐ 320. LEON DURHAM
☐ 361. RAY FONTENOT
☐ 388. DAVEY LOPES
☐ 411. GEORGE FRAZIER
☐ 433. BILLY HATCHER
☐ 442. SCOTT SANDERSON
☐ 483. THAD BOSLEY
☐ 510. STEVE ENGEL
☐ 533. RON MERIDITH
☐ 555. WARREN BRUSSTAR
☐ 564. DICK RUTHVEN
☐ 613. JAY BALLER

CHICAGO WHITE SOX

☐ 58. BRITT BURNS
☐ 86. DARYL BOSTON
☐ 122. DAN SPILLNER
☐ 135. GREG WALKER
☐ 160. RICHARD DOTSON
☐ 180. HAROLD BAINES
☐ 208. OZZIE GUILLEN
☐ 244. FLOYD BANNISTER
☐ 257. JULIO CRUZ
☐ 282. SCOTT FLETCHER
☐ 302. LUIS SALAZAR
☐ 330. JOEL SKINNER
☐ 366. CARLTON FISK
☐ 379. BOB JAMES
☐ 404. TIM HULETT
☐ 424. JERRY HAIRSTON
☐ 452. BRYAN LITTLE
☐ 488. JUAN AGOSTO
☐ 501. GENE NELSON
☐ 526. RON KITTLE
☐ 546. JOE DESA
☐ 574. REID NICHOLS
☐ 609. TOM SEAVER
☐ 623. JOEL DAVIS
☐ 632. RUDY LAW

CINCINNATI REDS

☐ 27. KAL DANIELS
☐ 37. PAUL O'NEILL
☐ 62. PETE ROSE
☐ 81. RON OESTER
☐ 121. RON ROBINSON
☐ 140. WAYNE KRENCHICKI
☐ 164. ERIC DAVIS
☐ 184. MARIO SOTO
☐ 203. DAVE PARKER
☐ 243. DAVE CONCEPCION
☐ 262. JAY TIBBS
☐ 286. NICK ESASKY
☐ 306. GARY REDUS
☐ 325. EDDIE MILNER
☐ 365. TOM HUME
☐ 384. TOM BROWNING
☐ 408. TED POWER
☐ 428. TONY PEREZ
☐ 447. BUDDY BELL
☐ 487. JOHN FRANCO
☐ 506. JOE PRICE
☐ 530. BO DIAZ
☐ 550. DAVE VAN GORDER
☐ 569. TOM RUNNELLS
☐ 650. MAX VENABLE

CLEVELAND INDIANS

☐ 29. CORY SNYDER
☐ 94. TOM WADDELL
☐ 102. BRETT BUTLER
☐ 129. PAT TABLER
☐ 154. BROOK JACOBY
☐ 216. JULIO FRANCO
☐ 224. JOE CARTER
☐ 251. ANDRE THORNTON
☐ 276. MEL HALL
☐ 338. NEAL HEATON
☐ 346. GEORGE VUKOVICH
☐ 373. CHRIS BANDO
☐ 398. JERRY WILLARD
☐ 460. CARMEN CASTILLO

☐ 468. ROY SMITH
☐ 495. RAMON ROMERO
☐ 520. TONY BERNAZARD
☐ 582. JAMIE EASTERLY
☐ 590. MIKE HARGROVE

DETROIT TIGERS

☐ 49. LOU WHITAKER
☐ 90. CHET LEMON
☐ 105. JACK MORRIS
☐ 125. KIRK GIBSON
☐ 150. CHRIS PITTARO
☐ 171. ALAN TRAMMELL
☐ 212. DAN PETRY
☐ 227. WILLIE HERNANDEZ
☐ 247. WALT TERRELL
☐ 272. NELSON SIMMONS
☐ 293. AURELIO LOPEZ
☐ 334. LANCE PARRISH
☐ 349. BARBARO GARBEY
☐ 369. DARRELL EVANS
☐ 394. RANDY O'NEAL
☐ 415. ALEJANDRO SANCHEZ
☐ 456. BOB MELVIN
☐ 471. DAVE BERGMAN
☐ 491. FRANK TANANA
☐ 516. BILL SCHERRER
☐ 537. TOM BROOKENS
☐ 578. MIKE LAGA
☐ 593. LARRY HERNDON
☐ 615. JOHN GRUBB

HOUSTON ASTROS

☐ 31. TY GAINEY
☐ 60. JOSE CRUZ
☐ 84. JERRY MUMPHREY
☐ 110. BILL DORAN
☐ 136. DENNY WALLING
☐ 161. BOB KNEPPER
☐ 182. JEFF HEATHCOCK
☐ 206. TERRY PUHL
☐ 232. CRAIG REYNOLDS
☐ 258. NOLAN RYAN
☐ 283. BILL DAWLEY
☐ 304. FRANK DIPINO
☐ 328. DAVE SMITH
☐ 354. MARK BAILEY
☐ 380. GLENN DAVIS
☐ 405. ALAN ASHBY
☐ 426. JEFF CALHOUN
☐ 450. JIM PANKOVITS
☐ 476. MIKE SCOTT
☐ 502. JOHN MIZEROCK
☐ 527. PHIL GARNER
☐ 548. KEVIN BASS
☐ 572. DICKIE THON

KANSAS CITY ROYALS

☐ 53. GEORGE BRETT
☐ 95. DANNY JACKSON
☐ 100. BRET SABERHAGEN
☐ 130. FRANK WHITE
☐ 155. PAT SHERIDAN
☐ 175. WILLIE WILSON
☐ 217. DARRYL MOTLEY
☐ 222. STEVE BALONI
☐ 252. ONIX CONCEPCION

☐ 277. JIM SUNDBERG
☐ 297. CHARLIE LEIBRANDT
☐ 339. JORGE ORTA
☐ 344. GREG PRYOR
☐ 374. BUD BLACK
☐ 399. LONNIE SMITH
☐ 419. MIKE JONES
☐ 461. DAVE LEEPER
☐ 466. LYNN JONES
☐ 496. JOHN WATHAN
☐ 521. HAL MCRAE
☐ 541. DAN QUISENBERRY
☐ 583. MARK GUBICZA
☐ 588. STEVE FARR
☐ 605. BUDDY BIANCALANA

LOS ANGELES DODGERS

☐ 52. MIKE MARSHALL
☐ 93. MIKE SCIOSCIA
☐ 104. JERRY REUSS
☐ 128. MARIANO DUNCAN
☐ 153. BILL RUSSELL
☐ 174. PEDRO GUERRERO
☐ 215. FERNANDO VALENZUELA
☐ 226. OREL HERSHISER
☐ 250. DENNIS POWELL
☐ 275. KEN HOWELL
☐ 296. GREG BROCK
☐ 337. TERRY WHITFIELD
☐ 348. CARLOS DIAZ
☐ 372. RICK HONEYCUTT
☐ 397. TOM NIEDENFUER
☐ 418. ENOS CABELL
☐ 459. BOB WELCH
☐ 470. KEN LANDREAUX
☐ 494. LEN MATUSZEK
☐ 519. STEVE YEAGER
☐ 540. STEVE SAX
☐ 581. GILBERTO REYES
☐ 592. FRANKLIN STUBBS
☐ 617. BILL MADLOCK

MILWAUKEE BREWERS

☐ 40. JUAN NIEVES
☐ 48. ROBIN YOUNT
☐ 89. DION JAMES
☐ 107. RAY BURRIS
☐ 115. JIM GANTNER
☐ 124. PAUL MOLITOR
☐ 149. DANNY DARWIN
☐ 170. CECIL COOPER
☐ 211. BILL SCHROEDER
☐ 229. ROLLIE FINGERS
☐ 237. MOOSE HAAS
☐ 246. CHARLIE MOORE
☐ 271. BOB GIBSON
☐ 292. TED SIMMONS
☐ 333. BEN OGLIVIE
☐ 351. TED HIGUERA
☐ 359. EARNEST RILES
☐ 368. RICK MANNING
☐ 393. JAIME COCANOWER
☐ 414. PAUL HOUSEHOLDER
☐ 455. ED ROMERO
☐ 473. PETE VUCKOVICH
☐ 481. RANDY READY
☐ 490. BILL WEGMAN
☐ 515. BILLY JO ROBIDOUX
☐ 536. RAY SEARAGE
☐ 577. TIM LEARY
☐ 595. CARLOS PONCE
☐ 634. MIKE FELDER

MINNESOTA TWINS

☐ 70. KENT HRBEK
☐ 72. KIRBY PUCKETT
☐ 120. JOHN BUTCHER
☐ 147. MIKE SMITHSON
☐ 192. TOM BRUNANSKY
☐ 194. FRANK VIOLA
☐ 242. TIM TEUFEL
☐ 269. MICKEY HATCHER
☐ 314. GARY GAETTI
☐ 316. MARK SALAS
☐ 364. RON DAVIS
☐ 391. TIM LAUDNER
☐ 436. PETE FILSON
☐ 438. DAVE ENGLE

☐ 486. ROY SMALLEY
☐ 513. FRANK EUFEMIA
☐ 558. GREG GAGNE
☐ 560. RON WASHINGTON
☐ 598. STEVE LOMBARDOZZI
☐ 630. MARK FUNDERBURK
☐ 635. KEN SCHROM
☐ 649. BERT BLYLEVEN

MONTREAL EXPOS

☐ 33. ANDRES GALARRAGA
☐ 55. HUBIE BROOKS
☐ 87. ANDRE DAWSON
☐ 97. MIKE FITZGERALD
☐ 132. VANCE LAW
☐ 157. JIM WOHLFORD
☐ 177. TIM RAINES
☐ 209. JEFF REARDON
☐ 219. TIM WALLACH
☐ 254. DAVID PALMER
☐ 279. HERMAN WINNINGHAM
☐ 299. BRYN SMITH
☐ 331. BILL GULLICKSON
☐ 341. JOE HESKETH
☐ 376. CHARLIE LEA
☐ 401. TERRY FRANCONA
☐ 421. TIM BURKE
☐ 453. GARY LUCAS
☐ 463. RANDY ST. CLAIRE
☐ 498. U.L. WASHINGTON
☐ 523. MITCH WEBSTER
☐ 543. FLOYD YOUMANS
☐ 575. BERT ROBERGE
☐ 585. BILL LASKEY

NEW YORK METS

☐ 68. GARY CARTER
☐ 75. DWIGHT GOODEN
☐ 116. GEORGE FOSTER
☐ 190. KEITH HERNANDEZ
☐ 197. DARRYL STRAWBERRY
☐ 238. WALLY BACKMAN
☐ 312. HOWARD JOHNSON
☐ 319. RAFAEL SANTANA
☐ 360. JOHN CHRISTENSEN
☐ 434. CLINT HURDLE
☐ 441. RICK AGUILERA
☐ 482. LENNY DYKSTRA
☐ 556. DANNY HEEP
☐ 563. RON DARLING
☐ 597. RAY KNIGHT
☐ 604. MOOKIE WILSON
☐ 625. SID FERNANDEZ
☐ 629. ROGER MCDOWELL
☐ 631. ED LYNCH
☐ 646. JESSE OROSCO
☐ 647. BILLY BEANE
☐ 652. CALVIN SCHIRALDI

NEW YORK YANKEES

☐ 51. RICKEY HENDERSON
☐ 92. WILLIE RANDOLPH
☐ 103. RON GUIDRY
☐ 126. KEN GRIFFEY
☐ 152. MIKE PAGLIARULO
☐ 173. DON MATTINGLY
☐ 214. DAVE RIGHETTI
☐ 225. ED WHITSON
☐ 248. DAVE WINFIELD
☐ 274. BUTCH WYNEGAR
☐ 295. DALE BERRA
☐ 336. DENNIS RASMUSSEN
☐ 347. DON BAYLOR
☐ 370. RON HASSEY
☐ 396. SCOTT BRADLEY
☐ 417. DAN PASQUA
☐ 458. BOB SHIRLEY
☐ 469. ANDRE ROBERTSON
☐ 492. BRIAN FISHER
☐ 518. RICH BORDI
☐ 539. BILLY SAMPLE
☐ 580. PHIL NIEKRO
☐ 591. MARTY BYSTROM
☐ 601. JOE NIEKRO
☐ 608. JOE COWLEY
☐ 610. NEIL ALLEN
☐ 638. BOBBY MEACHAM

1986 Donruss

OAKLAND A'S

- ☐ 39. JOSE CANSECO
- ☐ 54. DAVE KINGMAN
- ☐ 96. MIKE DAVIS
- ☐ 101. ALFREDO GRIFFIN
- ☐ 131. CARNEY LANSFORD
- ☐ 156. MIKE GALLEGO
- ☐ 176. DWAYNE MURPHY
- ☐ 218. DAVE COLLINS
- ☐ 223. JAY HOWELL
- ☐ 253. MIKE HEATH
- ☐ 278. CHRIS CODIROLI
- ☐ 298. BILL KRUEGER
- ☐ 340. DONNIE HILL
- ☐ 345. MICKEY TETTLETON
- ☐ 375. STEVE HENDERSON
- ☐ 400. BRUCE BOCHTE
- ☐ 420. STEVE KIEFER
- ☐ 462. TIM BIRTSAS
- ☐ 467. DUSTY BAKER
- ☐ 497. ROB PICCIOLO
- ☐ 522. JOSE RIJO
- ☐ 542. TONY PHILLIPS
- ☐ 584. STAN JAVIER
- ☐ 589. STEVE ONTIVEROS

PHILADELPHIA PHILLIES

- ☐ 34. DAVE SPIPANOFF
- ☐ 61. MIKE SCHMIDT
- ☐ 82. JOHN RUSSELL
- ☐ 111. KENT TEKULVE
- ☐ 137. OZZIE VIRGIL
- ☐ 163. GREG GROSS
- ☐ 183. STEVE CARLTON
- ☐ 204. JOHN DENNY
- ☐ 233. SHANE RAWLEY
- ☐ 259. JEFF STONE
- ☐ 285. GLENN WILSON
- ☐ 305. VON HAYES
- ☐ 326. JUAN SAMUEL
- ☐ 355. LARRY ANDERSON
- ☐ 381. TIM CORCORAN
- ☐ 407. GARRY MADDOX
- ☐ 427. DON CARMAN
- ☐ 448. DAVE RUCKER
- ☐ 477. DARREN DAULTON
- ☐ 503. LUIS AGUAYO
- ☐ 529. KEVIN GROSS
- ☐ 549. TOM FOLEY
- ☐ 570. RICK SCHU
- ☐ 612. FRED TOLIVER
- ☐ 619. DAVE STEWART
- ☐ 622. CHARLES HUDSON

PITTSBURGH PIRATES

- ☐ 44. BOB KIPPER
- ☐ 64. TONY PENA
- ☐ 78. BENNY DISTEFANO
- ☐ 113. MARVELL WYNNE
- ☐ 142. CECILIO GUANTE
- ☐ 166. RICK RHODEN
- ☐ 186. JOHNNY RAY
- ☐ 200. STEVE KEMP
- ☐ 235. JOSE DELEON
- ☐ 264. LARRY MCWILLIAMS
- ☐ 288. LEE MAZZILLI
- ☐ 308. SAM KHALIFA
- ☐ 322. JASON THOMPSON
- ☐ 357. DON ROBINSON
- ☐ 386. JIM MORRISON
- ☐ 410. DENNY GONZALEZ
- ☐ 430. BOB WALK
- ☐ 444. JOE ORSULAK
- ☐ 479. BILL ALMON
- ☐ 508. JUNIOR ORTIZ
- ☐ 532. RICK REUSCHEL
- ☐ 552. R.J. REYNOLDS
- ☐ 566. SID BREAM
- ☐ 600. PAT CLEMENTS
- ☐ 642. MIKE BROWN

ST. LOUIS CARDINALS

- ☐ 43. TODD WORRELL
- ☐ 59. OZZIE SMITH
- ☐ 83. TOMMY HERR
- ☐ 109. WILLIE MCGEE

- ☐ 138. RICKY HORTON
- ☐ 168. JACK CLARK
- ☐ 181. VINCE COLEMAN
- ☐ 205. TERRY PENDLETON
- ☐ 231. JOAQUIN ANDUJAR
- ☐ 260. JOHN TUDOR
- ☐ 290. DARRELL PORTER
- ☐ 303. KEN DAYLEY
- ☐ 327. TOM NIETO
- ☐ 353. BOB FORSCH
- ☐ 382. DANNY COX
- ☐ 412. ANDY VAN SLYKE
- ☐ 425. TITO LANDRUM
- ☐ 449. IVAN DEJESUS
- ☐ 475. JEFF LAHTI
- ☐ 504. KURT KEPSHIRE
- ☐ 534. STEVE BRAUN
- ☐ 547. BRIAN HARPER
- ☐ 571. BILL CAMPBELL
- ☐ 596. PAT PERRY
- ☐ 648. CESAR CEDENO

SAN DIEGO PADRES

- ☐ 41. LANCE MCCULLERS
- ☐ 63. STEVE GARVEY
- ☐ 80. KEVIN MCREYNOLDS
- ☐ 112. TONY GWYNN
- ☐ 139. LAMARR HOYT
- ☐ 162. DAVE DRAVECKY
- ☐ 185. GOOSE GOSSAGE
- ☐ 202. GARRY TEMPLETON
- ☐ 234. ERIC SHOW
- ☐ 261. MARK THURMOND
- ☐ 284. ANDY HAWKINS
- ☐ 307. CRAIG LEFFERTS
- ☐ 324. CARMELO MARTINEZ
- ☐ 356. TERRY KENNEDY
- ☐ 383. TIM FLANNERY
- ☐ 406. TIM STODDARD
- ☐ 429. JERRY DAVIS
- ☐ 446. JERRY ROYSTER
- ☐ 478. GRAIG NETTLES
- ☐ 505. ED WOJNA
- ☐ 528. KURT BEVACQUA
- ☐ 551. BRUCE BOCHY
- ☐ 568. MARIO RAMIREZ

SAN FRANCISCO GIANTS

- ☐ 46. MIKE WOODARD
- ☐ 65. CHILI DAVIS
- ☐ 79. JEFF LEONARD
- ☐ 114. DAVID GREEN
- ☐ 143. MIKE KRUKOW
- ☐ 187. DAN GLADDEN
- ☐ 201. MANNY TRILLO
- ☐ 236. JOSE URIBE
- ☐ 265. MARK DAVIS
- ☐ 309. SCOTT GARRELTS
- ☐ 323. BOB BRENLY
- ☐ 358. JIM GOTT
- ☐ 387. DAVE LAPOINT
- ☐ 431. BRAD WELLMAN
- ☐ 445. ATLEE HAMMAKER
- ☐ 480. GREG MINTON
- ☐ 509. VIDA BLUE
- ☐ 553. CHRIS BROWN
- ☐ 567. JOEL YOUNGBLOOD
- ☐ 633. ROGER MASON
- ☐ 641. DAN DRIESSEN

SEATTLE MARINERS

- ☐ 38. DANNY TARTABULL
- ☐ 69. ALVIN DAVIS
- ☐ 74. BOB KEARNEY
- ☐ 118. MARK LANGSTON
- ☐ 145. EDWIN NUNEZ
- ☐ 191. PHIL BRADLEY
- ☐ 196. JIM BEATTIE
- ☐ 240. MIKE MOORE
- ☐ 267. MATT YOUNG
- ☐ 313. JIM PRESLEY
- ☐ 318. DAVE HENDERSON
- ☐ 362. SPIKE OWEN
- ☐ 389. AL COWENS
- ☐ 435. IVAN CALDERON
- ☐ 440. GORMAN THOMAS
- ☐ 484. HAROLD REYNOLDS
- ☐ 511. KARL BEST

- ☐ 557. DARNELL COLES
- ☐ 562. BILLY SWIFT
- ☐ 628. JACK LAZORKO
- ☐ 637. ED VANDE BERG

TEXAS RANGERS

- ☐ 30. JOSE GUZMAN
- ☐ 42. RICK SURHOFF
- ☐ 56. ODDIBE MCDOWELL
- ☐ 98. GARY WARD
- ☐ 99. PETE O'BRIEN
- ☐ 134. WAYNE TOLLESON
- ☐ 159. TOBY HARRAH
- ☐ 178. LARRY PARRISH
- ☐ 220. GEORGE WRIGHT
- ☐ 221. TOMMY DUNBAR
- ☐ 256. CURTIS WILKERSON
- ☐ 281. DON SLAUGHT
- ☐ 300. BURT HOOTON
- ☐ 342. CHARLIE HOUGH
- ☐ 343. DAVE ROZEMA
- ☐ 378. DAVE SCHMIDT
- ☐ 403. BILL STEIN
- ☐ 422. MIKE MASON
- ☐ 464. CHRIS WELSH
- ☐ 465. GREG HARRIS
- ☐ 500. DUANE WALKER
- ☐ 525. ALAN BANNISTER
- ☐ 544. STEVE BUECHELE
- ☐ 586. JEFF RUSSELL
- ☐ 587. DICKIE NOLES
- ☐ 603. DWAYNE HENRY

AL OLIVER DH

TORONTO BLUE JAYS

- ☐ 28. FRED MCGRIFF
- ☐ 71. GEORGE BELL
- ☐ 73. LLOYD MOSEBY
- ☐ 119. TONY FERNANDEZ
- ☐ 146. DAVE STIEB
- ☐ 193. JESSE BARFIELD
- ☐ 195. WILLIE UPSHAW
- ☐ 241. DAMASO GARCIA
- ☐ 268. JIM CLANCY
- ☐ 315. LUIS LEAL
- ☐ 317. BILL CAUDILL
- ☐ 363. JIM ACKER
- ☐ 390. DOYLE ALEXANDER
- ☐ 437. TOM HENKE
- ☐ 439. TOM FILER
- ☐ 485. AL OLIVER
- ☐ 512. CECIL FIELDER
- ☐ 559. ERNIE WHITT
- ☐ 561. JIMMY KEY
- ☐ 606. RANCE MULLINIKS
- ☐ 621. GARY LAVELLE
- ☐ 626. DENNIS LAMP
- ☐ 639. CLIFF JOHNSON
- ☐ 640. GARTH IORG

1986 DONRUSS
ROOKIES (56)
2 1/2 X 3 1/2

TODD WORRELL P

ATLANTA BRAVES

☐ 10. ANDRES THOMAS
☐ 28. PAUL ASSENMACHER

BALTIMORE ORIOLES

NO CARDS ISSUED

BOSTON RED SOX

☐ 29. JEFF SELLERS
☐ 48. REY QUINONEZ
☐ 53. ROB WOODWARD

CALIFORNIA ANGELS

☐ 1. WALLY JOYNER

CHICAGO CUBS

NO CARDS ISSUED

CHICAGO WHITE SOX

☐ 30. BOBBY BONILLA
☐ 51. JOHN CANGELOSI
☐ 55. JOE MCKEON

CINCINNATI REDS

☐ 2. TRACY JONES

CLEVELAND INDIANS

☐ 15. CORY SNYDER
☐ 25. SCOTT BAILES
☐ 43. ANDY ALLANSON

CORY SNYDER IF

DETROIT TIGERS

☐ 27. ERIC KING

HOUSTON ASTROS

☐ 9. CHARLIE KERFELD
☐ 34. JIM DESHAIES

KANSAS CITY ROYALS

☐ 36. SCOTT BANKHEAD
☐ 38. BO JACKSON

LOS ANGELES DODGERS

☐ 5. REGGIE WILLIAMS

MILWAUKEE BREWERS

☐ 12. JUAN NIEVES
☐ 14. DAN PLESAC
☐ 37. DALE SVEUM

MINNESOTA TWINS

☐ 3. ALLAN ANDERSON
☐ 18. STEVE LOMBARDOZZI
☐ 44. MARK PORTUGAL

MONTREAL EXPOS

☐ 7. ANDRES GALARRAGA
☐ 9. AL NEWMAN

NEW YORK METS

☐ 17. KEVIN MITCHELL
☐ 54. ED HEARN

NEW YORK YANKEES

☐ 8. BOB TEWKSBURY
☐ 31. DOUG DRABEK

OAKLAND A'S

☐ 22. JOSE CANSECO
☐ 40. ERIC PLUNK
☐ 41. BILL BATHE
☐ 50. BILL MOONEYHAM

PHILADELPHIA PHILLIES

NO CARDS ISSUED

BARRY BONDS OF

PITTSBURGH PIRATES

☐ 11. BARRY BONDS
☐ 46. BOB KIPPER

ST. LOUIS CARDINALS

☐ 21. TODD WORRELL
☐ 26. GREG MATHEWS
☐ 35. MIKE LAVALLIERE

SAN DIEGO PADRES

☐ 33. BIP ROBERTS
☐ 42. JOHN KRUK
☐ 47. GENE WALTER

SAN FRANCISCO GIANTS

☐ 32. WILL CLARK
☐ 39. ROB THOMPSON

SEATTLE MARINERS

☐ 45. DANNY TARTABULL

TEXAS RANGERS

☐ 4. ED CORREA
☐ 19. MITCH WILLIAMS
☐ 23. PETE INCAVIGLIA
☐ 24. JOSE GUZMAN
☐ 49. BOBBY WITT
☐ 52. RUBEN SIERRA

TORONTO BLUE JAYS

☐ 13. MARK EICHHORN
☐ 16. KELLY GRUBER
☐ 20. JOHN CERUTTI

1987 DONRUSS (660)
2 1/2 X 3 1/2

BOB BRENLY C

ATLANTA BRAVES

☐ 67. OZZIE VIRGIL
☐ 78. DALE MURPHY
☐ 143. BILLY SAMPLE
☐ 167. ZANE SMITH
☐ 190. RICK MAHLER
☐ 202. RAFAEL RAMIREZ
☐ 266. ANDRES THOMAS
☐ 290. PAUL ASSENMACHER
☐ 314. JEFF DEDMON
☐ 325. DAVID PALMER
☐ 389. BOB HORNER
☐ 414. GENE GARBER
☐ 437. KEN OBERKFELL
☐ 448. BRUCE BENEDICT
☐ 513. KEN GRIFFEY
☐ 537. TED SIMMONS
☐ 560. ED OLWINE
☐ 571. CLIFF SPECK
☐ 634. GLENN HUBBARD
☐ 657. DOYLE ALEXANDER
☐ 659. JIM ACKER

BALTIMORE ORIOLES

☐ 30. KEN GERHART
☐ 39. ERIC BELL
☐ 48. EDDIE MURRAY
☐ 89. CAL RIPKEN
☐ 108. FRED LYNN
☐ 125. MIKE BODDICKER
☐ 150. MIKE YOUNG
☐ 171. KEN DIXON
☐ 213. RICH BORDI
☐ 231. DON AASE
☐ 248. LARRY SHEETS
☐ 273. STORM DAVIS
☐ 294. RICK DEMPSEY
☐ 336. LEE LACY
☐ 354. JOHN SHELBY
☐ 371. JUAN BENIQUEZ

☐ 396. NATE SNELL
☐ 418. JIM DWYER
☐ 459. MIKE FLANAGAN
☐ 477. JIM TRABER
☐ 494. JOHN HABYAN
☐ 520. SCOTT MCGREGOR
☐ 541. JOHN STEFERO
☐ 582. ODELL JONES
☐ 601. JACKIE GUTIERREZ

BOSTON RED SOX

☐ 44. PAT DODSON
☐ 51. OIL CAN BOYD
☐ 92. JIM RICE
☐ 129. DWIGHT EVANS
☐ 153. RICH GEDMAN
☐ 174. BRUCE HURST
☐ 216. BOB STANLEY
☐ 252. WADE BOGGS
☐ 276. ROGER CLEMENS
☐ 297. AL NIPPER
☐ 339. DON BAYLOR
☐ 375. TOM SEAVER
☐ 399. STEVE CRAWFORD
☐ 421. JOE SAMBITO
☐ 462. BILL BUCKNER
☐ 498. TONY ARMAS
☐ 523. MARTY BARRETT
☐ 544. JEFF SELLERS
☐ 585. MIKE GREENWELL
☐ 606. ED ROMERO
☐ 622. DAVE HENDERSON
☐ 633. SPIKE OWEN
☐ 641. CALVIN SCHIRALDI
☐ 643. MARC SULLIVAN
☐ 647. DAVE SAX
☐ 652. ROB WOODWARD
☐ 658. SAMMY STEWART

CALIFORNIA ANGELS

☐ 38. DEVON WHITE
☐ 40. WILL FRASER
☐ 58. MIKE WITT
☐ 86. BRIAN DOWNING
☐ 110. DONNIE MOORE
☐ 135. WALLY JOYNER
☐ 160. GARY PETTIS
☐ 181. DON SUTTON
☐ 210. REGGIE JACKSON
☐ 233. BOB BOONE
☐ 258. ROB WILFONG
☐ 283. DICK SCHOFIELD
☐ 305. JACK HOWELL
☐ 333. DOUG CORBETT
☐ 356. DOUG DECINCES
☐ 381. KIRK MCCASKILL
☐ 407. CHUCK FINLEY
☐ 428. RUPPERT JONES
☐ 456. BOBBY GRICH
☐ 479. MARK MCLEMORE
☐ 505. RAY CHADWICK
☐ 530. STU CLIBURN
☐ 551. JOHN CANDELARIA
☐ 579. GUS POLIDOR
☐ 583. MARK RYAL
☐ 603. JERRY NARRON
☐ 618. GARY LUCAS

CHICAGO CUBS

☐ 36. GREG MADDUX
☐ 43. RAFAEL PALMEIRO
☐ 68. RICK SUTCLIFFE
☐ 77. RYNE SANDBERG
☐ 119. SHAWON DUNSTON
☐ 146. BOB DERNIER
☐ 169. KEITH MORELAND
☐ 191. THAD BOSLEY
☐ 201. STEVE TROUT
☐ 242. LEON DURHAM
☐ 269. JODY DAVIS
☐ 292. LEE SMITH
☐ 315. JAMIE MOYER
☐ 324. JERRY MUMPHREY
☐ 365. DENNIS ECKERSLEY
☐ 392. CHRIS SPEIER
☐ 416. FRANK DIPINO
☐ 438. RON DAVIS
☐ 447. SCOTT SANDERSON

☐ 488. DAVE MARTINEZ
☐ 516. ED LYNCH
☐ 539. CHICO WALKER
☐ 570. MANNY TRILLO
☐ 594. DREW HALL

CHICAGO WHITE SOX

☐ 59. GREG WALKER
☐ 87. OZZIE GUILLEN
☐ 124. JOEL DAVIS
☐ 137. DARYL BOSTON
☐ 162. JOHN CANGELOSI
☐ 182. DAVE SCHMIDT
☐ 211. FLOYD BANNISTER
☐ 247. CARLTON FISK
☐ 260. TIM HULETT
☐ 285. JERRY HAIRSTON
☐ 306. RUSS MORMAN
☐ 334. RON KARKOVICE
☐ 370. BOBBY THIGPEN
☐ 383. RICH DOTSON
☐ 409. STEVE LYONS
☐ 429. HAROLD BAINES
☐ 457. JOSE DELEON
☐ 493. BOB JAMES
☐ 507. NEIL ALLEN
☐ 532. RON HASSEY
☐ 552. JOE COWLEY
☐ 580. GENE NELSON
☐ 617. STEVE CARLTON
☐ 628. BILL DAWLEY

JERRY HAIRSTON OF

CINCINNATI REDS

☐ 63. TOM BROWNING
☐ 82. MARIO SOTO
☐ 123. KURT STILLWELL
☐ 142. KAL DANIELS
☐ 166. NICK ESASKY
☐ 186. PETE ROSE(M)
☐ 206. RON OESTER
☐ 246. BO DIAZ
☐ 265. ERIC DAVIS
☐ 289. JOHN FRANCO
☐ 310. RON ROBINSON
☐ 329. JOHN DENNY
☐ 369. BILL GULLICKSON
☐ 388. DAVE PARKER
☐ 413. TRACY JONES
☐ 433. EDDIE MILNER
☐ 452. ROB MURPHY
☐ 492. BARRY LARKIN
☐ 512. TERRY MCGRIFF
☐ 536. TED POWER
☐ 556. BUDDY BELL

CLEVELAND INDIANS

☐ 32. GREG SWINDELL
☐ 95. ANDY ALLANSON
☐ 104. BROOK JACOBY
☐ 131. JULIO FRANCO
☐ 156. JOE CARTER
☐ 219. BRETT BUTLER
☐ 227. SCOTT BAILES
☐ 254. PAT TABLER
☐ 279. ANDRE THORNTON
☐ 342. TOM CANDIOTTI
☐ 350. ERNIE CAMACHO
☐ 377. TONY BERNAZARD

☐ 403. KEN SCHROM
☐ 465. PHIL NIEKRO
☐ 473. MEL HALL
☐ 501. CHRIS BANDO
☐ 526. CORY SNYDER
☐ 588. CARMEN CASTILLO
☐ 596. BRYAN OELKERS
☐ 623. DAVE CLARK

DETROIT TIGERS

☐ 47. BRUCE FIELDS
☐ 50. KIRK GIBSON
☐ 91. LANCE PARRISH
☐ 107. LOU WHITAKER
☐ 127. ALAN TRAMMELL
☐ 152. FRANK TANANA
☐ 173. JACK MORRIS
☐ 215. DAVE COLLINS
☐ 230. DARNELL COLES
☐ 250. ERIC KING
☐ 275. WALT TERRELL
☐ 296. TOM BROOKENS
☐ 338. DWIGHT LOWRY
☐ 353. CHET LEMON
☐ 373. DAN PETRY
☐ 398. DARRELL EVANS
☐ 420. DAVE BERGMAN
☐ 461. CHUCK CARY
☐ 476. JOHNNY GRUBB
☐ 496. MIKE HEATH
☐ 522. WILLIE HERNANDEZ
☐ 543. MARK THURMOND
☐ 584. RANDY O'NEAL

HOUSTON ASTROS

☐ 61. GLENN DAVIS
☐ 85. JOSE CRUZ
☐ 112. BOB KNEPPER
☐ 138. NOLAN RYAN
☐ 163. MIKE SCOTT
☐ 184. JIM DESHAIES
☐ 209. CHARLIE KERFELD
☐ 235. MARK BAILEY
☐ 261. DICKIE THON
☐ 286. BILL DORAN
☐ 308. DAVE SMITH
☐ 332. ALAN ASHBY
☐ 358. PHIL GARNER
☐ 384. CRAIG REYNOLDS
☐ 410. KEVIN BASS
☐ 431. TERRY PUHL
☐ 455. DAVEY LOPES
☐ 481. BILLY HATCHER
☐ 508. DANNY DARWIN
☐ 533. TY GAINEY
☐ 554. DENNY WALLING
☐ 578. JEFF CALHOUN
☐ 605. JIM PANKOVITS
☐ 629. AURELIO LOPEZ
☐ 640. LARRY ANDERSEN
☐ 653. JOHN MIZEROCK

KANSAS CITY ROYALS

☐ 35. BO JACKSON
☐ 54. GEORGE BRETT
☐ 96. WILLIE WILSON
☐ 102. STEVE BALBONI
☐ 132. BRET SABERHAGEN
☐ 157. DANNY JACKSON
☐ 177. DAN QUISENBERRY
☐ 220. CHARLIE LEIBRANDT
☐ 225. LONNIE SMITH
☐ 255. FRANK WHITE
☐ 280. JIM SUNDBERG
☐ 301. STEVE FARR
☐ 343. RUDY LAW
☐ 348. JORGE ORTA
☐ 378. GREG PRYOR
☐ 404. BUD BLACK
☐ 424. MIKE KINGERY
☐ 466. MARK GUBICZA
☐ 471. HAL MCRAE
☐ 502. DAVID CONE
☐ 527. BUDDY BIANCALANA
☐ 624. ANGEL SALAZAR

LOS ANGELES DODGERS

- [ ] 53. PEDRO GUERRERO
- [ ] 94. FERNANDO VALENZUELA
- [ ] 106. OREL HERSHISER
- [ ] 130. MIKE SCIOSCIA
- [ ] 155. BILL MADLOCK
- [ ] 176. MIKE MARSHALL
- [ ] 218. TOM NIEDENFUER
- [ ] 229. KEN HOWELL
- [ ] 253. MARIANO DUNCAN
- [ ] 278. STEVE SAX
- [ ] 299. FRANKLIN STUBBS
- [ ] 341. REGGIE WILLIAMS
- [ ] 352. KEN LANDREAUX
- [ ] 376. ED VANDE BERG
- [ ] 402. RICK HONEYCUTT
- [ ] 423. LEN MATUSZEK
- [ ] 464. JEFF HAMILTON
- [ ] 475. BOB WELCH
- [ ] 499. DENNIS POWELL
- [ ] 525. JOSE GONZALEZ
- [ ] 546. ALEX TREVINO
- [ ] 587. RALPH BRYANT
- [ ] 598. BRIAN HOLTON

MILWAUKEE BREWERS

- [ ] 28. B.J. SURHOFF
- [ ] 33. MIKE BIRKBECK
- [ ] 49. TED HIGUERA
- [ ] 90. JUAN NIEVES
- [ ] 109. BILL WEGMAN
- [ ] 117. PAUL MOLITOR
- [ ] 126. ROBIN YOUNT
- [ ] 151. ERNEST RILES
- [ ] 172. JIM GANTNER
- [ ] 214. DAN PLESAC
- [ ] 232. TIM LEARY
- [ ] 240. BILLY JO ROBIDOUX
- [ ] 249. JUAN CASTILLO
- [ ] 274. ROB DEER
- [ ] 295. MIKE FELDER
- [ ] 337. GLENN BRAGGS
- [ ] 355. MARK CLEAR
- [ ] 363. CECIL COOPER
- [ ] 372. CHARLIE MOORE
- [ ] 397. BRYAN CLUTTERBUCK
- [ ] 419. BEN OGLIVIE
- [ ] 460. JOEY MEYER
- [ ] 478. CHRIS BOSIO
- [ ] 486. BILL SCHROEDER
- [ ] 495. JIM ADDUCI
- [ ] 521. RICK MANNING
- [ ] 542. DALE SVEUM

MINNESOTA TWINS

- [ ] 71. BERT BLYLEVEN
- [ ] 73. KENT HRBEK
- [ ] 122. GARY GAETTI
- [ ] 149. KIRBY PUCKETT
- [ ] 194. TOM BRUNANSKY
- [ ] 196. FRANK VIOLA
- [ ] 245. MIKE SMITHSON
- [ ] 272. KEITH ATHERTON
- [ ] 318. STEVE LOMBARDOZZI
- [ ] 320. TIM LAUDNER
- [ ] 368. ALLAN ANDERSON
- [ ] 395. GREG GAGNE
- [ ] 441. RANDY BUSH
- [ ] 443. ROY SMALLEY
- [ ] 491. MICKEY HATCHER
- [ ] 519. ANDRE DAVID
- [ ] 564. GEORGE FRAZIER
- [ ] 566. MARK PORTUGAL
- [ ] 615. NEAL HEATON

MONTREAL EXPOS

- [ ] 56. TIM RAINES
- [ ] 88. HUBIE BROOKS
- [ ] 98. JEFF REARDON
- [ ] 134. JOE HESKETH
- [ ] 159. BRYN SMITH
- [ ] 179. TIM WALLACH
- [ ] 212. VANCE LAW
- [ ] 222. TIM BURKE
- [ ] 257. FLOYD YOUMANS
- [ ] 282. JAY TIBBS
- [ ] 303. ANDRES GALARRAGA

- [ ] 335. MITCH WEBSTER
- [ ] 345. MIKE FITZGERALD
- [ ] 380. ANDY MCGAFFIGAN
- [ ] 406. WAYNE KRENCHICKI
- [ ] 426. AL NEWMAN
- [ ] 458. ANDRE DAWSON
- [ ] 468. BOB SEBRA
- [ ] 504. TOM FOLEY
- [ ] 529. WILFREDO TEJADA
- [ ] 549. CASEY CANDAELE
- [ ] 625. RANDY HUNT

NEW YORK METS

- [ ] 29. RANDY MYERS
- [ ] 69. GARY CARTER
- [ ] 76. KEITH HERNANDEZ
- [ ] 118. DARRYL STRAWBERRY
- [ ] 192. RON DARLING
- [ ] 199. DWIGHT GOODEN
- [ ] 241. ROGER MCDOWELL
- [ ] 316. WALLY BACKMAN
- [ ] 323. SID FERNANDEZ
- [ ] 364. BOB OJEDA
- [ ] 439. JESSE OROSCO
- [ ] 446. ED HEARN
- [ ] 487. MOOKIE WILSON
- [ ] 562. LEE MAZZILLI
- [ ] 569. RAFAEL SANTANA
- [ ] 575. DAVE MAGADAN
- [ ] 581. TIM TEUFEL
- [ ] 586. RAY KNIGHT
- [ ] 599. KEVIN MITCHELL
- [ ] 611. LEN DYKSTRA
- [ ] 620. RICK AGUILERA
- [ ] 626. JOHN GIBBONS
- [ ] 635. KEVIN ELSTER
- [ ] 642. STAN JEFFERSON
- [ ] 646. HOWARD JOHNSON
- [ ] 649. DANNY HEEP

NEW YORK YANKEES

- [ ] 52. DON MATTINGLY
- [ ] 93. RON GUIDRY
- [ ] 105. DAVE WINFIELD
- [ ] 128. DAVE RIGHETTI
- [ ] 154. WILLIE RANDOLPH
- [ ] 175. DENNIS RASMUSSEN
- [ ] 217. JOE NIEKRO
- [ ] 228. RICKEY HENDERSON
- [ ] 251. DOUG DRABEK
- [ ] 277. MIKE EASLER
- [ ] 298. MIKE PAGLIARULO
- [ ] 340. BRIAN FISHER
- [ ] 351. RON KITTLE
- [ ] 374. ROD SCURRY
- [ ] 401. PHIL LOMBARDI
- [ ] 422. BOB TEWKSBURY
- [ ] 463. BOB SHIRLEY
- [ ] 474. DAN PASQUA
- [ ] 497. TIM STODDARD
- [ ] 524. WAYNE TOLLESON
- [ ] 545. JOEL SKINNER
- [ ] 597. SCOTT NIELSEN

OAKLAND A'S

- [ ] 34. TERRY STEINBACH
- [ ] 46. MARK MCGWIRE
- [ ] 55. JOSE RIJO
- [ ] 97. JOSE CANSECO
- [ ] 103. TONY PHILLIPS
- [ ] 133. MIKE DAVIS
- [ ] 158. CARNEY LANSFORD
- [ ] 178. ERIC PLUNK
- [ ] 221. STEVE ONTIVEROS
- [ ] 226. CHRIS CODIROLI
- [ ] 256. ALFREDO GRIFFIN
- [ ] 281. BILL BATHE
- [ ] 302. BILL MOONEYHAM
- [ ] 344. CURT YOUNG
- [ ] 349. MICKEY TETTLETON
- [ ] 379. DWAYNE MURPHY
- [ ] 405. DONNIE HILL
- [ ] 425. DAVE KINGMAN
- [ ] 467. JERRY WILLARD
- [ ] 472. DAVE LEIPER
- [ ] 503. JAY HOWELL
- [ ] 528. MOOSE HAAS
- [ ] 548. JOAQUIN ANDUJAR

- [ ] 590. STAN JAVIER
- [ ] 595. ROB NELSON
- [ ] 648. DAVE STEWART

PHILADELPHIA PHILLIES

- [ ] 42. CHRIS JAMES
- [ ] 62. GLENN WILSON
- [ ] 83. SHANE RAWLEY
- [ ] 113. VON HAYES
- [ ] 139. MIKE SCHMIDT
- [ ] 165. JUAN SAMUEL
- [ ] 185. STEVE BEDROSIAN
- [ ] 207. JOHN RUSSELL
- [ ] 236. KEVIN GROSS
- [ ] 262. DARREN DAULTON
- [ ] 288. GARY REDUS
- [ ] 309. JEFF STONE
- [ ] 330. MILT THOMPSON
- [ ] 359. STEVE JELTZ
- [ ] 385. GREG GROSS
- [ ] 412. RON ROENICKE
- [ ] 432. DON CARMAN
- [ ] 453. KENT TEKULVE
- [ ] 482. DAN SCHATZEDER
- [ ] 509. RICK SCHU
- [ ] 535. MIKE MADDUX
- [ ] 555. BRUCE RUFFIN
- [ ] 576. MARVIN FREEMAN
- [ ] 630. CHARLIE HUDSON

PITTSBURGH PIRATES

- [ ] 65. R.J. REYNOLDS
- [ ] 79. SID BREAM
- [ ] 115. TONY PENA
- [ ] 144. JOHNNY RAY
- [ ] 168. MIKE BROWN
- [ ] 188. RICK REUSCHEL
- [ ] 203. BOB WALK
- [ ] 238. CECILIO GUANTE
- [ ] 267. MIKE DIAZ
- [ ] 291. JOE ORSULAK
- [ ] 312. JIM WINN
- [ ] 326. BILL ALMON
- [ ] 361. BARRY BONDS
- [ ] 390. PAT CLEMENTS
- [ ] 415. MIKE BIELECKI
- [ ] 435. RICK RHODEN
- [ ] 449. JUNIOR ORTIZ
- [ ] 484. JIM MORRISON
- [ ] 514. BENNY DISTEFANO
- [ ] 538. RAFAEL BELLIARD
- [ ] 558. BOBBY BONILLA
- [ ] 572. BOB KIPPER
- [ ] 602. BARRY JONES
- [ ] 608. DON ROBINSON

ST. LOUIS CARDINALS

- [ ] 37. JIM LINDEMAN
- [ ] 60. OZZIE SMITH
- [ ] 84. WILLIE MCGEE
- [ ] 111. JACK CLARK
- [ ] 140. TOMMY HERR
- [ ] 170. JOHN TUDOR
- [ ] 183. TERRY PENDLETON
- [ ] 208. GREG MATHEWS
- [ ] 234. RICKY HORTON
- [ ] 263. VINCE COLEMAN

1987
BASEBALL ISSUES

Donruss Action All-Star (60 cards)
.....................................$6.75 ppd.
Donruss Pop-Ups (20 cards)
.....................................$5.75 ppd.
1987 Topps 22 card Glossy set
.....................................$5.50 ppd.
1987 Fleer Limited Edition (44 cards) ....$6.50 ppd.
1987 Eckerd Drug set (44 cards)
.....................................$7.25 ppd.

BREWER & PACKER
POLICE SETS

Complete Police Sets of the Milwaukee Brewers and Green Bay Packers. Brewer Police sets feature all the players from the 1983-86 season. Packers sets feature the 1985 & 1986 team.

1983 Brewer Police Set (30 cards) .... $10.00 ppd.
1984 Brewer Police Set (30 cards) .... $9.50 ppd.
1985 Brewer Police Set (30 cards) .... $9.00 ppd.
1986 Brewer Police Set (30 cards) .... $8.00 ppd.
All 4 Brewer sets purchased together (120 cards) .... $22.00 ppd.
1985 Packer Police (25 cards) .... $6.50 ppd.
1986 Packer Police (25 cards) .... $5.50 ppd.
Both Packer sets purchased together (50 cards) .... $10.95 ppd.

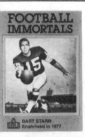

FOOTBALL IMMORTALS

For the first time ever a complete set of ALL of the football immortals enshrined in the Football Hall of Fame in Canton, Ohio. Even the 1985 inductees, Rozelle, Namath, Gatski, Simpson and Staubach are included. This beautiful black and white set with gold borders is a must for all football fans. Relive the days when these greats were running, tackling, blocking on the gridiron by reading the backs which include stats and biography. Also included are Jimmy Brown, Sayers, Lombardi, Butkus, Starr, Gregg. Complete set includes 135 cards, seven of which are shots of the Hall of Fame. A real nice set, don't miss it.

Complete set (135 cards)
$14.25 postpaid

ONE YEAR WINNERS
3 SERIES — NOW AVAILABLE

* These sets feature players whose Big League careers were very short. Most of the players in this set have not appeared on a baseball card previously.
* Each card contains the complete major league record of the player along with a short biography.
* Each series has a different front design.
* Great sets for Trivia Questions.
* Ideal for the TRUE baseball fan.
* Here's a chance to get cards of the players from your favorite team that were never before issued.
Series #1 (B&W) 18 cards (Numbered 1-18) **$3.75 ppd.**
Series #2 (Full Color) 36 cards (Numbered 19-54) **$7.50 ppd.**
New series #3 (Full Color) 64 cards (Numbered 55-118)
$10.00 ppd.
Special — (Here's your chance to get all 118 cards)
Order Series #2 and #3 and get Series #1 free!

Rick Herrscher

1953 BRAVES
Limited Edition Collectors Set

* Special limited edition collectors set marking the 30th anniversary of the Milwaukee Braves' move from Boston.
* 33-card set, custom-printed in two colors. Same 2⅝x3¾'' size as the great baseball cards of the mid-1950s.
* Made from original spring training photos. Includes nearly all of the 1953 Braves, from the greats — Mathews, Spahn, etc. — to obscure players who have never before appeared on any baseball card, like Virgil Jester and Luis Marquez.

Complete Set — Only $4.50 Postpaid

Eddie Mathews
third baseman

Baseball Immortals
Now All 196
Inductees Included

Now for the first time ever, a complete set of 196 cards in full color. The set, entitled, "BASEBALL IMMORTALS" features each and every member of Baseballs Hall of Fame including the 1986 inductees. The cards are extremely eye appealing with multi-colored borders: green, yellow, purple, blue, red, orange, etc. (similar to the 1975 Topps set). The banner indicates the year of induction to the Hall of Fame, with the pennant and inner border in a very vibrant metallic gold. The back is multi colored with biographies and statistics giving pertinent information about the Baseball Immortal.

The most unique feature of this incredible set is the varnish that was applied to each card that protects the card and gives it the glossy look and feel.

DON'T WAIT, ORDER YOUR HALL OF FAME SET NOW!!
ONLY $16.25 ppd.

Regular Card Size
2½''x3½''

CONLON SMITHSONIAN SETS #1 & #2

The premier Limited Edition Conlon Smithsonian set features 60 different stars from long ago. The sepia color cards are on the traditional 2½'' x 3½'' board. Set features stars such as Ruth, Gehrig, Cobb, Hornsby, Dean and many other stars of that era from the famous collection of Charles Conlon. A second series of the Conlon set is also available and contains many Hall of Famers and Superstars from the past. The Conlon Smithsonian Sets are very unique as they were printed from the original glass negatives.
Conlon Set Series #1 (60 cards) .... $15.95 ppd.
Conlon Set Series #2 (60 cards) .... $14.95 ppd.

Negro League
Baseball Stars

★ *Jackie Robinson* ★

NEGRO LEAGUE
BASEBALL STARS

For the first time ever, a set of cards on the Negro League using actual photographs. This set is of 119 cards includes: Satchel Paige, Josh Gibson, Cool Papa Bell, Buck Leonard, Monte Irvin, Judy Johnson, and more. Also shown are many historic Negro League uniforms including the Kansas City Monarchs, Homestead Grays and Pittsburgh Crawfords. The Negro Leagues are an important part of baseball history. Now you can experience some of its rich and exciting tradition.

Complete Set (119 Cards) $10.50 ppd.
2 Sets $19.50 ppd.

WANTED TOP PRICES PAID ESPECIALLY NEED:

Colgon Chips cards, Tobacco cards (1885-1915) Coupon, Kotton Cigarettes, T205 Gold Border, T206 White Border, T207 Brown Background, 1933-38 Goudey, 1939-41 Play Ball.
Any or all Milwaukee Braves, Green Bay Packers items.
We are buying cards (gum, tobacco, meats, bread, cereal, wieners, etc.) Issued prior to 1955.
Will pay premium prices for desirable items. Send description or list for immediate quote.

OUR 40th YEAR IN CARDS — AMERICA'S MOST RELIABLE CARD DEALER

With over 34 million cards in stock . . . we have America's MOST COMPLETE STOCK OF SPORTS TRADING CARDS. All sets and singles are available . . . 1948-1987. We also have thousands of pre-1948 cards available.
SUPER SERVICE!! We have six full-time employees ready and able to process your order with the maximum of efficiency and speed . . . TRY OUR SERVICE AND SEE . . . You'll agree . . . It's the best you've ever had. Full money back guarantee if you are not completely satisfied with our service and products. YOU, the customer are always number 1 to us!
To receive Super Service it is necessary to send a Postal Money Order with your order. (All personal checks are held 15 days for clearance). NOTE: All prices subject to change without notice.
See Our INSIDE FRONT COVER Ad For Other Items We Have In Stock!

MasterCard

COMPLETE 80 PAGE CATALOG
Please Send $1.00 for next 3 issues.

LARRY FRITSCH CARDS

735 OLD WAUSAU RD.
P.O. BOX 863, DEPT 579
STEVENS POINT, WI
54481
(715) 344-8687

VISA

(Charge orders add 5% to total —
Minimum charge order $10.00)

33

1987 Donruss

☐ 293. MIKE LAGA
☐ 307. TODD WORRELL
☐ 331. MIKE LAVALLIERE
☐ 357. KEN DAYLEY
☐ 386. TITO LANDRUM
☐ 417. ANDY VAN SLYKE
☐ 430. PAT PERRY
☐ 454. CURT FORD
☐ 480. JOHN MORRIS
☐ 510. JOSE OQUENDO
☐ 540. BOB FORSCH
☐ 553. DANNY COX
☐ 577. JEFF LAHTI
☐ 604. STEVE LAKE
☐ 631. RAY SOFF

SAN DIEGO PADRES

☐ 31. BENITO SANTIAGO
☐ 64. TONY GWYNN
☐ 81. STEVE GARVEY
☐ 114. LEON "BIP" ROBERTS
☐ 141. GARRY TEMPLETON
☐ 164. ERIC SHOW
☐ 187. DAVE DRAVECKY
☐ 205. TERRY KENNEDY
☐ 237. LANCE MCCULLERS
☐ 264. ANDY HAWKINS
☐ 287. TIM FLANNERY
☐ 311. BRUCE BOCHY
☐ 328. JOHN KRUK
☐ 360. ED WHITSON
☐ 387. CRAIG LEFFERTS
☐ 411. MARVELL WYNNE
☐ 434. LAMARR HOYT
☐ 451. KEVIN MCREYNOLDS
☐ 483. RICH GOSSAGE
☐ 511. GENE WALTER
☐ 534. JERRY ROYSTER
☐ 557. JIMMY JONES
☐ 574. RANDY ASADOOR
☐ 589. ED WOJNA
☐ 607. DAVE LAPOINT
☐ 632. RAY HAYWARD
☐ 654. TIM PYZNARSKI

SAN FRANCISCO GIANTS

☐ 66. WILL CLARK
☐ 80. CHRIS BROWN
☐ 116. SCOTT GARRELTS
☐ 145. ROB THOMPSON
☐ 189. DAN GLADDEN
☐ 204. ROGER MASON
☐ 239. BOB MELVIN
☐ 268. CHILI DAVIS
☐ 313. MARK DAVIS
☐ 327. CANDY MALDONADO
☐ 362. VIDA BLUE
☐ 391. JEFF LEONARD
☐ 436. JOSE URIBE
☐ 450. MIKE ALDRETE
☐ 485. BOB BRENLY
☐ 515. TERRY MULHOLLAND
☐ 547. RANDY KUTCHER
☐ 559. JEFF ROBINSON
☐ 573. KELLY DOWNS
☐ 609. MIKE KRUKOW
☐ 616. JUAN BERENGUER
☐ 636. MIKE LACOSS
☐ 644. MARK GRANT

SEATTLE MARINERS

☐ 70. MIKE MOORE
☐ 75. ALVIN DAVIS
☐ 120. JIM PRESLEY
☐ 147. DANNY TARTABULL
☐ 193. MATT YOUNG
☐ 198. KARL BEST
☐ 243. ED NUNEZ
☐ 270. PHIL BRADLEY
☐ 317. KEN PHELPS
☐ 322. LEE GUETTERMAN
☐ 366. MIKE MORGAN
☐ 393. JOHN MOSES
☐ 440. SCOTT BRADLEY
☐ 445. BOB KEARNEY
☐ 489. HAROLD REYNOLDS
☐ 517. BILL SWIFT
☐ 563. MIKE BROWN
☐ 568. MARK LANGSTON
☐ 610. DAVE VALLE
☐ 613. MIKE TRUJILLO
☐ 638. REY QUINONES
☐ 656. MICKEY BRANTLEY
☐ 660. PETE LADD

TEXAS RANGERS

☐ 41. JERRY BROWNE
☐ 57. ED CORREA
☐ 99. BOBBY WITT
☐ 101. JOSE GUZMAN
☐ 136. DON SLAUGHT
☐ 161. ODDIBE MCDOWELL
☐ 180. STEVE BUECHELE
☐ 223. CURTIS WILKERSON
☐ 224. PETE INCAVIGLIA
☐ 259. PETE O'BRIEN
☐ 284. MIKE MASON
☐ 304. SCOTT FLETCHER
☐ 346. RUBEN SIERRA
☐ 347. MITCH WILLIAMS
☐ 382. GREG HARRIS
☐ 408. TOBY HARRAH
☐ 427. GARY WARD
☐ 469. LARRY PARRISH
☐ 470. CHARLIE HOUGH
☐ 506. MIKE LOYND
☐ 531. DALE MOHORCIC
☐ 550. JEFF RUSSELL
☐ 592. MIKE STANLEY
☐ 593. DARRELL PORTER
☐ 619. GENO PETRALLI
☐ 627. KEVIN BROWN
☐ 637. DWAYNE HENRY
☐ 651. BOB BROWER

TORONTO BLUE JAYS

☐ 45. DUANE WARD
☐ 72. TONY FERNANDEZ
☐ 74. LLOYD MOSEBY
☐ 121. JESSE BARFIELD
☐ 148. ERNIE WHITT
☐ 195. DAVE STIEB
☐ 197. TOM HENKE
☐ 244. JIMMY KEY
☐ 271. GEORGE BELL
☐ 319. RANCE MULLINIKS
☐ 321. MARK EICHHORN
☐ 367. WILLIE UPSHAW
☐ 394. GARTH IORG
☐ 442. JOHN CERUTTI
☐ 444. KELLY GRUBER
☐ 490. JEFF HEARRON
☐ 518. MANNY LEE
☐ 561. GLENALLEN HILL
☐ 565. MIKE SHARPERSON
☐ 567. RICK LEACH
☐ 591. JEFF MUSSELMAN
☐ 614. DAMASO GARCIA
☐ 621. FRED MCGRIFF
☐ 639. JIM CLANCY
☐ 645. CLIFF JOHNSON
☐ 650. JOE JOHNSON
☐ 655. LUIS AQUINO

1963 FLEER (66)
2 1/2" X 3 1/2"

AL SPANGLER
Houston Colt .45's—Outfield

BALTIMORE ORIOLES

- ☐ 1. STEVE BARBER
- ☐ 2. RON HANSEN
- ☐ 3. MILT PAPPAS
- ☐ 4. BROOKS ROBINSON

BOSTON RED SOX

- ☐ 6. LOU CLINTON
- ☐ 7. BILL MONBOUQUETTE
- ☐ 8. CARL YASTRZEMSKI

CHICAGO CUBS

- ☐ 31. GLEN HOBBIE
- ☐ 32. RON SANTO

CHICAGO WHITE SOX

- ☐ 9. RAY HERBERT
- ☐ 10. JIM LANDIS

CINCINNATI REDS

- ☐ 33. GENE FREESE
- ☐ 34. VADA PINSON
- ☐ 35. BOB PURKEY

CLEVELAND INDIANS

- ☐ 11. DICK DONOVAN
- ☐ 12. TITO FRANCONA
- ☐ 13. JERRY KINDALL
- ☐ 46. JOE ADCOCK

DETROIT TIGERS

- ☐ 14. FRANK LARY

HOUSTON COLT .45'S

- ☐ 37. BOB ASPROMONTE
- ☐ 38. DICK FARRELL
- ☐ 39. AL SPANGLER

KANSAS CITY ATHLETICS

- ☐ 15. DICK HOWSER
- ☐ 16. JERRY LUMPE
- ☐ 17. NORM SIEBERN

LOS ANGELES ANGELS

- ☐ 18. DON LEE
- ☐ 19. ALBIE PEARSON
- ☐ 20. BOB RODGERS
- ☐ 21. LEON WAGNER

LOS ANGELES DODGERS

- ☐ 40. TOMMY DAVIS
- ☐ 41. DON DRYSDALE
- ☐ 42. SANDY KOUFAX
- ☐ 43. MAURY WILLS

WARREN SPAHN
Milwaukee Braves—Pitcher

MILWAUKEE BRAVES

- ☐ 44. FRANK BOLLING
- ☐ 45. WARREN SPAHN

MINNESOTA TWINS

- ☐ 22. JIM KAAT
- ☐ 23. VIC POWER
- ☐ 24. RICH ROLLINS

NEW YORK METS

- ☐ 47. ROGER CRAIG
- ☐ 48. AL JACKSON
- ☐ 49. ROD KANEHL

NEW YORK YANKEES

- ☐ 25. BOBBY RICHARDSON
- ☐ 26. RALPH TERRY

PHILADELPHIA PHILLIES

- ☐ 50. RUBEN AMARO
- ☐ 51. JOHN CALLISON
- ☐ 52. CLAY DALRYMPLE
- ☐ 53. DON DEMETER
- ☐ 54. ART MAHAFFEY

PITTSBURGH PIRATES

- ☐ 55. SMOKY BURGESS
- ☐ 56. ROBERTO CLEMENTE
- ☐ 57. ELROY FACE
- ☐ 58. VERNON LAW
- ☐ 59. BILL MAZEROSKI

ST. LOUIS CARDINALS

- ☐ 60. KEN BOYER
- ☐ 61. BOB GIBSON
- ☐ 62. GENE OLIVER
- ☐ 63. BILL WHITE

WILLIE MAYS
San Francisco Giants—Outfield

SAN FRANCISCO GIANTS

- ☐ 5. WILLIE MAYS
- ☐ 36. JOE AMALFITANO
- ☐ 64. ORLANDO CEPEDA
- ☐ 65. JIMMY DAVENPORT
- ☐ 66. BILLY O'DELL

WASHINGTON SENATORS

- ☐ 27. TOM CHENEY
- ☐ 28. CHUCK COTTIER
- ☐ 29. JIMMY PIERSALL
- ☐ 30. DAVE STENHOUSE

1981 FLEER (660)
2 1/2" X 3 1/2"

CHRIS CHAMBLISS
FIRST BASE

ATLANTA BRAVES

- ☐ 242. PHIL NIEKRO
- ☐ 243. DALE MURPHY
- ☐ 244. BOB HORNER
- ☐ 245. JEFF BURROUGHS
- ☐ 246. RICK CAMP
- ☐ 247. BOBBY COX(M)
- ☐ 248. BRUCE BENEDICT
- ☐ 249. GENE GARBER
- ☐ 250. JERRY ROYSTER
- ☐ 251. GARY MATTHEWS
- ☐ 252. CHRIS CHAMBLISS
- ☐ 253. LUIS GOMEZ
- ☐ 254. BILL NAHORODNY
- ☐ 255. DOYLE ALEXANDER
- ☐ 256. BRIAN ASSELSTINE
- ☐ 257. BIFF POCOROBA
- ☐ 258. MIKE LUM
- ☐ 259. CHARLIE SPIKES
- ☐ 260. GLENN HUBBARD
- ☐ 261. TOMMY BOGGS
- ☐ 262. AL HRABOSKY
- ☐ 263. RICK MATULA
- ☐ 264. PRESTON HANNA
- ☐ 265. LARRY BRADFORD
- ☐ 266. RAFAEL RAMIREZ
- ☐ 267. LARRY MCWILLIAMS
- ☐ 646. TEAM CHECKLIST(B)

BALTIMORE ORIOLES

- ☐ 169. JIM PALMER
- ☐ 170. STEVE STONE
- ☐ 171. MIKE FLANAGAN
- ☐ 172. AL BUMBRY
- ☐ 173. DOUG DECINCES
- ☐ 174. SCOTT MCGREGOR
- ☐ 175. MARK BELANGER
- ☐ 176. TIM STODDARD
- ☐ 177. RICK DEMPSEY
- ☐ 178. EARL WEAVER(M)
- ☐ 179. TIPPY MARTINEZ
- ☐ 180. DENNIS MARTINEZ
- ☐ 181. SAMMY STEWART
- ☐ 182. RICH DAUER
- ☐ 183. LEE MAY
- ☐ 184. EDDIE MURRAY
- ☐ 185. BENNY AYALA
- ☐ 186. JOHN LOWENSTEIN
- ☐ 187. GARY ROENICKE

☐ 188. KEN SINGLETON
☐ 189. DAN GRAHAM
☐ 190. TERRY CROWLEY
☐ 191. KIKO GARCIA
☐ 192. DAVE FORD
☐ 193. MARK COREY
☐ 194. LENN SAKATA
☐ 195. DOUG DECINCES
☐ 644. TEAM CHECKLIST(F)

BOSTON RED SOX

☐ 221. CARL YASTRZEMSKI
☐ 222. JIM RICE
☐ 223. FRED LYNN
☐ 224. CARLTON FISK
☐ 225. RICK BURLESON
☐ 226. DENNIS ECKERSLEY
☐ 227. BUTCH HOBSON
☐ 228. TOM BURGMEIER
☐ 229. GARRY HANCOCK
☐ 230. DON ZIMMER(M)
☐ 231. STEVE RENKO
☐ 232. DWIGHT EVANS
☐ 233. MIKE TORREZ
☐ 234. BOB STANLEY
☐ 235. JIM DWYER
☐ 236. DAVE STAPLETON
☐ 237. GLENN HOFFMAN
☐ 238. JERRY REMY
☐ 239. DICK DRAGO
☐ 240. BILL CAMPBELL
☐ 241. TONY PEREZ
☐ 638. CARL YASTRZEMSKI
☐ 646. TEAM CHECKLIST(F)

CALIFORNIA ANGELS

☐ 268. ROD CAREW
☐ 269. BOBBY GRICH
☐ 270. CARNEY LANSFORD
☐ 271. DON BAYLOR
☐ 272. JOE RUDI
☐ 273. DAN FORD
☐ 274. JIM FREGOSI(M)
☐ 275. DAVE FROST
☐ 276. FRANK TANANA
☐ 277. DICKIE THON
☐ 278. JASON THOMPSON
☐ 279. RICK MILLER
☐ 280. BERT CAMPANERIS
☐ 281. TOM DONOHUE
☐ 282. BRIAN DOWNING
☐ 283. FRED PATEK
☐ 284. BRUCE KISON
☐ 285. DAVE LAROCHE
☐ 286. DON AASE
☐ 287. JIM BARR
☐ 288. ALFREDO MARTINEZ
☐ 289. LARRY HARLOW
☐ 290. ANDY HASSLER
☐ 647. TEAM CHECKLIST(F)

CHICAGO CUBS

☐ 291. DAVE KINGMAN
☐ 292. BILL BUCKNER
☐ 293. RICK REUSCHEL
☐ 294. BRUCE SUTTER
☐ 295. JERRY MARTIN
☐ 296. SCOT THOMPSON
☐ 297. IVAN DEJUSUS
☐ 298. STEVE DILLARD
☐ 299. DICK TIDROW
☐ 300. RANDY MARTZ
☐ 301. LENNY RANDLE
☐ 302. LYNN MCGLOTHEN
☐ 303. CLIFF JOHNSON
☐ 304. TIM BLACKWELL
☐ 305. DENNIS LAMP
☐ 306. BILL CAUDILL
☐ 307. CARLOS LEZCANO
☐ 308. JIM TRACY
☐ 309. DOUG CAPILLA*
☐ 310. WILLIE HERNANDEZ
☐ 311. MIKE VAIL
☐ 312. MIKE KRUKOW
☐ 313. BARRY FOOTE
☐ 314. LARRY BIITTNER
☐ 315. MIKE TYSON
☐ 647. TEAM CHECKLIST(B)

CHICAGO WHITE SOX

☐ 339. ED FARMER
☐ 340. BOB MOLINARO
☐ 341. TODD CRUZ
☐ 342. BRITT BURNS
☐ 343. KEVIN BELL
☐ 344. TONY LARUSSA(M)
☐ 345. STEVE TROUT
☐ 346. HAROLD BAINES
☐ 347. RICH WORTHAM
☐ 348. WAYNE NORDHAGEN
☐ 349. MIKE SQUIRES
☐ 350. LAMAR JOHNSON
☐ 352. FRANCISCO BARRIOS
☐ 353. THAD BOSLEY
☐ 354. CHET LEMON
☐ 355. BRUCE KIMM
☐ 356. RICHARD DOTSON
☐ 357. JIM MORRISON
☐ 358. MIKE PROLY
☐ 359. GREG PRYOR
☐ 648. TEAM CHECKLIST(B)

CINCINNATI REDS

☐ 196. JOHNNY BENCH
☐ 197. DAVE CONCEPCION
☐ 198. RAY KNIGHT
☐ 199. KEN GRIFFEY
☐ 200. TOM SEAVER
☐ 201. DAVE COLLINS
☐ 202. GEORGE FOSTER
☐ 203. JUNIOR KENNEDY
☐ 204. FRANK PASTORE
☐ 205. DAN DRIESSEN
☐ 206. HECTOR CRUZ
☐ 207. PAUL MOSKAU
☐ 208. CHARLIE LEIBRANDT
☐ 209. HARRY SPILMAN
☐ 210. JOE PRICE
☐ 211. TOM HUME
☐ 212. JOE NOLAN
☐ 213. DOUG BAIR
☐ 214. MARIO SOTO
☐ 215. BILL BONHAM
☐ 216. GEORGE FOSTER
☐ 217. PAUL HOUSEHOLDER
☐ 218. RON OESTER
☐ 219. SAM MEJIAS
☐ 220. SHELDON BURNSIDE
☐ 644. TEAM CHECKLIST(B)

CLEVELAND INDIANS

☐ 387. MIKE HARGROVE
☐ 388. JORGE ORTA
☐ 389. TOBY HARRAH
☐ 390. TOM VERYZER
☐ 391. MIGUEL DILONE
☐ 392. DAN SPILLNER
☐ 393. JACK BROHAMER
☐ 394. WAYNE GARLAND
☐ 395. SID MONGE
☐ 396. RICK WAITS
☐ 397. JOE CHARBONEAU
☐ 398. GARY ALEXANDER
☐ 399. JERRY DYBZINSKI
☐ 400. MIKE STANTON
☐ 401. MIKE PAXTON
☐ 402. GARY GRAY
☐ 403. RICK MANNING
☐ 404. BO DIAZ
☐ 405. RON HASSEY
☐ 406. ROSS GRIMSLEY
☐ 407. VICTOR CRUZ
☐ 408. LEN BARKER
☐ 649. TEAM CHECKLIST(B)

DETROIT TIGERS

☐ 459. STEVE KEMP
☐ 460. SPARKY ANDERSON(M)
☐ 461. ALAN TRAMMELL
☐ 462. MARK FIDRYCH
☐ 463. LOU WHITAKER
☐ 464. DAVE ROZEMA
☐ 465. MILT WILCOX
☐ 466. CHAMP SUMMERS
☐ 467. LANCE PARRISH

☐ 468. DAN PETRY
☐ 469. PAT UNDERWOOD
☐ 470. RICK PETERS
☐ 471. AL COWENS
☐ 472. JOHN WOCKENFUSS
☐ 473. TOM BROOKENS
☐ 474. RICHIE HEBNER
☐ 475. JACK MORRIS
☐ 476. JIM LENTINE
☐ 477. BRUCE ROBBINS
☐ 478. MARK WAGNER
☐ 479. TIM CORCORAN
☐ 480. STAN PAPI
☐ 481. KIRK GIBSON
☐ 482. DAN SCHATZEDER
☐ 652. TEAM CHECKLIST(F)

HOUSTON ASTROS

☐ 51. ART HOWE
☐ 52. KEN FORSCH
☐ 53. VERN RUHLE
☐ 54. JOE NIEKRO
☐ 55. FRANK LACORTE
☐ 56. J.R. RICHARD
☐ 57. NOLAN RYAN
☐ 58. ENOS CABELL
☐ 59. CESAR CEDENO
☐ 60. JOSE CRUZ
☐ 61. BILL VIRDON(M)
☐ 62. TERRY PUHL
☐ 63. JOAQUIN ANDUJAR
☐ 64. ALAN ASHBY
☐ 65. JOE SAMBITO
☐ 66. DENNY WALLING
☐ 67. JEFF LEONARD
☐ 68. LUIS PUJOLS
☐ 69. BRUCE BOCHY
☐ 70. RAFAEL LANDESTOY
☐ 71. DAVE SMITH
☐ 72. DANNY HEEP
☐ 73. JULIO GONZALEZ
☐ 74. CRAIG REYNOLDS
☐ 75. GARY WOODS
☐ 76. DAVE BERGMAN
☐ 77. RANDY NIEMANN
☐ 78. JOE MORGAN
☐ 642. TEAM CHECKLIST(F)

KANSAS CITY ROYALS

☐ 28. GEORGE BRETT
☐ 29. WILLIE WILSON
☐ 30. PAUL SPLITTORFF
☐ 31. DAN QUISENBERRY
☐ 32. AMOS OTIS
☐ 33. STEVE BUSBY
☐ 34. U.L. WASHINGTON
☐ 35. DAVE CHALK
☐ 36. DARRELL PORTER
☐ 37. MARTY PATTIN
☐ 38. LARRY GURA
☐ 39. RENIE MARTIN
☐ 40. RICH GALE
☐ 41. HAL MCRAE
☐ 42. DENNIS LEONARD
☐ 43. WILLIE AIKENS
☐ 44. FRANK WHITE
☐ 45. CLINT HURDLE
☐ 46. JOHN WATHAN
☐ 47. PETE LACOCK
☐ 48. RANCE MULLINIKS
☐ 49. JEFF TWITTY
☐ 50. JAMIE QUIRK
☐ 483. AMOS OTIS
☐ 641. TEAM CHECKLIST(B)
☐ 653. WILLIE WILSON
☐ 655. GEORGE BRETT

LOS ANGELES DODGERS

☐ 110. STEVE GARVEY
☐ 111. REGGIE SMITH
☐ 112. DON SUTTON
☐ 113. BURT HOOTON
☐ 114. DAVE LOPES
☐ 115. DUSTY BAKER
☐ 116. TOM LASORDA(M)
☐ 117. BILL RUSSELL
☐ 118. JERRY REUSS
☐ 119. TERRY FORSTER

36

* Capilla appears with Braves on the back of
his card. This notation is in error as Capilla
did not play for the Braves. His card is not,
therefore, listed with the Braves.

☐ 120. BOB WELCH
☐ 121. DON STANHOUSE
☐ 122. RICK MONDAY
☐ 123. DERREL THOMAS
☐ 124. JOE FERGUSON
☐ 125. RICK SUTCLIFFE
☐ 126. RON CEY
☐ 127. DAVE GOLTZ
☐ 128. JAY JOHNSTONE
☐ 129. STEVE YEAGER
☐ 130. GARY WEISS
☐ 131. MIKE SCIOSCIA
☐ 132. VIC DAVALILLO
☐ 133. DOUG RAU
☐ 134. PEPE FRIAS
☐ 135. MICKEY HATCHER
☐ 136. STEVE HOWE
☐ 137. BOBBY CASTILLO
☐ 138. GARY THOMASSON
☐ 139. RUDY LAW
☐ 140. FERNANDO VALENZUELA
☐ 141. MANNY MOTA
☐ 606. STEVE GARVEY
☐ 643. TEAM CHECKLIST(F)

MILWAUKEE BREWERS(23)

☐ 507. GORMAN THOMAS
☐ 508. BEN OGLIVIE
☐ 509. LARRY HISLE
☐ 510. SAL BANDO
☐ 511. ROBIN YOUNT
☐ 512. MIKE CALDWELL
☐ 513. SIXTO LEZCANO
☐ 514. BILL TRAVERS
☐ 515. PAUL MOLITOR
☐ 516. MOSSE HAAS
☐ 517. BILL CASTRO
☐ 518. JIM SLATON
☐ 519. LARY SORENSEN
☐ 520. BOB MCCLURE
☐ 521. CHARLIE MOORE
☐ 522. JIM GANTNER
☐ 523. REGGIE CLEVELAND
☐ 524. DON MONEY
☐ 525. BILL TRAVERS
☐ 526. BUCK MARTINEZ
☐ 527. DICK DAVIS
☐ 639. CECIL COOPER
☐ 654. TEAM CHECKLIST(F)

MINNESOTA TWINS(22)

☐ 551. ROY SMALLEY
☐ 552. JERRY KOOSMAN
☐ 553. KEN LANDREAUX
☐ 554. JOHN CASTINO
☐ 555. DOUG CORBETT
☐ 556. BOMBO RIVERA
☐ 557. RON JACKSON
☐ 558. BUTCH WYNEGAR
☐ 559. HOSKEN POWELL
☐ 560. PETE REDFERN
☐ 561. ROGER ERICKSON
☐ 562. GLENN ADAMS
☐ 563. RICK SOFIELD
☐ 564. GEOFF ZAHN
☐ 565. PETE MACKANIN
☐ 566. MIKE CUBBAGE
☐ 567. DARRELL JACKSON
☐ 568. DAVE EDWARDS
☐ 569. ROB WILFONG
☐ 570. SAL BUTERA
☐ 571. JOSE MORALES
☐ 656. TEAM CHECKLIST(F)

MONTREAL EXPOS(28)

☐ 142. GARY CARTER
☐ 143. STEVE ROGERS
☐ 144. WARREN CROMARTIE
☐ 145. ANDRE DAWSON
☐ 146. LARRY PARRISH
☐ 147. ROWLAND OFFICE
☐ 148. ELLIS VALENTINE
☐ 149. DICK WILLIAMS(M)
☐ 150. BILL GULLICKSON
☐ 151. ELIAS SOSA
☐ 152. JOHN TAMARGO
☐ 153. CHRIS SPEIER
☐ 154. RON LEFLORE

☐ 155. RODNEY SCOTT
☐ 156. STAN BAHNSEN
☐ 157. BILL LEE
☐ 158. FRED NORMAN
☐ 159. WOODIE FRYMAN
☐ 160. DAVE PALMER
☐ 161. JERRY WHITE
☐ 162. ROBERTO RAMOS
☐ 163. JOHN D'ACQUISTO
☐ 164. TOMMY HUTTON
☐ 165. CHARLIE LEA
☐ 166. SCOTT SANDERSON
☐ 167. KEN MACHA
☐ 168. TONY BERNAZARD
☐ 643. TEAM CHECKLIST(B)

NEW YORK METS(24)

☐ 316. LEE MAZZILLI
☐ 317. JOHN STEARNS
☐ 318. ALEX TREVINO
☐ 319. CRAIG SWAN
☐ 320. FRANK TAVERAS
☐ 321. STEVE HANDERSON
☐ 322. NEIL ALLEN
☐ 323. MARK BOMBACK
☐ 324. MIKE JORGENSEN
☐ 325. JOE TORRE(M)
☐ 326. ELLIOTT MADDOX
☐ 327. PETE FALCONE
☐ 328. RAY BURRIS
☐ 329. CLAUDELL WASHINGTON
☐ 330. DOUG FLYNN
☐ 331. JOEL YOUNGBLOOD
☐ 332. BILL ALMON
☐ 333. TOM HAUSMAN
☐ 334. PAT ZACHRY
☐ 335. JEFF REARDON
☐ 336. WALLY BACKMAN
☐ 337. DAN NORMAN
☐ 338. JERRY MORALES
☐ 648. TEAM CHECKLIST(F)

NEW YORK YANKEES(33)

☐ 79. REGGIE JACKSON
☐ 80. BUCKY DENT
☐ 81. TOMMY JOHN
☐ 82. LUIS TIANT
☐ 83. RICK CERONE
☐ 84. DICK HOWSER(M)
☐ 85. LOU PINIELLA
☐ 86. RON DAVIS
☐ 87. GRAIG NETTLES
☐ 88. RON GUIDRY
☐ 89. RICH GOSSAGE
☐ 90. RUDY MAY
☐ 91. GAYLORD PERRY
☐ 92. ERIC SODERHOLM
☐ 93. BOB WATSON
☐ 94. BOBBY MURCER
☐ 95. BOBBY BROWN
☐ 96. JIM SPENCER
☐ 97. TOM UNDERWOOD
☐ 98. OSCAR GAMBLE
☐ 99. JOHNNY OATES
☐ 100. FRED STANLEY
☐ 101. RUPPERT JONES
☐ 102. DENNIS WERTH
☐ 103. JOE LEFEBVRE
☐ 104. BRIAN DOYLE
☐ 105. AURELIO RODRIGUEZ
☐ 106. DOUG BIRD
☐ 107. MIKE GRIFFIN
☐ 108. TIM LOLLAR
☐ 109. WILLIE RANDOLPH
☐ 642. TEAM CHECKLIST(B)
☐ 650. REGGIE JACKSON

OAKLAND A'S(24)

☐ 351. RICKEY HENDERSON
☐ 572. RICK LANGFORD
☐ 573. MIKE NORRIS
☐ 574. RICKEY HENDERSON
☐ 575. TONY ARMAS
☐ 576. DAVE REVERING
☐ 577. JEFF NEWMAN
☐ 578. BOB LACEY
☐ 579. BRIAN KINGMAN

☐ 580. MITCHELL PAGE
☐ 581. BILLY MARTIN(M)
☐ 582. ROB PICCIOLO
☐ 583. MIKE HEATH
☐ 584. MICKEY KLUTTS
☐ 585. ORLANDO GONZALEZ
☐ 586. MIKE DAVIS
☐ 587. WAYNE GROSS
☐ 588. MATT KEOUGH
☐ 589. STEVE MCCATTY
☐ 590. DWAYNE MURPHY
☐ 591. MARIO GUERRERO
☐ 592. DAVE MCKAY
☐ 593. JIM ESSIAN
☐ 656. TEAM CHECKLIST(B)

PHILADELPHIA PHILLIES(31)

☐ 1. PETE ROSE
☐ 2. LARRY BOWA
☐ 3. MANNY TRILLO
☐ 4. BOB BOONE
☐ 5. MIKE SCHMIDT
☐ 6. STEVE CARLTON
☐ 7. TUG MCGRAW
☐ 8. LARRY CHRISTENSON
☐ 9. BAKE MCBRIDE
☐ 10. GREG LUZINSKI
☐ 11. RON REED
☐ 12. DICKIE NOLES
☐ 13. KEITH MORELAND
☐ 14. BOB WALK
☐ 15. LONNIE SMITH
☐ 16. DICK RUTHVEN
☐ 17. SPARKY LYLE
☐ 18. GREG GROSS
☐ 19. GARRY MADDOX
☐ 20. NINO ESPINOSA
☐ 21. GEORGE VUKOVICH
☐ 22. JOHN VUKOVICH
☐ 23. RAMON AVILES
☐ 24. KEVIN SAUCIER
☐ 25. RANDY LERCH
☐ 26. DEL UNSER
☐ 27. TIM MCCARVER
☐ 640. MIKE SCHMIDT
☐ 641. TEAM CHECKLIST(F)
☐ 657. TUG MCGRAW
☐ 660. STEVE CARLTON

PITTSBURGH PIRATES(29)

☐ 360. DAVE PARKER
☐ 361. OMAR MORENO
☐ 362. KENT TEKULVA
☐ 363. WILLIE STARGELL
☐ 364. PHIL GARNER
☐ 365. ED OTT
☐ 366. DON ROBINSON
☐ 367. CHUCK TANNER(M)
☐ 368. JIM ROOKER
☐ 369. DALE BERRA
☐ 370. JIM BIBBY
☐ 371. STEVE NICOSIA
☐ 372. MIKE EASLER
☐ 373. BILL ROBINSON
☐ 374. LEE LACY
☐ 375. JOHN CANDELARIA
☐ 376. MANNY SANGUILLEN
☐ 377. RICK RHODEN
☐ 378. GRANT JACKSON

☐ 379. TIM FOLI
☐ 380. ROD SCURRY
☐ 381. BILL MADLOCK
☐ 382. KURT BEVACQUA
☐ 383. BERT BLYLEVEN
☐ 384. EDDIE SOLOMON
☐ 385. ENRIQUE ROMO
☐ 386. JOHN MILNER
☐ 419. JESSE JEFFERSON(B)
☐ 649. TEAM CHECKLIST(F)

ST. LOUIS CARDINALS

☐ 528. TED SIMMONS
☐ 529. GARRY TEMPLETON
☐ 530. KEN REITZ
☐ 531. TONY SCOTT
☐ 532. KEN OBERKFELL
☐ 533. BOB SYKES
☐ 534. KEITH SMITH
☐ 535. JOHN LITTLEFIELD
☐ 536. JIM KAAT
☐ 537. BOB FORSCH
☐ 538. MIKE PHILLIPS
☐ 539. TERRY LANDRUM
☐ 540. LEON DURHAM
☐ 541. TERRY KENNEDY
☐ 542. GEORGE HENDRICK
☐ 543. DANE IORG
☐ 544. MARK LITTELL
☐ 545. KEITH HERNANDEZ
☐ 546. SILVIO MARTINEZ
☐ 547. DON HOOD
☐ 548. BOBBY BONDS
☐ 549. MIKE RAMSEY
☐ 550. TOM HERR
☐ 654. TEAM CHECKLIST(B)

SAN DIEGO PADRES

☐ 484. DAVE WINFIELD
☐ 485. ROLLIE FINGERS
☐ 486. GENE RICHARDS
☐ 487. RANDY JONES
☐ 488. OZZIE SMITH
☐ 489. GENE TENACE
☐ 490. BILL FAHEY
☐ 491. JOHN CURTIS
☐ 492. DAVE CASH
☐ 493. TIM FLANNERY
☐ 494. JERRY MUMPHREY
☐ 495. BOB SHIRLEY
☐ 496. STEVE MURA
☐ 497. ERIC RASMUSSEN
☐ 498. BRODERICK PERKINS
☐ 499. BARRY EVANS
☐ 500. CHUCK BAKER
☐ 501. LUIS SALAZAR
☐ 502. GARY LUCAS
☐ 503. MIKE ARMSTRONG
☐ 504. JERRY TURNER
☐ 505. DENNIS KINNEY
☐ 506. WILLIE MONTANEZ
☐ 652. TEAM CHECKLIST(B)

SAN FRANCISCO GIANTS

☐ 432. VIDA BLUE
☐ 433. JACK CLARK
☐ 434. WILLIE MCCOVEY
☐ 435. MIKE IVIE
☐ 436. DARRELL EVANS
☐ 437. TERRY WHITFIELD
☐ 438. RENNIE STENNETT
☐ 439. JOHN MONTEFUSCO
☐ 440. JIM WOHLFORD
☐ 441. BILL NORTH
☐ 442. MILT MAY
☐ 443. MAX VENABLE
☐ 444. ED WHITSON
☐ 445. AL HOLLAND
☐ 446. RANDY MOFFITT
☐ 447. BOB KNEPPER
☐ 448. GARY LAVELLE
☐ 449. GREG MINTON
☐ 450. JOHNNIE LEMASTER
☐ 451. LARRY HERNDON
☐ 452. RICH MURRAY
☐ 453. JOE PETTINI
☐ 454. ALLEN RIPLEY

☐ 455. DENNIS LITTLEJOHN
☐ 456. TOM GRIFFIN
☐ 457. ALAN HARGESHEIMER
☐ 458. JOE STRAIN
☐ 651. TEAM CHECKLIST(B)

SEATTLE MARINERS

☐ 594. DAVE HEAVERLO
☐ 595. MUARY WILLS(M)
☐ 596. JUAN BENIQUEZ
☐ 597. RODNEY CRAIG
☐ 598. JIM ANDERSON
☐ 599. FLOYD BANNISTER
☐ 600. BRUCE BOCHTE
☐ 601. JULIO CRUZ
☐ 602. TED COX
☐ 603. DAN MEYER
☐ 604. LARRY COX
☐ 605. BILL STEIN
☐ 607. DAVE A. ROBERTS
☐ 608. LEON ROBERTS
☐ 609. REGGIE WALTON
☐ 610. DAVE ELDER
☐ 611. LARRY MILBOURNE
☐ 612. KIM ALLEN
☐ 613. MARIO MENDOZA
☐ 614. TOM PACIOREK
☐ 615. GLENN ABBOTT
☐ 616. JOE SIMPSON
☐ 658. TEAM CHECKLIST(F)

TEXAS RANGERS

☐ 617. MICKEY RIVERS
☐ 618. JIM KERN
☐ 619. JIM SUNDBERG
☐ 620. RICHIE ZISK
☐ 621. JON MATLACK
☐ 622. FERGUSON JENKINS
☐ 623. PAT CORRALES(M)
☐ 624. ED FIGUEROA
☐ 625. BUDDY BELL
☐ 626. AL OLIVER
☐ 627. DOC MEDICH
☐ 628. BUMP WILLS
☐ 629. RUSTY STAUB
☐ 630. PAT PUTNAM
☐ 631. JOHN GRUBB
☐ 632. DANNY DARWIN
☐ 633. KEN CLAY
☐ 634. JIM NORRIS
☐ 635. JOHN BUTCHER
☐ 636. DAVE W. ROBERTS
☐ 637. BILLY SAMPLE
☐ 658. TEAM CHECKLIST(B)

TORONTO BLUE JAYS

☐ 409. BOB BAILOR
☐ 410. OTTO VELEZ
☐ 411. ERNIE WHITT
☐ 412. JIM CLANCY
☐ 413. BARRY BONNELL
☐ 414. DAVE STIEB
☐ 415. DAMASO GARCIA
☐ 416. JOHN MAYBERRY
☐ 417. ROY HOWELL
☐ 418. DANNY AINGE
☐ 419. JESSE JEFFERSON(F)

☐ 420. JOEY MCLAUGHLIN
☐ 421. LLOYD MOSEBY
☐ 422. AL WOODS
☐ 423. GARTH IORG
☐ 424. DOUG AULT
☐ 425. KEN SCHROM
☐ 426. MIKE WILLIS
☐ 427. STEVE BRAUN
☐ 428. BOB DAVIS
☐ 429. JERRY GARVIN
☐ 430. ALFREDO GRIFFIN
☐ 431. BOB MATTICK(M)
☐ 651. TEAM CHECKLIST(F)

1982 FLEER (660)
2 1/2″ X 3 1/2″

ATLANTA BRAVES

☐ 428. BRIAN ASSELSTINE
☐ 429. BRUCE BENEDICT
☐ 430. TOM BOGGS
☐ 431. LARRY BRADFORD
☐ 432. RICK CAMP
☐ 433. CHRIS CHAMBLISS
☐ 434. GENE GARBER
☐ 435. PRESTON HANNA
☐ 436. BOB HORNER
☐ 437. GLENN HUBBARD
☐ 438. AL HRABOSKY
☐ 439. RUFINO LINARES
☐ 440. RICK MAHLER
☐ 441. ED MILLER
☐ 442. JOHN MONTEFUSCO
☐ 443. DALE MURPHY
☐ 444. PHIL NIEKRO
☐ 445. GAYLORD PERRY
☐ 446. BIFF POCOROBA
☐ 447. RAFAEL RAMIREZ
☐ 448. JERRY ROYSTER
☐ 449. CLAUDELL WASHINGTON
☐ 655. TEAM CHECKLIST(B)

BALTIMORE ORIOLES

☐ 157. BENNY AYALA
☐ 158. MARK BELANGER
☐ 159. AL BUMBRY
☐ 160. TERRY CROWLEY
☐ 161. RICH DAUER
☐ 162. DOUG DECINCES
☐ 163. RICK DEMPSEY
☐ 164. JIM DWYER
☐ 165. MIKE FLANAGAN
☐ 166. DAVE FORD
☐ 167. DAN GRAHAM
☐ 168. WAYNE KRENCHICKI
☐ 169. JOHN LOWENSTEIN
☐ 170. DENNIS MARTINEZ
☐ 171. TIPPY MARTINEZ
☐ 172. SCOTT MCGREGOR
☐ 173. JOSE MORALES
☐ 174. EDDIE MURRAY
☐ 175. JIM PALMER
☐ 176. CAL RIPKEN
☐ 177. GARY ROENICKE
☐ 178. LENN SAKATA
☐ 179. KEN SINGLETON
☐ 180. SAMMY STEWART

☐ 181. TIM STODDARD
☐ 182. STEVE STONE
☐ 650. TEAM CHECKLIST(F)

BOSTON RED SOX

☐ 287. GARY ALLENSON
☐ 288. TOM BURGMEIER
☐ 289. BILL CAMPBELL
☐ 290. MARK CLEAR
☐ 291. STEVE CRAWFORD
☐ 292. DENNIS ECKERSLEY
☐ 293. DWIGHT EVANS
☐ 294. RICH GEDMAN
☐ 295. GARRY HANCOCK
☐ 296. GLENN HOFFMAN
☐ 297. BRUCE HURST
☐ 298. CARNEY LANSFORD
☐ 299. RICK MILLER
☐ 300. REID NICHOLS
☐ 301. BOB OJEDA
☐ 302. TONY PEREZ
☐ 303. CHUCK RAINEY
☐ 304. JERRY REMY
☐ 305. JIM RICE
☐ 306. JOE RUDI
☐ 307. BOB STANLEY
☐ 308. DAVE STAPLETON
☐ 309. FRANK TANANA
☐ 310. MIKE TORREZ
☐ 311. JOHN TUDOR
☐ 312. CARL YASTRZEMSKI
☐ 652. TEAM CHECKLIST(B)

CALIFORNIA ANGELS

☐ 450. DON AASE
☐ 451. DON BAYLOR
☐ 452. JUAN BENIQUEZ
☐ 453. RICK BURLESON
☐ 454. BERT CAMPANERIS
☐ 455. ROD CAREW
☐ 456. BOB CLARK
☐ 457. BRIAN DOWNING
☐ 458. DAN FORD
☐ 459. KEN FORSCH
☐ 460. DAVE FROST
☐ 461. BOBBY GRICH
☐ 462. LARRY HARLOW
☐ 463. JOHN HARRIS
☐ 464. ANDY HASSLER
☐ 465. BUTCH HOBSON
☐ 466. JESSE JEFFERSON
☐ 467. BRUCE KISON
☐ 468. FRED LYNN
☐ 469. ANGEL MORENO
☐ 470. ED OTT
☐ 471. FRED PATEK
☐ 472. STEVE RENKO
☐ 473. MIKE WITT
☐ 474. GEOFF ZAHN
☐ 656. TEAM CHECKLIST(F)

CHICAGO CUBS

☐ 586. DOUG BIRD
☐ 587. TIM BLACKWELL
☐ 588. BOBBY BONDS
☐ 589. BILL BUCKNER
☐ 590. BILL CAUDILL
☐ 591. HECTOR CRUZ
☐ 592. JODY DAVID
☐ 593. IVAN DEJESUS
☐ 594. STEVE DILLARD
☐ 595. LEON DURHAM
☐ 596. RAWLY EASTWICK
☐ 597. STEVE HENDERSON
☐ 598. MIKE KRUKOW
☐ 599. MIKE LUM
☐ 600. RANDY MARTZ
☐ 601. JERRY MORALES
☐ 602. KEN REITZ
☐ 603. LEE SMITH
☐ 604. DICK TIDROW
☐ 605. JIM TRACY
☐ 606. MIKE TYSON
☐ 607. TY WALLER
☐ 659. TEAM CHECKLIST(F)

CHICAGO WHITE SOX

☐ 335. BILL ALMON
☐ 336. HAROLD BAINES
☐ 337. ROSS BAUMGARTEN
☐ 338. TONY BERNAZARD
☐ 339. BRITT BURNS
☐ 340. RICHARD DOTSON
☐ 341. JIM ESSIAN
☐ 342. ED FARMER
☐ 343. CARLTON FISK
☐ 344. KEVIN HICKEY
☐ 345. LAMARR HOYT
☐ 346. LAMAR JOHNSON
☐ 347. JERRY KOOSMAN
☐ 348. RUSTY KUNTZ
☐ 349. DENNIS LAMP
☐ 350. RON DEFLORE
☐ 351. CHET LEMON
☐ 352. GREG LUZINSKI
☐ 353. BOB MOLINARO
☐ 354. JIM MORRISON
☐ 355. WAYNE NORDHAGEN
☐ 356. GREG PRYOR
☐ 357. MIKE SQUIRES
☐ 358. STEVE TROUT
☐ 653. TEAM CHECKLIST(B)

CINCINNATI REDS

☐ 57. JOHNNY BENCH
☐ 58. BRUCE BERENYI
☐ 59. LARRY BIITTNER
☐ 60. SCOTT BROWN
☐ 61. DAVE COLLINS
☐ 62. GEOFF COMBE
☐ 63. DAVE CONCEPCION
☐ 64. DAN DRIESSEN
☐ 65. JOE EDELEN
☐ 66. GEORGE FÓSTER
☐ 67. KEN GRIFFEY
☐ 68. PAUL HOUSEHOLDER
☐ 69. TOM HUME
☐ 70. JUNIOR KENNEDY
☐ 71. RAY KNIGHT
☐ 72. MIKE LACOSS
☐ 73. RAFAEL LANDESTOY
☐ 74. CHARLIE LEIBRANDT
☐ 75. SAM MEJIAS
☐ 76. PAUL MOSKAU
☐ 77. JOE NOLAN
☐ 78. MIKE O'BERRY
☐ 79. RON OESTER
☐ 80. FRANK PASTORE
☐ 81. JOE PRICE
☐ 82. TOM SEAVER
☐ 83. MARIO SOTO
☐ 84. MIKE VAIL
☐ 648. TEAM CHECKLIST(F)

CLEVELAND INDIANS

☐ 359. ALAN BANNISTER
☐ 360. LEN BARKER
☐ 361. BERT BLYLEVEN
☐ 362. JOE CHARBONEAU
☐ 363. JOHN DENNY
☐ 364. BO DIAZ
☐ 365. MIGUEL DILONE
☐ 366. JERRY DYBZINSKI
☐ 367. WAYNE GARLAND
☐ 368. MIKE HARGROVE
☐ 369. TOBY HARRAH
☐ 370. RON HASSEY
☐ 371. VON HAYES
☐ 372. PAT KELLY
☐ 373. DUANE KUIPER
☐ 374. RICK MANNING
☐ 375. SID MONGE
☐ 376. JORGE ORTA
☐ 377. DAVE ROSELLO
☐ 378. DAN SPILLNER
☐ 379. MIKE STANTON
☐ 380. ANDRE THORNTON
☐ 381. TOM VERYZER
☐ 382. RICK WAITS
☐ 654. TEAM CHECKLIST(F)

DETROIT TIGERS

☐ 263. TOM BROOKENS
☐ 264. GEORGE CAPPUZZELLO
☐ 265. MARTY CASTILLO
☐ 266. AL COWENS
☐ 267. KIRK GIBSON
☐ 268. RICHIE HEBNER
☐ 269. RON JACKSON
☐ 270. LYNN JONES
☐ 271. STEVE KEMP
☐ 272. RICK LEACH
☐ 273. AURELIO LOPEZ
☐ 274. JACK MORRIS
☐ 275. KEVIN SAUCIER
☐ 276. LANCE PARRISH
☐ 277. RICK PETERS
☐ 278. DAN PETRY
☐ 279. DAVID ROZEMA
☐ 280. STAN PAPI
☐ 281. DAN SCHATZEDER
☐ 282. CHAMP SUMMERS
☐ 283. ALAN TRAMMELL
☐ 284. LOU WHITAKER
☐ 285. MILT WILCOX
☐ 286. JOHN WOCKENFUSS
☐ 652. TEAM CHECKLIST(F)

HOUSTON ASTROS

☐ 212. ALAN ASHBY
☐ 213. CESAR CEDENO
☐ 214. JOSE CRUZ
☐ 215. KIKO GARCIA
☐ 216. PHIL GARNER
☐ 217. DANNY HEEP
☐ 218. ART HOWE
☐ 219. BOB KNEPPER
☐ 220. FRANK LACORTE
☐ 221. JOE NIEKRO
☐ 222. JOE PITTMAN
☐ 223. TERRY PUHL
☐ 224. LUIS PUJOLS
☐ 225. CRAIG REYNOLDS
☐ 226. J.R. RICHARD
☐ 227. DAVE W. ROBERTS
☐ 228. VERN RUHLE
☐ 229. NOLAN RYAN
☐ 230. JOE SAMBITO
☐ 231. TONY SCOTT
☐ 232. DAVE SMITH
☐ 233. HARRY SPILMAN
☐ 234. DON SUTTON
☐ 235. DICKIE THON
☐ 236. DENNY WALLING
☐ 237. GARY WOODS
☐ 651. TEAM CHECKLIST(F)

George Brett
ROYALS • THIRD BASE

KANSAS CITY ROYALS

☐ 404. WILLIE AIKENS
☐ 405. GEORGE BRETT
☐ 406. KEN BRETT
☐ 407. DAVE CHALK
☐ 408. RICH GALE
☐ 409. CESAR GERONIMO
☐ 410. LARRY GURA
☐ 411. CLINT HURDLE

1982 Fleer

□ 412. MIKE JONES
□ 413. DENNIS LEONARD
□ 414. RENIE MARTIN
□ 415. LEE MAY
□ 416. HAL MCRAE
□ 417. DARRYL MOTLEY
□ 418. RANCE MULLINIKS
□ 419. AMOS OTIS
□ 420. KEN PHELPS
□ 421. JAMIE QUIRK
□ 422. DAN QUISENBERRY
□ 423. PAUL SPLITTORFF
□ 424. U.L. WASHINGTON
□ 425. JOHN WATHAN
□ 426. FRANK WHITE
□ 427. WILLIE WILSON
□ 655. TEAM CHECKLIST(F)

LOS ANGELES DODGERS

□   1. DUSTY BAKER
□   2. BOBBY CASTILLO
□   3. RON CEY
□   4. TERRY FORSTER
□   5. STEVE GARVEY
□   6. DAVE GOLTZ
□   7. PEDRO GUERRERO
□   8. BURT HOOTON
□   9. STEVE HOWE
□   10. JAY JOHNSTONE
□   11. KEN LANDREAUX
□   12. DAVEY LOPES
□   13. MIKE MARSHALL
□   14. BOBBY MITCHELL
□   15. RICK MONDAY
□   16. TOM NIEDENFUER
□   17. TED POWER
□   18. JERRY REUSS
□   19. RON ROENICKE
□   20. BILL RUSSELL
□   21. STEVE SAX
□   22. MIKE SCIOSCIA
□   23. REGGIE SMITH
□   24. DAVE STEWART
□   25. RICK SUTCLIFFE
□   26. DERREL THOMAS
□   27. FERNANDO VALENZUELA
□   28. BOB WELCH
□   29. STEVE YEAGER
□ 647. TEAM CHECKLIST(F)

MILWAUKEE BREWERS

□ 133. JERRY AUGUSTINE
□ 134. SAL BANDO
□ 135. MARK BROUHARD
□ 136. MIKE CALDWELL
□ 137. REGGIE CLEVELAND
□ 138. CECIL COOPER
□ 139. JAMIE EASTERLY
□ 140. MARSHALL EDWARDS
□ 141. ROLLIE FINGERS
□ 142. JIM GANTNER
□ 143. MOOSE HAAS
□ 144. LARRY HISLE
□ 145. ROY HOWELL
□ 146. RICKEY KEETON
□ 147. RANDY LERCH
□ 148. PAUL MOLITOR
□ 149. DON MONEY
□ 150. CHARLIE MOORE
□ 151. BEN OGLIVIE
□ 152. TED SIMMONS
□ 153. JIM SLATON
□ 154. GORMAN THOMAS
□ 155 ROBIN YOUNT
□ 156. PETE VUCKOVICH
□ 649. TEAM CHECKLIST(B)

MINNESOTA TWINS

□ 545. GLENN ADAMS
□ 546. FERNANDO ARROYO
□ 547. JOHN VERHOEVEN
□ 548. SAL BUTERA
□ 549. JOHN CASTINO
□ 550. DON COOPER
□ 551. DOUG CORBETT
□ 552. DAVE ENGLE
□ 553. ROGER ERICKSON

□ 554. DANNY GOODWIN
□ 555. DARRELL JACKSON
□ 556. PETE MACKANIN
□ 557. JACK O'CONNOR
□ 558. HOSKEN POWELL
□ 559. PETE REDFERN
□ 560. ROY SMALLEY
□ 561. CHUCK BAKER
□ 562. GARY WARD
□ 563. ROB WILFONG
□ 564. AL WILLIAMS
□ 565. BUTCH WYNEGAR
□ 658. TEAM CHECKLIST(F)

MONTREAL EXPOS

□ 183. STAN BAHNSEN
□ 184. RAY BURRIS
□ 185. GARY CARTER
□ 186. WARREN CROMARTIE
□ 187. ANDRE DAWSON
□ 188. TERRY FRANCONA
□ 189. WOODIE FRYMAN
□ 190. BILL GULLICKSON
□ 191. GRANT JACKSON
□ 192. WALLACE JOHNSON
□ 193. CHARLIE LEA
□ 194. BILL LEE
□ 195. JERRY MANUEL
□ 196. BRAD MILLS
□ 197. JOHN MILNER
□ 198. ROWLAND OFFICE
□ 199. DAVID PALMER
□ 200. LARRY PARRISH
□ 201. MIKE PHILLIPS
□ 202. TIM RAINES
□ 203. BOBBY RAMOS
□ 204. JEFF REARDON
□ 205. STEVE ROGERS
□ 206. SCOTT SANDERSON
□ 207. RODNEY SCOTT
□ 208. ELIAS SOSA
□ 209. CHRIS SPEIER
□ 210. TIM WALLACH
□ 211. JERRY WHITE
□ 630. TEAM CHECKLIST(B)

NEW YORK METS

□ 520. NEIL ALLEN
□ 521. BOB BAILOR
□ 522. HUBIE BROOKS
□ 523. MIKE CUBBAGE
□ 524. PETE FALCONE
□ 525. DOUG FLYNN
□ 526. TOM HAUSMAN
□ 527. RON HODGES
□ 528. RANDY JONES
□ 529. MIKE JORGENSEN
□ 530. DAVE KINGMAN
□ 531. ED LYNCH
□ 532. MIKE MARSHALL
□ 533. LEE MAZZILLI
□ 534. DYAR MILLER
□ 535. MIKE SCOTT
□ 536. RUSTY STAUB
□ 537. JOHN STEARNS
□ 538. CRAIG SWAN
□ 539. FRANK TAVERAS
□ 540. ALEX TREVINO
□ 541. ELLIS VALENTINE
□ 542. MOOKIE WILSON
□ 543. JOEL YOUNGBLOOD
□ 544. PAT ZACHRY
□ 657. TEAM CHECKLIST(B)

NEW YORK YANKEES

□   30. BOBBY BROWN
□   31. RICK CERONE
□   32. RON DAVIS
□   33. BUCKY DENT
□   34. BARRY FOOTE
□   35. GEORGE FRAZIER
□   36. OSCAR GAMBLE
□   37. RICH GOSSAGE
□   38. RON GUIDRY
□   39. REGGIE JACKSON
□   40. TOMMY JOHN
□   41. RUDY MAY

□   42. LARRY MILBOURNE
□   43. JERRY MUMPHREY
□   44. BOBBY MURCER
□   45. GENE NELSON
□   46. GRAIG NETTLES
□   47. JOHNNY OATES
□   48. LOU PINIELLA
□   49. WILLIE RANDOLPH
□   50. RICK REUSCHEL
□   51. DAVE REVERING
□   52. DAVE RIGHETTI
□   53. AURELIO RODRIGUEZ
□   54. BOB WATSON
□   55. DENNIS WERTH
□   56. DAVE WINFIELD
□ 647. TEAM CHECKLIST(B)

OAKLAND A'S

□   85. TONY ARMAS
□   86. SHOOTY BABBIT
□   87. DAVE BEARD
□   88. RICK BOSETTI
□   89. KEITH DRUMRIGHT
□   90. WAYNE GROSS
□   91. MIKE HEATH
□   92. RICKEY HENDERSON
□   93. CLIFF JOHNSON
□   94. JEFF JONES
□   95. MATT KEOUGH
□   96. BRIAN KINGMAN
□   97. MICKEY KLUTTS
□   98. RICK LANGFORD
□   99. STEVE MCCATTY
□ 100. DAVE MCKAY
□ 101. DWAYNE MURPHY
□ 102. JEFF NEWMAN
□ 103. MIKE NORRIS
□ 104. BOB OWCHINKO
□ 105. MITCHELL PAGE
□ 106. ROB PICCIOLO
□ 107. JIM SPENCER
□ 108. FRED STANLEY
□ 109. TOM UNDERWOOD
□ 648. TEAM CHECKLIST(B)

Mickey Klutts
A'S • THIRD BASE

PHILADELPHIA PHILLIES

□ 238. LUIS AGUAYO
□ 239. RAMON AVILES
□ 240. BOB BOONE
□ 241. LARRY BOWA
□ 242. WARREN BRUSSTAR
□ 243. STEVE CARLTON
□ 244. LARRY CHRISTENSON
□ 245. DICK DAVIS
□ 246. GREG GROSS
□ 247. SPARKY LYLE
□ 248. GARRY MADDOX
□ 249. GARY MATTHEWS
□ 250. BAKE MCBRIDE
□ 251. TUG MCGRAW
□ 252. KEITH MORELAND
□ 253. DICKIE NOLES
□ 254. MIKE PROLY
□ 255. RON REED
□ 256. PETE ROSE
□ 257. DICK RUTHVEN
□ 258. MIKE SCHMIDT
□ 259. LONNIE SMITH

1982 Fleer

□ 260. MANNY TRILLO
□ 261. DEL UNSER
□ 262. GEORGE VUKOVICH
□ 651. TEAM CHECKLIST(B)

PITTSBURGH PIRATES

□ 475. GARY ALEXANDER
□ 476. DALE BERRA
□ 477. KURT BEVACQUA
□ 478. JIM BIBBY
□ 479. JOHN CANDELARIA
□ 480. VICTOR CRUZ
□ 481. MIKE EASLER
□ 482. TIM FOLI
□ 483. LEE LACY
□ 484. VANCE LAW
□ 485. BILL MADLOCK
□ 486. WILLIE MONTANEZ
□ 487. OMAR MORENO
□ 488. STEVE NICOSIA
□ 489. DAVE PARKER
□ 490. TONY PENA
□ 491. PASCUAL PEREZ
□ 492. JOHNNY RAY
□ 493. RICK RHODEN
□ 494. BILL ROBINSON
□ 495. DON ROBINSON
□ 496. ENRIQUE ROMO
□ 497. ROD SCURRY
□ 498. EDDIE SOLOMON
□ 499. WILLIE STARGELL
□ 500. KENT TEKULVE
□ 501. JASON THOMPSON
□ 656. TEAM CHECKLIST(B)

ST. LOUIS CARDINALS

□ 110. JOAQUIN ANDUJAR
□ 111. STEVE BRAUN
□ 112. BOB FORSCH
□ 113. GEORGE HENDRICK
□ 114. KEITH HERNANDEZ
□ 115. TOM HERR
□ 116. DANE IORG
□ 117. JIM KAAT
□ 118. TITO LANDRUM
□ 119. SIXTO LEZCANO
□ 120. MARK LITTELL
□ 121. JOHN MARTIN
□ 122. SILVIO MARTINEZ
□ 123. KEN OBERKFELL
□ 124. DARRELL PORTER
□ 125. MIKE RAMSEY
□ 126. ORLANDO SANCHEZ
□ 127. BOB SHIRLEY
□ 128. LARY SORENSEN
□ 129. BRUCE SUTTER
□ 130. BOB SYKES
□ 131. GARRY TEMPLETON
□ 132. GENE TENACE
□ 649. TEAM CHECKLIST(F)

SAN FRANCISCO GIANTS

□ 383. DOYLE ALEXANDER
□ 384. VIDA BLUE
□ 385. FRED BREINING
□ 386. ENOS CABELL
□ 387. JACK CLARK
□ 388. DARRELL EVANS
□ 389. TOM GRIFFIN
□ 390. LARRY HERNDON
□ 391. AL HOLLAND
□ 392. GARY LAVELLE
□ 393. JOHNNIE LEMASTER
□ 394. JERRY MARTIN
□ 395. MILT MAY
□ 396. GREG MINTON
□ 397. JOE MORGAN
□ 398. JOE PETTINI
□ 399. ALAN RIPLEY
□ 400. BILLY E. SMITH
□ 401. RENNIE STENNETT
□ 402. ED WHITSON
□ 403. JIM WOHLFORD
□ 654. TEAM CHECKLIST(B)

SAN DIEGO PADRES

□ 566. RANDY BASS
□ 567. JUAN BONILLA
□ 568. DANNY BOONE
□ 569. JOHN CURTIS
□ 570. JUAN EICHELBERGER
□ 571. BARRY EVANS
□ 572. TIM FLANNERY
□ 573. RUPPERT JONES
□ 574. TERRY KENNEDY
□ 575. JOE LEFEBVRE
□ 576. JOHN LITTLEFIELD
□ 577. GARY LUCAS
□ 578. STEVE MURA
□ 579. BRODERICK PERKINS
□ 580. GENE RICHARDS
□ 581. LUIS SALAZAR
□ 582. OZZIE SMITH
□ 583. JOHN URREA
□ 584. CHRIS WELSH
□ 585. RICK WISE
□ 658. TEAM CHECKLIST

SEATTLE MARINERS

□ 502. GLENN ABBOTT
□ 503. JIM ANDERSON
□ 504. FLOYD BANNISTER
□ 505. BRUCE BOCHTE
□ 506. JEFF BURROUGHS
□ 507. BRYAN CLARK
□ 508. KEN CLAY
□ 509. JULIO CRUZ
□ 510. DICK DRAGO
□ 511. GARY GRAY
□ 512. DAN MEYER
□ 513. JERRY NARRON
□ 514. TOM PACIOREK
□ 515. CASEY PARSONS
□ 516. LENNY RANDLE
□ 517. SHANE RAWLEY
□ 518. JOE SIMPSON
□ 519. RICHIE ZISK
□ 657. TEAM CHECKLIST(F)

TEXAS RANGERS

□ 313. BUDDY BELL
□ 314. STEVE COMER
□ 315. DANNY DARWIN
□ 316. JOHN ELLIS
□ 317. JOHN GRUBB
□ 318. RICK HONEYCUTT
□ 319. CHARLIE HOUGH
□ 320. FERGUSON JENKINS
□ 321. JOHN HENRY JOHNSON
□ 322. JIM KERN
□ 323. JON MATLACK
□ 324. DOC MEDICH
□ 325. MARIO MENDOZA
□ 326. AL OLIVER
□ 327. PAT PUTNAM
□ 328. MICKEY RIVERS
□ 329. LEON ROBERTS
□ 330. BILLY SAMPLE
□ 331. BILL STEIN
□ 332. JIM SUNDBERG
□ 333. MARK WAGNER
□ 334. BUMP WILLS
□ 653. TEAM CHECKLIST(F)

TORONTO BLUE JAYS

□ 608. DANNY AINGE
□ 609. JORGE BELL
□ 610. MARK BOMBACK
□ 611. BARRY BONNELL
□ 612. JIM CLANCY
□ 613. DAMASO GARCIA
□ 614. JERRY GARVIN
□ 615. ALFREDO GRIFFIN
□ 616. GARTH IORG
□ 617. LUIS LEAL
□ 618. KEN MACHA
□ 619. JOHN MAYBERRY
□ 620. JOEY MCLAUGHLIN
□ 621. LLOYD MOSEBY
□ 622. DAVE STIEB
□ 623. JACKSON TODD

□ 624. WILLIE UPSHAW
□ 625. OTTO VELEZ
□ 626. ERNIE WHITT
□ 627. AL WOODS
□ 659. TEAM CHECKLIST(B)

1983 FLEER (660)
2 1/2" X 3 1/2"

Steve Garvey
FIRST BASE

ATLANTA BRAVES

□ 129. STEVE BEDROSIAN
□ 130. BRUCE BENEDICT
□ 131. TOMMY BOGGS
□ 132. BRETT BUTLER
□ 133. RICK CAMP
□ 134. CHRIS CHAMBLISS
□ 135. KEN DAYLEY
□ 136. GENE GARBER
□ 137. TERRY HARPER
□ 138. BOB HORNER
□ 139. GLENN HUBBARD
□ 140. RUFINO LINARES
□ 141. RICK MAHLER
□ 142. DALE MURPHY
□ 143. PHIL NIEKRO
□ 144. PASCUAL PEREZ
□ 145. BIFF POCOROBA
□ 146. RAFAEL RAMIREZ
□ 147. JERRY ROYSTER
□ 148. KEN SMITH
□ 149. BOB WALK
□ 150. CLAUDELL WASHINGTON
□ 151. BOB WATSON
□ 152. LARRY WHISENTON
□ 649. TEAM CHECKLIST(B)

BALTIMORE ORIOLES

□ 52. BENNY AYALA
□ 53. BOB BONNER
□ 54. AL BUMBRY
□ 55. TERRY CROWLEY
□ 56. STORM DAVIS
□ 57. RICH DAUER
□ 58. RICK DEMPSEY
□ 59. JIM DWYER
□ 60. MIKE FLANAGAN
□ 61. DAN FORD
□ 62. GLENN GULLIVER
□ 63. JOHN LOWENSTEIN
□ 64. DENNIS MARTINEZ
□ 65. TIPPY MARTINEZ
□ 66. SCOTT MCGREGOR
□ 67. EDDIE MURRAY
□ 68. JOE NOLAN
□ 69. JIM PALMER
□ 70. CAL RIPKEN
□ 71. GARY ROENICKE
□ 72. LENN SAKATA
□ 73. KEN SINGLETON
□ 74. SAMMY STEWART
□ 75. TIM STODDARD
□ 648. TEAM CHECKLIST(F)

1983 Fleer

BOSTON RED SOX

- [ ] 177. GARY ALLENSON
- [ ] 178. LUIS APONTE
- [ ] 179. WADE BOGGS
- [ ] 180. TOM BURGMEIER
- [ ] 181. MARK CLEAR
- [ ] 182. DENNIS ECKERSLEY
- [ ] 183. DWIGHT EVANS
- [ ] 184. RICH GEDMAN
- [ ] 185. GLENN HOFFMAN
- [ ] 186. BRUCE HURST
- [ ] 187. CARNEY LANSFORD
- [ ] 188. RICK MILLER
- [ ] 189. REID NICHOLS
- [ ] 190. BOB OJEDA
- [ ] 191. TONY PEREZ
- [ ] 192. CHUCK RAINEY
- [ ] 193. JERRY REMY
- [ ] 194. JIM RICE
- [ ] 195. BOB STANLEY
- [ ] 196. DAVE STAPLETON
- [ ] 197. MIKE TORREZ
- [ ] 198. JOHN TUDOR
- [ ] 199. JULIO VALDEZ
- [ ] 200. CARL YASTRZEMSKI
- [ ] 650. TEAM CHECKLIST(B)

CALIFORNIA ANGELS

- [ ] 76. DON AASE
- [ ] 77. DON BAYLOR
- [ ] 78. JUAN BENIQUEZ
- [ ] 79. BOB BOONE
- [ ] 80. RICK BURLESON
- [ ] 81. ROD CAREW
- [ ] 82. BOBBY CLARK
- [ ] 83. DOUG CORBETT
- [ ] 84. JOHN CURTIS
- [ ] 85. DOUG DECINCES
- [ ] 86. BRIAN DOWNING
- [ ] 87. JOE FERGUSON
- [ ] 88. TIM FOLI
- [ ] 89. KEN FORSCH
- [ ] 90. DAVE GOLTZ
- [ ] 91. BOBBY GRICH
- [ ] 92. ANDY HASSLER
- [ ] 93. REGGIE JACKSON
- [ ] 94. RON JACKSON
- [ ] 95. TOMMY JOHN
- [ ] 96. BRUCE KISON
- [ ] 97. FRED LYNN
- [ ] 98. ED OTT
- [ ] 99. STEVE RENKO
- [ ] 100. LUIS SANCHEZ
- [ ] 101. ROB WILFONG
- [ ] 102. MIKE WITT
- [ ] 103. GEOFF ZAHN
- [ ] 648. TEAM CHECKLIST(B)

CHICAGO CUBS

- [ ] 490. DOUG BIRD
- [ ] 491. LARRY BOWA
- [ ] 492. BILL BUCKNER
- [ ] 493. BILL CAMPBELL
- [ ] 494. JODY DAVIS
- [ ] 495. LEON DURHAM
- [ ] 496. STEVE HENDERSON
- [ ] 497. WILLIE HERNANDEZ
- [ ] 498. FERGUSON JENKINS
- [ ] 499. JAY JOHNSTONE
- [ ] 500. JUNIOR KENNEDY
- [ ] 501. RANDY MARTZ
- [ ] 502. JERRY MORALES
- [ ] 503. KEITH MORELAND
- [ ] 504. DICKIE NOLES
- [ ] 505. MIKE PROLY
- [ ] 506. ALLEN RIPLEY
- [ ] 507. RYNE SANDBERG
- [ ] 508. LEE SMITH
- [ ] 509. PAT TABLER
- [ ] 510. DICK TIDROW
- [ ] 511. BUMP WILLS
- [ ] 512. GARY WOODS
- [ ] 657. TEAM CHECKLIST(F)

CHICAGO WHITE SOX

- [ ] 228. BILL ALMON
- [ ] 229. HAROLD BAINES
- [ ] 230. SALOME BAROJAS
- [ ] 231. TONY BERNAZARD
- [ ] 232. BRITT BURNS
- [ ] 233. RICHARD DOTSON
- [ ] 234. ERNESTO ESCARREGA
- [ ] 235. CARLTON FISK
- [ ] 236. JERRY HAIRSTON
- [ ] 237. KEVIN HICKEY
- [ ] 238. LEMARR HOYT
- [ ] 239. STEVE KEMP
- [ ] 240. JIM KERN
- [ ] 241. RON KITTLE
- [ ] 242. JERRY KOOSMAN
- [ ] 243. DENNIS LAMP
- [ ] 244. RUDY LAW
- [ ] 245. VANCE LAW
- [ ] 246. RON LEFLORE
- [ ] 247. GREG LUZINSKI
- [ ] 248. TOM PACIOREK
- [ ] 249. AURELIO RODRIGUEZ
- [ ] 250. MIKE SQUIRES
- [ ] 251. STEVE TROUT
- [ ] 651. TEAM CHECKLIST(B)

CINCINNATI REDS

- [ ] 584. JOHNNY BENCH
- [ ] 585. BRUCE BERENYI
- [ ] 586. LARRY BIITTNER
- [ ] 587. CESAR CEDENO
- [ ] 588. DAVE CONCEPCION
- [ ] 589. DAN DRIESSEN
- [ ] 590. GREG HARRIS
- [ ] 591. BEN HAYES
- [ ] 592. PAUL HOUSEHOLDER
- [ ] 593. TOM HUME
- [ ] 594. WAYNE KRENCHICKI
- [ ] 595. RAFAEL LANDESTOY
- [ ] 596. CHARLIE LEIBRANDT
- [ ] 597. EDDIE MILNER
- [ ] 598. RON OESTER
- [ ] 599. FRANK PASTORE
- [ ] 600. JOE PRICE
- [ ] 601. TOM SEAVER
- [ ] 602. BOB SHIRLEY
- [ ] 603. MARIO SOTO
- [ ] 604. ALEX TREVINO
- [ ] 605. MIKE VAIL
- [ ] 606. DUANE WALKER
- [ ] 659. TEAM CHECKLIST(F)

CLEVELAND INDIANS

- [ ] 400. CHRIS BANDO
- [ ] 401. ALAN BANNISTER
- [ ] 402. LEN BARKER
- [ ] 403. TOM BRENNAN
- [ ] 404. CARMELO CASTILLO
- [ ] 405. MIGUEL DILONE
- [ ] 406. JERRY DYBZINSKI
- [ ] 407. MIKE FISCHLIN
- [ ] 408. ED GLYNN
- [ ] 409. MIKE HARGROVE
- [ ] 410. TOBY HARRAH
- [ ] 411. RON HASSEY
- [ ] 412. VON HAYES
- [ ] 413. RICK MANNING
- [ ] 414. BAKE MCBRIDE
- [ ] 415. LARRY MILBOURNE
- [ ] 416. BILL NAHORODNY
- [ ] 417. JACK PERCONTE
- [ ] 418. LARY SORENSEN
- [ ] 419. DAN SPILLNER
- [ ] 420. RICK SUTCLIFFE
- [ ] 421. ANDRE THORNTON
- [ ] 422. RICK WAITS
- [ ] 423. EDDIE WHITSON
- [ ] 655. TEAM CHECKLIST(F)

DETROIT TIGERS

- [ ] 327. TOM BROOKENS
- [ ] 328. ENOS CABELL
- [ ] 329. KIRK GIBSON
- [ ] 330. LARRY HERNDON
- [ ] 331. MIKE IVIE
- [ ] 332. HOWARD JOHNSON
- [ ] 333. LYNN JONES
- [ ] 334. RICK LEACH
- [ ] 335. CHET LEMON
- [ ] 336. JACK MORRIS
- [ ] 337. LANCE PARRISH
- [ ] 338. LARRY PASHNICK

- [ ] 339. DAN PETRY
- [ ] 340. DAVE ROZEMA
- [ ] 341. DAVE RUCKER
- [ ] 342. ELIAS SOSA
- [ ] 343. DAVE TOBIK
- [ ] 344. ALAN TRAMMELL
- [ ] 345. JERRY TURNER
- [ ] 346. JERRY UJDUR
- [ ] 347. PAT UNDERWOOD
- [ ] 348. LOU WHITAKER
- [ ] 349. MILT WILCOX
- [ ] 350. GLENN WILSON
- [ ] 351. JOHN WOCKENFUSS
- [ ] 653. TEAM CHECKLIST(B)

HOUSTON ASTROS

- [ ] 445. ALAN ASHBY
- [ ] 446. JOSE CRUZ
- [ ] 447. KIKO GARCIA
- [ ] 448. PHIL GARNER
- [ ] 449. DANNY HEEP
- [ ] 450. ART HOWE
- [ ] 451. BOB KNEPPER
- [ ] 452. ALAN KNICELY
- [ ] 453. RAY KNIGHT
- [ ] 454. FRANK LACORTE
- [ ] 455. MIKE LACOSS
- [ ] 456. RANDY MOFFITT
- [ ] 457. JOE NIEKRO
- [ ] 458. TERRY PUHL
- [ ] 459. LUIS PUJOLS
- [ ] 460. CRAIG REYNOLDS
- [ ] 461. BERT ROBERGE
- [ ] 462. VERN RUHLE
- [ ] 463. NOLAN RYAN
- [ ] 464. JOE SAMBITO
- [ ] 465. TONY SCOTT
- [ ] 466. DAVE SMITH
- [ ] 467. HARRY SPILMAN
- [ ] 468. DICKIE THON
- [ ] 469. DENNY WALLING
- [ ] 656. TEAM CHECKLIST(F)

LOS ANGELES DODGERS

- [ ] 201. DUSTY BAKER
- [ ] 202. JOE BECKWITH
- [ ] 203. GREG BROCK
- [ ] 204. RON CEY
- [ ] 205. TERRY FORSTER
- [ ] 206. STEVE GARVEY
- [ ] 207. PEDRO GUERRERO
- [ ] 208. BURT HOOTON
- [ ] 209. STEVE HOWE
- [ ] 210. KEN LANDREAUX
- [ ] 211. MIKE MARSHALL
- [ ] 212. CANDY MALDONADO
- [ ] 213. RICK MONDAY
- [ ] 214. TOM NIEDENFUER
- [ ] 215. JORGE ORTA
- [ ] 216. JERRY REUSS
- [ ] 217. RON ROENICKE
- [ ] 218. VINCENTE ROMO
- [ ] 219. BILL RUSSELL
- [ ] 220. STEVE SAX
- [ ] 221. MIKE SCIOSCIA
- [ ] 222. DAVE STEWART
- [ ] 223. DERREL THOMAS
- [ ] 224. FERNANDO VALENZUELA
- [ ] 225. BOB WELCH
- [ ] 226. RICKY WRIGHT
- [ ] 227. STEVE YEAGER
- [ ] 651. TEAM CHECKLIST(F)

KANSAS CITY ROYALS

- [ ] 104. WILLIE AIKENS
- [ ] 105. MIKE ARMSTRONG
- [ ] 106. VIDA BLUE
- [ ] 107. BUD BLACK
- [ ] 108. GEORGE BRETT
- [ ] 109. BILL CASTRO
- [ ] 110. ONIX CONCEPCION
- [ ] 111. DAVE FROST
- [ ] 112. CESAR GERONIMO
- [ ] 113. LARRY GURA
- [ ] 114. STEVE HAMMOND
- [ ] 115. DON HOOD
- [ ] 116. DENNIS LEONARD
- [ ] 117. JERRY MARTIN

☐ 118. LEE MAY
☐ 119. HAL MCRAE
☐ 120. AMOS OTIS
☐ 121. GREG PRYOR
☐ 122. DAN QUISENBERRY
☐ 123. DON SLAUGHT
☐ 124. PAUL SPLITTORFF
☐ 125. U.L. WASHINGTON
☐ 126. JOHN WATHAN
☐ 127. FRANK WHITE
☐ 128. WILLIE WILSON
☐ 649. TEAM CHECKLIST(F)

Rollie Fingers
PITCHER

MILWAUKEE BREWERS

☐ 26. JERRY AUGUSTINE
☐ 27. DWIGHT BERNARD
☐ 28. MARK BROUHARD
☐ 29. MIKE CALDWELL
☐ 30. CECIL COOPER
☐ 31. JAMIE EASTERLY
☐ 32. MARSHALL EDWARDS
☐ 33. ROLLIE FINGERS
☐ 34. JIM GANTNER
☐ 35. MOOSE HAAS
☐ 36. ROY HOWELL
☐ 37. PETER LADD
☐ 38. BOB MCCLURE
☐ 39. DOC MEDICH
☐ 40. PAUL MOLITOR
☐ 41. DON MONEY
☐ 42. CHARLIE MOORE
☐ 43. BEN OGLIVIE
☐ 44. ED ROMERO
☐ 45. TED SIMMONS
☐ 46. JIM SLATON
☐ 47. DON SUTTON
☐ 48. GORMAN THOMAS
☐ 49. PETE VUCKOVICH
☐ 50. NED YOST
☐ 51. ROBIN YOUNT
☐ 647. TEAM CHECKLIST(B)

MINNESOTA TWINS

☐ 607. TOM BRUNANSKY
☐ 608. BOBBY CASTILLO
☐ 609. JOHN CASTINO
☐ 610. RON DAVIS
☐ 611. LENNY FAEDO
☐ 612. TERRY FELTON
☐ 613. GARY GAETTI
☐ 614. MICKEY HATCHER
☐ 615. BRAD HAVENS
☐ 616. KENT HRBEK
☐ 617. RANDY JOHNSON
☐ 618. TIM LAUDNER
☐ 619. JEFF LITTLE
☐ 620. BOB MITCHELL
☐ 621. JACK O'CONNOR
☐ 622. JOHN PACELLA
☐ 623. PETE REDFERN
☐ 624. JESUS VEGA
☐ 625. FRANK VIOLA
☐ 626. RON WASHINGTON
☐ 627. GARY WARD
☐ 628. AL WILLIAMS
☐ 659. TEAM CHECKLIST(B)

Al Oliver
FIRST BASE

MONTREAL EXPOS

☐ 277. RAY BURRIS
☐ 278. GARY CARTER
☐ 279. WARREN CROMARTIE
☐ 280. ANDRE DAWSON
☐ 281. TERRY FRANCONA
☐ 282. DOUG FLYNN
☐ 283. WOODY FRYMAN
☐ 284. BILL GULLICKSON
☐ 285. WALLACE JOHNSON
☐ 286. CHARLIE LEA
☐ 287. RANDY LERCH
☐ 288. BRAD MILLS
☐ 289. DAN NORMAN
☐ 290. AL OLIVER
☐ 291. DAVID PALMER
☐ 292. TIM RAINES
☐ 293. JEFF REARDON
☐ 294. STEVE ROGERS
☐ 295. SCOTT SANDERSON
☐ 296. DAN SCHATZEDER
☐ 297. BRYN SMITH
☐ 298. CHRIS SPEIER
☐ 299. TIM WALLACH
☐ 300. JERRY WHITE
☐ 301. JOEL YOUNGBLOOD
☐ 652. TEAM CHECKLIST(B)

NEW YORK METS

☐ 536. NEIL ALLEN
☐ 537. WALLY BACKMAN
☐ 538. BOB BAILOR
☐ 539. HUBIE BROOKS
☐ 540. CARLOS DIAZ
☐ 541. PETE FALCONE
☐ 542. GEORGE FOSTER
☐ 543. RON GARDENHIRE
☐ 544. BRIAN GILES
☐ 545. RON HODGES
☐ 546. RANDY JONES
☐ 547. MIKE JORGENSEN
☐ 548. DAVE KINGMAN
☐ 549. ED LYNCH
☐ 550. JESSE OROSCO
☐ 551. RICK OWNBEY
☐ 552. CHARLIE PULEO
☐ 553. GARY RAJSICH
☐ 554. MIKE SCOTT
☐ 555. RUSTY STAUB
☐ 556. JOHN STEARNS
☐ 557. CRAIG SWAN
☐ 558. ELLIS VALENTINE
☐ 559. TOM VERYZER
☐ 560. MOOKIE WILSON
☐ 561. PAT ZACHRY
☐ 658. TEAM CHECKLIST(F)

NEW YORK YANKEES

☐ 376. RICK CERONE
☐ 377. DAVE COLLINS
☐ 378. ROGER ERICKSON
☐ 379. GEORGE FRAZIER
☐ 380. OSCAR GAMBLE
☐ 381. RICH GOSSAGE
☐ 382. KEN GRIFFEY
☐ 383. RON GUIDRY

☐ 384. DAVE LAROCHE
☐ 385. RUDY MAY
☐ 386. JOHN MAYBERRY
☐ 387. LEE MAZZILLI
☐ 388. MIKE MORGAN
☐ 389. JERRY MUMPHREY
☐ 390. BOBBY MURCER
☐ 391. GRAIG NETTLES
☐ 392. LOU PINIELLA
☐ 393. WILLIE RANDOLPH
☐ 394. SHANE RAWLEY
☐ 395. DAVE RIGHETTI
☐ 396. ANDRE ROBERTSON
☐ 397. ROY SMALLEY
☐ 398. DAVE WINFIELD
☐ 399. BUTCH WYNEGAR
☐ 654. TEAM CHECKLIST(B)

OAKLAND A'S

☐ 513. TONY ARMAS
☐ 514. DAVE BEARD
☐ 515. JEFF BURROUGHS
☐ 516. JOHN D'ACQUISTO
☐ 517. WAYNE GROSS
☐ 518. MIKE HEATH
☐ 519. RICKEY HENDERSON
☐ 520. CLIFF JOHNSON
☐ 521. MATT KEOUGH
☐ 522. BRIAN KINGMAN
☐ 523. RICK LANGFORD
☐ 524. DAVEY LOPES
☐ 525. STEVE MCCATTY
☐ 526. DAVE MCKAY
☐ 527. DAN MEYER
☐ 528. DWAYNE MURPHY
☐ 529. JEFF NEWMAN
☐ 530. MIKE NORRIS
☐ 531. BOB OWCHINKO
☐ 532. JOE RUDI
☐ 533. JIMMY SEXTON
☐ 534. FRED STANLEY
☐ 535. TOM UNDERWOOD
☐ 657. TEAM CHECKLIST(B)

PHILADELPHIA PHILLIES

☐ 153. PORFIORIO ALTAMIRANO
☐ 154. MARTY BYSTROM
☐ 155. STEVE CARLTON
☐ 156. LARRY CHRISTENSON
☐ 157. IVAN DEJESUS
☐ 158. JOHN DENNY
☐ 159. BOB DERNIER
☐ 160. BO DIAZ
☐ 161. ED FARMER
☐ 162. GREG GROSS
☐ 163. MIKE KRUKOW
☐ 164. GARRY MADDOX
☐ 165. GARY MATTHEWS
☐ 166. TUG MCGRAW
☐ 167. BOB MOLINARO
☐ 168. SID MONGE
☐ 169. RON REED
☐ 170. BILL ROBINSON
☐ 171. PETE ROSE
☐ 172. DICK RUTHVEN
☐ 173. MIKE SCHMIDT
☐ 174. MANNY TRILLO
☐ 175. OZZIE VIRGIL
☐ 176. GEORGE VUKOVICH
☐ 650. TEAM CHECKLIST(F)

PITTSBURGH PIRATES

☐ 302. ROSS BAUMGARTEN
☐ 303. DALE BERRA
☐ 304. JOHN CANDELARIA
☐ 305. DICK DAVIS
☐ 306. MIKE EASLER
☐ 307. RICHIE HEBNER
☐ 308. LEE LACY
☐ 309. BILL MADLOCK
☐ 310. LARRY MCWILLIAMS
☐ 311. JOHN MILNER
☐ 312. OMAR MORENO
☐ 313. JIM MORRISON
☐ 314. STEVE NICOSIA
☐ 315. DAVE PARKER

1983 Fleer

□ 316. TONY PENA
□ 317. JOHNNY RAY
□ 318. RICK RHODEN
□ 319. DON ROBINSON
□ 320. ENRIQUE ROMO
□ 321. MANNY SARMIENTO
□ 322. ROD SCURRY
□ 323. JIM SMITH
□ 324. WILLIE STARGELL
□ 325. JASON THOMPSON
□ 326. KENT TEKULVE
□ 653. TEAM CHECKLIST(F)

ST. LOUIS CARDINALS

□   1. JOAQUIN ANDUJAR
□   2. DOUG BAIR
□   3. STEVE BRAUN
□   4. GLENN BRUMMER
□   5. BOB FORSCH
□   6. DAVID GREEN
□   7. GEORGE HENDRICK
□   8. KEITH HERNANDEZ
□   9. TOM HERR
□ 10. DANE IORG
□ 11. JIM KAAT
□ 12. JEFF LAHTI
□ 13. TITO LANDRUM
□ 14. DAVE LAPOINT
□ 15. WILLIE MCGEE
□ 16. STEVE MURA
□ 17. KEN OBERKFELL
□ 18. DARRELL PORTER
□ 19. MIKE RAMSEY
□ 20. GENE ROOF
□ 21. LONNIE SMITH
□ 22. OZZIE SMITH
□ 23. JOHN STUPER
□ 24. BRUCE SUTTER
□ 25. GENE TENACE
□ 647. TEAM CHECKLIST(F)

SAN DIEGO PADRES

□ 352. KURT BEVACQUA
□ 353. JUAN BONILLA
□ 354. FLOYD CHIFFER
□ 355. LUIS DELEON
□ 356. DAVE DRAVECKY
□ 357. DAVE EDWARDS
□ 358. JUAN EICHELBERGER
□ 359. TIM FLANNERY
□ 360. TONY GWYNN
□ 361. RUPPERT JONES
□ 362. TERRY KENNEDY
□ 363. JOE LEFEBVRE
□ 364. SIXTO LEZCANO
□ 365. TIM LOLLAR
□ 366. GARY LUCAS
□ 367. JOHN MONTEFUSCO
□ 368. BRODERICK PERKINS
□ 369. JOE PITTMAN
□ 370. GENE RICHARDS
□ 371. LUIS SALAZAR
□ 372. ERIC SHOW
□ 373. GARRY TEMPLETON
□ 374. CHRIS WELSH
□ 375. ALAN WIGGINS
□ 654. TEAM CHECKLIST(F)

SAN FRANCISCO GIANTS

□ 252. JIM BARR
□ 253. DAVE BERGMANN
□ 254. FRED BREINING
□ 255. BOB BRENLY
□ 256. JACK CLARK
□ 257. CHILI DAVIS
□ 258. DARRELL EVANS
□ 259. ALAN FOWLKES
□ 260. RICH GALE
□ 261. ATLEE HAMMAKER
□ 262. AL HOLLAND
□ 263. DUANE KUIPER
□ 264. BILL LASKEY
□ 265. GARY LAVELLE
□ 266. JOHNNIE LEMASTER
□ 267. RENIE MARTIN
□ 268. MILT MAY
□ 269. GREG MINTO
□ 270. JOE MORGAN

□ 271. TOM O'MALLEY
□ 272. REGGIE SMITH
□ 273. GUY SULARZ
□ 274. CHAMP SUMMERS
□ 275. MAX VENABLE
□ 276. JIM WOHLFORD
□ 652. TEAM CHECKLIST(F)

SEATTLE MARINERS

□ 470. LARRY ANDERSEN
□ 471. FLOYD BANNISTER
□ 472. JIM BEATTIE
□ 473. BRUCE BOCHTE
□ 474. MANNY CASTILLO
□ 475. BILL CAUDILL
□ 476. BRYAN CLARK
□ 477. AL COWENS
□ 478. JULIO CRUZ
□ 479. TODD CRUZ
□ 480. GARY GRAY
□ 481. DAVE HENDERSON
□ 482. MIKE MOORE
□ 483. GAYLORD PERRY
□ 484. DAVE REVERING
□ 485. JOE SIMPSON
□ 486. MIKE STANTON
□ 487. RICK SWEET
□ 488. ED VANDEBERG
□ 489. RICHIE ZISK
□ 656. TEAM CHECKLIST(B)

TEXAS RANGERS

□ 562. BUDDY BELL
□ 563. JOHN BUTCHER
□ 564. STEVE COMER
□ 565. DANNY DARWIN
□ 566. BUCKY DENT
□ 567. JOHN GRUBB
□ 568. RICK HONEYCUTT
□ 569. DAVE HOSTETLER
□ 570. CHARLIE HOUGH
□ 571. LAMAR JOHNSON
□ 572. JON MATLACK
□ 573. PAUL MIRABELLA
□ 574. LARRY PARRISH
□ 575. MIKE RICHARDT
□ 576. MICKEY RIVERS
□ 577. BILLY SAMPLE
□ 578. DAVE J. SCHMIDT
□ 579. BILL STEIN
□ 580. JIM SUNDBERG
□ 581. FRANK TANANA
□ 582. MARK WAGNER
□ 583. GEORGE WRIGHT
□ 658. TEAM CHECKLIST(B)

TORONTO BLUE JAYS

□ 424 JESSIE BARFIELD
□ 425. BARRY BONNELL
□ 426. JIM CLANCY
□ 427. DAMASO GARCIA
□ 428. JERRY GARVIN
□ 429. ALFREDO GRIFFIN
□ 430. GARTH IORG
□ 431. ROY LEE JACKSON
□ 432. LUIS LEAL
□ 433. BUCK MARTINEZ
□ 434. JOE MCLAUGHLIN
□ 435. LLOYD MOSEBY
□ 436. RANCE MULLINIKS
□ 437. DALE MURRAY
□ 438. WAYNE NORDHAGEN
□ 439. GENE PETRALLI
□ 440. HOSKEN POWELL
□ 441. DAVE STIEB
□ 442. WILLIE UPSHAW
□ 443. ERNIE WHITT
□ 444. AL WOODS
□ 655 TEAM CHECKLIST(B)

1984 FLEER (660)
2 1/2" X 3 1/2"

ATLANTA BRAVES

□ 170. LEN BARKER
□ 171. STEVE BEDROSIAN
□ 172. BRUCE BENEDICT
□ 173. BRETT BUTLER
□ 174. RICK CAMP
□ 175. CHRIS CHAMBLISS
□ 176. KEN DAYLEY
□ 177. PETE FALCONE
□ 178. TERRY FORSTER
□ 179. GENE GARBER
□ 180. TERRY HARPER
□ 181. BOB HORNER
□ 182. GLENN HUBBARD
□ 183. RANDY JOHNSON
□ 184. CRAIG MCMURTRY
□ 185. DONNIE MOORE
□ 186. DALE MURPHY
□ 187. PHIL NIEKRO
□ 188. PASCUAL PEREZ
□ 189. BIFF POCOROBA
□ 190. RAFAEL RAMIREZ
□ 191. JERRY ROYSTER
□ 192. CLAUDELL WASHINGTON
□ 193. BOB WATSON
□ 654. TEAM(F) & TORRE(M)

BALTIMORE ORIOLES

□   1. MIKE BODDICKER
□   2. AL BUMBRY
□   3. TODD CRUZ
□   4. RICH DAUER
□   5. STORM DAVIS
□   6. RICK DEMPSEY
□   7. JIM DWYER
□   8. MIKE FLANAGAN
□   9. DAN FORD
□ 10. JOHN LOWENSTEIN
□ 11. DENNIS MARTINEZ
□ 12. TIPPY MARTINEZ
□ 13. SCOTT MCGREGOR
□ 14. EDDIE MURRAY
□ 15. JOE NOLAN
□ 16. JIM PALMER
□ 17. CAL RIPKEN
□ 18. GARY ROENICKE
□ 19. LENN SAKATA
□ 20. JOHN SHELBY
□ 21. KEN SINGLETON
□ 22. SAMMY STEWARD
□ 23. TIM STODDARD
□ 647. TEAM(F) & ALTOBELLI(M)

BOSTON RED SOX

□ 388. GARY ALLENSON
□ 389. LUIS APONTE
□ 390. TONY ARMAS
□ 391. DOUG BIRD
□ 392. WADE BOGGS
□ 393. DENNIS BOYD
□ 394. MIKE BROWN
□ 395. MARK CLEAR
□ 396. DENNIS ECKERSLEY

☐ 397. DWIGHT EVANS
☐ 398. RICH GEDMAN
☐ 399. GLENN HOFFMAN
☐ 400. BRUCE HURST
☐ 401. JOHN HENRY JOHNSON
☐ 402. ED JURAK
☐ 403. RICK MILLER
☐ 404. JEFF NEWMAN
☐ 405. REID NICHOLS
☐ 406. BOB OJEDA
☐ 407. JERRY REMY
☐ 408. JIM RICE
☐ 409. BOB STANELY
☐ 410. DAVE STAPLETON
☐ 411. JOHN TUDOR
☐ 412. CARL YASTRZMESKI
☐ 649. TEAM CHECKLIST(B)

CALIFORNIA ANGELS

☐ 508. JUAN BENIQUEZ
☐ 509. BOB BOONE
☐ 510. RICK BURLESON
☐ 511. ROD CAREW
☐ 512. BOBBY CLARK
☐ 513. JOHN CURTIS
☐ 514. DOUG DECINCES
☐ 515. BRIAN DOWNING
☐ 516. TIM FOLI
☐ 517. KEN FORSCH
☐ 518. BOBBY GRICH
☐ 519. ANDY HASSLER
☐ 520. REGGIE JACKSON
☐ 521. RON JACKSON
☐ 522. TOMMY JOHN
☐ 523. BRUCE KISON
☐ 524. STEVE LUBRATICH
☐ 525. FRED LYNN
☐ 526. GARY PETTIS
☐ 527. LUIS SANCHEZ
☐ 528. DARYL SCONIERS
☐ 529. ELLIS VALENTINE
☐ 530. ROB WILFONG
☐ 531. MIKE WITT
☐ 532. GEOFF ZAHN
☐ 654. TEAM CHECKLIST(B)

CHICAGO CUBS

☐ 486. LARRY BOWA
☐ 487. WARREN BRUSSTAR
☐ 488. BILL BUCKNER
☐ 489. BILL CAMPBELL
☐ 490. RON CEY
☐ 491. JODY DAVIS
☐ 492. LEON DURHAM
☐ 493. MEL HALL
☐ 494. FERGUSON JENKINS
☐ 495. JAY JOHNSTONE
☐ 496. CRAIG LEFFERTS
☐ 497. CARMELO MARTINEZ
☐ 498. JERRY MORALES
☐ 499. KEITH MORELAND
☐ 500. DICKIE NOLES
☐ 501. MIKE PROLY
☐ 502. CHUCK RAINEY
☐ 503. DICK RUTHVEN
☐ 504. RYNE SANDBERY
☐ 505. LEE SMITH
☐ 506. STEVE TROUT
☐ 507. GARY WOODS
☐ 653. TEAM CHECKLIST(B)

CHICAGO WHITE SOX

☐ 50. JUAN AGOSTO
☐ 51. HARROLD BAINES
☐ 52. FLOYD BANNISTER
☐ 53. SALOME BAROJAS
☐ 54. BRITT BURNS
☐ 55. JULIO CRUZ
☐ 56. RICHARD DOTSON
☐ 57. JERRY DYBZINSKI
☐ 58. CARLTON FISK
☐ 59. SCOTT FLETCHER
☐ 60. JERRY HAIRSTON
☐ 61. KEVIN HICKEY
☐ 62. MARC HILL
☐ 63. LA MARR HOYT
☐ 64. RON KITTLE
☐ 65. JERRY KOOSMAN

☐ 66. DENNIS LAMP
☐ 67. RUDY LAW
☐ 68. VANCE LAW
☐ 69. GREG LUZINSKI
☐ 70. TOM PACIOREK
☐ 71. MIKE SQUIRES
☐ 72. DICK TIDROW
☐ 73. GREG WALKER
☐ 649. TEAM(F) & LARUSSA(M)

CINCINNATI REDS

☐ 462. JOHNNY BENCY
☐ 463. BRUCE BERENYI
☐ 464. DANN BILARDELLO
☐ 465. CESAR CEDENO
☐ 466. DAVE CONCEPCION
☐ 467. DAN DRIESSEN
☐ 468. NICK ESASKY
☐ 469. RICH GALE
☐ 470. BEN HAYES
☐ 471. PAUL HOUSEHOLDER
☐ 471. TOM HUME
☐ 473. ALAN KNICELY
☐ 474. EDDIE MILNER
☐ 475. RON OESTER
☐ 476. KELLY PARIS
☐ 477. FRANK PASTORE
☐ 478. TED POWER
☐ 479. JOE PRICE
☐ 480. CHARLIE PULEO
☐ 481. GARY REDUS
☐ 482. BILL SCHERRER
☐ 483. MARIO SOTO
☐ 484. ALEX TREVINO
☐ 485. DUANE WALKER
☐ 652. TEAM CHECKLIST(B)

CLEVELAND INDIANS

☐ 533. BUD ANDERSON
☐ 534. CHRIS BANDO
☐ 535. ALAN BANNISTER
☐ 536. BERT BLYLEVEN
☐ 537. TOM BRENNAN
☐ 538. JAMIE EASTERLY
☐ 539. JUAN EICHELBERGER
☐ 540. JIM ESSIAN
☐ 541. MIKE FISCHLIN
☐ 542. JULIO FRANCO
☐ 543. MIKE HARGROVE
☐ 544. TOBY HARRAH
☐ 545. RON HASSEY
☐ 546. NEAL HEATON
☐ 547. BAKE MCBRIDE
☐ 548. BRODERICK PERKINS
☐ 549. LARY SORENSEN
☐ 550. DAN SPILLNER
☐ 551. RICK SUTCLIFFE
☐ 552. PAT TABLER
☐ 553. GORMAN THOMAS
☐ 554. ANDRE THORNTON
☐ 555. GEORGE VUKOVICH
☐ 655. TEAM CHECKLIST(B)

DETROIT TIGERS

☐ 74. GLENN ABBOTT
☐ 75. HOWARD BAILEY
☐ 76. DOUG BAIR
☐ 77. JUAN BERENGUER
☐ 78. TOM BROOKENS
☐ 79. ENOS CABELL
☐ 80. KIRK GIBSON
☐ 81. JOHN GRUBB
☐ 82. LARRY HERNDON
☐ 83. WAYNE KRENCHICKI
☐ 84. RICK LEACH
☐ 85. CHET LEMON
☐ 86. AURELIO LOPEZ
☐ 87. JACK MORRIS
☐ 88. LANCE PARRISH
☐ 89. DAN PETRY
☐ 90. DAVE ROZEMA
☐ 91. ALAN TRAMMELL
☐ 92. LOU WHITAKER
☐ 93. MILT WILCOX
☐ 94. GLENN WILSON
☐ 95. JOHN WOCKENFUSS
☐ 650. TEAM(F) & ANDERSON(M)

HOUSTON ASTROS

☐ 220. ALAN ASHBY
☐ 221. KEVIN BASS
☐ 222. JOSE CRUZ
☐ 223. BILL DAWLEY
☐ 224. FRANK DIPINO
☐ 225. BILL DORAN
☐ 226. PHIL GARNER
☐ 227. ART HOWE
☐ 228. BOB KNEPPER
☐ 229. RAY KNIGHT
☐ 230. FRANK LACORTE
☐ 231. MIKE LACOSS
☐ 232. MIKE MADDEN
☐ 233. JERRY MUMPHREY
☐ 234. JOE NIEKRO
☐ 235. TERRY PUHL
☐ 236. LUIS PUJOLS
☐ 237. CRAIG REYNOLDS
☐ 238. VERN RUHLE
☐ 239. NOLAN RYAN
☐ 240. MIKE SCOTT
☐ 241. TONY SCOTT
☐ 242. DAVE SMITH
☐ 243. DICKIE THON
☐ 244. DENNY WALLING
☐ 656. TEAM(F) & LILLIS(M)

KANSAS CITY ROYALS

☐ 341. WILLIE AIKENS
☐ 342. MIKE ARMSTRONG
☐ 343. BUD BLACK
☐ 344. GEORGE BRETT
☐ 345. ONIX CONCEPCION
☐ 346. KEITH CREEL
☐ 347. LARRY GURA
☐ 348. DON HOOD
☐ 349. DENNIS LEONARD
☐ 350. HAL MCRAE
☐ 351. AMOS OTIS
☐ 352. GAYLORD PERRY
☐ 353. GREG PRYOR
☐ 354. DAN QUISENBERRY
☐ 355. STEVE RENKO
☐ 356. LEON ROBERTS
☐ 357. PAT SHERIDAN
☐ 358. JOE SIMPSON
☐ 359. DON SLAUGHT
☐ 360. PAUL SPLITTORFF
☐ 361. U.L. WASHINGTON
☐ 362. JOHN WATHAN
☐ 363. FRANKE WHITE
☐ 364. WILLIE WILSON
☐ 647. TEAM CHECKLIST(B)

LOS ANGELES DODGERS

☐ 96. DUSTY BAKER
☐ 97. JOE BECKWITH
☐ 98. GREG BROCK
☐ 99. JACK FIMPLE
☐ 100. PEDRO GUERRERO
☐ 101. RICK HONEYCUTT
☐ 102. BURT HOOTON
☐ 103. STEVE HOWE
☐ 104. KEN LANDREAUX
☐ 105. MIKE MARSHALL
☐ 106. RICK MONDAY
☐ 107. JOSE MORALES
☐ 108. TOM NIENDENFUER
☐ 109. ALEJANDRO PENA
☐ 110. JERRY REUSS
☐ 111. BILL RUSSELL
☐ 112. STEVE SAX
☐ 113. MIKE SCIOSCIA
☐ 114. DERREL THOMAS
☐ 115. FERNANDO VALENZUELA
☐ 116. BOB WELCH
☐ 117. STEVE YEAGER
☐ 118. PAT ZACHRY
☐ 651. TEAM(F) & LASORDA(M)

MILWAUKEE BREWERS

☐ 194. JERRY AUGUSTINE
☐ 195. MARK BROUHARD
☐ 196. MIKE CALDWELL
☐ 197. TOM CANDIOTTI

- ☐ 198. CECIL COOPER
- ☐ 199. ROLLIE FINGERS
- ☐ 200. JIM GANTNER
- ☐ 201. BOB GIBSON
- ☐ 202. MOOSE HAAS
- ☐ 203. ROY HOWELL
- ☐ 204. PETE LADD
- ☐ 205. RICK MANNING
- ☐ 206. BOB MCCLURE
- ☐ 207. PAUL MOLITOR
- ☐ 208. DON MONEY
- ☐ 209. CHARLIE MOORE
- ☐ 210. BEN OGLIVIE
- ☐ 211. CHUCK PORTER
- ☐ 212. ED ROMERO
- ☐ 213. TED SIMMONS
- ☐ 214. JIM SLATON
- ☐ 215. DON SUTTON
- ☐ 216. TOM TELLMANN
- ☐ 217. PETE VUCKOVICH
- ☐ 218. NED YOST
- ☐ 219. ROBIN YOUNT
- ☐ 655. TEAM(F) & LACHEMANN(M)

MINNESOTA TWINS

- ☐ 556. DARRELL BROWN
- ☐ 557. TOM BRUNANSKY
- ☐ 558. RANDY BUSH
- ☐ 559. BOBBY CASTILLO
- ☐ 560. JOHN CASTINO
- ☐ 561. RON DAVIS
- ☐ 562. DAVE ENGLE
- ☐ 563. LENNY FAEDO
- ☐ 564. PETE FILSON
- ☐ 565. GARY GAETTI
- ☐ 566. MICKEY HATCHER
- ☐ 567. KENT HRBEK
- ☐ 568. RUSTY KUNTZ
- ☐ 569. TIM LAUDNER
- ☐ 570. RICK LYSANDER
- ☐ 571. BOBBY MITCHELL
- ☐ 572. KEN SCHROM
- ☐ 573. RAY SMITH
- ☐ 574. TIM TEUFEL
- ☐ 575. FRANK VIOLA
- ☐ 576. GARY WARD
- ☐ 577. RON WASHINGTON
- ☐ 578. LEN WHITEHOUSE
- ☐ 579. AL WILLIAMS
- ☐ 656. TEAM CHECKLIST(B)

MONTREAL EXPOS

- ☐ 270. RAY BURRIS
- ☐ 271. GARY CARTER
- ☐ 272. WARREN CROMARTIE
- ☐ 273. ANDRE DAWSON
- ☐ 274. DOUG FLYNN
- ☐ 275. TERRY FRANCONA
- ☐ 276. BILL GULLICKSON
- ☐ 277. BOB JAMES
- ☐ 278. CHARLIE LEA
- ☐ 279. BRYAN LITTLE
- ☐ 280. AL OLIVER
- ☐ 281. TIM RAINES
- ☐ 282. BOBBY RAMOS
- ☐ 283. JEFF REARDON
- ☐ 284. STEVE ROGERS
- ☐ 285. SCOTT SANDERSON
- ☐ 286. DAN SCHATZEDER
- ☐ 287. BRYN SMITH
- ☐ 288. CHRIS SPEIER
- ☐ 289. MANNY TRILLO
- ☐ 290. MIKE VAIL
- ☐ 291. TIM WALLACH
- ☐ 292. CHRIS WELSH
- ☐ 293. JIM WOHLFORD
- ☐ 658. TEAM(F) & VIRDON(M)

NEW YORK METS

- ☐ 580. BOB BAILOR
- ☐ 581. MARK BRADLEY
- ☐ 582. HUBIE BROOKS
- ☐ 583. CARLOS DIAZ
- ☐ 584. GEORGE FOSTER
- ☐ 585. BRIAN GILES
- ☐ 586. DANNY HEEP
- ☐ 587. KEITH HERNANDEZ
- ☐ 588. RON HODGES

- ☐ 589. SCOTT HOLMAN
- ☐ 590. DAVE KINGMAN
- ☐ 591. ED LYNCH
- ☐ 592. JOSE OQUENDO
- ☐ 593. JESSE OROSCO
- ☐ 594. JUNIOR ORTIZ
- ☐ 595. TOM SEAVER
- ☐ 596. DOUG SISK
- ☐ 597. RUSTY STAUB
- ☐ 598. JOHN STEARNS
- ☐ 599. DARRYL STRAWBERRY
- ☐ 600. CRAIG SWAN
- ☐ 601. WALT TERRELL
- ☐ 602. MIKE TORREZ
- ☐ 603. MOOKIE WILSON
- ☐ 657. TEAM CHECKLIST(B)

NEW YORK YANKEES

- ☐ 119. DON BAYLOR
- ☐ 120. BERT CAMPANERIS
- ☐ 121. RICK CERONE
- ☐ 122. RAY FONTENOT
- ☐ 123. GEORGE FRAZIER
- ☐ 124. OSCAR GAMBLE
- ☐ 125. GOOSE GOSSAGE
- ☐ 126. KEN GRIFFEY
- ☐ 127. RON GUIDRY
- ☐ 128. JAY HOWELL
- ☐ 129. STEVE KEMP
- ☐ 130. MATT KEOUGH
- ☐ 131. DON MATTINGLY
- ☐ 132. JOHN MONTEFUSCO
- ☐ 133. OMAR MORENO
- ☐ 134. DALE MURRAY
- ☐ 135. GRAIG NETTLES
- ☐ 136. LOU PINIELLA
- ☐ 137. WILLIE RANDOLPH
- ☐ 138. SHANE RAWLEY
- ☐ 139. DAVE RIGHETTI
- ☐ 140. ANDRE ROBERTSON
- ☐ 141. BOB SHIRLEY
- ☐ 142. ROY SMALLEY
- ☐ 143. DAVE WINFIELD
- ☐ 144. BUTCH WYNEGAR
- ☐ 652. TEAM(F) & MARTIN(M)

OAKLAND A'S

- ☐ 436. BILL ALMON
- ☐ 437. KEITH ATHERTON
- ☐ 438. DAVE BEARD
- ☐ 439. TOM BURGMEIER
- ☐ 440. JEFF BURROUGHS
- ☐ 441. CHRIS CONDIROLI
- ☐ 442. TIM CONROY
- ☐ 443. MIKE DAVIS
- ☐ 444. WAYNE GROSS
- ☐ 445. GARRY HANCOCK
- ☐ 446. MIKE HEATH
- ☐ 447. RICKEY HENDERSON
- ☐ 448. DON HILL
- ☐ 449. BOB KEARNEY
- ☐ 450. BILL KRUEGER
- ☐ 451. RICK LANGFORD
- ☐ 452. CARNEY LANSFORD
- ☐ 453. DAVEY LOPES
- ☐ 454. STEVE MCCATTY
- ☐ 455. DAN MEYER
- ☐ 456. DWAYNE MURPHY
- ☐ 457. MIKE NORRIS
- ☐ 458. RICKY PETERS
- ☐ 459. TONY PHILLIPS
- ☐ 460. TOM UNDERWOOD
- ☐ 461. MIKE WARREN
- ☐ 651. TEAM CHECKLIST(B)

PHILADELPHIA PHILLIES

- ☐ 24. MARTY BYSTROM
- ☐ 25. STEVE CARLTON
- ☐ 26. IVAN DEJESUS
- ☐ 27. JOHN DENNY
- ☐ 28. BOB DERNIER
- ☐ 29. BO DIAZ
- ☐ 30. KIKO GARCIA
- ☐ 31. GREG GROSS
- ☐ 32. KEVIN GROSS
- ☐ 33. VON HAYES
- ☐ 34. WILLIE HERNANDEZ

- ☐ 35. AL HOLLAND
- ☐ 36. CHARLES HUDSON
- ☐ 37. JOE LEFEBVRE
- ☐ 38. SIXTON LEZCANO
- ☐ 39. GARRY MADDOX
- ☐ 40. GARY MATTHEWS
- ☐ 41. LEN MATUSZEK
- ☐ 42. TUG MCGRAW
- ☐ 43. JOE MORGAN
- ☐ 44. TONY PEREZ
- ☐ 45. RON REED
- ☐ 46. PETE ROSE
- ☐ 47. JUAN SAMUEL
- ☐ 48. MIKE SCHMIDT
- ☐ 49. OZZIE VIRGIL
- ☐ 648. TEAM(F) & OWENS(M)

Steve Carlton
PITCHER

PITTSBURGH PIRATES

- ☐ 245. DALE BERRAY
- ☐ 246. JIM BIBBY
- ☐ 247. JOHN CANDELARIA
- ☐ 248. JOSE DELEON
- ☐ 249. MIKE EASLER
- ☐ 250. CECILIO GUANTE
- ☐ 251. RICHIE HEBNER
- ☐ 252. LEE LACY
- ☐ 253. BILL MADLOCK
- ☐ 254. MILT MAY
- ☐ 255. LEE MAZZILLI
- ☐ 256. LARRY MCWILLIAMS
- ☐ 257. JIM MORRISON
- ☐ 258. DAVE PARKER
- ☐ 259. TONY PENA
- ☐ 260. JOHNNY RAY
- ☐ 261. RICK RHODEN
- ☐ 262. DON ROBINSON
- ☐ 263. MANNY SARMIENTO
- ☐ 264. ROD SCURRY
- ☐ 265. KENT TEKULVE
- ☐ 266. GENE TENACE
- ☐ 267. JASON THOMPSON
- ☐ 268. LEE TUNNELL
- ☐ 269. MARVELL WYNNE
- ☐ 657. TEAM(F) & TANNER(M)

ST. LOUIS CARDINALS

- ☐ 318. NEIL ALLEN
- ☐ 319. JOAQUIN ANDUJAR
- ☐ 320. STEVE BRAUN
- ☐ 321. GLENN BRUMMER
- ☐ 322. BOB FORSCH
- ☐ 323. DAVID GREEN
- ☐ 324. GEORGE HENDRICK
- ☐ 325. TOM HERR
- ☐ 326. DANE IORG
- ☐ 327. JEFF LAHTI
- ☐ 328. DAVE LAPOINT
- ☐ 329. WILLIE MCGEE
- ☐ 330. KEN OBERKFELL
- ☐ 331. DARRELL PORTER
- ☐ 332. JAMIE QUIRK
- ☐ 333. MIKE RAMSEY
- ☐ 334. FLOYD RAYFORD
- ☐ 335. LONNIE SMITH
- ☐ 336. OZZIE SMITH
- ☐ 337. JOHN STUPER
- ☐ 338. BRUCE SUTTER

☐ 339. ANDY VAN SLYKE
☐ 340. DAVE VON OHLEN
☐ 660. TEAM(F) & HERZOG(M)

SAN DIEGO PADRES

☐ 294. KURT BEVACQUA
☐ 295. JUAN BONILLA
☐ 296. BOBBY BROWN
☐ 297. LUIS DELEON
☐ 298. DAVE DRAVECKY
☐ 299. TIM FLANNERY
☐ 300. STEVE GARVEY
☐ 301. TONY GWYNN
☐ 302. ANDY HAWKINS
☐ 303. RUPPERT JONES
☐ 304. TERRY KENNEDY
☐ 305. TIM LOLLAR
☐ 306. GARY LUCAS
☐ 307. KEVIN MCREYNOLDS
☐ 308. SID MONGE
☐ 309. MARIO RAMIREZ
☐ 310. GENE RICHARDS
☐ 311. LUIS SALAZAR
☐ 312. ERIC SHOW
☐ 313. ELIAS SOSA
☐ 314. GARRY TEMPLETON
☐ 315. MARK THURMOND
☐ 316. ED WHITSON
☐ 317. ALAN WIGGINS
☐ 659. TEAM(F) & WILLIAMS(M)

SAN FRANCISCO GIANTS

☐ 365. JIM BARR
☐ 366. DAVE BERGMAN
☐ 367. FRED BREINING
☐ 368. BOB BRENLY
☐ 369. JACK CLARK
☐ 370. CHILI DAVIS
☐ 371. MARK DAVIS
☐ 372. DARRELL EVANS
☐ 373. ATLEE HAMMAKER
☐ 374. MIKE KRUKOW
☐ 375. DUANE KUIPER
☐ 376. BILL LASKEY
☐ 377. GARY LAVELLE
☐ 378. JOHNNIE LEMASTER
☐ 379. JEFF LEONARD
☐ 380. RANDY LERCH
☐ 381. RENIE MARTIN
☐ 382. ANDY MCGAFFIGAN
☐ 383. GREG MINTON
☐ 384. TOM O'MALLEY
☐ 385. MAX VENABLE
☐ 386. BRAD WELLMAN
☐ 387. JOEL YOUNGBLOOD
☐ 648. TEAM CHECKLIST(B)

SEATTLE MARINERS

☐ 604. JAMIE ALLEN
☐ 605. JIM BEATTIE
☐ 606. TONY BERNAZARD
☐ 607. MANNY CASTILLO
☐ 608. BILL CAUDILL
☐ 609. BRYAN CLARK
☐ 610. AL COWENS
☐ 611. DAVE HENDERSON
☐ 612. STEVE HENDERSON
☐ 613. ORLANDO MERCADO
☐ 614. MIKE MOORE
☐ 615. RICKY NELSON
☐ 616. SPIKE OWEN
☐ 617. PAT PUTNAM
☐ 618. RON ROENICKE
☐ 619. MIKE STANTON
☐ 620. BOB STODDARD
☐ 621. RICK SWEET
☐ 622. ROY THOMAS
☐ 623. ED VANDEBERG
☐ 624. MATT YOUNG
☐ 625. RICHIE ZISK
☐ 658. TEAM CHECKLIST(B)

TEXAS RANGERS

☐ 413. BUDDY BELL
☐ 414. LARRY BITTNER
☐ 415. JOHN BUTCHER

☐ 416. DANNY DARWIN
☐ 417. BUCKY DENT
☐ 418. DAVE HOSTETLER
☐ 419. CHARLIE HOUGH
☐ 420. BOBBY JOHNSON
☐ 421. ODELL JONES
☐ 422. JON MATLACK
☐ 423. PETE O'BRIEN
☐ 424. LARRY PARRISH
☐ 425. MICKEY RIVERS
☐ 426. BILLY SAMPLE
☐ 427. DAVE SCHMIDT
☐ 428. MIKE SMITHSON
☐ 429. BILL STEIN
☐ 430. DAVE STEWART
☐ 431. JIM SUNDBERG
☐ 432. FRANK TANANA
☐ 433. DAVE TOBIK
☐ 434. WAYNE TOLLESON
☐ 435. GEORGE WRIGHT
☐ 650. TEAM CHECKLIST(B)

Bucky Dent
SHORTSTOP

TORONTO BLUE JAYS

☐ 145. JIM ACKER
☐ 146. DOYLE ALEXANDER
☐ 147. JESSE BARFIELD
☐ 148. JORGE BELL
☐ 149. BARRY BONNELL
☐ 150. JIM CLANCY
☐ 151. DAVE COLLINS
☐ 152. TONY FERNANDEZ
☐ 153. DAMASO GARCIA
☐ 154. DAVE GEISEL
☐ 155. JIM GOTT
☐ 156. ALFREDO GRIFFIN
☐ 157. GARTH IORG
☐ 158. ROY LEE JACKSON
☐ 159. CLIFF JOHNSON
☐ 160. LUIS LEAL
☐ 161. BUCK MARTINEZ
☐ 162. JOEY MCLAUGHLIN
☐ 163. RANDY MOFFIT
☐ 164. LLOYD MOSEBY
☐ 165. RANCE MULLINIKS
☐ 166. JORGE ORTA
☐ 167. DAVE STIEB
☐ 168. WILLIE UPSHAW
☐ 169. ERNIE WHITT
☐ 653. TEAM(F) & COX(M)

1984 FLEER TRADED (132) 2 1/2" X 3 1/2"

Graig Nettles
THIRD BASE

ATLANTA BRAVES

☐ 63U. BRAD KOMMINSK
☐ 84U. KEN OBERKFELL
☐ 92U. GERALD PERRY
☐ 118U. ALEX TREVINO

BALTIMORE ORIOLES

☐ 45U. WAYNE GROSS
☐ 95U. FLOYD RAYFORD
☐ 121U. TOM UNDERWOOD
☐ 131U. MIKE YOUNG

BOSTON RED SOX

☐ 8U. MARTY BARRETT
☐ 18U. BILL BUCKNER
☐ 27U. ROGER CLEMENS
☐ 33U. MIKE EASLER
☐ 41U. RICH GALE
☐ 47U. JACKIE GUTIERREZ

CALIFORNIA ANGELS

☐ 17U. MIKE BROWN
☐ 67U. FRANK LACORTE
☐ 101U. RON ROMANICK
☐ 105U. DICK SCHOFIELD
☐ 107U. JIM SLATON
☐ 115U. CRAIG SWAN

CHICAGO CUBS

☐ 31U. BOB DERNIER
☐ 34U. DENNIS ECKERSLEY
☐ 40U. GEORGE FRAZIER
☐ 49U. RON HASSEY
☐ 50U. RICHIE HEBNER
☐ 77U. GARY MATTHEWS
☐ 104U. SCOTT SANDERSON
☐ 110U. TIM STODDARD
☐ 114U. RICK SUTCLIFFE

CHICAGO WHITE SOX

☐ 96U. RON REED
☐ 106U. TOM SEAVER

CINCINNATI REDS

☐ 39U. JOHN FRANCO
☐ 65U. WAYNE KRENCHICKI
☐ 88U. BOB OWCHINKO
☐ 89U. DAVE PARKER
☐ 91U. TONY PEREZ

CLEVELAND INDIANS

☐ 2U. LUIS APONTE
☐ 12U. TONY BERNAZARD
☐ 21U. BRETT BUTLER
☐ 56U. BROOK JACOBY
☐ 58U. MIKE JEFFCOAT
☐ 123U. TOM WADDELL

1984 Fleer Traded

Willie Hernandez
PITCHER

Ray Burris
PITCHER

TORONTO BLUE JAYS

□ 1U. WILLIE AIKENS
□ 26U. BRYAN CLARK
□ 61U. JIMMY KEY
□ 68U. DENNIS LAMP
□ 71U. RICH LEACH

1985 FLEER
2 1/2" X 3 1/2"

DWIGHT GOODEN
PITCHER

DETROIT TIGERS

□ 11U. DAVE BERGMAN
□ 36U. DARRELL EVANS
□ 42U. BARBARO GARBEY
□ 51U. WILLIE HERNANDEZ
□ 59U. RUPPERT JONES
□ 66U. RUSTY KUNTZ

HOUSTON ASTROS

□ 3U. MARK BAILEY
□ 22U. ENOS CABELL

KANSAS CITY ROYALS

□ 6U. STEVE BALBONI
□ 10U. JOE BECKWITH
□ 46U. MARK GUBICZA
□ 55U. DANE IORG
□ 81U. DARRYL MOTLEY
□ 86U. JORGE ORTA
□ 103U. BRET SABERHAGEN

LOS ANGELES DODGERS

□ 4U. BOB BAILOR
□ 32U. CARLOS DIAZ
□ 97U. R.J. REYNOLDS
□ 122U. MIKE VAIL
□ 125U. TERRY WHITFIELD

MILWAUKEE BREWERS

□ 25U. BOBBY CLARK
□ 28U. JAIME COCANOWER
□ 57U. DION JAMES
□ 113U. JIM SUNDBERG

MINNESOTA TWINS

□ 20U. JOHN BUTCHER
□ 52U. ED HODGE
□ 93U. KIRBY PUCKETT
□ 108U. MIKE SMITHSON

MONTREAL EXPOS

□ 16U. FRED BREINING
□ 73U. GARY LUCAS
□ 78U. ANDY MCGAFFIGAN
□ 102U. PETE ROSE
□ 116U. DERREL THOMAS

NEW YORK METS

□ 29U. RON DARLING
□ 37U. MIKE FITZGERALD
□ 43U. DWIGHT GOODEN
□ 74U. JERRY MARTIN

NEW YORK YANKEES

□ 38U. TIM FOLI
□ 48U. TOBY HARRAH
□ 83U. PHIL NIEKRO
□ 99U. JOSE RIJO

OAKLAND A'S

□ 13U. BRUCE BOCHTE
□ 19U. RAY BURRIS
□ 24U. BILL CAUDILL
□ 35U. JIM ESSIAN
□ 62U. DAVE KINGMAN
□ 80U. JOE MORGAN
□ 109U. LARY SORENSEN

PHILADELPHIA PHILLIES

□ 23U. BILL CAMPBELL
□ 64U. JERRY KOOSMAN
□ 94U. SHANE RAWLEY
□ 111U. JEFF STONE
□ 128U. GLENN WILSON
□ 129U. JOHN WOCKENFUSS

PITTSBURGH PIRATES

□ 87U. AMOS OTIS
□ 120U. JOHN TUDOR

ST. LOUIS CARDINALS

□ 53U. RICKY HORTON
□ 54U. ART HOWE
□ 69U. TITO LANDRUM

SAN DIEGO PADRES

□ 44U. RICH GOSSAGE
□ 72U. CRAIG LEFFERTS
□ 75U. CARMELO MARTINEZ
□ 82U. GRAIG NETTLES
□ 112U. CHAMP SUMMERS

SAN FRANCISCO GIANTS

□ 5U. DUSTY BAKER
□ 85U. AL OLIVER
□ 98U. GENE RICHARDS
□ 100U. JEFF ROBINSON
□ 119U. MANNY TRILLO
□ 127U. FRANK WILLIAMS

SEATTLE MARINERS

□ 9U. DAVE BEARD
□ 14U. BARRY BONNELL
□ 15U. PHIL BRADLEY
□ 30U. ALVIN DAVIS
□ 60U. BOB KEARNEY
□ 70U. MARK LANGSTON
□ 90U. JACK PERCONTE
□ 117U. GORMAN THOMAS

TEXAS RANGERS

□ 7U. ALAN BANNISTER
□ 76U. MIKE MASON
□ 79U. JOEY MCLAUGHLIN
□ 124U. CURTIS WILKERSON
□ 130U. NED YOST

ATLANTA BRAVES

□ 318. LEN BARKER
□ 319. STEVE BEDROSIAN
□ 320. BRUCE BENEDICT
□ 321. RICK CAMP
□ 322. CHRIS CHAMBLISS
□ 323. JEFF DEDMON
□ 324. TERRY FORSTER
□ 325. GENE GARBER
□ 326. ALBERT HALL
□ 327. TERRY HARPER
□ 328. BOB HORNER
□ 329. GLENN HUBBARD
□ 330. RANDY JOHNSON
□ 331. BRAD KOMMINSK
□ 332. RICK MAHLER
□ 333. CRAIG MCMURTRY
□ 334. DONNIE MOORE
□ 335. DALE MURPHY
□ 336. KEN OBERKFELL
□ 337. PASCUAL PEREZ
□ 338. GERALD PERRY
□ 339. RAFAEL RAMIREZ
□ 340. JERRY ROYSTER
□ 341. ALEX TREVINO
□ 342. CLAUDELL WASHINGTON
□ 651. ZANE SMITH(P)
□ 651. PAUL ZUVELLA(P)
□ 657. TEAM CHECKLIST(F)

BALTIMORE ORIOLES

□ 170. MIKE BODDICKER
□ 171. AL BUMBRY
□ 172. TODD CRUZ
□ 173. RICH DAUER
□ 174. STORM DAVIS
□ 175. RICK DEMPSEY
□ 176. JIM DWYER
□ 177. MIKE FLANAGAN
□ 178. DAN FORD
□ 179. WAYNE GROSS
□ 180. JOHN LOWENSTEIN
□ 181. DENNIS MARTINEZ
□ 182. TIPPY MARTINEZ
□ 183. SCOTT MCGREGOR
□ 184. EDDIE MURRAY
□ 185. JOE NOLAN
□ 186. FLOYD RAYFORD
□ 187. CAL RIPKEN
□ 188. GARY ROENICKE
□ 189. LENN SAKATA
□ 190. JOHN SHELBY
□ 191. KEN SINGLETON
□ 192. SAMMY STEWART
□ 193. BILL SWAGGERTY
□ 194. TOM UNDERWOOD
□ 195. MIKE YOUNG
□ 655. TEAM CHECKLIST(B)

1985 Fleer

BOSTON RED SOX

- ☐ 148. GARY ALLENSON
- ☐ 149. TONY ARMAS
- ☐ 150. MARTY BARRETT
- ☐ 151. WADE BOGGS
- ☐ 152. DENNIS BOYD
- ☐ 153. BILL BUCKNER
- ☐ 154. MARK CLEAR
- ☐ 155. ROGER CLEMENS
- ☐ 156. STEVE CRAWFORD
- ☐ 157. MIKE EASLER
- ☐ 158. DWIGHT EVANS
- ☐ 159. RICH GEDMAN
- ☐ 160. JACKIE GUTIERREZ
- ☐ 161. BRUCE HURST
- ☐ 162. JOHN HENRY JOHNSON
- ☐ 163. RICK MILLER
- ☐ 164. REID NICHOLS
- ☐ 165. AL NIPPER
- ☐ 166. BOB OJEDA
- ☐ 167. JERRY REMY
- ☐ 168. JIM RICE
- ☐ 169. BOB STANLEY
- ☐ 655. TEAM CHECKLIST(B)

CALIFORNIA ANGELS

- ☐ 293. DON AASE
- ☐ 294. JUAN BENIQUEZ
- ☐ 295. BOB BOONE
- ☐ 296. MIKE BROWN
- ☐ 297. ROD CAREW
- ☐ 298. DOUG CORBETT
- ☐ 299. DOUG DECINCES
- ☐ 300. BRIAN DOWNING
- ☐ 301. KEN FORSCH
- ☐ 302. BOBBY GRICH
- ☐ 303. REGGIE JACKSON
- ☐ 304. TOMMY JOHN
- ☐ 305. CURT KAUFMAN
- ☐ 306. BRUCE KISON
- ☐ 307. FRED LYNN
- ☐ 308. GARY PETTIS
- ☐ 309. RON ROMANICK
- ☐ 310. LUIS SANCHEZ
- ☐ 311. DICK SCHOFIELD
- ☐ 312. DARYL SCONIERS
- ☐ 313. JIM SLATON
- ☐ 314. DERREL THOMAS
- ☐ 315. ROB WILFONG
- ☐ 316. MIKE WITT
- ☐ 317. GEOFF ZAHN
- ☐ 657. TEAM CHECKLIST(F)

CHICAGO CUBS

- ☐ 49. RICH BORDI
- ☐ 50. LARRY BOWA
- ☐ 51. WARREN BRUSSTAR
- ☐ 52. RON CEY
- ☐ 53. HENRY COTTO
- ☐ 54. JODY DAVIS
- ☐ 55. BOB DERNIER
- ☐ 56. LEON DURHAM
- ☐ 57. DENNIS ECKERSLEY
- ☐ 58. GEORGE FRAZIER
- ☐ 59. RICHIE HEBNER
- ☐ 60. DAVE LOPES
- ☐ 61. GARY MATTHEWS
- ☐ 62. KEITH MORELAND
- ☐ 63. RICK REUSCHEL
- ☐ 64. DICK RUTHVEN
- ☐ 65. RYNE SANDBERG
- ☐ 66. SCOTT SANDERSON
- ☐ 67. LEE SMITH
- ☐ 68. TIM STODDARD
- ☐ 69. RICK SUTCLIFFE
- ☐ 70. STEVE TROUT
- ☐ 71. GARY WOODS
- ☐ 649. BILL HATCHER(P)
- ☐ 649. SHAWON DUNSTON(P)
- ☐ 654. TEAM CHECKLIST(B)

CHICAGO WHITE SOX

- ☐ 506. JUAN AGOSTO
- ☐ 507. HAROLD BAINES
- ☐ 508. FLOYD BANNISTER
- ☐ 509. BRITT BURNS

- ☐ 510. JULIO CRUZ
- ☐ 511. RICHARD DOTSON
- ☐ 512. JERRY DYBZINSKI
- ☐ 513. CARLTON FISK
- ☐ 514. SCOTT FLETCHER
- ☐ 515. JERRY HAIRSTON
- ☐ 516. MARC HILL
- ☐ 517. LAMARR HOYT
- ☐ 518. RON KITTLE
- ☐ 519. RUDY LAW
- ☐ 520. VANCE LAW
- ☐ 521. GREG LUZINSKI
- ☐ 522. GENE NELSON
- ☐ 523. TOM PACIOREK
- ☐ 524. RON REED
- ☐ 525. BERT ROBERGE
- ☐ 526. TOM SEAVER
- ☐ 527. ROY SMALLEY
- ☐ 528. DAN SPILLNER
- ☐ 529. MIKE SQUIRES
- ☐ 530. GREG WALKER
- ☐ 646. JOEL SKINNER(P)
- ☐ 659. TEAM CHECKLIST(F)

CINCINNATI REDS

- ☐ 531. CESAR CEDENO
- ☐ 532. DAVE CONCEPCION
- ☐ 533. ERIC DAVIS
- ☐ 534. NICK ESASKY
- ☐ 535. TOM FOLEY
- ☐ 536. JOHN FRANCO
- ☐ 537. BRAD GULDEN
- ☐ 538. TOM HUME
- ☐ 539. WAYNE KRENCHICKI
- ☐ 540. ANDY MCGAFFIGAN
- ☐ 541. EDDIE MILNER
- ☐ 542. RON OESTER
- ☐ 543. BOB OWCHINKO
- ☐ 544. DAVE PARKER
- ☐ 545. FRANK PASTORE
- ☐ 546. TONY PEREZ
- ☐ 547. TED POWER
- ☐ 548. JOE PRICE
- ☐ 549. GARY REDUS
- ☐ 550. PETE ROSE(M)
- ☐ 551. JEFF RUSSELL
- ☐ 552. MARIO SOTO
- ☐ 553. JAY TIBBS
- ☐ 554. DUANE WALKER
- ☐ 650. RON ROBINSON(P)
- ☐ 659. TEAM CHECKLIST(B)

CLEVELAND INDIANS

- ☐ 437. LUIS APONTE
- ☐ 438. CHRIS BANDO
- ☐ 439. TONY BERNAZARD
- ☐ 440. BERT BLYLEVEN
- ☐ 441. BRETT BUTLER
- ☐ 442. ERNIE CAMACHO
- ☐ 443. JOE CARTER
- ☐ 444. CARMELO CASTILLO
- ☐ 445. JAMIE EASTERLY
- ☐ 446. STEVE FARR
- ☐ 447. MIKE FISCHLIN
- ☐ 448. JULIO FRANCO
- ☐ 449. MEL HALL
- ☐ 450. MIKE HARGROVE
- ☐ 451. NEAL HEATON
- ☐ 452. BROOK JACOBY
- ☐ 453. MIKE JEFFCOAT
- ☐ 454. DON SCHULZE
- ☐ 455. ROY SMITH
- ☐ 456. PAT TABLER
- ☐ 457. ANDRE THORNTON
- ☐ 458. GEORGE VUKOVICH
- ☐ 459. TOM WADDELL
- ☐ 460. JERRY WILLARD
- ☐ 646. JOSE ROMAN(P)
- ☐ 658. TEAM CHECKLIST(B)

DETROIT TIGERS

- ☐ 1. DOUG BAIR
- ☐ 2. JUAN BERENGUER
- ☐ 3. DAVE BERGMAN
- ☐ 4. TOM BROOKENS
- ☐ 5. MARTY CASTILLO
- ☐ 6. DARRELL EVANS
- ☐ 7. BARBARO GARBEY

- ☐ 8. KIRK GIBSON
- ☐ 9. JOHN GRUBB
- ☐ 10. WILLIE HERNANDEZ
- ☐ 11. LARRY HERNDON
- ☐ 12. HOWARD JOHNSON
- ☐ 13. RUPPERT JONES
- ☐ 14. RUSTY KUNTZ
- ☐ 15. CHET LEMON
- ☐ 16. AURELIO LOPEZ
- ☐ 17. SID MONGE
- ☐ 18. JACK MORRIS
- ☐ 19. LANCE PARRISH
- ☐ 20. DAN PETRY
- ☐ 21. DAVE ROZEMA
- ☐ 22. BILL SCHERRER
- ☐ 23. ALAN TRAMMELL
- ☐ 24. LOU WHITAKER
- ☐ 25. MILT WILCOX
- ☐ 654. RANDY O'NEAL(P)
- ☐ 654. TEAM CHECKLIST(F)

HOUSTON ASTROS

- ☐ 343. ALAN ASHBY
- ☐ 344. MARK BAILEY
- ☐ 345. KEVIN BASS
- ☐ 346. ENOS CABELL
- ☐ 347. JOSE CRUZ
- ☐ 348. BILL DAWLEY
- ☐ 349. FRANK DIPINO
- ☐ 350. BILL DORAN
- ☐ 351. PHIL GARNER
- ☐ 352. BOB KNEPPER
- ☐ 353. MIKE LACOSS
- ☐ 354. JERRY MUMPHREY
- ☐ 355. JOE NIEKRO
- ☐ 356. TERRY PUHL
- ☐ 357. CRAIG REYNOLDS
- ☐ 358. VERN RUHLE
- ☐ 359. NOLAN RYAN
- ☐ 360. JOE SAMBITO
- ☐ 361. MIKE SCOTT
- ☐ 362. DAVE SMITH
- ☐ 363. JULIO SOLANO
- ☐ 364. DICKIE THON
- ☐ 365. DENNY WALLING
- ☐ 652. GLENN DAVIS(P)
- ☐ 657. TEAM CHECKLIST(B)

KANSAS CITY ROYALS

- ☐ 196. STEVE BALBONI
- ☐ 197. JOE BECKWITH
- ☐ 198. BUD BLACK
- ☐ 199. GEORGE BRETT
- ☐ 200. ONIX CONCEPCION
- ☐ 201. MARK GUBICZA
- ☐ 202. LARRY GURA
- ☐ 203. MARK HUISMANN
- ☐ 204. DANE IORG
- ☐ 205. DANNY JACKSON
- ☐ 206. CHARLIE LEIBRANDT
- ☐ 207. HAL MCRAE
- ☐ 208. DARRYL MOTLEY
- ☐ 209. JORGE ORTA
- ☐ 210. GREG PRYOR
- ☐ 211. DAN QUISENBERRY
- ☐ 212. BRET SABERHAGEN
- ☐ 213. PAT SHERIDAN

1985 Fleer

☐ 214. DON SLAUGHT
☐ 215. U.L. WASHINGTON
☐ 216. JOHN WATHAN
☐ 217. FRANK WHITE
☐ 218. WILLIE WILSON
☐ 656. TEAM CHECKLIST(F)

LOS ANGELES DODGERS

☐ 366. DAVE ANDERSON
☐ 367. BOB BAILOR
☐ 368. GREG BROCK
☐ 369. CARLOS DIAZ
☐ 370. PEDRO GUERRERO
☐ 371. OREL HERSHISER
☐ 372. RICK HONEYCUTT
☐ 373. BURT HOOTON
☐ 374. KEN HOWELL
☐ 375. KEN LANDREQUX
☐ 376. CANDY MALDONADO
☐ 377. MIKE MARSHALL
☐ 378. TOM NIEDENFUER
☐ 379. ALEJANDRO PENA
☐ 380. JERRY REUSS
☐ 381. R.J. REYNOLDS
☐ 382. GERMAN RIVERA
☐ 383. BILL RUSSELL
☐ 384. STEVE SAX
☐ 385. MIKE SCIOSCIA
☐ 386. FRANKLIN STUBBS
☐ 387. FERNANDO VALENZUELA
☐ 388. BOB WELCH
☐ 389. TERRY WHITFIELD
☐ 390. STEVE YEAGER
☐ 391. PAT ZACHRY
☐ 657. TEAM CHECKLIST(B)

MILWAUKEE BREWERS

☐ 576. MARK BROUHARD
☐ 577. MIKE CALDWELL
☐ 578. BOBBY CLARK
☐ 579. JAIME COCANOWER
☐ 580. CECIL COOPER
☐ 581. ROLLIE FINGERS
☐ 582. JIM GANTNER
☐ 583. MOOSE HAAS
☐ 584. DION JAMES
☐ 585. PETE LADD
☐ 586. RICK MANNING
☐ 587. BOB MCCLURE
☐ 588. PAUL MOLITOR
☐ 589. CHARLIE MOORE
☐ 590. BEN OGLIVIE
☐ 591. CHUCK PORTER
☐ 592. RANDY READY
☐ 593. ED ROMERO
☐ 594. BILL SCHROEDER
☐ 595. RAY SEARAGE
☐ 596. TED SIMMONS
☐ 597. JIM SUNDBERG
☐ 598. DON SUTTON
☐ 599. TOM TELLMAN
☐ 600. RICK WAITS
☐ 601. ROBIN YOUNT
☐ 644. WILLIE LOZADO(P)
☐ 660 TEAM CHECKLIST(F)

MINNESOTA TWINS

☐ 270. DARRELL BROWN
☐ 271. TOM BRUNANSKY
☐ 272. RANDY BUSH
☐ 273. JOHN BUTCHER
☐ 274. BOBBY CASTILLO
☐ 275. RON DAVIS
☐ 276. DAVE ENGLE
☐ 277. PETE FILSON
☐ 278. GARY GAETTI
☐ 279. MICKEY HATCHER
☐ 280. ED HODGE
☐ 281. KENT HRBEK
☐ 282. HOUSTON JIMENEZ
☐ 283. TIM LAUDNER
☐ 284. RICK LYSANDER
☐ 285. DAVE MEIER
☐ 286. KIRBY PUCKETT
☐ 287. PAT PUTNAM
☐ 288. KEN SCHROM
☐ 289. MIKE SMITHSON

☐ 290. TIM TEUFEL
☐ 291. FRANK VIOLA
☐ 292. RON WASHINGTON
☐ 656. TEAM CHECKLIST(B)

MONTREAL EXPOS

☐ 392. FRED BREINING
☐ 393. GARY CARTER
☐ 394. ANDRE DAWSON
☐ 395. MIGUEL DILONE
☐ 396. DAN DRIESSEN
☐ 397. DOUG FLYNN
☐ 398. TERRY FRANCONA
☐ 399. BILL GULLICKSON
☐ 400. BOB JAMES
☐ 401. CHARLIE LEA
☐ 402. BRYAN LITTLE
☐ 403. GARY LUCAS
☐ 404. DAVID PALMER
☐ 405. TIM RAINES
☐ 406. MIKE RAMSEY
☐ 407. JEFF REARDON
☐ 408. STEVE ROGERS
☐ 409. DAN SCHATZEDER
☐ 410. BRYN SMITH
☐ 411. MIKE STENHOUSE
☐ 412. TIM WALLACH
☐ 413. JIM WOHLFORD
☐ 652. JOE HESKETH(P)
☐ 658. TEAM CHECKLIST(F)

NEW YORK METS

☐ 72. WALLY BACKMAN
☐ 73. BRUCE BERENYI
☐ 74. HUBIE BROOKS
☐ 75. KELVIN CHAPMAN
☐ 76. RON DARLING
☐ 77. SID FERNANDEZ
☐ 78. MIKE FITZGERALD
☐ 79. GEORGE FOSTER
☐ 80. BRENT GAFF
☐ 81. RON GARDENHIRE
☐ 82. DWIGHT GOODEN
☐ 83. TOM GORMAN
☐ 84. DANNY HEEP
☐ 85. KEITH HERNANDEZ
☐ 86. RAY KNIGHT
☐ 87. ED LYNCH
☐ 88. JOSE OQUENDO
☐ 89. JESSE OROSCO
☐ 90. RAFAEL SANTANA
☐ 91. DOUG SISK
☐ 92. RUSTY STAUB
☐ 93. DARRYL STRAWBERRY
☐ 94. WALT TERRELL
☐ 95. MOOKIE WILSON
☐ 654. TEAM CHECKLIST(B)

NEW YORK YANKEES

☐ 120. MIKE ARMSTRONG
☐ 121. DON BAYLOR
☐ 122. MARTY BYSTROM
☐ 123. RICK CERONE
☐ 124. JOE COWLEY
☐ 125. BRIAN DAYETT
☐ 126. TIM FOLI
☐ 127. RAY FONTENOT

☐ 128. KEN GRIFFEY
☐ 129. RON GUIDRY
☐ 130. TOBY HARRAH
☐ 131. JAY HOWELL
☐ 132. STEVE KEMP
☐ 133. DON MATTINGLY
☐ 134. BOBBY MEACHAM
☐ 135. JOHN MONTEFUSCO
☐ 136. OMAR MORENO
☐ 137. DALE MURRAY
☐ 138. PHIL NIEKRO
☐ 139. MIKE PAGLIARULO
☐ 140. WILLIE RANDOLPH
☐ 141. DENNIS RASMUSSEN
☐ 142. DAVE RIGHETTI
☐ 143. JOSE RIJO
☐ 144. ANDRE ROBERTSON
☐ 145. BOB SHIRLEY
☐ 146. DAVE WINFIELD
☐ 147. BUTCH WYNEGAR
☐ 644. VIC MATA(P)
☐ 655. TEAM CHECKLIST(F)

OAKLAND A'S

☐ 414. BILL ALMON
☐ 415. KEITH ATHERTON
☐ 416. BRUCE BOCHTE
☐ 417. TOM BURGMEIER
☐ 418. RAY BURRIS
☐ 419. BILL CAUDILL
☐ 420. CHRIS CODIROLI
☐ 421. TIM CONROY
☐ 422. MIKE DAVIS
☐ 423. JIM ESSIAN
☐ 424. MIKE HEATH
☐ 425. RICKEY HENDERSON
☐ 426. DONNIE HILL
☐ 427. DAVE KINGMAN
☐ 428. BILL KRUEGER
☐ 429. CARNEY LANSFORD
☐ 430. STEVE MCCATTY
☐ 431. JOE MORGAN
☐ 432. DWAYNE MURPHY
☐ 433. TONY PHILLIPS
☐ 434. LARY SORENSEN
☐ 435. MIKE WARREN
☐ 436. CURT YOUNG
☐ 647. STEVE KIEFER(P)
☐ 658. TEAM CHECKLIST(F)

PHILADELPHIA PHILLIES

☐ 244. LARRY ANDERSON
☐ 245. BILL CAMPBELL
☐ 246. STEVE CARLTON
☐ 247. TIM CORCORAN
☐ 248. IVAN DEJESUS
☐ 249. JOHN DENNY
☐ 250. BO DIAZ
☐ 251. GREG GROSS
☐ 252. KEVIN GROSS
☐ 253. VON HAYES
☐ 254. AL HOLLAND
☐ 255. CHARLES HUDSON
☐ 256. JERRY KOOSMAN
☐ 257. JOE LEFEBVRE
☐ 258. SIXTO LEZCANO
☐ 259. GARRY MADDOX
☐ 260. LEN MATUSZEK
☐ 261. TUG MCGRAW
☐ 262. AL OLVIER
☐ 263. SHANE RAWLEY
☐ 264. JUAN SAMUEL
☐ 265. MIKE SCHMIDT
☐ 266. JEFF STONE
☐ 267. OZZIE VIRGIL
☐ 268. GLENN WILSON
☐ 269. JOHN WOCKENFUSS
☐ 653. JOHN RUSSELL(P)
☐ 653. STEVE JELTZ(P)
☐ 656. TEAM CHECKLIST(B)

PITTSBURGH PIRATES

☐ 461. DALE BERRA
☐ 462. JOHN CANDELARIA
☐ 463. JOSE DELEON
☐ 464. DOUG FROBEL
☐ 465. CECILLIO GUANTE

☐ 466. BRIAN HARPER
☐ 467. LEE LACY
☐ 468. BILL MADLOCK
☐ 469. LEE MAZZILLI
☐ 470. LARRY MCWILLIAMS
☐ 471. JIM MORRISON
☐ 472. TONY PENA
☐ 473. JOHNNY RAY
☐ 474. RICK RHODEN
☐ 475. DON ROBINSON
☐ 476. ROD SCURRY
☐ 477. KENT TEKULVE
☐ 478. JASON THOMPSON
☐ 479. JOHN TUDOR
☐ 480. LEE TUNNELL
☐ 481. MARVELL WYNNE
☐ 650. MIKE BIELECKI(P)
☐ 658. TEAM CHECKLIST(B)

ST. LOUIS CARDINALS

☐ 219. NEIL ALLEN
☐ 220. JOAQUIN ANDUJAR
☐ 221. STEVE BRAUN
☐ 222. DANNY COX
☐ 223. BOB FORSCH
☐ 224. DAVID GREEN
☐ 225. GEORGE HENDRICK
☐ 226. TOM HERR
☐ 227. RICKY HORTON
☐ 228. ART HOWE
☐ 229. MIKE JORGENSEN
☐ 230. KURT KEPSHIRE
☐ 231. JEFF LAHTI
☐ 232. TITO LANDRUM
☐ 233. DAVE LAPOINT
☐ 234. WILLIE MCGEE
☐ 235. TOM NIETO
☐ 236. TERRY PENDLETON
☐ 237. DARRELL PORTER
☐ 238. DAVE RUCKER
☐ 239. LONNIE SMITH
☐ 240. OZZIE SMITH
☐ 241. BRUCE SUTTER
☐ 242. ANDY VAN SLYKE
☐ 243. DAVE VON OHLEN
☐ 656. TEAM CHECKLIST(F)

SAN DIEGO PADRES

☐ 26. KURT BEVACQUA
☐ 27. GREG BOOKER
☐ 28. BOBBY BROWN
☐ 29. LUIS DELEON
☐ 30. DAVE DRAVECKY
☐ 31. TIM FLANNERY
☐ 32. STEVE GARVEY
☐ 33. GOOSE GOSSAGE
☐ 34. TONY GWYNN
☐ 35. GREG HARRIS
☐ 36. ANDY HAWKINS
☐ 37. TERRY KENNEDY
☐ 38. CRAIG LEFFERTS
☐ 39. TIM LOLLAR
☐ 40. CARMELO MARTINEZ
☐ 41. KEVIN MCREYNOLDS
☐ 42. GRAIG NETTLES
☐ 43. LUIS SALAZAR
☐ 44. ERIC SHOW
☐ 45. GARRY TEMPLETON
☐ 46. MARK THURMOND
☐ 47. ED WHITSON
☐ 48. ALAN WIGGINS
☐ 654. TEAM CHECKLIST(F)

SAN FRANCISCO GIANTS

☐ 602. DUSTY BAKER
☐ 603. BOB BRENLY
☐ 604. JACK CLARK
☐ 605. CHILI DAVIS
☐ 606. MARK DAVIS
☐ 607. DAN GLADDEN
☐ 608. ATLEE HAMMAKER
☐ 609. MIKE KRUKOW
☐ 610. DUANE KUIPER
☐ 611. BOB LACEY
☐ 612. BILL LASKEY
☐ 613. GARY LAVELLE
☐ 614. JOHNNIE LEMASTER
☐ 615. JEFF LEONARD

☐ 616. RANDY LERCH
☐ 617. GREG MINTON
☐ 618. STEVE NICOSIA
☐ 619. GENE RICHARDS
☐ 620. JEFF ROBINSON
☐ 621. SCOT THOMPSON
☐ 622. MANNY TRILLO
☐ 623. BRAD WELLMAN
☐ 624. FRANK WILLIAMS
☐ 625. JOEL YOUNGBLOOD
☐ 648. ROB DEER(P)
☐ 648. ALEJANDRO SANCHEZ(P)
☐ 660. TEAM CHECKLIST(F)

SEATTLE MARINERS

☐ 482. SALOME BAROJAS
☐ 483. DAVE BEARD
☐ 484. JIM BEATTIE
☐ 485. BARRY BONNELL
☐ 486. PHIL BRADLEY
☐ 487. AL COWENS
☐ 488. ALVIN DAVIS
☐ 489. DAVE HENDERSON
☐ 490. STEVE HENDERSON
☐ 491. BOB KEARNEY
☐ 492. MARK LANGSTON
☐ 493. LARRY MILBOURNE
☐ 494. PAUL MIRABELLA
☐ 495. MIKE MOORE
☐ 496. EDWIN NUNEZ
☐ 497. SPIKE OWEN
☐ 498. JACK PERCONTE
☐ 499. KEN PHELPS
☐ 500. JIM PRESLEY
☐ 501. MIKE STANTON
☐ 502. BOB STODDARD
☐ 503. GORMAN THOMAS
☐ 504. ED VANDE BERG
☐ 505. MATT YOUNG
☐ 647. DANNY TARTABULL(P)
☐ 659. TEAM CHECKLIST(F)

TEXAS RANGERS

☐ 555. ALAN BANNISTER
☐ 556. BUDDY BELL
☐ 557. DANNY DARWIN
☐ 558. CHARLIE HOUGH
☐ 559. BOBBY JONES
☐ 560. ODELL JONES
☐ 561. JEFF KUNKEL
☐ 562. MIKE MASON
☐ 563. PETE O'BRIEN
☐ 564. LARRY PARRISH
☐ 565. MICKEY RIVERS
☐ 566. BILLY SAMPLE
☐ 567. DAVE SCHMIDT
☐ 568. DONNIE SCOTT
☐ 569. DAVE STEWART
☐ 570. FRANK TANANA
☐ 571. WAYNE TOLLESON
☐ 572. GARY WARD
☐ 573. CURTIS WILKERSON
☐ 574. GEORGE WRIGHT
☐ 575. NED YOST
☐ 659. TEAM CHECKLIST(B)

TORONTO BLUE JAYS

☐ 96. JIM ACKER
☐ 97. WILLIE AIKENS
☐ 98. DOYLE ALEXANDER
☐ 99. JESSE BARFIELD
☐ 100. GEORGE BELL
☐ 101. JIM CLANCY
☐ 102. DAVE COLLINS
☐ 103. TONY FERNANDEZ
☐ 104. DAMASO GARCIA
☐ 105. JIM GOTT
☐ 106. ALFREDO GRIFFIN
☐ 107. GARTH IORG
☐ 108. ROY LEE JACKSON
☐ 109. CLIFF JOHNSON
☐ 110. JIMMY KEY
☐ 111. DENNIS LAMPE
☐ 112. RICK LEACH
☐ 113. LUIS LEAL
☐ 114. BUCK MARTINEZ
☐ 115. LLOYD MOSEBY

☐ 116. RANCE MULLINIKS
☐ 117. DAVE STIEB
☐ 118. WILLIE UPSHAW
☐ 119. ERNIE WHITT
☐ 645. KELLY GRUBER(P)
☐ 655 TEAM CHECKLIST(F)

1985 FLEER
TRADED (132)
2 1/2 X 3 1/2

ATLANTA BRAVES

☐ 24U. RICK CERONE
☐ 114U. BRUCE SUTTER

BALTIMORE ORIOLES

☐ 1U. DON AASE
☐ 30U. FRITZ CONNALLY
☐ 36U. KEN DIXON
☐ 67U. LEE LACY
☐ 75U. FRED LYNN
☐ 101U. LARRY SHEETS
☐ 107U. NATE SNELL

BOSTON RED SOX

☐ 65U. BRUCE KISON
☐ 76U. STEVE LYONS

CALIFORNIA ANGELS

☐ 26U. PAT CLEMENTS
☐ 27U. STEWART CLIBURN
☐ 63U. RUPPERT JONES
☐ 74U. URBANO LUGO
☐ 82U. DONNIE MOORE

CHICAGO CUBS

☐ 35U. BRIAN DAYETT
☐ 42U. RAY FONTENOT
☐ 108U. LARY SORENSEN
☐ 109U. CHRIS SPEIER

CHICAGO WHITE SOX

☐ 9U. DARYL BOSTON
☐ 39U. BOB FALLON
☐ 44U. OSCAR GAMBLE
☐ 48U. OZZIE GUILLEN
☐ 59U. TIM HULETT
☐ 60U. BOB JAMES
☐ 73U. TIM LOLLAR
☐ 95U. LUIS SALAZAR
☐ 116U. BRUCE TANNER

CINCINNATI REDS

☐ 12U. TOM BROWNING
☐ 112U. JOHN STUPER

CLEVELAND INDIANS

☐ 93U. VERN RUHLE
☐ 120U. RICH THOMPSON
☐ 126U. DAVE VON OHLEN

1985 Fleer Traded

DETROIT TIGERS

- [ ] 87U. CHRIS PITTARO
- [ ] 98U. ALEX SANCHEZ
- [ ] 103U. NELSON SIMMONS
- [ ] 118U. WALT TERRELL

HOUSTON ASTROS

- [ ] 18U. JEFF CALHOUN
- [ ] 78U. RON MATHIS

KANSAS CITY ROYALS

- [ ] 66U. MIKE LACOSS
- [ ] 106U. LONNIE SMITH
- [ ] 113U. JIM SUNDBERG

LOS ANGELES DODGERS

- [ ] 22U. BOBBY CASTILLO
- [ ] 38U. MARIANO DUNCAN
- [ ] 84U. AL OLIVER

MILWAUKEE BREWERS

- [ ] 15U. RAY BURRIS
- [ ] 32U. DANNY DARWIN
- [ ] 54U. TEDDY HIGUERA
- [ ] 89U. EARNIE RILES

MINNESOTA TWINS

- [ ] 43U. GREG GAGNE
- [ ] 94U. MARK SALAS
- [ ] 105U. ROY SMALLEY
- [ ] 110U. MIKE STENHOUSE
- [ ] 127U. CURT WARDLE
- [ ] 131U. RICH YETT

MONTREAL EXPOS

- [ ] 10U. HUBIE BROOKS
- [ ] 14U. TIM BURKE
- [ ] 41U. MIKE FITZGERALD
- [ ] 70U. VANCE LAW
- [ ] 77U. MICKEY MAHLER
- [ ] 128U. U.L. WASHINGTON
- [ ] 130U. HERM WINNINGHAM

NEW YORK METS

- [ ] 21U. GARY CARTER
- [ ] 62U. HOWARD JOHNSON
- [ ] 81U. ROGER MCDOWELL
- [ ] 96U. JOE SAMBITO
- [ ] 99U. CALVIN SCHIRALDI

NEW YORK YANKEES

- [ ] 4U. DALE BERRA
- [ ] 8U. RICH BORDI
- [ ] 31U. HENRY COTTO
- [ ] 40U. BRIAN FISHER
- [ ] 50U. RON HASSEY
- [ ] 51U. RICKEY HENDERSON
- [ ] 86U. DAN PASQUA
- [ ] 97U. BILLY SAMPLE
- [ ] 129U. ED WHITSOM

OAKLAND A'S

- [ ] 3U. DUSTY BAKER
- [ ] 6U. TIM BIRTSAS
- [ ] 29U. DAVE COLLINS
- [ ] 47U. ALFREDO GRIFFIN
- [ ] 52U. STEVE HENDERSON
- [ ] 57U. JAY HOWELL
- [ ] 115U. DON SUTTON
- [ ] 119U. MICKEY TETTLETON

PHILADELPHIA PHILLIES

- [ ] 20U. DON CARMAN
- [ ] 33U. DARREN DAULTON
- [ ] 92U. DAVE RUCKER
- [ ] 100U. RICK SCHU
- [ ] 117U. KENT TEKULVE

PITTSBURGH PIRATES

- [ ] 2U. BILL ALMON
- [ ] 53U. GEORGE HENDRICK
- [ ] 55U. AL HOLLAND
- [ ] 64U. STEVE KEMP
- [ ] 72U. SIXTO LEZCANO
- [ ] 85U. JOE ORSULAK
- [ ] 88U. RICK REUSCHEL

ST. LOUIS CARDINALS

- [ ] 19U. BILL CAMPBELL
- [ ] 25U. JACK CLARK
- [ ] 28U. VINCE COLEMAN
- [ ] 123U. JOHN TUDOR

SAN DIEGO PADRES

- [ ] 13U. AL BUMBRY
- [ ] 34U. JERRY DAVIS
- [ ] 58U. LAMARR HOYT
- [ ] 90U JERRY ROYSTER
- [ ] 111U. TIM STODDARD

SAN FRANCISCO GIANTS

- [ ] 7U. VIDA BLUE
- [ ] 11U. CHRIS BROWN
- [ ] 45U. JIM GOTT
- [ ] 46U. DAVID GREEN
- [ ] 68U. DAVE LAPOINT
- [ ] 122U. ALEX TREVINO
- [ ] 124U. JOSE URIBE

SEATTLE MARINERS

- [ ] 5U. KARL BEST
- [ ] 17U. IVAN CALDERON
- [ ] 125U. DAVE VALLE

TEXAS RANGERS

- [ ] 37U. TOMMY DUNBAR
- [ ] 49U. TOBY HARRAH
- [ ] 56U. BURT HOOTON
- [ ] 61U. CLIFF JOHNSON
- [ ] 80U. ODDIBE MCDOWELL
- [ ] 91U. DAVE ROZEMA
- [ ] 104U. DON SLAUGHT

TORONTO BLUE JAYS

- [ ] 16U. JEFF BURROUGHS
- [ ] 23U. BILL CAUDILL
- [ ] 69U. GARY LAVELLE
- [ ] 71U. MANNY LEE
- [ ] 79U. LEN MATUSZEK
- [ ] 83U. RON MUSSELMAN
- [ ] 102U. RON SHEPHERD
- [ ] 121U. LOUIS THORNTON

1986 FLEER (660)
2 1/2 X 3 1/2

ATLANTA BRAVES

- [ ] 507. LEN BARKER
- [ ] 508. STEVE BEDROSIAN
- [ ] 509. BRUCE BENEDICT
- [ ] 510. RICK CAMP
- [ ] 511. RICK CERONE
- [ ] 512. CHRIS CHAMBLISS
- [ ] 513. JEFF DEDMON
- [ ] 514. TERRY FORSTER
- [ ] 515. GENE GARBER
- [ ] 516. TERRY HARPER
- [ ] 517. BOB HORNER
- [ ] 518. GLENN HUBBARD
- [ ] 519. JOE JOHNSON
- [ ] 520. BRAD KOMMINSK
- [ ] 521. RICK MAHLER
- [ ] 522. DALE MURPHY
- [ ] 523. KEN OBERKFELL
- [ ] 524. PASCUAL PEREZ
- [ ] 525. GERALD PERRY
- [ ] 526. RAFAEL RAMIREZ
- [ ] 527. STEVE SHIELDS
- [ ] 528. ZANE SMITH
- [ ] 529. BRUCE SUTTER
- [ ] 530. MILT THOMPSON
- [ ] 531. CLAUDELL WASHINGTON
- [ ] 532. PAUL ZUVELLA
- [ ] 659. TEAM CHECKLIST(F)

BALTIMORE ORIOLES

- [ ] 268. DON AASE
- [ ] 269. MIKE BODDICKER
- [ ] 270. RICH DAUER
- [ ] 271. STORM DAVIS
- [ ] 272. RICK DEMPSEY
- [ ] 273. KEN DIXON
- [ ] 274. JIM DWYER
- [ ] 275. MIKE FLANAGAN
- [ ] 276. WAYNE GROSS
- [ ] 277. LEE LACY
- [ ] 278. FRED LYNN
- [ ] 279. DENNIS MARTINEZ
- [ ] 280. TIPPY MARTINEZ
- [ ] 281. SCOTT MCGREGOR
- [ ] 282. EDDIE MURRAY
- [ ] 283. FLOYD RAYFORD
- [ ] 284. CAL RIPKEN
- [ ] 285. GARY ROENICKE
- [ ] 286. LARRY SHEETS
- [ ] 287. JOHN SHELBY
- [ ] 288. NATE SNELL
- [ ] 289. SAMMY STEWART
- [ ] 290. ALAN WIGGINS
- [ ] 291. MIKE YOUNG
- [ ] 656. TEAM CHECKLIST(B)

BOSTON RED SOX

- ☐ 339. TONY ARMAS
- ☐ 340. MARTY BARRETT
- ☐ 341. WADE BOGGS
- ☐ 342. DENNIS BOYD
- ☐ 343. BILL BUCKNER
- ☐ 344. MARK CLEAR
- ☐ 345. ROGER CLEMENS
- ☐ 346. STEVE CRAWFORD
- ☐ 347. MIKE EASLER
- ☐ 348. DWIGHT EVANS
- ☐ 349. RICH GEDMAN
- ☐ 350. JACKIE GUTIERREZ
- ☐ 351. GLENN HOFFMAN
- ☐ 352. BRUCE HURST
- ☐ 353. BRUCE KISON
- ☐ 354. TIM LOLLAR
- ☐ 355. STEVE LYONS
- ☐ 356. AL NIPPER
- ☐ 357. BOB OJEDA
- ☐ 358. JIM RICE
- ☐ 359. BOB STANLEY
- ☐ 360. MIKE TRUJILLO
- ☐ 651. ROB WOODWARD(P)
- ☐ 657. TEAM CHECKLIST(B)

CALIFORNIA ANGELS

- ☐ 148. JUAN BENIQUEZ
- ☐ 149. BOB BOONE
- ☐ 150. JOHN CANDELARIA
- ☐ 151. ROD CAREW
- ☐ 152. STEWARD CLIBURN
- ☐ 153. DOUG DECINCES
- ☐ 154. BRIAN DOWNING
- ☐ 155. KEN FORSCH
- ☐ 156. CRAIG GERBER
- ☐ 157. BOBBY GRICH
- ☐ 158. GEORGE HENDRICK
- ☐ 159. AL HOLLAND
- ☐ 160. REGGIE JACKSON
- ☐ 161. RUPPERT JONES
- ☐ 162. URBANO LUGO
- ☐ 163. KIRK MCCASKILL
- ☐ 164. DONNIE MOORE
- ☐ 165. GARY PETTIS
- ☐ 166. RON ROMANICK

CALIFORNIA ANGELS

- ☐ 148. JUAN BENIQUEZ
- ☐ 149. BOB BOONE
- ☐ 150. JOHN CANDELARIA
- ☐ 151. ROD CAREW
- ☐ 152. STEWART CLIBURN
- ☐ 153. DOUG DECINCES
- ☐ 154. BRIAN DOWNING
- ☐ 155. KEN FORSCH ·
- ☐ 156. CRAIG GERBER
- ☐ 157. BOBBY GRICH
- ☐ 158. GEORGE HENDRICK
- ☐ 159. AL HOLLAND
- ☐ 160. REGGIE JACKSON
- ☐ 161. RUPPERT JONES
- ☐ 162. URBANO LUGO
- ☐ 163. KIRK MCCASKILL
- ☐ 164. DONNIE MOORE
- ☐ 165. GARY PETTIS
- ☐ 166. RON ROMANICK
- ☐ 167. DICK SCHOFIELD
- ☐ 168. DARYL SCONIERS
- ☐ 169. JIM SLATON
- ☐ 170. DON SUTTON
- ☐ 171. MIKE WITT
- ☐ 650. GUS POLIDOR(P)
- ☐ 650. MARK MCLEMORE(P)
- ☐ 655. TEAM CHECKLIST(B)

CHICAGO CUBS

- ☐ 361. THAD BOSLEY
- ☐ 362. WARREN BRUSSTAR
- ☐ 363. RON CEY
- ☐ 364. JODY DAVIS
- ☐ 365. BOB DERNIER
- ☐ 366. SHAWON DUNSTON
- ☐ 367. LEON DURHAM
- ☐ 368. DENNIS ECKERSLEY
- ☐ 369. RAY FONTENOT
- ☐ 370. GEORGE FRAZIER

- ☐ 371. BILL HATCHER
- ☐ 372. DAVE LOPES
- ☐ 373. GARY MATTHEWS
- ☐ 374. RON MEREDITH
- ☐ 375. KEITH MORELAND
- ☐ 376. REGGIE PATTERSON
- ☐ 377. DICK RUTHVEN
- ☐ 378. RYNE SANDBERG
- ☐ 379. SCOTT SANDERSON
- ☐ 380. LEE SMITH
- ☐ 381. LARY SORENSEN
- ☐ 382. CHRIS SPEIER
- ☐ 383. RICK SUTCLIFFE
- ☐ 384. STEVE TROUT
- ☐ 385. GARY WOODS
- ☐ 657. TEAM CHECKLIST(B)

CHICAGO WHITE SOX

- ☐ 197. JUAN AGOSTO
- ☐ 198. HAROLD BAINES
- ☐ 199. FLOYD BANNISTER
- ☐ 200. BRITT BURNS
- ☐ 201. JULIO CRUZ
- ☐ 202. JOEL DAVIS
- ☐ 203. RICHARD DOTSON
- ☐ 204. CARLTON FISK
- ☐ 205. SCOTT FLETCHER
- ☐ 206. OZZIE GUILLEN
- ☐ 207. JERRY HAIRSTON
- ☐ 208. TIM HULETT
- ☐ 209. BOB JAMES
- ☐ 210. RON KITTLE
- ☐ 211. RUDY LAW
- ☐ 212. BRYAN LITTLE
- ☐ 213. GENE NELSON
- ☐ 214. REID NICHOLS
- ☐ 215. LUIS SALAZAR
- ☐ 216. TOM SEAVER
- ☐ 217. DAN SPILLNER
- ☐ 218. BRUCE TANNER
- ☐ 219. GREG WALKER
- ☐ 220. DAVE WEHRMEISTER
- ☐ 656. TEAM CHECKLIST(F)

CINCINNATI REDS

- ☐ 172. BUDDY BELL
- ☐ 173. TOM BROWNING
- ☐ 174. DAVE CONCEPCION
- ☐ 175. ERIC DAVIS
- ☐ 176. BO DIAZ
- ☐ 177. NICK ESASKY
- ☐ 178. JOHN FRANCO
- ☐ 179. TOM HUME
- ☐ 180. WAYNE KRENCHICKI
- ☐ 181. ANDY MCGAFFIGAN
- ☐ 182. EDDIE MILNER
- ☐ 183. RON OESTER
- ☐ 184. DAVE PARKER
- ☐ 185. FRANK PASTORE
- ☐ 186. TONY PEREZ
- ☐ 187. TED POWER
- ☐ 188. JOE PRICE
- ☐ 189. GARY REDUS
- ☐ 190. RON ROBINSON
- ☐ 191. PETE ROSE(M)
- ☐ 192. MARIO SOTO
- ☐ 193. JOHN STUPER
- ☐ 194. JAY TIBBS
- ☐ 195. DAVE VAN GORDER
- ☐ 196. MAX VENABLE
- ☐ 646. KAL DANIELS(P)
- ☐ 646. PAUL O'NEILL(P)
- ☐ 655. TEAM CHECKLIST(B)

CLEVELAND INDIANS

- ☐ 579. CHRIS BANDO
- ☐ 580. TONY BERNAZARD
- ☐ 581. BRETT BUTLER
- ☐ 582. ERNIE CAMACHO
- ☐ 583. JOE CARTER
- ☐ 584. CARMEN CASTILLO
- ☐ 585. JAMIE EASTERLY
- ☐ 586. JULIO FRANCO
- ☐ 587. MEL HALL
- ☐ 588. MIKE HARGROVE
- ☐ 589. NEAL HEATON
- ☐ 590. BROOK JACOBY

- ☐ 591. OTIS NIXON
- ☐ 592. JERRY REED
- ☐ 593. VERN RUHLE
- ☐ 594. PAT TABLER
- ☐ 595. RICH THOMPSON
- ☐ 596. ANDRE THORNTON
- ☐ 597. DAVE VON OHLEN
- ☐ 598. GEORGE VUKOVICH
- ☐ 599. TOM WADDELL
- ☐ 600. CURT WARDLE
- ☐ 601. JERRY WILLARD
- ☐ 653. CORY SNYDER(P)
- ☐ 660. TEAM CHECKLIST(F)

DETROIT TIGERS

- ☐ 221. JUAN BERENGUER
- ☐ 222. DAVE BERGMAN
- ☐ 223. TOM BROOKENS
- ☐ 224. DARRELL EVANS
- ☐ 225. BARBARO GARBEY
- ☐ 226. KIRK GIBSON
- ☐ 227. JOHN GRUBB
- ☐ 228. WILLIE HERNANDEZ
- ☐ 229. LARRY HERNDON
- ☐ 230. CHET LEMON
- ☐ 231. AURELIO LOPEZ
- ☐ 232. JACK MORRIS
- ☐ 233. RANDY O'NEAL
- ☐ 234. LANCE PARRISH
- ☐ 235. DAN PETRY
- ☐ 236. ALEX SANCHEZ
- ☐ 237. BILL SCHERRER
- ☐ 238. NELSON SIMMONS
- ☐ 239. FRANK TANANA
- ☐ 240. WALT TERRELL
- ☐ 241. ALAN TRAMMELL
- ☐ 242. LOU WHITAKER
- ☐ 243. MILT WILCOX
- ☐ 656. TEAM CHECKLIST(F)

BARBARO GARBEY
OUTFIELD • DN

HOUSTON ASTROS

- ☐ 292. ALAN ASHBY
- ☐ 293. MARK BAILEY
- ☐ 294. KEVIN BASS
- ☐ 295. JEFF CALHOUN
- ☐ 296. JOSE CRUZ
- ☐ 297. GLENN DAVIS
- ☐ 298. BILL DAWLEY
- ☐ 299. FRANK DIPINO
- ☐ 300. BILL DORAN
- ☐ 301. PHIL GARNER
- ☐ 302. JEFF HEATHCOCK
- ☐ 303. CHARLIE KERFELD
- ☐ 304. BOB KNEPPER
- ☐ 305. RON MATHIS
- ☐ 306. JERRY MUMPHREY
- ☐ 307. JIM PANKOVITS
- ☐ 308. TERRY PUHL
- ☐ 309. CRAIG REYNOLDS
- ☐ 310. NOLAN RYAN
- ☐ 311. MIKE SCOTT
- ☐ 312. DAVE SMITH
- ☐ 313. DICKIE THON
- ☐ 314. DENNY WALLING
- ☐ 657. TEAM CHECKLIST(F)

KANSAS CITY ROYALS

- ☐ 1. STEVE BALBONI
- ☐ 2. JOE BECKWITH
- ☐ 3. BUDDY BIANCALANA
- ☐ 4. BUD BLACK
- ☐ 5. GEORGE BRETT
- ☐ 6. ONIX CONCEPCION
- ☐ 7. STEVE FARR
- ☐ 8. MARK GUBICZA
- ☐ 9. DANE IORG
- ☐ 10. DANNY JACKSON
- ☐ 11. LYNN JONES
- ☐ 12. MIKE JONES
- ☐ 13. CHARLIE LEIBRANDT
- ☐ 14. HAL MCRAE
- ☐ 15. OMAR MORENO
- ☐ 16. DARRYL MOTLEY
- ☐ 17. JORGE ORTA
- ☐ 18. DAN QUISENBERRY
- ☐ 19. BRET SABERHAGEN
- ☐ 20. PAT SHERIDAN
- ☐ 21. LONNIE SMITH
- ☐ 22. JIM SUNDBERG
- ☐ 23. JOHN WATHAN
- ☐ 24. FRANK WHITE
- ☐ 25. WILLIE WILSON
- ☐ 654. TEAM CHECKLIST(F)

LOS ANGELES DODGERS

- ☐ 123. DAVE ANDERSON
- ☐ 124. BOB BAILOR
- ☐ 125. GREG BROCK
- ☐ 126. ENOS CABELL
- ☐ 127. BOBBY CASTILLO
- ☐ 128. CARLOS DIAZ
- ☐ 129. MARIANO DUNCAN
- ☐ 130. PEDRO GUERRERO
- ☐ 131. OREL HERSHISER
- ☐ 132. RICK HONEYCUTT
- ☐ 133. KEN HOWELL
- ☐ 134. KEN LANDREAUX
- ☐ 135. BILL MADLOCK
- ☐ 136. CANDY MALDONADO
- ☐ 137. MIKE MARSHALL
- ☐ 138. LEN MATUSZEK
- ☐ 139. TOM NIEDENFUER
- ☐ 140. ALEJANDRO PENA
- ☐ 141. JERRY REUSS
- ☐ 142. BILL RUSSELL
- ☐ 143. STEVE SAX
- ☐ 144. MIKE SCIOSCIA
- ☐ 145. FERNANDO VALENZUELA
- ☐ 146. BOB WELCH
- ☐ 147. TERRY WHITFIELD
- ☐ 655. TEAM CHECKLIST(F)

MILWAUKEE BREWERS

- ☐ 482. RAY BURRIS
- ☐ 483. JAIME COCANOWER
- ☐ 484. CECIL COOPER
- ☐ 485. DANNY DARWIN
- ☐ 486. ROLLIE FINGERS
- ☐ 487. JIM GANTNER
- ☐ 488. BOB GIBSON
- ☐ 489. MOOSE HAAS
- ☐ 490. TEDDY HIGUERA
- ☐ 491. PAUL HOUSEHOLDER
- ☐ 492. PETE LADD
- ☐ 493. RICK MANNING
- ☐ 494. BOB MCCLURE
- ☐ 495. PAUL MOLITOR
- ☐ 496. CHARLIE MOORE
- ☐ 497. BEN OGLIVIE
- ☐ 498. RANDY READY
- ☐ 499. EARNIE RILES
- ☐ 500. ED ROMERO
- ☐ 501. BILL SCHROEDER
- ☐ 502. RAY SEARAGE
- ☐ 503. TED SIMMONS
- ☐ 504. PETE VUCKOVICH
- ☐ 505. RICK WAITS
- ☐ 506. ROBIN YOUNT
- ☐ 652. BILLY JOE ROBIDOUX(P)
- ☐ 659. TEAM CHECKLIST(F)

KIRBY PUCKETT

MINNESOTA TWINS

- ☐ 386. BERT BLYLEVEN
- ☐ 387. TOM BRUNANSKY
- ☐ 388. RANDY BUSH
- ☐ 389. JOHN BUTCHER
- ☐ 390. RON DAVIS
- ☐ 391. DAVE ENGLE
- ☐ 392. FRANK EUFEMIA
- ☐ 393. PETE FILSON
- ☐ 394. GARY GAETTI
- ☐ 395. GREG GAGNE
- ☐ 396. MICKEY HATCHER
- ☐ 397. KENT HRBEK
- ☐ 398. TIM LAUDNER
- ☐ 399. RICK LYSANDER
- ☐ 400. DAVE MEIER
- ☐ 401. KIRBY PUCKETT
- ☐ 402. MARK SALAS
- ☐ 403. KEN SCHROM
- ☐ 404. ROY SMALLEY
- ☐ 405. MIKE SMITHSON
- ☐ 406. MIKE STENHOUSE
- ☐ 407. TIM TEUFEL
- ☐ 408. FRANK VIOLA
- ☐ 409. RON WASHINGTON
- ☐ 652. MARK FUNDERBURK(P)
- ☐ 658. TEAM CHECKLIST(F)

MONTREAL EXPOS

- ☐ 244. HUBIE BROOKS
- ☐ 245. TIM BURKE
- ☐ 246. ANDRE DAWSON
- ☐ 247. MIKE FITZGERALD
- ☐ 248. TERRY FRANCONA
- ☐ 249. BILL GULLICKSON
- ☐ 250. JOE HESKETH
- ☐ 251. BILL LASKEY
- ☐ 252. VANCE LAW
- ☐ 253. CHARLIE LEA
- ☐ 254. GARY LUCAS
- ☐ 255. DAVID PALMER
- ☐ 256. TIM RAINES
- ☐ 257. JEFF REARDON
- ☐ 258. BERT ROBERGE
- ☐ 259. DAN SCHATZEDER
- ☐ 260. BRYN SMITH
- ☐ 261. RANDY ST. CLAIRE
- ☐ 262. SCOT THOMPSON
- ☐ 263. TIM WALLACH
- ☐ 264. U.L. WASHINGTON
- ☐ 265. MITCH WEBSTER
- ☐ 266. HERM WINNINGHAM
- ☐ 267. FLOYD YOUMANS
- ☐ 647. ANDRES GALARRAGA(P)
- ☐ 656. TEAM CHECKLIST(B)

NEW YORK METS

- ☐ 74. RICK AGUILERA
- ☐ 75. WALLY BACKMAN
- ☐ 76. GARY CARTER
- ☐ 77. RON DARLING
- ☐ 78. LEN DYKSTRA
- ☐ 79. SID FERNANDEZ
- ☐ 80. GEORGE FOSTER
- ☐ 81. DWIGHT GOODEN
- ☐ 82. TOM GORMAN
- ☐ 83. DANNY HEEP

- ☐ 84. KEITH HERNANDEZ
- ☐ 85. HOWARD JOHNSON
- ☐ 86. RAY KNIGHT
- ☐ 87. TERRY LEACH
- ☐ 88. ED LYNCH
- ☐ 89. ROGER MCDOWELL
- ☐ 90. JESSE OROSCO
- ☐ 91. TOM PACIOREK
- ☐ 92. RONN REYNOLDS
- ☐ 93. RAFAEL SANTANA
- ☐ 94. DOUG SISK
- ☐ 95. RUSTY STAUB
- ☐ 96. DARRYL STRAWBERRY
- ☐ 97. MOOKIE WILSON
- ☐ 654. TEAM CHECKLIST

NEW YORK YANKEES

- ☐ 98. NEIL ALLEN
- ☐ 99. DON BAYLOR
- ☐ 100. DALE BERRA
- ☐ 101. RICH BORDI
- ☐ 102. MARTY BYSTROM
- ☐ 103. JOE COWLEY
- ☐ 104. BRIAN FISHER
- ☐ 105. KEN GRIFFEY
- ☐ 106. RON GUIDRY
- ☐ 107. RON HASSEY
- ☐ 108. RICKEY HENDERSON
- ☐ 109. DON MATTINGLY
- ☐ 110. BOBBY MEACHAM
- ☐ 111. JOHN MONTEFUSCO
- ☐ 112. PHIL NIEKRO
- ☐ 113. MIKE PAGLIARULO
- ☐ 114. DAN PASQUA
- ☐ 115. WILLIE RANDOLPH
- ☐ 116. DAVE RIGHETTI
- ☐ 117. ANDRE ROBERTSON
- ☐ 118. BILLY SAMPLE
- ☐ 119. BOB SHIRLEY
- ☐ 120. ED WHITSON
- ☐ 121. DAVE WINFIELD
- ☐ 122. BUTCH WYNEGAR
- ☐ 655. TEAM CHECKLIST(F)

OAKLAND A'S

- ☐ 410. KEITH ATHERTON
- ☐ 411. DUSTY BAKER
- ☐ 412. TIM BIRTSAS
- ☐ 413. BRUCE BOCHTE
- ☐ 414. CHRIS CODIROLLI
- ☐ 415. DAVE COLLINS
- ☐ 416. MIKE DAVIS
- ☐ 417. ALFREDO GRIFFIN
- ☐ 418. MIKE HEATH
- ☐ 419. STEVE HENDERSON
- ☐ 420. DONNIE HILL
- ☐ 421. JAY HOWELL
- ☐ 422. TOMMY JOHN
- ☐ 423. DAVE KINGMAN
- ☐ 424. BILL KRUEGER
- ☐ 425. RICK LANGFORD
- ☐ 426. CARNEY LANSFORD
- ☐ 427. STEVE MCCATTY
- ☐ 428. DWAYNE MURPHY
- ☐ 429. STEVE ONTIVEROS
- ☐ 430. TONY PHILLIPS
- ☐ 431. JOSE RIJO
- ☐ 432. MICKEY TETTLETON
- ☐ 649. ERIC PLUNK(P)
- ☐ 649. JOSE CANSECO(P)
- ☐ 658. TEAM CHECKLIST(F)

PHILADELPHIA PHILLIES

- ☐ 433. LUIS AGUAYO
- ☐ 434. LARRY ANDERSEN
- ☐ 435. STEVE CARLTON
- ☐ 436. DON CARMAN
- ☐ 437. TIM CORCORAN
- ☐ 438. DARREN DAULTON
- ☐ 439. JOHN DENNY
- ☐ 440. TOM FOLEY
- ☐ 441. GREG GROSS
- ☐ 442. KEVIN GROSS
- ☐ 443. VON HAYES
- ☐ 444. CHARLES HUDSON
- ☐ 445. GARRY MADDOX
- ☐ 446. SHANE RAWLEY

□ 447. DAVE RUCKER
□ 448. JOHN RUSSELL
□ 449. JUAN SAMUEL
□ 450. MIKE SCHMIDT
□ 451. RICH SCHU
□ 452. DAVE SHIPANOFF
□ 453. DAVE STEWART
□ 454. JEFF STONE
□ 455. KENT TEKULVE
□ 456. OZZIE VIRGIL
□ 457. GLENN WILSON
□ 647. FRED TOLIVER(P)
□ 658. TEAM CHECKLIST(B)

PITTSBURGH PIRATES

□ 602. BILL ALMON
□ 603. MIKE BIELECKI
□ 604. SID BREAM
□ 605. MIKE BROWN
□ 606. PAT CLEMENTS
□ 607. JOSE DELEON
□ 608. DENNY GONZALEZ
□ 609. CECILIO GUANTE
□ 610. STEVE KEMP
□ 611. SAM KHALIFA
□ 612. LEE MAZZILLI
□ 613. LARRY MCWILLIAMS
□ 614. JIM MORRISON
□ 615. JOE ORSULAK
□ 616. TONY PENA
□ 617. JOHNNY RAY
□ 618. RICK REUSCHEL
□ 619. R.J. REYNOLDS
□ 620. RICK RHODEN
□ 621. DON ROBINSON
□ 622. JASON THOMPSON
□ 623. LEE TUNNELL
□ 624. JIM WINN
□ 625. MARVELL WYNNE
□ 648. BOB KIPPER(P)
□ 660. TEAM CHECKLIST(F)

ST. LOUIS CARDINALS

□ 26. JOAQUIN ANDUJAR
□ 27. STEVE BRAUN
□ 28. BILL CAMPBELL
□ 29. CESAR CEDENO
□ 30. JACK CLARK
□ 31. VINCE COLEMAN
□ 32. DANNY COX
□ 33. KEN DAYLEY
□ 34. IVAN DEJESUS
□ 35. BOB FORSCH
□ 36. BRIAN HARPER
□ 37. TOM HERR
□ 38. RICKY HORTON
□ 39. KURT KEPSHIRE
□ 40. JEFF LAHTI
□ 41. TITO LANDRUM
□ 42. WILLIE MCGEE
□ 43. TOM NIETO
□ 44. TERRY PENDLETON
□ 45. DARRELL PORTER
□ 46. OZZIE SMITH
□ 47. JOHN TUDOR
□ 48. ANDY VAN SLYKE
□ 49. TODD WORRELL
□ 648. CURT FORD(P)
□ 654. TEAM CHECKLIST(F)

SAN DIEGO PADRES

□ 315. KURT BEVACQUA
□ 316. AL BUMBRY
□ 317. JERRY DAVIS
□ 318. LUIS DELEON
□ 319. DAVE DRAVECKY
□ 320. TIM FLANNERY
□ 321. STEVE GARVEY
□ 322. GOOSE GOSSAGE
□ 323. TONY GWYNN
□ 324. ANDY HAWKINS
□ 325. LAMARR HOYT
□ 326. ROY LEE JACKSON
□ 327. TERRY KENNEDY
□ 328. CRAIG LEFFERTS
□ 329. CARMELO MARTINEZ
□ 330. LANCE MCCULLERS
□ 331. KEVIN MCREYNOLDS

□ 332. GRAIG NETTLES
□ 333. JERRY ROYSTER
□ 334. ERIC SHOW
□ 335. TIM STODDARD
□ 336. GARRY TEMPLETON
□ 337. MARK THURMOND
□ 338. ED WOJNA
□ 644. BENITO SANTIAGO(P)
□ 644. GENE WALTER(P)
□ 651. TEAM CHECKLIST(F)

SAN FRANCISCO GIANTS

□ 533. VIDA BLUE
□ 534. BOB BRENLEY
□ 535. CHRIS BROWN
□ 536. CHILI DAVIS
□ 537. MARK DAVIS
□ 538. ROB DEER
□ 539. DAN DRIESSEN
□ 540. SCOTT GARRELTS
□ 541. DAN GLADDEN
□ 542. JIM GOTT
□ 543. DAVID GREEN
□ 544. ATLEE HAMMAKER
□ 545. MIKE JEFFCOAT
□ 546. MIKE KRUKOW
□ 547. DAVE LAPOINT
□ 548. JEFF LEONARD
□ 549. GREG MINTON
□ 550. ALEX TREVINO
□ 551. MANNY TRILLO
□ 552. JOSE URIBE
□ 553. BRAD WELLMAN
□ 554. FRANK WILLIAMS
□ 555. JOEL YOUNGBLOOD
□ 645. MIKE WOODARD(P)
□ 645. COLIN WARD(P)
□ 659. TEAM CHECKLIST(B)

SEATTLE MARINERS

□ 458. JIM BEATTIE
□ 459. KARL BEST
□ 460. BARRY BONNELL
□ 461. PHIL BRADLEY
□ 462. IVAN CALDERON
□ 463. AL COWENS
□ 464. ALVIN DAVIS
□ 465. DAVE HENDERSON
□ 466. BOB KEARNEY
□ 467. MARK LANGSTON
□ 468. BOB LONG
□ 469. MIKE MOORE
□ 470. EDWIN NUNEZ
□ 471. SPIKE OWEN
□ 472. JACK PERCONTE
□ 473. JIM PRESLEY
□ 474. DONNIE SCOTT
□ 475. BILL SWIFT
□ 476. DANNY TARTABULL
□ 477. GORMAN THOMAS
□ 478. ROY THOMAS
□ 479. ED VANDE BERG
□ 480. FRANK WILLS
□ 481. MATT YOUNG
□ 651. MICKEY BRANTLEY(P)
□ 658. TEAM CHECKLIST(B)

TEXAS RANGERS

□ 556. ALAN BANNISTER
□ 557. GLENN BRUMMER
□ 558. STEVE BUECHELE
□ 559. JOSE GUZMAN
□ 560. TOBY HARRAH
□ 561. GREG HARRIS
□ 562. DWAYNE HENRY
□ 563. BURT HOOTON
□ 564. CHARLIE HOUGH
□ 565. MIKE MASON
□ 566. ODDIBE MCDOWELL
□ 567. DICKIE NOLES
□ 568. PETE O'BRIEN
□ 569. LARRY PARRISH
□ 570. DAVE ROZEMA
□ 571. DAVE SCHMIDT
□ 572. DON SLAUGHT
□ 573. WAYNE TOLLESON
□ 574. DUANE WALKER

□ 575. GARY WARD
□ 576. CHRIS WELSH
□ 577. CURTIS WILKERSON
□ 578. GEORGE WRIGHT
□ 659. TEAM CHECKLIST(B)

TORONTO BLUE JAYS

□ 50. JIM ACKER
□ 51. DOYLE ALEXANDER
□ 52. JESSE BARFIELD
□ 53. GEORGE BELL
□ 54. JEFF BURROUGHS
□ 55. BILL CAUDILL
□ 56. JIM CLANCY
□ 57. TONY FERNANDEZ
□ 58. TOM FILER
□ 59. DAMASO GARCIA
□ 60. TOM HENKE
□ 61. GARTH IORG
□ 62. CLIFF JOHNSON
□ 63. JIMMY KEY
□ 64. DENNIS LAMP
□ 65. GARY LAVELLE
□ 66. BUCK MARTINEZ
□ 67. LLOYD MOSEBY
□ 68. RANCE MULLINIKS
□ 69. AL OLIVER
□ 70. DAVE STIEB
□ 71. LOUIS THORNTON
□ 72. WILLIE UPSHAW
□ 73. ERNIE WHITT
□ 653. CECIL FIELDER(P)
□ 654. TEAM CHECKLIST(B)

1986 FLEER TRADED (132) 2 1/2 X 3 1/2

ATLANTA BRAVES

□ 5U. PAUL ASSENMACHER
□ 78U. OMAR MORENO
□ 87U. DAVID PALMER
□ 102U. BILLY SAMPLE
□ 106U. TED SIMMONS
□ 112U. ANDRES THOMAS
□ 122U. OZZIE VIRGIL
□ 125U. DUANE WARD

BALTIMORE ORIOLES

□ 13U. JUAN BENIQUEZ
□ 16U. RICH BORDI
□ 47U. JACKIE GUTIERREZ

BOSTON RED SOX

□ 10U. DON BAYLOR
□ 93U. REY QUINONEZ
□ 101U. JOE SAMBITO
□ 107U. SAMMY STEWART

CALIFORNIA ANGELS

□ 42U. TERRY FORSTER
□ 59U. WALLY JOYNER

CHICAGO CUBS

- [ ] 7U. JAY BALLER
- [ ] 43U. TERRY FRANCONA
- [ ] 51U. GUY HOFFMAN
- [ ] 79U. JERRY MUMPHREY
- [ ] 120U. MANNY TRILLO

CHICAGO WHITE SOX

- [ ] 3U. NEIL ALLEN
- [ ] 15U. BOBBY BONILLA
- [ ] 19U. JOHN CANGELOSI
- [ ] 31U. JOE COWLEY
- [ ] 32U. BILL DAWLEY
- [ ] 75U. JOEL MCKEON
- [ ] 103U. DAVE SCHMIDT
- [ ] 118U. WAYNE TOLLESON

CINCINNATI REDS

- [ ] 34U. JOHN DENNY
- [ ] 46U. BILL GULLICKSON
- [ ] 58U. TRACY JONES
- [ ] 108U. KURT STILLWELL

CLEVELAND INDIANS

- [ ] 2U. ANDY ALLANSON
- [ ] 6U. SCOTT BAILES
- [ ] 18U. TOM CANDIOTTI
- [ ] 81U. PHIL NIEKRO
- [ ] 104U. KEN SCHROM

DETROIT TIGERS

- [ ] 17U. BILL CAMPBELL
- [ ] 21U. CHUCK CARY
- [ ] 28U. DAVE COLLINS
- [ ] 27U. DARNELL COLES
- [ ] 39U. DAVE ENGLE
- [ ] 64U. DAVE LAPOINT

HOUSTON ASTROS

- [ ] 35U. JIM DESHAIES
- [ ] 49U. BILLY HATCHER
- [ ] 69U. AURELIO LOPEZ
- [ ] 123U. TONY WALKER

KANSAS CITY ROYALS

- [ ] 8U. SCOTT BANKHEAD
- [ ] 66U. RUDY LAW
- [ ] 67U. DENNIS LEONARD
- [ ] 100U. ANGEL SALAZAR

LOS ANGELS DODGERS

- [ ] 119U. ALEX TREVINO
- [ ] 121U. ED VANDE BERG
- [ ] 128U. REGGIE WILLIAMS

BILLY JOE ROBIDOUX
FIRST BASE • OUTFIELD

MILWAUKEE BREWERS

- [ ] 22U. JUAN CASTILLO
- [ ] 23U. RICK CERONE
- [ ] 26U. MARK CLEAR
- [ ] 33U. ROB DEER
- [ ] 83U. JUAN NIEVES

- [ ] 90U. DAN PLASAC
- [ ] 97U. BILLY JOE ROBIDOUX
- [ ] 109U. DALE SVEUM

MINNESOTA TWINS

- [ ] 11U. BILLY BEANE
- [ ] 68U. STEVE LOMBARDOZZI
- [ ] 95U. JEFF REED

MONTREAL EXPOS

- [ ] 44U. ANDRES GALARRAGA
- [ ] 60U. WAYNE KRENCHICKI
- [ ] 74U. ANDY MCGAFFIGAN
- [ ] 80U. AL NEWMAN
- [ ] 88U. JEFF PARRETT
- [ ] 113U. JASON THOMPSON
- [ ] 116U. JAY TIBBS

NEW YORK METS

- [ ] 76U. KEVIN MITCHELL
- [ ] 82U. RANDY NIEMANN
- [ ] 84U. BOB OJEDA
- [ ] 110U. TIM TEUFEL

NEW YORK YANKEES

- [ ] 36U. DOUG DRABEK
- [ ] 37U. MIKE EASLER
- [ ] 40U. MIKE FISCHLIN
- [ ] 57U. TOMMY JOHN
- [ ] 98U. GARY ROENICKE
- [ ] 111U. BOB TEWKSBURY

OAKLAND A'S

- [ ] 4U. JOAQUIN ANDUJAR
- [ ] 9U. BILL BATHE
- [ ] 20U. JOSE CANSECO
- [ ] 48U. MOOSE HAAS
- [ ] 56U. STAN JAVIER
- [ ] 77U. BILL MOONEYHAM
- [ ] 126U. JERRY WILLARD

PHILADELPHIA PHILLIES

- [ ] 12U. STEVE BEDROSIAN
- [ ] 52U. TOM HUME
- [ ] 55U. CHRIS JAMES
- [ ] 94U. GARY REDUS
- [ ] 99U. RON ROENICKE
- [ ] 114U. MILT THOMPSON
- [ ] 117U. FRED TOLIVER

PITTSBURGH PIRATES

- [ ] 14U. BARRY BONDS

ST. LOUIS CARDINALS

- [ ] 29U. TIM CONROY
- [ ] 50U. MIKE HEATH
- [ ] 65U. MIKE LA VALLIERE
- [ ] 73U. GREG MATHEWS
- [ ] 85U. RICK OWNBEY
- [ ] 89U. PAT PERRY

SAN DIEGO PADRES

- [ ] 54U. DANE IORG
- [ ] 61U. JOHN KRUK
- [ ] 96U. BIP ROBERTS
- [ ] 124U. GENE WALTER
- [ ] 130U. MARVELL WYNNE

SAN FRANCISCO GIANTS

- [ ] 1U. MIKE ALDRETE
- [ ] 25U. WILL CLARK
- [ ] 62U. MIKE LACOSS
- [ ] 71U. CANDY MALDONADO
- [ ] 72U. ROGER MASON
- [ ] 92U. LUIS QUINONES
- [ ] 115U. ROB THOMPSON

SEATTLE MARINERS

- [ ] 45U. LEE GUETTERMAN
- [ ] 63U. PETER LADD
- [ ] 131U. STEVE YEAGER

PETE LADD
PITCHER

TEXAS RANGERS

- [ ] 30U. ED CORREA
- [ ] 41U. SCOTT FLETCHER
- [ ] 53U. PETE INCAVIGLIA
- [ ] 70U. MICKEY MAHLER
- [ ] 86U. TOM PACIOREK
- [ ] 91U. DARRELL PORTER
- [ ] 105U. RUBEN SIERRA
- [ ] 127U. MITCH WILLIAMS
- [ ] 129U. BOBBY WITT

TORONTO BLUE JAYS

- [ ] 24U. JOHN CERUTTI
- [ ] 38U. MARK EICHHORN

1987 FLEER (660)
2 1/2 X 3 1/2

Jimmy Key
BLUE JAYS

ATLANTA BRAVES

- [ ] 509. JIM ACKER
- [ ] 510. DOYLE ALEXANDER
- [ ] 511. PAUL ASSENMACHER
- [ ] 512. BRUCE BENEDICT
- [ ] 513. CHRIS CHAMBLISS
- [ ] 514. JEFF DEDMON
- [ ] 515. GENE GARBER
- [ ] 516. KEN GRIFFEY
- [ ] 517. TERRY HARPER
- [ ] 518. BOB HORNER
- [ ] 519. GLENN HUBBARD
- [ ] 520. RICK MAHLER
- [ ] 521. OMAR MORENO
- [ ] 522. DALE MURPHY
- [ ] 523. KEN OBERKFELL
- [ ] 524. ED OLWINE
- [ ] 525. DAVID PALMER
- [ ] 526. RAFAEL RAMIREZ
- [ ] 527. BILLY SAMPLE
- [ ] 528. TED SIMMONS
- [ ] 529. ZANE SMITH
- [ ] 530. BRUCE SUTTER
- [ ] 531. ANDRES THOMAS
- [ ] 532. OZZIE VIRGIL
- [ ] 659. TEAM CHECKLIST(F)

BALTIMORE ORIOLES

- [ ] 461. DON AASE
- [ ] 462. JUAN BENIQUEZ
- [ ] 463. MIKE BODDICKER
- [ ] 464. JUAN BONILLA
- [ ] 465. RICH BORDI
- [ ] 466. STORM DAVIS
- [ ] 467. RICK DEMPSEY
- [ ] 468. KEN DIXON
- [ ] 469. JIM DWYER
- [ ] 470. MIKE FLANAGAN
- [ ] 471. JACKIE GUTIERREZ
- [ ] 472. BRAD HAVENS
- [ ] 473. LEE LACY
- [ ] 474. FRED LYNN
- [ ] 475. SCOTT MCGREGOR
- [ ] 476. EDDIE MURRAY
- [ ] 477. TOM O'MALLEY
- [ ] 478. CAL RIPKEN
- [ ] 479. LARRY SHEETS
- [ ] 480. JOHN SHELBY
- [ ] 481. NATE SNELL
- [ ] 482. JIM TRABER
- [ ] 483. MIKE YOUNG
- [ ] 652. JOHN STEFERO(P)
- [ ] 658. TEAM CHECKLIST(B)

BOSTON RED SOX

- [ ] 26. TONY ARMAS
- [ ] 27. MARTY BARRETT
- [ ] 28. DON BAYLOR
- [ ] 29. WADE BOGGS
- [ ] 30. OIL CAN BOYD
- [ ] 31. BILL BUCKNER
- [ ] 32. ROGER CLEMENS
- [ ] 33. STEVE CRAWFORD
- [ ] 34. DWIGHT EVANS
- [ ] 35. RICH GEDMAN
- [ ] 36. DAVE HENDERSON
- [ ] 37. BRUCE HURST
- [ ] 38. TIM LOLLAR
- [ ] 39. AL NIPPER
- [ ] 40. SPIKE OWEN
- [ ] 41. JIM RICE
- [ ] 42. ED ROMERO
- [ ] 43. JOE SAMBITO
- [ ] 44. CALVIN SCHIRALDI
- [ ] 45. TOM SEAVER
- [ ] 46. JEFF SELLERS
- [ ] 47. BOB STANLEY
- [ ] 48. SAMMY STEWART
- [ ] 654. TEAM CHECKLIST(F)

CALIFORNIA ANGELS

- [ ] 73. BOB BOONE
- [ ] 74. RICK BURLESON
- [ ] 75. JOHN CANDELARIA
- [ ] 76. DOUG CORBETT
- [ ] 77. DOUG DECINCES
- [ ] 78. BRIAN DOWNING
- [ ] 79. CHUCK FINLEY
- [ ] 80. TERRY FORSTER
- [ ] 81. BOBBY GRICH
- [ ] 82. GEORGE HENDRICK
- [ ] 83. JACK HOWELL
- [ ] 84. REGGIE JACKSON
- [ ] 85. RUPPERT JONES
- [ ] 86. WALLY JOYNER
- [ ] 87. GARY LUCAS
- [ ] 88. KIRK MCCASKILL
- [ ] 89. DONNIE MOORE
- [ ] 90. GARY PETTIS
- [ ] 91. VERN RUHLE
- [ ] 92. DICK SCHOFIELD
- [ ] 93. DON SUTTON
- [ ] 94. ROB WILFONG
- [ ] 95. MIKE WITT
- [ ] 646. WILLIE FRASER(P)
- [ ] 646. DEVON WHITE(P)
- [ ] 654. TEAM CHECKLIST(B)

CINCINNATI REDS

- [ ] 193. BUDDY BELL
- [ ] 194. TOM BROWNING
- [ ] 195. SAL BUTERA
- [ ] 196. DAVE CONCEPCION
- [ ] 197. KAL DANIELS
- [ ] 198. ERIC DAVIS
- [ ] 199. JOHN DENNY
- [ ] 200. BO DIAZ
- [ ] 201. NICK ESASKY
- [ ] 202. JOHN FRANCO
- [ ] 203. BILL GULLICKSON
- [ ] 204. BARRY LARKIN
- [ ] 205. EDDIE MILNER
- [ ] 206. ROB MURPHY
- [ ] 207. RON OESTER
- [ ] 208. DAVE PARKER
- [ ] 209. TONY PEREZ
- [ ] 210. TED POWER
- [ ] 211. JOE PRICE
- [ ] 212. RON ROBINSON
- [ ] 213. PETE ROSE(M)
- [ ] 214. MARIO SOTO
- [ ] 215. KURT STILLWELL
- [ ] 216. MAX VENABLE
- [ ] 217. CHRIS WELSH
- [ ] 218. CARL WILLIS
- [ ] 651. TRACY JONES(P)
- [ ] 656. TEAM CHECKLIST(F)

CLEVELAND INDIANS

- [ ] 241. ANDY ALLANSON
- [ ] 242. SCOTT BAILES
- [ ] 243. CHRIS BANDO
- [ ] 244. TONY BERNAZARD
- [ ] 245. JOHN BUTCHER
- [ ] 246. BRETT BUTLER
- [ ] 247. ERNIE CAMACHO
- [ ] 248. TOM CANDIOTTI
- [ ] 249. JOE CARTER
- [ ] 250. CARMEN CASTILLO
- [ ] 251. JULIO FRANCO
- [ ] 252. MEL HALL
- [ ] 253. BROOK JACOBY
- [ ] 254. PHIL NIEKRO
- [ ] 255. OTIS NIXON
- [ ] 256. DICKIE NOLES
- [ ] 257. BRYAN OELKERS
- [ ] 258. KEN SCHROM
- [ ] 259. DON SCHULZE
- [ ] 260. CORY SNYDER
- [ ] 261. PAT TABLER
- [ ] 262. ANDERE THORNTON
- [ ] 263. RICH YETT
- [ ] 644. DAVE CLARK(P)
- [ ] 644. GREG SWINDELL(P)
- [ ] 656. TEAM CHECKLIST(B)

CHICAGO CUBS

- [ ] 555. THAD BOSLEY
- [ ] 556. RON CEY
- [ ] 557. JODY DAVIS
- [ ] 558. RON DAVIS
- [ ] 559. BOB DERNIER
- [ ] 560. FRANK DIPINO
- [ ] 561. SHAWON DUNSTON
- [ ] 562. LEON DURHAM
- [ ] 563. DENNIS ECKERSLEY
- [ ] 564. TERRY FRANCONA
- [ ] 565. DAVE GUMPERT
- [ ] 566. GUY HOFFMAN
- [ ] 567. ED LYNCH
- [ ] 568. GARY MATTHEWS
- [ ] 569. KEITH MORELAND
- [ ] 570. JAMIE MOYER

- [ ] 571. JERRY MUMPHREY
- [ ] 572. RYNE SANDBERG
- [ ] 573. SCOTT SANDERSON
- [ ] 574. LEE SMITH
- [ ] 575. CHRIS SPEIER
- [ ] 576. RICK SUTCLIFFE
- [ ] 577. MANNY TRILLO
- [ ] 578. STEVE TROUT
- [ ] 659. TEAM CHECKLIST(B)

CHICAGO WHITE SOX

- [ ] 484. NEIL ALLEN
- [ ] 485. HAROLD BAINES
- [ ] 486. FLOYD BANNISTER
- [ ] 487. DARYL BOSTON
- [ ] 488. IVAN CALDERON
- [ ] 489. JOHN CANGELOSI
- [ ] 490. STEVE CARLTON
- [ ] 491. JOE COWLEY
- [ ] 492. JULIO CRUZ
- [ ] 493. BILL DAWLEY
- [ ] 494. JOSE DELEON
- [ ] 495. RICHARD DOTSON
- [ ] 496. CARLTON FISK
- [ ] 497. OZZIE GUILLEN
- [ ] 498. JERRY HAIRSTON
- [ ] 499. RON HASSEY
- [ ] 500. TIM HULETT
- [ ] 501. BOB JAMES
- [ ] 502. STEVE LYONS
- [ ] 503. JOEL MCKEON
- [ ] 504. GENE NELSON
- [ ] 505. DAVE SCHMIDT
- [ ] 506. RAY SEARAGE
- [ ] 507. BOBBY THIGPEN
- [ ] 508. GREG WALKER
- [ ] 645. RUSS MORMAN(P)
- [ ] 645. RON KARKOVICE(P)
- [ ] 659. TEAM CHECKLIST(F)

DETROIT TIGERS

- [ ] 144. DAVE BERGMAN
- [ ] 145. TOM BROOKENS
- [ ] 146. BILL CAMPBELL
- [ ] 147. CHUCK CARY
- [ ] 148. DARNELL COLES
- [ ] 149. DAVE COLLINS
- [ ] 150. DARRELL EVANS
- [ ] 151. KIRK GIBSON
- [ ] 152. JOHN GRUBB
- [ ] 153. WILLIE HERNANDEZ
- [ ] 154. LARRY HERNDON
- [ ] 155. ERIC KING
- [ ] 156. CHET LEMON
- [ ] 157. DWIGHT LOWRY
- [ ] 158. JACK MORRIS
- [ ] 159. RANDY O'NEAL
- [ ] 160. LANCE PARRIS
- [ ] 161. DAN PETRY
- [ ] 162. PAT SHERIDAN
- [ ] 163. JIM SLATON
- [ ] 164. FRANK TANANA
- [ ] 165. WALT TERRELL
- [ ] 166. MARK THURMOND
- [ ] 167. ALLAN TRAMMELL
- [ ] 168. LOU WHITAKER
- [ ] 655. TEAM CHECKLIST(B)

HOUSTON ASTROS

- [ ] 49. LARRY ANDERSON
- [ ] 50. ALAN ASHBY
- [ ] 51. KEVIN BASS
- [ ] 52. JEFF CALHOUN
- [ ] 53. JOSE CRUZ
- [ ] 54. DANNY DARWIN
- [ ] 55. GLENN DAVIS
- [ ] 56. JIM DESHAIES
- [ ] 57. BILL DORAN
- [ ] 58. PHIL GARNER
- [ ] 59. BILLY HATCHER
- [ ] 60. CHARLIE KERFELD
- [ ] 61. BOB KNEPPER
- [ ] 62. DAVE LOPES
- [ ] 63. AURELIO LOPEZ
- [ ] 64. JIM PANKOVITS
- [ ] 65. TERRY PUHL
- [ ] 66. CRAIG REYNOLDS
- [ ] 67. NOLAN RYAN

- ☐ 68. MIKE SCOTT
- ☐ 69. DAVE SMITH
- ☐ 70. DICKIE THON
- ☐ 71. TONY WALKER
- ☐ 72. DENNY WALLING
- ☐ 654. TEAM CHECKLIST(B)

KANSAS CITY ROYALS

- ☐ 362. STEVE BALBONI
- ☐ 363. SCOTT BANKHEAD
- ☐ 364. BUDDY BIANCALANA
- ☐ 365. BUD BLACK
- ☐ 366. GEORGE BRETT
- ☐ 367. STEVE FARR
- ☐ 368. MARK GUBICZA
- ☐ 369. BO JACKSON
- ☐ 370. DANNY JACKSON
- ☐ 371. MIKE KINGERY
- ☐ 372. RUDY LAW
- ☐ 373. CHARLIE LEIBRANDT
- ☐ 374. DENNIS LEONARD
- ☐ 375. HAL MCRAE
- ☐ 376. JORE ORTA
- ☐ 377. JAMIE QUIRK
- ☐ 378. DAN QUISENBERRY
- ☐ 379. BRET SABERHAGEN
- ☐ 380. ANGEL SALAZAR
- ☐ 381. LONNIE SMITH
- ☐ 382. JIM SUNDBERG
- ☐ 383. FRANK WHITE
- ☐ 384. WILLIE WILSON
- ☐ 652. KEVIN SEITZER(P)
- ☐ 657. TEAM CHECKLIST(B)

LOS ANGELES DODGERS

- ☐ 436. DAVE ANDERSON
- ☐ 437. GREG BROCK
- ☐ 438. ENOS CABELL
- ☐ 439. MARIANO DUNCAN
- ☐ 440. PEDRO GUERRERO
- ☐ 441. OREL HERSHISER
- ☐ 442. RICK HONEYCUTT
- ☐ 443. KEN HOWELL
- ☐ 444. KEN LANDREAUX
- ☐ 445. BILL MADLOCK
- ☐ 446. MIKE MARSHALL
- ☐ 447. LEN MATUSZEK
- ☐ 448. TOM NIEDENFUER
- ☐ 449. AJEJANDRO PENA
- ☐ 450. DENNIS POWELL
- ☐ 451. JERRY REUSS
- ☐ 452. BUD RUSSELL
- ☐ 453. STEVE SAX
- ☐ 454. MIKE SCIOSCIA
- ☐ 455. FRANKLIN STUBBS
- ☐ 456. ALEX TREVINO
- ☐ 457. FERNANDO VALENZUELA
- ☐ 458. ED VANDE BERG
- ☐ 459. BOB WELCH
- ☐ 460. REGGIE WILLIAMS
- ☐ 649. RALPH BRYANT(P)
- ☐ 649. JOSE GONZALEZ(P)
- ☐ 658. TEAM CHECKLIST(B)

MILWAUKEE BREWERS

- ☐ 338. CHRIS BOSIO
- ☐ 339. GLENN BRAGGS
- ☐ 340. RICK CERONE
- ☐ 341. MARK CLEAR
- ☐ 342. BRYAN CLUTTERBUCK
- ☐ 343. CECIL COOPER
- ☐ 344. ROB DEER
- ☐ 345. JIM GANTNER
- ☐ 346. TED HIGUERA
- ☐ 347. JOHN HENRY JOHNSON
- ☐ 348. TIM LEARY
- ☐ 349. RICK MANNING
- ☐ 350. PAUL MOLITOR
- ☐ 351. CHARLIE MOORE
- ☐ 352. JUAN NIEVES
- ☐ 353. BEN OGLIVIE
- ☐ 354. DAN PLESAC
- ☐ 355. ERNEST RILES
- ☐ 356. BILLY JOE ROBIDOUX
- ☐ 357. BILL SCHROEDER
- ☐ 358. DALE SVEUM
- ☐ 359. GORMAN THOMAS

- ☐ 360. BILL WEGMAN
- ☐ 361. ROBIN YOUNT
- ☐ 657. TEAM CHECKLIST(B)

MINNESOTA TWINS

- ☐ 533. ALLAN ANDERSON
- ☐ 534. KEITH ATHERTON
- ☐ 535. BILLY BEANE
- ☐ 536. BERT BLYLEVEN
- ☐ 537. TOM BRUNANSKY
- ☐ 538. RANDY BUSH
- ☐ 539. GEORGE FRAZIER
- ☐ 540. GARY GAETTI
- ☐ 541. GREG GAGNE
- ☐ 542. MICKEY HATCHER
- ☐ 543. NEAL HEATON
- ☐ 544. KENT HRBEK
- ☐ 545. ROY LEE JACKSON
- ☐ 546. TIM LAUDNER
- ☐ 547. STEVE LOMBARDOZZI
- ☐ 548. MARK PORTUGAL
- ☐ 549. KIRBY PUCKETT
- ☐ 550. JEFF REED
- ☐ 551. MARK SALAS
- ☐ 552. ROY SMALLEY
- ☐ 553. MIKE SMITHSON
- ☐ 554. FRANK VIOLA
- ☐ 659. TEAM CHECKLIST(B)

MONTREAL EXPOS

- ☐ 313. DANN BILARDELLO
- ☐ 314. HUBIE BROOKS
- ☐ 315. TIM BURKE
- ☐ 316. ANDRE DAWSON
- ☐ 317. MIKE FITZGERALD
- ☐ 318. TOM FOLEY
- ☐ 319. ANDRES GALARRAGA
- ☐ 320. JOE HESKETH
- ☐ 321. WALLACE JOHNSON
- ☐ 322. WAYNE KRENCHICKI
- ☐ 323. VANCE LAW
- ☐ 324. DENNIS MARTINEZ
- ☐ 325. BOB MCCLURE
- ☐ 326. ANDY MCGAFFIGAN
- ☐ 327. AL NEWMAN
- ☐ 328. TIM RAINES
- ☐ 329. JEFF REARDON
- ☐ 330. LUIS RIVERA
- ☐ 331. BOB SEBRA
- ☐ 332. BRYN SMITH
- ☐ 333. JAY TIBBS
- ☐ 334. TIM WALLACH
- ☐ 335. MITCH WEBSTER
- ☐ 336. JIM WOHLFORD
- ☐ 337. FLOYD YOUMANS
- ☐ 657. TEAM CHECKLIST(F)

NEW YORK METS

- ☐ 1. RICK AGUILERA
- ☐ 2. RICHARD ANDERSON
- ☐ 3. WALLY BACKMAN
- ☐ 4. GARY CARTER
- ☐ 5. RON DARLING
- ☐ 6. LEN DYKSTRA
- ☐ 7. KEVIN ELSTER
- ☐ 8. SID FERNANDEZ
- ☐ 9. DWIGHT GOODEN
- ☐ 10. ED HEARN
- ☐ 11. DANNY HEEP
- ☐ 12. KEITH HERNANDEZ
- ☐ 13. HOWARD JOHNSON
- ☐ 14. RAY KNIGHT
- ☐ 15. LEE MAZZILLI
- ☐ 16. ROGER MCDOWELL
- ☐ 17. KEVIN MITCHELL
- ☐ 18. RANDY NIEMANN
- ☐ 19. BOB OJEDA
- ☐ 20. JESSE OROSCO
- ☐ 21. RAFAEL SANTANA
- ☐ 22. DOUG SISK
- ☐ 23. DARRYL STRAWBERRY
- ☐ 24. TIM TEUFEL
- ☐ 25. MOOKIE WILSON
- ☐ 648. DAVE MAGADAN(P)
- ☐ 654. TEAM CHECKLIST(F)

Danny Heep
OUTFIELD

NEW YORK YANKEES

- ☐ 96. DOUG DRABEK
- ☐ 97. MIKE EASLER
- ☐ 98. MIKE FISCHLIN
- ☐ 99. BRIAN FISHER
- ☐ 100. RON GUIDRY
- ☐ 101. RICKEY HENDERSON
- ☐ 102. TOMMY JOHN
- ☐ 103. RON KITTLE
- ☐ 104. DON MATTINGLY
- ☐ 105. BOBBY MEACHAM
- ☐ 106. JOE NIEKRO
- ☐ 107. MIKE PAGLIARULO
- ☐ 108. DAN PASQUA
- ☐ 109. WILLIE RANDOLPH
- ☐ 110. DENNIS RASMUSSEN
- ☐ 111. DAVE RIGHETTI
- ☐ 112. GARY ROENICKE
- ☐ 113. ROD SCURRY
- ☐ 114. BOB SHIRLEY
- ☐ 115. JOEL SKINNER
- ☐ 116. TIM STODDARD
- ☐ 117. BOB TEWKSBURY
- ☐ 118. WAYNE TOLLESON
- ☐ 119. CLAUDELL WASHINGTON
- ☐ 120. DAVE WINFIELD
- ☐ 648. PHIL LOMBARDI(P)
- ☐ 655. TEAM CHECKLIST(F)

OAKLAND A'S

- ☐ 385. JOAQUIN ANDUJAR
- ☐ 386. DOUG BAIR
- ☐ 387. DUSTY BAKER
- ☐ 388. BRUCE BOCHTE
- ☐ 389. JOSE CANSECO
- ☐ 390. CHRIS CONDIROLI
- ☐ 391. MIKE DAVIS
- ☐ 392. ALFREDO GRIFFIN
- ☐ 393. MOOSE HAAS
- ☐ 394. DONNIE HILL
- ☐ 395. JAY HOWELL
- ☐ 396. DAVE KINGMAN
- ☐ 397. CARNEY LANSFORD
- ☐ 398. DAVID LEIPER
- ☐ 399. BILL MOONEYHAM
- ☐ 400. DWAYNE MURPHY
- ☐ 401. STEVE ONTIVEROS
- ☐ 402. TONY PHILLIPS
- ☐ 403. ERIC PLUNK
- ☐ 404. JOSE RIJO
- ☐ 405. TERRY STEINBACH
- ☐ 406. DAVE STEWART
- ☐ 407. MICKEY TETTLETON
- ☐ 408. DAVE VON OHLEN
- ☐ 409. JERRY WILLARD
- ☐ 410. CURT YOUNG
- ☐ 653. ROB NELSON(P)
- ☐ 658. TEAM CHECKLIST(F)

PHILADELPHIA PHILLIES

- ☐ 169. LUIS AGUAYO
- ☐ 170. STEVE BEDROSIAN
- ☐ 171. DON CARMAN
- ☐ 172. DARREN DAULTON
- ☐ 173. GREG GROSS
- ☐ 174. KEVIN GROSS
- ☐ 175. VON HAYES

SPORT AMERICANA PUBLICATIONS

The Number One Publisher of Reference Works for Sports Memorabilia and Trading Card Collectors

Baseball Card Price Guide No. 9 . . . .$ 12.95
Football, Hockey, Basketball & Boxing
   Card Price Guide No. 5 (Available late 1987) . . . .$ 12.95
Baseball Memorabilia & Autograph Price Guide . . . . . .$ 8.95
Baseball Address List No. 4 (The Autograph
   Hunter's Best Friend) . . . .$ 9.95
Price Guide to the Non-Sports Cards No. 3
   (Available late 1987). . . . .$ 12.95
Alphabetical Baseball Card Checklist No. 3
   (Avialable late 1987). . . . .$ 9.95
Baseball Collectibles Price Guide. . . . .$ 9.95
Team Baseball Card Checklist No. 3 . . . .$ 9.95

All SPORT AMERICANA publications are available at better bookstores across the country. If you don't see the publication that you want, ask the bookstore attendant.

- [ ] 176. CHARLES HUDSON
- [ ] 177. TOM HUME
- [ ] 178. STEVE JELTZ
- [ ] 179. MIKE MADDUX
- [ ] 180. SHANE RAWLEY
- [ ] 181. GARY REDUS
- [ ] 182. RON ROENICKE
- [ ] 183. BRUCE RUFFIN
- [ ] 184. JOHN RUSSELL
- [ ] 185. JUAN SAMUEL
- [ ] 186. DAN SCHATZEDER
- [ ] 187. MIKE SCHMIDT
- [ ] 188. RICK SCHU
- [ ] 189. JEFF STONE
- [ ] 190. KENT TEKULVE
- [ ] 191. MILT THOMPSON
- [ ] 192. GLENN WILSON
- [ ] 651. MARVIN FREEMAN(P)
- [ ] 655 TEAM CHECKLIST(B)

PITTSBURGH PIRATES

- [ ] 601. BILL ALMON
- [ ] 602. RAFAEL BELLIARD
- [ ] 603. MIKE BIELECKI
- [ ] 604. BARRY BONDS
- [ ] 605. BOBBY BONILLA
- [ ] 606. SID BREAM
- [ ] 607. MIKE BROWN
- [ ] 608. PAT CLEMENTS
- [ ] 609. MIKE DIAZ
- [ ] 610. CECILIO GUANTE
- [ ] 611. BARRY JONES
- [ ] 612. BOB KIPPER
- [ ] 613. LARRY MCWILLIAMS
- [ ] 614. JIM MORRISON
- [ ] 615. JOE ORSULAK
- [ ] 616. JUNIOR ORTIZ
- [ ] 617. TONY PENA
- [ ] 618. JOHNNY RAY
- [ ] 619. RICK REUSCHEL
- [ ] 620. R. J. REYNOLDS
- [ ] 621. RICK RHODEN
- [ ] 622. DON ROBINSON
- [ ] 623. BOB WALK
- [ ] 624. JIM WINN
- [ ] 660. TEAM CHECKLIST(F)

ST. LOUIS CARDINALS

- [ ] 289. JACK CLARK
- [ ] 290. VINCE COLEMAN
- [ ] 291. TIM CONROY
- [ ] 292. DANNY COX
- [ ] 293. KEN DAYLEY
- [ ] 294. CURT FORD
- [ ] 295. BOB FORSCH
- [ ] 296. TOM HERR
- [ ] 297. RICKY HORTON
- [ ] 298. CLINT HURDLE
- [ ] 299. JEFF LAHTI
- [ ] 300. STEVE LAKE
- [ ] 301. TITO LANDRUM
- [ ] 302. MIKE LAVALLIERE
- [ ] 303. GREG MATHEWS
- [ ] 304. WILLIE MCGEE
- [ ] 305. JOSE OQUENDO
- [ ] 306. TERRY PENDLETON
- [ ] 307. PAT PERRY
- [ ] 308. OZZIE SMITH
- [ ] 309. RAY SOFF
- [ ] 310. JOHN TUDOR
- [ ] 311. ANDY VAN SLYKE
- [ ] 312. TODD WORRELL
- [ ] 657. TEAM CHECKLIST(F)

SAN DIEGO PADRES

- [ ] 411. BRUCE BOCHY
- [ ] 412. DAVE DRAVECKY
- [ ] 413. TIM FLANNERY
- [ ] 414. STEVE GARVEY
- [ ] 415. GOOSE GOSSAGE
- [ ] 416. TONY GWYNN
- [ ] 417. ANDY HAWKINS
- [ ] 418. LAMARR HOYT
- [ ] 419. TERRY KENNEDY
- [ ] 420. JOHN KRUK
- [ ] 421. DAVE LAPOINT
- [ ] 422. CRAIG LEFFERTS
- [ ] 423. CARMELO MARTINEZ

- [ ] 424. LANCE MCCULLERS
- [ ] 425. KEVIN MCREYNOLDS
- [ ] 426. GRAIG NETTLES
- [ ] 427. BIP ROBERTS
- [ ] 428. JERRY ROYSTER
- [ ] 429. BENITO SANTIAGO
- [ ] 430. ERIC SHOW
- [ ] 431. BOB STODDARD
- [ ] 432. GARRY TEMPLETON
- [ ] 433. GENE WALTER
- [ ] 434. ED WHITSON
- [ ] 435. MARVELL WYNNE
- [ ] 650. JIMMY JONES(P)
- [ ] 650. RANDY ASADOOR(P)
- [ ] 658. TEAM CHECKLIST(F)

SAN FRANCISCO GIANTS

- [ ] 264. MIKE ALDRETE
- [ ] 265. JUAN BERENGUER
- [ ] 266. VIDA BLUE
- [ ] 267. BOB BRENLY
- [ ] 268. CHRIS BROWN
- [ ] 269. WILL CLARK
- [ ] 270. CHILI DAVIS
- [ ] 271. MARK DAVIS
- [ ] 272. KELLY DOWNS
- [ ] 273. SCOTT GARRELTS
- [ ] 274. DAN GLADDEN
- [ ] 275. MIKE KRUKOW
- [ ] 276. RANDY KUTCHER
- [ ] 277. MIKE LACOSS
- [ ] 278. JEFF LEONARD
- [ ] 279. CANDY MALDONADO
- [ ] 280. ROGER MASON
- [ ] 281. BOB MELVIN
- [ ] 282. GREG MINTON
- [ ] 283. JEFF ROBINSON
- [ ] 284. HARRY SPILMAN
- [ ] 285. ROB THOMPSON
- [ ] 286. JOSE URIBE
- [ ] 287. FRANK WILLIAMS
- [ ] 288. JOEL YOUNGBLOOD
- [ ] 656. TEAM CHECKLIST(B)

SEATTLE MARINERS

- [ ] 579. KARL BEST
- [ ] 580. PHIL BRADLEY
- [ ] 581. SCOTT BRADLEY
- [ ] 582. MICKEY BRANTLEY
- [ ] 583. MIKE BROWN
- [ ] 584. ALVIN DAVIS
- [ ] 585. LEE GUETTERMAN
- [ ] 586. MARK HUISMANN
- [ ] 587. BOB KEARNEY
- [ ] 588. PETE LADD
- [ ] 589. MARK LANGSTON
- [ ] 590. MIKE MOORE
- [ ] 591. MIKE MORGAN
- [ ] 592. JOHN MOSES
- [ ] 593. KEN PHELPS
- [ ] 594. JIM PRESLEY
- [ ] 595. REY QUINONEZ
- [ ] 596. HAROLD REYNOLDS
- [ ] 597. BILLY SWIFT
- [ ] 598. DANNY TARTABULL
- [ ] 599. STEVE YEAGER
- [ ] 600. MATT YOUNG
- [ ] 653. STEVE FIREOVID(P)
- [ ] 660. TEAM CHECKLIST(F)

TEXAS RANGERS

- [ ] 121. STEVE BUECHELE
- [ ] 122. ED CORREA
- [ ] 123. SCOTT FLETCHER
- [ ] 124. JOSE GUZMAN
- [ ] 125. TOBY HARRAH
- [ ] 126. GREG HARRIS
- [ ] 127. CHARLIE HOUGH
- [ ] 128. PETE INCAVIGLIA
- [ ] 129. MIKE MASON
- [ ] 130. ODDIBE MCDOWELL
- [ ] 131. DALE MOHORCIC
- [ ] 132. PETE O'BRIEN
- [ ] 133. TOM PACIOREK
- [ ] 134. LARRY PARRISH
- [ ] 135. GENO PETRALLI
- [ ] 136. DARRELL PORTER

- [ ] 137. JEFF RUSSELL
- [ ] 138. RUBEN SIERRA
- [ ] 139. DON SLAUGHT
- [ ] 140. GARY WARD
- [ ] 141. CURTIS WILKERSON
- [ ] 142. MITCH WILLIAMS
- [ ] 143. BOBBY WITT
- [ ] 647. JERRY BROWNE(P)
- [ ] 647. MIKE STANLEY(P)
- [ ] 655. TEAM CHECKLIST(F)

TORONTO BLUE JAYS

- [ ] 219. JESSE BARFIELD
- [ ] 220. GEORGE BELL
- [ ] 221. BILL CAUDILL
- [ ] 222. JOHN CERUTTI
- [ ] 223. CLANCY
- [ ] 224. MARK EICHHORN
- [ ] 225. TONY FERNANDEZ
- [ ] 226. DAMASO GARCIA
- [ ] 227. KELLY GRUBER
- [ ] 228. TOM HENKE
- [ ] 229. GARTH IORG
- [ ] 230. CLIFF JOHNSON
- [ ] 231. JOE JOHNSON
- [ ] 232. JIMMY KEY
- [ ] 233. DENNIS LAMP
- [ ] 234. RICK LEACH
- [ ] 235. BUCK MARTINEZ
- [ ] 236. LLOYD MOSEBY
- [ ] 237. RANCE MULLINIKS
- [ ] 238. DAVE STIEB
- [ ] 239. WILLIE UPSHAW
- [ ] 240. ERNIE WHITT
- [ ] 656. TEAM CHECKLIST(F)

FRITSCH

JEREMY

1A — Jeremy Fritsch
Height: 3'0"
Weight: 34 lbs.
Born: 9/19/84
Stevens Point, Wisconsin

Jeremy visited the zoo last year.

Jeremy recently celebrated his second birthday with a party which all of his friends and relatives attended. He was a tire chief with a fireman cake and theme. Over the past few months his favorite activities have included collecting and playing with matchbox cars, playing football, riding his bike, watching cartoons (Yogi Bear, Felix the Cat and Mickey Mouse are his favorites), dancing to music on the radio, playing with his dog, B.G. and turning on and off light switches. According to the doctor's charts Jeremy, who has blonde hair and blue eyes, is above average in both height and weight. A new sister, Jaycie has recently been added to Jeremy's family. She keeps Jeremy very busy as he helps his mother care for her. He had a little trouble adapting to Jaycie's arrival at his home but now has adjusted completely and loves his new sister very much. Jeremy is anxiously awaiting the summer months so he can play outside with all of his friends in the neighborhood.

J.F.F.—Printed in U.S.A.

1933 GOUDEY (240)
2 3/8″ X 2 7/8″

BOSTON BRAVES

- [ ] 24. HORACE FORD
- [ ] 30. FRANK HOGAN
- [ ] 50. ED BRANDT
- [ ] 69. RANDY MOORE
- [ ] 91. TOM ZACHARY
- [ ] 98. WALTER BERGER
- [ ] 117. RABBIT MARANVILLE
- [ ] 131. FRED FRANKHOUSE
- [ ] 139. BEN CANTWELL
- [ ] 161. AL SPOHRER
- [ ] 162. LEO MANGUM
- [ ] 172. BILLY HARGRAVE
- [ ] 179. FRED LEACH
- [ ] 185. BOB SMITH
- [ ] 212. BILLY URBANSKI

BOSTON RED SOX

- [ ] 8. ROY JOHNSON
- [ ] 14. HENRY JOHNSON
- [ ] 42. EDDIE COLLINS
- [ ] 48. MARTY MCMANUS
- [ ] 93. JOHN WELCH
- [ ] 105. BERNIE FRIBERG
- [ ] 197. RICK FERRELL
- [ ] 221. DALE ALEXANDER

BROOKLYN DODGERS

- [ ] 2. DAZZY VANCE(F)
- [ ] 13. LAFAYETTE THOMPSON
- [ ] 17. WATSON CLARK
- [ ] 32. JOHN CLANCY
- [ ] 58. LEFTY O'DOUL
- [ ] 72. OWEN CARROLL
- [ ] 78. JACK QUINN
- [ ] 99. TONY CUCCINELLO
- [ ] 118. VAL PICINICH
- [ ] 141. RAY BENGE
- [ ] 143. GLENN WRIGHT
- [ ] 151. JAKE FLOWERS
- [ ] 155. JOE JUDGE
- [ ] 211. HACK WILSON

CHICAGO CUBS

- [ ] 5. BABE HERMAN
- [ ] 23. KIKI CUYLER
- [ ] 39. MARK KOENIG
- [ ] 51. CHARLIE GRIMM
- [ ] 55. PAT MALONE
- [ ] 64. BURLEIGH GRIMES

- [ ] 67. GUY BUSH
- [ ] 135. WOODY ENGLISH
- [ ] 152. ZACK TAYLOR
- [ ] 186. JOHN SCHULTE(C)
- [ ] 202. GABBY HARTNETT
- [ ] 203. LON WARNEKE
- [ ] 204. RIGGS STEPHENSON
- [ ] 224. FRANK DEMAREE
- [ ] 225. BILL JURGES
- [ ] 226. CHARLEY ROOT
- [ ] 227. BILL HERMAN

CHICAGO WHITE SOX

- [ ] 6. JIMMY DYKES
- [ ] 7. TED LYONS
- [ ] 33. RALPH KRESS
- [ ] 35. AL SIMMONS
- [ ] 43. LEW FONSECA
- [ ] 65. MILTON GASTON
- [ ] 79. RED FABER
- [ ] 81. SAM JONES
- [ ] 184. CHARLEY BERRY
- [ ] 195. EVAR SWANSON
- [ ] 219. MULE HAAS

CINCINNATI REDS

- [ ] 40. TAYLOR DOUTHIT
- [ ] 44. JIM BOTTOMLEY
- [ ] 45. LARRY BENTON
- [ ] 66. GEORGE GRANTHAM
- [ ] 74. EPPA RIXEY
- [ ] 80. CLYDE MANION
- [ ] 97. JOE MORRISSEY
- [ ] 137. FRED LUCAS
- [ ] 150. RAY KOLP
- [ ] 213. EARL ADAMS

CLEVELAND INDIANS

- [ ] 10. GLENN MYATT
- [ ] 26. CHALMER CISSELL
- [ ] 27. GEORGE CONNALLY
- [ ] 75. WILLIE KAMM
- [ ] 96. WILLIS HUDLIN
- [ ] 116. EDDIE MORGAN
- [ ] 171. CHARLEY JAMIESON
- [ ] 194. EARL AVERILL
- [ ] 218. WESLEY FERRELL

DETROIT TIGERS

- [ ] 4. HEINIE SCHUBLE
- [ ] 11. BILLY ROGELL
- [ ] 15. VICTOR SORRELL
- [ ] 100. GEORGE UHLE
- [ ] 104. FRED MARBERRY
- [ ] 199. TOM BRIDGES
- [ ] 222. CHARLEY GEHRINGER

NEW YORK GIANTS

- [ ] 3. HUGH GRITZ
- [ ] 20. BILLY TERRY
- [ ] 41. GUS MANCUSO
- [ ] 52. ANDY COHEN
- [ ] 84. GLENN SPENCER
- [ ] 102. TRAVIS JACKSON
- [ ] 125. BILL TERRY (M)
- [ ] 126. JOE MOORE
- [ ] 127. MEL OTT
- [ ] 129. HAROLD SCHUMACHER
- [ ] 130. FRED FITZSIMMONS
- [ ] 142. PAUL RICHARDS

- [ ] 207. MEL OTT
- [ ] 208. BERNIE JAMES
- [ ] 209. ADOLFO LUQUE
- [ ] 230. CARL HUBBELL
- [ ] 231. JOE MOORE
- [ ] 232. LEFTY O'DOUL
- [ ] 233. JOHNNY VERGEZ
- [ ] 234. CARL HUBBELL
- [ ] 235. FRED FITZSIMMONS
- [ ] 236. GEORGE DAVIS
- [ ] 237. GUS MANCUSO
- [ ] 238. HUGH CRITZ
- [ ] 239. LEROY PARMELEE
- [ ] 240. HAROLD SCHUMACHER

NEW YORK YANKEES

- [ ] 12. GEORGE PIPGRAS
- [ ] 19. BILL DICKEY
- [ ] 31. TONY LAZZERI
- [ ] 53. BABE RUTH
- [ ] 56. RED RUFFING
- [ ] 83. PETE JABLONOWSKI
- [ ] 92. LOU GEHRIG
- [ ] 103. EARLE COMBS
- [ ] 138. HERB PENNOCK
- [ ] 144. BABE RUTH
- [ ] 148. EDDIE FARRELL
- [ ] 149. BABE RUTH
- [ ] 156. DANNY MACFAYDEN
- [ ] 157. SAM BYRD
- [ ] 160. LOU GEHRIG
- [ ] 165. JOE SEWELL
- [ ] 181. BABE RUTH
- [ ] 191. BEN CHAPMAN
- [ ] 192. WALTER BROWN
- [ ] 193. LYNFORD LARY
- [ ] 215. RUSSELL VAN ATTA
- [ ] 216. LEFTY GOMEZ
- [ ] 217. FRANK CROSETTI

PHILADELPHIA ATHLETICS

- [ ] 29. JIMMY FOXX
- [ ] 59. BING MILLER
- [ ] 61. MAX BISHOP
- [ ] 76. MICKEY COCHRANE
- [ ] 82. DIB WILLIAMS
- [ ] 145. GEORGE WALBERT
- [ ] 154. JIMMY FOXX
- [ ] 183. GEORGE WALBERG
- [ ] 196. LEROY MAHAFFEY
- [ ] 220. LEFTY GROVE

PHILADELPHIA PHILLIES

- [ ] 21. PHIL COLLINS
- [ ] 28. DICK BARTELL
- [ ] 38. FRED BRICKELL
- [ ] 115. CLIFF HEATHCOTE
- [ ] 128. CHUCK KLEIN
- [ ] 132. JIM ELLIOTT
- [ ] 136. FLINT RHEM
- [ ] 170. HARRY MCCURDY
- [ ] 178. JACKIE WARNER
- [ ] 210. VIRGIL DAVIS

PITTSBURGH PIRATES

- [ ] 22. PIE TRAYNOR
- [ ] 25. PAUL WANER
- [ ] 36. TOMMY THEVENOW
- [ ] 54. RAY KREMER
- [ ] 60. WAITE HOYT
- [ ] 77. ADAM COMOROSKY
- [ ] 133. FRED LINDSTROM
- [ ] 164. LLOYD WANER
- [ ] 205. HEINIE MEINE
- [ ] 206. GUS SUHR
- [ ] 228. TONY PIET
- [ ] 229. FLOYD VAUGHAN

ST. LOUIS BROWNS

- [ ] 1. BENNY BENGOUGH
- [ ] 16. GEORGE BLAEHOLDER
- [ ] 18. MUDDY RUEL
- [ ] 101. DICK COFFMAN
- [ ] 120. CARL REYNOLDS
- [ ] 140. IRVING HADLEY
- [ ] 166. SAM WEST
- [ ] 188. ROGERS HORNSBY(M)
- [ ] 198. IRVING BURNS

ST. LOUIS CARDINALS

- ☐ 2. DAZZY VANCE(B)
- ☐ 34. BOB O'FARRELL
- ☐ 37. JIMMY WILSON
- ☐ 46. ETHAN ALLEN
- ☐ 49. FRANK FRISCH
- ☐ 62. PEPPER MARTIN
- ☐ 73. JESSE HAINES
- ☐ 94. BILL WALKER
- ☐ 119. ROGERS HORNSBY
- ☐ 147. LEO DUROCHER
- ☐ 173. ROSCOE HOLM
- ☐ 200. BILL HALLAHAN
- ☐ 201. ERNIE ORSATTI
- ☐ 223. DIZZY DEAN

WASHINGTON SENATORS

- ☐ 9. DAVE HARRIS
- ☐ 47. HEINIE MANUSH
- ☐ 63. JOE CRONIN(M)
- ☐ 71. ROBERT BURKE
- ☐ 95. ALVIN CROWDER
- ☐ 107. HEINIE MANUSH
- ☐ 108. JOE KUHEL
- ☐ 109. JOE CRONIN(M)
- ☐ 110. GOOSE GOSLIN
- ☐ 111. MONTE WEAVER
- ☐ 112. FRED SCHULTE
- ☐ 113. OSWALD BLUEGE
- ☐ 114. LUKE SEWELL
- ☐ 121. WALTER STEWART
- ☐ 122. ALVIN CROWDER
- ☐ 123. JACK RUSSELL
- ☐ 124. EARL WHITEHILL
- ☐ 134. SAM RICE
- ☐ 146. WALTER STEWART
- ☐ 153. BUDDY MYER
- ☐ 158. MOE BERG
- ☐ 159. OSWALD BLUEGE
- ☐ 163. LUKE SEWELL
- ☐ 167. JACK RUSSELL
- ☐ 168. GOOSE GOSLIN
- ☐ 169. AL THOMAS
- ☐ 187. HEINIE MANUSH
- ☐ 189. JOE CRONIN(M)
- ☐ 190. FRED SCHULTE
- ☐ 214. JOHN KERR

1934 GOUDEY (96)
2 3/8" X 2 7/8"

JOHN MARCUM

Lou Gehrig says...

BOSTON BRAVES

- ☐ 5. ED BRANDT
- ☐ 20. FRANK HOGAN
- ☐ 31. BAXTER JORDAN
- ☐ 36. WALTER BETTS
- ☐ 59. JOE MOWRY
- ☐ 80. MARTY MCMANUS
- ☐ 81. BOB BROWN

BOSTON RED SOX

- ☐ 19. LEFTY GROVE
- ☐ 30. JULIUS SOLTERS
- ☐ 75. BILL WERBER
- ☐ 93. FRED OSTERMUELLER

BROOKLYN DODGERS

- ☐ 24. RAY BENGE
- ☐ 46. JOE STRIPP
- ☐ 47. JOHN FREDERICK

- ☐ 49. SAM LESLIE
- ☐ 50. WALTER BECK
- ☐ 89. LINUS FREY

CHICAGO CUBS

- ☐ 3. CHARLIE GRIMM(M)
- ☐ 4. WOODY ENGLISH
- ☐ 10. CHUCK KLEIN
- ☐ 60. LYNN NELSON
- ☐ 71. LYLE TINNING
- ☐ 90. KI KI CUYLER

CHICAGO WHITE SOX

- ☐ 27. LUKE APPLING
- ☐ 41. GEORGE EARNSHAW(B)
- ☐ 63. MINTER HAYES
- ☐ 74. BOB BOKEN
- ☐ 79. EDDIE DURHAM

CINCINNATI REDS

- ☐ 8. TONY PIET
- ☐ 34. CHICK HAFEY
- ☐ 35. ERNIE LOMBARDI
- ☐ 54. WESLEY SCHULMERICH(B)
- ☐ 56. MARK KOENIG
- ☐ 84. PAUL DERRINGER
- ☐ 85. ADAM COMOROSKY

CLEVELAND INDIANS

- ☐ 14. WILLIE KAMM
- ☐ 38. ORAL HILDEBRAND
- ☐ 43. DICK PORTER
- ☐ 66. MEL HARDER
- ☐ 67. BOB WEILAND
- ☐ 76. HAL TROSKY
- ☐ 77. JOE VOSMIK

DETROIT TIGERS

- ☐ 2. MICKEY COCHRANE(M)
- ☐ 23. CHARLEY GEHRINGER
- ☐ 26. GERALD WALKER
- ☐ 44. TOM BRIDGES
- ☐ 62. HANK GREENBERG
- ☐ 70. PETE FOX
- ☐ 92. STEVE LARKIN

NEW YORK GIANTS

- ☐ 12. CARL HUBBELL
- ☐ 17. HUGH CRITZ
- ☐ 21. BILL TERRY(M)
- ☐ 32. BLONDY RYAN
- ☐ 52. HERMAN BELL
- ☐ 53. GEORGE WATKINS
- ☐ 88. HOMER PEEL

GEORGE WATKINS

Lou Gehrig says...

NEW YORK YANKEES

- ☐ 9. BEN CHAPMAN
- ☐ 37. LOU GEHRIG
- ☐ 39. FRED WALKER
- ☐ 42. JOHN ALLEN
- ☐ 61. LOU GEHRIG
- ☐ 72. ARNDT JORGENS
- ☐ 94. RED ROLFE
- ☐ 95. MYRIL HOAG
- ☐ 96. JIM DESHONG

PHILADELPHIA ATHLETICS

- ☐ 1. JIMMY FOXX
- ☐ 25. ROGER CRAMER
- ☐ 28. ED COLEMAN
- ☐ 41. GEORGE EARNSHAW(F)
- ☐ 68. BOB JOHNSON
- ☐ 69. JOHN MARCUM
- ☐ 78. PINKEY HIGGINS

PHILADELPHIA PHILLIES

- ☐ 33. FRANK HURST
- ☐ 54. WESLEY SCHULMERICH(F)
- ☐ 55. ED HOLLEY
- ☐ 87. GEORGE DARROW
- ☐ 91. DOLPH CAMILLI

PITTSBURGH PIRATES

- ☐ 11. PAUL WANER
- ☐ 22. FLOYD VAUGHAN
- ☐ 29. LARRY FRENCH
- ☐ 57. BILL SWIFT
- ☐ 58. EARL GRACE
- ☐ 86. LLOYD JOHNSON

ST. LOUIS BROWNS

- ☐ 45. OSCAR MELILLO
- ☐ 64. FRANK GRUBE
- ☐ 73. ED WELLS

ST. LOUIS CARDINALS

- ☐ 6. DIZZY DEAN
- ☐ 7. LEO DUROCHER
- ☐ 13. FRANK FRISCH
- ☐ 48. TEX CARLETON
- ☐ 51. RIP COLLINS
- ☐ 82. BILL HALLAHAN
- ☐ 83. JIM MOONEY

CLIFF BOLTON

Lou Gehrig says...

WASHINGTON SENATORS

- ☐ 15. ALVIN CROWDER
- ☐ 16. JOE KUHEL
- ☐ 18. HEINIE MANUSH
- ☐ 40. JOHN STONE
- ☐ 65. CLIFF BOLTON

1935 GOUDEY
PUZZLE (36)
2 3/8" X 2 7/8"

Each of the 1935 Goudey cards has four players depicted on the card. While most cards portray four players from the same team, several cards portray players from different teams. Players in parentheses are not on the same team as the subject player(s), but are on the same card.

1935 Goudey

BOSTON BRAVES

- ☐ MOORE, HOGAN, FRANKHOUSE, BRANDT
- ☐ RUTH, MCMANUS, BRANDT, MARANVILLE
- ☐ SPOHRER, RHEM, CANTWELL, BENTON

BOSTON RED SOX

- ☐ CRONIN, REYNOLDS, BISHOP, CISSELL
- ☐ WERBER, R. FERRELL, W. FERRELL, OSTERMUELLER

BROOKLYN DODGERS

- ☐ LESLIE, FREY, STRIPP, W. CLARK
- ☐ BENGE, ZACHARY (KOENIG, FITZSIMMONS)
- ☐ VANCE (BERRY, BURKE, KRESS)

CHICAGO CUBS

- ☐ GRIMES, KLEIN, CUYLER, ENGLISH

CHICAGO WHITE SOX

- ☐ EARNSHAW, DYKES, L. SEWELL, APPLINE
- ☐ HAYES, LYONS, HAAS, BONURA
- ☐ RUEL, SIMMONS (KAMM, COCHRANE)
- ☐ WRIGHT (TRAYNOR, LUCAS THEVENOW

CINCINNATI REDS

- ☐ CAMPBELL, MEYERS, GOODMAN, KAMPOURIS
- ☐ PIET, COMORDSKY, BOTTOMLEY, ADAMS
- ☐ BYRD, MACFAYDEN (MARTIN, O'FARRELL)
- ☐ COMOROSKY, BOTTOMLEY (HUDLIN, MYATT)

CLEVELAND INDIANS

- ☐ KAMM, HILDEBRAND, AVERILL, TROSKY
- ☐ VOSMIK, KNICKERBOCKER, HARDER, STEWART
- ☐ HUDLIN, MYATT (COMOROSKY, BOTTOMLEY
- ☐ KAMM (RUEL, SIMMONS, COCHRANE)

DETROIT TIGERS

- ☐ COCHRANE, GEHRINGER, BRIDGES, ROGELL
- ☐ FOX, GREENBERG, WALKER, ROWE
- ☐ SCHUBLE, MARBERRY, GOSLIN, CROWDER
- ☐ COCHRANE (RUEL, SIMMONS, KAMM)

NEW YORK GIANTS

- ☐ CRITZ, BARTELL, OTT, MANCUSO
- ☐ TERRY, SCHUMACHER, MANCUSO, JACKSON
- ☐ KOENIG FITZSIMMONS (BENGE, ZACHARY)

NEW YORK YANKEES

- ☐ DESHONG, ALLEN, ROLFE, WALKER
- ☐ RUFFING, MALONE, LAZZERI, DICKEY

PHILADELPHIA ATHLETICS

- ☐ JOHNSON, COLEMAN, MARCUM, CRAMER
- ☐ MAHAFFEY, FOXX, WILLIAMS, HIGGINS
- ☐ BERRY (VANCE, BURKE, KRESS)

PHILADELPHIA PHILLIES

- ☐ WILSON, ALLEN, JONNARD, BRICKELL

PITTSBURGH PIRATES

- ☐ HERMAN, SUHR, PADDEN, BLANTON
- ☐ P. WANER, BUSH, W. HOYT, L. WANER
- ☐ TRAYNOR, LUCAS, THEVENOW (WRIGHT)

ST. LOUIS BROWNS

- ☐ BURNS, HEMSLEY, GRUBE, WEILAND
- ☐ WEST, MELILLO, BLAEHOLDER, COFFMAN

ST. LOUIS CARDINALS

- ☐ FRISCH, J. DEAN, ORSATTI, TEX CARLETON
- ☐ MARTIN, O'FARRELL (BYRD, MACFAYDEN

WASHINGTON SENATORS

- ☐ KUHEL, WHITEHILL, MEYER, STONE
- ☐ MANUSH, LARY, M. WEAVER, HADLEY
- ☐ BURKE, KRESS (BERRY, VANCE)

1936 GOUDEY
GAME (25)
2 3/8" X 2 7/8"
BLACK & WHITE

BOSTON BRAVES

- ☐ 1. WALLY BERGER
- ☐ 8. JOE COSCARART

BOSTON RED SOX

- ☐ 13. RICK FERRELL
- ☐ 25. BILL WERBER

BROOKLYN DODGERS

- ☐ 3. FRENCHI BORDAGARAY

CHICAGO CUBS

- ☐ 20. CHUCK KLEIN

CHICAGO WHITE SOX

- ☐ 2. ZEKE BONURA
- ☐ 12. JIMMY DYKES

CINCINNATI REDS

- ☐ 10. KIKI CUYLER
- ☐ 11. PAUL DERRINGER

CLEVELAND INDIANS

- ☐ 19. ORAL HILDEBRAND
- ☐ 23. JOE VOSMIK

DETROIT TIGERS

- ☐ 7. MICKEY COCHRANE
- ☐ 15. HANK GREENBERG

NEW YORK GIANTS

- ☐ 6. CLYDE CASTLEMAN

NEW YORK YANKEES

- ☐ 9. FRANK CROSETTI
- ☐ 14. LEFTY GOMEZ

PHILADELPHIA ATHLETICS

- ☐ 18. PINKY HIGGINS

PHILADELPHIA PHILLIES

- ☐ 5. DOLPH CAMILLI

PITTSBURGH PIRATES

- ☐ 4. BILL BRUBAKER
- ☐ 24. PAUL WANER

ST. LOUIS BROWNS

- ☐ 17. ROLLIE HEMSLEY

ST. LOUIS CARDINALS

☐ 21. PEPPER MARTIN

WASHINGTON SENATORS

☐ 16. BUCKY HARRIS
☐ 22. BOBO NEWSOM

1938 GOUDEY HEADS UP (48)
2 3/8" X 2 7/8"

BOSTON BEES

☐ 257. AL LOPEZ
☐ 281. AL LOPEZ

JOE VOSMIK, Red Sox

BOSTON RED SOX

☐ 247. JOE VOSMIK
☐ 249. JIMMIE FOXX
☐ 258. BOBBY DOERR
☐ 271. JOE VOSMIK
☐ 273. JIMMIE FOXX
☐ 282. BOBBY DOERR

BROOKLYN DODGERS

☐ 254. VAN LINGLE MUNGO
☐ 278. VAN LINGLE MUNGO

CHICAGO CUBS

☐ 244. FRANK DEMAREE
☐ 268. FRANK DEMAREE

CHICAGO WHITE SOX

☐ 243. JOE KUHEL
☐ 261. RIP RADCLIFF
☐ 263. MARVIN OWEN
☐ 267. JOE KUHEL
☐ 285. RIP RADCLIFF
☐ 287. MARVIN OWEN

CINCINNATI REDS

☐ 246. ERNIE LOMBARDI
☐ 270. ERNIE LOMBARDI

CLEVELAND INDIANS

☐ 245. FRANK PYTLAK
☐ 255. MOOSE SOLTERS
☐ 264. BOB FELLER

☐ 269. FRANK PYTLAK
☐ 279. MOOSE SOLTERS
☐ 288. BOB FELLER

DETROIT TIGERS

☐ 241. CHARLIE GEHRINGER
☐ 242. PETE FOX
☐ 253. HANK GREENBERG
☐ 256. VERNON KENNEDY
☐ 260. RUDY YORK
☐ 265. CHARLIE GEHRINGER
☐ 266. PETE FOX
☐ 277. HANK GREENBERG
☐ 280. VERNON KENNEDY
☐ 284. RUDY YORK

ERVIN FOX, Tigers

NEW YORK GIANTS

☐ 248. DICK BARTELL
☐ 272. DICK BARTELL

NEW YORK YANKEES

☐ 250. JOE DIMAGGIO
☐ 251. BUMP HADLEY
☐ 274. JOE DIMAGGIO
☐ 275. BUMP HADLEY

PHILADELPHIA ATHLETICS

☐ 259. BILL WERBER
☐ 283. BILL WERBER

PHILADELPHIA PHILLIES

NO CARDS ISSUED

PITTSBURGH PIRATES

NO CARDS ISSUED

ST. LOUIS BROWNS

NO CARDS ISSUED

ST. LOUIS CARDINALS

☐ 262. JOE MEDWICK
☐ 286. JOE MEDWICK

WASHINGTON SENATORS

☐ 252. ZEKE BONURA
☐ 276. ZEKE BONURA

1941 GOUDEY (33)
2 3/8" X 2 7/8"

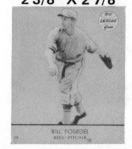

BILL POSEDEL
BEES—PITCHER

BOSTON BEES

☐ 19. BILL POSEDEL
☐ 22. JOE SULLIVAN
☐ 24. STANLEY ANDREWS
☐ 30. JIM TOBIN
☐ 31. CHESTER ROSS

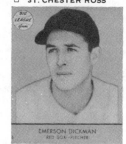

EMERSON DICKMAN
RED SOX—PITCHER

BOSTON RED SOX

☐ 6. EMERSON DICKMAN

BROOKLYN DODGERS

☐ 18. WHITLOW WYATT

CHICAGO CUBS

☐ 21. HAROLD WARSTLER
☐ 28. AL TODD

CHICAGO WHITE SOX

☐ 9. BILL DIETRICH
☐ 10. TAFT WRIGHT
☐ 15. DARIO LODIGIANI

DARIO LODIGIANI
WHITE SOX—INFIELDER

CINCINNATI REDS

☐ 7. WAYNE AMBLER

CLEVELAND INDIANS

NO CARDS ISSUED

DETROIT TIGERS

☐ 32. GEORGE COFFMAN

NEW YORK GIANTS

☐ 3. LOUIS CHIOZZA
☐ 20. CARL HUBBELL
☐ 23. BABE YOUNG
☐ 25. MORRIS ARNOVICH
☐ 33. MELT OTT

NEW YORK YANKEES

☐ 4. BUDDY ROSAR

PHILADELPHIA ATHLETICS

☐ 13. FRANK HAYES

PHILADELPHIA PHILLIES

☐ 1. HUGH MULCAHY
☐ 17. VITO TAMULIS
☐ 27. BILL CROUCH

1941 Goudey

PITTSBURGH PIRATES

- [ ] 26. ELBERT FLETCHER
- [ ] 29. DEBS GARMS

ST. LOUIS BROWNS

- [ ] 2. HARLAND CLIFT
- [ ] 5. GEORGE MCQUINN
- [ ] 8. BOB MUNCRIEF
- [ ] 11. DON HEFFNER
- [ ] 12. FRITZ OSTERMUELLER
- [ ] 14. JACK KRAMER

ST. LOUIS CARDINALS

NO CARDS ISSUED

WASHINGTON SENATORS

- [ ] 16. GEORGE CASE

1939 PLAY BALL AMERICA (162) 2 1/2" X 3 1/8" BLACK & WHITE

BOSTON BEES

- [ ] 49. EDDIE MILLER
- [ ] 57. BUDDY HASSETT
- [ ] 61. TONY CUCCINELLO
- [ ] 69. ELBIE FLETCHER
- [ ] 70. FRED FRANKHOUSE
- [ ] 72. DEBS GARMS
- [ ] 85. JOHN COONEY
- [ ] 87. MILBURN SHOFFNER
- [ ] 120. RABBIT WARSTLER
- [ ] 121. BILL POSEDEL
- [ ] 149. MAX WEST
- [ ] 155. JIM OUTLAW

BOSTON RED SOX

- [ ] 4. ELDEN AUKER
- [ ] 7. BOBBY DOERR
- [ ] 14. JIM TABOR
- [ ] 16. JOHN PEACOCK
- [ ] 17. EMERSON DICKMAN
- [ ] 20. JOE HEVING
- [ ] 27. FRED OSTERMUELLER
- [ ] 29. JACK WILSON
- [ ] 40. JIM BAGBY
- [ ] 62. TOM CAREY
- [ ] 92. TED WILLIAMS
- [ ] 101. ROGER CRAMER
- [ ] 103. MOE BERG
- [ ] 107. JOE VOSMIK
- [ ] 116. GENE DESAUTELS

BROOKLYN DODGERS

- [ ] 6. LEO DUROCHER(M)
- [ ] 13. LUKE HAMLIN
- [ ] 68. FRED SINGTON
- [ ] 74. COOKIE LAVAGETTO
- [ ] 76. GOODY ROSEN
- [ ] 86. DOLPH CAMILLI
- [ ] 95. WHIT WYATT
- [ ] 96. BABE PHELPS

- [ ] 110. FRED FITZSIMMONS
- [ ] 111. VAN LINGLE MUNGO
- [ ] 134. FORREST PRESSNELL
- [ ] 139. VITO TAMULIS
- [ ] 140. RAY HAYWORTH
- [ ] 141. PETE COSCARART
- [ ] 142. IRA HUTCHINSON
- [ ] 151. HUGH CASEY
- [ ] 154. JOHN HUDSON
- [ ] 159. RED EVANS
- [ ] 160. GENE MOORE

CHICAGO CUBS

NO CARDS ISSUED

CHICAGO WHITE SOX

- [ ] 91. JOHN KNOTT
- [ ] 105. ERIC MCNAIR

CINCINNATI REDS

- [ ] 2. LEE GRISSOM
- [ ] 15. PAUL DERRINGER
- [ ] 22. BUCKY WALTERS
- [ ] 36. FRANK MCCORMICK
- [ ] 38. BILL MYERS
- [ ] 65. HARRY CRAFT
- [ ] 67. ED JOOST
- [ ] 75. STAN BORDAGARAY
- [ ] 77. LEW RIGGS
- [ ] 99. WALLY BERGER
- [ ] 119. BILL HERSHBERGER
- [ ] 123. RAY DAVIS
- [ ] 161. LONNIE FREY
- [ ] 162. WHITEY MOORE

CLEVELAND INDIANS

- [ ] 5. LUKE SEWELL
- [ ] 78. JAKE SOLTERS
- [ ] 143. EARL AVERILL
- [ ] 152. ROY WEATHERLY

DETROIT TIGERS

- [ ] 50. CHARLIE GEHRINGER
- [ ] 56. HANK GREENBERG
- [ ] 60. SCHOOLBOY ROWE
- [ ] 80. PETE FOX
- [ ] 104. TOM BRIDGES
- [ ] 115. RALPH KRESS

- [ ] 136. ROY BELL
- [ ] 147. GEORGE COFFMAN
- [ ] 150. JIM WALKUP
- [ ] 153. DIZZY TROUT
- [ ] 158. BUD THOMAS

NEW YORK GIANTS

- [ ] 18. HARRY DANNING
- [ ] 23. BURGESS WHITEHEAD
- [ ] 24. RICHARD COFFMAN
- [ ] 32. BOB SEEDS
- [ ] 34. FRANK DEMAREE
- [ ] 35. BILL JURGES
- [ ] 51. MEL OTT
- [ ] 53. CARL HUBBELL
- [ ] 54. HARRY GUMBERT
- [ ] 58. LOU CHIOZZA
- [ ] 66. JIM RIPPLE
- [ ] 73. HAL SCHUMACHER
- [ ] 79. JOJO MOORE
- [ ] 124. WALTER BROWN
- [ ] 125. CLIFF MELTON
- [ ] 144. ZEKE BONURA

NEW YORK YANKEES

- [ ] 1. JAKE POWELL
- [ ] 3. RED RUFFING
- [ ] 25. GEORGE SELKIRK
- [ ] 26. JOE DIMAGGIO
- [ ] 30. BILL DICKEY
- [ ] 42. ARNDT JORGENS
- [ ] 48. LEFTY GOMEZ
- [ ] 52. TOMMY HENRICH
- [ ] 71. MONTE PEARSON
- [ ] 81. BABE DAHLGREN
- [ ] 88. CHARLIE KELLER

PHILADELPHIA PHILLIES

- [ ] 12. HERSHEL MARTIN
- [ ] 28. SYLVESTER JOHNSON
- [ ] 33. DEL YOUNG
- [ ] 37. VIRGIL DAVIS
- [ ] 45. MERRILL MAY
- [ ] 46. MORRIS ARNOVICH
- [ ] 63. EMMETT MUELLER
- [ ] 82. CHUCK KLEIN(F)
- [ ] 98. PINKEY WHITNEY
- [ ] 127. GIL BRACK
- [ ] 145. HUGH MULCAHY

PHILADELPHIA ATHLETCS

- [ ] 8. HENRY PIPPEN
- [ ] 64. WALLY MOSES
- [ ] 84. SKEETER NEWSOME
- [ ] 97. BOB JOHNSON
- [ ] 108. FRANK HAYES
- [ ] 117. WAYNE AMBLER
- [ ] 118. LYNN NELSON

PITTSBURGH PIRATES

- [ ] 9. JIM TOBIN
- [ ] 11. JOHN RIZZO
- [ ] 55. ARKIE VAUGHAN
- [ ] 82. CHUCK KLEIN(B)
- [ ] 83. GUS SUHR
- [ ] 89. LLOYD WANER
- [ ] 90. BOB KLINGER
- [ ] 94. HEINIE MANUSH
- [ ] 102. PEP YOUNG
- [ ] 112. PAUL WANER
- [ ] 128. JOE BOWMAN
- [ ] 129. BILL SWIFT
- [ ] 130. BILL BRUBAKER
- [ ] 156. RAY BERRES

ST. LOUIS BROWNS

- [ ] 43. MELO ALMADA
- [ ] 44. DON HEFFNER
- [ ] 109. MYRIL HOAG
- [ ] 122. GEORGE MCQUINN
- [ ] 148. BILL TROTTER

ST. LOUIS CARDINALS

- [ ] 19. DAFFY DEAN
- [ ] 41. LON WARNEKE
- [ ] 131. MORT COOPER

☐ 132. JIM BROWN
☐ 133. LYNN MYERS
☐ 135. MICKEY OWEN
☐ 146. TOM SUNKEL
☐ 157. DON PADGETT

WASHINGTON SENATORS

☐ 10. JIM DESHONG
☐ 21. DUTCH LEONARD
☐ 31. SAM WEST
☐ 39. RICK FERRELL
☐ 47. BUDDY LEWIS
☐ 59. KEN CHASE
☐ 93. CHARLIE GELBERT
☐ 100. BUDDY MYER
☐ 114. CECIL TRAVIS
☐ 137. PETE APPLETON
☐ 138. GEORGE CASE

1940 PLAY BALL (240)
2 1/2" X 3 1/8"
BLACK & WHITE

"TWINKLETOES" SELKIRK

BOSTON BEES

☐ 56. EDDIE MILLER
☐ 57. MAX WEST
☐ 58. BILL POSEDEL
☐ 59. RABBITT WARTSLER
☐ 60. JOHN COONEY
☐ 61. TONY CUCCINELLO
☐ 62. BUDDY HASSETT
☐ 140. DICK COFFMAN
☐ 141. CASEY STENGEL(M)
☐ 142. GEORGE KELLY(C)
☐ 143. GENE MOORE(B)

BOSTON RED SOX

☐ 27. TED WILLIAMS
☐ 28. GENE DESAUTELS
☐ 29. ROGER CRAMER
☐ 30. MOE BERG(C)
☐ 31. JACK WILSON
☐ 32. JIM BAGBY
☐ 33. FRED OSTERMUELLER
☐ 34. JOHN PEACOCK
☐ 35. JOE HEVING
☐ 36. JIM TABOR
☐ 37. EMERSON DICKMAN
☐ 38. BOBBY DOERR
☐ 39. TOM CAREY
☐ 133. JIMMIE FOXX
☐ 134. JOE CRONIN(M)
☐ 196. LEO NONNENKAMP
☐ 197. LOU FINNEY
☐ 198. DENNY GALEHOUSE

BROOKLYN DODGERS

☐ 63. PETE COSCARART
☐ 64. VAN LINGO MUNGO
☐ 65. FRED FITZSIMMONS
☐ 66. BABE PHELPS
☐ 67. WHIT WYATT
☐ 68. DOLPH CAMILLI
☐ 69. COOKIE LAVAGETTO
☐ 70. LUKE HAMLIN
☐ 71. MELO ALMADA
☐ 72. CHUCK DRESSEN(C)
☐ 143. GENE MOORE(F)

☐ 144. JOE VOSMIK
☐ 145. VITO TAMULIS
☐ 146. FORREST PRESSNELL
☐ 147. JOHN HUDSON
☐ 148. HUGH CASEY
☐ 207. GUS MANCUSO

"CHUCK" DRESSEN

CHICAGO CUBS

☐ 239. GEORGE UHLE(C)

CHICAGO WHITE SOX

☐ 13. JOHN KNOTT
☐ 14. ERIC MCNAIR
☐ 126. JAKE SOLTERS
☐ 127. MUDDY RUEL(C)
☐ 128. PETE APPLETON
☐ 184. MULE HAAS(C)
☐ 185. JOE JUHEL
☐ 186. TAFT WRIGHT
☐ 187. JIMMY DYKES(M)

"WILDFIRE" CRAFT

CINCINNATI REDS

☐ 73. BUCKY WALTERS
☐ 74. PAUL DERRINGER
☐ 75. FRANK MCCORMICK
☐ 76. LONNIE FREY
☐ 77. BILL HERSHBERGER
☐ 78. LEW RIGGS
☐ 79. HARRY CRAFT
☐ 80. BILL MYERS
☐ 81. WALLY BERGER
☐ 82. HANK GOWDY(C)
☐ 149. MILBURN SHOFFNER
☐ 150. WHITEY MOORE
☐ 151. ED JOOST
☐ 152. JIMMY WILSON(C)
☐ 153. BILL MCKECHNIE(M)
☐ 208. LEE GAMBLE

CLEVELAND INDIANS

☐ 47. OSCAR VITT(M)
☐ 48. LUKE SEWELL(C)
☐ 49. ROY WEATHERLY
☐ 50. HAL TROSKY
☐ 138. BEAU BELL
☐ 202. AL MILNAR
☐ 203. ODELL HALE
☐ 204. HARRY EISENSTAT
☐ 205. ROLLIE HEMSLEY

DETROIT TIGERS

☐ 40. HANK GREENBERG
☐ 41. CHARLIE GEHRINGER
☐ 42. BUD THOMAS
☐ 43. PETE FOX
☐ 44. DIZZY TROUT
☐ 45. RALPH KRESS
☐ 46. EARL AVERILL
☐ 135. LYNN NELSON
☐ 136. COTTON PIPPEN
☐ 137. BING MILLER(C)
☐ 199. PINKY HIGGINS
☐ 200. BRUCE CAMPBELL
☐ 201. BARNEY MCCOSKY

NEW YORK GIANTS

☐ 83. CLIFF MELTON
☐ 84. JOJO MOORE
☐ 85. HAL SCHUMACHER
☐ 86. HARRY GUMBERT
☐ 87. CARL HUBBELL
☐ 88. MEL OTT
☐ 89. BILL JURGES
☐ 90. FRANK DEMAREE
☐ 91. BOB SEEDS
☐ 92. BURGESS WHITEHEAD
☐ 93. HARRY DANNING
☐ 154. WALTER BROWN
☐ 155. RAY HAYWORTH
☐ 156. DAFFY DEAN
☐ 157. LOU CHIOZZA
☐ 158. TRAVIS JACKSON(C)
☐ 159. FRANK SNYDER(C)
☐ 209. HY VANDENBERG
☐ 210. BILL LOHRMAN
☐ 211. ROY JOINER
☐ 212. BABE YOUNG
☐ 213. JOHN RUCKER
☐ 214. KEN O'DEA
☐ 215. JOHNNIE MCCARTHY

NEW YORK YANKEES

☐ 1. JOE DIMAGGIO
☐ 2. ARNDT JORGENS
☐ 3. BABE DAHLGREN
☐ 4. TOMMY HENRICH
☐ 5. MONTE PEARSON
☐ 6. LEFTY GOMEZ
☐ 7. BILL DICKEY
☐ 8. GEORGE SELKIRK
☐ 9. CHARLIE KELLER
☐ 10. RED RUFFING
☐ 11. JAKE POWELL
☐ 12. JOHNNY SCHULTE(C)
☐ 121. ATLEY DONALD
☐ 122. STEVE SUNDRA
☐ 123. ORAL HILDEBRAND
☐ 124. EARLE COMBS(C)
☐ 125. ART FLETCHER(C)
☐ 181. SPUD CHANDLER
☐ 182. BILL KNICKERBOCKER
☐ 183. MARVIN BREUER

PHILADELPHIA ATHLETICS

☐ 24. FRANK HAYES
☐ 25. BOB JOHNSON
☐ 26. WALLY MOSES
☐ 132. CONNIE MACK(M)
☐ 190. CHARLEY BERRY(C)
☐ 191. JOHNNY BABICH
☐ 192. DICK SIEBERT
☐ 193. CHUBBY DEAN
☐ 194. SAM·CHAPMAN
☐ 195. DEE MILES

PHIADELPHIA PHILLIES

☐ 94. GUS SUHR
☐ 95. HUGH MULCAHY
☐ 96. EMMETT MUELLER
☐ 97. MORRIS ARNOVICH
☐ 98. MERRILL MAY
☐ 99. SYLVESTER JOHNSON
☐ 100. HERSHEL MARTIN
☐ 101. DEL YOUNG
☐ 102. CHUCK KLEIN
☐ 160. HANS LOBERT(C)
☐ 216. JOE MARTY

☐ 217. WALTER BECK
☐ 218. WALTER MILLIES
☐ 240. BILL ATWOOD

PITTSBURGH PIRATES

☐ 103. ELBIE FLETCHER
☐ 104. PAUL WANER
☐ 105. LLOYD WANER
☐ 106. PEP YOUNG
☐ 107. ARKY VAUGHAN
☐ 108. JOHN RIZZO
☐ 161. DEBS GARMS
☐ 162. JOE BOWMAN
☐ 163. SPUD DAVIS
☐ 164. RAY BERRES
☐ 165. BOB KLINGER
☐ 166. BILL BRUBAKER
☐ 167. FRANK FRISCH(M)
☐ 168. HONUS WAGNER(C)
☐ 219. RUSS BAUERS
☐ 220. MACE BROWN
☐ 221. LEE HANDLEY
☐ 222. MAX BUTCHER

ST. LOUIS BROWNS

☐ 51. DON HEFFNER
☐ 52. MYRIL HOAG
☐ 53. GEORGE MCQUINN
☐ 54. BILL TROTTER
☐ 55. GEORGE COFFMAN
☐ 139. ELDEN AUKER
☐ 206. CHET LAABS

ST. LOUIS CARDINALS

☐ 109. DON PADGETT
☐ 110. TOM SUNKEL
☐ 111. MICKEY OWEN
☐ 112. JIM BROWN
☐ 113. MORT COOPER
☐ 114. LON WARNEKE
☐ 115. MIKE GONZALES(C)

WASHINGTON SENATORS

☐ 15. GEORGE CASE
☐ 16. CECIL TRAVIS
☐ 17. BUDDY MYER
☐ 18. CHARLIE GELBERT
☐ 19. KEN CHASE
☐ 20. BUDDY LEWIS
☐ 21. RICK FERRELL
☐ 22. SAM WEST
☐ 23. DUTCH LEONARD
☐ 129. BUCKY HARRIS(M)
☐ 130. CLYDE MILAN(C)
☐ 131. ZEKE BONURA
☐ 188. JOE KRAKAUSKAS
☐ 189. JIM BLOODWORTH

1941 PLAY BALL SPORTS HALL OF FAME (72) 2 1/2″ X 3 1/8″

BARNEY McCOSKY

BOSTON BRAVES

☐ 1. EDDIE MILLER*
☐ 2. MAX WEST*
☐ 25. GENE MOORE

* Nos. 1 and 2 appear with Boston Bees on the back of the card.

☐ 49. BABE DAHLGREN
☐ 50. JOHN COONEY
☐ 58. FRANK DEMAREE

BOSTON RED SOX

☐ 13. JIMMIE FOXX
☐ 14. TED WILLIAMS
☐ 15. JOE CRONIN(M)
☐ 29. JACK WILSON
☐ 30. LOU FINNEY
☐ 63. DOM DIMAGGIO
☐ 64. BOBBY DOERR

BROOKLYN DODGERS

☐ 51. DOLPH CAMILLI
☐ 52. KIRBY HIGBE
☐ 53. LUKE HAMLIN
☐ 54. PEE WEE REESE
☐ 55. WHIT WYATT

CHICAGO CUBS

NO CARDS ISSUED

CHICAGO WHITE SOX

☐ 31. JOE KUHEL
☐ 32. TAFT WRIGHT

CLEVELAND INDIANS

☐ 16. HAL TROSKY
☐ 17. ROY WEATHERLY
☐ 33. AL MILNAR
☐ 34. ROLLIE HEMSLEY

DETROIT TIGERS

☐ 18. HANK GREENBERG
☐ 19. CHARLIE GEHRINGER
☐ 35. PINKY HIGGINS
☐ 36. BARNEY MCCOSKY
☐ 37. BRUCE CAMPBELL
☐ 65. TOMMY BRIDGES

CARL HUBBELL

NEW YORK GIANTS

☐ 6. CARL HUBBELL
☐ 7. HARRY DANNING
☐ 8. MEL OTT
☐ 26. HARRY GUMBERT
☐ 27. BABE YOUNG
☐ 57. MORRIS ARNOVICH
☐ 59. BILL JURGES

NEW YORK YANKEES

☐ 20. RED RUFFING
☐ 21. CHARLIE KELLER
☐ 38. ATLEY DONALD
☐ 39. TOMMY HENRICH
☐ 70. BILL DICKEY
☐ 71. JOE DIMAGGIO
☐ 72. LEFTY GOMEZ

PHILADELPHIA ATHLETICS

☐ 22. BOB JOHNSON
☐ 40. JOHN BABICH
☐ 41. FRANK HAYES
☐ 42. WALLY MOSES

☐ 43. AL BRANCATO
☐ 44. SAM CHAPMAN
☐ 68. JOHN KNOTT

"PINKY" MAY

PHILADELPHIA PHILLIES

☐ 9. MERRILL MAY
☐ 28. JOE MARTY
☐ 60. CHUCK KLEIN

PITTSBURGH PIRATES

☐ 10. ARKY VAUGHAN
☐ 11. DEBS GARMS
☐ 61. VINCE DIMAGGIO
☐ 62. ELBIE FLETCHER

ST. LOUIS BROWNS

☐ 23. GEORGE MCQUINN
☐ 45. ELDEN AUKER
☐ 66. HARLAND CLIFT
☐ 67. WALT JUDNICH

ST. LOUIS CARDINALS

☐ 12. JIM BROWN

WASHINGTON SENATORS

☐ 24. DUTCH LEONARD
☐ 46. SID HUDSON
☐ 47. BUDDY LEWIS
☐ 48. CECIL TRAVIS*
☐ 69. GEORGE CASE

67

SPORTFLICS

The technology of the Sportflics cards allows them to portray more than one player per card. Because the purpose of this team checklist is to account for the cards of all players on a particular team in a particular year, it is necessary to list the card numbers more than once if more than one player is on a given card. The conventions below are used to denote a card with more than one player on it.

BS — Big Six Card
TS — Tri-Star Card
BT — Big Twelve Card

1986 SPORTFLICS (200)
2 1/2 X 3 1/2

ATLANTA BRAVES

- [ ] 5. DALE MURPHY
- [ ] 47. BRUCE SUTTER
- [ ] 62. DALE MURPHY(TS)
- [ ] 65. BRUCE SUTTER(TS)
- [ ] 66. BOB HORNER(TS)
- [ ] 115. BOB HORNER
- [ ] 135. PHIL NIEKRO(TS)
- [ ] 179. DALE MURPHY(BS)
- [ ] 183. DALE MURPHY(BS)

BALTIMORE ORIOLES

- [ ] 4. EDDIE MURRAY
- [ ] 8. CAL RIPKEN
- [ ] 38. FRED LYNN
- [ ] 54. CAL RIPKEN(TS)
- [ ] 57. CAL RIPKEN(TS)
- [ ] 59. MIKE FLANAGAN(TS)
- [ ] 63. FRED LYNN(TS)
- [ ] 69. CAL RIPKEN(TS)
- [ ] 71. FRED LYNN(TS)
- [ ] 73. FRED LYNN(TS)
- [ ] 73. EDDIE MURRAY(TS)
- [ ] 73. CAL RIPKEN(TS)
- [ ] 87. LEE LACY
- [ ] 104. MIKE BODDICKER
- [ ] 128. CAL RIPKEN(TS)
- [ ] 137. FRED LYNN(TS)
- [ ] 145. EDDIE MURRAY(TS)
- [ ] 147. RICK DEMPSEY(TS)
- [ ] 149. MIKE BODDICKER(TS)
- [ ] 150. FRED LYNN(TS)
- [ ] 177. LARRY SHEETS(BS)
- [ ] 199. MIKE YOUNG

BOSTON RED SOX

- [ ] 3. WADE BOGGS
- [ ] 17. JIM RICE
- [ ] 32. DWIGHT EVANS
- [ ] 52. JIM RICE(TS)
- [ ] 61. JIM RICE(TS)
- [ ] 61. TONY ARMAS(TS)
- [ ] 75. WADE BOGGS(TS)
- [ ] 81. BILL BUCKNER
- [ ] 84. RICH GEDMAN
- [ ] 139. JIM RICE(TS)
- [ ] 140. BILL BUCKNER(TS)
- [ ] 145. TONY ARMAS(TS)
- [ ] 146. JIM RICE(TS)
- [ ] 152. DENNIS BOYD
- [ ] 169. BOB STANLEY
- [ ] 178. MIKE GREENWELL(BS)
- [ ] 180. WADE BOGGS(BS)
- [ ] 183. WADE BOGGS(BS)
- [ ] 184. WADE BOGGS(BS)

CALIFORNIA ANGELS

- [ ] 37. REGGIE JACKSON
- [ ] 53. MIKE WITT(TS)
- [ ] 57. REGGIE JACKSON(TS)
- [ ] 61. REGGIE JACKSON(TS)
- [ ] 69. ROD CAREW(TS)
- [ ] 71. REGGIE JACKSON(TS)
- [ ] 74. ROD CAREW(TS)
- [ ] 106. ROD CAREW
- [ ] 129. JOHN CANDELARIA(TS)
- [ ] 135. DON SUTTON(TS)
- [ ] 146. ROD CAREW(TS)
- [ ] 147. REGGIE JACKSON(TS)
- [ ] 150. REGGIE JACKSON(TS)
- [ ] 154. BRIAN DOWNING
- [ ] 173. DOUG DECINCES
- [ ] 175. DON SUTTON
- [ ] 177. STEWART CLIBURN(BS)
- [ ] 180. ROD CAREW(BS)
- [ ] 182. ROD CAREW(BS)

CHICAGO CUBS

- [ ] 20. RYNE SANDBERG
- [ ] 45. LEE SMITH
- [ ] 46. RICK SUTCLIFFE
- [ ] 51. RYNE SANDBERG(TS)
- [ ] 55. LEE SMITH(TS)
- [ ] 60. RICK SUTCLIFFE(TS)
- [ ] 66. GARY MATTHEWS(TS)
- [ ] 70. RICK SUTCLIFFE(TS)
- [ ] 72. RICK SUTCLIFFE(TS)
- [ ] 90. KEITH MORELAND
- [ ] 111. LEON DURHAM
- [ ] 127. RYNE SANDBERG(TS)
- [ ] 129. DENNIS ECKERSLEY(TS)
- [ ] 130. RON CEY(TS)
- [ ] 134. RICK SUTCLIFFE(TS)
- [ ] 144. DAVEY LOPES(TS)
- [ ] 149. RICK SUTCLIFFE(TS)
- [ ] 155. SHAWON DUNSTON
- [ ] 194. DAVEY LOPES

CHICAGO WHITE SOX

- [ ] 7. HAROLD BAINES
- [ ] 22. OZZIE GUILLEN
- [ ] 25. TOM SEAVER
- [ ] 52. HAROLD BAINES(TS)
- [ ] 60. TOM SEAVER(TS)
- [ ] 67. RON KITTLE(TS)
- [ ] 67. CARLTON FISK(TS)
- [ ] 67. TOM SEAVER(TS)
- [ ] 70. TOM SEAVER(TS)
- [ ] 86. RON KITTLE
- [ ] 105. BRITT BURNS
- [ ] 125. CARLTON FISK
- [ ] 133. RICHARD DOTSON(TS)
- [ ] 134. TOM SEAVER(TS)
- [ ] 135. TOM SEAVER(TS)
- [ ] 142. TOM SEAVER(TS)
- [ ] 158. BOB JAMES
- [ ] 174. GREG WALKER
- [ ] 176. OZZIE GUILLEN(BS)
- [ ] 182. TOM SEAVER(BS)

CINCINNATI REDS

- [ ] 23. DAVE PARKER
- [ ] 50. PETE ROSE
- [ ] 51. PETE ROSE(TS)
- [ ] 56. PETE ROSE(TS)
- [ ] 58. DAVE PARKER(TS)
- [ ] 58. PETE ROSE(TS)
- [ ] 69. PETE ROSE(TS)
- [ ] 79. TOM BROWNING
- [ ] 130. PETE ROSE(TS)
- [ ] 131. DAVE CONCEPCION(TS)
- [ ] 138. TONY PEREZ(TS)
- [ ] 138. PETE ROSE(TS)
- [ ] 151. BUDDY BELL
- [ ] 153. DAVE CONCEPCION
- [ ] 156. JOHN FRANCO
- [ ] 166. TED POWER
- [ ] 168. MARIO SOTO
- [ ] 181. DAVE PARKER(BS)
- [ ] 181. PETE ROSE(BS)
- [ ] 182. PETE ROSE(BS)
- [ ] 183. DAVE PARKER(BS)
- [ ] 185. TOM BROWNING(BS)

CLEVELAND INDIANS

- [ ] 26. BRETT BUTLER
- [ ] 33. JULIO FRANCO
- [ ] 171. ANDRE THORNTON

DETROIT TIGERS

- [ ] 21. KIRK GIBSON
- [ ] 48. LOU WHITAKER
- [ ] 65. WILLIE HERNANDEZ(TS)
- [ ] 74. LOU WHITAKER(TS)
- [ ] 85. WILLIE HERNANDEZ
- [ ] 92. LANCE PARRISH
- [ ] 117. JACK MORRIS
- [ ] 141. JACK MORRIS(TS)
- [ ] 147. ALAN TRAMMELL(TS)
- [ ] 172. ALAN TRAMMELL
- [ ] 183. DARRELL EVANS(BS)
- [ ] 189. DARRELL EVANS

HOUSTON ASTROS

- [ ] 30. JOSE CRUZ
- [ ] 43. NOLAN RYAN
- [ ] 141. NOLAN RYAN(TS)
- [ ] 143. NOLAN RYAN(TS)
- [ ] 182. NOLAN RYAN(BS)
- [ ] 188. GLENN DAVIS
- [ ] 195. MIKE SCOTT

KANSAS CITY ROYALS

- [ ] 1. GEORGE BRETT
- [ ] 10. BRET SABERHAGEN
- [ ] 52. GEORGE BRETT(TS)
- [ ] 55. DAN QUISENBERRY(TS)
- [ ] 63. GEORGE BRETT(TS)
- [ ] 118. DAN QUISENBERRY
- [ ] 124. WILLIE WILSON
- [ ] 128. WILLIE WILSON(TS)
- [ ] 144. WILLIE WILSON(TS)

☐ 159. CHARLIE LEIBRANDT
☐ 176. BRET SABERHAGEN(BS)
☐ 179. GEORGE BRETT(BS)
☐ 180. GEORGE BRETT(BS)
☐ 180. WILLIE WILSON(BS)
☐ 185. BRET SABERHAGEN(BS)
☐ 186. BRET SABERHAGEN(BT)
☐ 186. LONNIE SMITH(BT)
☐ 186. DANNY JACKSON(BT)
☐ 186. DANE IORG(BT)
☐ 186. JIM SUNDBERG(BT)
☐ 186. CHARLIE LEIBRANDT(BT)
☐ 186. DAN QUISENBERRY(BT)
☐ 186. DARRYL MOTLEY(BT)
☐ 186. GEORGE BRETT(BT)
☐ 186. STEVE BALBONI(BT)
☐ 186. WILLIE WILSON(BT)
☐ 186. FRANK WHITE(BT)
☐ 200. BUDDY BIANCALANA

LOS ANGELES DODGERS

☐   9. OREL HERSHISER
☐ 12. FERNANDO VALENZUELA
☐ 14. PEDRO GUERRERO
☐ 53. JERRY REUSS(TS)
☐ 56. STEVE SAX(TS)
☐ 58. BILL MADLOCK(TS)
☐ 60. FERNANDO VALENZUELA(TS)
☐ 72. FERNANDO VALENZUELA(TS)
☐ 88. BILL MADLOCK
☐ 89. MIKE MARSHALL
☐ 95. STEVE SAX
☐ 131. BILL MADLOCK(TS)
☐ 132. FERNANDO VALENZUELA(TS)
☐ 143. FERNANDO VALENZUELA(TS)
☐ 148. PEDRO GUERRERO(TS)
☐ 167. MIKE SCIOSCIA
☐ 181. BILL MADLOCK(BS)
☐ 181. PEDRO GUERRERO(BS)
☐ 198. BOB WELCH

MILWAUKEE BREWERS

☐ 16. ERNEST RILES
☐ 29. CECIL COOPER
☐ 39. PAUL MOLITOR
☐ 42. ROBIN YOUNT
☐ 54. ROBIN YOUNT(TS)
☐ 63. ROBIN YOUNT(TS)
☐ 65. ROLLIE FINGERS(TS)
☐ 71. ROBIN YOUNT(TS)
☐ 114. TEDDY HIGUERA
☐ 128. PAUL MOLITOR(TS)
☐ 130. ROLLIE FINGERS(TS)
☐ 145. CECIL COOPER(TS)
☐ 146. ROLLIE FINGERS(TS)
☐ 178. BILLY JO ROBIDOUX(BS)
☐ 180. CECIL COOPER(BS)
☐ 196. TED SIMMONS

MINNESOTA TWINS

☐ 36. KENT HRBEK
☐ 64. BERT BLYLEVEN(TS)
☐ 80. TOM BRUNANSKY
☐ 93. KIRBY PUCKETT
☐ 99. FRANK VIOLA
☐ 103. BERT BLYLEVEN
☐ 142. BERT BLYLEVEN(TS)
☐ 177. MARK SALAS(BS)
☐ 178. MARK FUNDERBURK(BS)
☐ 178. STEVE LOMBARDOZZI(BS)

MONTREAL EXPOS

☐ 11. TIM RAINES
☐ 66. ANDRE DAWSON(TS)
☐ 110. ANDRE DAWSON
☐ 119. JEFF REARDON
☐ 120. BRYN SMITH
☐ 123. TIM WALLACH
☐ 127. TIM RAINES(TS)
☐ 144. TIM RAINES(TS)
☐ 177. JOE HESKETH(BS)
☐ 187. HUBIE BROOKS

NEW YORK METS

☐ 15. KEITH HERNANDEZ
☐ 28. GARY CARTER
☐ 56. DARRYL STRAWBERRY(TS)

☐ 62. KEITH HERNANDEZ(TS)
☐ 68. GEORGE FOSTER(TS)
☐ 97. DARRYL STRAWBERRY
☐ 100. DWIGHT GOODEN
☐ 109. RON DARLING
☐ 126. GARY CARTER(TS)
☐ 126. GEORGE FOSTER(TS)
☐ 127. KEITH HERNANDEZ(TS)
☐ 131. GEORGE FOSTER(TS)
☐ 136. DWIGHT GOODEN(TS)
☐ 137. GARY CARTER(TS)
☐ 138. RUSTY STAUB(TS)
☐ 139. GEORGE FOSTER(TS)
☐ 143. DWIGHT GOODEN(TS)
☐ 161. ROGER MCDOWELL
☐ 176. DWIGHT GOODEN(BS)
☐ 179. KEITH HERNANDEZ(BS)
☐ 181. KEITH HERNANDEZ(BS)
☐ 184. DWIGHT GOODEN(BS)
☐ 185. DWIGHT GOODEN(BS)

NEW YORK YANKEES

☐   2. DON MATTINGLY
☐   6. RICKEY HENDERSON
☐ 18. RON GUIDRY
☐ 41. DAVE RIGHETTI
☐ 49. DAVE WINFIELD
☐ 53. PHIL NIEKRO(TS)
☐ 54. DON MATTINGLY(TS)
☐ 57. DON BAYLOR(TS)
☐ 59. RON GUIDRY(TS)
☐ 72. DAVE RIGHETTI(TS)
☐ 75. DON MATTINGLY(TS)
☐ 141. DAVE RIGHETTI(TS)
☐ 149. RON GUIDRY(TS)
☐ 163. PHIL NIEKRO
☐ 176. DON MATTINGLY(BS)
☐ 177. BRIAN FISHER(BS)
☐ 179. RON GUIDRY(BS)
☐ 179. DON MATTINGLY(BS)
☐ 180. DON MATTINGLY(BS)
☐ 182. PHIL NIEKRO(BS)
☐ 183. DON MATTINGLY(BS)
☐ 184. RICKEY HENDERSON(BS)
☐ 184. DON MATTINGLY(BS)
☐ 185. RON GUIDRY(BS)

OAKLAND A'S

☐ 68. DAVE KINGMAN(TS)
☐ 75. CARNEY LANSFORD(TS)
☐ 83. MIKE DAVIS
☐ 116. DAVE KINGMAN
☐ 136. ALFREDO GRIFFIN(TS)
☐ 150. DAVE KINGMAN(TS)
☐ 178. JOSE CANSECO(BS)
☐ 192. JAY HOWELL

PHILADELPHIA PHILLIES

☐ 27. STEVE CARLTON
☐ 44. MIKE SCHMIDT
☐ 62. MIKE SCHMIDT(TS)
☐ 64. JERRY KOOSMAN(TS)
☐ 64. JOHN DENNY(TS)
☐ 68. MIKE SCHMIDT(TS)
☐ 70. STEVE CARLTON(TS)
☐ 94. JUAN SAMUEL
☐ 132. JOHN DENNY(TS)

☐ 134. JOHN DENNY(TS)
☐ 139. MIKE SCHMIDT(TS)
☐ 148. MIKE SCHMIDT(TS)

PITTSBURGH PIRATES

☐ 165. TONY PENA
☐ 177. JOE ORSULAK(BS)

ST. LOUIS CARDINALS

☐ 19. WILLIE MCGEE
☐ 24. VINCE COLEMAN
☐ 101. JOAQUIN ANDUJAR
☐ 107. JACK CLARK
☐ 108. DANNY COX
☐ 113. TOM HERR
☐ 121. OZZIE SMITH
☐ 122. JOHN TUDOR
☐ 129. BOB FORSCH(TS)
☐ 133. JOAQUIN ANDUJAR(TS)
☐ 136. VINCE COLEMAN(TS)
☐ 148. DARRELL PORTER(TS)
☐ 176. VINCE COLEMAN(BS)
☐ 176. WILLIE MCGEE(BS)
☐ 179. WILLIE MCGEE(BS)
☐ 183. WILLIE MCGEE(BS)
☐ 184. WILLIE MCGEE(BS)
☐ 184. JOHN TUDOR(BS)
☐ 185. JOHN TUDOR(BS)
☐ 185. JOAQUIN ANDUJAR(BS)

SAN DIEGO PADRES

☐ 13. TONY GWYNN
☐ 35. STEVE GARVEY
☐ 51. STEVE GARVEY(TS)
☐ 55. GOOSE GOSSAGE(TS)
☐ 59. LAMARR HOYT(TS)
☐ 91. GRAIG NETTLES
☐ 137. STEVE GARVEY(TS)
☐ 140. TONY GWYNN(TS)
☐ 170. GARRY TEMPLETON
☐ 181. TONY GWYNN(BS)
☐ 190. GOOSE GOSSAGE
☐ 191. ANDY HAWKINS
☐ 193. LAMARR HOYT

SAN FRANCISCO GIANTS

☐ 78. CHRIS BROWN
☐ 82. CHILI DAVIS
☐ 132. VIDA BLUE(TS)
☐ 142. VIDA BLUE(TS)
☐ 157. SCOTT GARRELTS

SEATTLE MARINERS

☐ 31. ALVIN DAVIS
☐ 40. JIM PRESLEY
☐ 74. ALVIN DAVIS(TS)
☐ 77. PHIL BRADLEY
☐ 162. MIKE MOORE
☐ 178. DAN TARTABULL(BS)

TEXAS RANGERS

☐ 160. ODDIBE MCDOWELL
☐ 197. GARY WARD

TORONTO BLUE JAYS

☐ 34. DAMASO GARCIA
☐ 76. JESSE BARFIELD
☐ 96. DAVE STIEB
☐ 98. WILLIE UPSHAW
☐ 102. GEORGE BELL
☐ 112. TONY FERNANDEZ
☐ 126. AL OLIVER(TS)
☐ 133. DOYLE ALEXANDER(TS)
☐ 140. AL OLIVER(TS)
☐ 164. AL OLIVER

1986 SPORTFLICS ROOKIES (50)
2 1/2 X 3 1/2

ATLANTA BRAVES

☐ 14. ANDRES THOMAS
☐ 24. PAUL ASSENMACHER

BALTIMORE ORIOLES

☐ 32. JIM TRABER
☐ 46. FRED LYNN(TS)
☐ 48. EDDIE MURRAY(BS)
☐ 48. CAL RIPKEN(BS)

BOSTON RED SOX

☐ 44. CALVIN SCHIRALDI

CALIFORNIA ANGELS

☐ 7. WALLY JOYNER

CHICAGO CUBS

NO CARDS ISSUED

CHICAGO WHITE SOX

☐ 31. JOHN CANGELOSI
☐ 33. RUSS MORMAN

CINCINNATI REDS

☐ 34. BARRY LARKIN
☐ 43. KAL DANIELS
☐ 46. PETE ROSE(TS)

CLEVELAND INDIANS

☐ 9. SCOTT BAILES
☐ 18. CORY SNYDER
☐ 30. GREG SWINDELL

DETROIT TIGERS

☐ 42. ERIC KING
☐ 48. LOU WHITAKER(BS)

HOUSTON ASTROS

☐ 15. JIM DESHAIES
☐ 23. CHARLIE KERFELD

KANSAS CITY ROYALS

☐ 37. MIKE KINGERY
☐ 39. SCOTT BANKHEAD
☐ 40. BO JACKSON

LOS ANGELES DODGERS

☐ 19. REGGIE WILLIAMS
☐ 47. FERNANDO VALENZUELA(TS)
☐ 48. STEVE SAX(BS)

MILWAUKEE BREWERS

☐ 4. DALE SVEUM
☐ 5. JUAN NIEVES
☐ 10. DAN PLESAC
☐ 21. GLENN BRAGGS
☐ 28. BILLY JO ROBIDOUX

MINNESOTA TWINS

☐ 17. STEVE LOMBARDOZZI

MONTREAL EXPOS

☐ 27. ANDRES GALARRAGA

NEW YORK METS

☐ 47. TOM SEAVER(TS)
☐ 47. DWIGHT GOODEN(TS)
☐ 48. DARRYL STRAWBERRY(BS)
☐ 49. KEVIN MITCHELL

NEW YORK YANKEES

☐ 48. DAVE RIGHETTI(BS)

OAKLAND A'S

☐ 11. JOSE CANSECO

PHILADELPHIA PHILLIES

☐ 29. BRUCE RUFFIN

PITTSBURGH PIRATES

☐ 13. BARRY BONDS
☐ 26. BOBBY BONILLA
☐ 50. MIKE DIAZ

ST. LOUIS CARDINALS

☐ 35. TODD WORRELL
☐ 41. GREG MATHEWS

SAN DIEGO PADRES

☐ 1. JOHN KRUK
☐ 8. LANCE MCCULLERS

SAN FRANCISCO GIANTS

☐ 6. WILL CLARK
☐ 25. ROBBY THOMPSON
☐ 46. WILLIE MAYS(TS)

SEATTLE MARINERS

☐ 22. DANNY TARTABULL
☐ 45. MICKEY BRANTLEY

TEXAS RANGERS

☐ 2. EDWIN CORREA
☐ 3. PETE INCAVIGLIA
☐ 12. BOBBY WITT
☐ 16. RUBEN SIERRA
☐ 20. MITCH WILLIAMS

TORONTO BLUE JAYS

☐ 36. JOHN CERUTTI
☐ 38. MARK EICHHORN

1987 SPORTFLICS (200)
2 1/2 X 3 1/2

ATLANTA BRAVES

☐ 3. DALE MURPHY
☐ 73. BOB HORNER
☐ 155. DALE MURPHY(TS)
☐ 159. DALE MURPHY(BS)
☐ 196. BOB HORNER(TS)

BALTIMORE ORIOLES

☐ 6. EDDIE MURRAY
☐ 9. CAL RIPKEN
☐ 49. FRED LYNN
☐ 56. MIKE BODDICKER
☐ 75. EDDIE MURRAY(TS)
☐ 86. LEE LACY
☐ 113. CAL RIPKEN(TS)
☐ 159. EDDIE MURRAY(BS)
☐ 165. DON AASE
☐ 194. DON AASE(TS)
☐ 198. FRED LYNN(TS)

BOSTON RED SOX

☐ 2. WADE BOGGS
☐ 10. ROGER CLEMENS
☐ 28. TOM SEAVER
☐ 38. BRUCE HURST
☐ 47. DENNIS BOYD
☐ 70. BILL BUCKNER
☐ 80. JIM RICE(TS)
☐ 97. JIM RICE
☐ 111. ROGER CLEMENS(TS)
☐ 112. MARTY BARRETT(TS)
☐ 114. WADE BOGGS(TS)
☐ 118. PAT DODSON(BS)
☐ 128. DWIGHT EVANS
☐ 149. RICH GEDMAN
☐ 154. RICH GEDMAN(TS)
☐ 159. ROGER CLEMENS(BS)
☐ 163. DON BAYLOR
☐ 182. MARTY BARRETT
☐ 196. ROGER CLEMENS(TS)
☐ 197. WADE BOGGS(BS)

CALIFORNIA ANGELS

- ☐ 26. WALLY JOYNER
- ☐ 44. REGGIE JACKSON
- ☐ 59. MIKE WITT
- ☐ 75. WALLY JOYNER(TS)
- ☐ 99. DON SUTTON
- ☐ 106. DOUG DECINCES
- ☐ 127. KIRK McCASKILL
- ☐ 148. JOHN CANDELARIA
- ☐ 156. DON SUTTON(TS)
- ☐ 157. GARY PETTIS(TS)
- ☐ 161. BRIAN DOWNING
- ☐ 184. BOBBY GRICH

CHICAGO CUBS

- ☐ 8. RYNE SANDBERG
- ☐ 79. SHAWON DUNSTON(TS)
- ☐ 98. SHAWON DUNSTON
- ☐ 104. LEE SMITH
- ☐ 116. RYNE SANDBERG(TS)
- ☐ 122. KEITH MORELAND
- ☐ 158. RAFAEL PALMEIRO(BS)
- ☐ 170. JODY DAVIS
- ☐ 185. LEON DURHAM
- ☐ 197. RYNE SANDBERG(BS)

CHICAGO WHITE SOX

- ☐ 140. CARLTON FISK
- ☐ 153. HAROLD BAINES(TS)
- ☐ 157. JOHN CANGELOSI(TS)
- ☐ 158. DAVE COCHRANE(BS)
- ☐ 171. HAROLD BAINES
- ☐ 186. OZZIE GUILLEN
- ☐ 196. JOE COWLEY(TS)
- ☐ 200. STEVE CARLTON

CINCINNATI REDS

- ☐ 22. ERIC DAVIS
- ☐ 25. PETE ROSE
- ☐ 35. DAVE PARKER
- ☐ 117. DAVE PARKER(TS)
- ☐ 141. BUDDY BELL
- ☐ 155. ERIC DAVIS(TS)
- ☐ 192. JOHN FRANCO
- ☐ 199. ERIC DAVIS(TS)

CLEVELAND INDIANS

- ☐ 24. CORY SNYDER
- ☐ 60. TONY BERNAZARD
- ☐ 66. PAT TABLER
- ☐ 69. BRETT BUTLER
- ☐ 84. JULIO FRANCO
- ☐ 107. KEN SCHROM
- ☐ 109. BROOK JACOBY
- ☐ 112. TONY BERNAZARD(TS)
- ☐ 118. DAVID CLARK(BS)
- ☐ 147. PHIL NIEKRO
- ☐ 176. JOE CARTER
- ☐ 180. MEL HALL

DETROIT TIGERS

- ☐ 48. KIRK GIBSON
- ☐ 87. JACK MORRIS
- ☐ 101. LANCE PARRISH
- ☐ 105. WILLIE HERNANDEZ
- ☐ 111. JACK MORRIS(TS)
- ☐ 112. LOU WHITAKER(TS)
- ☐ 132. DARRELL EVANS
- ☐ 137. LOU WHITAKER
- ☐ 154. LANCE PARRISH(TS)
- ☐ 188. ALAN TRAMMELL

HOUSTON ASTROS

- ☐ 17. GLENN DAVIS
- ☐ 19. MIKE SCOTT
- ☐ 29. BOB KNEPPER
- ☐ 42. JOSE CRUZ
- ☐ 77. DAVE SMITH(TS)
- ☐ 94. DAVE SMITH
- ☐ 116. BILL DORAN(TS)
- ☐ 117. KEVIN BASS(TS)
- ☐ 118. TY GAINEY(BS)
- ☐ 119. MIKE SCOTT(TS)
- ☐ 120. MIKE SCOTT(TS)
- ☐ 125. NOLAN RYAN
- ☐ 146. CHARLIE KERFELD
- ☐ 152. JOSE CRUZ(TS)
- ☐ 156. JIM DESHAIES(TS)
- ☐ 162. BILL DORAN
- ☐ 175. KEVIN BASS
- ☐ 195. GLENN DAVIS(TS)

KANSAS CITY ROYALS

- ☐ 5. GEORGE BRETT
- ☐ 85. WILLIE WILSON
- ☐ 114. GEORGE BRETT(TS)
- ☐ 145. BRET SABERHAGEN
- ☐ 158. KEVIN SEITZER(BS)
- ☐ 167. DAN QUISENBERRY
- ☐ 168. FRANK WHITE
- ☐ 190. BO JACKSON
- ☐ 197. GEORGE BRETT(BS)

LOS ANGELES DODGERS

- ☐ 12. STEVE SAX
- ☐ 27. PEDRO GUERRERO
- ☐ 43. OREL HERSHISER
- ☐ 67. MIKE SCIOSCIA
- ☐ 82. MIKE MARSHALL
- ☐ 119. FERNANDO VALENZUELA(TS)
- ☐ 120. FERNANDO VALENZUELA(TS)
- ☐ 130. BILL MADLOCK
- ☐ 150. FERNANDO VALENZUELA
- ☐ 151. MIKE SCIOSCIA(TS)

MILWAUKEE BREWERS

- ☐ 11. TEDDY HIGUERA
- ☐ 16. ROBIN YOUNT
- ☐ 54. PAUL MOLITOR
- ☐ 111. TEDDY HIGUERA(TS)
- ☐ 169. CECIL COOPER
- ☐ 172. ROB DEER

MINNESOTA TWINS

- ☐ 7. KIRBY PUCKETT
- ☐ 15. KENT HRBEK
- ☐ 64. GARY GAETTI
- ☐ 81. BERT BLYLEVEN
- ☐ 114. GARY GAETTI(TS)
- ☐ 134. TOM BRUNANSKY
- ☐ 198. KIRBY PUCKETT(TS)

MONTREAL EXPOS

- ☐ 18. HUBIE BROOKS
- ☐ 34. TIM RAINES
- ☐ 72. TIM WALLACH
- ☐ 77. JEFF REARDON(TS)
- ☐ 79. HUBIE BROOKS(TS)
- ☐ 103. FLOYD YOUMANS
- ☐ 115. TIM WALLACH(TS)
- ☐ 139. ANDRE DAWSON
- ☐ 152. TIM RAINES(TS)
- ☐ 158. CASEY CANDAELE(BS)
- ☐ 177. MITCH WEBSTER
- ☐ 197. HUBIE BROOKS(BS)
- ☐ 197. TIM RAINES(BS)
- ☐ 199. TIM RAINES(TS)

NEW YORK METS

- ☐ 20. DARRYL STRAWBERRY
- ☐ 36. BOB OJEDA
- ☐ 50. GARY CARTER
- ☐ 53. RON DARLING
- ☐ 58. LEN DYKSTRA
- ☐ 63. SID FERNANDEZ
- ☐ 76. JESSIE OROSCO
- ☐ 88. RAY KNIGHT
- ☐ 100. DWIGHT GOODEN
- ☐ 120. DWIGHT GOODEN(TS)
- ☐ 124. WALLY BACKMAN
- ☐ 133. KEITH HERNANDEZ
- ☐ 144. KEVIN MITCHELL
- ☐ 151. GARY CARTER(TS)
- ☐ 159. DWIGHT GOODEN(BS)
- ☐ 160. ROGER McDOWELL
- ☐ 195. KEITH HERNANDEZ(TS)

NEW YORK YANKEES

- ☐ 1. DON MATTINGLY
- ☐ 4. RICKEY HENDERSON
- ☐ 41. DAVE WINFIELD
- ☐ 55. MIKE PAGLIARULO
- ☐ 57. DAVE RIGHETTI
- ☐ 71. DENNIS RASMUSSEN
- ☐ 75. DON MATTINGLY(TS)
- ☐ 83. RON GUIDRY
- ☐ 92. MIKE EASLER
- ☐ 118. PHIL LOMBARDI(BS)
- ☐ 119. DAVE RIGHETTI(TS)
- ☐ 143. DAN PASQUA
- ☐ 153. DAVE WINFIELD(TS)
- ☐ 157. RICKEY HENDERSON(TS)
- ☐ 159. DON MATTINGLY(BS)
- ☐ 159. RICKEY HENDERSON(BS)
- ☐ 194. DAVE RIGHETTI(TS)
- ☐ 198. RICKEY HENDERSON(TS)

OAKLAND A'S

- ☐ 80. JOSE CANSECO(TS)
- ☐ 90. JOSE CANSECO
- ☐ 118. TERRY STEINBACH(BS)
- ☐ 138. CARNEY LANSFORD
- ☐ 164. ALFREDO GRIFFIN
- ☐ 178. DAVE KINGMAN

PHILADELPHIA PHILLIES

- ☐ 30. MIKE SCHMIDT
- ☐ 108. DON CARMAN
- ☐ 110. STEVE BEDROSIAN
- ☐ 115. MIKE SCHMIDT(TS)
- ☐ 123. JUAN SAMUEL
- ☐ 156. MIKE SCHMIDT(TS)
- ☐ 166. GLENN WILSON
- ☐ 181. SHANE RAWLEY
- ☐ 193. VON HAYES

PITTSBURGH PIRATES

- ☐ 93. TONY PENA
- ☐ 116. JOHNNY RAY(TS)
- ☐ 121. JOHNNY RAY
- ☐ 129. RICK RHODEN
- ☐ 151. TONY PENA(TS)

ST. LOUIS CARDINALS

- ☐ 33. TODD WORRELL
- ☐ 65. VINCE COLEMAN
- ☐ 74. WILLIE McGEE
- ☐ 77. TODD WORRELL(TS)
- ☐ 79. OZZIE SMITH(TS)
- ☐ 142. OZZIE SMITH
- ☐ 152. VINCE COLEMAN(TS)
- ☐ 173. JOHN TUDOR
- ☐ 191. BOB FORSCH
- ☐ 199. VINCE COLEMAN(TS)

SAN DIEGO PADRES

- ☐ 31. TONY GWYNN
- ☐ 40. STEVE GARVEY
- ☐ 61. JOHN KRUK
- ☐ 117. TONY GWYNN(TS)
- ☐ 118. BENITO SANTIAGO(BS)
- ☐ 135. KEVIN McREYNOLDS

☐ 155. KEVIN MCREYNOLDS(TS)
☐ 158. RANDY ASADOOR(BS)
☐ 158. TIM PYZNARSKI(BS)
☐ 197. TONY GWYNN(BS)

SAN FRANCISCO GIANTS

☐ 13. CHRIS BROWN
☐ 45. CHILI DAVIS
☐ 46. ROBBY THOMPSON
☐ 62. MIKE KRUKOW
☐ 68. SCOTT GARRELTS
☐ 78. CANDY MALDONADO
☐ 95. WILL CLARK
☐ 115. CHRIS BROWN(TS)
☐ 195. WILL CLARK(TS)

SEATTLE MARINERS

☐ 21. ALVIN DAVIS
☐ 23. DANNY TARTABULL
☐ 89. PHIL BRADLEY
☐ 102. MARK LANGSTON
☐ 179. JIM PRESLEY

TEXAS RANGERS

☐ 32. DON SLAUGHT
☐ 37. PETE INCAVIGLIA
☐ 39. BOBBY WITT
☐ 52. PETE O'BRIEN
☐ 91. GARY WARD
☐ 113. SCOTT FLETCHER(TS)
☐ 126. GREG HARRIS
☐ 131. ODDIBE MCDOWELL
☐ 136. SCOTT FLETCHER
☐ 154. DON SLAUGHT(TS)
☐ 174. LARRY PARRISH

TORONTO BLUE JAYS

☐ 14. JESSE BARFIELD
☐ 51. GEORGE BELL
☐ 80. GEORGE BELL(TS)
☐ 96. LLOYD MOSEBY
☐ 113. TONY FERNANDEZ(TS)
☐ 153. JESSE BARFIELD(TS)
☐ 183. DAMASO GARCIA
☐ 187. TONY FERNANDEZ
☐ 189. JIM CLANCY
☐ 194. MARK EICHHORN(TS)

TRY **DEN'S**

DEN'S
COLLECTORS DEN

PLASTIC CARD PROTECTING PAGES
LARGEST SELECTION IN THE HOBBY

FINEST QUALITY PLASTIC SHEETS

SEND ONLY $1.00 for DEN'S BIG CATALOGUE CATALOGUE sent FREE with each ORDER

Featuring:

NON—MIGRATING PLASTIC IN ALL SHEETS
PLASTIC THAT DOES NOT STICK TOGETHER
STIFFNESS TO RESIST CARD CURLING
INTELLIGENT DESIGN
RESISTANCE TO CRACKING
FULL COVERAGE OF CARDS, PHOTOS, ENVELOPES

NO MIX & MATCH

STYLE	POCKETS CAPACITY	RECOMMENDED FOR	1•24	25•99	100•299	300•600
9 / 9T (TOP LOAD)	9 / 18	TOPPS (1957–PRESENT), FLEER, DONRUSS, TCMA, KELLOGG, POST CEREAL, LEAF (1960), RECENT NON-SPORTS CARDS, ALL STANDARD 2½" X 3½" CARDS	.25	.23	.21	.19
8	8 / 16	TOPPS (1952–1956), BOWMAN (1953–55)	.25	.23	.21	.19
12	12 / 24	BOWMAN (1948–50), TOPPS (1951 RED AND BLUE), RECENT TOPPS AND FLEER STICKERS	.25	.23	.21	.19
1	1 / 2	PHOTOGRAPHS (8X10)	.25	.23	.21	.19
2	2 / 4	PHOTOGRAPHS (5x7), TOPPS SUPERSTAR PHOTOS	.25	.23	.21	.19
4	4 / 8	POSTCARDS, TOPPS SUPER (1964,70,71), EXHIBITS, DONRUSS (ACTION ALL STARS), PEREZ STEELE HOF	.25	.23	.21	.19
18	18 / 36	T CARDS, TOPPS COINS, BAZOOKA (1963–67 INDIVIDUAL CARDS)	.35	.35	.30	.27
9G	9 / 18	GOUDEY, DIAMOND STARS, LEAF (1948)	.35	.35	30	27
9PB	9 / 18	PLAY BALL, BOWMAN (1951–52), DOUBLE PLAY, TOPPS MINIS, ALL GUM, INC. SPORT AND NON–SPORT	.35	.35	.30	.27
1C	1 / 2	TURKEY REDS (T3), PEPSI (1977), PRESS GUIDES, MOST WRAPPERS SPORT AND NON–SPORT	.35	.35	.30	.27
3	3 / 6	HOSTESS PANELS, HIRES, ZELLERS PANELS	.30	.25	.25	.20
6V	6 / 12	TOPPS (DOUBLE HEADERS, GREATEST MOMENTS, 1951 TEAM, CONNIE MACK, CURRENT STARS, 1965 FOOTBALL AND HOCKEY, BUCKS, 1969–70 BASKETBALL), DADS HOCKEY, DOUBLE FOLDERS, TRIPLE FOLDERS	.35	.35	.30	.27
6D	6 / 12	RED MAN (WITH OR WITHOUT TABS), DISC, KAHN'S (1955–67)	.35	.35	.30	.27
1Y	1 / 1	YEARBOOKS, PROGRAMS, MAGAZINES, HOBBYPAPERS TABLOIDS POCKET SIZE 9"X12"	.35	.35	.30	.27
1S	1 / 2	SMALL PROGRAMS, MAGAZINE PAGES AND PHOTOS, CRACKER JACK SHEETS, POCKET SIZE 8½" X 11"	.30	.30	25	.20
10	10 / 10	MATCHBOOK COVERS, POCKET SIZE 1 3/4" X 4 3/4"	.35	.35	.30	.27
3E	3 / 3	FIRST DAY COVERS, BASEBALL COMMEMORATIVE ENVELOPES, STANDARD SIZED ENVELOPES	.35	.35	.30	.27
3L	3 / 6	SQUIRT, PEPSI (1963), FLEER (STAMPS IN STRIPS), TOPPS (1964 AND 1969 STAMPS IN STRIPS),	.35	.35	.30	.27
6P	6 / 12	POLICE OR SAFETY CARDS (ALL SPORTS)	.25	.23	.21	.19

PRICE EACH (DOES NOT INCLUDE P & H)

1951 TOPPS
TEAM CARDS
DATED (9)
2 1/16" X 5 1/4"

- ☐ BOSTON RED SOX
- ☐ BROOKLYN DODGERS
- ☐ CHICAGO WHITE SOX
- ☐ CINCINNATI REDS
- ☐ NEW YORK GIANTS
- ☐ PHILADELPHIA ATHLETICS
- ☐ PHILADELPHIA PHILLIES
- ☐ ST. LOUIS CARDINALS
- ☐ WASHINGTON SENATORS

1951 TOPPS
TEAM CARDS
UNDATED (9)
2 1/16" X 5 1/4"

- ☐ BOSTON RED SOX
- ☐ BROOKLYN DODGERS
- ☐ CHICAGO WHITE SOX
- ☐ CINCINNATI REDS
- ☐ NEW YORK GIANTS
- ☐ PHILADELPHIA ATHLETICS
- ☐ PHILADELPHIA PHILLIES
- ☐ ST. LOUIS CARDINALS
- ☐ WASHINGTON SENATORS

1951 TOPPS
RED BACKS (52)
2" X 2 5/8"

BOSTON BRAVES

- ☐ 2. SID GORDON
- ☐ 30. WARREN SPAHN
- ☐ 52. TOMMY HOLMES

BOSTON RED SOX

- ☐ 4. VERN STEPHENS
- ☐ 10. MEL PARNELL
- ☐ 20. DOM DIMAGGIO

- ☐ 42. RAY SCARBOROUGH
- ☐ 43. MICKEY MCDERMOTT
- ☐ 46. BILLY GOODMAN

BROOKLYN DODGERS

- ☐ 11. GENE HERMANSKI
- ☐ 16. PREACHER ROE
- ☐ 31. GIL HODGES
- ☐ 38. DUKE SNIDER

CHICAGO CUBS

- ☐ 14. WAYNE TERWILLIGER

CHICAGO WHITE SOX

- ☐ 36. GUS ZERNIAL
- ☐ 49. AL ZARILLA
- ☐ 51. EDDIE ROBINSON

CINCINNATI REDS

- ☐ 34. GRADY HATTON
- ☐ 39. TED KLUSZEWSKI

CLEVELAND INDIANS

- ☐ 8. EARLY WYNN
- ☐ 12. JIM HEGAN
- ☐ 13. DALE MITCHELL
- ☐ 22. BOB FELLER
- ☐ 23. RAY BOONE

- ☐ 26. LUKE EASTER
- ☐ 29. BOB KENNEDY
- ☐ 35. AL ROSEN
- ☐ 40. MIKE GARCIA

DETROIT TIGERS

NO CARDS ISSUED

NEW YORK GIANTS

- ☐ 21. LARRY JANSEN
- ☐ 32. HENRY THOMPSON
- ☐ 37. WES WESTRUM
- ☐ 41. WHITEY LOCKMAN
- ☐ 48. EDDIE STANKY
- ☐ 50. MONTE IRVIN

NEW YORK YANKEES

- ☐ 1. YOGI BERRA
- ☐ 5. PHIL RIZZUTO
- ☐ 6. ALLIE REYNOLDS
- ☐ 18. GERRY COLEMAN
- ☐ 24. HANK BAUER

PHILADELPHIA ATHLETICS

- ☐ 3. FERRIS FAIN
- ☐ 28. ELMER VALO
- ☐ 36. GUS ZERNIAL

PHILADELPHIA PHILLIES

- ☐ 45. ANDY SEMINICK

PITTSBURGH PIRATES

- ☐ 15. RALPH KINER
- ☐ 17. GUS BELL
- ☐ 25. CLIFF CHAMBERS
- ☐ 27. WALLY WESTLAKE
- ☐ 33. BILL WERLE

ST. LOUIS BROWNS

- ☐ 9. ROY SIEVERS
- ☐ 19. DICK KOKOS

ST. LOUIS CARDINALS

- ☐ 7. HOWIE POLLET
- ☐ 47. TOMMY GLAVIANO

WASHINGTON SENATORS

- ☐ 44. SID HUDSON

1951 TOPPS
BLUE BACKS (52)
2″ X 2 5/8″

BOSTON BRAVES

- ☐ 9. JOHNNY SAIN
- ☐ 12. SAM JETHROE
- ☐ 32. BOB ELLIOTT
- ☐ 34. EARL TORGESON

BOSTON RED SOX

- ☐ 5. JOHNNY PESKY
- ☐ 37. BOBBY DOERR

BROOKLYN DODGERS

- ☐ 20. RALPH BRANCA
- ☐ 42. BRUCE EDWARDS
- ☐ 48. BILLY COX

CHICAGO CUBS

- ☐ 17. ROY SMALLEY
- ☐ 27. ANDY PAFKO
- ☐ 41. JOHNNY SCHMITZ
- ☐ 49. HANK SAUER

CHICAGO WHITE SOX

- ☐ 2. HANK MAJESKI
- ☐ 19. PHIL MASI
- ☐ 26. CHICO CARRASQUEL
- ☐ 45. BILLY PIERCE

CINCINNATI REDS

- ☐ 44. JOHNNY WYROSTEK
- ☐ 47. HERM WEHMEIER

CLEVELAND INDIANS

- ☐ 31. LOU BRISSIE
- ☐ 52. SAM CHAPMAN

DETROIT TIGERS

- ☐ 11. JOHNNY GROTH
- ☐ 23. DIZZY TROUT
- ☐ 40. VIC WERTZ
- ☐ 46. GERRY PRIDDY

NEW YORK GIANTS

NO CARDS ISSUED

NEW YORK YANKEES

- ☐ 10. JOE PAGE
- ☐ 35. TOMMY BYRNE
- ☐ 39. ED LOPAT
- ☐ 50. JOHNNY MIZE

PHILADELPHIA ATHLETICS

- ☐ 15. EDDIE JOOST

PHILADELPHIA PHILLIES

- ☐ 3. RICHIE ASHBURN
- ☐ 4. DEL ENNIS
- ☐ 8. DICK SISLER
- ☐ 29. GRANNY HAMNER
- ☐ 43. WILLIE JONES
- ☐ 51. EDDIE WAITKUS

PITTSBURGH PIRATES

- ☐ 16. MURRY DICKSON

ST. LOUIS BROWNS

- ☐ 18. NED GARVER
- ☐ 24. SHERMAN LOLLAR
- ☐ 33. DON LENHARDT
- ☐ 36. CLIFF FANNIN

ST. LOUIS CARDINALS

- ☐ 6. RED SCHOENDIENST
- ☐ 7. GERRY STALEY
- ☐ 14. GEORGE MUNGER
- ☐ 21. BILLY JOHNSON
- ☐ 28. HARRY BRECHEEN
- ☐ 30. ENOS SLAUGHTER

WASHINGTON SENATORS

- ☐ 1. EDDIE YOST
- ☐ 13. MICKEY VERNON
- ☐ 22. BOB KUZAVA
- ☐ 25. SAM MELE
- ☐ 38. IRV NOREN

1952 TOPPS (407)
2 5/8″ X 3 3/4″

BOSTON BRAVES

- ☐ 14. BOB ELLIOTT
- ☐ 27. SAM JETHROE
- ☐ 33. WARREN SPAHN
- ☐ 96. WILLARD MARSHALL
- ☐ 97. EARL TORGESON
- ☐ 140. JOHN ANTONELLI
- ☐ 162. DEL CRANDALL
- ☐ 252. VERN BICKFORD
- ☐ 264. ROY HARTSFIELD
- ☐ 267. SID GORDON
- ☐ 276. JIM WILSON
- ☐ 288. CHET NICHOLS
- ☐ 289. TOMMY HOLMES(M)
- ☐ 293. SIBBY SISTI
- ☐ 294. WALKER COOPER
- ☐ 302. MAX SURKONT
- ☐ 360. GEORGE CROWE
- ☐ 367. BOB THORPE
- ☐ 388. BOB CHIPMAN
- ☐ 393. EBBA ST. CLAIRE
- ☐ 407. ED MATHEWS

BOSTON RED SOX

- ☐ 4. DON LENHARDT
- ☐ 15. JOHNNY PESKY
- ☐ 22. DOM DIMAGGIO
- ☐ 23. BILLY GOODMAN
- ☐ 30. MEL PARNELL
- ☐ 43. RAY SCARBOROUGH
- ☐ 54. LEO KIELY
- ☐ 72. KARL OLSON
- ☐ 78. ELLIS KINDER
- ☐ 84. VERN STEPHENS
- ☐ 119. MICKEY McDERMOTT
- ☐ 121. GUS NIARHOS
- ☐ 139. KEN WOOD
- ☐ 152. AL EVANS

1952 Topps

☐ 177. BILL WIGHT
☐ 180. CHARLEY MAXWELL
☐ 186. WALT MASTERSON
☐ 235. WALT DROPO
☐ 247. RANDY GUMPERT
☐ 255. CLYDE VOLLMER
☐ 269. WILLARD NIXON
☐ 327. ARCHIE WILSON
☐ 329. IVAN DELOCK
☐ 335. TED LEPCIO
☐ 343. DICK GERNERT
☐ 345. SAM WHITE
☐ 374. AL BENTON
☐ 376. FAYE THRONEBERRY
☐ 383. DEL WILBER
☐ 404. DICK BRODOWSKI

BROOKLYN DODGERS

☐   1. ANDY PAFKO
☐   7. WAYNE TERWILLIGER
☐ 20. BILLY LOES
☐ 36. GIL HODGES
☐ 37. DUKE SNIDER
☐ 51. JIM RUSSEL
☐ 53. CHRIS VAN CUYK
☐ 66. PREACHER ROE
☐ 136. JOHNNY SCHMITZ
☐ 188. CLARENCE PODBIELAN
☐ 198. PHIL HAUGSTAD
☐ 205. CLYDE KING
☐ 232. BILLY COX
☐ 239. ROCKY BRIDGES
☐ 250. CARL ERSKINE
☐ 273. ERV PALICA
☐ 274. RALPH BRANCA
☐ 312. JACKIE ROBINSON
☐ 314. ROY CAMPANELLA
☐ 319. RUBE WALKER
☐ 320. JOHN RUTHERFORD
☐ 321. JOE BLACK
☐ 326. GEORGE SHUBA
☐ 333. PEE WEE REESE
☐ 342. CLEM LABINE
☐ 355. BOBBY MORGAN
☐ 365. COOKIE LAVAGETTO(C)
☐ 377. CHUCK DRESSEN(M)
☐ 389. BEN WADE
☐ 390. ROCKY NELSON
☐ 394. BILLY HERMAN(C)
☐ 395. JAKE PITLER(C)
☐ 396. DICK WILLIAMS

CHICAGO CUBS

☐ 16. GENE HERMANSKI
☐ 35. HANK SAUER
☐ 105. JOHN PRAMESA
☐ 110. DUTCH LEONARD
☐ 114. WILLARD RAMSDELL
☐ 127. PAUL MINNER
☐ 148. JOHNNY KLIPPSTEIN
☐ 153. BOB RUSH
☐ 157. BOB USHER
☐ 164. WALT DUBIEL
☐ 172. EDDIE MIKSIS
☐ 173. ROY SMALLEY
☐ 184. BOB RAMAZZOTTI
☐ 194. JOE HATTEN
☐ 204. RON NORTHEY
☐ 224. BRUCE EDWARDS
☐ 225. FRANK BAUMHOLTZ
☐ 259. BOB ADDIS
☐ 295. PHIL CAVARRETTA(M)
☐ 322. RANDY JACKSON
☐ 324. WARREN HACKER
☐ 325. BILL SERENA
☐ 330. TURK LOWN
☐ 341. HAL JEFFCOAT
☐ 348. BOB KELLY
☐ 356. TOBY ATWELL
☐ 359. DEE FONDY
☐ 401. BOB SCHULTZ

CHICAGO WHITE SOX

☐ 32. EDDIE ROBINSON
☐ 42. LOU KRETLOW
☐ 50. MARV RICKERT
☐ 62. CHUCK STOBBS
☐ 70. AL ZARILLA
☐ 95. KEN HOLCOMBE
☐ 98. BILL PIERCE
☐ 102. BILL KENNEDY(B)
☐ 117. SHERMAN LOLLAR
☐ 133. AL WIDMAR
☐ 159. SAUL ROGOVIN
☐ 169. HOWIE JUDSON
☐ 195. MINNIE MINOSO
☐ 211. RAY COLEMAN
☐ 251. CHICO CARRASQUEL

☐ 254. JOE DOBSON
☐ 279. ED STEWART
☐ 283. PHIL MASI
☐ 303. HARRY DORISH
☐ 304. SAM DENTE
☐ 305. PAUL RICHARDS(M)
☐ 308. LUIS ALOMA

CINCINNATI REDS

☐   6. GRADY HATTON
☐ 13. JOHNNY WYROSTEK
☐ 29. TED KLUSZEWSKI
☐ 69. VIRGIL STALLCUP
☐ 80. HERM WEHMEIER
☐ 113. DICK SISLER
☐ 118. KEN RAFFENSBERGER
☐ 135. DIXIE HOWELL
☐ 137. ROY MCMILLAN
☐ 142. HARRY PERKOWSKI
☐ 144. ED BLAKE
☐ 151. WALLY POST
☐ 156. FRANK HILLER
☐ 161. BUD BYERLY
☐ 171. ED ERAUTT
☐ 176. HANK EDWARDS
☐ 179. FRANK SMITH
☐ 249. BOBBY ADAMS
☐ 297. ANDY SEMINICK
☐ 323. BUBBA CHURCH
☐ 328. BOB BORKOWSKI
☐ 344. EWELL BLACKWELL
☐ 347. JOE ADCOCK
☐ 350. CAL ABRAMS
☐ 379. JOE ROSSI
☐ 391. BEN CHAPMAN(C)
☐ 405. ED PELLAGRINI
☐ 406. JOE NUXHALL

CLEVELAND INDIANS

☐ 10. AL ROSEN
☐ 17. JIM HEGAN
☐ 18. MERRILL COMBS
☐ 24. LUKE EASTER
☐ 55. RAY BOONE
☐ 77. BOB KENNEDY
☐ 88. BOB FELLER
☐ 92. DALE MITCHELL
☐ 120. BOB CHAKALES
☐ 189. PETE REISER
☐ 193. HARRY SIMPSON
☐ 199. GEORGE ZUVERINK
☐ 207. MICKEY HARRIS
☐ 217. GEORGE STIRNWEISS
☐ 243. LARRY DOBY
☐ 253. JOHN BERARDINO
☐ 257. BOBBY AVILA
☐ 258. STEVE GROMEK
☐ 268. BOB LEMON
☐ 270. LOU BRISSIE
☐ 272. MIKE GARCIA
☐ 277. EARLY WYNN
☐ 282. BIRDIE TEBBETTS
☐ 300. BARNEY MCCOSKY
☐ 363. DICK ROZEK
☐ 382. SAM JONES
☐ 399. JIM FRIDLEY

DETROIT TIGERS

☐ 25. JOHN GROTH
☐ 28. JERRY PRIDDY
☐ 39. DIZZY TROUT
☐ 86. TED GRAY
☐ 89. JOHNNY LIPON
☐ 103. CLIFF MAPES
☐ 104. DON KOLLOWAY
☐ 126. FRED HUTCHINSON
☐ 146. FRANK HOUSE
☐ 181. BOB SWIFT
☐ 192. MYRON GINSBERG
☐ 208. MARLIN STUART
☐ 222. HOOT EVERS
☐ 230. MATT BATTS
☐ 234. STEVE SOUCHOCK
☐ 238. ART HOUTTEMAN
☐ 244. VIC WERTZ
☐ 246. GEORGE KELL
☐ 262. VIRGIL TRUCKS
☐ 275. PAT MULLIN
☐ 296. RED ROLFE(M)
☐ 354. FRED HATFIELD
☐ 370. BILLY HOEFT

NEW YORK GIANTS

☐   3. HANK THOMPSON
☐   5. LARRY JANSEN
☐ 26. MONTY IRVIN
☐ 52. DON MUELLER

☐ 61. TOOKIE GILBERT
☐ 75. WES WESTRUM
☐ 101. MAX LANIER
☐ 124. MONTE KENNEDY
☐ 125. BILL RIGNEY
☐ 130. SHELDON JONES
☐ 141. CLINT HARTUNG
☐ 261. WILLIE MAYS
☐ 265. CHUCK DIERING
☐ 313. BOBBY THOMSON
☐ 315. LEO DUROCHER(M)
☐ 316. DAVEY WILLIAMS
☐ 318. HAL GREGG
☐ 336. DAVE KOSLO
☐ 337. JIM HEARN
☐ 338. SAL YVARS
☐ 346. GEORGE SPENCER
☐ 351. AL DARK
☐ 371. BOB HOFMAN
☐ 385. HERMAN FRANKS(C)
☐ 392. HOYT WILHELM

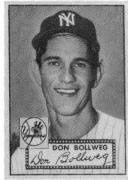

DON BOLLWEG
Don Bollweg

NEW YORK YANKEES

☐   9. BOB HOGUE
☐ 11. PHIL RIZZUTO
☐ 48. JOE PAGE
☐ 49. JOHNNY SAIN
☐ 57. ED LOPAT
☐ 67. ALLIE REYNOLDS
☐ 85. BOB KUZAVA
☐ 99. GENE WOODLING
☐ 122. JACK JENSEN
☐ 128. DON BOLLWEG
☐ 129. JOHNNY MIZE
☐ 155. FRANK OVERMIRE
☐ 168. CHARLIE SILVERA
☐ 175. BILLY MARTIN
☐ 191. YOGI BERRA
☐ 200. RALPH HOUK
☐ 202. JOE COLLINS
☐ 206. JOE OSTROWSKI
☐ 214. JOHNNY HOPP
☐ 215. HANK BAUER
☐ 237. JERRY COLEMAN
☐ 248. FRANK SHEA(F)
☐ 311. MICKEY MANTLE
☐ 331. TOM MORGAN
☐ 372. GIL MCDOUGALD
☐ 373. JIM TURNER(C)
☐ 384. FRANK CROSETTI(C)
☐ 400. BILL DICKEY(C)
☐ 403. BILL MILLER

PHILADELPHIA ATHLETICS

☐ 21. FERRIS FAIN
☐ 31. GUS ZERNIAL
☐ 34. ELMER VALO
☐ 41. BOB WELLMAN
☐ 45. EDDIE JOOST
☐ 112. HENRY MAJESKI
☐ 116. CARL SCHEIB
☐ 131. MORRIE MARTIN
☐ 134. JOE TIPTON
☐ 182. BILLY HITCHCOCK
☐ 201. ALEX KELLNER
☐ 210. DICK FOWLER
☐ 219. BOBBY SHANTZ
☐ 226. DAVE PHILLEY
☐ 231. SAM ZOLDAK
☐ 256. PETE SUDER
☐ 278. AL CLARK
☐ 290. JOE ASTROTH
☐ 299. RAY MURRAY
☐ 340. BOB HOOPER
☐ 358. JOHN KUCAB
☐ 368. ED WRIGHT

PHILADELPHIA PHILLIES

- ☐ 44. CON DEMPSEY
- ☐ 47. WILLIE JONES
- ☐ 59. ROBIN ROBERTS
- ☐ 74. ANDY HANSEN
- ☐ 107. CONNIE RYAN
- ☐ 108. JIM KONSTANTY
- ☐ 158. EDDIE WAITKUS
- ☐ 185. BILL NICHOLSON
- ☐ 187. BOB J. MILLER
- ☐ 203. CURT SIMMONS
- ☐ 209. HOWIE FOX
- ☐ 213. NIPPY JONES
- ☐ 216. RICHIE ASHBURN
- ☐ 221. GRANNY HAMNER
- ☐ 223. DEL ENNIS
- ☐ 281. TOMMY BROWN
- ☐ 339. RUSS MEYER
- ☐ 352. KARL DREWS
- ☐ 357. SMOKY BURGESS
- ☐ 362. KEN HEINTZELMAN

DALE COOGAN

PITTSBURGH PIRATES

- ☐ 12. MONTY BASGALL
- ☐ 63. HOWIE POLLET
- ☐ 73. BILL WERLE
- ☐ 81. VERNON LAW
- ☐ 87. DALE COOGAN
- ☐ 109. TED WILKS
- ☐ 138. BILL MACDONALD
- ☐ 150. TED BEARD
- ☐ 154. JOE MUIR
- ☐ 166. PAUL LEPALME
- ☐ 167. BILL HOWERTON
- ☐ 170. GUS BELL
- ☐ 183. ERV DUSAK
- ☐ 197. GEORGE STRICKLAND
- ☐ 218. CLYDE MCCULLOUGH
- ☐ 227. JOE GARAGIOLA
- ☐ 233. BOB FRIEND
- ☐ 236. ED FITZ GERALD
- ☐ 240. JACK PHILLIPS
- ☐ 260. PETE CASTIGLIONE
- ☐ 266. MURRY DICKSON
- ☐ 310. GEORGE METKOVICH
- ☐ 332. TONY BARTIROME
- ☐ 353. BOBBY DEL GRECO
- ☐ 361. BILL POSEDEL(C)
- ☐ 364. CLYDE SUKEFORTH(C)
- ☐ 369. DICK GROAT
- ☐ 375. JACK MERSON
- ☐ 380. CLEM KOSHOREK
- ☐ 381. MILT STOCK(C)
- ☐ 387. BILLY MEYER(M)
- ☐ 397. FORREST MAIN

ST. LOUIS BROWNS

- ☐ 8. FRED MARSH
- ☐ 46. GORDON GOLDSBERRY
- ☐ 58. BOB MAHONEY
- ☐ 64. ROY SIEVERS
- ☐ 82. DUANE PILLETTE
- ☐ 102. BILLY KENNEDY(F)
- ☐ 143. LES MOSS
- ☐ 147. BOB YOUNG
- ☐ 149. DICK KRYHOSKI
- ☐ 160. OWEN FRIEND
- ☐ 163. STAN ROJEK
- ☐ 174. CLARENCE MARSHALL
- ☐ 212. NED GARVER
- ☐ 229. GENE BEARDEN
- ☐ 241. TOMMY BYRNE
- ☐ 271. JIM DELSING

- ☐ 284. HANK ARFT
- ☐ 285. CLIFF FANNIN
- ☐ 286. JOE DEMAESTRI
- ☐ 349. BOB CAIN
- ☐ 366. DAVE MADISON
- ☐ 402. EARL HARRIST

ST. LOUIS CARDINALS

- ☐ 19. JOHNNY BUCHA
- ☐ 38. WALLY WESTLAKE
- ☐ 56. TOMMY GLAVIANO
- ☐ 65. ENOS SLAUGHTER
- ☐ 68. CLIFF CHAMBERS
- ☐ 76. EDDIE STANKY
- ☐ 79. GERRY STALEY
- ☐ 83. BILLY JOHNSON
- ☐ 91. RED SCHOENDIENST
- ☐ 100. DEL RICE
- ☐ 111. HARRY LOWREY
- ☐ 115. GEORGE MUNGER
- ☐ 165. EDDIE KAZAK
- ☐ 196. SOLLY HEMUS
- ☐ 220. JOE PRESKO
- ☐ 228. AL BRAZLE
- ☐ 242. TOM POHOLSKY
- ☐ 263. HARRY BRECHEEN
- ☐ 280. CLOYD BOYER
- ☐ 287. STEVE BILKO
- ☐ 334. WILMER MIZELL
- ☐ 378. LES FUSSELMAN
- ☐ 386. EDDIE YUHAS
- ☐ 398. HAL RICE

WASHINGTON SENATORS

- ☐ 2. PETE RUNNELS
- ☐ 40. IRV NOREN
- ☐ 60. SID HUDSON
- ☐ 71. TOM UPTON
- ☐ 90. MICKEY GRASSO
- ☐ 93. AL SIMA
- ☐ 94. SAM MELE
- ☐ 106. MICKEY VERNON
- ☐ 123. EDDIE YOST
- ☐ 132. CLYDE KLUTTZ
- ☐ 145. JOE HAYNES
- ☐ 178. CASS MICHAELS
- ☐ 190. DON JOHNSON
- ☐ 245. SHERRY ROBERTSON
- ☐ 248. FRANK SHEA(B)
- ☐ 291. GIL COAN
- ☐ 292. FLOYD BAKER
- ☐ 298. BOB ROSS
- ☐ 301. BOB PORTERFIELD
- ☐ 306. LOU SLEATER
- ☐ 307. FRANK CAMPOS
- ☐ 309. JIM BUSBY
- ☐ 317. CONNIE MARRERO

1953 TOPPS (274)
2 5/8" X 3 3/4"

ED MATHEWS
3rd base BOSTON BRAVES

BOSTON RED SOX

- ☐ 18. TED LEPCIO
- ☐ 19. MEL PARNELL
- ☐ 30. WILLARD NIXON
- ☐ 32. CLYDE VOLLMER
- ☐ 40. JOHN LIPON
- ☐ 44. ELLIS KINDER
- ☐ 49. FAYE THRONEBERRY
- ☐ 55. MICKEY MCDERMOTT

- ☐ 63. GUS NIARHOS
- ☐ 69. DICK BRODOWSKI
- ☐ 94. BILL KENNEDY
- ☐ 138. GEORGE KELL
- ☐ 139. SAMMY WHITE
- ☐ 149. DOM DIMAGGIO
- ☐ 169. DIZZY TROUT
- ☐ 170. BILL WERLE
- ☐ 181. AL ZARILLA
- ☐ 184. HAL BROWN
- ☐ 248. GENE STEPHENS
- ☐ 251. SID HUDSON
- ☐ 280. MILT BOLLING

BROOKLYN DODGERS

- ☐ 1. JACKIE ROBINSON
- ☐ 4. BEN WADE
- ☐ 14. CLEM LABINE
- ☐ 27. ROY CAMPANELLA
- ☐ 34. GEORGE SHUBA
- ☐ 50. CHUCK DRESSEN(M)
- ☐ 76. PEE WEE REESE
- ☐ 81. JOE BLACK
- ☐ 85. BOBBY MORGAN
- ☐ 125. DICK WILLIAMS
- ☐ 134. RUBE WALKER
- ☐ 137. JOHN RUTHERFORD
- ☐ 174. BILLY LOES
- ☐ 176. DON HOAK
- ☐ 216. JIM HUGHES
- ☐ 221. BOB MILLIKEN
- ☐ 254. PREACHER ROE
- ☐ 255. DIXIE HOWELL
- ☐ 258. JIM GILLIAM
- ☐ 263. JOHN PODRES
- ☐ 272. BILL ANTONELLO

CHICAGO CUBS

- ☐ 23. TOBY ATWELL
- ☐ 29. HAL JEFFCOAT
- ☐ 39. EDDIE MIKSIS
- ☐ 46. JOHNNY KLIPPSTEIN
- ☐ 92. PAUL MINNER
- ☐ 111. HANK SAUER
- ☐ 130. TURK LOWN
- ☐ 144. BOB SCHULTZ
- ☐ 155. DUTCH LEONARD
- ☐ 157. BOB ADDIS
- ☐ 173. PRESTON WARD
- ☐ 179. GENE HERMANSKI
- ☐ 202. CARL SAWATSKI

CHICAGO WHITE SOX

- ☐ 5. JOE DOBSON
- ☐ 53. SHERMAN LOLLAR
- ☐ 66. MINNIE MINOSO
- ☐ 73. EDDIE ROBINSON
- ☐ 123. TOMMY BYRNE
- ☐ 143. BILLY PIERCE
- ☐ 156. JIM RIVERA
- ☐ 196. BOB KEEGAN
- ☐ 229. ROCKY KRSNICH
- ☐ 240. FRED MARSH
- ☐ 250. BOB WILSON
- ☐ 257. BOB BOYD
- ☐ 270. VERN STEPHENS

CINCINNATI REDS

- ☐ 7. BOB BORKOWSKI
- ☐ 12. HOWIE JUDSON
- ☐ 28. EDDIE PELLAGRINI
- ☐ 45. GRADY HATTON
- ☐ 47. BUBBA CHURCH
- ☐ 95. WILLARD MARSHALL
- ☐ 105. JOE NUXHALL
- ☐ 110. HERM WEHMEIER
- ☐ 116. FRANK SMITH
- ☐ 118. GUS BELL
- ☐ 152. BOB ADAMS
- ☐ 153. ANDY SEMINICK
- ☐ 162. TED KLUSZEWSKI
- ☐ 206. ED BAILEY
- ☐ 209. JIM GREENGRASS
- ☐ 226. ED ERAUTT
- ☐ 236. HARRY PERKOWSKI
- ☐ 237. BUD PODBIELAN
- ☐ 252. HANK FOILES
- ☐ 259. ROY MCMILLAN
- ☐ 276. KEN RAFFENSBERGER

CLEVELAND INDIANS

- ☐ 2. LUKE EASTER
- ☐ 6. SAM JONES
- ☐ 25. RAY BOONE
- ☐ 26. DALE MITCHELL

1953 Topps

- ☐ 33. BOB KENNEDY
- ☐ 54. BOB FELLER
- ☐ 61. EARLY WYNN
- ☐ 75. MIKE GARCIA
- ☐ 80. JIM HEGAN
- ☐ 84. BOB HOOPER
- ☐ 101. TED WILKS
- ☐ 135. AL ROSEN
- ☐ 150. HARRY SIMPSON
- ☐ 171. BILL GLYNN
- ☐ 187. JIM FRIDLEY
- ☐ 192. WALLY WESTLAKE
- ☐ 233. AL ABER

DETROIT TIGERS

- ☐ 52. TED GRAY
- ☐ 72. FRED HUTCHINSON(M)
- ☐ 99. DAVE MADISON
- ☐ 112. NED GARVER
- ☐ 113. JERRY PRIDDY
- ☐ 121. WALT DROPO
- ☐ 163. FRED HATFIELD
- ☐ 165. BILLY HOEFT
- ☐ 194. EDDIE KAZAK
- ☐ 211. J. W. PORTER
- ☐ 228. HAL NEWHOUSER
- ☐ 239. JIM DELSING
- ☐ 277. DON LUND

MILWAUKEE BRAVES

- ☐ 3. GEORGE CROWE*
- ☐ 37. ED MATHEWS*
- ☐ 91. EBBA ST. CLAIRE*
- ☐ 106. JOHNNY ANTONELLI*
- ☐ 117. SID GORDON*
- ☐ 124. SIBBY SISTI*
- ☐ 147. WARREN SPAHN*
- ☐ 158. JOHN LOGAN*
- ☐ 161. VERN BICKFORD*
- ☐ 185. JIM PENDLETON
- ☐ 197. DEL CRANDALL
- ☐ 208. JIM WILSON
- ☐ 212. JACK DITTMER
- ☐ 214. BILL BRUTON
- ☐ 215. GENE CONLEY
- ☐ 217. MURRAY WALL

NEW YORK GIANTS

- ☐ 11. SAL YVARS
- ☐ 20. HANK THOMPSON
- ☐ 38. JIM HEARN
- ☐ 62. MONTE IRVIN
- ☐ 109. AL DARK
- ☐ 115. GEORGE SPENCER
- ☐ 120. DAVEY WILLIAMS
- ☐ 126. BILL CONNELLY
- ☐ 151. HOYT WILHELM
- ☐ 182. BOBBY HOFMAN
- ☐ 244. WILLIE MAYS
- ☐ 260. SAM CALDERONE

NEW YORK YANKEES

- ☐ 9. JOE COLLINS
- ☐ 31. EWELL BLACKWELL
- ☐ 35. IRV NOREN
- ☐ 43. GIL MCDOUGALD
- ☐ 77. JOHNNY MIZE
- ☐ 82. MICKEY MANTLE
- ☐ 86. BILLY MARTIN
- ☐ 87. ED LOPAT
- ☐ 100. BILL MILLER

* Nos. 3, 37, 91, 106, 117, 124, 147, 158 & 161 appear with Boston Braves on the front of the card.

- ☐ 104. YOGI BERRA
- ☐ 114. PHIL RIZZUTO
- ☐ 119. JOHNNY SAIN
- ☐ 132. TOM MORGAN
- ☐ 141. ALLIE REYNOLDS
- ☐ 167. ART SCHULT
- ☐ 188. ANDY CAREY
- ☐ 207. WHITEY FORD
- ☐ 210. BOB CERV
- ☐ 213. RAY SCARBOROUGH
- ☐ 242. CHARLIE SILVERA
- ☐ 264. GENE WOODLING

PHILADELPHIA ATHLETICS

- ☐ 15. BOBO NEWSOM
- ☐ 17. BILLY HITCHCOCK
- ☐ 24. FERRIS FAIN
- ☐ 42. GUS ZERNIAL
- ☐ 57. CARL SCHEIB
- ☐ 64. DAVE PHILLEY
- ☐ 97. DON KOLLOWAY
- ☐ 103. JOE ASTROTH
- ☐ 122. ELMER VALO
- ☐ 129. KEITH THOMAS
- ☐ 131. HARRY BYRD
- ☐ 186. CHARLIE BISHOP
- ☐ 195. ED MCGHEE
- ☐ 199. MARION FRICANO
- ☐ 225. BOBBY SHANTZ
- ☐ 227. MORRIS MARTIN
- ☐ 234. RAY MURRAY
- ☐ 279. JOE COLEMAN

PHILADELPHIA PHILLIES

- ☐ 10. SMOKY BURGESS
- ☐ 22. HOWIE FOX
- ☐ 59. KARL DREWS
- ☐ 79. JOHNNY WYROSTEK
- ☐ 88. WILLIE JONES
- ☐ 102. CONNIE RYAN
- ☐ 136. KEN HEINTZELMAN
- ☐ 140. TOMMY GLAVIANO
- ☐ 146. GRANNY HAMNER

PITTSBURGH PIRATES

- ☐ 8. CLEM KOSHOREK
- ☐ 48. BOB DEL GRECO
- ☐ 58. GEORGE METKOVICH
- ☐ 71. TONY BARTIROME
- ☐ 74. JOE ROSSI
- ☐ 83. HOWIE POLLET
- ☐ 98. CAL ABRAMS
- ☐ 107. DANNY O'CONNELL
- ☐ 154. DICK GROAT
- ☐ 175. RON KLINE
- ☐ 178. JIM WAUGH
- ☐ 191. RALPH KINER
- ☐ 198. FORREST MAIN
- ☐ 201. PAUL LA PALME
- ☐ 222. VIC JANOWICZ
- ☐ 223. JOHN O'BRIEN
- ☐ 230. JOHNNY LINDELL
- ☐ 235. JOHN HETKI
- ☐ 238. CAL HOGUE
- ☐ 243. CARLOS BERNIER
- ☐ 246. ROY FACE
- ☐ 247. MIKE SANDLOCK
- ☐ 249. ED O'BRIEN

ST. LOUIS BROWNS

- ☐ 36. JOHNNY GROTH
- ☐ 65. EARL HARRIST
- ☐ 67. ROY SIEVERS
- ☐ 90. HANK EDWARDS
- ☐ 96. VIRGIL TRUCKS
- ☐ 127. CLINT COURTNEY
- ☐ 142. VIC WERTZ
- ☐ 160. BOB YOUNG
- ☐ 166. BILL HUNTER
- ☐ 177. JIM DYCK
- ☐ 200. GORDON GOLDSBERRY
- ☐ 203. CLIFF FANNIN
- ☐ 220. SATCHEL PAIGE
- ☐ 232. DICK KOKOS
- ☐ 245. BILL NORMAN(C)
- ☐ 266. BOB CAIN
- ☐ 269. DUANE PILLETTE
- ☐ 278. WILLIE MIRANDA

ST. LOUIS CARDINALS

- ☐ 16. HARRY LOWREY
- ☐ 21. BILLY JOHNSON
- ☐ 41. ENOS SLAUGHTER
- ☐ 56. GERALD STALEY
- ☐ 60. CLOYD BOYER

- ☐ 68. DEL RICE
- ☐ 70. ED YUHAS
- ☐ 78. RED SCHOENDIENST
- ☐ 93. HAL RICE
- ☐ 128. WILMER MIZELL
- ☐ 168. WILLARD SCHMIDT
- ☐ 172. RIP REPULSKI
- ☐ 180. VIRGIL STALLCUP
- ☐ 183. STU MILLER
- ☐ 189. RAY JABLONSKI
- ☐ 190. DIXIE WALKER(C)
- ☐ 193. MIKE CLARK
- ☐ 204. DICK BOKELMANN
- ☐ 205. VERN BENSON
- ☐ 218. LES FUSSELMAN
- ☐ 231. SOLLY HEMUS
- ☐ 273. HARVEY HADDIX
- ☐ 274. JOHN RIDDLE(C)

Connie MARRERO pitcher WASHINGTON SENATORS

WASHINGTON SENATORS

- ☐ 13. CONNIE MARRERO
- ☐ 51. FRANK CAMPOS
- ☐ 89. CHUCK STOBBS
- ☐ 108. BOB PORTERFIELD
- ☐ 133. GIL COAN
- ☐ 148. MICKEY GRASSO
- ☐ 159. WAYNE TERWILLIGER
- ☐ 164. FRANK SHEA
- ☐ 219. PETE RUNNELS
- ☐ 224. LOU SLEATER
- ☐ 241. AL SIMA
- ☐ 256. LES PEDEN
- ☐ 262. BOB OLDIS
- ☐ 265. JACKIE JENSEN

1954 TOPPS (250)
2 5/8" X 3 3/4"

ERNIE BANKS shortstop CHICAGO CUBS

BALTIMORE ORIOLES

- ☐ 8. BOB YOUNG
- ☐ 19. JOHNNY LIPON(F)
- ☐ 48. BILLY HUNTER
- ☐ 54. VERN STEPHENS
- ☐ 85. BOB TURLEY
- ☐ 106. DICK KOKOS
- ☐ 107. DUANE PILLETTE
- ☐ 150. DICK KRYHOSKI

77

1954 Topps

- ☐ 152. MIKE BLYZKA
- ☐ 156. JOE COLEMAN
- ☐ 157. DON LENHARDT
- ☐ 203. HARRY BRECHEEN(C)
- ☐ 207. TOM OLIVER(C)
- ☐ 226. JEHOSIE HEARD
- ☐ 240. SAM MELE
- ☐ 246. HOWIE FOX

BOSTON RED SOX

- ☐ 1. TED WILLIAMS
- ☐ 40. MEL PARNELL
- ☐ 47. ELLIS KINDER
- ☐ 66. TED LEPCIO
- ☐ 80. JACKIE JENSEN
- ☐ 82. MILT BOLLING
- ☐ 93. SID HUDSON
- ☐ 133. DEL BAKER(C)
- ☐ 144. BILL WERLE
- ☐ 171. LEO KIELY
- ☐ 172. HAL BROWN
- ☐ 186. KARL OLSON
- ☐ 195. BILL CONSOLO
- ☐ 217. PAUL SCHREIBER(C)
- ☐ 221. DICK BRODOWSKI
- ☐ 227. BUSTER MILLS(C)
- ☐ 250. TED WILLIAMS

BROOKLYN DODGERS

- ☐ 10. JACKIE ROBINSON
- ☐ 14. PREACHER ROE
- ☐ 32. DUKE SNIDER
- ☐ 35. JIM GILLIAM
- ☐ 86. BILLY HERMAN(C)
- ☐ 98. JOE BLACK
- ☐ 102. GIL HODGES
- ☐ 121. CLEM LABINE
- ☐ 126. BEN WADE
- ☐ 132. TOM LASORDA
- ☐ 153. RUBE WALKER
- ☐ 166. JOHNNY PODRES
- ☐ 169. JIM HUGHES
- ☐ 177. BOB MILLIKEN
- ☐ 209. CHARLIE THOMPSON
- ☐ 211. DON HOAK

CHICAGO CUBS

- ☐ 4. HANK SAUER
- ☐ 28. PAUL MINNER
- ☐ 31. JOHNNY KLIPPSTEIN
- ☐ 55. PHIL CAVARRETTA(M)
- ☐ 60. FRANK BAUMHOLTZ
- ☐ 67. JIM WILLIS
- ☐ 76. BOB SCHEFFING(C)
- ☐ 89. HOWIE POLLET
- ☐ 94. ERNIE BANKS
- ☐ 229. BOB TALBOT
- ☐ 243. RAY BLADES(C)

CHICAGO WHITE SOX

- ☐ 19. JOHNNY LIPON(B)
- ☐ 27. FERRIS FAIN
- ☐ 34. JIM RIVERA
- ☐ 39. SHERM LOLLAR
- ☐ 57. LUIS ALOMA
- ☐ 58. BOB WILSON
- ☐ 100. BOB KEEGAN
- ☐ 110. HARRY DORISH
- ☐ 113. BOB BOYD
- ☐ 146. DON JOHNSON
- ☐ 154. MIKE FORNIELES
- ☐ 173. JACK HARSHMAN
- ☐ 198. CARL SAWATSKI
- ☐ 216. AL SIMA
- ☐ 218. FRED MARSH
- ☐ 222. BILL WILSON

CINCINNATI REDS

- ☐ 7. TED KLUSZEWSKI
- ☐ 22. JIM GREENGRASS
- ☐ 46. KEN RAFFENSBERGER
- ☐ 69. BUD PODBIELAN
- ☐ 71. FRANK SMITH
- ☐ 120. ROY McMILLAN
- ☐ 123. BOBBY ADAMS
- ☐ 125. HARRY PERKOWSKI
- ☐ 136. CONNIE RYAN
- ☐ 138. BOB BORKOWSKI
- ☐ 162. HERMAN WEHMEIER
- ☐ 182. CHUCK HARMON
- ☐ 184. ED BAILEY
- ☐ 208. GRADY HATTON

CLEVELAND INDIANS

- ☐ 15. AL ROSEN
- ☐ 23. LUKE EASTER
- ☐ 29. JIM HEGAN
- ☐ 70. LARRY DOBY
- ☐ 81. DAVE HOSKINS
- ☐ 92. WALLY WESTLAKE
- ☐ 103. JIM LEMON
- ☐ 155. BOB KENNEDY
- ☐ 159. DAVE PHILLEY
- ☐ 160. RALPH KRESS(C)
- ☐ 178. BILL GLYNN
- ☐ 199. ROCKY NELSON
- ☐ 248. AL SMITH

DETROIT TIGERS

- ☐ 18. WALT DROPO
- ☐ 25. HARVEY KUENN
- ☐ 44. NED GARVER
- ☐ 63. JOHNNY PESKY
- ☐ 65. BOB SWIFT(C)
- ☐ 77. RAY BOONE
- ☐ 88. MATT BATTS
- ☐ 111. JIM DELSING
- ☐ 131. RENO BERTOIA
- ☐ 163. FRANK HOUSE
- ☐ 167. DON LUND
- ☐ 190. RAY HERBERT
- ☐ 193. JOHNNY HOPP(C)
- ☐ 197. SCHOOLBOY ROWE(C)
- ☐ 201. AL KALINE
- ☐ 219. CHUCK KRESS
- ☐ 224. DICK WEIK
- ☐ 238. AL ABER
- ☐ 241. BOB G. MILLER

MILWAUKEE BRAVES

- ☐ 12. DEL CRANDALL
- ☐ 20. WARREN SPAHN
- ☐ 30. ED MATHEWS
- ☐ 53. JACK DITTMER
- ☐ 59. GENE CONLEY
- ☐ 68. SAMMY CALDERONE
- ☐ 79. ANDY PAFKO
- ☐ 109. BILL BRUTON
- ☐ 122. JOHNNY LOGAN
- ☐ 128. HANK AARON
- ☐ 141. JOEY JAY
- ☐ 165. JIM PENDLETON
- ☐ 176. BOB KEELY(C)
- ☐ 181. MEL ROACH
- ☐ 188. DAVE JOLLY
- ☐ 206. RAY CRONE
- ☐ 210. BOB BUHL
- ☐ 231. ROY SMALLEY

NEW YORK GIANTS

- ☐ 3. MONTE IRVIN
- ☐ 36. HOYT WILHELM
- ☐ 42. DON MUELLER
- ☐ 64. HANK THOMPSON
- ☐ 74. BILL TAYLOR
- ☐ 90. WILLIE MAYS
- ☐ 99. BOB HOFMAN
- ☐ 119. JOHNNY ANTONELLI
- ☐ 170. DUSTY RHODES
- ☐ 180. WES WESTRUM
- ☐ 200. LARRY JANSEN
- ☐ 220. RUBEN GOMEZ
- ☐ 225. DON LIDDLE

NEW YORK YANKEES

- ☐ 5. ED LOPAT
- ☐ 13. BILLY MARTIN
- ☐ 17. PHIL RIZZUTO
- ☐ 37. WHITEY FORD
- ☐ 50. YOGI BERRA
- ☐ 56. WILLIE MIRANDA
- ☐ 62. EDDIE ROBINSON
- ☐ 83. JOE COLLINS
- ☐ 96. CHARLIE SILVERA
- ☐ 101. GENE WOODLING
- ☐ 105. ANDY CAREY
- ☐ 130. HANK BAUER
- ☐ 175. FRANK LEJA
- ☐ 205. JOHNNY SAIN
- ☐ 230. BOB KUZAVA
- ☐ 239. BILL SKOWRON

PHILADELPHIA ATHLETICS

- ☐ 2. GUS ZERNIAL
- ☐ 21. BOBBY SHANTZ
- ☐ 49. RAY MURRAY
- ☐ 52. VIC POWER
- ☐ 61. BOB CAIN
- ☐ 112. BILL RENNA
- ☐ 118. CARL SCHEIB
- ☐ 124. MARION FRICANO
- ☐ 129. FORREST JACOBS
- ☐ 143. ROLLIE HEMSLEY(C)
- ☐ 145. ELMER VALO
- ☐ 148. BOB TRICE
- ☐ 149. JIM ROBERTSON
- ☐ 168. MORRIE MARTIN
- ☐ 214. ARNOLD PORTOCARRERO
- ☐ 215. ED McGHEE
- ☐ 232. LOU LIMMER
- ☐ 233. AUGIE GALAN(C)
- ☐ 244. LEROY WHEAT

PHILADELPHIA PHILLIES

- ☐ 24. GRANNY HAMNER
- ☐ 41. WILLIE JONES
- ☐ 45. RICHIE ASHBURN
- ☐ 51. JOHNNY LINDELL
- ☐ 78. TED KAZANSKI
- ☐ 104. MIKE SANDLOCK
- ☐ 108. THORNTON KIPPER
- ☐ 127. STEVE O'NEILL(M)
- ☐ 174. TOM QUALTERS
- ☐ 183. EARLE COMBS(C)
- ☐ 196. STAN JOK
- ☐ 212. BOB MICELOTTA
- ☐ 236. PAUL PENSON
- ☐ 247. ED MAYO(C)

PITTSBURGH PIRATES

- ☐ 11. PAUL SMITH
- ☐ 16. VIC JANOWICZ
- ☐ 43. DICK GROAT
- ☐ 72. PRESTON WARD
- ☐ 75. FRED HANEY(M)
- ☐ 84. DICK COLE
- ☐ 87. ROY FACE
- ☐ 95. HAL RICE
- ☐ 134. CAL HOGUE
- ☐ 139. ED O'BRIEN
- ☐ 139. JOHN O'BRIEN
- ☐ 161. JOHN HETKI
- ☐ 179. GAIR ALLIE
- ☐ 202. BOB PURKEY
- ☐ 213. JOHN FITZPATRICK(C)
- ☐ 228. GENE HERMANSKI
- ☐ 234. JERRY LYNCH
- ☐ 235. VERN LAW
- ☐ 242. CURT ROBERTS

ST. LOUIS CARDINALS

- ☐ 9. HARVEY HADDIX
- ☐ 26. RAY JABLONSKI
- ☐ 38. EDDIE STANKY(M)
- ☐ 115. RIP REPULSKI
- ☐ 116. STEVE BILKO
- ☐ 117. SOLLY HEMUS
- ☐ 135. JOE PRESKO
- ☐ 137. WALLY MOON
- ☐ 142. TOM POHOLSKY
- ☐ 147. JOHN RIDDLE(C)
- ☐ 151. ALEX GRAMMAS
- ☐ 158. PEANUTS LOWREY
- ☐ 164. STU MILLER
- ☐ 191. DICK SCHOFIELD
- ☐ 192. COT DEAL
- ☐ 194. BILL SARNI
- ☐ 237. MIKE RYBA(C)
- ☐ 249. WILMER MIZELL

WASHINGTON SENATORS

- ☐ 6. PETE RUNNELS
- ☐ 33. JOHNNY SCHMITZ
- ☐ 73. WAYNE TERWILLIGER
- ☐ 91. BOB OLDIS
- ☐ 97. JERRY LANE
- ☐ 114. DEAN STONE
- ☐ 140. TOM WRIGHT
- ☐ 185. CHUCK STOBBS
- ☐ 187. HEINIE MANUSH(C)
- ☐ 189. BOB ROSS
- ☐ 204. ANGEL SCULL
- ☐ 223. JOE HAYNES(C)
- ☐ 245. ROY SIEVERS

1955 TOPPS (206)
2 5/8" X 3 3/4"

AL KALINE *outfield* DETROIT TIGERS

BALTIMORE ORIOLES

- ☐ 8. HAL W. SMITH
- ☐ 13. FRED MARSH
- ☐ 48. BOB KENNEDY
- ☐ 57. BILLY O'DELL
- ☐ 64. GUS TRIANDOS
- ☐ 105. CHUCK DIERING
- ☐ 113. HARRY BRECHEEN(C)
- ☐ 154. WILLIE MIRANDA
- ☐ 162. JOE COLEMAN
- ☐ 165. DON JOHNSON
- ☐ 168. DUANE PILLETTE
- ☐ 185. DON FERRARESE
- ☐ 190. GENE WOODLING
- ☐ 208. RAY MOORE

BOSTON RED SOX

- ☐ 2. TED WILLIAMS
- ☐ 18. RUSS KEMMERER
- ☐ 36. LEO KIELY
- ☐ 72. KARL OLSON
- ☐ 83. TOM BREWER
- ☐ 91. MILT BOLLING
- ☐ 106. FRANK SULLIVAN
- ☐ 115. ELLIS KINDER
- ☐ 116. TOM HURD
- ☐ 128. TED LEPCIO
- ☐ 131. GRADY HATTON
- ☐ 140. MEL PARNELL
- ☐ 148. HAL BROWN
- ☐ 150. MIKE HIGGINS(M)
- ☐ 152. HARRY AGGANIS
- ☐ 163. FAYE THRONEBERRY
- ☐ 171. DICK BRODOWSKI
- ☐ 176. NORM ZAUCHIN
- ☐ 200. JACK JENSEN
- ☐ 206. PETE DALEY
- ☐ 207. BILL CONSOLO

JACKIE ROBINSON

BROOKLYN DODGERS

- ☐ 5. JIM GILLIAM
- ☐ 19. BILLY HERMAN(C)
- ☐ 25. JOHNNY PODRES
- ☐ 40. DON HOAK
- ☐ 50. JACKIE ROBINSON
- ☐ 51. JIM HUGHES
- ☐ 75. SANDY AMOROS
- ☐ 90. KARL SPOONER
- ☐ 92. DON ZIMMER
- ☐ 108. RUBE WALKER
- ☐ 111. BOB MILLIKEN
- ☐ 123. SANDY KOUFAX
- ☐ 156. JOE BLACK
- ☐ 180. CLEM LABINE
- ☐ 187. GIL HODGES
- ☐ 195. ED ROEBUCK
- ☐ 199. BERT HAMRIC
- ☐ 210. DUKE SNIDER

CHICAGO CUBS

- ☐ 6. STAN HACK(M)
- ☐ 28. ERNIE BANKS
- ☐ 45. HANK SAUER
- ☐ 52. BILL TREMEL
- ☐ 68. JIM DAVIS
- ☐ 76. HOWIE POLLET
- ☐ 93. STEVE BILKO
- ☐ 129. ELVIN TAPPE
- ☐ 172. FRANK BAUMHOLTZ
- ☐ 179. JIM BOLGER
- ☐ 184. HARRY PERKOWSKI
- ☐ 196. GALE WADE

CHICAGO WHITE SOX

- ☐ 10. BOB KEEGAN
- ☐ 32. ED MCGHEE
- ☐ 58. JIM RIVERA
- ☐ 66. RON JACKSON
- ☐ 104. JACK HARSHMAN
- ☐ 122. CARL SAWATSKI
- ☐ 146. DICK DONOVAN
- ☐ 201. SHERM LOLLAR

CINCINNATI REDS

- ☐ 3. ART FOWLER
- ☐ 44. CORKY VALENTINE
- ☐ 56. RAY JABLONSKI
- ☐ 69. ED BAILEY
- ☐ 74. BOB BORKOWSKI
- ☐ 82. CHUCK HARMON
- ☐ 120. TED KLUSZEWSKI
- ☐ 153. BUD PODBIELAN
- ☐ 170. JIM PEARCE
- ☐ 174. RUDY MINARCIN
- ☐ 178. BOBBY ADAMS
- ☐ 181. ROY MCMILLAN

CLEVELAND INDIANS

- ☐ 7. JIM HEGAN
- ☐ 24. HAL NEWHOUSER
- ☐ 39. BILLY GLYNN
- ☐ 70. AL ROSEN
- ☐ 85. DON MOSSI
- ☐ 102. WALLY WESTLAKE
- ☐ 133. DAVE HOSKINS
- ☐ 151. RED KRESS(C)
- ☐ 160. RAY NARLESKI
- ☐ 197. AL SMITH

DETROIT TIGERS

- ☐ 4. AL KALINE
- ☐ 9. BOB G. MILLER
- ☐ 11. FERRIS FAIN
- ☐ 49. J.W. PORTER
- ☐ 65. RAY BOONE

- ☐ 87. FRANK HOUSE
- ☐ 94. RENO BERTOIA
- ☐ 138. RAY HERBERT
- ☐ 192. JIM DELSING

KANSAS CITY ATHLETICS

- ☐ 14. JIM FINIGAN
- ☐ 30. VIC POWER
- ☐ 54. LOU LIMMER
- ☐ 61. SPOOK JACOBS
- ☐ 77. ARNOLD PORTOCARRERO
- ☐ 86. BILL WILSON
- ☐ 96. CHARLIE BISHOP
- ☐ 101. JOHNNY GRAY
- ☐ 110. GUS ZERNIAL
- ☐ 121. BILL RENNA
- ☐ 132. BOB TRICE
- ☐ 145. ELMER VALO
- ☐ 177. JIM ROBERTSON

MILWAUKEE BRAVES

- ☐ 15. JIM PENDLETON
- ☐ 23. JACK PARKS
- ☐ 31. WARREN SPAHN
- ☐ 35. DAVE JOLLY
- ☐ 47. HANK AARON
- ☐ 81. GENE CONLEY
- ☐ 103. CHARLIE WHITE
- ☐ 117. MEL ROACH
- ☐ 134. JOE JAY
- ☐ 149. RAY CRONE
- ☐ 155. ED MATHEWS
- ☐ 161. CHUCK TANNER
- ☐ 182. HUMBERTO ROBINSON

NEW YORK GIANTS

- ☐ 1. DUSTY RHODES
- ☐ 17. BOBBY HOFMAN
- ☐ 27. BILLY GARDNER
- ☐ 42. WINDY MCCALL
- ☐ 53. BILL TAYLOR
- ☐ 71. RUBEN GOMEZ
- ☐ 100. MONTE IRVIN
- ☐ 119. BOB LENNON
- ☐ 144. JOE AMALFITANO
- ☐ 194. WILLIE MAYS

NEW YORK YANKEES

- ☐ 20. ANDY CAREY
- ☐ 22. BILL SKOWRON
- ☐ 38. BOB TURLEY
- ☐ 63. JOE COLLINS
- ☐ 80. BOB GRIM
- ☐ 99. FRANK LEJA
- ☐ 109. ED LOPAT
- ☐ 139. STEVE KRALY
- ☐ 158. TOM CARROLL
- ☐ 166. HANK BAUER
- ☐ 188. CHARLIE SILVERA
- ☐ 189. PHIL RIZZUTO
- ☐ 193. JOHNNY SAIN
- ☐ 198. YOGI BERRA

PHILADELPHIA PHILLIES

- ☐ 29. HERMAN WEHMEIER
- ☐ 33. TOM QUALTERS
- ☐ 46. TED KAZANSKI
- ☐ 62. THORNTON KIPPER
- ☐ 79. DANNY SCHELL
- ☐ 114. LOU ORTIZ
- ☐ 130. MAYO SMITH(M)
- ☐ 157. BOB J. MILLER
- ☐ 167. TOM CASAGRANDE
- ☐ 202. JIM OWENS

PITTSBURGH PIRATES

- ☐ 12. JAKE THIES
- ☐ 26. DICK GROAT
- ☐ 59. GAIR ALLIE
- ☐ 73. JACK SHEPARD
- ☐ 88. BOB SKINNER
- ☐ 95. PRESTON WARD
- ☐ 107. CURT ROBERTS
- ☐ 112. NELSON KING
- ☐ 118. BOB PURKEY
- ☐ 126. DICK HALL
- ☐ 127. DALE LONG
- ☐ 135. JOHNNY O'BRIEN
- ☐ 142. JERRY LYNCH
- ☐ 147. LAURIN PEPPER
- ☐ 164. ROBERTO CLEMENTE
- ☐ 205. GENE FREESE

ST. LOUIS CARDINALS

- ☐ 21. ALEX GRAMMAS
- ☐ 37. JOE CUNNINGHAM
- ☐ 43. HARVEY HADDIX
- ☐ 55. RIP REPULSKI
- ☐ 67. WALLY MOON
- ☐ 78. GORDON JONES
- ☐ 89. JOE FRAZIER
- ☐ 98. JOHNNY RIDDLE(C)
- ☐ 125. KEN BOYER
- ☐ 137. HARRY ELLIOTT
- ☐ 143. DICK SCHOFIELD
- ☐ 183. TONY JACOBS
- ☐ 191. ED STANKY(M)
- ☐ 204. FRANK SMITH

ROY SIEVERS   outfield   WASHINGTON NATIONALS

WASHINGTON SENATORS

- ☐ 16. ROY SIEVERS
- ☐ 34. WAYNE TERWILLIGER
- ☐ 41. CHUCK STOBBS
- ☐ 60. DEAN STONE
- ☐ 84. CAMILO PASCUAL
- ☐ 97. CARLOS PAULA
- ☐ 124. HARMON KILLEBREW
- ☐ 136. BUNKY STEWART
- ☐ 141. TOM WRIGHT
- ☐ 159. JOHNNY SCHMITZ
- ☐ 169. BOB OLDIS
- ☐ 173. BOB KLINE

1956 TOPPS (340)
2 5/8″ X 3 3/4″

GUS TRIANDOS

BALTIMORE ORIOLES

- ☐ 19. CHUCK DIERING
- ☐ 23. FRED MARSH
- ☐ 43. RAY MOORE
- ☐ 62. HAL W. SMITH
- ☐ 80. GUS TRIANDOS
- ☐ 100. TEAM CARD
- ☐ 103. WILLIE MIRANDA
- ☐ 154. DAVE POPE
- ☐ 167. HARRY DORISH
- ☐ 169. BOB NELSON
- ☐ 171. JIM WILSON
- ☐ 206. ERV PALICA
- ☐ 222. DAVE PHILLEY
- ☐ 229. HARRY BRECHEEN(C)
- ☐ 231. BOB HALE
- ☐ 266. DON FERRARESE
- ☐ 276. GEORGE ZUVERINK
- ☐ 286. BILL WIGHT
- ☐ 287. BOBBY ADAMS
- ☐ 303. JIM DYCK

BOSTON RED SOX

- ☐ 5. TED WILLIAMS
- ☐ 26. GRADY HATTON
- ☐ 34. TOM BREWER
- ☐ 71. FRAMK SULLIVAN

- ☐ 89. NORM ZAUCHIN
- ☐ 93. GEORGE SUSCE
- ☐ 111. TEAM CARD
- ☐ 115. JACKIE JENSEN
- ☐ 122. WILLARD NIXON
- ☐ 143. JIM PIERSALL
- ☐ 168. SAMMY WHITE
- ☐ 217. BILLY KLAUS
- ☐ 228. MICKEY VERNON
- ☐ 245. BILLY GOODMAN
- ☐ 248. BOB PORTERFIELD
- ☐ 256. TOM HURD
- ☐ 284. IKE DELOCK
- ☐ 298. JOHNNY SCHMITZ
- ☐ 304. FRANK MALZONE
- ☐ 313. GENE STEPHENS
- ☐ 315. MILT BOLLING

BROOKLYN DODGERS

- ☐ 8. WALTER ALSTON(M)
- ☐ 30. JACKIE ROBINSON
- ☐ 42. SANDY AMOROS
- ☐ 58. ED ROEBUCK
- ☐ 63. ROGER CRAIG
- ☐ 79. SANDY KOUFAX
- ☐ 83. KARL SPOONER
- ☐ 99. DON ZIMMER
- ☐ 101. ROY CAMPANELLA
- ☐ 145. GIL HODGES
- ☐ 150. DUKE SNIDER
- ☐ 166. TEAM CARD
- ☐ 173. JOHNNY PODRES
- ☐ 184. DON BESSENT
- ☐ 190. CARL FURILLO
- ☐ 223. RANDY JACKSON
- ☐ 233. CARL ERSKINE
- ☐ 235. DON NEWCOMBE
- ☐ 260. PEE WEE REESE
- ☐ 270. BILLY LOES
- ☐ 280. JIM GILLIAM
- ☐ 295. CLEM LABINE
- ☐ 299. CHARLEY NEAL
- ☐ 333. RUBE WALKER

CHICAGO CUBS

- ☐ 11. TEAM CARD
- ☐ 15. ERNIE BANKS
- ☐ 41. HANK SAUER
- ☐ 66. BOB SPEAKE
- ☐ 74. JIM KING
- ☐ 96. BILL TREMEL
- ☐ 102. JIM DAVIS
- ☐ 112. DEE FONDY
- ☐ 124. DON KAISER
- ☐ 142. GENE BAKER
- ☐ 179. HARRY CHITI
- ☐ 182. PAUL MINNER
- ☐ 194. MONTE IRVIN
- ☐ 214. BOB RUSH
- ☐ 227. RUSS MEYER
- ☐ 259. SAM JONES
- ☐ 282. WARREN HACKER
- ☐ 285. EDDIE MIKSIS
- ☐ 291. FRANK KELLERT
- ☐ 314. HOBIE LANDRITH
- ☐ 335. DON HOAK

CHICAGO WHITE SOX

- ☐ 18. DICK DONOVAN
- ☐ 29. JACK HARSHMAN
- ☐ 38. BOB KENNEDY
- ☐ 54. BOB KEEGAN
- ☐ 70. JIM RIVERA
- ☐ 118. NELLIE FOX
- ☐ 125. MINNIE MINOSO
- ☐ 144. BOB POWELL
- ☐ 149. DIXIE HOWELL
- ☐ 160. BILLY PIERCE
- ☐ 186. RON JACKSON
- ☐ 188. TEAM CARD
- ☐ 195. GEORGE KELL
- ☐ 238. WALT DROPO
- ☐ 243. SHERM LOLLAR
- ☐ 250. LARRY DOBY
- ☐ 262. HOWIE POLLET
- ☐ 265. SANDY CONSUEGRA
- ☐ 267. BOB NIEMAN
- ☐ 292. LUIS APARICIO
- ☐ 326. CONNIE JOHNSON

CINCINNATI REDS

- ☐ 25. TED KLUSZEWSKI
- ☐ 36. RUDY MINARCIN
- ☐ 47. ART FOWLER
- ☐ 86. RAY JABLONSKI
- ☐ 90. TEAM CARD

- ☐ 123. ROY MCMILLAN
- ☐ 137. AL SILVERA
- ☐ 158. WALLY POST
- ☐ 162. GUS BELL
- ☐ 178. JOE BLACK
- ☐ 192. SMOKY BURGESS
- ☐ 212. JOHNNY TEMPLE
- ☐ 218. JOE NUXHALL
- ☐ 224. BUD PODBIELAN
- ☐ 242. HERSHELL FREEMAN
- ☐ 249. JOHNNY KLIPPSTEIN
- ☐ 289. HAL JEFFCOAT
- ☐ 305. BROOKS LAWRENCE
- ☐ 308. CHUCK HARMON
- ☐ 324. ROCKY BRIDGES

CLEVELAND INDIANS

- ☐ 35. AL ROSEN
- ☐ 39. DON MOSSI
- ☐ 48. JIM HEGAN
- ☐ 59. JOSE SANTIAGO
- ☐ 85. TEAM CARD
- ☐ 105. AL SMITH
- ☐ 132. BOBBY AVILA
- ☐ 133. RAY NARLESKI
- ☐ 140. HERB SCORE
- ☐ 163. GENE WOODLING
- ☐ 187. EARLY WYNN
- ☐ 200. BOB FELLER
- ☐ 210. MIKE GARCIA
- ☐ 230. CHICO CARRASQUEL
- ☐ 255. BOB LEMON
- ☐ 268. DALE MITCHELL
- ☐ 281. ART HOUTTEMAN
- ☐ 300. VIC WERTZ
- ☐ 311. HAL NARAGON
- ☐ 330. JIM BUSBY

DETROIT TIGERS

- ☐ 6. RAY BOONE
- ☐ 20. AL KALINE
- ☐ 32. FRANK HOUSE
- ☐ 57. DUKE MAAS
- ☐ 84. BABE BIRRER
- ☐ 92. RED WILSON
- ☐ 117. VIRGIL TRUCKS
- ☐ 126. JIM BRADY
- ☐ 147. EARL TORGESON
- ☐ 152. BILLY HOEFT
- ☐ 155. HARVEY KUENN
- ☐ 189. NED GARVER
- ☐ 191. FRANK LARY
- ☐ 203. BILL TUTTLE
- ☐ 207. JIM SMALL
- ☐ 213. TEAM CARD
- ☐ 263. BOB G. MILLER
- ☐ 310. STEVE GROMEK
- ☐ 317. AL ABER
- ☐ 318. FRED HATFIELD
- ☐ 338. JIM DELSING

GUS ZERNIAL   outfield KANSAS CITY ATHLETICS

KANSAS CITY ATHLETICS

- ☐ 3. ELMER VALO
- ☐ 16. HECTOR LOPEZ
- ☐ 22. JIM FINIGAN
- ☐ 45. GUS ZERNIAL
- ☐ 53. ARNOLD PORTOCARRERO
- ☐ 67. VIC POWER
- ☐ 82. BILL RENNA
- ☐ 106. JOE ASTROTH
- ☐ 109. ENOS SLAUGHTER
- ☐ 151. SPOOK JACOBS
- ☐ 161. JOE DEMAESTRI
- ☐ 176. ALEX KELLNER
- ☐ 236. TEAM CARD
- ☐ 239. HARRY SIMPSON
- ☐ 246. TOM GORMAN
- ☐ 258. ART DITMAR
- ☐ 261. BOBBY SHANTZ
- ☐ 279. JOHNNY GROTH
- ☐ 319. JACK CRIMIAN
- ☐ 339. RANCE PLESS

MILWAUKEE BRAVES

FRONT ROW: Pendleton, Robinson, Trowbridge, Cave, Vargas, Blazkewicz, Queen, Jay, Spahn. 2nd ROW: O'Connell, Spangler, Keeley, Cooney, Grimm, Walters, Gorin, Whisenant, Logan, Jolly, Taylor, Davidson. 3rd ROW: Locks, Dittmer, Malkmus, Facchini, Koslo, Patko, Mathews, Paine, Crone, White, Torre, Bruton, Adcock, Ferguson, Lewis. BACK ROW: Crandall, Smalley, Caro, Buhl, Burdette, Wilson, MacMahon, Ciggie, Roland, Aaron, Tanner, Parks, Johnson, Nichols, Thompson, Conley, Thomson.

MILWAUKEE BRAVES

- ☐ 10. WARREN SPAHN
- ☐ 17. GENE CONLEY
- ☐ 31. HANK AARON
- ☐ 69. CHUCK TANNER
- ☐ 76. RAY CRONE
- ☐ 95. TEAM CARD
- ☐ 107. ED MATHEWS
- ☐ 131. BOB ROSELLI
- ☐ 136. JOHNNY LOGAN
- ☐ 172. FRANK TORRE
- ☐ 175. DEL CRANDALL
- ☐ 185. BILL BRUTON
- ☐ 219. LEW BURDETTE
- ☐ 244. BOB BUHL
- ☐ 254. GEORGE CROWE
- ☐ 257. BOBBY THOMSON
- ☐ 272. DANNY O'CONNELL
- ☐ 278. CHET NICHOLS
- ☐ 294. ERNIE JOHNSON
- ☐ 312. ANDY PAFKO
- ☐ 320. JOE ADCOCK

NEW YORK GIANTS

- ☐ 9. RUBEN GOMEZ
- ☐ 28. BOBBY HOFMAN
- ☐ 44. WINDY MCCALL
- ☐ 50. DUSTY RHODES
- ☐ 73. WAYNE TERWILLIGER
- ☐ 91. GAIL HARRIS
- ☐ 104. BOB LENNON
- ☐ 130. WILLIE MAYS
- ☐ 138. JOHNNY ANTONELLI
- ☐ 148. ALVIN DARK
- ☐ 156. WES WESTRUM
- ☐ 199. HANK THOMPSON
- ☐ 202. JIM HEARN
- ☐ 205. WHITEY LOCKMAN
- ☐ 226. TEAM CARD
- ☐ 241. DON MUELLER
- ☐ 264. RAY MONZANT
- ☐ 271. FOSTER CASTLEMAN
- ☐ 277. DARYL SPENCER
- ☐ 301. MARV GRISSOM
- ☐ 307. HOYT WILHELM
- ☐ 325. DON LIDDLE

NEW YORK YANKEES

- ☐ 12. ANDY CAREY
- ☐ 21. JOE COLLINS
- ☐ 40. BOB TURLEY
- ☐ 52. BOB GRIM
- ☐ 61. BILL SKOWRON
- ☐ 88. JOHNNY KUCKS
- ☐ 110. YOGI BERRA
- ☐ 113. PHIL RIZZUTO
- ☐ 135. MICKEY MANTLE
- ☐ 139. TOMMY CARROLL
- ☐ 177. HANK BAUER
- ☐ 181. BILLY MARTIN
- ☐ 208. ELSTON HOWARD
- ☐ 215. TOMMY BYRNE
- ☐ 225. GIL MCDOUGALD
- ☐ 240. WHITEY FORD
- ☐ 251. TEAM CARD
- ☐ 253. IRV NOREN
- ☐ 288. BOB CERV
- ☐ 302. EDDIE ROBINSON
- ☐ 316. JERRY COLEMAN
- ☐ 321. JIM KONSTANTY
- ☐ 332. DON LARSEN
- ☐ 340. MICKEY MCDERMOTT

PHILADELPHIA PHILLIES

- ☐ 7. RON NEGRAY
- ☐ 60. MAYO SMITH(M)
- ☐ 72. TEAM CARD
- ☐ 78. HERM WEHMEIER
- ☐ 81. WALLY WESTLAKE
- ☐ 114. JIM OWENS
- ☐ 120. RICHIE ASHBURN
- ☐ 127. WILLIE JONES
- ☐ 174. GLEN GORBOUS
- ☐ 180. ROBIN ROBERTS
- ☐ 183. STAN LOPATA
- ☐ 197. GRANNY HAMNER
- ☐ 211. MURRY DICKSON
- ☐ 220. DEL ENNIS
- ☐ 269. JACK MEYER
- ☐ 274. FRANK BAUMHOLTZ
- ☐ 275. JIM GREENGRASS
- ☐ 290. CURT SIMMONS
- ☐ 296. ANDY SEMINICK
- ☐ 334. BOB J. MILLER
- ☐ 337. BOBBY MORGAN

PITTSBURGH PIRATES

- ☐ 13. ROY FACE
- ☐ 24. DICK GROAT
- ☐ 33. ROBERTO CLEMENTE
- ☐ 46. GENE FREESE
- ☐ 56. DALE LONG
- ☐ 65. JOHNNY O'BRIEN
- ☐ 94. RON KLINE
- ☐ 97. JERRY LYNCH
- ☐ 108. LAURIN PEPPER
- ☐ 116. EDDIE O'BRIEN
- ☐ 121. TEAM CARD
- ☐ 129. JAKE MARTIN
- ☐ 153. FRANK THOMAS
- ☐ 204. ART SWANSON
- ☐ 209. MAX SURKONT
- ☐ 221. BOB FRIEND
- ☐ 232. TOBY ATWELL
- ☐ 252. VERNON LAW
- ☐ 297. BOB SKINNER
- ☐ 306. CURT ROBERTS
- ☐ 328. PRESTON WARD
- ☐ 331. DICK HALL

ST. LOUIS CARDINALS

- ☐ 14. KEN BOYER
- ☐ 27. NELSON BURBRINK
- ☐ 37. ALEX GRAMMAS
- ☐ 55. WALLY MOON
- ☐ 64. LUIS ARROYO
- ☐ 77. HARVEY HADDIX
- ☐ 119. LARRY JACKSON
- ☐ 134. TEAM CARD
- ☐ 141. JOE FRAZIER
- ☐ 165. RED SCHOENDIENST
- ☐ 170. BILL VIRDON
- ☐ 193. WILMER MIZELL
- ☐ 196. TOM POHOLSKY
- ☐ 201. RIP REPULSKI
- ☐ 247. BILL SARNI
- ☐ 273. WALKER COOPER
- ☐ 283. HAL R. SMITH
- ☐ 293. STU MILLER
- ☐ 309. DON BLASINGAME
- ☐ 323. WILLARD SCHMIDT.
- ☐ 336. ELLIS KINDER

WASHINGTON SENATORS

- ☐ 4. CARLOS PAULA
- ☐ 49. PEDRO RAMOS
- ☐ 51. ERNIE ORAVETZ
- ☐ 68. CHUCK STOBBS
- ☐ 75. ROY SIEVERS
- ☐ 87. DEAN STONE
- ☐ 98. CAMILO PASCUAL
- ☐ 128. EDDIE YOST
- ☐ 146. TEAM CARD
- ☐ 157. DICK BRODOWSKI
- ☐ 159. CLINT COURTNEY
- ☐ 164. HARMON KILLEBREW
- ☐ 198. ED FITZ GERALD
- ☐ 216. JERRY SCHOONMAKER
- ☐ 234. PETE RUNNELS
- ☐ 237. JOSE VALDIVIELSO
- ☐ 322. KARL OLSON
- ☐ 327. BOB WIESLER
- ☐ 329. LOU BERBERET

1957 TOPPS (407)
2 1/2" X 3 1/2"

BALTIMORE ORIOLES

- ☐ 11. GEORGE ZUVERINK
- ☐ 14. BOB NIEMAN
- ☐ 17. BILLY GARDNER
- ☐ 26. BOB BOYD
- ☐ 43. CONNIE JOHNSON
- ☐ 59. DICK WILLIAMS
- ☐ 106. RAY MOORE
- ☐ 116. MIKE FORNIELES
- ☐ 146. DON FERRARESE
- ☐ 151. WILLIE MIRANDA
- ☐ 156. GUS TRIANDOS
- ☐ 184. TITO FRANCONA
- ☐ 194. HAL BROWN
- ☐ 230. GEORGE KELL
- ☐ 236. JOE GINSBERG
- ☐ 244. BILLY LOES
- ☐ 251. TEAM CARD
- ☐ 276. JIM PYBURN
- ☐ 311. AL PILARCIK
- ☐ 316. BILLY O' DELL
- ☐ 328. BROOKS ROBINSON
- ☐ 340. BILL WIGHT
- ☐ 382. JIM BRIDEWESER
- ☐ 406. BOB HALE

BOSTON RED SOX

- ☐ 1. TED WILLIAMS
- ☐ 21. FRANK SULLIVAN
- ☐ 56. DAVE SISLER
- ☐ 63. IKE DELOCK
- ☐ 75. JIM PIERSALL
- ☐ 92. MICKEY VERNON
- ☐ 112. TOM BREWER
- ☐ 118. BOB PORTERFIELD
- ☐ 131. MILT BOLLING
- ☐ 163. SAMMY WHITE
- ☐ 171. TEAM CARD
- ☐ 189. WILLARD NIXON
- ☐ 202. DICK GERNERT
- ☐ 217. GENE STEPHENS
- ☐ 220. JACKIE JENSEN
- ☐ 229. GEORGE SUSCE
- ☐ 288. TED LEPCIO
- ☐ 292. BILLY KLAUS
- ☐ 303. BILLY GOODMAN
- ☐ 313. MEL PARNELL
- ☐ 336. HAYWOOD SULLIVAN
- ☐ 342. GENE MAUCH
- ☐ 355. FRANK MALZONE
- ☐ 372. NORM ZAUCHIN
- ☐ 381. DEAN STONE
- ☐ 388. PETE DALEY
- ☐ 399. BILLY CONSOLO

BROOKLYN DODGERS

- ☐ 5. SAL MAGLIE
- ☐ 18. DON DRYSDALE
- ☐ 30. PEE WEE REESE
- ☐ 45. CARL FURILLO
- ☐ 53. CLEM LABINE
- ☐ 80. GIL HODGES
- ☐ 115. JIM GILLIAM
- ☐ 130. DON NEWCOMBE
- ☐ 147. AL WALKER
- ☐ 170. DUKE SNIDER
- ☐ 173. ROGER CRAIG
- ☐ 178. DON BESSENT
- ☐ 190. RANDY JACKSON

☐ 201. SANDY AMOROS
☐ 210. ROY CAMPANELLA
☐ 242. CHARLEY NEAL
☐ 252. CARL ERSKINE
☐ 277. JOHNNY PODRES
☐ 284. DON ZIMMER
☐ 302. SANDY KOUFAX
☐ 319. GINO CIMOLI
☐ 324. TEAM CARD
☐ 337. RENE VALDES
☐ 366. KEN LEHMAN
☐ 376. DON ELSTON

CHICAGO CUBS

☐ 16. WALT MORYN
☐ 42. DEE FONDY
☐ 55. ERNIE BANKS
☐ 74. VITO VALENTINETTI
☐ 84. MOE DRABOWSKY
☐ 134. DON KAISER
☐ 137. BOB RUSH
☐ 155. JIM BROSNAN
☐ 159. SOLLY DRAKE
☐ 176. GENE BAKER
☐ 183. TEAM CARD
☐ 186. JIM KING
☐ 218. RAY JABLONSKI
☐ 235. TOM POHOLSKY
☐ 247. TURK LOWN
☐ 255. CHARLIE SILVERA
☐ 268. JACKIE COLLUM
☐ 289. JIM BOLGER
☐ 339. BOB SPEAKE
☐ 346. DICK LITTLEFIELD
☐ 351. DAVE HILLMAN
☐ 353. CAL NEEMAN
☐ 371. BOB LENNON
☐ 378. ELMER SINGLETON
☐ 396. CASEY WISE

LUIS Aparicio
CHICAGO. WHITE SOX S.S.

CHICAGO WHITE SOX

☐   7. LUIS APARICIO
☐ 23. SHERM LOLLAR
☐ 31. RON NORTHEY
☐ 38. NELLIE FOX
☐ 85. LARRY DOBY
☐ 99. BOB KEEGAN
☐ 107. JIM RIVERA
☐ 124. DAVE PHILLEY
☐ 138. MINNIE MINOSO
☐ 152. JACK HARSHMAN
☐ 160. BILL PIERCE
☐ 181. DICK DONOVAN
☐ 213. LES MOSS
☐ 221. DIXIE HOWELL
☐ 227. JERRY STALEY
☐ 257. WALT DROPO
☐ 278. FRED HATFIELD
☐ 301. SAM ESPOSITO
☐ 329. TEAM CARD
☐ 330. JIM WILSON
☐ 344. PAUL LAPALME
☐ 352. ELLIS KINDER
☐ 375. JIM LANDIS
☐ 395. BUBBA PHILLIPS
☐ 401. EARL BATTEY

CINCINNATI REDS

☐   9. JOHNNY TEMPLE
☐ 32. HERSH FREEMAN
☐ 35. FRANK ROBINSON
☐ 66. BROOKS LAWRENCE
☐ 69. ROY MCMILLAN
☐ 73. GEORGE CROWE

☐ 93. HAL JEFFCOAT
☐ 103. JOE NUXHALL
☐ 128. ED BAILEY
☐ 157. WALLY POST
☐ 165. TED KLUSZEWSKI
☐ 180. GUS BELL
☐ 219. TOM ACKER
☐ 222. ALEX GRAMMAS
☐ 228. SMOKY BURGESS
☐ 233. ART FOWLER
☐ 274. DON HOAK
  ☐ 279. BOB THURMAN
☐ 294. ROCKY BRIDGES
☐ 296. JOHNNY KLIPPSTEIN
☐ 322. TEAM CARD
☐ 341. DON GROSS
☐ 358. JERRY LYNCH
☐ 370. WARREN HACKER
☐ 373. PETE WHISENANT
☐ 393. RAUL SANCHEZ

CLEVELAND INDIANS

☐   8. DON MOSSI
☐ 40. EARLY WYNN
☐ 50. HERB SCORE
☐ 67. CHICO CARRASQUEL
☐ 78. VIC WERTZ
☐ 96. HANK AGUIRRE
☐ 120. BOB LEMON
☐ 136. JIM HEGAN
☐ 144. RAY NARLESKI
☐ 145. AL SMITH
☐ 172. GENE WOODLING
☐ 195. BOBBY AVILA
☐ 212. ROCKY COLAVITO
☐ 226. PRESTON WARD
☐ 249. DAVE POPE
☐ 263. GEORGE STRICKLAND
☐ 266. KEN KUHN
☐ 275. TEAM CARD
☐ 300. MIKE GARCIA
☐ 309. JIM BUSBY
☐ 347. HAL NARAGON
☐ 364. CAL MCLISH
☐ 385. ART HOUTTEMAN

DETROIT TIGERS

☐ 19. BOB WILSON
☐ 33. JIM SMALL
☐ 60. BILLY HOEFT
☐ 72. BILL TUTTLE
☐ 77. PAUL FOYTACK
☐ 88. HARVEY KUENN
☐ 102. RAY BOONE
☐ 125. AL KALINE
☐ 141. AL ABER
☐ 149. BOB KENNEDY
☐ 168. FRANK LARY
☐ 198. TEAM CARD
☐ 205. CHARLEY MAXWELL
☐ 223. FRANK HOUSE
☐ 238. EDDIE ROBINSON
☐ 248. JIM FINIGAN
☐ 258. STEVE GROMEK
☐ 282. JACK DITTMER
☐ 297. JACK CRIMIAN
☐ 307. JACK PHILLIPS
☐ 325. FRANK BOLLING
☐ 338. JIM BUNNING
☐ 357. EARL TORGESON
☐ 379. DON LEE
☐ 390. RENO BERTOIA
☐ 405. DUKE MAAS

KANSAS CITY ATHLETICS

☐   6. HECTOR LOPEZ
☐ 13. WALLY BURNETTE
☐ 41. HAL W. SMITH
☐ 44. JOE DEMAESTRI
☐ 83. LOU SKIZAS
☐ 87. TOM GORMAN
☐ 121. CLETE BOYER
☐ 139. LOU KRETLOW
☐ 142. CHARLEY THOMPSON
☐ 167. VIC POWER
☐ 187. VIRGIL TRUCKS
☐ 204. TEAM CARD
☐ 207. BILLY HUNTER
☐ 225. HARRY SIMPSON
☐ 239. TOM MORGAN
☐ 253. GUS ZERNIAL
☐ 269. BOB CERV
☐ 280. ALEX KELLNER
☐ 285. NED GARVER
☐ 298. IRV NOREN
☐ 318. MICKEY MCDERMOTT
☐ 354. RIP COLEMAN

☐ 360. JOHNNY GROTH
☐ 369. MILT GRAFF
☐ 402. JIM PISONI

JOHNNY Logan
MILWAUKEE BRAVES

MILWAUKEE BRAVES

☐   4. JOHNNY LOGAN
☐ 20. HANK AARON
☐ 28. GENE CONLEY
☐ 37. FRANK TORRE
☐ 48. BILL BRUTON
☐ 68. RAY CRONE
☐ 90. WARREN SPAHN
☐ 114. TEAM CARD
☐ 117. JOE ADCOCK
☐ 127. BOB BUHL
☐ 133. DEL CRANDALL
☐ 143. ANDY PAFKO
☐ 188. FELIX MANTILLA
☐ 193. DEL RICE
☐ 208. LEW BURDETTE
☐ 250. ED MATHEWS
☐ 262. BOBBY THOMSON
☐ 271. DANNY O'CONNELL
☐ 283. WES COVINGTON
☐ 321. RED MURFF
☐ 333. ERNIE JOHNSON
☐ 343. TAYLOR PHILLIPS
☐ 383. JUAN PIZARRO
☐ 389. DAVE JOLLY
☐ 392. CHUCK TANNER

NEW YORK GIANTS

☐ 10. WILLIE MAYS
☐ 39. AL WORTHINGTON
☐ 49. DARYL SPENCER
☐ 58. RUBEN GOMEZ
☐ 61. DUSTY RHODES
☐ 86. BILL SARNI
☐ 105. JOHNNY ANTONELLI
☐ 109. HANK THOMPSON
☐ 123. STEVE RIDZIK
☐ 148. DON MUELLER
☐ 154. RED SCHOENDIENST
☐ 191. JOE MARGONERI
☐ 197. HANK SAUER
☐ 216. MARV GRISSOM
☐ 232. WHITEY LOCKMAN
☐ 237. FOSTER CASTLEMAN
☐ 281. GAIL HARRIS
☐ 291. WINDY MCCALL
☐ 310. MAX SURKONT
☐ 317. TEAM CARD
☐ 323. WES WESTRUM
☐ 331. RAY KATT
☐ 361. CURT BARCLAY
☐ 365. OSSIE VIRGIL
☐ 377. ANDRE RODGERS

NEW YORK YANKEES

☐   2. YOGI BERRA
☐ 25. WHITEY FORD
☐ 34. TOM STURDIVANT
☐ 36. BOB GRIM
☐ 62. BILLY MARTIN
☐ 82. ELSTON HOWARD
☐ 95. MICKEY MANTLE
☐ 97. TEAM CARD
☐ 108. TOMMY BYRNE
☐ 132. ART DITMAR
☐ 135. BILL SKOWRON
☐ 164. TOMMY CARROLL
☐ 175. DON LARSEN
☐ 185. JOHNNY KUCKS
☐ 192. JERRY COLEMAN

☐ 200. GIL MCDOUGALD
☐ 215. ENOS SLAUGHTER
☐ 240. HANK BAUER
☐ 264. BOB TURLEY
☐ 272. BOBBY SHANTZ
☐ 286. BOBBY RICHARDSON
☐ 290. ANDY CAREY
☐ 295. JOE COLLINS
☐ 306. DARRELL JOHNSON
☐ 312. TONY KUBEK
☐ 391. RALPH TERRY
☐ 398. AL CICOTTE

PHILADELPHIA PHILLIES

☐ 15. ROBIN ROBERTS
☐ 27. TED KAZANSKI
☐ 46. BOB J. MILLER
☐ 54. ELMER VALO
☐ 70. RICHIE ASHBURN
☐ 91. MACK BURK
☐ 119. STAN LOPATA
☐ 129. SAUL ROGOVIN
☐ 158. CURT SIMMONS
☐ 162. JACK MEYER
☐ 174. WILLIE JONES
☐ 214. TEAM CARD
☐ 224. MARV BLAYLOCK
☐ 231. SOLLY HEMUS
☐ 241. JOE LONNETT
☐ 245. RIP REPULSKI
☐ 254. RON NEGRAY
☐ 265. HARVEY HADDIX
☐ 305. CHICO FERNADEZ
☐ 314. ED BOUCHEE
☐ 332. BOB BOWMAN
☐ 335. GRANNY HAMNER
☐ 348. JIM HEARN
☐ 374. DON CARDWELL
☐ 387. JACK SANFORD
☐ 397. ROY SMALLEY
☐ 404. HARRY ANDERSON

PITTSBURGH PIRATES

☐ 3. DALE LONG
☐ 12. DICK GROAT
☐ 24. BILL MAZEROSKI
☐ 52. LEE WALLS
☐ 76. BOB CLEMENTE
☐ 104. HANK FOILES
☐ 110. BILL VIRDON
☐ 140. FRANK THOMAS
☐ 150. BOB FRIEND
☐ 161. TEAM CARD
☐ 166. ROY FACE
☐ 199. VERNON LAW
☐ 209. BOB SKINNER
☐ 234. DICK COLE
☐ 256. RON KLINE
☐ 259. EDDIE O'BRIEN
☐ 267. DANNY KRAVITZ
☐ 308. DICK HALL
☐ 327. JIM PENDLETON
☐ 345. PAUL SMITH
☐ 349. NELSON KING
☐ 362. ROMAN MEJIAS
☐ 368. BOB PURKEY
☐ 394. LUIS ARROYO

ST. LOUIS CARDINALS

☐ 47. DON BLASINGAME
☐ 65. WALLY MOON
☐ 71. MURRY DICKSON
☐ 79. LINDY MCDANIEL
☐ 81. HERM WEHMEIER
☐ 94. BOBBY DEL GRECO
☐ 98. AL DARK
☐ 111. HAL R. SMITH
☐ 113. WILMER MIZELL
☐ 122. KEN BOYER
☐ 182. HOBIE LANDRITH
☐ 196. LARRY JACKSON
☐ 203. HOYT WILHELM
☐ 206. WILLARD SCHMIDT
☐ 243. TEAM CARD
☐ 260. DEL ENNIS
☐ 273. JIM DAVIS
☐ 287. SAM JONES
☐ 299. CHUCK HARMON
☐ 304. JOE CUNNINGHAM
☐ 350. EDDIE MIKSIS
☐ 359. TOM CHENEY
☐ 363. EDDIE KASKO
☐ 380. WALKER COOPER
☐ 384. BOBBY GENE SMITH

WASHINGTON SENATORS

☐ 22. JERRY SNYDER
☐ 29. WHITEY HERZOG
☐ 51. CLINT COURTNEY
☐ 57. JIM LEMON
☐ 64. PETE RUNNELS
☐ 89. ROY SIEVERS
☐ 101. CHUCK STOBBS
☐ 126. BOB WIESLER
☐ 153. KARL OLSON
☐ 169. HERB PLEWS
☐ 177. EDDIE YOST
☐ 179. ERNIE ORAVETZ
☐ 211. CAMILO PASCUAL
☐ 246. JOSE VALDIVIELSO
☐ 261. BOB CHAKALES
☐ 270. TEAM CARD
☐ 293. TED ABERNATHY
☐ 315. LOU BERBERET
☐ 320. NEIL CHRISLEY
☐ 326. PEDRO RAMOS
☐ 334. JERRY SCHOONMAKER
☐ 356. FAYE THRONEBERRY
☐ 367. ED FITZ GERALD
☐ 386. LYLE LUTTRELL
☐ 403. DICK HYDE

1958 TOPPS (494)
2 1/2" X 3 1/2"

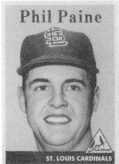

Phil Paine
ST. LOUIS CARDINALS

BALTIMORE ORIOLES

☐ 6. GEORGE ZUVERINK
☐ 28. JIM BUSBY
☐ 40. GEORGE KELL
☐ 67. JOE GINSBERG
☐ 84. BILLY O'DELL
☐ 96. JOE DURHAM
☐ 105. BILLY GARDNER
☐ 113. JERRY WALKER
☐ 121. EDDIE MIKSIS
☐ 141. KEN LEHMAN
☐ 165. BOB NIEMAN
☐ 179. WILLIE MIRANDA
☐ 191. ART CECCARELLI
☐ 217. JACK HARSHMAN
☐ 229. FRANK ZUPO
☐ 259. AL PILARCIK
☐ 266. CONNIE JOHNSON
☐ 279. BOB BOYD
☐ 307. BROOKS ROBINSON
☐ 336. BERT HAMRIC
☐ 359. BILLY LOES
☐ 381. HAL BROWN
☐ 398. GENE WOODLING
☐ 408. TEAM CARD
☐ 416. FOSTER CASTLEMAN
☐ 429. GUS TRIANDOS
☐ 441. JIM MARSHALL
☐ 457. MILT PAPPAS
☐ 465. ARNIE PORTOCARRERO
☐ 471. LENNY GREEN

BOSTON RED SOX

☐ 1. TED WILLIAMS
☐ 18. FRANK SULLIVAN
☐ 29. TED LEPCIO
☐ 38. DICK GERNERT
☐ 59. DAVE SISLER
☐ 73. PETE DALEY
☐ 89. BILLY KLAUS
☐ 130. JACKIE JENSEN
☐ 148. BILLY CONSOLO

☐ 167. FRANK BAUMANN
☐ 189. GEORGE SUSCE
☐ 197. HAYWOOD SULLIVAN
☐ 204. LEO KIELY
☐ 220. TOM BREWER
☐ 227. GENE STEPHENS
☐ 260. FRANK MALZONE
☐ 265. PETE RUNNELS
☐ 280. JIM PIERSALL
☐ 297. DON BUDDIN
☐ 312. TEAM CARD
☐ 328. IKE DELOCK
☐ 344. BOB PORTERFIELD
☐ 361. MIKE FORNIELES
☐ 371. MARTY KEOUGH
☐ 383. LOU BERBERET
☐ 395. WILLARD NIXON
☐ 410. MURRAY WALL
☐ 414. SAMMY WHITE
☐ 445. BOB W. SMITH
☐ 473. BILL RENNA

CHICAGO CUBS

☐ 7. DALE LONG
☐ 33. CAL NEEMAN
☐ 41. DAVE HILLMAN
☐ 66. LEE WALLS
☐ 80. DICK DROTT
☐ 91. CHUCK TANNER
☐ 99. BOBBY ADAMS
☐ 122. WALT MORYN
☐ 135. MOE BRABOWSKY
☐ 144. BOBBY MORGAN
☐ 159. TAYLOR PHILLIPS
☐ 184. ELVIN TAPPE
☐ 201. JIM BOLGER
☐ 209. BOB ANDERSON
☐ 221. JERRY KINDALL
☐ 241. DICK LITTLEFIELD
☐ 261. TURK LOWN
☐ 281. SAM TAYLOR
☐ 310. ERNIE BANKS
☐ 327. TEAM CARD
☐ 342. JIM BROSNAN
☐ 363. DON ELSTON
☐ 384. JOHN GORYL
☐ 411. TONY TAYLOR
☐ 430. BOBBY THOMSON
☐ 449. GENE FODGE
☐ 461. ED MAYER
☐ 467. GLEN HOBBIE

CHICAGO WHITE SOX

☐ 11. JIM RIVERA
☐ 26. RON JACKSON
☐ 50. BILLY PIERCE
☐ 56. BILL FISCHER
☐ 85. LUIS APARICIO
☐ 100. EARLY WYNN
☐ 108. JIM LANDIS
☐ 129. JIM DERRINGTON
☐ 138. EARL TORGESON
☐ 153. LES MOSS
☐ 163. JIM WILSON
☐ 177. AL SMITH
☐ 200. BOB KEEGAN
☐ 212. BUBBA PHILLIPS
☐ 225. BILLY GOODMAN
☐ 249. RAY MOORE
☐ 256. TEAM CARD
☐ 267. SHERM LOLLAR
☐ 290. DICK DONOVAN
☐ 316. TITO FRANCONA
☐ 338. WALT DROPO
☐ 347. DON RUDOLPH
☐ 364. EARL BATTEY
☐ 400. NELLIE FOX
☐ 412. JERRY STALEY
☐ 421. DIXIE HOWELL
☐ 425. SAM ESPOSITO
☐ 453. TOM QUALTERS

CINCINNATI REDS

☐ 12. GEORGE CROWE
☐ 27. BUD FREEMAN
☐ 34. BOB THURMAN
☐ 49. SMOKY BURGESS
☐ 63. JOE NUXHALL
☐ 75. GUS BELL
☐ 103. JERRY LYNCH
☐ 118. HARVEY HADDIX
☐ 126. STAN PALYS
☐ 131. BOB HENRICH
☐ 149. TOM ACKER
☐ 157. DEE FONDY
☐ 160. DON HOAK
☐ 205. JOHNNY TEMPLE
☐ 214. WILLARD SCHMIDT

☐ 237. BILL WIGHT	☐ 257. HAL W. SMITH	☐ 147. DON MCMAHON
☐ 242. JOHNNY KLIPPSTEIN	☐ 277. VIRGIL TRUCKS	☐ 164. BOB TAYLOR
☐ 254. ALEX GRAMMAS	☐ 292. NED GARVER	☐ 176. BOB BUHL
☐ 285. FRANK ROBINSON	☐ 302. MIKE BAXES	☐ 190. RED SCHOENDIENST
☐ 294. HAL JEFFCOAT	☐ 318. FRANK HOUSE	☐ 223. ANDY PAFKO
☐ 311. BOB PURKEY	☐ 329. BOB CERV	☐ 234. CARL SAWATSKI
☐ 330. ED BAILEY	☐ 349. MURRY DICKSON	☐ 247. CASEY WISE
☐ 346. STEVE BILKO	☐ 367. JACK URBAN	☐ 252. BOB TROWBRIDGE
☐ 360. ROY MCMILLAN	☐ 379. RAY HERBERT	☐ 270. WARREN SPAHN
☐ 374. BROOKS LAWRENCE	☐ 391. DAVE MELTON	☐ 283. RAY SHEARER
☐ 376. CHARLEY RABE	☐ 406. VIC POWER	☐ 313. BOB RUSH
☐ 396. DUTCH DOTTERER	☐ 450. PRESTON WARD	☐ 325. JOE ADCOCK
☐ 420. VADA PINSON		☐ 355. BILL BRUTON
☐ 428. TEAM CARD		☐ 377. TEAM CARD
☐ 466. PETE WHISENANT		☐ 390. DEL CRANDALL
		☐ 407. CARLTON WILLEY

CLEVELAND INDIANS

Sandy Koufax

L. A. DODGERS

☐ 2. BOB LEMON	☐ 431. GENE CONLEY
☐ 22. HAL NARAGON	☐ 440. ED MATHEWS
☐ 35. DON MOSSI	☐ 454. HARRY HANEBRINK
☐ 47. ROGER MARIS	☐ 472. JOE JAY
☐ 55. CHICO CARRASQUEL	
☐ 79. DICK WILLIAMS	

NEW YORK YANKEES

☐ 102. GEORGE STRICKLAND	☐ 9. HANK BAUER
☐ 123. DICK TOMANEK	☐ 20. GIL MCDOUGALD
☐ 133. RUSS NIXON	☐ 43. SAL MAGLIE
☐ 158. TEAM CARD	☐ 54. NORM SIEBERN
☐ 170. VIC WERTZ	☐ 61. DARRELL JOHNSON
☐ 182. JOE CAFFIE	☐ 87. JOHNNY KUCKS
☐ 196. MIKE GARCIA	☐ 101. BOBBY RICHARDSON
☐ 208. CAL MCLISH	☐ 127. TOM STURDIVANT
☐ 222. BUD DALEY	☐ 142. ENOS SLAUGHTER
☐ 233. MICKEY VERNON	☐ 150. MICKEY MANTLE
☐ 243. LARRY RAINES	☐ 161. DON LARSEN
☐ 276. BOBBY AVILA	☐ 175. MARV THRONEBERRY
☐ 295. MINNIE MINOSO	☐ 193. JERRY LUMPE
☐ 324. HOYT WILHELM	☐ 224. BOB GRIM
☐ 339. FRED HATFIELD	☐ 240. BILL SKOWRON
☐ 352. HERB SCORE	☐ 246. TEAM CARD
☐ 368. ROCKY COLAVITO	☐ 255. BOB TURLEY
☐ 388. BILLY MORAN	☐ 275. ELSTON HOWARD
☐ 394. JIM GRANT	☐ 296. RYNE DUREN
☐ 424. LARRY DOBY	☐ 299. HARRY SIMPSON
☐ 439. RAY NARLESKI	☐ 320. WHITEY FORD
☐ 443. BILLY HARRELL	☐ 333. ANDY CAREY
☐ 446. CARROLL HARDY	☐ 354. ART DITMAR
☐ 456. DICK BROWN	☐ 370. YOGI BERRA
☐ 462. GARY GEIGER	☐ 382. AL CICOTTE
☐ 469. DON FERRARESE	☐ 393. TONY KUBEK
	☐ 419. BOBBY SHANTZ

DETROIT TIGERS

LOS ANGELES DODGERS

PHILADELPHIA PHILLIES

☐ 13. BILLY HOEFT	☐ 16. CHARLEY NEAL	☐ 14. RIP REPULSKI
☐ 32. J.W. PORTER	☐ 25. DON DRYSDALE	☐ 36. TED KAZANSKI
☐ 46. LOU SLEATER	☐ 42. JOHN ROSEBORO	☐ 48. CHUCK HARMON
☐ 57. TIM THOMPSON	☐ 71. TEAM CARD	☐ 64. JOE LONNETT
☐ 70. AL KALINE	☐ 77. DON ZIMMER	☐ 76. DICK FARRELL
☐ 81. STEVE BOROS	☐ 88. DUKE SNIDER	☐ 90. ROBIN ROBERTS
☐ 95. FRANK BOLLING	☐ 93. SANDY AMOROS	☐ 116. DAVE PHILLEY
☐ 112. GUS ZERNIAL	☐ 120. JOHNNY PODRES	☐ 134. TEAM CARD
☐ 115. JIM BUNNING	☐ 146. DICK GRAY	☐ 171. HARRY ANDERSON
☐ 154. HARRY BYRD	☐ 162. GIL HODGES	☐ 181. WILLIE JONES
☐ 185. RAY BOONE	☐ 187. SANDY KOUFAX	☐ 186. JACK MEYER
☐ 206. BOB SHAW	☐ 194. ROGER CRAIG	☐ 207. SOLLY HEMUS
☐ 213. RED WILSON	☐ 203. AL WALKER	☐ 230. RICHIE ASHBURN
☐ 232. RENO BERTOIA	☐ 215. JIM GILLIAM	☐ 251. WARREN HACKER
☐ 245. FRANK LARY	☐ 244. DON DEMETER	☐ 264. JACK SANFORD
☐ 262. JOHNNY GROTH	☐ 258. CARL ERSKINE	☐ 268. GRANNY HAMNER
☐ 271. BILLY MARTIN	☐ 286. GINO CIMOLI	☐ 278. MACK BURK
☐ 282. PAUL FOYTACK	☐ 301. RANDY JACKSON	☐ 291. DON LANDRUM
☐ 309. GAIL HARRIS	☐ 305. CLEM LABINE	☐ 298. JIM HEARN
☐ 319. LOU SKIZAS	☐ 323. ELMER VALO	☐ 326. BOB J. MILLER
☐ 337. HANK AGUIRRE	☐ 340. DON NEWCOMBE	☐ 348. CHICO FERNANDEZ
☐ 345. JIM HEGAN	☐ 357. DANNY MCDEVITT	☐ 353. STAN LOPATA
☐ 365. TOM MORGAN	☐ 373. JOE PIGNATANO	☐ 372. DON CARDWELL
☐ 380. CHARLEY MAXWELL	☐ 375. PEE WEE REESE	☐ 387. WALLY POST
☐ 389. BILL TAYLOR	☐ 401. DON BESSENT	☐ 404. CURT SIMMONS
☐ 397. TEAM CARD	☐ 417. CARL FURILLO	☐ 415. BOB BOWMAN
☐ 434. HARVEY KUENN	☐ 435. ED ROEBUCK	☐ 433. PANCHO HERRERA
☐ 448. CHARLIE LAU		☐ 460. CHUCK ESSEGIAN
☐ 463. VITO VALENTINETTI		☐ 474. ROMAN SEMPROCH

KANSAS CITY ATHLETICS

Wes Covington
M
OUTFIELD   MILWAUKEE BRAVES

PITTSBURGH PIRATES

☐ 3. ALEX KELLNER		☐ 4. HANK FOILES
☐ 23. BILL TUTTLE		☐ 45. DICK GROAT
☐ 39. BOB MARTYN		☐ 52. BOB CLEMENTE
☐ 62. JOE DEMAESTRI		☐ 74. ROY FACE
☐ 69. WALLY BURNETTE		☐ 82. RON KLINE
☐ 98. BILLY HUNTER		☐ 94. BOB SKINNER
☐ 119. HARRY CHITI		☐ 104. JIM PENDLETON
☐ 139. GEORGE BRUNET		☐ 132. VERN LAW
☐ 155. HECTOR LOPEZ	## MILWAUKEE BRAVES	☐ 151. BUDDY PRITCHARD
☐ 169. RALPH TERRY		☐ 172. DON GROSS
☐ 174. TEAM CARD	☐ 10. LEW BURDETTE	☐ 178. TED KLUSZEWSKI
☐ 192. MILT GRAFF	☐ 17. FELIX MANTILLA	☐ 198. BILL VIRDON
☐ 202. WOODY HELD	☐ 30. HANK AARON	☐ 218. DICK RAND
☐ 228. DUKE MAAS	☐ 51. DEL RICE	☐ 226. BOB G. SMITH
☐ 235. TOM GORMAN	☐ 78. ERNIE JOHNSON	☐ 238. BILL MAZEROSKI
	☐ 83. BOB HAZLE	
	☐ 110. JOHNNY LOGAN	
	☐ 117. FRANK TORRE	
	☐ 140. WES COVINGTON	

☐ 269. PAUL SMITH
☐ 293. GENE FREESE
☐ 306. WHAMMY DOUGLAS
☐ 315. BOB FRIEND
☐ 322. HARDING PETERSON
☐ 341. TEAM CARD
☐ 358. GENE BAKER
☐ 392. BENNIE DANIELS
☐ 409. FRANK THOMAS
☐ 426. JOHNNY O'BRIEN
☐ 432. JOHN POWERS
☐ 444. DANNY KRAVITZ
☐ 452. ROMAN MEJIAS
☐ 459. RON BLACKBURN
☐ 470. R.C. STEVENS

ST. LOUIS CARDINALS

☐ 8. EDDIE KASKO
☐ 24. HOBIE LANDRITH
☐ 53. MORRIE MARTIN
☐ 60. DEL ENNIS
☐ 65. VON MCDANIEL
☐ 97. LARRY JACKSON
☐ 106. DICK SCHOFIELD
☐ 114. IRV NOREN
☐ 125. AL DARK
☐ 143. BILLY MUFFETT
☐ 168. JOE CUNNINGHAM
☐ 180. LINDY MCDANIEL
☐ 199. DON BLASINGAME
☐ 210. WALLY MOON
☐ 216. TEAM CARD
☐ 231. LLOYD MERRITT
☐ 248. HERM WEHMEIER
☐ 273. HAL R. SMITH
☐ 287. SAM JONES
☐ 350. KEN BOYER
☐ 366. GENE GREEN
☐ 385. WILMER MIZELL
☐ 402. BOBBY GENE SMITH
☐ 423. PHIL CLARK
☐ 442. PHIL PAINE
☐ 451. JOE TAYLOR
☐ 464. CURT FLOOD

SAN FRANCISCO GIANTS

☐ 5. WILLIE MAYS
☐ 19. TEAM CARD
☐ 21. CURT BARCLAY
☐ 37. MIKE MCCORMICK
☐ 68. DARYL SPENCER
☐ 86. VALMY THOMAS
☐ 107. OSSIE VIRGIL
☐ 111. STU MILLER
☐ 128. WILLIE KIRKLAND
☐ 136. JIM FINIGAN
☐ 152. JOHNNY ANTONELLI
☐ 166. DANNY O'CONNELL
☐ 183. DAVE JOLLY
☐ 195. WHITEY LOCKMAN
☐ 211. PETE BURNSIDE
☐ 253. DON MUELLER
☐ 263. EDDIE BRESSOUD
☐ 272. RAY CRONE
☐ 284. RAY KATT
☐ 308. PAUL GIEL
☐ 332. JIM KING
☐ 335. RUBEN GOMEZ
☐ 343. ORLANDO CEPEDA
☐ 362. RAY JABLONSKI
☐ 378. HANK SAUER
☐ 399. MARV GRISSOM
☐ 413. JIM DAVENPORT
☐ 427. AL WORTHINGTON
☐ 437. BOB SPEAKE
☐ 447. RAY MONZANT
☐ 468. BOB SCHMIDT

WASHINGTON SENATORS

☐ 15. JIM LEMON
☐ 31. TEX CLEVENGER
☐ 44. TEAM CARD
☐ 58. ART SCHULT
☐ 72. BUD BYERLY
☐ 92. CLINT COURTNEY
☐ 109. HERB PLEWS
☐ 124. BOBBY USHER
☐ 137. RUSS KEMMERER
☐ 156. DICK HYDE
☐ 173. EDDIE YOST
☐ 188. MILT BOLLING
☐ 219. CAMILO PASCUAL
☐ 236. ED FITZ GERALD
☐ 239. CHUCK STOBBS
☐ 250. ROY SIEVERS
☐ 274. ROCKY BRIDGES
☐ 288. HARMON KILLEBREW
☐ 303. NEIL CHRISLEY

☐ 317. ALBIE PEARSON
☐ 331. PEDRO RAMOS
☐ 356. BOB MALKMUS
☐ 369. RALPH LUMENTI
☐ 403. STEVE KORCHECK
☐ 405. KEN ASPROMONTE
☐ 422. NORM ZAUCHIN
☐ 438. WHITEY HERZOG
☐ 455. HAL GRIGGS
☐ 458. JULIO BECQUER

1959 TOPPS (572)
2 1/2" X 3 1/2"

BALTIMORE ORIOLES

☐ 7. AL PILARCIK
☐ 21. CONNIE JOHNSON
☐ 47. JIM FINIGAN
☐ 48. TEAM CARD
☐ 66. JOE GINSBERG
☐ 82. BOB BOYD
☐ 89. BILLY GARDNER
☐ 98. ARNIE PORTOCARRERO
☐ 143. WILLIE TASBY
☐ 144. JERRY WALKER
☐ 170. GENE WOODLING
☐ 192. CHARLEY BEAMON
☐ 209. LENNY GREEN
☐ 219. GEORGE ZUVERINK
☐ 250. BILLY O'DELL
☐ 264. CHICO CARRASQUEL
☐ 279. ERNIE JOHNSON
☐ 299. BILLY KLAUS
☐ 330. GUS TRIANDOS
☐ 336. BILLY LOES
☐ 349. HOYT WILHELM
☐ 363. BOBBY AVILA
☐ 375. BOB NIEMAN
☐ 391. MILT PAPPAS
☐ 411. WHITEY LOCKMAN
☐ 439. BROOKS ROBINSON
☐ 444. RON HANSEN
☐ 475. JACK HARSHMAN
☐ 487. HAL BROWN
☐ 507. BOB HALE
☐ 529. GEORGE BAMBERGER
☐ 540. WILLY MIRANDA

BOSTON RED SOX

☐ 13. DICK GERNERT
☐ 32. DON BUDDING
☐ 42. MURRAY WALL
☐ 55. TOM BREWER
☐ 72. BILL RENNA
☐ 91. HERB MOFORD
☐ 112. BILLY CONSOLO
☐ 139. ED SADOWSKI
☐ 146. JERRY ZIMMERMAN
☐ 161. FRANK BAUMANN
☐ 173. BILL MONBOUQUETTE
☐ 185. JIM BUSBY
☐ 199. LEO KIELY
☐ 220. FRANK MALZONE
☐ 236. TED BOWSFIELD
☐ 248. TEAM CARD
☐ 261. GENE STEPHENS
☐ 276. PETE DALEY
☐ 286. DEAN STONE
☐ 303. MARTY KEOUGH
☐ 323. FRANK SULLIVAN
☐ 348. TED LEPCIO
☐ 361. WILLARD NIXON
☐ 370. PETE RUNNELS
☐ 384. DAVE SISLER
☐ 400. JACKIE JENSEN

☐ 416. HAYWOOD SULLIVAN
☐ 437. IKE DELOCK
☐ 456. JERRY CASALE
☐ 473. MIKE FORNIELES
☐ 486. SAMMY WHITE
☐ 500. VIC WERTZ
☐ 521. GARY GEIGER

CHICAGO CUBS

☐ 15. DICK DROTT
☐ 29. JIM BOLGER
☐ 46. BILL R. HENRY
☐ 62. TONY TAYLOR
☐ 77. JOHN GORYL
☐ 105. LEE WALLS
☐ 113. TAYLOR PHILLIPS
☐ 118. JOHN BUZHARDT
☐ 130. LOU JACKSON
☐ 153. JIM MARSHALL
☐ 177. JOHNNY BRIGGS
☐ 193. SAMMY TAYLOR
☐ 214. MARCELINO SOLIA
☐ 226. ART CECCARELLI
☐ 234. CHUCK TANNER
☐ 249. BOBBY ADAMS
☐ 274. JERRY KINDALL
☐ 301. EARL AVERILL
☐ 304. TEAM CARD
☐ 319. DAVE HILLMAN
☐ 334. GLEN HOBBIE
☐ 350. ERNIE BANKS
☐ 362. DOLAN NICHOLS
☐ 367. CAL NEEMAN
☐ 388. BOB WILL
☐ 407. MOE DRABOWSKY
☐ 414. DALE LONG
☐ 429. BOBBY THOMSON
☐ 447. BOB ANDERSON
☐ 474. MOE THACKER
☐ 488. WALT MORYN
☐ 502. AL DARK
☐ 512. GEORGE ALTMAN
☐ 520. DON ELSTON
☐ 538. CHICK KING
☐ 548. ELMER SINGLETON

CHICAGO WHITE SOX

☐ 5. DICK DONOVAN
☐ 22. AL SMITH
☐ 30. NELLIE FOX
☐ 73. RON JACKSON
☐ 86. BOB KEEGAN
☐ 94. TEAM CARD
☐ 103. BILLY GOODMAN
☐ 114. EARL BATTEY
☐ 119. JOHN CALLISON
☐ 138. JOHN ROMANO
☐ 159. BOB SHAW
☐ 179. DON RUDOLPH
☐ 187. BUBBA PHILLIPS
☐ 213. JIM RIVERA
☐ 252. RAY BOONE
☐ 260. EARLY WYNN
☐ 277. TURK LOWN
☐ 293. RAY MOORE
☐ 310. LUIS APARICIO
☐ 328. LOU SKIZAS
☐ 341. TOM QUALTERS
☐ 351. EARL TORGESON
☐ 368. DON MUELLER
☐ 385. SHERM LOLLAR
☐ 410. BILLY PIERCE
☐ 426. JERRY STALEY
☐ 438. SAM ESPOSITO
☐ 453. LES MOSS
☐ 477. BARRY LATMAN
☐ 493. JIM LANDIS
☐ 509. NORM CASH
☐ 537. RODOLFO ARIAS

CINCINNATI REDS

☐ 14. PETE WHISENANT
☐ 25. DON HOAK
☐ 58. EDDIE MIKSIS
☐ 67. BROOKS LAWRENCE
☐ 81. HAL JEFFCOAT
☐ 97. JERRY LYNCH
☐ 111. TEAM CARD
☐ 120. CHUCK COLES
☐ 136. JIM O'TOOLE
☐ 158. WALT DROPO
☐ 171. WILLARD SCHMIDT
☐ 184. HARVEY HADDIX
☐ 201. TOM ACKER
☐ 210. ED BAILEY
☐ 224. CLAUDE OSTEEN
☐ 232. EDDIE KASKO
☐ 255. DEL ENNIS

☐ 271. ORLANDO PENA
☐ 288. DUTCH DOTTERER
☐ 312. DON NEWCOMBE
☐ 335. JOHNNY TEMPLE
☐ 356. BOB MABE
☐ 365. GUS BELL
☐ 389. JOE NUXHALL
☐ 405. ROY MCMILLAN
☐ 431. WHAMMY DOUGLAS
☐ 435. FRANK ROBINSON
☐ 448. VADA PINSON
☐ 489. JOHN POWERS
☐ 490. FRANK THOMAS
☐ 494. DON PAVLETICH
☐ 506. BOB PURKEY
☐ 518. MIKE CUELLER
☐ 541. BOB THURMAN

CLEVELAND INDIANS

☐ 11. BILLY HUNTER
☐ 38. MORRIE MARTIN
☐ 57. AL CICOTTE
☐ 61. DICK BROWN
☐ 80. MINNIE MINOSO
☐ 88. HERB SCORE
☐ 106. HAL WOODESHICK
☐ 115. MICKEY VERNON
☐ 123. DON DILLARD
☐ 142. DICK STIGMAN
☐ 168. CARROLL HARDY
☐ 186. JIM GRANT
☐ 196. BILLY MORAN
☐ 207. GEORGE STRICKLAND
☐ 229. VIC POWER
☐ 247. DON FERRARESE
☐ 266. WOODY HELD
☐ 283. RUSS HEMAN
☐ 295. BILLY MARTIN
☐ 327. GARY BELL
☐ 344. RUSS NIXON
☐ 355. JIM PIERSALL
☐ 371. DICK BRODOWSKI
☐ 376. HAL NARAGON
☐ 394. RANDY JACKSON
☐ 420. HECTOR LOPEZ
☐ 445. CAL MCLISH
☐ 476. TEAM CARD
☐ 501. BOBBY TIEFENAUER
☐ 516. MIKE GARCIA
☐ 531. RAY WEBSTER
☐ 542. JIM PERRY

DETROIT TIGERS

☐ 2. EDDIE YOST
☐ 24. RED WILSON
☐ 36. HANK AGUIRRE
☐ 52. COOT VEAL
☐ 70. HARVEY KUENN
☐ 96. LOU BERBERET
☐ 132. DON LEE
☐ 149. JIM BUNNING
☐ 164. JOHNNY GROTH
☐ 189. NEIL CHRISLEY
☐ 203. OSSIE VIRGIL
☐ 233. PAUL FOYTACK
☐ 256. JERRY DAVIE
☐ 268. TITO FRANCONA
☐ 280. FRANK BOLLING
☐ 302. DON MOSSIE
☐ 318. ROCKY BRIDGES
☐ 329. TEAM CARD
☐ 331. STEVE BOROS
☐ 343. BILLY HOEFT
☐ 354. PETE BURNSIDE
☐ 360. AL KALINE
☐ 378. GAIL HARRIS
☐ 393. FRANK LARY
☐ 409. GUS ZERNIAL
☐ 421. HERM WEHMEIER
☐ 442. RAY NARLESKI
☐ 455. LARRY DOBY
☐ 481. CHARLEY MAXWELL
☐ 504. OSSIE ALVAREZ
☐ 511. GEORGE SUSCE
☐ 524. LARRY OSBORNE
☐ 545. TOM MORGAN

KANSAS CITY ATHLETICS

☐ 18. JACK URBAN
☐ 41. BOB MARTYN
☐ 51. RIP COLEMAN
☐ 64. JOE DEMAESTRI
☐ 79. HARRY CHITI
☐ 100. BOB CERV
☐ 127. KENT HADLEY
☐ 140. CHARLIE SECREST
☐ 154. RAY HERBERT

☐ 172. TEAM CARD
☐ 176. PRESTON WARD
☐ 182. MILT GRAFF
☐ 202. ROGER MARIS
☐ 227. HAL W. SMITH
☐ 245. NED GARVER
☐ 254. ZEKE BELLA
☐ 263. BUDDY DALEY
☐ 281. WALT CRADDOCK
☐ 292. DICK WILLIAMS
☐ 313. FRANK HOUSE
☐ 333. HARRY SIMPSON
☐ 358. RALPH TERRY
☐ 369. DICK TOMANEK
☐ 381. MIKE BAXES
☐ 392. WHITEY HERZOG
☐ 402. HECTOR LOPEZ
☐ 423. BOB GRIM
☐ 449. TOM GORMAN
☐ 459. BILL TUTTLE
☐ 482. RUSS MEYER
☐ 496. WAYNE TERWILLIGER
☐ 513. TOM CARROLL
☐ 532. MARK FREEMAN

duke snider

OUTFIELD

LOS ANGELES DODGERS

☐ 16. JOE PIGNATANO
☐ 20. DUKE SNIDER
☐ 43. STEVE BILKO
☐ 53. STAN WILLIAMS
☐ 71. DON BESSENT
☐ 107. NORM LARKER
☐ 125. RON FAIRLY
☐ 133. BOB LILLIS
☐ 152. JOHNNY KLIPPSTEIN
☐ 163. SANDY KOUFAX
☐ 195. RIP REPULSKI
☐ 206. CARL FURILLO
☐ 217. CARL ERSKINE
☐ 244. DICK GRAY
☐ 258. FRED KIPP
☐ 270. GIL HODGES
☐ 287. DON ZIMMER
☐ 306. JIM GILLIAM
☐ 321. BOB GIALLOMBARDO
☐ 324. DON DEMETER
☐ 364. DANNY MCDEVITT
☐ 387. DON DRYSDALE
☐ 403. CLEM LABINE
☐ 406. SOLLY DRAKE
☐ 427. CHARLIE NEAL
☐ 441. JOHN ROSEBORO
☐ 457. TEAM CARD
☐ 495. JOHNNY PODRES
☐ 508. ART FOWLER
☐ 522. GENE SNYDER
☐ 530. WALLY MOON
☐ 547. JIM BAXES

MILWAUKEE BRAVES

☐ 3. DON MCMAHON
☐ 27. ANDY PAFKO
☐ 40. WARREN SPAHN
☐ 54. MEL ROACH
☐ 65. FRANK TORRE
☐ 95. CARL WILLEY
☐ 104. DEL RICE
☐ 126. EDDIE HAAS
☐ 128. BOB HARTMAN
☐ 157. FELIX MANTILLA
☐ 165. BILL BRUTON
☐ 188. JUAN PIZARRO
☐ 204. CASEY WISE
☐ 225. JOHNNY LOGAN
☐ 239. BOB TROWBRIDGE

☐ 259. JIM PISONI
☐ 273. JOE JAY
☐ 290. WES COVINGTON
☐ 315. JOE ADCOCK
☐ 322. HARRY HANEBRINK
☐ 347. BOB BUHL
☐ 366. HUMBERTO ROBINSON
☐ 380. HANK AARON
☐ 396. BOB RUSH
☐ 419. TEAM CARD
☐ 425. DEL CRANDALL
☐ 440. LOU BURDETTE
☐ 450. ED MATHEWS
☐ 480. RED SCHOENDIENST
☐ 499. JOHNNY O'BRIEN

NEW YORK YANKEES

☐ 10. MICKEY MANTLE
☐ 23. MURRY DICKSON
☐ 45. ANDY CAREY
☐ 60. BOB TURLEY
☐ 76. BOBBY RICHARDSON
☐ 90. BILL SKOWRON
☐ 108. ZACK MONROE
☐ 117. JOHN BLANCHARD
☐ 131. DERON JOHNSON
☐ 155. ENOS SLAUGHTER
☐ 167. DUKE MAAS
☐ 180. YOGI BERRA
☐ 205. DON LARSEN
☐ 222. BOBBY SHANTZ
☐ 240. HANK BAUER
☐ 251. CLETIS BOYER
☐ 272. JERRY LUMPE
☐ 289. JOHNNY KUCKS
☐ 308. NORM SIEBERN
☐ 326. MARV THRONEBERRY
☐ 345. GIL MCDOUGALD
☐ 374. ART DITMAR
☐ 395. ELSTON HOWARD
☐ 417. VIRGIL TRUCKS
☐ 430. WHITEY FORD
☐ 471. TOM STURDIVANT
☐ 485. RYNE DUREN
☐ 505. TONY KUBEK
☐ 510. TEAM CARD
☐ 525. JIM COATES
☐ 533. DARRELL JOHNSON

PHILADELPHIA PHILLIES

☐ 8. TEAM CARD
☐ 31. KEN LEHMAN
☐ 39. ED BOUCHEE
☐ 56. CARL SAWATSKI
☐ 63. JIM HEARN
☐ 85. HARRY ANDERSON
☐ 92. DAVE PHILLEY
☐ 99. TED KAZANSKI
☐ 121. BOB CONLEY
☐ 129. FRANK HERRERA
☐ 175. DICK FARRELL
☐ 178. RUBEN AMARO
☐ 197. RAY SEMPROCH
☐ 208. WILLIE JONES
☐ 221. BOB BOWMAN
☐ 235. VALMY THOMAS
☐ 253. SETH MOREHEAD
☐ 269. JACK MEYER
☐ 300. RICHIE ASHBURN
☐ 314. DON CARDWELL
☐ 338. SPARKY ANDERSON
☐ 352. ROBIN ROBERTS
☐ 372. JIM HEGAN
☐ 382. CURT SIMMONS
☐ 398. WALLY POST
☐ 412. STAN LOPATA
☐ 436. GRANNY HAMNER
☐ 452. CHICO FERNANDEZ
☐ 472. GENE FREESE
☐ 492. GENE CONLEY
☐ 503. JIM OWENS
☐ 517. JOE KOPPE
☐ 535. RUBEN GOMEZ
☐ 546. AL SCHROLL

PITTSBURGH PIRATES

☐ 12. VERN LAW
☐ 35. TED KLUSZEWSKI
☐ 49. BILL HALL
☐ 68. DICK SCHOFIELD
☐ 83. BOB G. SMITH
☐ 110. GEORGE WITT
☐ 122. BENNIE DANIELS
☐ 134. JIM MCDANIEL
☐ 160. DICK GROAT
☐ 174. JIM PENDLETON

☐ 181. BOB PORTERFIELD
☐ 190. BILL VIRDON
☐ 218. ROMAN MEJIAS
☐ 228. DON GROSS
☐ 238. GENE BAKER
☐ 265. RON KLINE
☐ 282. R.C. STEVENS
☐ 294. HANK FOILES
☐ 305. CURT RAYDON
☐ 320. BOB SKINNER
☐ 339. ROY FACE
☐ 357. DICK STUART
☐ 401. RON BLACKBURN
☐ 415. BILL MAZEROSKI
☐ 432. SMOKY BURGESS
☐ 446. ROCKY NELSON
☐ 460. BOB FRIEND
☐ 478. BOB CLEMENTE
☐ 523. HARRY BRIGHT
☐ 528. TEAM CARD
☐ 536. DAN KRAVITZ

ST. LOUIS CARDINALS

☐ 6. ALEX GRAMMAS
☐ 26. CHUCK STOBBS
☐ 37. GENE GREEN
☐ 59. IRV NOREN
☐ 75. SAM JONES
☐ 101. ALEX KELLNER
☐ 135. GENE OLIVER
☐ 137. DICK RICKETTS
☐ 150. STAN MUSIAL
☐ 162. BOBBY GENE SMITH
☐ 194. JIM BROSNAN
☐ 211. BOB BLAYLOCK
☐ 223. TEAM CARD
☐ 231. ELLIS BURTON
☐ 243. MARV GRISSOM
☐ 278. CHUCK ESSEGIAN
☐ 285. JOE CUNNINGHAM
☐ 296. ERNIE BROGLIO
☐ 309. SAL MAGLIE
☐ 325. KEN BOYER
☐ 337. GEORGE CROWE
☐ 353. CURT FLOOD
☐ 379. BOB J. MILLER
☐ 399. LARRY JACKSON
☐ 418. GINO CIMOLI
☐ 433. BILLY HARRELL
☐ 454. PHIL CLARK
☐ 479. LINDY MCDANIEL
☐ 491. DON BLASINGAME
☐ 497. HAL R. SMITH
☐ 514. BOB GIBSON
☐ 527. SOLLY HEMUS(M)
☐ 539. GARY BLAYLOCK
☐ 544. LEE TATE
☐ 549. HOWIE NUNN

willie mays

SAN FRANCISCO GIANTS
OUTFIELD

SAN FRANCISCO GIANTS

☐ 9. PAUL GIEL
☐ 19. ED BRESSOUD
☐ 28. RED WORTHINGTON
☐ 50. WILLIE MAYS
☐ 69. TEAM CARD
☐ 87. DANNY O'CONNELL
☐ 102. FELIPE ALOU
☐ 109. BOB SCHMIDT
☐ 141. JOE SHIPLEY
☐ 145. DOM ZANNI
☐ 148. MIKE MCCORMICK
☐ 183. STU MILLER
☐ 198. JIM DAVENPORT
☐ 216. ANDRE RODGERS
☐ 241. BILLY MUFFETT

☐ 257. LEON WAGNER
☐ 275. JACK SANFORD
☐ 297. JACKIE BRANDT
☐ 307. CURT BARCLAY
☐ 332. RAY MONZANT
☐ 342. RAY JABLONSKI
☐ 359. BILL WHITE
☐ 377. JOHNNY ANTONELLI
☐ 390. ORLANDO CEPEDA
☐ 404. HANK SAUER
☐ 422. HOBIE LANDRITH
☐ 443. DARYL SPENCER
☐ 458. GORDON JONES
☐ 484. WILLIE KIRKLAND
☐ 526. BOB SPEAKE

WASHINGTON SENATORS

☐ 4. ALBIE PEARSON
☐ 33. ED FITZ GERALD
☐ 44. VITO VALENTINETTI
☐ 78. PEDRO RAMOS
☐ 84. RENO BERTOIA
☐ 93. JULIO BECQUER
☐ 116. BOB ALLISON
☐ 124. DAN DOBBEK
☐ 151. BOB MALKMUS
☐ 169. TED ABERNATHY
☐ 191. RUSS KEMMERER
☐ 215. JIM LEMON
☐ 230. BILL FISCHER
☐ 242. RON SAMFORD
☐ 246. J.W. PORTER
☐ 267. JOHN ROMONOSKY
☐ 284. STEVE KORCHECK
☐ 298. TEX CLEVENGER
☐ 311. NORM ZAUCHIN
☐ 316. RALPH LUMENTI
☐ 340. ROY SIEVERS
☐ 373. HERB PLEWS
☐ 386. JIM DELSING
☐ 397. TEAM CARD
☐ 413. CAMILO PASCUAL
☐ 424. KEN ASPROMONTE
☐ 434. HAL GRIGGS
☐ 451. JIMMY CONSTABLE
☐ 483. CLINT COURTNEY
☐ 498. DICK HYDE
☐ 515. HARMON KILLEBREW
☐ 534. FAYE THRONEBERRY

1960 TOPPS (572)
2 1/2" X 3 1/2"

ELIO CHACON
CINCINNATI REDS   INFIELD

BALTIMORE ORIOLES

☐ 12. MILT PAPPAS
☐ 28. BROOKS ROBINSON
☐ 46. JACK FISHER
☐ 53. JACKIE BRANDT
☐ 60. GUS TRIANDOS
☐ 79. WALT DROPO
☐ 89. HAL BROWN
☐ 98. GORDON JONES
☐ 106. BILLY GARDNER
☐ 126. CHUCK ESTRADA
☐ 127. RON HANSEN
☐ 179. RIP COLEMAN
☐ 190. GENE WOODLING
☐ 207. BOB BOYD
☐ 224. PAUL RICHARDS(M)
☐ 241. ALBIE PEARSON
☐ 254. ARNIE PORTOCARRERO
☐ 269. GENE GREEN
☐ 288. BOB MABE
☐ 304. JOE GINSBERG
☐ 322. WILLIE TASBY
☐ 348. BARRY SHETRONE
☐ 369. BILLY HOEFT
☐ 395. HOYT WILHELM
☐ 406. BILLY KLAUS
☐ 422. JOHNNY POWERS

☐ 448. JIM GENTILE
☐ 455. COACHES CARD
☐ 481. WES STOCK
☐ 494. TEAM CARD
☐ 498. AL PILARCIK
☐ 514. STEVE BARBER
☐ 525. MARV BREEDING
☐ 540. JERRY WALKER

BOSTON RED SOX

☐ 15. PETE RUNNELS
☐ 38. JERRY CASALE
☐ 54. MIKE FORNIELES
☐ 68. DAVE HILLMAN
☐ 71. MARTY KEOUGH
☐ 94. LEO KIELY
☐ 111. VIC WERTZ
☐ 117. TOM BORLAND
☐ 148. CARL YASTRZEMSKI
☐ 153. BOBBY THOMSON
☐ 184. GARY GEIGER
☐ 203. SAMMY WHITE
☐ 220. BILLY JURGES(M)
☐ 232. JIM BUSBY
☐ 249. EARL WILSON
☐ 267. JIM MARSHALL
☐ 280. FRANK SULLIVAN
☐ 296. NELSON CHITTUM
☐ 310. FRANK MALZONE
☐ 317. PUMPSIE GREEN
☐ 336. IKE DELOCK
☐ 363. GENE STEPHENS
☐ 382. TED BOWSFIELD
☐ 403. ED SADOWSKI
☐ 426. RON JACKSON
☐ 439. TOM BREWER
☐ 452. RAY WEBSTER
☐ 456. COACHES CARD
☐ 474. HAYWOOD SULLIVAN
☐ 487. TOM STURDIVANT
☐ 520. DON BUDDIN
☐ 533. LU CLINTON
☐ 537. TEAM CARD
☐ 544. BILL MONBOUQUETTE

CHICAGO CUBS

☐ 10. ERNIE BANKS
☐ 27. DICK DROTT
☐ 39. EARL AVERILL
☐ 74. WALT MORYN
☐ 86. DICK GERNERT
☐ 93. ART SCHULT
☐ 95. FRANK THOMAS
☐ 125. DICK ELLSWORTH
☐ 147. BOB WILL
☐ 156. ART CECCARELLI
☐ 162. SAMMY TAYLOR
☐ 182. GLEN HOBBIE
☐ 217. CHARLEY GRIMM(M)
☐ 233. DON ELSTON
☐ 248. DEL RICE
☐ 259. GEORGE ALTMAN
☐ 277. HARRY BRIGHT
☐ 294. TONY TAYLOR
☐ 305. RICHIE ASHBURN
☐ 337. CAL NEEMAN
☐ 349. MOE DRABOWSKY
☐ 357. AL SCHROLL
☐ 375. DALE LONG
☐ 412. BOB ANDERSON
☐ 433. IRV NOREN
☐ 444. JERRY KINDALL
☐ 457. COACHES CARD
☐ 476. LOU JOHNSON
☐ 489. STEVE RIDZIK
☐ 504. SETH MOREHEAD
☐ 513. TEAM CARD
☐ 528. BEN JOHNSON

CHICAGO WHITE SOX

☐ 1. EARLY WYNN
☐ 31. SAMMY ESPOSITO
☐ 41. BARRY LATMAN
☐ 69. BILLY GOODMAN
☐ 100. NELLIE FOX
☐ 116. JIM RIVERA
☐ 121. CAMILO CARREON
☐ 131. ED HOBAUGH
☐ 150. BILLY PIERCE
☐ 169. JAKE STRIKER
☐ 180. HARRY SIMPSON
☐ 199. DICK DONOVAN
☐ 208. TEAM CARD
☐ 222. AL LOPEZ(M)
☐ 240. LUIS APARICIO
☐ 256. DICK BROWN
☐ 276. KEN MCBRIDE

1960 Topps

- 299. EARL TORGESON
- 306. FRANK BAUMANN
- 313. TURK LOWN
- 328. EARL BATTEY
- 346. J.C. MARTIN
- 365. MINNIE MINOSO
- 380. BOB SHAW
- 407. GARY PETERS
- 428. AL SMITH
- 435. GENE FREESE
- 447. RAY MOORE
- 458. COACHES CARD
- 477. DON FERRARESE
- 495. SHERM LOLLAR
- 505. TED KLUSZEWSKI
- 510. JERRY STALEY
- 532. MIKE GARCIA
- 538. FRANK BARNES
- 550. JIM LANDIS

CINCINNATI REDS

- 4. BOB PURKEY
- 21. DUTCH DOTTERER
- 45. ROY MCMILLAN
- 61. EDDIE KASKO
- 110. CAL MCLISH
- 119. CHICO CARDENAS
- 146. TED WIEAND
- 164. TEAM CARD
- 173. BILLY MARTIN
- 176. VADA PINSON
- 187. JAY HOOK
- 198. JERRY LYNCH
- 206. CLAUDE OSTEEN
- 219. FRED HUTCHINSON(M)
- 235. GUS BELL
- 257. GORDY COLEMAN
- 282. JOE NUXHALL
- 289. WILLIE JONES
- 311. RAUL SANCHEZ
- 325. JIM O'TOOLE
- 345. DON NEWCOMBE
- 359. BUDDY GILBERT
- 372. FRANK HOUSE
- 398. MIKE CUELLAR
- 411. ED BAILEY
- 424. PETE WHISENANT
- 434. BROOKS LAWRENCE
- 449. JIM BROSNAN
- 459. COACHES CARD
- 490. FRANK ROBINSON
- 506. LEE WALLS
- 518. TONY GONZALEZ
- 524. BILL R. HENRY
- 535. WHITEY LOCKMAN
- 543. ELIO CHACON

CLEVELAND INDIANS

- 14. JIM GRANT
- 30. TITO FRANCONA
- 36. RUSS NIXON
- 44. BOBBY LOCKE
- 63. GEORGE STRICKLAND
- 75. VIC POWER
- 112. JACK HARSHMAN
- 122. DON DILLARD
- 139. CARL MATHIAS
- 159. JIM PIERSALL
- 174. TEAM CARD
- 178. WOODY HELD
- 216. JOE GORDON
- 228. ERNIE JOHNSON
- 243. BUBBA PHILLIPS
- 279. CHUCK TANNER
- 309. BOB HALE
- 318. JIM BAXES
- 323. JOHNNY ROMANO
- 324. JIM PERRY
- 341. CARROLL HARDY
- 360. HERBY SCORE
- 376. JOHNNY BRIGGS
- 400. ROCKY COLAVITO
- 423. ED FITZ GERALD
- 441. GARY BELL
- 460. COACHES CARD
- 473. AL CICOTTE
- 500. JOHNNY TEMPLE
- 507. DICK STIGMAN
- 521. MIKE LEE
- 536. WYNN HAWKINS
- 552. WALT BOND

DETROIT TIGERS

- 6. LOU BERBERET
- 22. ROCKY BRIDGES
- 33. TOM MORGAN
- 50. AL KALINE
- 72. TEAM CARD
- 85. FRANK LARY
- 118. BOB BRUCE
- 141. JIM PROCTOR
- 152. GAIL HARRIS
- 161. RAY NARLESKI
- 171. JOHNNY GROTH
- 186. DAVE SISLER
- 201. LARRY OSBORNE
- 214. JIMMIE DYKES(M)
- 245. EDDIE YOST
- 261. PETE BURNSIDE

- 273. NEIL CHRISLEY
- 286. RAY SEMPROCH
- 301. JERRY DAVIE
- 314. CHICO FERNADEZ
- 330. HARVEY KUENN
- 342. CASEY WISE
- 364. PAUL FOYTACK
- 379. RED WILSON
- 396. STEVE BILKO
- 418. DON MOSSI
- 443. CHARLIE MAXWELL
- 461. COACHES CARD
- 482. FRANK BOLLING
- 488. NORM CASH
- 502. JIM BUNNING
- 531. SANDY AMOROS
- 546. HANK AGUIRRE

KANSAS CITY ATHLETICS

- 8. BUD DALEY
- 11. NORM SIEBERN
- 26. WAYNE TERWILLIGER
- 66. BOB TROWBRIDGE
- 77. HANK FOILES
- 78. BOB GRIM
- 81. RUSS SNYDER
- 92. WHITEY HERZOG
- 108. PETE DALEY
- 135. KEN JOHNSON
- 137. LOU KLIMCHOCK
- 177. JOHNNY KUCKS
- 188. DICK WILLIAMS
- 215. BOB ELLIOTT(M)
- 229. JOE MORGAN
- 252. RAY HERBERT
- 262. HANK BAUER
- 274. TOM ACKER
- 290. JERRY LUMPE
- 308. DICK HALL
- 339. HARRY CHITI
- 353. DON LARSEN
- 367. BILL TUTTLE
- 413. TEAM CARD
- 415. BOB CERV
- 427. AL GRUNWALD
- 436. MARV THRONEBERRY
- 462. COACHES CARD
- 471. NED GARVER
- 497. JOHN TSITOURIS
- 516. MARTY KUTYNA
- 542. KEN HAMLIN

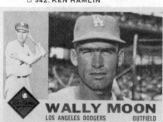

WALLY MOON
LOS ANGELES DODGERS OUTFIELD

LOS ANGELES DODGERS

- 5. WALLY MOON
- 18. TEAM CARD
- 29. CLEM LABINE
- 47. DON ZIMMER
- 62. ROGER CRAIG
- 88. JOHN ROSEBORO
- 105. LARRY SHERRY
- 128. BILL HARRIS
- 132. FRANK HOWARD
- 155. CHARLIE NEAL
- 166. CHUCK ESSEGIAN
- 191. JOHNNY KLIPPSTEIN
- 202. FRED KIPP
- 212. WALT ALSTON(M)
- 234. DON DEMETER
- 255. JIM GILLIAM
- 265. RIP REPULSKI
- 278. STAN WILLIAMS
- 295. GIL HODGES
- 321. RON FAIRLY
- 333. DANNY MCDEVITT
- 343. SANDY KOUFAX
- 354. BOB LILLIS
- 394. NORM LARKER
- 408. CARL FURILLO
- 425. JOHNNY PODRES
- 442. JOE PIGNATANO
- 463. COACHES CARD
- 475. DON DRYSDALE
- 493. DUKE SNIDER
- 509. TOMMY DAVIS
- 519. ED ROEBUCK
- 529. NORM SHERRY
- 547. BOB ASPROMONTE
- 551. ED RAKOW

MILWAUKEE BRAVES

- 3. JOE ADCOCK
- 19. FELIX MANTILLA
- 37. BILL BRUTON

- 59. JUAN PIZARRO
- 70. LOU BURDETTE
- 90. BOBBY AVILA
- 107. CARL WILLEY
- 129. BOB HARTMAN
- 143. AL SPANGLER
- 158. WES COVINGTON
- 170. DEL CRANDALL
- 189. DON MCMAHON
- 205. JOHNNY LOGAN
- 213. CHUCK DRESSEN(M)
- 246. LEE MAYE
- 266. JOE JAY
- 281. RAY BOONE
- 300. HANK AARON
- 312. CHARLIE LAU
- 335. RED SCHOENDIENST
- 351. DON NOTTEBART
- 374. BOB BUHL
- 381. TEAM CARD
- 404. BOB RUSH
- 417. CHUCK COTTIER
- 420. ED MATHEWS
- 445. WARREN SPAHN
- 464. COACHES CARD
- 478. FRANK TORRE
- 491. MEL ROACH
- 515. STAN LOPATA
- 534. KEN MACKENZIE

NEW YORK YANKEES

- 35. WHITEY FORD
- 51. JIM COATES
- 65. ELSTON HOWARD
- 83. TONY KUBEK
- 96. RALPH TERRY
- 102. KENT HADLEY
- 109. CLETIS BOYER
- 134. DERON JOHNSON
- 142. BILL SHORT
- 163. HECTOR LOPEZ
- 183. ELI GRBA
- 196. ANDY CAREY
- 204. RYNE DUREN
- 227. CASEY STENGEL(M)
- 237. ELMER VALO
- 247. GIL MCDOUGALD
- 270. BOB TURLEY
- 283. JOHN BLANCHARD
- 315. BOBBY SHANTZ
- 329. ZACK MONROE
- 332. TEAM CARD
- 350. MICKEY MANTLE
- 358. JOE DEMAESTRI
- 370. BILL SKOWRON
- 377. ROGER MARIS
- 405. BOBBY RICHARDSON
- 421. DUKE MAAS
- 430. ART DITMAR
- 465. COACHES CARD
- 480. YOGI BERRA
- 499. JOHNNY JAMES
- 522. KEN L. HUNT

PHILADELPHIA PHILLIES

- 13. WALLY POST
- 17. JOHNNY CALLISON
- 34. SPARKY ANDERSON
- 52. DAVE PHILLEY
- 64. JACK MEYER
- 82. RUBEN GOMEZ
- 97. TED LEPCIO
- 103. DICK FARRELL
- 130. FRANK HERRERA
- 138. ART MAHAFFEY
- 167. VALMY THOMAS
- 185. JIM OWENS
- 194. BOBBY GENE SMITH
- 211. TAYLOR PHILLIPS
- 226. EDDIE SAWYER(M)
- 251. BOBBY MALKMUS
- 264. ROBIN ROBERTS
- 285. HARRY ANDERSON
- 293. GENE CONLEY
- 302. TEAM CARD
- 319. JOE KOPPE
- 331. HENRY MASON
- 347. ED BOUCHEE
- 366. DALLAS GREEN
- 384. DON CARDWELL
- 416. HUMBERTO ROBINSON
- 438. JIM COKER
- 451. CURT SIMMONS
- 466. COACHES CARD
- 472. AL DARK
- 486. BOBBY DEL GRECO
- 511. KEN WALTERS
- 523. CLAY DALRYMPLE
- 541. TONY CURRY
- 549. JOHN BUZHARDT

PITTSBURGH PIRATES

- 2. ROMAN MEJIAS
- 20. ROY FACE
- 48. HAL W. SMITH
- 49. CURT RAYDON
- 55. BILL MAZEROSKI
- 58. GINO CIMOLI

88

☐ 91. BENNIE DANIELS
☐ 104. DICK SCHOFIELD
☐ 113. BOB SKINNER
☐ 133. JULIAN JAVIER
☐ 145. JIM UMBRICHT
☐ 157. ROCKY NELSON
☐ 209. RON BLACKBURN
☐ 223. DANNY MURTAUGH(M)
☐ 238. DANNY KRAVITZ
☐ 258. DICK GROAT
☐ 272. FRED GREEN
☐ 284. DON GROSS
☐ 298. GEORGE WITT
☐ 326. BOB CLEMENTE
☐ 340. HARVEY HADDIX
☐ 361. BOB OLDIS
☐ 373. DON HOAK
☐ 393. SMOKY BURGESS
☐ 402. DICK STUART
☐ 414. DON WILLIAMS
☐ 437. BOB FRIEND
☐ 453. VERN LAW
☐ 467. COACHES CARD
☐ 484. TEAM CARD
☐ 496. BILL VIRDON
☐ 512. JOE GIBBON
☐ 526. PAUL GIEL
☐ 539. GENE BAKER

ST. LOUIS CARDINALS

☐ 16. ERNIE BROGLIO
☐ 24. DICK GRAY
☐ 40. JOE CUNNINGHAM
☐ 73. BOB GIBSON
☐ 84. HAL R. SMITH
☐ 101. BOB L. MILLER
☐ 120. DUKE CARMEL
☐ 124. JIM DONOHUE
☐ 149. BOB NIEMAN
☐ 168. ALEX GRAMMAS
☐ 195. LINDY MCDANIEL
☐ 197. RON KLINE
☐ 218. SOLLY HEMUS(M)
☐ 236. DICK RICKETTS
☐ 242. TEAM CARD
☐ 250. STAN MUSIAL
☐ 263. DARRELL JOHNSON
☐ 275. CURT FLOOD
☐ 291. BOB KEEGAN
☐ 307. GENE OLIVER
☐ 327. RAY SADECKI
☐ 355. BILL WHITE
☐ 368. DARYL SPENCER
☐ 383. LEON WAGNER
☐ 401. BOB DULIBA
☐ 419. GEORGE CROWE
☐ 446. ELLIS BURTON
☐ 468. COACHES CARD
☐ 485. KEN BOYER
☐ 492. LARRY JACKSON
☐ 517. CHARLEY JAMES
☐ 545. CARL SAWATSKI

JIM DAVENPORT
SAN FRANCISCO GIANTS   THIRD BASE

SAN FRANCISCO GIANTS

☐ 23. EDDIE FISHER
☐ 42. HOBIE LANDRITH
☐ 67. JOSE PAGAN
☐ 80. JOHNNY ANTONELLI
☐ 140. JULIO NAVARRO
☐ 144. AL STIEGLITZ
☐ 151. TEAM CARD
☐ 154. JIM DAVENPORT
☐ 165. JACK SANFORD
☐ 172. WILLIE KIRKLAND
☐ 181. BILLY LOES
☐ 192. DANNY O'CONNELL
☐ 200. WILLIE MAYS
☐ 225. BILL RIGNEY(M)
☐ 239. JOE SHIPLEY
☐ 253. EDDIE BRESSOUD
☐ 268. AL WORTHINGTON

☐ 287. FELIPE ALOU
☐ 303. BILLY O'DELL
☐ 316. WILLIE MCCOVEY
☐ 338. RAY MONZANT
☐ 356. JOE AMALFITANO
☐ 371. BUD BYERLY
☐ 378. STU MILLER
☐ 397. DON BLASINGAME
☐ 410. SAM JONES
☐ 431. ANDRE RODGERS
☐ 450. ORLANDO CEPEDA
☐ 469. COACHES CARD
☐ 479. GEORGES MARANDA
☐ 501. BOB SCHMIDT
☐ 530. MIKE MCCORMICK

WASHINGTON SENATORS

☐ 9. FAYE THRONEBERRY
☐ 25. ROY SIEVERS
☐ 43. TEAM CARD
☐ 56. STEVE KORCHECK
☐ 76. BILL FISCHER
☐ 87. JOHN ROMONOSKY
☐ 99. LENNY GREEN
☐ 114. KEN ASPROMONTE
☐ 123. DAN DOBBEK
☐ 136. JIM KAAT
☐ 175. PEDRO RAMOS
☐ 193. DICK HYDE
☐ 210. HARMON KILLEBREW
☐ 221. COOKIE LAVAGETTO(M)
☐ 231. HAL NARAGON
☐ 244. HAL GRIGGS
☐ 271. JULIO BECQUER
☐ 297. RENO BERTOIA
☐ 320. BOB ALLISON
☐ 334. TED ABERNATHY
☐ 344. CLINT COURTNEY
☐ 362. RUSS KEMMERER
☐ 392. TEX CLEVENGER
☐ 409. RON SAMFORD
☐ 432. CHUCK STOBBS
☐ 440. JIM LEMON
☐ 454. HAL WOODESHICK
☐ 470. COACHES CARD
☐ 483. CAMILO PASCUAL
☐ 503. DON LEE
☐ 508. BILLY CONSOLO
☐ 527. JOSE VALDIVIELSO
☐ 548. DON MINCHER

1961 TOPPS (587)
2 1/2" X 3 1/2"

HANK AARON
Outfield

BALTIMORE ORIOLES

☐ 10. BROOKS ROBINSON
☐ 26. WES STOCK
☐ 62. AL PILARCIK
☐ 71. JERRY ADAIR
☐ 85. JERRY WALKER
☐ 102. GENE STEPHENS
☐ 125. STEVE BARBER
☐ 131. PAUL RICHARDS
☐ 140. GUS TRIANDOS
☐ 143. RUSS SNYDER(B)
☐ 159. TEAM CARD
☐ 182. DAVE NICHOLSON
☐ 218. HAL BROWN
☐ 240. RON HANSEN
☐ 256. BILLY HOEFT
☐ 277. HANK FOILES
☐ 295. MILT PAPPAS
☐ 321. MARV BREEDING

☐ 343. EARL ROBINSON
☐ 369. DAVE PHILLEY
☐ 395. CHUCK ESTRADA
☐ 428. RAY BARKER
☐ 442. GORDON JONES
☐ 463. JACK FISHER
☐ 489. WALT DROPO
☐ 515. JACKIE BRANDT
☐ 545. HOYT WILHELM
☐ 559. JIM GENTILE

BOSTON RED SOX

☐ 16. BILLY MUFFETT
☐ 33. GARY GEIGER
☐ 53. RUSS NIXON
☐ 69. EARL WILSON
☐ 81. TRACY STALLARD
☐ 99. DON BUDDIN
☐ 113. MIKE FORNIELES
☐ 128. RIP REPULSKI
☐ 193. GENE CONLEY
☐ 210. PETE RUNNELS
☐ 221. MIKE HIGGINS(M)
☐ 236. DON GILE
☐ 257. CARROLL HARDY
☐ 268. IKE DELOCK
☐ 287. CARL YASTRZEMSKI
☐ 301. CHET NICHOLS
☐ 326. DAVE HILLMAN
☐ 340. VIC WERTZ
☐ 354. BILLY HARRELL
☐ 373. TEAM CARD
☐ 419. TOM BORLAND
☐ 434. TOM BREWER
☐ 445. FRANK MALZONE
☐ 454. PUMPSIE GREEN
☐ 499. CHUCK SCHILLING
☐ 519. JIM PAGLIARONI
☐ 540. JACKIE JENSEN
☐ 548. TED WILLS
☐ 562. BILL MONBOUQUETTE

CHICAGO CUBS

☐ 12. MOE THACKER
☐ 27. JERRY KINDALL
☐ 35. RON SANTO
☐ 58. JOE SCHAFFERNOTH
☐ 88. RICHIE ASHBURN
☐ 107. SETH MOREHEAD
☐ 122. TEAM CARD
☐ 141. BILLY WILLIAMS
☐ 169. DON ELSTON
☐ 196. ED BOUCHEE
☐ 214. DANNY MURPHY
☐ 231. DICK DROTT
☐ 253. SAMMY TAYLOR
☐ 264. GLEN HOBBIE
☐ 283. BOB ANDERSON
☐ 302. AL HEIST
☐ 317. JIM BREWER
☐ 350. ERNIE BANKS
☐ 364. MOE DRABOWSKY
☐ 382. FRANK THOMAS
☐ 427. DICK ELLSWORTH
☐ 441. DICK BERTELL
☐ 493. DON ZIMMER
☐ 512. BOB WILL
☐ 533. JACK CURTIS
☐ 551. GEORGE ALTMAN
☐ 564. DON CARDWELL

CHICAGO WHITE SOX

☐ 7. TEAM CARD
☐ 30. NELLIE FOX
☐ 56. RUSS KEMMERER
☐ 79. JOE GINSBERG
☐ 90. JERRY STALEY
☐ 124. J.C. MARTIN
☐ 132. AL LOPEZ(M)
☐ 152. EARL TORGESON
☐ 157. CAL MCLISH
☐ 170. AL SMITH
☐ 185. HERB SCORE
☐ 205. BILL PIERCE
☐ 227. JUAN PIZARRO
☐ 247. BILLY GOODMAN
☐ 271. JIM LANDIS
☐ 285. SHERM LOLLAR
☐ 303. GARY PETERS
☐ 323. SAMMY ESPOSITO
☐ 352. BOB SHAW
☐ 367. JIM RIVERA
☐ 380. MINNIE MINOSO
☐ 391. WINSTON BROWN
☐ 424. TURK LOWN
☐ 440. LUIS APARICIO
☐ 455. EARLY WYNN

☐ 470. ROY SIEVERS
☐ 509. CAMILO CARREON
☐ 529. BOB ROSELLI
☐ 550. FRANK BAUMANN

CINCINNATI REDS

☐ 9. BOB PURKEY
☐ 66. BILL R. HENRY
☐ 76. HARRY ANDERSON
☐ 97. JERRY LYNCH
☐ 110. VADA PINSON
☐ 135. FRED HUTCHINSON(M)
☐ 162. JAY HOOK
☐ 166. DANNY KRAVITZ
☐ 175. GENE FREESE
☐ 194. GORDY COLEMAN
☐ 215. GUS BELL
☐ 233. JOE JAY
☐ 244. CHICO CARDENAS
☐ 249. TEAM CARD
☐ 276. RAY RIPPELMEYER
☐ 292. JIM BAUMER
☐ 328. JIM O'TOOLE
☐ 346. HOWIE NUNN
☐ 360. FRANK ROBINSON
☐ 378. WALLY POST
☐ 399. CLIFF COOK
☐ 418. ED BAILEY
☐ 436. JIM MALONEY
☐ 456. HAL BEVAN
☐ 497. WILLIE JONES
☐ 513. JIM BROSNAN
☐ 534. EDDIE KASKO
☐ 556. KEN R. HUNT

CLEVELAND INDIANS

☐ 5. JOHN ROMANO
☐ 15. WILLIE KIRKLAND
☐ 18. JIM GRANT
☐ 34. WYNN HAWKINS
☐ 60. WOODIE HELD
☐ 77. DICK STIGMAN
☐ 101. BUBBA PHILLIPS
☐ 115. JOHNNY ANTONELLI
☐ 155. JOHNNY TEMPLE
☐ 172. DON DILLARD
☐ 191. MIKE DE LA HOZ
☐ 222. JIMMIE DYKES(M)
☐ 255. VIC POWER
☐ 274. GARY BELL
☐ 319. VALMY THOMAS
☐ 334. WALT BOND
☐ 345. JIM PIERSALL
☐ 362. FRANK FUNK
☐ 385. JIM PERRY
☐ 421. TY CLINE
☐ 452. BOB ALLEN
☐ 467. TEAM CARD
☐ 503. TITO FRANCONA
☐ 511. JOE MORGAN
☐ 532. BOB HALE
☐ 537. BOBBY LOCKE
☐ 560. BARRY LATMAN

DETROIT TIGERS

☐ 13. CHUCK COTTIER
☐ 14. DON MOSSI
☐ 37. CHARLIE MAXWELL
☐ 51. TEAM CARD
☐ 67. OSSIE VIRGIL
☐ 83. BOB BRUCE
☐ 95. NORM CASH
☐ 112. CHICO FERNANDEZ
☐ 151. JIM DONOHUE
☐ 171. PAUL FOYTACK
☐ 192. DICK BROWN
☐ 208. LARRY OSBORNE
☐ 223. BOB SCHEFFING(M)
☐ 239. DAVE SISLER(B)
☐ 243. FRANK LARY
☐ 251. BILL BRUTON
☐ 269. HARRY CHITI
☐ 284. DICK GERNERT
☐ 324. HANK AGUIRRE
☐ 330. ROCKY COLAVITO
☐ 348. STEVE BOROS
☐ 376. MIKE ROARKE
☐ 429. AL KALINE
☐ 439. PHIL REGAN
☐ 459. TERRY FOX
☐ 490. JIM BUNNING
☐ 514. JAKE WOOD
☐ 544. GEORGE THOMAS
☐ 553. BILL FISCHER

KANSAS CITY ATHLETICS

☐ 8. DICK WILLIAMS
☐ 24. KEN JOHNSON
☐ 39. LEO POSADA
☐ 57. MARV THRONEBERRY
☐ 94. JOHNNY KUCKS
☐ 106. WHITEY HERZOG
☐ 143. RUSS SNYDER(F)
☐ 177. DON LARSEN
☐ 197. DICK HALL
☐ 199. BOB BOYD
☐ 212. HAYWOOD SULLIVAN
☐ 224. JOE GORDON(M)
☐ 248. ED KEEGAN
☐ 267. NORM SIEBERN
☐ 297. TEAM CARD
☐ 322. BILL KUNKEL
☐ 342. CLINT COURTNEY
☐ 365. JERRY LUMPE
☐ 381. DAVE WICKERSHAM
☐ 384. CHUCK ESSEGIAN
☐ 398. HANK BAUER
☐ 416. DICK HOWSER
☐ 422. BUD DALEY
☐ 444. JOE NUXHALL
☐ 462. LOU KLIMCHOCK
☐ 498. RAY HERBERT
☐ 518. ANDY CAREY
☐ 536. BILL TUTTLE(F)
☐ 552. JIM ARCHER

ROCKY BRIDGES Shortstop — Los Angeles Angels

LOS ANGELES ANGELS

☐ 65. TED KLUSZEWSKI
☐ 121. ELI GRBA
☐ 156. KEN L. HUNT
☐ 163. ED SADOWSKI
☐ 176. KEN ASPROMONTE
☐ 184. STEVE BILKO
☐ 195. JERRY CASALE
☐ 209. KEN MCBRIDE
☐ 216. TED BOWSFIELD
☐ 225. BILL RIGNEY(M)
☐ 246. BOB DAVIS
☐ 263. KEN HAMLIN
☐ 272. TOM MORGAN
☐ 282. FAYE THRONEBERRY
☐ 288. ALBIE PEARSON
☐ 291. TEX CLEVENGER
☐ 329. JULIO BECQUER
☐ 331. NED GARVER
☐ 358. EARL AVERILL
☐ 413. EDDIE YOST
☐ 448. DEL RICE
☐ 457. JOHNNY JAMES
☐ 464. LEROY THOMAS
☐ 466. RON MOELLER
☐ 508. ROCKY BRIDGES
☐ 527. GENE LEEK
☐ 547. LEON WAGNER

LOS ANGELES DODGERS

☐ 6. ED ROEBUCK
☐ 23. DON DEMETER
☐ 38. BOB LILLIS
☐ 74. JOE PIGNATANO
☐ 86. TEAM CARD
☐ 109. JOHNNY PODRES
☐ 130. NORM LARKER
☐ 136. WALT ALSTON(M)
☐ 147. ED RAKOW
☐ 168. TOMMY DAVIS
☐ 190. STAN WILLIAMS
☐ 238. JIM GILLIAM
☐ 260. DON DRYSDALE
☐ 280. FRANK HOWARD

☐ 298. JIM GOLDEN
☐ 325. WALLY MOON
☐ 344. SANDY KOUFAX
☐ 363. JOHN ROSEBORO
☐ 396. BOB ASPROMONTE
☐ 412. LARRY SHERRY
☐ 423. CHARLIE NEAL
☐ 443. DUKE SNIDER
☐ 460. GIL HODGES
☐ 492. RON FAIRLY
☐ 506. WILLIE DAVIS
☐ 522. DICK FARRELL
☐ 525. RON PERRANOSKI
☐ 543. ROGER CRAIG

MILWAUKEE BRAVES

☐ 29. DON NOTTEBART
☐ 61. RON PICHE
☐ 73. AL SPANGLER
☐ 84. LEE MAYE
☐ 89. BILLY MARTIN
☐ 105. CARL WILLEY
☐ 120. ED MATHEWS
☐ 137. CHUCK DRESSEN(M)
☐ 145. BOB BUHL
☐ 164. FELIX MANTILLA
☐ 183. ANDRE RODGERS
☐ 200. WARREN SPAHN
☐ 217. MEL ROACH
☐ 245. JOE ADCOCK
☐ 261. CHARLIE LAU
☐ 278. DON MCMAHON
☐ 296. WES COVINGTON
☐ 320. LOU BURDETTE
☐ 335. FRANK BOLLING
☐ 353. HOWIE BEDELL
☐ 372. BOB HENDLEY
☐ 390. DEL CRANDALL
☐ 415. HANK AARON
☐ 446. BOB TAYLOR
☐ 463. TEAM CARD
☐ 465. ROY MCMILLAN
☐ 496. KEN MACKENZIE
☐ 501. JOHN DEMERIT
☐ 524. JOHNNY LOGAN

MINNESOTA TWINS

☐ 4. LENNY GREEN
☐ 21. ZORRO VERSALLES
☐ 36. JACK KRALICK
☐ 63. JIM KAAT
☐ 80. HARMON KILLEBREW
☐ 92. HAL NARAGON
☐ 108. DAN DOBBEK
☐ 123. BILLY GARDNER
☐ 153. DON LEE
☐ 186. ELMER VALO
☐ 201. PETE WHISENANT
☐ 226. COOKIE LAVAGETTO(M)
☐ 235. CAMILO PASCUAL
☐ 254. TED SADOWSKI
☐ 289. RAY MOORE
☐ 315. EARL BATTEY
☐ 336. DON MINCHER
☐ 355. BOB ALLISON
☐ 374. PAUL GIEL
☐ 392. RENO BERTOIA
☐ 431. CHUCK STOBBS
☐ 450. JIM LEMON
☐ 469. RALPH LUMENTI
☐ 504. BILLY CONSOLO
☐ 528. PEDRO RAMOS
☐ 536. BILL TUTTLE(B)
☐ 542. TEAM CARD
☐ 557. JOSE VALDIVIELSO

NEW YORK YANKEES

☐ 2. ROGER MARIS
☐ 19. CLETIS BOYER
☐ 28. HECTOR LOPEZ
☐ 40. BOB TURLEY
☐ 68. DERON JOHNSON
☐ 104. JOHN BLANCHARD
☐ 116. JOE DEMAESTRI
☐ 133. RALPH HOUK(M)
☐ 142. LUIS ARROYO
☐ 160. WHITEY FORD
☐ 180. BOBBY RICHARDSON
☐ 213. BILL STAFFORD
☐ 228. TEAM CARD
☐ 252. BILL SHORT
☐ 265. TONY KUBEK
☐ 300. MICKEY MANTLE
☐ 333. FRITZ BRICKELL
☐ 349. DANNY MCDEVITT
☐ 356. RYNE DUREN

☐ 371. BILL SKOWRON
☐ 387. DUKE MAAS
☐ 389. RALPH TERRY
☐ 425. YOGI BERRA
☐ 495. ELSTON HOWARD
☐ 510. ART DITMAR
☐ 531. JIM COATES
☐ 541. ROLAND SHELDON
☐ 563. BOB CERV

PHILADELPHIA PHILLIES

☐   3. JOHN BUZHARDT
☐ 20. ROBIN ROBERTS
☐ 59. JIM WOODS
☐ 78. LEE WALLS
☐ 93. TONY GONZALEX
☐ 103. RUBEN AMARO
☐ 111. JACK MEYER
☐ 144. JIM COKER
☐ 154. BOBBY DEL GRECO
☐ 179. JOE KOPPE
☐ 202. AL NEIGER
☐ 219. GENE MAUCH(M)
☐ 234. TED LEPCIO
☐ 262. TONY CURRY
☐ 281. FRANK SULLIVAN
☐ 299. CLAY DALRYMPLE
☐ 316. BOBBY GENE SMITH
☐ 341. JIM OWENS
☐ 359. DALLAS GREEN
☐ 377. RUBEN GOMEZ
☐ 394. KEN WALTERS
☐ 411. TONY TAYLOR
☐ 433. ART MAHAFFEY
☐ 468. JOHNNY CALLISON
☐ 491. TEAM CARD
☐ 502. CLARENCE COLEMAN
☐ 530. BOBBY MALKMUS
☐ 558. DON FERRARESE

PITTSBURGH PIRATES

☐   1. DICK GROAT
☐ 22. CLEM LABINE
☐ 54. EARL FRANCIS
☐ 70. BILL VIRDON
☐ 82. JOE CHRISTOPHER
☐ 100. HARVEY HADDIX
☐ 126. DICK STUART
☐ 138. DANNY MURTAUGH(M)
☐ 149. BOB OLDIS
☐ 165. GINO CIMOLI
☐ 181. FRED GREEN
☐ 204. BOB SKINNER
☐ 230. DON HOAK
☐ 242. HAL W. SMITH
☐ 270. BOB FRIEND
☐ 286. GEORGE WITT
☐ 304. ROCKY NELSON
☐ 339. GENE BAKER
☐ 370. ROY FACE
☐ 379. BOBBY SHANTZ
☐ 388. BOB CLEMENTE
☐ 400. VERN LAW
☐ 430. BILL MAZEROSKI
☐ 453. DICK SCHOFIELD
☐ 461. SMOKY BURGESS
☐ 494. TOM CHENEY
☐ 523. JOE GIBBON
☐ 554. TEAM CARD

ST. LOUIS CARDINALS

☐ 11. CURT SIMMONS
☐ 32. RAY SADECKI
☐ 52. GEORGE CROWE
☐ 64. ALEX GRAMMAS
☐ 91. WALT MORYN
☐ 118. CHRIS CANNIZZARO
☐ 127. RON KLINE
☐ 139. SOLLY HEMUS(M)
☐ 148. JULIAN JAVIER
☐ 178. BOB NIEMAN
☐ 198. CARL SAWATSKI
☐ 211. BOB GIBSON
☐ 232. BILL WHITE
☐ 241. AL CICOTTE
☐ 266. LINDY MCDANIEL
☐ 290. STAN MUSIAL
☐ 314. BOB L. MILLER
☐ 338. DON LANDRUM
☐ 347. TEAM CARD
☐ 357. DARYL SPENCER
☐ 375. KEN BOYER
☐ 420. ERNIE BROGLIO
☐ 438. CURT FLOOD
☐ 487. GENE OLIVER
☐ 505. RED SCHOENDIENST

☐ 520. JOE CUNNINGHAM
☐ 535. LARRY JACKSON
☐ 549. HAL R. SMITH
☐ 561. CHARLEY JAMES

SAN FRANCISCO GIANTS

☐ 31. BOB SCHMIDT
☐ 55. JIM DAVENPORT
☐ 72. STU MILLER
☐ 87. JOE AMALFITANO
☐ 96. BILLY O'DELL
☐ 114. HOBIE LANDRITH
☐ 150. WILLIE MAYS
☐ 161. SHERMAN JONES
☐ 167. TEAM CARD
☐ 188. JIM MARSHALL
☐ 203. EDDIE BRESSOUD
☐ 220. AL DARK(M)
☐ 237. BILLY LOES
☐ 258. JACK SANFORD
☐ 279. JOSE PAGAN
☐ 294. DON BLASINGAME
☐ 305. MIKE MCCORMICK
☐ 327. MATTY ALOU
☐ 366. EDDIE FISHER
☐ 417. JUAN MARICHAL
☐ 435. ORLANDO CEPEDA
☐ 449. BOBBY BOLIN
☐ 500. HARVEY KUEEN
☐ 517. WILLIE MCCOVEY
☐ 538. CHUCK HILLER
☐ 555. SAM JONES
☐ 565. FELIPE ALOU

WASHINGTON SENATORS

☐ 117. DALE LONG
☐ 129. ED HOBAUGH
☐ 134. MICKEY VERNON(M)
☐ 146. MARTY KEOUGH
☐ 158. PETE DALEY
☐ 174. RAY SEMPROCH
☐ 187. BILLY KLAUS
☐ 206. GENE GREEN
☐ 229. RUDY HERNANDEX
☐ 239. DAVE SISLER(F)
☐ 259. JOHN SCHAIVE
☐ 275. GENE WOODLING
☐ 293. TOM STURDIVANT
☐ 318. DANNY O'CONNELL
☐ 332. DUTCH DOTTERER
☐ 351. JIM KING
☐ 368. BENNIE DANIELS
☐ 386. JOE HICKS
☐ 397. HAL WOODESHICK
☐ 414. DICK DONOVAN
☐ 432. COOT VEAL
☐ 447. HARRY BRIGHT
☐ 458. WILLIE TASBY
☐ 488. JOE MCCLAIN
☐ 507. PETE BURNSIDE
☐ 526. R.C. STEVENS
☐ 539. JOHNNY KLIPPSTEIN
☐ 546. MARTY KUTYNA

1962 TOPPS (598)
2 1/2" X 3 1/2"

BALTIMORE ORIOLES

☐   6. MARV BREEDING
☐ 34. JOHNNY TEMPLE
☐ 45. BROOKS ROBINSON
☐ 64. RUSS SNYDER
☐ 75. MILT PAPPAS
☐ 99. BOOG POWELL
☐ 112. HANK FOILES
☐ 121. BILLY HITCHCOCK(M)
☐ 134. BILLY HOEFT
☐ 165. JACKIE BRANDT
☐ 189. DICK HALL
☐ 203. JACK FISHER
☐ 221. BILL SHORT
☐ 245. RON HANSEN
☐ 272. EARL ROBINSON
☐ 290. JIM GENTILE
☐ 327. OSSIE VIRGIL
☐ 355. STEVE BARBER
☐ 382. DICK WILLIAMS
☐ 420. GUS TRIANDOS
☐ 442. WES STOCK
☐ 449. JERRY ADAIR
☐ 476. TEAM CARD
☐ 488. HAL BROWN
☐ 513. WHITEY HERZOG
☐ 533. CHARLEY LAU
☐ 545. HOYT WILHELM
☐ 560. CHUCK ESTRADA
☐ 577. DAVE NICHOLSON
☐ 591. ART QUIRK(R)

BOSTON RED SOX

☐   3. PETE RUNNELS
☐ 35. DON SCHWALL
☐ 81. JIM PAGLIARONI
☐ 101. CARROLL HARDY
☐ 117. GARY GEIGER
☐ 153. PUMPSIE GREEN
☐ 187. GENE CONLEY
☐ 201. IKE DELOCK
☐ 225. FRANK MALZONE
☐ 244. DON GILE
☐ 276. HAL KOLSTAD
☐ 301. GALEN CISCO
☐ 334. TEAM CARD
☐ 336. BILLY MUFFETT
☐ 345. CHUCK SCHILLING
☐ 368. BOB TILLMAN
☐ 403. CHET NICHOLS
☐ 425. CARL YASTRZEMSKI
☐ 444. TED WILLS
☐ 457. LOU CLINTON
☐ 504. EDDIE BRESSOUD
☐ 512. MIKE FORNIELES
☐ 523. RUSS NIXON
☐ 542. DAVE PHILLEY
☐ 559. MIKE HIGGINS(M)
☐ 567. TRACY STALLARD
☐ 580. BILL MONBOUQUETTE
☐ 591. DICK RADATZ(R)

CHICAGO CUBS

☐ 25. ERNIE BANKS
☐ 47. BOB WILL
☐ 66. CUNO BARRAGON
☐ 89. BARNEY SCHULTZ
☐ 119. DANNY MURPHY

☐ 170. RON SANTO
☐ 191. JIM BREWER
☐ 240. GEORGE ALTMAN
☐ 264. DICK ELLSWORTH
☐ 274. SAMMY TAYLOR
☐ 288. BILLY WILLIAMS
☐ 309. MOE MORHARDT
☐ 359. BOBBY LOCKE
☐ 372. JACK CURTIS
☐ 387. LOU BROCK
☐ 446. DON ELSTON
☐ 458. BOB BUHL
☐ 461. KEN HUBBS
☐ 477. ANDRE RODGERS
☐ 495. DON CARDWELL
☐ 546. MOE THACKER
☐ 552. TEAM CARD
☐ 557. BOB ANDERSON
☐ 585. GLEN HOBBIE
☐ 597. JIM MCKNIGHT(R)

CHICAGO WHITE SOX

☐ 8. RAY HERBERT
☐ 73. NELLIE FOX
☐ 91. J.C. MARTIN
☐ 113. TEAM CARD
☐ 116. HERB SCORE
☐ 161. FRANK BAUMANN
☐ 178. CAMILO CARREON
☐ 195. JOE CUNNINGHAM
☐ 214. DON ZANNI
☐ 255. JUAN PIZARRO
☐ 283. CHARLIE SMITH
☐ 286. AL LOPEZ(M)
☐ 325. LUIS APARICIO
☐ 341. MIKE HERSHBERGER
☐ 363. BOB ROSELLI
☐ 385. EARLY WYNN
☐ 410. AL SMITH
☐ 426. BOB FARLEY
☐ 454. FLOYD ROBINSON
☐ 479. JOEL HORLEN
☐ 514. SHERM LOLLAR
☐ 528. TURK LOWN
☐ 540. JIM LANDIS
☐ 555. JOHN BUZHARDT
☐ 576. RUSS KEMMERER
☐ 586. SAMMY ESPOSITO
☐ 595. BOB FRANK SADOWSKI(R)

CINCINNATI REDS

☐ 2. JIM BROSNAN
☐ 16. DARRELL JOHNSON
☐ 41. CLIFF COOK
☐ 80. VADA PINSON
☐ 103. DON BLASINGAME
☐ 120. BOB PURKEY
☐ 148. WALLY POST
☐ 151. JOHNNY KLIPPSTEIN
☐ 171. DAVE SISLER
☐ 172. FRED HUTCHINSON(M)
☐ 193. EDDIE KASKO
☐ 205. GENE FREESE
☐ 258. MARTY KEOUGH
☐ 267. DAN DOBBEK
☐ 282. DAVE HILLMAN
☐ 302. JOHN EDWARDS
☐ 331. MOE DRABOWSKY
☐ 350. FRANK ROBINSON
☐ 364. KEN R. HUNT
☐ 381. CHICO CARDENAS
☐ 414. JOE GAINES
☐ 440. JOE JAY
☐ 450. JIM O'TOOLE
☐ 465. TEAM CARD
☐ 478. DON ZIMMER
☐ 487. JERRY LYNCH
☐ 508. GORDY COLEMAN
☐ 524. HOWIE NUNN
☐ 562. BILL R. HENRY
☐ 594. DON PAVLETICH(R)

CLEVELAND INDIANS

☐ 15. DICK DONOVAN
☐ 49. HAL JONES
☐ 78. GENE GREEN
☐ 97. TITO FRANCONA
☐ 123. MIKE DE LA HOZ
☐ 145. BARRY LATMAN
☐ 182. BOB NIEMAN
☐ 215. WOODY HELD
☐ 224. DON RUDOLPH
☐ 242. MEL MCGAHA(M)
☐ 253. HARRY CHITI
☐ 273. GARY BELL
☐ 292. JERRY KINDALL
☐ 307. JIM GRANT

☐ 330. JOHNNY ROMANO
☐ 362. TY CLINE
☐ 379. CHUCK ESSEGIAN
☐ 405. JIM PERRY
☐ 447. WILLIE KIRKLAND
☐ 462. WILLIE TASBY
☐ 485. PEDRO RAMOS
☐ 511. BUBBA PHILLIPS
☐ 537. TEAM CARD
☐ 543. BOB ALLEN
☐ 563. KEN ASPROMONTE
☐ 587. FRANK FUNK
☐ 591. SAM MCDOWELL(R)
☐ 591. RON TAYLOR(R)
☐ 594. DOC EDWARDS(R)
☐ 598. AL LUPLOW(R)

DETROIT TIGERS

☐ 20. ROCKY COLAVITO
☐ 24. TEAM CARD
☐ 62. STEVE BOROS
☐ 87. MIKE ROARKE
☐ 92. SAM JONES
☐ 105. DON MOSSI
☐ 114. HOWIE KOPLITZ
☐ 150. AL KALINE
☐ 173. CHICO FERNANDEZ
☐ 196. TERRY FOX
☐ 216. RON KLINE
☐ 250. NORM CASH
☐ 261. GEORGE ALUSIK
☐ 299. DON WERT
☐ 335. BILL BRUTON
☐ 349. PAUL FOYTACK
☐ 366. PHIL REGAN
☐ 407. HANK AGUIRRE
☐ 416. BOB SCHEFFING(M)
☐ 427. JAKE WOOD
☐ 438. DICK BROWN
☐ 460. JIM BUNNING
☐ 481. VIC WERTZ
☐ 506. CHARLIE MAXWELL
☐ 527. DICK MCAULIFFE
☐ 554. BUBBA MORTON
☐ 583. LARRY OSBORNE
☐ 591. RON NISCHWITZ(R)

JOHNSON

HOUSTON COLT .45'S

☐ 12. HARRY CRAFT(M)
☐ 23. NORM LARKER
☐ 44. DON TAUSSIG
☐ 74. BOB LILLIS
☐ 126. AL CICOTTE
☐ 156. MERRITT RANEW
☐ 177. BOBBY SHANTZ
☐ 204. JOHNNY WEEKLY
☐ 227. BOBBY TIEFENAUER
☐ 248. BOB ASPROMONTE
☐ 278. KEN JOHNSON
☐ 304. DICK FARRELL
☐ 332. DON BUDDIN
☐ 354. ROMAN MEJIAS
☐ 373. AL HEIST
☐ 419. BOB BRUCE
☐ 432. JIM PENDLETON
☐ 459. JOE AMALFITANO
☐ 483. DON MCMAHON(B)
☐ 492. HAL W. SMITH
☐ 509. DAVE GIUSTI
☐ 526. HAL WOODESHICK
☐ 536. DICK GERNERT
☐ 556. AL SPANGLER
☐ 568. JIM GOLDEN
☐ 574. DEAN STONE
☐ 598. ED OLIVARES(R)

KANSAS CITY ATHLETICS

☐ 13. DICK HOWSER
☐ 38. GENE STEPHENS
☐ 82. DERON JOHNSON
☐ 122. NORM BASS
☐ 147. BILL KUNKEL
☐ 168. LEO POSADA
☐ 184. HAYWOOD SULLIVAN
☐ 246. ART DITMAR
☐ 254. GORDON WINDHORN
☐ 275. NORM SIEBERN
☐ 305. JERRY LUMPE
☐ 333. FRANK CIPRIANI
☐ 342. ED RAKOW
☐ 357. JERRY WALKER
☐ 384. TEAM CARD
☐ 402. GINO CIMOLI
☐ 417. JOE AZCUE
☐ 433. JIM ARCHER
☐ 451. JOSE TARTABULL
☐ 463. HANK BAUER(M)
☐ 493. DANNY MCDEVITT
☐ 496. WAYNE CAUSEY
☐ 517. DAVE WICKERSHAM
☐ 548. BOBBY DEL GRECO
☐ 564. BOB GRIM
☐ 592. DAN PFISTER(R)
☐ 595. MARLAN COUGHTRY(R)
☐ 598. MANNY JIMENEZ(R)

LOS ANGELES ANGELS

☐ 11. TOM MORGAN
☐ 39. JOE KOPPE
☐ 68. KEN L. HUNT
☐ 96. ELI GRBA
☐ 128. ART FOWLER
☐ 132. TEAM CARD
☐ 154. LEE THOMAS
☐ 176. EDDIE YOST
☐ 194. DEAN CHANCE
☐ 209. JIM FREGOSI
☐ 257. JACK SPRING
☐ 268. KEN MCBRIDE
☐ 287. GEORGE WITT
☐ 343. ALBIE PEARSON
☐ 369. TED BOWSFIELD
☐ 388. RYNE DUREN
☐ 422. STEVE BILKO
☐ 431. BOB RODGERS
☐ 452. EARL AVERILL
☐ 491. LEON WAGNER
☐ 498. JIM DONOHUE
☐ 525. GEORGE THOMAS
☐ 539. BILLY MORAN
☐ 549. BILL RIGNEY(M)
☐ 569. ED SADOWSKI
☐ 592. BO BELINSKY(R)
☐ 595. FELIX TORRES(R)

LOS ANGELES DODGERS

☐ 5. SANDY KOUFAX
☐ 32. JOHN ROSEBORO
☐ 43. TEAM CARD
☐ 69. PHIL ORTEGA
☐ 108. WILLIE DAVIS
☐ 129. LEE WALLS
☐ 131. PETE RICHERT
☐ 175. FRANK HOWARD
☐ 190. WALLY MOON
☐ 197. DARYL SPENCER
☐ 217. WALT ALSTON(M)
☐ 238. NORM SHERRY
☐ 280. JOHNNY PODRES
☐ 297. RON PERRANOSKI
☐ 340. DON DRYSDALE
☐ 348. LARRY BURRIGHT
☐ 358. TOMMY DAVIS
☐ 375. RON FAIRLY
☐ 404. TIM HARKNESS
☐ 418. ANDY CAREY
☐ 435. LARRY SHERRY
☐ 486. JIM GILLIAM
☐ 500. DUKE SNIDER
☐ 515. STAN WILLIAMS
☐ 535. ED ROEBUCK
☐ 594. DOUG CAMILLI(R)

MILWAUKEE BRAVES

☐ 30. ED MATHEWS
☐ 63. TONY CLONINGER
☐ 76. HOWIE BEDELL
☐ 100. WARREN SPAHN
☐ 109. BOB SHAW
☐ 130. FRANK BOLLING
☐ 158. TEAM CARD
☐ 174. CARL WILLEY

☐ 186. MACK JONES
☐ 218. JOE TORRE
☐ 239. CECIL BUTLER
☐ 259. LOU KLIMCHOCK
☐ 265. JOE ADCOCK
☐ 289. MIKE KRSNICH
☐ 320. HANK AARON
☐ 361. BOB HENDLEY
☐ 380. LOU BURDETTE
☐ 406. BOB TAYLOR
☐ 443. DEL CRANDALL
☐ 483. DON MCMAHON(F)
☐ 518. LEE MAVE
☐ 541. DON NOTTEBART
☐ 582. RON PICHE
☐ 588. BIRDIE TEBBETTS(M)
☐ 594. BOB UECKER(R)
☐ 597. DENIS MENKE(R)
☐ 597. AMADO SAMUEL(R)

MINNESOTA TWINS

☐ 21. JIM KAAT
☐ 70. HARMON KILLEBREW
☐ 84. LENNY GREEN
☐ 102. AL SCHROLL
☐ 124. BILL PLEIS
☐ 164. HAL NARAGON
☐ 166. DON LEE
☐ 180. BOB ALLISON
☐ 208. BILLY MARTIN
☐ 222. JERRY ZIMMERMAN
☐ 230. CAMILO PASCUAL
☐ 298. BILL TUTTLE
☐ 321. LEE STANGE
☐ 339. JOSE VALDIVIELSO
☐ 346. JACK KRALICK
☐ 371. EARL BATTEY
☐ 386. DON MINCHER
☐ 437. RAY MOORE
☐ 445. VIC POWER
☐ 482. SAM MELE(M)
☐ 499. ZOILO VERSALLES
☐ 510. JIM LEMON
☐ 532. DICK STIGMAN
☐ 558. JOHN GORYL
☐ 584. TEAM CARD
☐ 592. JOE BONIKOWSKI(R)
☐ 596. BERNIE ALLEN(R)
☐ 596. RICH ROLLINS(R)

NEW YORK METS

■ 4. JOHN DEMERIT
■ 7. FRANK THOMAS
■ 26. CHRIS CANNIZZARO
☐ 29. CASEY STENGEL(M)
☐ 85. GIL HODGES
■ 94. JAY HOOK
■ 162. SAMMY DRAKE
■ 183. ROGER CRAIG
☐ 213. RICHIE ASHBURN
■ 256. ELIO CHACON
■ 279. HOBIE LANDRITH
■ 293. BOB L. MILLER
■ 308. NEIL CHRISLEY
■ 337. JIM MARSHALL
■ 365. CHARLEY NEAL
■ 408. GUS BELL
☐ 421. KEN MACKENZIE
☐ 436. FELIX MANTILLA
☐ 464. AL JACKSON
☐ 497. ED BOUCHEE
☐ 572. BOB G. MILLER
☐ 593. CRAIG ANDERSON(R)
☐ 593. BOB MOORHEAD(R)
☐ 597. ROD KANEHL(R)
☐ 598. JIM HICKMAN(R)

NEW YORK YANKEES

☐ 1. ROGER MARIS
☐ 31. TOM TRESH
☐ 48. RALPH TERRY
☐ 65. BOBBY RICHARDSON
☐ 88. RALPH HOUK(M)
☐ 93. JOHN BLANCHARD
☐ 110. BILL SKOWRON
☐ 159. HAL RENIFF
☐ 169. BOB CERV
☐ 185. ROLAND SHELDON
☐ 200. MICKEY MANTLE
☐ 219. AL DOWNING
☐ 243. ROBIN ROBERTS
☐ 251. TEAM CARD
☐ 281. JAKE GIBBS
☐ 291. HAL STOWE
☐ 310. WHITEY FORD
☐ 338. BILLY GARDNER
☐ 360. YOGI BERRA

☐ 376. BUD DALEY
☐ 400. ELSTON HOWARD
☐ 430. TONY KUBEK
☐ 455. LUIS ARROYO
☐ 490. CLETE BOYER
☐ 502. HECTOR LOPEZ
☐ 553. JIM COATES
☐ 570. BILL STAFFORD
☐ 589. BOB TURLEY
☐ 592. JIM BOUTON(R)
☐ 596. PHIL LINZ(R)
☐ 596. JOE PEPITONE(R)

PHILADELPHIA PHILLIES

☐ 17. JOHN CALLISON
☐ 46. JACK BALDSCHUN
☐ 77. TONY TAYLOR
☐ 104. TED SAVAGE
☐ 111. DALLAS GREEN
☐ 146. DON DEMETER
☐ 157. WES COVINGTON
☐ 181. PAUL BROWN
☐ 212. JIM OWENS
☐ 220. ROY SIEVERS
☐ 249. ED KEEGAN
☐ 269. BOB OLDIS
☐ 284. RUBEN AMARO
☐ 294. TEAM CARD
☐ 303. FRANK TORRE
☐ 328. KEN WALTERS
☐ 352. FRANK SULLIVAN
☐ 374. GENE MAUCH(M)
☐ 434. CLAY DALRYMPLE
☐ 453. CAL MCLISH
☐ 494. SAMMY WHITE
☐ 521. JACKIE DAVIS
☐ 534. TONY GONZALEZ
☐ 550. ART MAHAFFEY
☐ 571. BILLY KLAUS
☐ 581. MEL ROACH
☐ 593. JACK HAMILTON(R)

PITTSBURGH PIRATES

☐ 10. ROBERTO CLEMENTE
☐ 36. DON LEPPERT
☐ 67. HARVEY HADDIX
☐ 86. DONN CLENDENON
☐ 95. DON HOAK
☐ 115. BOB SKINNER
☐ 160. DICK STUART
☐ 179. TOM STURDIVANT
☐ 210. ROY FACE
☐ 229. JESUS MCFARLANE
☐ 252. EARL FRANCIS
☐ 270. DICK GROAT
☐ 295. VERN LAW
☐ 326. TOM PARSONS
☐ 353. BILL MAZEROSKI
☐ 389. SMOKY BURGESS
☐ 409. TEAM CARD
☐ 415. BILL VIRDON
☐ 424. AL MCBEAN
☐ 448. JOE GIBBON
☐ 484. DICK SCHOFIELD
☐ 503. DANNY MURTAUGH(M)
☐ 520. BOB FRIEND
☐ 573. JOHNNY LOGAN
☐ 593. JACK LAMABE(R)
☐ 593. BOB VEALE(R)
☐ 598. HOWIE GOSS(R)

ST. LOUIS CARDINALS

☐ 14. BILL WHITE
☐ 19. RAY WASHBURN
☐ 28. MINNIE MINOSO
☐ 50. STAN MUSIAL
☐ 61. TEAM CARD
☐ 83. LARRY JACKSON
☐ 106. CARL SAWATSKI
☐ 118. JULIAN JAVIER
☐ 149. BOB DULIBA
☐ 167. TIM MCCARVER
☐ 198. JOHNNY KEANE(M)
☐ 202. CARL WARWICK
☐ 223. ALEX GRAMMAS
☐ 241. JOHNNY KUCKS
☐ 266. JOHN ANDERSON
☐ 285. CURT SIMMONS
☐ 323. DON LANDRUM
☐ 344. ED BAUTA
☐ 370. KEN BOYER
☐ 383. RAY SADECKI
☐ 412. CHARLIE JAMES
☐ 439. JERRY BUCHEK
☐ 489. JULIO GOTAY
☐ 507. ERNIE BROGLIO

☐ 522. LINDY MCDANIEL
☐ 530. BOB GIBSON
☐ 531. BOBBY GENE SMITH
☐ 547. DON FERRARESE
☐ 561. GENE OLIVER
☐ 575. RED SCHOENDIENST
☐ 579. JIM SCHAFFER
☐ 590. CURT FLOOD

SAN FRANCISCO GIANTS

☐ 9. JIM DAVENPORT
☐ 33. DON LARSEN
☐ 40. ORLANDO CEPEDA
☐ 71. DICK LEMAY
☐ 107. MIKE MCCORMICK
☐ 133. FELIPE ALOU
☐ 155. STU MILLER
☐ 188. CHUCK HILLER
☐ 199. GAYLORD PERRY
☐ 226. TEAM CARD
☐ 231. ERNIE BOWMAN
☐ 247. JOE PIGNATANO
☐ 260. BILL PIERCE
☐ 300. WILLIE MAYS
☐ 322. AL DARK(M)
☐ 329. BOB BOLIN
☐ 356. TOM HALLER
☐ 377. JOHNNY ORSINO
☐ 413. MATTY ALOU
☐ 429. BILLY O'DELL
☐ 459. ED BAILEY
☐ 480. HARVEY KUENN
☐ 505. JUAN MARICHAL
☐ 538. JACK SANFORD
☐ 544. WILLIE MCCOVEY
☐ 565. JOSE PAGAN
☐ 578. JIM DUFFALO

McCLAIN
WASH. SENATORS P

WASHINGTON SENATORS

☐ 27. CHUCK COTTIER
☐ 42. JIM KING
☐ 79. ED HOBAUGH
☐ 90. JIM PIERSALL
☐ 125. GENE WOODLING
☐ 152. MICKEY VERNON(M)
☐ 206. TEAM CARD
☐ 207. PETE BURNSIDE
☐ 228. DALE LONG
☐ 262. BOB SCHMIDT
☐ 271. RAY RIPPELMEYER
☐ 296. KEN HAMLIN
☐ 324. JOE MCCLAIN
☐ 347. CHUCK HINTON
☐ 378. BENNIE DANIELS
☐ 411. DANNY O'CONNELL
☐ 428. JOE HICKS
☐ 501. CLAUDE OSTEEN
☐ 519. BOB W. JOHNSON
☐ 529. JOHN SCHAIVE
☐ 551. HARRY BRIGHT
☐ 566. MARTY KUTYNA
☐ 592. DAVE STENHOUSE(R)
☐ 594. KEN RETZER(R)

1963 TOPPS (576)
2 1/2" X 3 1/2"

BOB UECKER
MILWAUKEE BRAVES C

BALTIMORE ORIOLES

- [ ] 12. STEVE BARBER
- [ ] 19. PETE BURNSIDE
- [ ] 41. CHARLIE LAU
- [ ] 65. JACKIE BRANDT
- [ ] 88. RON HANSEN
- [ ] 108. HOYT WILHELM
- [ ] 112. DICK BROWN
- [ ] 125. ROBIN ROBERTS
- [ ] 158. BOB SAVERINE(R)
- [ ] 205. LUIS APARICIO
- [ ] 208. JOHN MILLER(R)
- [ ] 209. HOBIE LANDRITH
- [ ] 213. BILLY HITCHCOCK(M)
- [ ] 260. JIM GENTILE
- [ ] 286. STU MILLER
- [ ] 319. JOE GAINES
- [ ] 345. BROOKS ROBINSON
- [ ] 358. MILT PAPPAS
- [ ] 377. TEAM CARD
- [ ] 398. BOOG POWELL
- [ ] 418. JOHNNY ORSINO
- [ ] 438. WES STOCK
- [ ] 465. CHUCK ESTRADA
- [ ] 488. JERRY ADAIR
- [ ] 496. STEVE DALKOWSKI(R)
- [ ] 504. BOB W. JOHNSON
- [ ] 526. DICK HALL
- [ ] 543. RUSS SNYDER
- [ ] 562. DAVE MCNALLY(R)
- [ ] 563. MIKE MCCORMICK

BOSTON RED SOX

- [ ] 28. MIKE FORNIELES
- [ ] 52. CHUCK SCHILLING
- [ ] 76. EARL WILSON
- [ ] 96. LOU CLINTON
- [ ] 115. CARL YASTRZEMSKI
- [ ] 136. IKE DELOCK
- [ ] 168. RUSS NIXON
- [ ] 188. EDDIE BRESSOUD
- [ ] 202. TEAM CARD
- [ ] 216. GENE CONLEY
- [ ] 232. FRANK MALZONE
- [ ] 251. JACK LAMABE
- [ ] 253. PETE JERNIGAN(R)
- [ ] 285. DICK STUART
- [ ] 299. DAVE MOREHEAD(R)
- [ ] 307. CHET NICHOLS
- [ ] 328. DICK WILLIAMS
- [ ] 343. JOHNNY PESKY(M)
- [ ] 363. DICK RADATZ
- [ ] 384. BOB TILLMAN
- [ ] 408. BILLY GARDNER
- [ ] 432. ROMAN MEJIAS
- [ ] 447. FELIX MANTILLA
- [ ] 480. BILL MONBOUQUETTE
- [ ] 513. GARY GEIGER
- [ ] 553. JIM GOSGER(R)
- [ ] 574. HAL KOLSTAD

CHICAGO CUBS

- [ ] 15. KEN HUBBS
- [ ] 31. CAL KOONCE
- [ ] 54. NELSON MATHEWS(R)
- [ ] 58. BOB WILL
- [ ] 81. JIMMIE SCHAFFER
- [ ] 95. LARRY JACKSON

- [ ] 113. DON LANDRUM
- [ ] 175. BOB BUHL
- [ ] 193. ANDRE RODGERS
- [ ] 212. GLEN HOBBIE
- [ ] 222. TEAM CARD
- [ ] 252. RON SANTO
- [ ] 272. DANNY MURPHY
- [ ] 287. DICK BERTELL
- [ ] 309. JIM BREWER
- [ ] 329. LINDY MCDANIEL
- [ ] 353. BILLY WILLIAMS
- [ ] 380. ERNIE BANKS
- [ ] 399. DICK ELLSWORTH
- [ ] 416. ALEX GRAMMAS
- [ ] 452. BARNEY SCHULTZ
- [ ] 459. DICK LEMAY
- [ ] 464. KEN ASPROMONTE
- [ ] 472. LOU BROCK
- [ ] 489. PAUL TOTH
- [ ] 515. DON ELSTON
- [ ] 532. STEVE BOROS
- [ ] 557. CUNO BARRAGAN

CHICAGO WHITE SOX

- [ ] 16. AL SMITH
- [ ] 35. JOHN BUZHARDT
- [ ] 54. DAVE DEBUSSCHERE(R)
- [ ] 66. MIKE JOYCE
- [ ] 86. CHARLEY MAXWELL
- [ ] 100. JOE CUNNINGHAM
- [ ] 118. SHERM LOLLAR
- [ ] 160. JUAN PIZARRO
- [ ] 181. SAMMY ESPOSITO
- [ ] 223. EDDIE FISHER
- [ ] 234. DAVE NICHOLSON
- [ ] 253. DEACON JONES(R)
- [ ] 254. MIKE HERSHBERGER
- [ ] 271. DEAN STONE
- [ ] 288. TEAM CARD
- [ ] 308. CAMILO CARREON
- [ ] 324. PETE WARD(R)
- [ ] 332. JOEL HORLEN
- [ ] 354. DOM ZANNI
- [ ] 381. FRANK BAUMANN
- [ ] 405. FLOYD ROBINSON
- [ ] 424. CHARLEY SMITH
- [ ] 458. AL LOPEZ(M)
- [ ] 485. JIM LANDIS
- [ ] 499. J.C. MARTIN
- [ ] 522. GARY PETERS(R)
- [ ] 525. NELLIE FOX
- [ ] 537. AL WEIS(R)
- [ ] 560. RAY HERBERT

CINCINNATI REDS

- [ ] 21. MARTY KEOUGH
- [ ] 29. SAMMY ELLIS(R)
- [ ] 29. JESSE GONDER(R)
- [ ] 37. JERRY LYNCH
- [ ] 63. TEAM CARD
- [ ] 70. JIM O'TOOLE
- [ ] 90. GORDY COLEMAN
- [ ] 116. JIM BROSNAN
- [ ] 133. GENE FREESE
- [ ] 158. TOMMY HARPER(R)
- [ ] 178. JOHNNY EDWARDS
- [ ] 194. JOE NUXHALL
- [ ] 203. CHICO CARDENAS
- [ ] 225. JOE JAY
- [ ] 244. JOHN TSITOURIS
- [ ] 265. VADA PINSON
- [ ] 284. DAVE SISLER
- [ ] 304. HARRY BRIGHT
- [ ] 326. HANK FOILES
- [ ] 350. BOB PURKEY
- [ ] 378. BILL R. HENRY
- [ ] 400. FRANK ROBINSON
- [ ] 407. CHICO RUIZ(R)
- [ ] 422. FRED HUTCHINSON(M)
- [ ] 444. JIM MALONEY
- [ ] 462. WALLY POST
- [ ] 483. JIM OWENS
- [ ] 498. EDDIE KASKO
- [ ] 518. DON BLASINGAME
- [ ] 534. KEN WALTERS
- [ ] 537. PETE ROSE(R)
- [ ] 556. AL WORTHINGTON

CLEVELAND INDIANS

- [ ] 14. PEDRO RAMOS
- [ ] 36. JERRY KINDALL
- [ ] 48. BIRDIE TEBBETTS(M)
- [ ] 72. JOHNNY ROMANO
- [ ] 103. CHUCK ESSEGIAN
- [ ] 129. GARY BELL
- [ ] 152. RON NISCHWITZ

- [ ] 170. JOE ADCOCK
- [ ] 187. WILLIE KIRKLAND
- [ ] 211. FRED WHITFIELD
- [ ] 227. JIM GRANT
- [ ] 228. MAX ALVIS(R)
- [ ] 248. TITO FRANCONA
- [ ] 266. BOB ALLEN
- [ ] 296. DOC EDWARDS
- [ ] 317. SAM MCDOWELL
- [ ] 324. VIC DAVALILLO(R)
- [ ] 351. AL LUPLOW
- [ ] 370. DICK DONOVAN
- [ ] 391. BILL DAILEY
- [ ] 413. JERRY WALKER
- [ ] 426. BARRY LATMAN
- [ ] 435. WOODY HELD
- [ ] 451. TEAM CARD
- [ ] 463. JOE SCHAFFERNOTH
- [ ] 466. TONY MARTINEZ(R)
- [ ] 493. WALT BOND
- [ ] 506. GENE GREEN
- [ ] 558. BOB LIPSKI(R)
- [ ] 561. MIKE DE LA HOZ

DETROIT TIGERS

- [ ] 25. AL KALINE
- [ ] 44. TERRY FOX
- [ ] 64. DICK MCAULIFFE
- [ ] 84. RON KLINE
- [ ] 134. BOB SCHEFFING(M)
- [ ] 140. FRANK LARY
- [ ] 164. BUBBA MORTON
- [ ] 169. DICK EGAN(R)
- [ ] 177. BUBBA PHILLIPS
- [ ] 224. MIKE ROARKE
- [ ] 240. ROCKY COLAVITO
- [ ] 257. HANK AGUIRRE
- [ ] 278. CHICO FERNANDEZ
- [ ] 299. BOB DUSTAL(R)
- [ ] 302. WHITEY HERZOG
- [ ] 327. PAUL FOYTACK
- [ ] 348. VIC WERTZ
- [ ] 365. JIM BUNNING
- [ ] 379. BOB ANDERSON
- [ ] 406. HOWIE KOPLITZ
- [ ] 407. FRANK KOSTRO(R)
- [ ] 437. BILL BRUTON
- [ ] 445. NORM CASH
- [ ] 453. JAKE WOOD
- [ ] 466. BILL FREEHAN(R)
- [ ] 475. GUS TRIANDOS
- [ ] 494. PHIL REGAN
- [ ] 516. PURNAL GOLDY
- [ ] 530. DON MOSSI
- [ ] 552. TEAM CARD
- [ ] 558. BILL FAUL(R)
- [ ] 573. COOT VEAL

BOB LILLIS

HOUSTON COLT .45'S

- [ ] 24. BOB BRUCE
- [ ] 45. BOB ASPROMONTE
- [ ] 77. AL SPANGLER
- [ ] 99. JIM UMBRICHT
- [ ] 119. BOB LILLIS
- [ ] 141. MANNY MOTA
- [ ] 153. HAL W. SMITH
- [ ] 158. DAVE L. ROBERTS(R)
- [ ] 189. DAVE GIUSTI
- [ ] 204. DON NOTTEBART
- [ ] 208. WALLY WOLF(R)
- [ ] 230. PETE RUNNELS
- [ ] 262. ELLIS BURON
- [ ] 277. DICK FARRELL

☐ 297. JIM GOLDEN
☐ 312. TEAM CARD
☐ 324. GEORGE WILLIAMS(R)
☐ 333. CARL WARWICK
☐ 338. RUSS KEMMERER
☐ 352. KEN JOHNSON
☐ 373. JIM CAMPBELL
☐ 386. JOHN BATEMAN(R)
☐ 395. DON MCMAHON
☐ 442. J.C. HARTMAN
☐ 468. CARROLL HARDY
☐ 491. HARRY CRAFT(M)
☐ 517. HAL WOODESHICK
☐ 538. GEORGE BRUNET
☐ 544. RUSTY STAUB(R)
☐ 553. BROCK DAVIS(R)
☐ 562. RANDY CARDINAL(R)
☐ 576. JOHNNY TEMPLE

KANSAS CITY ATHLETICS

☐ 23. ED LOPAT(M)
☐ 51. GEORGE ALUSIK
☐ 67. ED CHARLES
☐ 82. ED RAKOW
☐ 104. LEW KRAUSSE
☐ 124. DICK HOWSER
☐ 157. DIEGO SEGUI
☐ 195. MANNY JIMENEZ
☐ 214. ORLANDO PENA
☐ 236. BILL BRYAN
☐ 253. JOHN WOJCIK(R)
☐ 256. JERRY LUMPE
☐ 282. BOB DEL GRECO
☐ 301. BILL FISCHER
☐ 321. GINO CIMOLI
☐ 339. TED BOWSFIELD
☐ 359. HAYWOOD SULLIVAN
☐ 376. JOHNNIE WYATT
☐ 397. TEAM CARD
☐ 430. NORM SIEBERN
☐ 449. JOSE TARTABULL
☐ 461. NORM BASS
☐ 492. DAVE WICKERSHAM
☐ 501. JOE AZCUE
☐ 521. DAN PFISTER
☐ 539. WAYNE CAUSEY
☐ 549. PETE LOVRICH(R)

JIM FREGOSI
LOS ANGELES ANGELS SS

LOS ANGELES ANGELS

☐ 17. RYNE DUREN
☐ 33. BO BELINSKY
☐ 39. TEAM CARD
☐ 57. BILLY MORAN
☐ 98. GEORGE THOMAS
☐ 114. DAN OSINSKI
☐ 117. JACKE DAVIS
☐ 167. JIM FREGOSI
☐ 169. JULIO NAVARRO(R)
☐ 182. ALBIE PEARSON
☐ 207. KEN L. HUNT
☐ 231. ELI GRBA
☐ 249. LEO BURKE
☐ 280. BOB RODGERS
☐ 294. BILL RIGNEY(M)
☐ 322. BOB TURLEY
☐ 335. LEON WAGNER
☐ 355. DEAN CHANCE
☐ 372. DON LEE

☐ 386. ED KIRKPATRICK(R)
☐ 396. JOE KOPPE
☐ 407. DICK SIMPSON(R)
☐ 421. TOM MORGAN
☐ 441. LEE THOMAS
☐ 454. ART FOWLER
☐ 482. FELIX TORRES
☐ 496. FRED NEWMAN(R)
☐ 510. KEN MCBRIDE
☐ 522. MEL NELSON(R)
☐ 527. ED SADOWSKI
☐ 541. RON MOELLER
☐ 548. TOM SATRIANO
☐ 568. BOB FRANK SADOWSKI
☐ 572. JACK SPRING

LOS ANGELES DODGERS

☐ 11. LEE WALLS
☐ 53. JOE MOELLER
☐ 80. JIM GILLIAM
☐ 105. RON FAIRLY
☐ 123. FRANK HOWARD
☐ 150. JOHNNY PODRES
☐ 154. WALTER ALSTON(M)
☐ 180. BILL SKOWRON
☐ 196. DOUG CAMILLI
☐ 210. SANDY KOUFAX
☐ 229. WILLIE DAVIS
☐ 261. BOB L. MILLER
☐ 279. WALLY MOON
☐ 295. ED ROEBUCK
☐ 310. TOMMY DAVIS
☐ 337. TEAM CARD
☐ 360. DON DRYSDALE
☐ 383. PETE RICHERT
☐ 403. RON PERRANOSKI
☐ 439. DON ZIMMER
☐ 466. NATE OLIVER(R)
☐ 467. PHIL ORTEGA
☐ 487. JOHN ROSEBORO
☐ 496. JACK SMITH(R)
☐ 502. DARYL SPENCER
☐ 537. KEN MCMULLEN(R)
☐ 544. BILL HAAS(R)
☐ 562. KEN ROWE(R)
☐ 565. LARRY SHERRY

MILWAUKEE BRAVES

☐ 46. TOMMIE AARON
☐ 62. BOB HENDLEY
☐ 73. BOBBY BRAGAN(M)
☐ 74. DENVER LEMASTER
☐ 109. LEE MAYE
☐ 126. BOB UECKER
☐ 137. MACK JONES
☐ 156. ROY MCMILLAN
☐ 179. RON PICHE
☐ 201. CECIL BUTLER
☐ 238. LOU JOHNSON
☐ 253. LEN GABRIELSON(R)
☐ 255. BOB SHAW
☐ 275. ED MATHEWS
☐ 298. DON DILLARD
☐ 299. DAN SCHNEIDER(R)
☐ 320. WARREN SPAHN
☐ 324. PHILL ROOF(R)
☐ 347. JOE TORRE
☐ 367. TONY CLONINGER
☐ 390. HANK AARON
☐ 411. JIM CONSTABLE
☐ 414. TY CLINE
☐ 429. LOU BURDETTE
☐ 433. DENIS MENKE
☐ 460. DEL CRANDALL
☐ 476. FRANK FUNK
☐ 481. BOB TAYLOR
☐ 503. TEAM CARD
☐ 519. CLAUDE RAYMOND
☐ 536. NORM LARKER
☐ 547. GUS BELL
☐ 554. HANK FISCHER
☐ 570. FRANK BOLLING

MINNESOTA TWINS

☐ 26. RAY MOORE
☐ 40. VIC POWER
☐ 75. BOB ALLISON

☐ 89. DICK STIGMAN
☐ 110. RICH ROLLINS
☐ 127. BILL TUTTLE
☐ 162. TEAM CARD
☐ 165. JIM KAAT
☐ 186. JERRY ZIMMERMAN
☐ 198. LENNY GREEN
☐ 220. CAMILO PASCUAL
☐ 228. TONY OLIVA(R)
☐ 246. LEE STANGE
☐ 269. DON MINCHER
☐ 293. BILL PLEIS
☐ 314. JOHN GORYL
☐ 349. ZOILO VERSALLES
☐ 369. JIM LEMON
☐ 386. GARRY ROGGENBURK(R)
☐ 389. FRANK SULLIVAN
☐ 410. EARL BATTEY
☐ 427. BERNIE ALLEN
☐ 448. JACK KRALICK
☐ 500. HARMON KILLEBREW
☐ 522. JIM ROLAND(R)
☐ 531. SAM MELE(M)
☐ 535. JIM PERRY
☐ 549. PAUL RATLIFF(R)
☐ 564. GEORGE BANKS

NEW YORK METS

⚫ 27. CHOO CHOO COLEMAN
⚫ 59. CRAIG ANDERSON
⚫ 78. MARV THRONEBERRY
⚫ 93. GALEN CISCO
⚫ 107. JIM HICKMAN
⚫ 111. AL JACKSON
☐ 135. RICHIE ASHBURN
⚫ 174. LARRY BURRIGHT
⚫ 197. ROGER CRAIG
⚫ 217. JOE CHRISTOPHER
⚫ 228. ED KRANEPOOL(R)
⚫ 233. CASEY STENGEL(M)
⚫ 245. GIL HODGES
⚫ 273. SAMMY TAYLOR
⚫ 292. PUMPSIE GREEN
⚫ 316. NORM SHERRY
⚫ 334. WYNN HAWKINS
⚫ 342. GENE WOODLING
☐ 371. ROD KANEHL
☐ 386. LARRY BEARNARTH(R)
⚫ 393. KEN MACKENZIE
⚫ 419. TRACY STALLARD
⚫ 436. TIM HARKNESS
⚫ 469. JAY HOOK
☐ 473. TEAM CARD
⚫ 495. FRANK THOMAS
⚫ 511. CHARLIE NEAL
☐ 528. CARL WILLEY
☐ 550. DUKE SNIDER
☐ 558. AL MORAN(R)
☐ 558. RON HUNT(R)
☐ 562. DON ROWE(R)
⚫ 566. CLIFF COOK

NEW YORK YANKEES

☐ 20. TONY KUBEK
☐ 38. BUD DALEY
☐ 42. STAN WILLIAMS
☐ 54. JACK CULLEN(R)
☐ 60. ELSTON HOWARD
☐ 92. HECTOR LOPEZ
☐ 120. ROGER MARIS
☐ 155. BILL STAFFORD
☐ 183. JOE PEPITONE
☐ 200. MICKEY MANTLE
☐ 237. JIM COATES
☐ 247. TEAM CARD
☐ 264. PHIL LINZ
☐ 289. HAL BROWN
☐ 315. RALPH TERRY
☐ 340. YOGI BERRA
☐ 361. CLETE BOYER
☐ 382. RALPH HOUK(M)
☐ 401. JIM BOUTON
☐ 420. BOBBY RICHARDSON
☐ 446. WHITEY FORD
☐ 457. TEX CLEVENGER
☐ 470. TOM TRESH
☐ 484. DALE LONG
☐ 507. ROLAND SHELDON

□ 523. BILL KUNKEL
□ 537. PEDRO GONZALEZ(R)
□ 546. HAL RENIFF
□ 555. JOHN BLANCHARD
□ 569. LUIS ARROYO

PHILADELPHIA PHILLIES

□ 13. TEAM CARD
□ 29. JOHN BOOZER(R)
□ 29. RAY CULP(R)
□ 32. TONY GONZALEZ
□ 56. DENNIS BENNETT
□ 71. BOBBY WINE
□ 91. DALLAS GREEN
□ 132. JACK HAMILTON
□ 139. EARL AVERILL
□ 161. FRANK TORRE
□ 192. CLAY DALRYMPLE
□ 221. COOKIE ROJAS
□ 241. BILLY SMITH
□ 268. DON DEMETER
□ 283. ROY SIEVERS
□ 305. DON HOAK
□ 318. GENE MAUCH(M)
□ 341. JACK BALDSCHUN
□ 366. TONY TAYLOR
□ 385. ART MAHAFFEY
□ 404. BOB OLDIS
□ 434. JOHNNY CALLISON
□ 455. RUBEN AMARO
□ 478. PAUL BROWN
□ 512. CAL MCLISH
□ 529. WES COVINGTON
□ 549. MARCELINO LOPEZ(R)
□ 551. BILLY KLAUS
□ 553. JOHN HERNSTEIN(R)
□ 571. JOHNNY KLIPPSTEIN

PITTSBURGH PIRATES

□ 34. DICK SCHOFIELD
□ 55. BILL VIRDON
□ 87. BOB VEALE
□ 101. JOE GIBBON
□ 122. JULIO GOTAY
□ 151. TEAM CARD
□ 159. JIM PAGLIARONI
□ 169. TOMMIE SISK(R)
□ 184. VERNON LAW
□ 215. BOB SKINNER
□ 228. BOB BAILEY(R)
□ 239. HARVEY HADDIX
□ 259. JOHNNY LOGAN
□ 281. TOM STURDIVANT
□ 299. TOM BUTTERS(R)
□ 303. EARL FRANCIS
□ 323. BILL MAZEROSKI
□ 344. DON SCHWALL
□ 364. HOWIE GOSS
□ 387. AL MCBEAN
□ 407. LARRY ELLIOT(R)
□ 409. ROY FACE
□ 425. SMOKY BURGESS
□ 450. BOB FRIEND
□ 477. DONN CLENDENON
□ 508. TED SAVAGE
□ 540. BOB CLEMENTE
□ 549. RON PLASKETT(R)
□ 553. WILLIE STARGELL(R)
□ 559. DANNY MURTAUGH(M)
□ 575. DON CARDWELL

ST. LOUIS CARDINALS

□ 22. CURT SIMMONS
□ 49. DAL MAXVILL
□ 54. HARRY FANOK(R)
□ 83. CHARLEY JAMES
□ 97. BOB DULIBA
□ 130. DICK GROAT
□ 166. JOHNNY KEANE(M)
□ 172. GENE OLIVER
□ 190. MINNIE MINOSO
□ 206. RAY WASHBURN
□ 208. RON TAYLOR(R)
□ 226. JULIAN JAVIER
□ 250. STAN MUSIAL
□ 267. CARL SAWATSKI
□ 290. BILL WHITE

□ 313. ERNIE BROGLIO
□ 336. ED BAUTA
□ 357. GEORGE ALTMAN
□ 375. KEN BOYER
□ 394. TIM MCCARVER
□ 415. BOB GIBSON
□ 486. RAY SADECKI
□ 505. CURT FLOOD
□ 524. TEAM CARD
□ 533. BOBBY SHANTZ
□ 544. DUKE CARMEL(R)

SAN FRANCISCO GIANTS

□ 30. HARVEY KUEEN
□ 50. BILL PIERCE
□ 61. ERNIE BOWMAN
□ 85. TOM HALLER
□ 106. BOB BOLIN
□ 128. MATTY ALOU
□ 163. DON LARSEN
□ 169. GAYLORD PERRY(R)
□ 185. CHUCK HILLER
□ 199. JOE AMALFITANO
□ 208. RON HERBEL(R)
□ 235. BILLY O'DELL
□ 258. ALVIN DARK(M)
□ 270. FELIPE ALOU
□ 300. WILLIE MAYS
□ 325. JACK SANFORD
□ 346. BILLY HOEFT
□ 368. ED BAILEY
□ 388. JIM DAVENPORT
□ 417. TEAM CARD
□ 428. CARL BOLES
□ 440. JUAN MARICHAL
□ 456. JIM COKER
□ 466. JERRY ROBINSON(R)
□ 474. JACK FISHER
□ 490. WILLIE MCCOVEY
□ 520. ORLANDO CEPEDA
□ 545. JOSE PAGAN
□ 567. JIM DUFFALO

WASHINGTON SENATORS

□ 47. DON LOCK
□ 69. BUD ZIPFEL
□ 94. BOB SCHMIDT
□ 121. JIM HANNAN
□ 131. TEAM CARD
□ 149. MARV BREEDING
□ 158. ROGELIO ALVAREZ(R)
□ 171. STEVE HAMILTON
□ 176. JIM KING
□ 219. CHUCK COTTIER
□ 243. DON LEPPERT
□ 263. DAVE STENHOUSE
□ 276. BARRY SHETRONE
□ 291. DON RUDOLPH
□ 311. JOE MCCLAIN
□ 330. CHUCK HINTON
□ 356. JOHN SCHAIVE
□ 374. CLAUDE OSTEEN
□ 402. MICKEY VERNON(M)
□ 423. ED HOBAUGH
□ 443. JIM PIERSALL
□ 471. KEN RETZER
□ 479. ED BRINKMAN
□ 496. CARL BOULDIN(R)
□ 497. BENNIE DANIELS
□ 514. LARRY OSBORNE
□ 522. ART QUIRK(R)
□ 542. LOU KLIMCHOCK
□ 544. DICK PHILLIPS(R)

1964 TOPPS (587)
2 1/2" X 3 1/2"

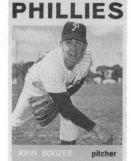

PHILLIES

JOHN BOOZER   pitcher

BALTIMORE ORIOLES

□ 17. WILLIE KIRKLAND
□ 22. JERRY ADAIR
□ 45. MILT PAPPAS
□ 63. JOHNNY ORSINO
□ 89. BOOG POWELL
□ 126. RUSS SNYDER
□ 145. NORM SIEBERN
□ 161. DAVE MCNALLY
□ 178. HANK BAUER(M)
□ 201. SAM BOWENS(R)
□ 201. WALLY BUNKER(R)
□ 221. BOB SAVERINE
□ 230. BROOKS ROBINSON
□ 239. HERM STARRETTE
□ 263. CHUCK ESTRADA
□ 285. ROBIN ROBERTS
□ 304. BOB W. JOHNSON
□ 322. GEORGE BRUNET
□ 364. JOE GAINES
□ 382. WES STOCK
□ 399. JACKIE BRANDT
□ 418. DAROLD KNOWLES(R)
□ 418. LES NARUM(R)
□ 439. HARVEY HADDIX
□ 450. STEVE BARBER
□ 473. TEAM CARD
□ 487. MIKE MCCORMICK
□ 511. LOU JACKSON
□ 540. LUIS APARICIO
□ 565. STU MILLER

BOSTON RED SOX

□ 25. BILL MONBOUQUETTE
□ 60. FRANK MALZONE
□ 79. BOB HEFFNER
□ 93. GARY GEIGER
□ 112. BOB TILLMAN
□ 153. DICK WILLIAMS
□ 170. DICK RADATZ
□ 186. ROMAN MEJIAS
□ 210. CARL YASTRZEMSKI
□ 228. FELIX MANTILLA
□ 248. JOHNNY PESKY(M)
□ 267. WILBUR WOOD
□ 287. TONY CONIGLIARO(R)
□ 287. BILL SPANSWICK(R)
□ 305. JACK LAMABE
□ 329. RUSS NIXON
□ 352. ED BRESSOUD
□ 376. DAVE MOREHEAD
□ 410. DICK STUART
□ 428. ARCHIE SKEEN(R)
□ 428. PETE SMITH(R)
□ 459. PETE CHARTON(R)
□ 459. DALTON JONES(R)
□ 481. CHUCK SCHILLING
□ 503. EARL WILSON
□ 526. LOU CLINTON
□ 572. DAVE GRAY(R)
□ 579. TEAM CARD

CHICAGO CUBS

- ☐ 29. LOU BROCK
- ☐ 55. ERNIE BANKS
- ☐ 78. MERRITT RANEW
- ☐ 96. BOB BUHL
- ☐ 111. DON ELSTON
- ☐ 131. STEVE BOROS
- ☐ 175. BILLY WILLIAMS
- ☐ 192. JOHN BOCCABELLA(R)
- ☐ 192. BILLY COWAN(R)
- ☐ 220. DICK ELLSWORTH
- ☐ 237. TEAM CARD
- ☐ 252. KEN ASPROMONTE
- ☐ 269. ELLIS BURTON
- ☐ 286. DON LANDRUM
- ☐ 309. PAUL TOTH
- ☐ 336. ANDRE RODGERS
- ☐ 359. JIM SCHAFFER
- ☐ 375. RON SANTO
- ☐ 408. JIM STEWART(R)
- ☐ 408. FRED BURDETTE(R)
- ☐ 424. DICK BERTELL
- ☐ 444. LARRY JACKSON
- ☐ 451. JOE AMALFITANO
- ☐ 469. FRED NORMAN(R)
- ☐ 469. STERLING SLAUGHTER(R)
- ☐ 486. BOB KENNEDY(HC)
- ☐ 510. LINDY MCDANIEL
- ☐ 548. WAYNE SCHURR(R)
- ☐ 557. LEO BURKE
- ☐ 578. GLEN HOBBIE

CHICAGO WHITE SOX

- ☐ 13. HOYT WILHELM
- ☐ 31. DAVE NICHOLSON
- ☐ 66. EDDIE FISHER
- ☐ 85. PETE WARD
- ☐ 107. BRUCE HOWARD
- ☐ 107. FRANK KREUTZER(R)
- ☐ 130. GARY PETERS
- ☐ 148. J.C. MARTIN
- ☐ 168. AL WEIS
- ☐ 195. FLOYD ROBINSON
- ☐ 215. RAY HERBERT
- ☐ 232. AL LOPEZ(M)
- ☐ 247. DAVE DEBUSSCHERE
- ☐ 264. JIM LANDIS
- ☐ 283. TOMMY MCCRAW
- ☐ 308. GENE STEPHENS
- ☐ 323. JOHN BUZHARDT
- ☐ 340. JOE CUNNINGHAM
- ☐ 368. FRITZ ACKLEY(R)
- ☐ 368. DON BUFORD(R)
- ☐ 384. RON HANSEN
- ☐ 401. CHARLIE MAXWELL
- ☐ 421. CAMILO CARREON
- ☐ 430. JUAN PIZARRO
- ☐ 453. FRANK BAUMANN
- ☐ 465. MIKE HERSHBERGER
- ☐ 496. TEAM CARD
- ☐ 538. MINNIE MINOSO
- ☐ 564. JERRY MCNERTNEY(R)
- ☐ 584. JOEL HORLEN

CINCINNATI REDS

- ☐ 33. SAMMY ELLIS(R)
- ☐ 33. MEL QUEEN(R)
- ☐ 49. BILL R. HENRY
- ☐ 72. CHICO CARDENAS
- ☐ 80. VADA PINSON
- ☐ 106. JOE NUXHALL
- ☐ 125. PETE ROSE
- ☐ 144. AL WORTHINGTON
- ☐ 166. MARTY KEOUGH
- ☐ 185. JIM O'TOOLE
- ☐ 207. FRED HUTCHINSON(M)
- ☐ 233. HAL W. SMITH
- ☐ 260. FRANK ROBINSON
- ☐ 275. JOHN TSITOURIS
- ☐ 303. JIM CAMPBELL
- ☐ 330. TOMMY HARPER
- ☐ 346. JOE JAY
- ☐ 356. BILL MCCOOL(R)
- ☐ 356. CHICO RUIZ(R)
- ☐ 377. BOB SKINNER
- ☐ 403. TEAM CARD

- ☐ 420. JIM MALONEY
- ☐ 436. CHARLIE NEAL
- ☐ 449. DERON JOHNSON
- ☐ 480. BOB PURKEY
- ☐ 507. JOHN EDWARDS
- ☐ 524. JIM DICKSON(R)
- ☐ 524. BOBBY KLAUS(R)
- ☐ 577. GORDY COLEMAN

CLEVELAND INDIANS

- ☐ 64. TED ABERNATHY
- ☐ 77. JERRY WALKER
- ☐ 105. WOODY HELD
- ☐ 122. DON MCMAHON
- ☐ 133. JIM GRANT
- ☐ 146. TOMMY JOHN(R)
- ☐ 146. BOB CHANCE(R)
- ☐ 172. TEAM CARD
- ☐ 184. AL LUPLOW
- ☐ 199. JOSE AZCUE
- ☐ 216. MIKE DE LA HOZ
- ☐ 234. GARY BELL
- ☐ 253. WALLY POST
- ☐ 301. LARRY BROWN
- ☐ 317. AL SMITH
- ☐ 338. JACK KRALICK
- ☐ 367. FRED WHITFIELD
- ☐ 391. SAM MCDOWELL
- ☐ 404. TONY MARTINEZ
- ☐ 435. VIC DAVALILLO
- ☐ 462. BIRDIE TEBBETTS(M)
- ☐ 478. DICK HOWSER
- ☐ 499. CHICO SALMON(R)
- ☐ 499. GORDON SEYFRIED(R)
- ☐ 515. JOHN ROMANO
- ☐ 530. LEON WAGNER
- ☐ 545. MAX ALVIS
- ☐ 552. TOM KELLEY(R)
- ☐ 552. SONNY SIEBERT(R)
- ☐ 562. PEDRO RAMOS
- ☐ 571. GENE CONLEY
- ☐ 583. TITO FRANCONA

DETROIT TIGERS

- ☐ 19. DON WERT
- ☐ 39. HANK AGUIRRE
- ☐ 58. DON DEMETER
- ☐ 67. TEAM CARD
- ☐ 98. BILL BRUTON
- ☐ 128. MICKEY LOLICH
- ☐ 143. BUBBA PHILLIPS
- ☐ 165. JERRY LUMPE
- ☐ 181. DAVE WICKERSHAM
- ☐ 197. FRANK LARY
- ☐ 236. BILL FAUL
- ☐ 250. AL KALINE
- ☐ 272. JAKE WOOD
- ☐ 292. MIKE ROARKE
- ☐ 312. FRITZ FISHER(R)
- ☐ 312. FRED GLADDING(R)
- ☐ 335. DON MOSSI
- ☐ 363. DICK MCAULIFFE
- ☐ 387. TERRY FOX
- ☐ 407. BILL FREEHAN
- ☐ 425. NORM CASH
- ☐ 443. CHARLIE DRESSEN(M)
- ☐ 461. GEORGE THOMAS
- ☐ 471. GATES BROWN
- ☐ 474. LARRY SHERRY
- ☐ 489. JULIO NAVARRO
- ☐ 491. ED RAKOW
- ☐ 512. WILLIE HORTON(R)
- ☐ 512. JOE SPARMA(R)
- ☐ 535. PHIL REGAN
- ☐ 572. DICK EGAN(R)

HOUSTON COLT .45'S

- ☐ 23. CHRIS ZACHARY
- ☐ 38. JIM WYNN
- ☐ 56. HAL BROWN
- ☐ 109. RUSTY STAUB
- ☐ 121. PETE RUNNELS
- ☐ 142. JOHN BATEMAN
- ☐ 158. KEN JOHNSON
- ☐ 179. CARL WARWICK
- ☐ 205. NELLIE FOX

- ☐ 226. JERRY GROTE(R)
- ☐ 226. LARRY YELLEN(R)
- ☐ 241. JIM OWENS
- ☐ 256. JOHNNY WEEKLY
- ☐ 282. BOB BRUCE
- ☐ 298. HARRY CRAFT(M)
- ☐ 321. BOB LILLIS
- ☐ 339. WALT BOND
- ☐ 354. DAVE GIUSTI
- ☐ 370. HAL WOODESHICK
- ☐ 389. JIM UMBRICHT
- ☐ 406. AL SPANGLER
- ☐ 434. DON NOTTEBART
- ☐ 467. BOB ASPROMONTE
- ☐ 492. JIM BEAUCHAMP(R)
- ☐ 492. MIKE WHITE(R)
- ☐ 504. CLAUDE RAYMOND
- ☐ 544. STEVE HERTZ(R)
- ☐ 544. JOE HOERNER(R)
- ☐ 560. DICK FARRELL

ATHLETICS

ORLANDO PENA   pitcher

KANSAS CITY ATHLETICS

- ☐ 26. GINO CIMOLI
- ☐ 42. MOE DRABOWSKY
- ☐ 75. WAYNE CAUSEY
- ☐ 108. JOHN WYATT
- ☐ 124. ORLANDO PENA
- ☐ 151. TEAM CARD
- ☐ 174. DOC EDWARDS
- ☐ 196. JIM GENTILE
- ☐ 212. PETE LOVRICH
- ☐ 229. CHARLEY LAU
- ☐ 244. TONY LARUSSA
- ☐ 276. JOSE TARTABULL
- ☐ 302. DAN PFISTER
- ☐ 320. ROCKY COLAVITO
- ☐ 334. LEW KRAUSSE
- ☐ 348. ED LOPAT(M)
- ☐ 366. NELSON MATHEWS
- ☐ 388. JOHN O'DONOGHUE(R)
- ☐ 388. GEORGE WILLIAMS(R)
- ☐ 402. TOM STURDIVANT
- ☐ 419. KEN HARRELSON
- ☐ 431. GEORGE ALUSIK
- ☐ 447. TED BOWSFIELD
- ☐ 466. DICK GREEN(R)
- ☐ 466. AURELIO MONTEAGUDO(R)
- ☐ 475. ED CHARLES
- ☐ 508. DIEGO SEGUI
- ☐ 528. DAVE DUNCAN(R)
- ☐ 528. TOM REYNOLDS(R)
- ☐ 574. MANNY JIMENEZ

LOS ANGELES ANGELS

- ☐ 32. DEAN CHANCE
- ☐ 48. BOB PERRY
- ☐ 71. JACK SPRING
- ☐ 97. JIM FREGOSI
- ☐ 110. ALBIE PEARSON
- ☐ 127. AUBREY GATEWOOD(R)
- ☐ 127. DICK SIMPSON(R)
- ☐ 149. PAUL FOYTACK
- ☐ 159. CHARLIE DEES
- ☐ 213. TEAM CARD
- ☐ 227. BARRY LATMAN
- ☐ 255. LEE THOMAS
- ☐ 273. MEL NELSON

☐ 279. JOE KOPPE
☐ 296. ED KIRKPATRICK
☐ 315. BO BELINSKY
☐ 333. BILLY MORAN
☐ 349. ART FOWLER
☐ 383. BILL RIGNEY
☐ 405. KEN McBRIDE
☐ 426. BOB RODGERS
☐ 441. BOB DULIBA
☐ 493. DON LEE
☐ 502. BOBBY KNOOP(R)
☐ 502. BOB LEE(R)
☐ 521. TOM SATRIANO
☐ 537. DAN OSINSKI
☐ 554. HANK FOILES
☐ 569. FRED NEWMAN
☐ 586. JIM PIERSALL

LOS ANGELES DODGERS

☐ 14. DICK NEN(R)
☐ 14. NICK WILLHITE(R)
☐ 30. RON PERRANOSKI
☐ 51. PETE RICHERT
☐ 68. WILLIE DAVIS
☐ 88. JOHN ROSEBORO
☐ 101. WALT ALSTON(M)
☐ 120. DON DRYSDALE
☐ 154. DICK TRACEWSKI
☐ 180. TOMMY DAVIS
☐ 200. SANDY KOUFAX
☐ 214. KEN McMULLEN
☐ 231. DICK CALMUS
☐ 249. DOUG CAMILLI
☐ 291. PHIL ORTEGA
☐ 310. JIM GILLIAM
☐ 337. AL FERRARA(R)
☐ 337. JEFF TORBORG(R)
☐ 353. WALLY MOON
☐ 371. FRANK HOWARD
☐ 394. BOB L. MILLER
☐ 411. LEE WALLS
☐ 456. WES PARKER(R)
☐ 456. JOHN WERHAS(R)
☐ 490. RON FAIRLY
☐ 531. TEAM CARD
☐ 548. PAUL SPECKENBACH(R)
☐ 549. JOE MOELLER
☐ 553. JIM BREWER
☐ 580. JOHNNY PODRES

MILWAUKEE BRAVES

☐ 35. ED MATHEWS
☐ 53. DENIS MENKE
☐ 65. FELIPE ALOU
☐ 70. JOE TORRE
☐ 94. JIM BRITTON(R)
☐ 94. LARRY MAXIE(R)
☐ 115. FRANK BOLLING
☐ 132. TEAM CARD
☐ 152. DENVER LEMASTER
☐ 171. TY CLINE
☐ 198. LEN GABRIELSON
☐ 218. HANK FISCHER
☐ 238. ROY McMILLAN
☐ 271. BOB SADOWSKI
☐ 289. FRANK FUNK
☐ 300. HANK AARON
☐ 316. GENE OLIVER
☐ 351. DAN SCHNEIDER
☐ 378. WOODY WOODWARD(R)
☐ 378. JACK SMITH(R)
☐ 400. WARREN SPAHN
☐ 416. LEE MAYE
☐ 437. ED BAILEY
☐ 454. TOMMIE AARON
☐ 476. RICO CARTY(R)
☐ 476. DICK·KELLEY(R)
☐ 506. BOBBY BRAGAN(M)
☐ 522. BOB TIEFENAUER
☐ 534. GUS BELL
☐ 541. PHIL ROOF(R)
☐ 541. PHIL NIEKRO(R)
☐ 551. BILLY HOEFT
☐ 575. TONY CLONINGER

MINNESOTA TWINS

☐ 15. ZOILO VERSALLES
☐ 34. JIM PERRY
☐ 54. SAM MELE(M)
☐ 73. JIMMIE HALL
☐ 90. EARL BATTEY
☐ 116. JAY WARD(R)
☐ 116. TONY OLIVA(R)
☐ 156. BILL DAILEY
☐ 177. HARMON KILLEBREW
☐ 194. JOHN GORYL
☐ 223. GEORGE BANKS
☐ 245. DICK STIGMAN
☐ 258. GARRY ROGGENBURK
☐ 270. RICH ROLLINS
☐ 290. BOB ALLISON
☐ 318. TEAM CARD
☐ 341. JIM ROLAND
☐ 355. VIC POWER
☐ 369. JERRY ZIMMERMAN
☐ 386. LENNY GREEN
☐ 409. BILL FISCHER
☐ 455. BERNIE ALLEN
☐ 484. BILL PLEIS
☐ 500. CAMILO PASCUAL
☐ 516. JERRY ARRIGO(R)
☐ 516. DWIGHT SIEBLER(R)
☐ 532. BUD BLOOMFIELD(R)
☐ 532. JOE NOSSEK(R)
☐ 542. DON MINCHER
☐ 555. LEE STANGE
☐ 564. JOE McCABE(R)
☐ 567. JIM KAAT

NEW YORK METS

■ 27. TEAM CARD
■ 44. DUKE CARMEL
■ 57. TIM HARKNESS
■ 84. CARL WILLEY
☐ 95. GEORGE ALTMAN
■ 113. GROVER POWELL
■ 129. AMADO SAMUEL
■ 155. DUKE SNIDER
☐ 176. TRACY STALLARD
■ 202. GALEN CISCO
■ 235. RON HUNT
☐ 251. CHOO CHOO COLEMAN
■ 288. AL MORAN
■ 324. CASEY STENGEL(M)
■ 345. FRANK THOMAS
☐ 361. JAY HOOK
■ 381. BOB TAYLOR
☐ 398. BILL HAAS(R)
☐ 398. DICK SMITH(R)
■ 422. JACK FISHER
■ 442. PUMPSIE GREEN
■ 457. JESSE GONDER
■ 477. MIKE JOYCE
☐ 494. AL JACKSON
☐ 514. JIM HICKMAN
■ 519. CHARLIE SMITH
■ 527. LARRY BEARNARTH
■ 536. LARRY ELLIOT(R)
■ 536. JOHN STEPHENSON(R)
☐ 546. JOE CHRISTOPHER
■ 556. STEVE DILLON(R)
■ 556. RON LOCKE(R)
☐ 566. ED KRANEPOOL
■ 576. JERRY HINSLEY(R)
■ 576. BILL WAKEFIELD
■ 582. ROD KANEHL

NEW YORK YANKEES

☐ 21. YOGI BERRA(M)
☐ 36. HAL RENIFF
☐ 50. MICKEY MANTLE
☐ 69. CLETE BOYER
☐ 86. AL DOWNING
☐ 100. ELSTON HOWARD
☐ 118. JOHN BLANCHARD
☐ 164. BUD DALEY
☐ 190. BOBBY RICHARDSON
☐ 206. STEVE HAMILTON
☐ 225. ROGER MARIS
☐ 259. HARRY BRIGHT
☐ 281. JAKE GIBBS(R)
☐ 281. TOM METCALF(R)

☐ 299. BILL STAFFORD
☐ 325. HECTOR LOPEZ
☐ 344. PHIL LINZ
☐ 360. JOE PEPITONE
☐ 380. WHITEY FORD
☐ 395. TOM TRESH
☐ 415. TONY KUBEK
☐ 433. TEAM CARD
☐ 458. RALPH TERRY
☐ 470. JIM BOUTON
☐ 488. PETE MIKKELSEN(R)
☐ 488. BOB MEYER(R)
☐ 505. STAN WILLIAMS
☐ 581. PEDRO GONZALEZ(R)
☐ 581. ARCHIE MOORE(R)

PHILADELPHIA PHILLIES

☐ 16. JOHN BOOZER
☐ 43. ROY SIEVERS
☐ 83. GUS TRIANDOS
☐ 104. ART MAHAFFEY
☐ 135. JOHNNY CALLISON
☐ 157. GENE MAUCH(M)
☐ 173. RYNE DUREN
☐ 191. CLAY DALRYMPLE
☐ 208. WES COVINGTON
☐ 243. RICHIE ALLEN
☐ 243. JOHN HERRNSTEIN(R)
☐ 254. DON HOAK
☐ 265. JIM BUNNING
☐ 293. TEAM CARD
☐ 319. PAUL BROWN
☐ 347. BOBBY WINE
☐ 365. CAL McLISH
☐ 379. TONY GONZALEZ
☐ 396. DENNIS BENNETT
☐ 412. RAY CULP
☐ 432. RUBEN AMARO
☐ 448. COOKIE ROJAS
☐ 464. DALLAS GREEN
☐ 482. JOHN BRIGGS(R)
☐ 482. DANNY CARTER(R)
☐ 520. JACK BALDSCHUN
☐ 533. JOHNNY KLIPPSTEIN
☐ 561. DAVE BENNETT(R)
☐ 561. RICK WISE(R)
☐ 585. TONY TAYLOR

PITTSBURGH PIRATES

☐ 20. BOB FRIEND
☐ 37. SMOKY BURGESS
☐ 62. TED SAVAGE
☐ 74. BOB PRIDDY(R)
☐ 74. TOM BUTTERS(R)
☐ 91. BOB BAILEY
☐ 117. EARL FRANCIS
☐ 141. DANNY MURTAUGH(M)
☐ 163. DONN CLENDENON
☐ 193. JERRY LYNCH
☐ 209. BOB ALLEN
☐ 224. TOMMIE SISK
☐ 246. MANNY MOTA
☐ 266. GENE FREESE
☐ 284. DICK SCHOFIELD
☐ 307. JOE GIBBON
☐ 326. RON BRAND
☐ 342. WILLIE STARGELL
☐ 373. TEAM CARD
☐ 392. JIM PAGLIARONI
☐ 417. DON CARDWELL
☐ 440. BOB CLEMENTE
☐ 472. VERNON LAW
☐ 495. BILL VIRDON
☐ 501. BOB VEALE
☐ 509. GENE ALLEY(R)
☐ 509. ORLANDO McFARLANE(R)
☐ 525. AL McBEAN
☐ 539. ROY FACE
☐ 558. DON SCHWALL
☐ 570. BILL MAZEROSKI

ST. LOUIS CARDINALS

☐ 24. CARL SAWATSKI
☐ 40. DICK GROAT
☐ 59. ERNIE BROGLIO
☐ 87. TEAM CARD
☐ 103. CURT FLOOD

1964 Topps

- ☐ 119. GARY KOLB
- ☐ 147. RAY SADECKI
- ☐ 160. KEN BOYER
- ☐ 183. RON TAYLOR
- ☐ 211. JIM COKER
- ☐ 240. BILL WHITE
- ☐ 262. MIKE SHANNON(R)
- ☐ 262. HARRY FANOK(R)
- ☐ 278. BOBBY SHANTZ
- ☐ 295. ROGER CRAIG
- ☐ 314. JERRY BUCHEK
- ☐ 332. RAY WASHBURN
- ☐ 357. CHARLIE JAMES
- ☐ 385. CURT SIMMONS
- ☐ 413. JOHNNY KEANE(M)
- ☐ 429. TIM MCCARVER
- ☐ 446. JULIAN JAVIER
- ☐ 460. BOB GIBSON
- ☐ 479. DAVE BAKENHASTER(R)
- ☐ 479. JOHNNY LEWIS(R)
- ☐ 497. JEOFF LONG
- ☐ 523. LOU BURDETTE
- ☐ 543. BOB UECKER
- ☐ 563. DAL MAXVILL
- ☐ 568. PHIL GAGLIANO(R)

SAN FRANCISCO GIANTS

- ☐ 18. BILLY O'DELL
- ☐ 47. JESUS ALOU(R)
- ☐ 47. RON HERBEL(R)
- ☐ 82. JIM DAVENPORT
- ☐ 99. AL STANEK
- ☐ 123. JOSE PAGAN
- ☐ 150. WILLIE MAYS
- ☐ 169. DEL CRANDALL
- ☐ 189. BOB HENDLEY
- ☐ 204. MATTY ALOU
- ☐ 222. BILL PIERCE
- ☐ 242. HARVEY KUENN
- ☐ 257. TEAM CARD
- ☐ 280. JUAN MARICHAL
- ☐ 297. KEN MACKENZIE
- ☐ 313. CHUCK HILLER
- ☐ 328. BOB SHAW
- ☐ 350. WILLIE MCCOVEY
- ☐ 374. BOBBY BOLIN
- ☐ 390. ORLANDO CEPEDA
- ☐ 414. JACK SANFORD
- ☐ 452. GIL GARRIDO(R)
- ☐ 452. JIM HART(R)
- ☐ 468. GAYLOR PERRY
- ☐ 485. TOM HALLER
- ☐ 513. DON LARSEN
- ☐ 529. AL DARK(M)
- ☐ 568. CAP PETERSON(R)
- ☐ 573. JIM DUFFALO

DON ZIMMER   3rd base

WASHINGTON SENATORS

- ☐ 28. CLAUDE OSTEEN
- ☐ 46. ED BRINKMAN
- ☐ 52. CHUCK HINTON
- ☐ 92. STEVE RIDZIK
- ☐ 114. DON LOCK
- ☐ 134. DON ZIMMER
- ☐ 167. MIKE BRUMLEY(R)
- ☐ 167. LOU PINIELLA(R)
- ☐ 187. ED ROEBUCK
- ☐ 203. JOHN KENNEDY

- ☐ 217. JIM KING
- ☐ 261. JIM HANNAN
- ☐ 277. KEN RETZER
- ☐ 294. KEN L. HUNT
- ☐ 311. TOM BROWN
- ☐ 327. DON BLASINGAME
- ☐ 343. TEAM CARD
- ☐ 358. RON KLINE
- ☐ 372. HOWIE KOPLITZ
- ☐ 397. CHUCK COTTIER
- ☐ 427. DON RUDOLPH
- ☐ 445. BILL SKOWRON
- ☐ 463. DON LEPPERT
- ☐ 483. FRED VALENTINE
- ☐ 498. DAVE STENHOUSE
- ☐ 518. CARL BOULDIN
- ☐ 547. GIL HODGES(M)
- ☐ 559. DICK PHILLIPS
- ☐ 587. BENNIE DANIELS

1965 TOPPS (598)
2 1/2'' X 3 1/2''

PITCHER
ROBIN ROBERTS

BALTIMORE ORIOLES

- ☐ 15. ROBIN ROBERTS
- ☐ 33. JACKIE BRANDT
- ☐ 49. CURT BLEFARY(R)
- ☐ 49. JOHN MILLER()R
- ☐ 67. HARVEY HADDIX
- ☐ 94. CHARLIE LAU
- ☐ 113. STEVE BARBER
- ☐ 150. BROOKS ROBINSON
- ☐ 169. DAVE VINEYARD
- ☐ 188. SAM BOWENS
- ☐ 204. RUSS SNYDER
- ☐ 231. JERRY ADAIR
- ☐ 249. DAVE MCNALLY
- ☐ 270. MILT PAPPAS
- ☐ 290. WALLY BUNKER
- ☐ 303. JOHNNY ORSINO
- ☐ 323. HANK BAUER
- ☐ 343. MIKE MCCORMICK
- ☐ 363. BOB W. JOHNSON
- ☐ 378. CHUCK ESTRADA
- ☐ 396. FRANK BERTAINA
- ☐ 410. LUIS APARICIO
- ☐ 427. BOB SAVERINE
- ☐ 455. NORM SIEBERN
- ☐ 473. PAUL BLAIR(R)
- ☐ 473. DAVE A. JOHNSON(R)
- ☐ 499. STU MILLER
- ☐ 518. KEN ROWE
- ☐ 539. HERM STARRETTE
- ☐ 560. BOOG POWELL
- ☐ 572. TEAM CARD
- ☐ 577. DAROLD KNOWLES(R)

BOSTON RED SOX

- ☐ 29. FELIX MANTILLA
- ☐ 42. EARL WILSON
- ☐ 55. TONY CONIGLIARO
- ☐ 74. RICO PETROCELLI(R)
- ☐ 74. JERRY STEPHENSON(R)
- ☐ 88. JACK LAMABE
- ☐ 111. LEE THOMAS
- ☐ 142. BILL MONBOUQUETTE

- ☐ 147. DENNIS BENNETT
- ☐ 162. RUSS NIXON
- ☐ 178. DALTON JONES
- ☐ 199. BOB HEFFNER
- ☐ 222. BOB TILLMAN
- ☐ 251. BILLY HERMAN(M)
- ☐ 272. CHUCK SCHILLING
- ☐ 295. DICK RADATZ
- ☐ 315. FRANK MALZONE
- ☐ 356. BILL SPANSWICK
- ☐ 385. CARL YASTRZEMSKI
- ☐ 403. TEAM CARD
- ☐ 434. DAVE MOREHEAD
- ☐ 452. GARY GEIGER
- ☐ 494. JAY RITCHIE
- ☐ 509. BOB GUINDON(R)
- ☐ 509. GERRY VEZENDY(R)
- ☐ 525. ED BRESSOUD
- ☐ 543. ED CONNOLLY
- ☐ 573. JIM LONBORG(R)
- ☐ 573. GERRY MOSES(R)
- ☐ 573. MIKE RYAN(R)
- ☐ 573. BILL SCHLESINGER(R)
- ☐ 588. LENNY GREEN

CALIFORNIA ANGELS*

- ☐ 26. BOBBY KNOOP
- ☐ 46. BOB LEE
- ☐ 66. BILL RIGNEY(M)
- ☐ 85. WILLIE SMITH
- ☐ 101. FRED NEWMAN
- ☐ 124. TOM SATRIANO
- ☐ 140. DEAN CHANCE
- ☐ 172. JIM PIERSALL
- ☐ 194. BILL KELSO(R)
- ☐ 194. RICK REICHARDT(R)
- ☐ 210. JIM FREGOSI
- ☐ 229. LOU CLINTON
- ☐ 242. GEORGE BRUNET
- ☐ 268. KEN MCBRIDE
- ☐ 293. TEAM CARD
- ☐ 307. BARRY LATMAN
- ☐ 324. BOBBY LOCKE
- ☐ 342. BOB RODGERS
- ☐ 358. ALBIE PEARSON
- ☐ 374. JOSE CARDENAL(R)
- ☐ 374. DICK SIMPSON
- ☐ 393. ED KIRKPATRICK
- ☐ 422. AUBREY GATEWOOD
- ☐ 442. VIC POWER
- ☐ 464. RON PICHE
- ☐ 486. TOM EGAN(R)
- ☐ 486. PAT ROGAN(R)
- ☐ 517. PAUL SCHAAL(R)
- ☐ 517. JACKIE J. WARNER(R)
- ☐ 537. MARCELINO LOPEZ(R)
- ☐ 537. RUDY MAY(R)
- ☐ 537. PHIL ROOF(R)
- ☐ 552. JULIO GOTAY
- ☐ 569. GINO CIMOLI
- ☐ 595. DON LEE

CHICAGO CUBS

- ☐ 14. LEN GABRIELSON
- ☐ 27. DICK BERTELL
- ☐ 34. CAL KOONCE
- ☐ 64. LOU BURDETTE
- ☐ 91. TEAM CARD
- ☐ 110. RON SANTO
- ☐ 149. WAYNE SCHURR
- ☐ 161. FRANK BAUMANN
- ☐ 165. DICK ELLSWORTH
- ☐ 186. BILLY COWAN
- ☐ 202. LEO BURKE
- ☐ 220. BILLY WILLIAMS
- ☐ 244. LINDY MCDANIEL
- ☐ 264. BOB BUHL
- ☐ 298. JIM STEWART
- ☐ 314. STERLING SLAUGHTER
- ☐ 334. VIC ROZNOVSKY
- ☐ 354. BILLY OTT(R)
- ☐ 354. JACK D. WARNER(R)
- ☐ 386. PAUL JAECKEL(R)
- ☐ 386. FRED NORMAN(R)
- ☐ 402. JOE AMALFITANO
- ☐ 420. LARRY JACKSON
- ☐ 436. DON ELSTON
- ☐ 457. BOB KENNEDY(HC)

* All of the cards appear as Los Angeles Angels.

- ☐ 510. ERNIE BANKS
- ☐ 528. GEORGE ALTMAN
- ☐ 549. ROBERTA PENA(R)
- ☐ 549. GLENN BECKERT(R)
- ☐ 565. ERNIE BROGLIO
- ☐ 584. HARRY BRIGHT
- ☐ 596. DON LANDRUM

CHICAGO WHITE SOX

- ☐ 41. BRUCE HOWARD(R)
- ☐ 41. MARV STAEHLE(R)
- ☐ 58. FRED TALBOT
- ☐ 70. BILL SKOWRON
- ☐ 81. DON BUFORD
- ☐ 89. MIKE HERSHBERGER
- ☐ 125. JUAN PIZARRO
- ☐ 146. RON HANSEN
- ☐ 183. DAVE NICHOLSON
- ☐ 198. SMOKY BURGESS
- ☐ 208. TOMMY JOHN
- ☐ 215. PETE WARD
- ☐ 234. TEAM CARD
- ☐ 253. DANNY CATER
- ☐ 276. HOYT WILHELM
- ☐ 297. DAVE DEBUSSCHERE
- ☐ 313. JIMMIE SCHAFFTER
- ☐ 328. EDDIE FISHER
- ☐ 345. FLOYD ROBINSON
- ☐ 368. KEN BERRY
- ☐ 368. JOEL GIBSON(R)
- ☐ 382. J.C. MARTIN
- ☐ 414. AL LOPEZ(M)
- ☐ 430. GARY PETERS
- ☐ 458. JOHN BUZHARDT
- ☐ 480. JOEL HORLEN
- ☐ 498. GENE STEPHENS
- ☐ 516. AL WEIS
- ☐ 541. GREG BOLLO(R)
- ☐ 541. BOB LOCKER(R)
- ☐ 586. TOMMY MCCRAW

CINCINNATI REDS

- ☐ 18. BILL MCCOOL
- ☐ 47. TOMMY HARPER
- ☐ 60. JIM O'TOOLE
- ☐ 75. DERON JOHNSON
- ☐ 102. STEVE BOROS
- ☐ 120. FRANK ROBINSON
- ☐ 141. CHARLIE JAMES
- ☐ 158. DICK SISLER(M)
- ☐ 174. JOE JAY
- ☐ 192. JIM COKER
- ☐ 207. PETE ROSE
- ☐ 221. JOHN TSITOURIS
- ☐ 243. TED DAVIDSON(R)
- ☐ 243. TOMMY HELMS(R)
- ☐ 263. MARTY KEOUGH
- ☐ 289. GORDY COLEMAN
- ☐ 312. JOE NUXHALL
- ☐ 316. TEAM CARD
- ☐ 339. RYNE DUREN
- ☐ 355. VADA PINSON
- ☐ 398. DAN NEVILLE(R)
- ☐ 398. ART SHAMSKY(R)
- ☐ 411. ROGER CRAIG
- ☐ 418. JOHNNY EDWARDS
- ☐ 437. CHICO CARDENAS
- ☐ 456. BILL R. HENRY
- ☐ 472. DON PAVLETICH
- ☐ 488. TED WILLS
- ☐ 507. SAMMY ELLIS
- ☐ 530. JIM MALONEY
- ☐ 554. CHICO RUIZ
- ☐ 581. TONY PEREZ(R)

CLEVELAND INDIANS

- ☐ 17. JOHNNY ROMANO
- ☐ 76. SAM MCDOWELL
- ☐ 92. DICK HOWSER
- ☐ 96. SONNY SIEBERT
- ☐ 105. CHICO SALMON
- ☐ 128. VIC DAVALILLO
- ☐ 145. LUIS TIANT
- ☐ 166. GEORGE CULVER(R)
- ☐ 166. TOMMIE AGEE
- ☐ 185. MAX ALVIS

- ☐ 235. CHUCK HINTON
- ☐ 262. BUD DALEY
- ☐ 283. FRED WHITFIELD
- ☐ 301. BIRDIE TEBBETTS(M)
- ☐ 317. DON MCMAHON
- ☐ 332. TED ABERNATHY
- ☐ 348. GEORGE BANKS
- ☐ 367. LEON WAGNER
- ☐ 380. ROCKY COLAVITO
- ☐ 404. STAN WILLIAMS
- ☐ 406. RALPH TERRY
- ☐ 424. GARY BELL
- ☐ 448. LEE STANGE
- ☐ 468. LARRY BROWN
- ☐ 481. TEAM CARD
- ☐ 501. RALPH GAGLIANO(R)
- ☐ 501. JIM RITTWAGE(R)
- ☐ 514. JOE AZCUE
- ☐ 535. JACK KRALICK
- ☐ 546. BILL DAVIS(R)
- ☐ 546. MIKE HEDLUND(R)
- ☐ 546. FLOYD WEAVER(R)
- ☐ 546. RAY BARKER(R)
- ☐ 562. BILLY MORAN
- ☐ 577. RICHIE SCHEINBLUM(R)
- ☐ 578. CAMILO CARREON

DETROIT TIGERS

- ☐ 19. GATES BROWN
- ☐ 37. FRED GLADDING
- ☐ 53. DICK MCAULIFFE
- ☐ 83. GEORGE THOMAS
- ☐ 130. AL KALINE
- ☐ 153. NORM CASH
- ☐ 173. TEAM CARD
- ☐ 191. PHIL REGAN
- ☐ 206. WILLIE HORTON
- ☐ 236. DENNIS MCLAIN
- ☐ 259. JIM NORTHRUP(R)
- ☐ 259. RAY OYLER(R)
- ☐ 271. DON WERT
- ☐ 288. JACK HAMILTON
- ☐ 306. BUBBA PHILLIPS
- ☐ 335. MICKEY LOLICH
- ☐ 353. JERRY LUMPE
- ☐ 375. DAVE WICKERSHAM
- ☐ 390. BILL FREEHAN
- ☐ 408. LARRY SHERRY
- ☐ 429. DON DEMETER
- ☐ 454. ED RAKOW
- ☐ 471. BILLY HOEFT
- ☐ 483. GEORGE SMITH
- ☐ 493. BILL ROMAN(R)
- ☐ 493. BRUCE BRUBAKER(R)
- ☐ 522. HANK AGUIRRE
- ☐ 538. CHUCK DRESSEN(M)
- ☐ 547. JAKE WOOD
- ☐ 563. JULIO NAVARRO
- ☐ 576. TERRY FOX
- ☐ 587. JOE SPARMA
- ☐ 593. JACKIE MOORE(R)
- ☐ 593. JOHN SULLIVAN(R)

HOUSTON ASTROS

- ☐ 16. JOE MORGAN(R)
- ☐ 16. SONNY JACKSON(R)
- ☐ 31. MIKE WHITE
- ☐ 48. CLAUDE RAYMOND
- ☐ 80. TURK FARRELL
- ☐ 109. WALT BOND
- ☐ 164. AL SPANGLER
- ☐ 175. BOB ASPROMONTE
- ☐ 179. HAL WOODESHICK
- ☐ 212. RON BRAND
- ☐ 240. BOB BRUCE
- ☐ 257. JIM WYNN
- ☐ 274. LUM HARRIS(M)
- ☐ 292. LARRY YELLEN
- ☐ 321. RUSTY STAUB
- ☐ 359. KEN JOHNSON
- ☐ 389. DON LARSEN
- ☐ 409. JIM BEAUCHAMP(R)
- ☐ 409. LARRY DIERKER(R)
- ☐ 433. JOHN BATEMAN
- ☐ 451. JIM OWENS
- ☐ 469. DON NOTTEBART
- ☐ 485. NELLIE FOX
- ☐ 504. JERRY GROTE

- ☐ 524. DAVE GIUSTI
- ☐ 553. DAN COOMBS(R)
- ☐ 553. JACK MCCLURE(R)
- ☐ 553. GENE RATLIFF(R)
- ☐ 594. JOE GAINES

KANSAS CITY ATHLETICS

- ☐ 35. ED CHARLES
- ☐ 51. BILLY BRYAN
- ☐ 71. JOHN O'DONOGHUE
- ☐ 87. NELSON MATHEWS
- ☐ 117. WES STOCK
- ☐ 151. TEAM CARD
- ☐ 168. DICK GREEN
- ☐ 197. DIEGO SEGUI
- ☐ 219. BOB MEYER
- ☐ 239. DOC EDWARDS
- ☐ 266. BERT CAMPANERIS
- ☐ 286. JIM DICKSON
- ☐ 286. AURELIO MONTEAGUDO(R)
- ☐ 311. ORLANDO PENA
- ☐ 333. TOMMIE REYNOLDS
- ☐ 365. JIM GENTILE
- ☐ 376. JIM LANDIS
- ☐ 391. MEL MCGAHA(M)
- ☐ 425. WAYNE CAUSEY
- ☐ 439. MOE DRABOWSKY
- ☐ 462. LEW KRAUSSE
- ☐ 479. KEN HARRELSON
- ☐ 526. RENE LACHEMANN(R)
- ☐ 526. JOHN ODOM(R)
- ☐ 526. SKIP LOCKWOOD(R)
- ☐ 526. JIM HUNTER(R)
- ☐ 557. JOSE SANTIAGO
- ☐ 577. DON BUSCHHORN(R)
- ☐ 590. JOHN WYATT

LOS ANGELES DODGERS

- ☐ 40. FRANK HOWARD
- ☐ 59. NATE OLIVER
- ☐ 77. DOUG CAMILLI
- ☐ 98. BOB L. MILLER
- ☐ 112. DERRELL GRIFFITH
- ☐ 119. JOHN KENNEDY
- ☐ 126. TEAM CARD
- ☐ 196. RON FAIRLY
- ☐ 217. WALT ALSTON(M)
- ☐ 238. JOE MOELLER
- ☐ 247. WALLY MOON
- ☐ 260. DON DRYSDALE
- ☐ 279. DICK TRACEWSKI
- ☐ 300. SANDY KOUFAX
- ☐ 331. AL FERRARA(R)
- ☐ 331. JOHN PURDIN(R)
- ☐ 344. WES PARKER
- ☐ 370. TOMMY DAVIS
- ☐ 387. JOHNNY PODRES
- ☐ 405. JOHN ROSEBORO
- ☐ 416. JIM BREWER
- ☐ 435. WILLIE DAVIS
- ☐ 453. WILLIE CRAWFORD(R)
- ☐ 453. JOHN WERHAS(R)
- ☐ 484. RON PERRANOSKI
- ☐ 527. JEFF TORBORG
- ☐ 544. HOWIE REED
- ☐ 561. DENNIS DABOLL(R)
- ☐ 561. MIKE KEKICH(R)

☐ 561. JIM LEFEBVRE(R)
☐ 561. HECTOR VALLE(R)
☐ 570. CLAUDE OSTEEN
☐ 579. DICK SMITH

MILWAUKEE BRAVES

☐ 23. BOB TIEFENAUER
☐ 44. WADE BLASINGAME
☐ 63. TY CLINE
☐ 82. SANDY ALOMAR(R)
☐ 82. JOHN BRAUN(R)
☐ 106. GENE OLIVER
☐ 127. FRANK LARY
☐ 156. BOB SADOWSKI
☐ 170. HANK AARON
☐ 182. MIKE DE LA HOZ
☐ 200. JOE TORRE
☐ 223. DAN OSINSKI
☐ 241. MACK JONES
☐ 269. FRANK BOLLING
☐ 287. GARY KOLB
☐ 305. RICO CARTY
☐ 327. DENIS MENKE
☐ 346. BOBBY BRAGAN(M)
☐ 366. DAN SCHNEIDER
☐ 383. FELIPE ALOU
☐ 407. LEE MAYE
☐ 426. TEAM CARD
☐ 441. DENNY LEMASTER
☐ 461. CLAY CARROLL(R)
☐ 461. PHIL NIEKRO(R)
☐ 476. BILLY O'DELL
☐ 487. WOODY WOODWARD
☐ 500. EDDIE MATHEWS
☐ 520. TONY CLONINGER
☐ 542. LOU KLIMCHOCK
☐ 567. TOMMIE AARON
☐ 585. HANK FISCHER

MINNESOTA TWINS

☐ 24. TEAM CARD
☐ 39. GERRY ARRIGO
☐ 62. JIM KAAT
☐ 90. RICH ROLLINS
☐ 108. DON MINCHER
☐ 122. BILL PLEIS
☐ 157. ZOILO VERSALLES
☐ 171. JIM ROLAND
☐ 180. BOB ALLISON
☐ 201. SANDY VALDESPINO(R)
☐ 201. CESAR TOVAR(R)
☐ 216. AL WORTHINGTON
☐ 237. BERNIE ALLEN
☐ 255. CAMILO PASCUAL
☐ 278. KEN RETZER
☐ 299. JERRY ZIMMERMAN
☐ 326. DWIGHT SIEBLER
☐ 340. TONY OLIVA
☐ 351. JIM PERRY
☐ 384. JOHNNY KLIPPSTEIN
☐ 400. HARMON KILLEBREW
☐ 421. GARY DOTTER(R)
☐ 421. JAY WARD(R)
☐ 432. JIM GRANT
☐ 459. FRANK KOSTRO
☐ 490. EARL BATTEY
☐ 506. SAM MELE(M)
☐ 529. JERRY FOSNOW
☐ 548. DICK STIGMAN
☐ 564. MEL NELSON
☐ 580. JIMMIE HALL
☐ 597. JOE NOSSEK(R)
☐ 597. RICH REESE(R)
☐ 597. JOHN SEVCIK(R)

NEW YORK METS

☐ 22. CHARLIE SMITH
■ 45. ROY MCMILLAN
■ 61. CHRIS CANNIZZARO
■ 73. DENNIS RIBANT
☐ 93. JACK FISHER
■ 114. JIM HICKMAN
☐ 144. ED KRANEPOOL
■ 167. BILLY WAKEFIELD
■ 187. CASEY STENGEL(M)
■ 205. WARREN SPAHN
■ 227. BOBBY KLAUS

■ 258. LARRY BEARNARTH
■ 277. JOHNNY LEWIS
■ 285. RON HUNT
■ 308. CLEON JONES(R)
■ 308. TOM PARSONS(R)
☐ 329. HAWK TAYLOR
☐ 349. LARRY MILLER
■ 364. GALEN CISCO
☐ 381. AL JACKSON
☐ 401. CARL WILLEY
☐ 423. JESSE GONDER
☐ 449. JERRY HINSLEY(R)
☐ 449. GARY KROLL(R)
☐ 470. YOGI BERRA
■ 495. JOE CHRISTOPHER
☐ 511. RON LOCKE
☐ 533. DAN NAPOLEON(R)
☐ 533. RON SWOBODA(R)
☐ 533. JIM BETHKE(R)
☐ 533. TUG MCGRAW(R)
☐ 551. TEAM CARD
☐ 581. KEVIN COLLINS(R)

NEW YORK YANKEES

☐ 13. PEDRO RAMOS
☐ 30. JIM BOUTON
☐ 65. TONY KUBEK
☐ 97. PEDRO GONZALEZ
☐ 115. BOBBY RICHARDSON
☐ 131. JOHNNY KEANE(M)
☐ 155. ROGER MARIS
☐ 177. PETE MIKKELSEN
☐ 226. ELVIO JIMENEZ(R)
☐ 226. JAKE GIBBS(R)
☐ 245. JOE PEPITONE
☐ 254. ROLAND SHELDON
☐ 261. DUKE CARMEL
☐ 281. BILL STAFFORD
☐ 309. STEVE HAMILTON
☐ 330. WHITEY FORD
☐ 350. MICKEY MANTLE
☐ 369. PHIL LINZ
☐ 388. JOHN BLANCHARD
☐ 413. HAL RENIFF
☐ 440. TOM TRESH
☐ 450. ELSTON HOWARD
☐ 475. CLETE BOYER
☐ 513. TEAM CARD
☐ 532. HECTOR LOPEZ
☐ 550. MEL STOTTLEMYRE
☐ 566. GIL BLANCO(R)
☐ 566. ART LOPEZ(R)
☐ 566. ROSS MOSCHITTO(R)
☐ 582. BOB SCHMIDT
☐ 598. AL DOWNING

PHILADELPHIA PHILLIES

☐ 20. JIM BUNNING
☐ 36. BOBBY WINE
☐ 52. ED ROEBUCK
☐ 72. TONY GONZALEZ
☐ 107. PAT CORRALES(R)
☐ 107. COSTEN SHOCKLEY(R)
☐ 123. FRANK THOMAS
☐ 163. JOHN BRIGGS
☐ 184. JOHN BOOZER
☐ 203. DALLAS GREEN
☐ 225. BOB BELINSKY
☐ 248. GUS TRIANDOS
☐ 280. DICK STUART
☐ 296. TONY TAYLOR
☐ 310. JOHNNY CALLISON
☐ 322. RICK WISE
☐ 338. TEAM CARD
☐ 352. ALEX JOHNSON
☐ 372. CLAY DALRYMPLE
☐ 399. RAY HERBERT
☐ 419. RUBEN AMARO
☐ 446. ART MAHAFFEY
☐ 460. RICHIE ALLEN
☐ 474. COOKIE ROJAS
☐ 489. GENE MAUCH(M)
☐ 505. RAY CULP
☐ 521. DAVE BENNETT(R)
☐ 521. MORRIE STEEVENS(R)
☐ 534. JOHN HERRNSTEIN
☐ 555. JACK BALDSCHUN
☐ 583. WES COVINGTON

PITTSBURGH PIRATES

☐ 25. AL MCBEAN
☐ 54. JOE GIBBON
☐ 69. BILL VIRDON
☐ 95. BILL MAZEROSKI
☐ 121. GENE ALLEY
☐ 143. JOHN GELNAR(R)
☐ 143. JERRY MAY(R)
☐ 160. BOB CLEMENTE
☐ 195. BOB VEALE
☐ 209. TEAM CARD
☐ 218. DICK SCHOFIELD
☐ 232. STEVE BLASS
☐ 246. TOM BUTTERS
☐ 265. JIM PAGLIARONI
☐ 291. JERRY LYNCH
☐ 325. DONN CLENDENON
☐ 347. ROY FACE
☐ 362. DON SCHWALL
☐ 377. WILLIE STARGELL
☐ 392. BOB FRIEND
☐ 412. BOB BAILEY
☐ 438. HARRY WALKER(M)
☐ 463. MANNY MOTA
☐ 478. WILBUR WOOD
☐ 492. GENE FREESE
☐ 502. DON CARDWELL
☐ 515. VERN LAW
☐ 536. ANDRE RODGERS
☐ 558. TOMMIE SISK
☐ 571. OSSIE VIRGIL
☐ 592. FRANK BORK

ST. LOUIS CARDINALS

☐ 28. BARNEY SCHULTZ
☐ 43. MIKE SHANNON
☐ 57. TEAM CARD
☐ 78. DAL MAXVILL
☐ 100. KEN BOYER
☐ 116. DAVE DOWLING(R)
☐ 116. BOB TOLAN(R)
☐ 154. BOB HUMPHREYS
☐ 190. BILL WHITE
☐ 214. BOB PURKEY
☐ 230. RAY SADECKI
☐ 256. TITO FRANCONA
☐ 275. DICK GROAT
☐ 294. TIM MCCARVER
☐ 320. BOB GIBSON
☐ 337. MIKE CUELLAR
☐ 357. CARL WARWICK
☐ 373. CURT SIMMONS
☐ 397. JERRY BUCHEK
☐ 415. CURT FLOOD
☐ 431. NELSON BRILES(R)
☐ 431. ED SPIEZIO(R)
☐ 447. JULIAN JAVIER
☐ 467. RAY WASHBURN
☐ 477. FRITZ ACKLEY(R)
☐ 477. STEVE CARLTON(R)
☐ 491. TRACY STALLARD
☐ 503. PHIL GAGLIANO
☐ 519. BOB UECKER
☐ 540. LOU BROCK
☐ 556. RED SCHOENDIENST(M)
☐ 568. RON TAYLOR
☐ 581. DAVE RICKETTS(R)
☐ 591. BOB SKINNER

SAN FRANCISCO GIANTS

☐ 32. HERMAN FRANKS(M)
☐ 50. JUAN MARICHAL
☐ 68. DEL CRANDALL
☐ 84. RON HERBEL
☐ 103. HARVEY KUENN
☐ 118. HAL LANIER
☐ 159. JIM DUFFALO
☐ 176. WILLIE MCCOVEY
☐ 193. GAYLORD PERRY
☐ 213. JIM DAVENPORT
☐ 228. JACK SANFORD
☐ 250. WILLIE MAYS
☐ 282. DICK ESTELLE(R)
☐ 282. MASANORI MURAKAMI(R)
☐ 302. AL STANEK
☐ 318. MATTY ALOU
☐ 341. BOBBY BOLIN

☐ 360. ORLANDO CEPEDA
☐ 379. TEAM CARD
☐ 395. JIM HART
☐ 428. BOB SHAW
☐ 444. BOB HENDLEY
☐ 465. TOM HALLER
☐ 482. BOB PRIDDY
☐ 497. KEN HENDERSON(R)
☐ 497. JACK HIATT(R)
☐ 512. CAP PETERSON
☐ 531. CHUCK HILLER
☐ 545. JESUS ALOU
☐ 559. ED BAILEY
☐ 575. JOSE PAGAN
☐ 589. FRANK LINZY(R)
☐ 589. BOB SCHRODER(R)

OUTFIELD
DON LOCK

WASHINGTON SENATORS

☐ 21. DON BLASINGAME
☐ 38. JIM KING
☐ 56. RON KLINE
☐ 86. LES NARUM
☐ 99. GIL HODGES(M)
☐ 129. BENNIE DANIELS
☐ 148. WILLIE KIRKLAND
☐ 152. PHIL ORTEGA
☐ 181. DON LOUN(R)
☐ 181. JOE MCCABE(R)
☐ 211. STEVE RIDZIK
☐ 224. BOB CHANCE
☐ 233. DON ZIMMER
☐ 252. PETE RICHERT
☐ 267. TEAM CARD
☐ 284. NICK WILLHITE
☐ 304. DAVE STENHOUSE
☐ 319. KEN MCMULLEN
☐ 336. WOODY HELD
☐ 371. FRANK KREUTZER
☐ 394. JIM HANNAN
☐ 417. ED BRINKMAN
☐ 445. DON LOCK
☐ 466. PETE CRAIG(R)
☐ 466. DICK NEN(R)
☐ 496. JOE CUNNINGHAM
☐ 523. MIKE BRUMLEY
☐ 574. ROY SIEVERS

1966 TOPPS (598)
2 1/2" X 3 1/2"

HANK AARON outfield

ATLANTA BRAVES

☐ 10. TONY CLONINGER
☐ 28. PHIL NIEKRO
☐ 49. WOODY WOODWARD
☐ 84. JIM BEAUCHAMP(R)
☐ 84. DICK KELLEY(R)
☐ 96. FELIPE ALOU
☐ 130. JOE TORRE
☐ 153. RICO CARTY
☐ 168. DAN OSINSKI
☐ 184. DENIS MENKE
☐ 200. EDDIE MATHEWS
☐ 237. BILLY O'DELL
☐ 252. DENVER LEMASTER
☐ 268. JOHN BLANCHARD
☐ 286. GARY GEIGER
☐ 307. CLAY CARROLL
☐ 326. TEAM CARD
☐ 346. MIKE DE LA HOZ
☐ 355. WADE BLASINGAME
☐ 381. HANK FISCHER
☐ 408. LEE THOMAS
☐ 428. SANDY ALOMAR
☐ 446. MACK JONES
☐ 466. KEN JOHNSON
☐ 476. BOBBY BRAGAN(M)
☐ 497. CHRIS CANNIZZARO
☐ 500. HANK AARON
☐ 518. HERB HIPPAUF(R)
☐ 518. ARNIE UMBACH(R)
☐ 541. GENE OLIVER
☐ 553. PAT GARRETT(R)
☐ 578. CHI CHI OLIVO

BALTIMORE ORIOLES

☐ 14. NORM SIEBERN
☐ 27. DAROLD KNOWLES(R)
☐ 27. ANDY ETCHEBARREN(R)
☐ 48. PAUL BLAIR
☐ 90. LUIS APARICIO
☐ 105. MILT PAPPAS
☐ 126. JIM PALMER
☐ 136. WOODY HELD
☐ 148. BOB W. JOHNSON
☐ 167. BOOG POWELL
☐ 193. DAVE MCNALLY
☐ 229. HANK BAUER(M)
☐ 247. CARL WARWICK
☐ 265. STU MILLER
☐ 291. MOE DRABOWSKY
☐ 310. FRANK ROBINSON
☐ 348. TEAM CARD
☐ 368. CHARLIE LAU
☐ 390. BROOKS ROBINSON
☐ 412. SAM BOWENS
☐ 427. JOHN MILLER
☐ 442. EDDIE BARNOWSKI(R)
☐ 442. EDDIE WATT(R)
☐ 460. CURT BLEFARY
☐ 467. VIC ROZNOVSKY
☐ 477. STEVE BARBER
☐ 499. WALLY BUNKER

☐ 513. CAMILO CARREON
☐ 533. JERRY ADAIR
☐ 562. RUSS SNYDER
☐ 579. FRANK BERTAINA(R)
☐ 579. GENE BRABENDER(R)
☐ 579. DAVE A. JOHNSON

BOSTON RED SOX

☐ 6. CHUCK SCHILLING
☐ 37. BILLY HERMAN(M)
☐ 53. BOB DULIBA
☐ 70. CARL YASTRZEMSKI
☐ 93. JIM LONBORG
☐ 114. JIM GOSGER
☐ 135. DAVE MOREHEAD
☐ 178. BOB TILLMAN
☐ 203. JOSE SANTIAGO
☐ 227. RUSS NIXON
☐ 259. TEAM CARD
☐ 277. GEORGE THOMAS
☐ 298. RICO PETROCELLI
☐ 317. DALTON JONES
☐ 329. PETE CHARTON
☐ 343. JOE CHRISTOPHER
☐ 356. OWEN JOHNSON(R)
☐ 356. KEN SANDERS(R)
☐ 380. TONY CONIGLIARO
☐ 396. JERRY STEPHENSON
☐ 419. MIKE RYAN
☐ 456. DARRELL BRANDON(R)
☐ 456. JOE FOY(R)
☐ 475. DICK RADATZ
☐ 491. DENNIS BENNETT
☐ 502. LENNY GREEN
☐ 512. DICK STIGMAN(F)
☐ 523. BOB SADOWSKI
☐ 542. GEORGE SMITH
☐ 558. GUIDO GRILLI(R)
☐ 558. PETE MAGRINI(R)
☐ 558. GEORGE SCOTT(R)
☐ 575. EARL WILSON

CALIFORNIA ANGELS

☐ 5. JIM FREGOSI
☐ 23. JACK SANFORD
☐ 42. AUBREY GATEWOOD
☐ 62. MERRITT RANEW
☐ 83. ALBIE PEARSON
☐ 102. ED KIRKPATRICK
☐ 131. TEAM CARD
☐ 152. FRANK MALZONE
☐ 155. MARCELINO LOPEZ
☐ 173. AL SPANGLER
☐ 192. VIC POWER
☐ 213. FRED NEWMAN
☐ 249. BILL RIGNEY(M)
☐ 263. TOM EGAN
☐ 280. BOBBY KNOOP
☐ 299. LOU BURDETTE
☐ 321. RICK REICHARDT
☐ 340. DEAN CHANCE
☐ 361. TOM SATRIANO
☐ 376. PAUL SCHAAL
☐ 393. GEORGE BRUNET
☐ 417. ED SUKLA(R)
☐ 417. JIM MCGLOTHLIN(R)
☐ 438. WILLIE SMITH
☐ 462. BOB RODGERS
☐ 481. BOB LEE
☐ 505. JOSE CARDENAL
☐ 536. DICK EGAN
☐ 553. JACKIE J. WARNER(R)
☐ 565. JIMMY PIERSALL

CHICAGO CUBS

☐ 2. TED ABERNATHY
☐ 24. DON KESSINGER
☐ 43. DON LANDRUM
☐ 63. JIM STEWART
☐ 82. BOB HENDLEY
☐ 110. ERNIE BANKS
☐ 139. BYRON BROWNE(R)
☐ 139. DON YOUNG(R)
☐ 146. GEORGE ALTMAN
☐ 166. CHRIS KRUG
☐ 185. BUB BUHL

- □ 204. TEAM CARD
- □ 232. GLENN BECKERT
- □ 246. ED BAILEY
- □ 278. CALVIN KOONCE
- □ 290. RON SANTO
- □ 306. TY CLINE
- □ 322. BILL FAUL
- □ 342. BOB HUMPHREYS
- □ 372. HARVEY KUENN
- □ 392. BILL HANDS(R)
- □ 392. RANDY HUNDLEY(R)
- □ 409. BILLY HOEFT
- □ 423. ERNIE BROGLIO
- □ 447. DICK ELLSWORTH
- □ 482. JOHN BOCCABELLA(R)
- □ 482. DAVE DOWLING(R)
- □ 484. WES COVINGTON
- □ 559. ROBERTO PENA
- □ 580. BILLY WILLIAMS

CHICAGO WHITE SOX

- □ 8. FLOYD ROBINSON
- □ 25. PETE WARD
- □ 47. J.C. MARTIN
- □ 66. AL WEIS
- □ 85. EDDIE FISHER
- □ 111. GARY PETERS
- □ 127. KEN BERRY
- □ 141. TOM MCCRAW
- □ 164. TOMMY AGEE(R)
- □ 164. MARV STAEHLE(R)
- □ 245. JOHN BUZHARDT
- □ 261. RON HANSEN
- □ 281. BRUCE HOWARD
- □ 301. GREG BOLLO
- □ 319. GENE FREESE
- □ 335. JUAN PIZARRO
- □ 354. SMOKY BURGESS
- □ 374. BOB LOCKER
- □ 398. DANNY CATER
- □ 413. JOHN ROMANO
- □ 426. TEAM CARD
- □ 448. EDDIE STANKY(M)
- □ 465. DON BUFORD
- □ 486. TOMMY JOHN
- □ 510. HOYT WILHELM
- □ 529. LEE ELIA
- □ 529. DENNIS HIGGINS(R)
- □ 529. BILL VOSS(R)
- □ 560. JOEL HORLEN
- □ 577. JACK LAMABE
- □ 590. BILL SKOWRON

CINCINNATI REDS

- □ 12. JOHN TSITOURIS
- □ 30. PETE ROSE
- □ 59. TEAM CARD
- □ 72. TONY PEREZ
- □ 89. TED DAVIDSON
- □ 119. ART SHAMSKY
- □ 140. JIM MALONEY
- □ 159. CHICO RUIZ
- □ 180. VADA PINSON
- □ 196. DON PAVLETICH
- □ 214. TOMMY HARPER
- □ 233. DOM ZANNI
- □ 250. SAM ELLIS
- □ 269. DON HEFFNER(M)
- □ 272. JACK BALDSCHUN
- □ 292. JIM COKER
- □ 311. TOMMY HELMS(R)
- □ 311. DICK SIMPSON(R)
- □ 334. MARTY KEOUGH
- □ 357. GERRY ARRIGO
- □ 370. LEO CARDENAS
- □ 389. JIM O'TOOLE
- □ 406. JOE JAY
- □ 424. LEE MAY(R)
- □ 424. DARRELL OSTEEN(R)
- □ 440. DERON JOHNSON
- □ 459. BILL MCCOOL
- □ 483. JOE NUXHALL
- □ 494. GORDY COLEMAN
- □ 507. JOHN EDWARDS
- □ 556. MEL QUEEN

CLEVELAND INDIANS

- □ 16. LARRY BROWN
- □ 44. BILL DAVIS(R)
- □ 44. TOM KELLEY(R)
- □ 65. LEON WAGNER
- □ 88. FRED WHITFIELD
- □ 109. RALPH TERRY
- □ 128. JIM LANDIS
- □ 129. JACK KRALICK
- □ 133. DON MCMAHON
- □ 150. ROCKY COLAVITO
- □ 169. DUKE SIMS
- □ 197. SONNY SIEBERT
- □ 231. FLOYD WEAVER
- □ 266. PEDRO GONZALES
- □ 285. LUIS TIANT
- □ 303. TEAM CARD
- □ 325. VIC DAVALILLO
- □ 339. DEL CRANDALL
- □ 371. LEE STANGE
- □ 391. CHUCK HINTON
- □ 415. MAX ALVIS
- □ 432. BOB HEFFNER
- □ 452. JOE AZCUE
- □ 470. SAM MCDOWELL
- □ 488. GEORGE BANKS
- □ 501. JOHN O'DONOGHUE
- □ 508. STEVE HARGAN
- □ 525. GARY BELL
- □ 538. BOB ALLEN
- □ 552. BIRDIE TEBBETTS
- □ 567. DICK HOWSER
- □ 581. TONY MARTINEZ
- □ 594. CHICO SALMON

DETROIT TIGERS

- □ 20. WILLIE HORTON
- □ 38. RON NISCHWITZ
- □ 58. DAVE WICKERSHAM
- □ 81. RAY OYLER
- □ 98. DON DEMETER
- □ 113. HANK AGUIRRE
- □ 145. BILL FREEHAN
- □ 161. JERRY LUMPE
- □ 187. CHUCK DRESSEN(M)
- □ 198. MICKEY STANLEY
- □ 209. FRITZ FISHER(R)
- □ 209. JOHN HILLER(R)
- □ 239. ORLANDO PENA
- □ 253. DON WERT
- □ 267. JOE SPARMA
- □ 289. LARRY SHERRY
- □ 315. NORM CASH
- □ 337. FRED GLADDING
- □ 362. GATES BROWN
- □ 378. DICK TRACEWSKI
- □ 410. AL KALINE
- □ 429. BILL MONBOUQUETTE
- □ 455. MICKEY LOLICH
- □ 472. TERRY FOX
- □ 495. DICK MCAULIFFE
- □ 509. JAKE WOOD
- □ 527. JULIO NAVARRO
- □ 540. DENNY MCLAIN
- □ 554. JIM NORTHRUP
- □ 569. ORLANDO MCFARLANE
- □ 583. TEAM CARD
- □ 597. JOHN SULLIVAN

HOUSTON ASTROS

- □ 21. DON NOTTEBART
- □ 45. JIM GENTILE
- □ 64. BOB BRUCE
- □ 86. JOHN BATEMAN
- □ 106. RUSTY STAUB
- □ 122. JOE GAINES
- □ 147. LUM HARRIS(M)
- □ 162. LEE MAYE
- □ 174. RON TAYLOR
- □ 195. JOE MORGAN
- □ 228. LARRY DIERKER
- □ 244. CHUCK HARRISON(R)
- □ 244. SONNY JACKSON(R)
- □ 258. DAVE GIUSTI
- □ 297. JIM OWENS
- □ 313. CHRIS ZACHARY

- □ 352. BOB ASPROMONTE
- □ 377. TURK FARRELL
- □ 394. RON BRAND
- □ 414. DAN COOMBS
- □ 431. WALT BOND
- □ 451. BARRY LATMAN
- □ 504. GRADY HATTON(M)
- □ 520. JIM WYNN
- □ 530. ROBIN ROBERTS
- □ 539. BILL HEATH(R)
- □ 539. CARROLL SEMBERA(R)
- □ 548. GARY KROLL
- □ 557. FELIX MANTILLA
- □ 566. MIKE CUELLAR
- □ 576. DAVE NICHOLSON
- □ 586. CLAUDE RAYMOND
- □ 596. NATE COLBERT(R)
- □ 596. GREG SIMS(R)

JIM HUNTER pitcher

KANSAS CITY ATHLETICS

- □ 18. ROLAND SHELDON
- □ 36. JIM HUNTER
- □ 55. KEN HARRELSON
- □ 74. DON MOSSI
- □ 107. LARRY STAHL(R)
- □ 107. RON TOMPKINS(R)
- □ 143. JOSE TARTABULL
- □ 157. RENE LACHEMANN
- □ 175. BERT CAMPANERIS
- □ 201. JIM DICKSON
- □ 236. MIKE HERSHBERGER
- □ 256. LEW KRAUSSE
- □ 287. JACK AKER
- □ 309. DIEGO SEGUI
- □ 332. BILLY BRYAN
- □ 366. WAYNE CAUSEY
- □ 382. PHIL ROOF
- □ 403. FRED TALBOT
- □ 422. ED CHARLES
- □ 433. ALVIN DARK(M)
- □ 458. MANNY JIMENEZ
- □ 492. TEAM CARD
- □ 521. JOHN WYATT
- □ 532. AURELIO MONTEAGUDO
- □ 545. DICK GREEN
- □ 568. PAUL LINDBLAD(R)
- □ 568. RON STONE(R)
- □ 588. CHUCK DOBSON(R)
- □ 588. KEN SUAREZ(R)

LOS ANGELES DODGERS

- □ 13. LOU JOHNSON
- □ 41. DON LE JOHN
- □ 57. JIM LEFEBVRE
- □ 75. TOMMY DAVIS
- □ 100. SANDY KOUFAX
- □ 116. WALTER ALSTON(M)
- □ 134. WES PARKER
- □ 158. JIM BREWER
- □ 171. NICK WILLHITE
- □ 189. JOHN ROSEBORO
- □ 208. BOB L. MILLER
- □ 238. TEAM CARD
- □ 257. JEFF TORBORG
- □ 270. CLAUDE OSTEEN
- □ 288. BILL SINGER(R)

☐ 288. DON SUTTON(R)
☐ 314. HECTOR VALLE
☐ 330. RON FAIRLY
☐ 347. PHIL REGAN
☐ 364. NATE OLIVER
☐ 387. HOWIE REED
☐ 407. JOHN KENNEDY
☐ 430. DON DRYSDALE
☐ 449. JOE MOELLER
☐ 468. JOHNNY PODRES
☐ 487. AL FERRARA
☐ 535. WILLIE DAVIS
☐ 555. RON PERRANOSKI
☐ 573. DERRELL GRIFFITH
☐ 591. BART SHIRLEY(R)

MINNESOTA TWINS

☐   3. SAM MELE(M)
☐ 22. JOE NOSSEK
☐ 40. JIM GRANT
☐ 56. SANDY VALDESPINO
☐ 73. JERRY ZIMMERMAN
☐ 97. JIM MERRITT
☐ 120. HARMON KILLEBREW
☐ 181. AL WORTHINGTON
☐ 190. JIMMIE HALL
☐ 207. FRANK QUILICI
☐ 240. EARL BATTEY
☐ 264. ANDY KOSCO(R)
☐ 264. TED UHLAENDER(R)
☐ 283. JIM PERRY
☐ 305. CAMILO PASCUAL
☐ 327. BERNIE ALLEN
☐ 345. BOB ALLISON
☐ 367. MEL NELSON
☐ 388. DON MINCHER
☐ 400. ZOILO VERSALLES
☐ 445. JIM KAAT
☐ 450. TONY OLIVA
☐ 473. RICH ROLLINS
☐ 493. JOHN KLIPPSTEIN
☐ 512. DICK STIGMAN(B)
☐ 526. TEAM CARD
☐ 546. DWIGHT SIEBLER
☐ 563. PETE CIMINO(R)
☐ 563. CESAR TOVAR(R)
☐ 582. GARRY ROGGENBURK

NEW YORK METS

■ 17. JOHN STEPHENSON
☐ 35. RON SWOBODA
■ 51. GORDON RICHARDSON
☐ 67. CLEON JONES(R)
☐ 67. DICK SELMA(R)
■ 87. DAN NAPOLEON
☐ 108. BOBBY KLAUS
☐ 124. TUG MCGRAW
☐ 154. CHUCK HILLER
☐ 172. TEAM CARD
■ 188. AL LUPLOW
☐ 191. DARRELL SUTHERLAND
☐ 212. ED KRANEPOOL
☐ 241. DENNIS RIBANT
■ 262. JACK HAMILTON
☐ 282. JOHNNY LEWIS
☐ 302. ERNIE BOWMAN
☐ 316. JACK FISHER
☐ 328. JERRY GROTE
☐ 341. WES WESTRUM(M)
☐ 360. RON HUNT
☐ 385. KEN BOYER
☐ 402. JIM HICKMAN
☐ 421. ROY MCMILLAN
☐ 443. BILL WAKEFIELD
☐ 464. LARRY BEARNARTH
☐ 480. DICK STUART
☐ 516. EDDIE BRESSOUD
☐ 534. DAVE EILERS(R)
☐ 534. ROB GARDNER(R)
☐ 561. CHOO CHOO COLEMAN
☐ 574. BILL HELPER(R)
☐ 574. BILL MURPHY(R)
☐ 589. LOU KLIMCHOCK

NEW YORK YANKEES

☐   9. CLETE BOYER
☐ 31. JACK CULLEN
☐ 50. MICKEY MANTLE
☐ 68. HAL RENIFF
☐ 79. JOE PEPITONE
☐ 92. TEAM CARD
☐ 117. JAKE GIBBS
☐ 138. ROGER REPOZ
☐ 160. WHITEY FORD
☐ 177. HECTOR LOPEZ
☐ 186. RUBEN AMARO
☐ 205. TOM TRESH
☐ 234. RICH BECK(R)
☐ 234. ROY WHITE(R)
☐ 276. JIM BOUTON
☐ 296. JOHNNY KEANE(M)
☐ 323. RAY BARKER
☐ 350. MEL STOTTLEMYRE
☐ 365. ROGER MARIS
☐ 384. AL DOWNING
☐ 405. ELSTON HOWARD
☐ 439. PEDRO RAMOS
☐ 469. BOBBY MURCER(R)
☐ 469. DOOLEY WOMACK(R)
☐ 490. BOBBY RICHARDSON
☐ 503. STEVE HAMILTON
☐ 519. BOB FRIEND
☐ 547. HORACE CLARKE
☐ 584. FRANK FERNANDEZ(R)
☐ 584. FRITZ PETERSON(R)

PHILADELPHIA PHILLIES

☐   4. RAY CULP
☐ 32. ADOLFO PHILLIPS
☐ 80. RICHIE ALLEN
☐ 104. ALEX JOHNSON
☐ 121. RAY HERBERT
☐ 151. GARY WAGNER
☐ 170. COOKIE ROJAS
☐ 202. CLAY DALRYMPLE
☐ 230. JOHNNY CALLISON
☐ 254. FERGUSON JENKINS(R)
☐ 254. BILL SORRELL(R)
☐ 284. BOBBY WINE
☐ 304. JOHN HERRNSTEIN
☐ 324. JOHN BOOZER
☐ 359. JOHN BRIGGS
☐ 383. JACKIE BRANDT
☐ 397. BILL WHITE
☐ 411. GENE MAUCH(M)
☐ 435. JIM BUNNING
☐ 463. TEAM CARD
☐ 478. TONY GONZALEZ
☐ 506. BO BELINSKY
☐ 522. PHIL LINZ
☐ 543. ROGER CRAIG
☐ 585. TONY TAYLOR
☐ 591. GRANT JACKSON(R)
☐ 595. LARRY JACKSON

PITTSBURGH PIRATES

☐ 15. VERN LAW
☐ 33. JIM PAGLIARONI
☐ 54. JOSE PAGAN
☐ 71. FRANK CARPIN
☐ 112. MANNY MOTA
☐ 123. FRANK BORK(R)
☐ 123. JERRY MAY(R)
☐ 144. DON SCHWALL
☐ 182. JERRY LYNCH
☐ 210. BILL MAZEROSKI
☐ 235. DON CARDWELL
☐ 248. PETE MIKKELSEN
☐ 255. WILLIE STARGELL
☐ 300. BOB CLEMENTE
☐ 318. HARRY WALKER(M)
☐ 336. GENE ALLEY
☐ 344. STEVE BLASS
☐ 353. AL MCBEAN
☐ 375. DONN CLENDENON
☐ 404. TEAM CARD
☐ 425. BOB VEALE
☐ 441. TOMMIE SISK
☐ 461. ROY FACE
☐ 485. BOB BAILEY

☐ 498. LUKE WALKER(R)
☐ 498. WOODY FRYMAN(R)
☐ 528. JESSE GONDER
☐ 551. BOB PURKEY
☐ 571. DAVE L. ROBERTS
☐ 592. ANDRE RODGERS

ST. LOUIS CARDINALS

☐   7. TRACY STALLARD
☐ 26. RAY SADECKI
☐ 60. CURT FLOOD
☐ 76. RED SCHOENDIENST(M)
☐ 91. BOB UECKER
☐ 103. DICK GROAT
☐ 125. LOU BROCK
☐ 137. PAT CORRALES
☐ 142. DON DENNIS
☐ 163. TITO FRANCONA
☐ 179. DENNIS AUST(R)
☐ 179. BOB TOLAN
☐ 206. ALVIN JACKSON
☐ 243. NELSON BRILES
☐ 275. TIM MCCARVER
☐ 293. MIKE SHANNON
☐ 320. BOB GIBSON
☐ 338. DAL MAXVILL
☐ 358. CHARLIE SMITH
☐ 379. TEAM CARD
☐ 399. RAY WASHBURN
☐ 418. PHIL GAGLIANO
☐ 436. JULIAN JAVIER
☐ 454. JERRY BUCHEK
☐ 471. BOB SKINNER
☐ 489. CURT SIMMONS
☐ 514. HAL WOODESHICK
☐ 544. JOE HOERNER(R)
☐ 544. GEORGE KERNEK(R)
☐ 544. JIMMY WILLIAMS(R)
☐ 570. ART MAHAFFEY

SAN FRANCISCO GIANTS

☐   1. WILLIE MAYS
☐ 19. TEAM CARD
☐ 39. KEN HENDERSON
☐ 61. BOB BOLIN
☐ 78. FRANK LINZY
☐ 94. MATTY ALOU
☐ 115. BILL R. HENRY
☐ 132. ORLANDO CEPEDA
☐ 176. JIM DAVENPORT
☐ 242. JESUS ALOU
☐ 260. BOB SHAW
☐ 271. HAL LANIER
☐ 295. JIM HART
☐ 308. TOM HALLER
☐ 331. RON HERBEL
☐ 349. CAP PETERSON
☐ 373. JACK HIATT(R)
☐ 373. DICK ESTELLE(R)
☐ 395. LEN GABRIELSON
☐ 420. JUAN MARICHAL
☐ 437. AL STANEK
☐ 457. JOE GIBBON
☐ 474. DICK SCHOFIELD
☐ 496. LINDY MCDANIEL
☐ 511. BOB BARTON(R)
☐ 511. TITO FUENTES(R)
☐ 524. OLLIE BROWN(R)
☐ 524. DON MASON(R)
☐ 537. HERMAN FRANKS(M)
☐ 550. WILLIE MCCOVEY
☐ 572. BOB PRIDDY
☐ 587. DICK BERTELL
☐ 598. GAYLORD PERRY

WASHINGTON SENATORS

☐ 11. BRANT ALYEA(R)
☐ 11. PETE CRAIG(R)
☐ 29. MIKE BRUMLEY
☐ 46. HOWIE KOPLITZ
☐ 69. KEN HAMLIN
☐ 77. JOHNNY ORSINO
☐ 95. PETE RICHERT
☐ 118. MIKE MCCORMICK
☐ 149. DICK NEN
☐ 165. DON LOCK

☐ 194. TEAM CARD
☐ 211. FRANK KREUTZER
☐ 251. ED BRINKMAN
☐ 274. BUSTER NARUM
☐ 294. STEVE RIDZIK
☐ 312. BOB SAVERINE
☐ 333. JOE COLEMAN
☐ 333. JIM FRENCH(R)
☐ 351. FRED VALENTINE
☐ 369. JIM KING
☐ 386. GIL HODGES(M)
☐ 401. KEN MCMULLEN
☐ 416. PHIL ORTEGA
☐ 434. WILLIE KIRKLAND
☐ 453. RON KLINE
☐ 479. JIM HANNAN
☐ 515. FRANK HOWARD
☐ 531. JOE CUNNINGHAM
☐ 549. AL CLOSTER(R)
☐ 549. CASEY COX(R)
☐ 564. BOB CHANCE
☐ 593. DOUG CAMILLI

FRED VALENTINE   outfield

1967 TOPPS (609)
2 1/2″ X 3 1/2″

RICK REICHARDT OUTFIELD

ANGELS

ATLANTA BRAVES

☐ 18. GENE OLIVER
☐ 35. RICO CARTY
☐ 57. PAT JARVIS
☐ 89. FELIX MILLAN
☐ 101. KEN JOHNSON
☐ 113. DAVE NICHOLSON
☐ 119. WADE BLASINGAME
☐ 138. DICK KELLEY
☐ 179. CHARLEY VAUGHN(R)
☐ 179. CECIL UPSHAW(R)
☐ 199. BILLY HITCHCOCK(M)
☐ 219. CLAY CARROLL
☐ 250. HANK AARON
☐ 267. DON SCHWALL
☐ 288. DENVER LEMASTER
☐ 307. JIM BEAUCHAMP
☐ 328. CLETE BOYER
☐ 350. JOE TORRE

☐ 372. MIKE DE LA HOZ
☐ 417. BOB BRUCE
☐ 435. MACK JONES
☐ 456. PHIL NIEKRO
☐ 477. TEAM CARD
☐ 490. TONY CLONINGER
☐ 504. ORLANDO MARTINEZ
☐ 518. DENIS MENKE
☐ 530. FELIPE ALOU
☐ 546. WOODY WOODWARD
☐ 566. GARY GEIGER
☐ 576. RAMON HERNANDEZ(R)
☐ 591. TY CLINE

BALTIMORE ORIOLES

☐ 22. GENE BRABENDER
☐ 38. BOB W. JOHNSON
☐ 60. LUIS APARICIO
☐ 82. STEVE BARBER
☐ 100. FRANK ROBINSON
☐ 125. MOE DRABOWSKY
☐ 141. JOHN MILLER
☐ 163. VIC ROZNOVSKY
☐ 180. CURT BLEFARY
☐ 204. MIKE EPSTEIN(R)
☐ 204. TOM PHOEBUS(R)
☐ 230. BOOG POWELL
☐ 251. WOODY HELD
☐ 271. EDDIE WATT
☐ 302. TEAM CARD
☐ 319. PAUL BLAIR
☐ 329. CHARLEY LAU
☐ 345. STU MILLER
☐ 363. DAVE A. JOHNSON
☐ 382. DAVE MCNALLY
☐ 405. RUSS SNYDER
☐ 434. EDDIE FISHER
☐ 457. ANDY ETCHEBARREN
☐ 475. JIM PALMER
☐ 491. SAM BOWENS
☐ 507. ED BARNOWSKI(R)
☐ 507. LARRY HANEY(R)
☐ 534. HANK BAUER(M)
☐ 558. MARK BELANGER(R)
☐ 558. BILL DILLMAN(R)
☐ 585. WALLY BUNKER
☐ 600. BROOKS ROBINSON

BOSTON RED SOX

☐ 7. DON MCMAHON
☐ 36. BOB TILLMAN
☐ 56. JOSE TARTABULL
☐ 75. GEORGE SCOTT
☐ 99. LEE STANGE
☐ 117. DARRELL BRANDON
☐ 139. DALTON JONES
☐ 161. DICK WILLIAMS(M)
☐ 184. GEORGE THOMAS
☐ 206. DENNIS BENNETT
☐ 223. MIKE RYAN
☐ 261. JOHN WYATT
☐ 280. TONY CONIGLIARO
☐ 297. DAVE MOREHEAD
☐ 314. MIKE ANDREWS(R)
☐ 314. REGGIE SMITH(R)
☐ 331. JOE FOY
☐ 342. HANK FISCHER
☐ 355. CARL YASTRZEMSKI
☐ 371. JIM LONBORG
☐ 429. GARRY ROGGENBURK
☐ 444. GEORGE SMITH
☐ 473. JOSE SANTIAGO
☐ 528. RICO PETROCELLI
☐ 547. RUSS GIBSON(R)
☐ 547. BILL ROHR(R)
☐ 572. DON DEMETER
☐ 594. DAN OSINSKI
☐ 596. GALEN CISCO
☐ 604. TEAM CARD

CALIFORNIA ANGELS

☐ 19. JIM MCGLOTHLIN
☐ 34. PETE CIMINO
☐ 40. RICK REICHARDT
☐ 58. PAUL SCHAAL
☐ 79. BUBBA MORTON
☐ 104. MINNIE ROJAS

☐ 122. GEORGE BRUNET
☐ 147. TOM EGAN
☐ 175. BOBBY KNOOP
☐ 193. JOSE CARDENAL
☐ 213. JAY JOHNSTONE
☐ 249. NICK WILLHITE
☐ 265. LOU BURDETTE
☐ 281. BOB RODGERS
☐ 293. ED KIRKPATRICK
☐ 312. DON MINCHER
☐ 327. TEAM CARD
☐ 343. TOM SATRIANO
☐ 367. BILL KELSO(R)
☐ 367. DON WALLACE(R)
☐ 385. JIM FREGOSI
☐ 401. JIM COATES
☐ 432. JIMMIE HALL
☐ 451. FRED NEWMAN
☐ 469. LEN GABRIELSON
☐ 494. BILL RIGNEY(M)
☐ 496. ORLANDO MCFARLANE
☐ 513. MARCELINO LOPEZ
☐ 549. JACK SANFORD
☐ 584. JIM PIERSALL

CHICAGO CUBS

☐ 16. BILL HANDS
☐ 39. CURT SIMMONS
☐ 70. RON SANTO
☐ 87. GEORGE ALTMAN
☐ 106. RANDY HUNDLEY
☐ 124. JIM STEWART
☐ 148. ADOLFO PHILLIPS
☐ 168. RAY CULP
☐ 171. CAL KOONCE
☐ 185. KEN HOLTZMAN
☐ 215. ERNIE BANKS
☐ 256. BOB HENDLEY
☐ 272. BILL CONNORS(R)
☐ 272. DAVE DOWLING(R)
☐ 296. GLENN BECKERT
☐ 315. BILLY WILLIAMS
☐ 333. FERGUSON JENKINS
☐ 354. TEAM CARD
☐ 388. ARNOLD EARLEY
☐ 419. DON KESSINGER
☐ 439. BYRON BROWNE
☐ 458. LEE THOMAS
☐ 481. LEO DUROCHER(M)
☐ 497. RON CAMPBELL
☐ 524. FELIX MANTILLA
☐ 536. JOE NIEKRO(R)
☐ 536. PAUL POPOVICH(R)
☐ 552. TED SAVAGE
☐ 576. NORM GIGON(R)
☐ 578. JOHN BOCCABELLA
☐ 608. RICH NYE(R)
☐ 608. JOHN UPHAM(R)

CHICAGO WHITE SOX

☐ 9. RON HANSEN
☐ 29. TOMMY MCCRAW
☐ 52. DENNIS HIGGINS
☐ 67. KEN BERRY
☐ 81. EDDIE STANKY(M)
☐ 107. JOEL HORLEN
☐ 159. BRUCE HOWARD
☐ 178. JOHN BUZHARDT.
☐ 208. JACK LAMABE
☐ 232. DON BUFORD
☐ 259. DON DENNIS
☐ 286. WAYNE CAUSEY
☐ 310. GARY PETERS
☐ 338. BOB LOCKER
☐ 357. BILL SKOWRON
☐ 373. DUANE JOSEPHSON(R)
☐ 373. FRED KLAGES(R)
☐ 391. WILBUR WOOD
☐ 406. LEE ELIA
☐ 422. HOYT WILHELM
☐ 436. PETE WARD
☐ 455. TOMMIE AGEE
☐ 467. JIM O'TOOLE
☐ 484. JERRY ADAIR
☐ 506. SMOKY BURGESS
☐ 532. JIM HICKS
☐ 538. J.C. MARTIN

☐ 556. AL WEIS
☐ 573. TEAM CARD
☐ 598. WALT WILLIAMS(R)
☐ 598. ED STROUD(R)
☐ 609. TOMMY JOHN

CINCINNATI REDS

☐ 6. DICK SIMPSON
☐ 21. DAVE BRISTOL(M)
☐ 44. JOE NUXHALL
☐ 61. GORDY COLEMAN
☐ 80. JIM MALONEY
☐ 96. ART SHAMSKY
☐ 114. JACK BALDSCHUN
☐ 120. FLOYD ROBINSON
☐ 135. DERON JOHNSON
☐ 158. JIMMIE COKER
☐ 176. SAMMY ELLIS
☐ 202. JOHNNY EDWARDS
☐ 222. DARRELL OSTEEN(R)
☐ 222. LEE MAY(R)
☐ 254. MILT PAPPAS
☐ 269. DON NOTTEBART
☐ 292. DON PAVLETICH
☐ 325. CHICO CARDENAS
☐ 339. CHICO RUIZ
☐ 353. BILL MCCOOL
☐ 374. MEL QUEEN
☐ 392. TOMMY HARPER
☐ 407. TEAM CARD
☐ 430. PETE ROSE
☐ 453. AURELIO MONTEAGUDO
☐ 476. TONY PEREZ
☐ 488. GERRY ARRIGO
☐ 505. TOMMY HELMS
☐ 519. TED DAVIDSON
☐ 550. VADA PINSON
☐ 597. TED ABERNATHY

CLEVELAND INDIANS

☐ 3. DUKE SIMS
☐ 24. BOB ALLEN
☐ 43. CHICO SALMON
☐ 69. VIC DAVALILLO
☐ 95. SONNY SIEBERT
☐ 127. JOHN O'DONOGHUE
☐ 145. LARRY BROWN
☐ 174. DICK RADATZ
☐ 189. CHUCK HINTON
☐ 214. TOM KELLEY
☐ 253. BILL DAVIS(R)
☐ 253. GUS GIL(R)
☐ 258. LEE MAYE
☐ 275. FRED WHITFIELD
☐ 295. SAM MCDOWELL
☐ 316. JACK KRALICK
☐ 336. JOE AZCUE
☐ 360. LEON WAGNER
☐ 377. LUIS TIANT
☐ 397. WILLIE SMITH
☐ 424. PEDRO GONZALEZ
☐ 440. STEVE HARGAN
☐ 479. GARY BELL
☐ 499. GEORGE CULVER(R)
☐ 499. JOSE VIDAL(R)
☐ 520. MAX ALVIS
☐ 544. TEAM CARD
☐ 563. JOE ADCOCK
☐ 580. ROCKY COLAVITO

DETROIT TIGERS

☐ 13. JOE SPARMA
☐ 30. AL KALINE
☐ 48. BILL FREEHAN
☐ 72. GEORGE KORINCE(R)
☐ 72. JOHN MATCHICK(R)
☐ 88. MICKEY LOLICH
☐ 112. DAVE WICKERHAM
☐ 134. GATES BROWN
☐ 170. DICK MCAULIFFE
☐ 192. FRED GLADDING
☐ 247. JERRY LUMPE
☐ 263. HANK AGUIRRE
☐ 284. JOHNNY PODRES
☐ 305. EARL WILSON
☐ 321. MAYO SMITH(M)

☐ 352. RAY OYLER
☐ 378. TEAM CARD
☐ 394. JAKE WOOD
☐ 408. JIM NORTHRUP
☐ 420. DENNIS MCLAIN
☐ 449. ORLANDO PENA
☐ 465. WILLIE HORTON
☐ 482. BILL MONBOUQUETTE
☐ 511. DON WERT
☐ 526. PAT DOBSON(R)
☐ 526. GEORGE KORINCE(R)
☐ 540. NORM CASH
☐ 559. DICK TRACEWSKI
☐ 571. LARRY SHERRY
☐ 588. JOHNNY KLIPPSTEIN
☐ 607. MICKEY STANLEY

HOUSTON ASTROS

☐ 8. CHUCK HARRISON
☐ 28. BARRY LATMAN
☐ 51. DAVE ADLESH(R)
☐ 51. WES BALES(R)
☐ 73. RUSTY STAUB
☐ 97. MIKE CUELLAR
☐ 136. CARROLL SEMBERA
☐ 166. ED MATHEWS
☐ 172. BILL HEATH
☐ 190. TURK FARRELL
☐ 212. CHRIS ZACHARY
☐ 231. JOHN BATEMAN
☐ 274. BOB ASPROMONTE
☐ 298. RON DAVIS
☐ 318. DAVE GUISTI
☐ 337. JOE MORGAN
☐ 347. GRADY HATTON(M)
☐ 364. CLAUDE RAYMOND
☐ 390. JIM WYNN
☐ 412. NORM MILLER(R)
☐ 412. DOUG RADER(R)
☐ 415. SONNY JACKSON
☐ 447. BOB BELINSKY
☐ 464. DAN COOMBS
☐ 483. JIM LANDIS
☐ 498. LARRY DIERKER
☐ 502. DERRELL GRIFFITH
☐ 543. DAN SCHNEIDER
☐ 564. ALONZO HARRIS(R)
☐ 564. AARON POINTER(R)
☐ 582. JIM OWENS

KANSAS CITY ATHLETICS

☐ 17. JIM GOSGER
☐ 33. SAL BANDO(R)
☐ 33. RANDY SCHWARTZ(R)
☐ 54. DICK GREEN
☐ 74. WES STOCK
☐ 90. JIM NASH
☐ 110. JACK AKER
☐ 129. PHIL ROOF
☐ 157. DANNY CATER
☐ 182. ED CHARLES
☐ 209. JOE NOSSEK
☐ 227. PAUL LINDBLAD
☐ 262. TEAM CARD
☐ 282. JOHNNY ODOM
☐ 303. GIL BLANCO

☐ 323. MIKE HERSHBERGER
☐ 344. OSSIE CHAVARRIA
☐ 369. JIM HUNTER
☐ 389. AL DARK(M)
☐ 416. ROGER REPOZ
☐ 438. CHUCK DOBSON
☐ 471. RENE LACHEMANN
☐ 515. BERT CAMPANERIS
☐ 542. RICK MONDAY(R)
☐ 542. TONY PIERCE(R)
☐ 565. LEW KRAUSSE
☐ 599. BOB DULIBA
☐ 603. TIM TALTON(R)
☐ 603. RAMON WEBSTER(R)

LOS ANGELES DODGERS

☐ 12. JIMMY CAMPANIS(R)
☐ 12. BILL SINGER(R)
☐ 31. JIM BREWER
☐ 32. BOB BAILEY
☐ 55. DON DRYSDALE
☐ 76. JIM BARBIERI
☐ 94. RON FAIRLY
☐ 111. JOHN KENNEDY
☐ 130. PHIL REGAN
☐ 149. JOE MOELLER
☐ 160. WILLIE DAVIS
☐ 197. RON PERRANOSKI
☐ 218. WES PARKER
☐ 260. JIM LEFEBVRE
☐ 276. BRUCE BRUBAKER
☐ 294. WALT ALSTON(M)
☐ 313. BOB LEE
☐ 330. CLAUDE OSTEEN
☐ 346. JIM HICKMAN
☐ 365. JOHN ROSEBORO
☐ 381. DICK SCHOFIELD
☐ 398. JEFF TORBORG
☐ 410. LOU JOHNSON
☐ 428. TOM HUTTON(R)
☐ 428. GENE MICHAEL(R)
☐ 445. DON SUTTON
☐ 461. BOB L. MILLER
☐ 503. TEAM CARD
☐ 514. JOHN WERHAS
☐ 525. RON HUNT
☐ 539. DICK EGAN
☐ 557. AL FERRARA

MINNESOTA TWINS

☐ 15. EARL BATTEY
☐ 50. TONY OLIVA
☐ 98. RICH ROLLINS
☐ 133. RON KLINE
☐ 137. RON CLARK(R)
☐ 137. JIM OLLOM(R)
☐ 164. DWIGHT SIEBLER
☐ 194. BOB ALLISON
☐ 211. TEAM CARD
☐ 224. WALT BOND
☐ 246. JIM PERRY
☐ 270. ZOILO VERSALLES
☐ 300. JIM KAAT
☐ 317. CESAR TOVAR
☐ 366. ANDY KOSCO
☐ 380. DEAN CHANCE
☐ 399. AL WORTHINGTON
☐ 418. SAM MELE(M)
☐ 431. TEN UHLAENDER
☐ 446. RUSS NIXON
☐ 460. HARMON KILLEBREW
☐ 486. RICH REESE(R)
☐ 486. BILL WHITBY(R)
☐ 501. JERRY ZIMMERMAN
☐ 523. JIM MERRITT
☐ 545. JIM GRANT
☐ 569. ROD CAREW(R)
☐ 575. DAVE BOSWELL

NEW YORK METS

☐ 2. JACK HAMILTON
■ 23. LARRY ELLIOT
☐ 42. TEAM CARD
◆ 59. RALPH TERRY
☐ 91. JOHNNY LEWIS
▲ 105. KEN BOYER

1967 Topps

■ 121. ED BRESSOUD
■ 144. BILL HEPLER
☐ 165. CLEON JONES
■ 198. CHUCK HILLER
☐ 217. ROB GARDNER
■ 264. RON SWOBODA
☐ 287. GREG GOOSSEN(R)
☐ 287. BART SHIRLEY(R)
☐ 306. BUD HARRELSON
☐ 348. TUG MCGRAW
■ 370. TOMMY DAVIS
■ 386. DICK SELMA
☐ 413. JERRY GROTE
☐ 433. AL LUPLOW
☐ 452. ED KRANEPOOL
☐ 470. BOB SHAW
☐ 487. TOMMIE REYNOLDS
☐ 522. JOHN STEPHENSON
☐ 533. JACK FISHER
☐ 537. CHUCK ESTRADA
☐ 555. DON CARDWELL
☐ 561. SANDY ALOMAR
☐ 568. JACKIE SULLIVAN
☐ 574. JERRY BUCHEK
☐ 581. BILL DENEHY(R)
☐ 581. TOM SEAVER(R)
☐ 587. DON SHAW(R)
☐ 593. WES WESTRUM(M)
☐ 606. RON TAYLOR

NEW YORK YANKEES

☐   5. WHITEY FORD
☐   25. ELSTON HOWARD
☐   77. DOOLEY WOMACK
☐   93. STAN BAHNSEN(R)
☐   93. BOBBY MURCER(R)
☐ 131. TEAM CARD
☐ 150. MICKEY MANTLE
☐ 169. HORACE CLARKE
☐ 201. HAL RENIFF
☐ 225. MEL STOTTLEMYRE
☐ 257. CHARLEY SMITH
☐ 277. STEVE WHITAKER
☐ 289. TOM TRESH
☐ 308. AL DOWNING
☐ 340. JOE PEPITONE
☐ 358. RUBEN AMARO
☐ 375. JAKE GIBBS
☐ 393. JIM BOUTON
☐ 411. DICK HOWSER
☐ 426. LOU CLINTON
☐ 442. BILL ROBINSON(R)
☐ 442. JOE VERBANIC(R)
☐ 468. RALPH HOUK(M)
☐ 495. FRITZ PETERSON
☐ 517. FRED TALBOT
☐ 553. MIKE HEGAN(R)
☐ 553. THAD TILLOTSON(R)
☐ 567. STEVE HAMILTON
☐ 583. RAY BARKER
☐ 601. BILL BRYAN

PHILADELPHIA PHILLIES

☐   14. PHIL LINZ
☐   37. RICK WISE
☐   53. CLAY DALRYMPLE
☐   68. BOB BUHL
☐   85. JOHNNY CALLISON
☐ 102. TEAM CARD
☐ 126. TONY TAYLOR
☐ 142. JACKIE BRANDT
☐ 181. TERRY FOX
☐ 187. PEDRO RAMOS
☐ 205. DICK GROAT
☐ 229. LARRY JACKSON
☐ 248. GENE MAUCH(M)
☐ 268. JOHN BRIGGS
☐ 290. BILL WHITE
☐ 326. BOB UECKER
☐ 359. DICK ELLSWORTH
☐ 376. DON LOCK
☐ 395. CHRIS SHORT
☐ 402. GRANT JACKSON(R)
☐ 402. BILLY WILSON(R)
☐ 427. RUBEN GOMEZ
☐ 443. TITO FRANCONA
☐ 450. RICHIE ALLEN

☐ 466. BOBBY WINE
☐ 489. DOUG CLEMENS
☐ 508. DICK HALL
☐ 529. GARY WAGNER
☐ 548. TONY GONZALEZ
☐ 560. JIM BUNNING
☐ 587. GARY SUTHERLAND(R)
☐ 595. COOKIE ROJAS

PITTSBURGH PIRATES

☐   10. MATTY ALOU
☐   49. ROY FACE
☐   66. MANNY MOTA
☐   84. TOMMIE SISK
☐ 123. JIMMIE PRICE(R)
☐ 123. LUKE WALKER(R)
☐ 140. WILLIE STARGELL
☐ 162. BILLY O'DELL
☐ 183. JIM PAGLIARONI
☐ 203. AL MCBEAN
☐ 221. WOODY FRYMAN
☐ 283. GENE ALLEY
☐ 301. JESSE GONDER
☐ 322. JOSE PAGAN
☐ 335. BOB VEALE
☐ 351. VERN LAW
☐ 379. JERRY MAY
☐ 400. BOB CLEMENTE
☐ 425. PETE MIKKELSON
☐ 448. HARRY WALKER(M)
☐ 472. JOHN GELNAR(R)
☐ 472. GEORGE SPRIGGS(R)
☐ 492. TEAM CARD
☐ 510. BILL MAZEROSKI
☐ 527. DENNIS RIBANT
☐ 535. DONN CLENDENON
☐ 554. ANDRE RODGERS
☐ 562. STEVE BLASS
☐ 570. MAURY WILLS
☐ 577. BILL SHORT
☐ 586. MANNY JIMENEZ
☐ 592. JIM SHELLENBACK(R)
☐ 602. JUAN PIZARRO

ST. LOUIS CARDINALS

☐   20. ORLANDO CEPEDA
☐   41. JOE HOERNER
☐   45. ROGER MARIS
☐   78. PAT CORRALES
☐   92. RAY WASHBURN
☐ 108. ALEX JOHNSON
☐ 128. ED SPIEZIO
☐ 146. STEVE CARLTON
☐ 173. TEAM CARD
☐ 195. AL JACKSON
☐ 196. JOHN ROMANO
☐ 210. BOB GIBSON
☐ 226. JULIAN JAVIER
☐ 245. CURT FLOOD
☐ 285. LOU BROCK
☐ 304. PHIL GAGLIANO
☐ 324. HAL WOODESHICK
☐ 356. LARRY JASTER
☐ 384. JIM COSMAN(R)
☐ 384. DICK HUGHES(R)
☐ 404. NELSON BRILES
☐ 421. DAL MAXVILL
☐ 474. BOB TOLAN
☐ 485. TIM MCCARVER
☐ 512. RED SCHOENDIENST(M)
☐ 589. DAVE RICKETTS
☐ 592. RON WILLIS(R)
☐ 605. MIKE SHANNON

SAN FRANCISCO GIANTS

☐   4. HAL LANIER
☐   26. BOB PRIDDY(R)
☐   46. LINDY MCDANIEL
☐   65. TOM HALLER
☐   83. OLLIE BROWN
☐   86. MIKE MCCORMICK(B)
☐ 116. HERMAN FRANKS(M)
☐ 132. OSSIE VIRGIL
☐ 156. RON HERBEL
☐ 177. TITO FUENTES

☐ 200. WILLIE MAYS
☐ 220. JIM HART
☐ 252. BOB BOLIN
☐ 279. FRANK LINZY
☐ 299. NORM SIEBERN
☐ 320. GAYLORD PERRY
☐ 332. JESUS ALOU
☐ 341. DICK DIETZ(R)
☐ 341. BILL SORRELL(R)
☐ 368. JACK HIATT
☐ 383. KEN HENDERSON
☐ 409. RAY SADECKI
☐ 441. JIM DAVENPORT
☐ 462. BOB BARTON
☐ 480. WILLIE MCCOVEY
☐ 500. JUAN MARICHAL
☐ 516. TEAM CARD
☐ 541. JOE GIBBON
☐ 579. BILL R. HENRY

WASHINGTON SENATORS

☐   11. BARRY MOORE
☐   26. BOB PRIDDY
☐   27. BOB SAVERINE
☐   47. KEN MCMULLEN
☐   64. FRED VALENTINE
☐   71. CAMILO PASCUAL
☐   86. MIKE MCCORMICK(R)
☐ 115. PAUL CASANOVA
☐ 118. BERNIE ALLEN
☐ 167. JOE COLEMAN
☐ 167. TIM CULLEN(R)
☐ 188. KEN HARRELSON
☐ 207. JOHN ORSINO
☐ 228. GIL HODGES(M)
☐ 255. FRANK HOWARD
☐ 273. DICK LINES
☐ 291. JIM HANNAN
☐ 311. ED BRINKMAN
☐ 349. BOB CHANCE
☐ 362. DAROLD KNOWLES
☐ 387. CAP PETERSTON
☐ 403. DICK NEN
☐ 414. CASEY COX
☐ 437. TEAM CARD
☐ 459. DICK BOSMAN(R)
☐ 459. PETE CRAIG(R)
☐ 478. BOB HUMPHREYS
☐ 493. PHIL ORTEGA
☐ 509. JIM KING
☐ 551. DOUG CAMILLI
☐ 569. HANK ALLEN(R)
☐ 590. PETE RICHERT

1968 TOPPS (598)
2 1/2" X 3 1/2"

TOMMIE
AARON

ATLANTA BRAVES

- [ ] 30. JOE TORRE
- [ ] 55. FELIPE ALOU
- [ ] 76. JIM BRITTON(R)
- [ ] 76. RON REED(R)
- [ ] 93. TONY CLONINGER
- [ ] 110. HANK AARON
- [ ] 134. PAT JARVIS
- [ ] 166. CLAUDE RAYMOND
- [ ] 174. BOB TILLMAN
- [ ] 187. SONNY JACKSON
- [ ] 203. DICK KELLEY
- [ ] 221. TEAM CARD
- [ ] 241. FELIX MILLAN
- [ ] 257. PHIL NIEKRO
- [ ] 286. CECIL UPSHAW
- [ ] 304. SANDY VALDESPINO
- [ ] 323. DERON JOHNSON
- [ ] 342. KEN JOHNSON
- [ ] 394. TOMMIE AARON
- [ ] 412. CLAY CARROLL
- [ ] 439. LUMAN HARRIS(M)
- [ ] 455. RICO CARTY
- [ ] 476. WOODY WOODWARY
- [ ] 527. TITO FRANCONA
- [ ] 550. CLETE BOYER
- [ ] 578. ORLANDO MARTINEZ
- [ ] 579. MIKE LUM(R)

BALTIMORE ORIOLES

- [ ] 20. BROOKS ROBINSON
- [ ] 42. LARRY HANEY
- [ ] 56. DAVE LEONHARD(R)
- [ ] 56. DAVE MAY(R)
- [ ] 82. SAM BOWENS
- [ ] 97. TOM PHOEBUS
- [ ] 118. MARK BELANGER
- [ ] 135. PAUL BLAIR
- [ ] 163. GENE BRABENDER
- [ ] 186. EDDIE WATT
- [ ] 194. DON BUFORD
- [ ] 204. ANDY ETCHEBARREN
- [ ] 222. JIM HARDIN
- [ ] 242. MOE DRABOWSKY
- [ ] 273. DAVE A. JOHNSON
- [ ] 293. BRUCE HOWARD
- [ ] 312. CURT BLEFARY
- [ ] 334. TEAM CARD
- [ ] 354. PETE RICHERT
- [ ] 381. BOOG POWELL
- [ ] 409. FRANK PETERS(R)
- [ ] 409. RON STONE(R)
- [ ] 428. VIC ROZNOVSKY
- [ ] 456. JOHN O'DONOGHUE
- [ ] 466. BILL DILLMAN
- [ ] 478. DAVE MCNALLY
- [ ] 489. WALLY BUNKER
- [ ] 500. FRANK ROBINSON
- [ ] 513. HANK BAUER(M)
- [ ] 549. CURT MOTTON(R)
- [ ] 549. ROGER NELSON(R)
- [ ] 575. JIM PALMER

BOSTON RED SOX

- [ ] 26. DARRELL BRANDON
- [ ] 43. GARY BELL
- [ ] 61. REGGIE SMITH
- [ ] 87. DICK WILLIAMS(M)
- [ ] 106. DALTON JONES
- [ ] 123. JOSE SANTIAGO
- [ ] 140. TONY CONIGLIARO
- [ ] 167. ELSTON HOWARD
- [ ] 189. BILL LANDIS
- [ ] 212. DAVE MOREHEAD
- [ ] 233. GEORGE SCOTT
- [ ] 250. CARL YASTRZEMSKI
- [ ] 272. RAY CULP
- [ ] 297. RUSS GIBSON
- [ ] 314. BILL ROHR(R)
- [ ] 314. GEORGE SPRIGGS(R)
- [ ] 331. DAN OSINSKI
- [ ] 346. JERRY ADAIR
- [ ] 387. JOE FOY
- [ ] 406. DICK ELLSWORTH
- [ ] 430. RICO PETROCELLI
- [ ] 449. GENE OLIVER
- [ ] 460. JIM LONBORG
- [ ] 481. JOHN WYATT
- [ ] 502. MIKE ANDREWS
- [ ] 519. JERRY STEPHENSON
- [ ] 537. NORM SIEBERN
- [ ] 555. JOSE TARTABULL
- [ ] 566. KEN HARRELSON
- [ ] 581. GARRY ROGGENBURK
- [ ] 593. LEE STANGE

CALIFORNIA ANGELS

- [ ] 24. BOBBY LOCKE
- [ ] 52. HAWK TAYLOR
- [ ] 75. DON MINCHER
- [ ] 102. JOSE CARDENAL
- [ ] 121. JIMMIE HALL
- [ ] 143. PETE CIMINO
- [ ] 170. JIM FREGOSI
- [ ] 193. JACK HAMILTON
- [ ] 216. BUBBA MORTON
- [ ] 238. TOM SATRIANO
- [ ] 252. TEAM CARD
- [ ] 271. BOBBY KNOOP
- [ ] 289. WOODY HELD
- [ ] 305. MINNIE ROJAS
- [ ] 328. CHUCK VINSON(R)
- [ ] 328. JIM WEAVER(R)
- [ ] 347. GEORGE BRUNET
- [ ] 389. JAY JOHNSTONE
- [ ] 416. BILL RIGNEY(M)
- [ ] 433. BOB RODGERS
- [ ] 453. SAMMY ELLIS
- [ ] 474. PAUL SCHAAL
- [ ] 493. JIM MCGLOTHLIN
- [ ] 531. CHUCK HINTON
- [ ] 552. ED KIRKPATRICK
- [ ] 570. RICK REICHARDT
- [ ] 587. ROGER REPOZ

BILLY
WILLIAMS

OUTFIELD
CUBS

CHICAGO CUBS

- [ ] 13. CHUCK HARTENSTEIN
- [ ] 37. BILLY WILLIAMS
- [ ] 60. KEN HOLTZMAN
- [ ] 83. JOHN STEPHENSON

- [ ] 101. GLENN BECKERT
- [ ] 119. TED SAVAGE
- [ ] 136. RANDY HUNDLEY
- [ ] 159. DON KESSINGER
- [ ] 179. BILL STONEMAN
- [ ] 184. LOU JOHNSON
- [ ] 202. ADOLFO PHILLIPS
- [ ] 219. ROB GARDNER
- [ ] 235. RON SANTO
- [ ] 258. JOSE ARCIA(R)
- [ ] 258. BILL SCHLESINGER(R)
- [ ] 279. BILL HANDS
- [ ] 296. BYRON BROWNE
- [ ] 321. LEO DUROCHER(M)
- [ ] 339. RICH NYE
- [ ] 355. ERNIE BANKS
- [ ] 382. RAMON HERNANDEZ
- [ ] 410. FERGUSON JENKINS
- [ ] 427. DICK CALMUS
- [ ] 451. AL SPANGLER
- [ ] 475. JOE NIEKRO
- [ ] 506. CLARENCE JONES
- [ ] 516. PETE MIKKELSON
- [ ] 542. JOHN BOCCABELLA
- [ ] 561. LEE ELIA
- [ ] 591. DICK NEN

CHICAGO WHITE SOX

- [ ] 14. JERRY MCNERTNEY
- [ ] 33. PETE WARD
- [ ] 51. BOB LOCKER
- [ ] 72. TOMMY JOHN
- [ ] 99. ROCKY COLAVITO
- [ ] 125. JOE HORLEN
- [ ] 142. BUDDY BRADFORD(R)
- [ ] 142. BILL VOSS(R)
- [ ] 172. WALT WILLIAMS
- [ ] 210. GARY PETERS
- [ ] 229. FRED KLAGES
- [ ] 259. KEN BOYER
- [ ] 265. TOMMY DAVIS
- [ ] 287. MICKEY ABARBANEL(R)
- [ ] 287. CISCO CARLOS(R)
- [ ] 310. LUIS APARICIO
- [ ] 329. DUANE JOSEPHSON
- [ ] 350. HOYT WILHELM
- [ ] 391. BOB PRIDDY
- [ ] 413. TOMMY MCCRAW
- [ ] 424. TEAM CARD
- [ ] 444. JACK FISHER
- [ ] 464. DON MCMAHON
- [ ] 485. KEN BERRY
- [ ] 504. RUSS SNYDER
- [ ] 522. WAYNE CAUSEY
- [ ] 541. SANDY ALOMAR
- [ ] 564. EDDIE STANKY(M)
- [ ] 585. WILBUR WOOD

CINCINNATI REDS

- [ ] 23. CHICO CARDENAS
- [ ] 48. TED DAVIDSON
- [ ] 74. MILT PAPPAS
- [ ] 90. VADA PINSON
- [ ] 108. DON PAVLETICH
- [ ] 130. TONY PEREZ
- [ ] 133. FRED WHITFIELD
- [ ] 148. DAVE BRISTOL(M)
- [ ] 171. DON NOTTEBART
- [ ] 196. GARY NOLAN
- [ ] 213. CHICO RUIZ
- [ ] 230. PETE ROSE
- [ ] 247. JOHNNY BENCH(R)
- [ ] 247. RON TOMPKINS(R)
- [ ] 264. TED ABERNATHY
- [ ] 283. MEL QUEEN
- [ ] 302. GERRY ARRIGO
- [ ] 319. GEORGE CULVER
- [ ] 338. BOB W. JOHNSON
- [ ] 353. MACK JONES
- [ ] 384. BILL F. HENRY(R)
- [ ] 384. HAL MCRAE(R)
- [ ] 405. TOMMY HELMS
- [ ] 425. JIM MALONEY
- [ ] 441. ALEX JOHNSON
- [ ] 463. JIMMIE SCHAFFER
- [ ] 487. LEE MAY
- [ ] 511. BILL KELSO
- [ ] 523. JOHN TSITOURIS

☐ 543. BOB LEE
☐ 574. TEAM CARD
☐ 597. BILL MCCOOL

CLEVELAND INDIANS

☐ 16. LOU PINIELLA(R)
☐ 16. RICHIE SCHEINBLUM(R)
☐ 35. STEVE HARGAN
☐ 54. STAN WILLIAMS
☐ 71. VERN FULLER
☐ 94. LEE MAYE
☐ 115. SAM MCDOWELL
☐ 176. BOB ALLEN
☐ 197. LARRY BROWN
☐ 218. KEN SUAREZ
☐ 237. ALVIN DARK(M)
☐ 269. BOB TIEFENAUER
☐ 295. SONNY SIEBERT
☐ 318. CHICO SALMON
☐ 340. MAX ALVIS
☐ 397. VIC DAVALILLO
☐ 418. EDDIE FISHER
☐ 432. BILL DAVIS(R)
☐ 432. JOSE VIDAL(R)
☐ 443. JOE AZCUE
☐ 471. ORLANDO PENA
☐ 495. LEON WAGNER
☐ 508. DUKE SIMS
☐ 532. LUIS TIANT
☐ 551. DARRELL SUTHERLAND
☐ 568. WILLIE SMITH
☐ 590. TOMMY HARPER

DETROIT TIGERS

☐ 22. PAT DOBSON
☐ 40. DENNY MCLAIN
☐ 58. ED MATHEWS
☐ 78. JIM NORTHRUP
☐ 113. TOM MATCHICK(R)
☐ 113. DARYL PATTERSON(R)
☐ 129. MICKEY STANLEY
☐ 160. EARL WILSON
☐ 178. DON WERT
☐ 201. MIKE MARSHALL
☐ 226. JIMMIE PRICE
☐ 240. AL KALINE
☐ 256. NORM CASH
☐ 285. DICK MCAULIFFE
☐ 307. JOHN HILLER
☐ 326. DENNIS RIBANT
☐ 360. WILLIE HORTON
☐ 399. RAY OYLER
☐ 414. MICKEY LOLICH
☐ 447. GEORGE KORINCE(R)
☐ 447. FRED LASHER(R)
☐ 470. BILL FREEHAN
☐ 488. DICK TRACEWSKI
☐ 505. JOE SPARMA
☐ 528. TEAM CARD
☐ 544. MAYO SMITH(M)
☐ 583. GATES BROWN

HOUSTON ASTROS

☐ 21. RON DAVIS
☐ 41. JULIO GOTAY
☐ 57. DAN SCHNEIDER
☐ 77. DON WILSON
☐ 95. BOB ASPROMONTE
☐ 128. TOM DUKES(R)
☐ 128. ALONZO HARRIS(R)
☐ 144. JOE MORGAN
☐ 161. NORM MILLER
☐ 182. DAVE GIUSTI
☐ 207. CARROLL SEMBERA
☐ 232. DENIS MENKE
☐ 260. JIM WYNN
☐ 274. MIKE CUELLAR
☐ 300. RUSTY STAUB
☐ 317. RON BRAND
☐ 332. DOUG RADER
☐ 359. JOE MOELLER
☐ 392. GRADY HATTON(M)
☐ 403. JOHN BUZHARDT
☐ 423. FRED GLADDING
☐ 438. LEE THOMAS
☐ 468. LARRY SHERRY

☐ 491. DENNY LEMASTER
☐ 507. WADE BLASINGAME
☐ 529. BRUCE VON HOFF
☐ 539. JIM RAY(R)
☐ 547. DAN COOMBS
☐ 565. LARRY DIERKER
☐ 569. IVAN MURRELL(R)
☐ 576. DAVE ADLESH
☐ 592. JOHN BATEMAN

LOS ANGELES DODGERS

☐ 15. RON HUNT
☐ 34. AL FERRARA
☐ 65. JOHN ROSEBORO
☐ 88. PHIL REGAN
☐ 103. DON SUTTON
☐ 124. NATE OLIVER
☐ 145. DON DRYSDALE
☐ 168. TEAM CARD
☐ 208. WILLIE DAVIS
☐ 228. JACK BILLINGHAM(R)
☐ 228. JIM FAIREY(R)
☐ 249. BILL SINGER
☐ 266. PAUL POPOVICH
☐ 281. JIM CAMPANIS
☐ 298. JIM BREWER
☐ 315. ZOILO VERSALLES
☐ 336. JOHN PURDIN
☐ 357. LEN GABRIELSON
☐ 398. JIM GRANT
☐ 417. WILLIE CRAWFORD
☐ 440. CLAUDE OSTEEN
☐ 457. JIM LEFEBVRE
☐ 472. WALT ALSTON(M)
☐ 492. JEFF TORBORG
☐ 510. RON FAIRLY
☐ 533. WES PARKER
☐ 553. HANK AGUIRRE
☐ 580. BOB BAILEY

FRANK
QUILICI

MINNESOTA TWINS

☐ 28. TED UHLAENDER
☐ 44. FRANK KOSTRO
☐ 64. JIM MERRITT
☐ 80. ROD CAREW
☐ 91. JIM OLLOM
☐ 111. RICH REESE
☐ 137. TEAM CARD
☐ 165. TONY OLIVA
☐ 181. JERRY ZIMMERMAN
☐ 206. CAL ERMER(M)
☐ 220. HARMON KILLEBREW
☐ 243. RICH ROLLINS
☐ 255. DEAN CHANCE
☐ 276. JIM ROLAND
☐ 301. GEORGE MITTERWALD(R)
☐ 301. RICH RENICK(R)
☐ 322. DAVE BOSWELL
☐ 335. BOB ALLISON
☐ 352. JACKIE HERNANDEZ
☐ 393. JIM PERRY
☐ 420. CESAR TOVAR
☐ 435. RON PERRANOSKI
☐ 450. JIM KAAT
☐ 473. AL WORTHINGTON
☐ 515. RUSS NIXON

☐ 534. BOB L. MILLER
☐ 557. FRANK QUILICI
☐ 589. RON CLARK(R)
☐ 589. MOE OGIER(R)

NEW YORK METS

◼ 27. GIL HODGES(M)
◼ 45. TOM SEAVER
◼ 63. DICK KENWORTHY
◼ 92. ED KRANEPOOL
◼ 114. RON SWOBODA
◼ 132. BUD HARRELSON
☐ 177. JERRY KOOSMAN(R)
☐ 177. NOLAN RYAN(R)
◼ 191. DAN FRISELLA
◼ 211. J.C. MARTIN
◼ 236. TUG MCGRAW
◼ 254. CLEON JONES
◼ 277. JERRY BUCHEK
◼ 292. ART SHAMSKY
◼ 313. AL WEIS
☐ 345. BOB HENDLEY
◼ 386. GREG GOOSSEN
◼ 401. TEAM CARD
◼ 421. RON TAYLOR
◼ 437. DON CARDWELL
◼ 465. TOMMIE AGEE
◼ 486. CAL KOONCE
◼ 503. AL JACKSON
◼ 521. DON SHAW
☐ 536. BILL SHORT
☐ 556. DICK SELMA
☐ 563. ED CHARLES
☐ 569. LESS ROHR(R)
☐ 572. DON BOSCH
☐ 582. JERRY GROTE
☐ 594. PHIL LINZ

NEW YORK YANKEES

☐ 29. JOE VERBANIC
☐ 47. RALPH HOUK(M)
☐ 69. TOM TRESH
☐ 89. JAKE GIBBS
☐ 105. AL DOWNING
☐ 120. MEL STOTTLEMYRE
☐ 138. RUBEN AMARO
☐ 195. JOE PEPITONE
☐ 214. STAN BAHNSEN(R)
☐ 214. FRANK FERNANDEZ(R)
☐ 234. BILL MONBOUQUETTE
☐ 246. FRITZ PETERSON
☐ 263. HORACE CLARKE
☐ 280. MICKEY MANTLE
☐ 299. GENE MICHAEL
☐ 316. STEVE BARBER
☐ 337. BILL ROBINSON
☐ 383. STEVE WHITAKER
☐ 402. MIKE HEGAN
☐ 431. DOOLEY WOMACK
☐ 467. DICK HOWSER
☐ 496. STEVE HAMILTON
☐ 524. ANDY KOSCO
☐ 539. MIKE FERRARO(R)
☐ 546. ROY WHITE
☐ 562. JIM BOUTON
☐ 577. FRED TALBOT
☐ 596. CHARLIE SMITH

OAKLAND A'S

☐ 18. MIKE HERSHBERGER
☐ 38. TONY PIERCE
☐ 62. CHUCK DOBSON
☐ 79. TED KUBIAK
☐ 109. BERT CAMPANERIS
☐ 127. PAUL LINDBLAD
☐ 146. SAL BANDO
☐ 164. RAMON WEBSTER
☐ 183. BOB KENNEDY(M)
☐ 199. ROBERTO RODRIQUEZ(R)
☐ 199. DARRELL OSTEEN(R)
☐ 224. JACK AKER
☐ 244. JOHN DONALDSON
☐ 261. DAVE DUNCAN
☐ 282. RICK MONDAY
☐ 303. DICK GREEN
☐ 324. JIM NASH

1968 Topps

- ☐ 343. JIM GOSGER
- ☐ 385. JIM HUNTER
- ☐ 404. FLOYD ROBINSON
- ☐ 422. RENE LACHEMANN
- ☐ 458. LEW KRAUSSE
- ☐ 484. PHIL ROOF
- ☐ 501. JOHN ODOM
- ☐ 517. DIEGO SEGUI
- ☐ 535. DANNY CATER
- ☐ 554. TEAM CARD
- ☐ 571. TONY LARUSSA
- ☐ 586. JIM PAGLIARONI

PHILADELPHIA PHILLIES

- ☐ 17. DICK HALL
- ☐ 39. COOKIE ROJAS
- ☐ 59. DON LOCK
- ☐ 81. LARRY JACKSON
- ☐ 98. GARY SUTHERLAND
- ☐ 112. WOODY FRYMAN
- ☐ 122. GENE MAUCH(M)
- ☐ 139. CHRIS SHORT
- ☐ 173. JOHN BOOZER
- ☐ 190. BILL WHITE
- ☐ 217. TURK FARRELL
- ☐ 225. RICHIE ALLEN
- ☐ 245. TONY GONZALEZ
- ☐ 262. RICK WISE
- ☐ 284. JOHN BRIGGS
- ☐ 306. MIKE RYAN
- ☐ 327. TONY TAYLOR
- ☐ 348. LARRY COLTON(R)
- ☐ 348. DICK THOENEN(R)
- ☐ 396. BOBBY WINE
- ☐ 415. JOHNNY CALLISON
- ☐ 434. RICK JOSEPH
- ☐ 448. GARY WAGNER
- ☐ 477. TEAM CARD
- ☐ 512. GRANT JACKSON
- ☐ 567. CLAY DALRYMPLE
- ☐ 579. LARRY HISLE(R)

PITTSBURGH PIRATES

- ☐ 19. JUAN PIZARRO
- ☐ 36. BOB MOOSE(R)
- ☐ 36. BOB ROBERTSON(R)
- ☐ 53. GENE ALLEY
- ☐ 70. BOB VEALE
- ☐ 86. WILLIE STARGELL
- ☐ 150. BOB CLEMENTE
- ☐ 175. MAURY WILLS
- ☐ 198. ROY FACE
- ☐ 215. JIM BUNNING
- ☐ 251. MANNY SANGUILLEN
- ☐ 270. MATTY ALOU
- ☐ 288. DAVE WICKERSHAM
- ☐ 308. TEAM CARD
- ☐ 325. MANNY MOTA
- ☐ 344. DONN CLENDENON
- ☐ 390. BILL MAZEROSKI
- ☐ 407. GARY KOLB
- ☐ 429. TOMMIE SISK
- ☐ 446. RON KLINE
- ☐ 461. CHUCK HILLER
- ☐ 482. JOSE PAGAN
- ☐ 499. STEVE BLASS
- ☐ 514. AL MCBEAN
- ☐ 538. MANNY JIMENEZ
- ☐ 559. CARL TAYLOR(R)
- ☐ 559. LUKE WALKER(R)
- ☐ 584. LARRY SHEPARD(M)
- ☐ 598. JERRY MAY

ST. LOUIS CARDINALS

- ☐ 25. JULIAN JAVIER
- ☐ 46. DAVE RICKETTS
- ☐ 68. RON WILLIS
- ☐ 84. BOB TOLAN
- ☐ 100. BOB GIBSON
- ☐ 117. LARRY JASTER
- ☐ 141. DAL MAXVILL
- ☐ 162. HAL GILSON(R)
- ☐ 162. MIKE TORREZ(R)
- ☐ 180. CURT FLOOD
- ☐ 200. ORLANDO CEPEDA
- ☐ 227. JOE HOERNER

- ☐ 253. DICK HUGHES
- ☐ 275. TIM MCCARVER
- ☐ 294. RED SCHOENDIENST(M)
- ☐ 311. JACK LAMABE
- ☐ 330. ROGER MARIS
- ☐ 349. ED SPIEZIO
- ☐ 388. RAY WASHBURN
- ☐ 408. STEVE CARLTON
- ☐ 445. MIKE SHANNON
- ☐ 459. DICK SIMPSON
- ☐ 479. PHIL GAGLIANO
- ☐ 497. TEAM CARD
- ☐ 520. LOU BROCK
- ☐ 540. NELSON BRILES
- ☐ 558. JOHN EDWARDS
- ☐ 588. DICK SCHOFIELD

SAN FRANCISCO GIANTS

- ☐ 32. JOE GIBBON
- ☐ 50. WILLIE MAYS
- ☐ 73. JIM HART
- ☐ 85. GAYLORD PERRY
- ☐ 104. DICK DIETZ
- ☐ 126. BOBBY ETHERIDGE
- ☐ 147. FRANK LINZY
- ☐ 169. BOB BOLIN
- ☐ 185. TOM HALLER
- ☐ 205. JUAN MARICAHL
- ☐ 223. OLLIE BROWN
- ☐ 239. BILL R. HENRY
- ☐ 267. HERMAN FRANKS(M)
- ☐ 290. WILLIE MCCOVEY
- ☐ 309. KEN HENDERSON
- ☐ 333. RON HERBEL
- ☐ 351. BOB BARTON
- ☐ 400. MIKE MCCORMICK
- ☐ 419. JACK HIATT
- ☐ 436. HAL LANIER
- ☐ 452. JESUS ALOU
- ☐ 469. TY CLINE
- ☐ 494. RAY SADECKI
- ☐ 525. JIM DAVENPORT
- ☐ 545. LINDY MCDANIEL

WASHINGTON SENATORS

- ☐ 31. ED STROUD
- ☐ 49. ED BRINKMAN
- ☐ 66. CASEY COX
- ☐ 96. FRANK COGGINS(R)
- ☐ 96. DICK NOLD(R)
- ☐ 116. KEN MCMULLEN
- ☐ 131. FRANK BERTAINA
- ☐ 149. BOB SAVERINE
- ☐ 188. CAP PETERSON
- ☐ 209. TIM CULLEN
- ☐ 231. DAVE BALDWIN
- ☐ 248. FRED VALENTINE
- ☐ 268. BOB HUMPHREYS
- ☐ 291. DICK LINES
- ☐ 320. FRANK HOWARD
- ☐ 341. JIM LEMON(M)
- ☐ 358. MIKE EPSTEIN
- ☐ 395. CAMILO PASCUAL
- ☐ 411. RON HANSEN
- ☐ 426. HANK ALLEN
- ☐ 442. DICK BOSMAN
- ☐ 462. BARRY MOORE
- ☐ 483. DAROLD KNOWLES
- ☐ 498. BILL BRYAN
- ☐ 509. DENNIS HIGGINS
- ☐ 526. BILL DENEHY
- ☐ 548. BERNIE ALLEN
- ☐ 560. PAUL CASANOVA
- ☐ 573. JOE COLEMAN
- ☐ 595. PHIL ORTEGA

1969 TOPPS (664) 2 1/2'' X 3 1/2''

ATLANTA BRAVES

- ☐ 33. WAYNE CAUSEY
- ☐ 53. SONNY JACKSON
- ☐ 79. MILT PAPPAS
- ☐ 100. HANK AARON
- ☐ 128. TOMMIE AARON
- ☐ 154. JIM BRITTON
- ☐ 177. RON REED
- ☐ 196. LUM HARRIS(M)
- ☐ 210. FELIX MILLAN
- ☐ 238. KEN JOHNSON
- ☐ 261. BOB W. JOHNSON
- ☐ 282. PAT JARVIS
- ☐ 300. FELIPE ALOU
- ☐ 331. GIL GARRIDO(R)
- ☐ 331. TOM HOUSE(R)
- ☐ 355. PHIL NIEKRO
- ☐ 374. BOB TILLMAN
- ☐ 385. ORLANDO CEPEDA
- ☐ 398. TITO FRANCONA
- ☐ 446. CLAUDE RAYMOND
- ☐ 489. CLETE BOYER
- ☐ 514. MIKE LUM
- ☐ 542. BOB ASPROMONTE
- ☐ 568. CECIL UPSHAW
- ☐ 590. RICO CARTY
- ☐ 611. BOB DIDIER(R)
- ☐ 611. WALT HRINIAK(R)
- ☐ 611. GARY NEIBAUER(R)
- ☐ 627. GEORGE STONE

BALTIMORE ORIOLES

- ☐ 15. BOOG POWELL
- ☐ 37. CURT MOTTON
- ☐ 66. MIKE ADAMSON(R)
- ☐ 66. MERV RETTENMUND(R)
- ☐ 86. PETE RICHERT
- ☐ 113. DAVE MAY
- ☐ 141. BILL DILLMAN
- ☐ 151. CLAY DALRYMPLE
- ☐ 185. TOM PHOEBUS
- ☐ 203. DAVE A. JOHNSON
- ☐ 228. DAVE LEONHARD
- ☐ 250. FRANK ROBINSON
- ☐ 277. ELROD HENDRICKS
- ☐ 299. MARK BELANGER
- ☐ 323. LARRY MILLER
- ☐ 340. DAVE MCNALLY
- ☐ 368. VIC ROZNOVSKY
- ☐ 393. GENE BRABENDER
- ☐ 453. MIKE CUELLAR
- ☐ 478. DON BUFORD
- ☐ 506. PAUL BLAIR
- ☐ 516. EARL WEAVER(M)
- ☐ 550. BROOKS ROBINSON
- ☐ 573. JIM PALMER
- ☐ 597. BOBBY FLOYD(R)
- ☐ 610. JIM HARDIN
- ☐ 634. ANDY ETCHEBARREN
- ☐ 652. EDDIE WATT

BOSTON RED SOX

- ☐ 21. JOSE SANTIAGO
- ☐ 52. MIKE ANDREWS
- ☐ 89. RUSS GIBSON
- ☐ 109. JIM LONBORG
- ☐ 130. CARL YASTRZEMSKI
- ☐ 148. LEE STANGE
- ☐ 172. JERRY STEPHENSON
- ☐ 189. JOE LAHOUD(R)
- ☐ 189. JOHN THIBDEAU(R)
- ☐ 215. RICO PETROCELLI
- ☐ 240. KEN HARRELSON
- ☐ 264. BILL LANDIS
- ☐ 287. JOSE TARTABULL
- ☐ 311. SPARKY LYLE
- ☐ 330. TONY CONIGLIARO
- ☐ 349. DICK WILLIAMS(M)
- ☐ 391. RAY CULP
- ☐ 457. DALTON JONES
- ☐ 476. KEN BRETT(R)
- ☐ 476. GERRY MOSES(R)
- ☐ 498. JUAN PIZARRO
- ☐ 521. GEORGE THOMAS
- ☐ 543. FRED NEWMAN
- ☐ 574. GEORGE SCOTT
- ☐ 628. BILL CONIGLIARO(R)
- ☐ 628. SYD O'BRIEN(R)
- ☐ 628. FRED WENZ(R)
- ☐ 660. REGGIE SMITH

CALIFORNIA ANGELS

- ☐ 32. SAMMY ELLIS
- ☐ 59. JAY JOHNSTONE
- ☐ 78. TOM SATRIANO
- ☐ 103. ROGER REPOZ
- ☐ 134. JIM WEAVER
- ☐ 157. BOB RODGERS
- ☐ 182. BILL RIGNEY(M)
- ☐ 205. RICK REICHARDT.
- ☐ 224. BILL HARRELSON(R)
- ☐ 224. STEVE KEALEY(R)
- ☐ 252. CHUCK COTTIER
- ☐ 275. VIC DAVALILLO
- ☐ 296. ANDY MESSERSMITH
- ☐ 315. EDDIE FISHER
- ☐ 342. BUBBA MORTON
- ☐ 365. JIM FREGOSI
- ☐ 386. JIM MCGLOTHLIN
- ☐ 407. TOM EGAN
- ☐ 445. BOBBY KNOOP
- ☐ 474. TOM MURPHY
- ☐ 502. MINNIE ROJAS
- ☐ 523. BOB CHANCE
- ☐ 565. HOYT WILHELM
- ☐ 583. CLYDE WRIGHT
- ☐ 598. RUBEN AMARO
- ☐ 621. BILL VOSS
- ☐ 645. GEORGE BRUNET
- ☐ 653. AURELIO RODRIGUEZ

CHICAGO CUBS

- ☐ 20. ERNIE BANKS
- ☐ 43. JOE NIEKRO
- ☐ 63. JIM HICKMAN
- ☐ 88. RICH NYE
- ☐ 115. BILL HANDS
- ☐ 147. LEO DUROCHER(M)
- ☐ 171. GLENN BECKERT
- ☐ 198. WILLIE SMITH
- ☐ 225. DON KESSINGER
- ☐ 247. GENE OLIVER
- ☐ 268. AL SPANGLER
- ☐ 288. KEN HOLTZMAN
- ☐ 312. LEE ELIA
- ☐ 347. RANDY HUNDLEY
- ☐ 372. ADOLFO PHILLIPS
- ☐ 404. VIC LAROSE(R)
- ☐ 404. GARY ROSS(R)
- ☐ 450. BILLY WILLIAMS
- ☐ 483. TED ABERNATHY
- ☐ 535. PHIL REGAN
- ☐ 538. CHARLIE SMITH
- ☐ 570. RON SANTO
- ☐ 593. DON NOTTEBART
- ☐ 602. ALEC DISTASO(R)
- ☐ 602. DON YOUNG(R)
- ☐ 602. JIM QUALLS(R)
- ☐ 640. FERGIE JENKINS

CHICAGO WHITE SOX

- ☐ 34. GARY PETERS
- ☐ 54. CISCO CARLOS
- ☐ 75. LUIS APARICIO
- ☐ 97. BUDDY BRADFORD
- ☐ 123. WILBUR WOOD
- ☐ 155. PETE WARD
- ☐ 173. BOB CHRISTIAN(R)
- ☐ 173. GERRY NYMAN(R)
- ☐ 179. DON PAVLETICH
- ☐ 222. DUANE JOSEPHSON
- ☐ 248. BOB PRIDDY
- ☐ 283. SANDY ALOMAR
- ☐ 309. WALT WILLIAMS
- ☐ 328. JOE HORLEN
- ☐ 363. RUSS NIXON
- ☐ 388. TOM MCCRAW
- ☐ 439. ED HERRMANN(R)
- ☐ 439. DAN LAZAR(R)
- ☐ 465. TOMMY JOHN
- ☐ 481. BILL MELTON
- ☐ 494. KEN BERRY
- ☐ 527. AL LOPEZ(M)
- ☐ 548. BOB LOCKER
- ☐ 566. RON HANSEN
- ☐ 622. DAN OSINSKI
- ☐ 636. WOODIE HELD
- ☐ 654. CARLOS MAY(R)
- ☐ 654. DON SECRIST(R)
- ☐ 654. RICH MORALES(R)

CINCINNATI REDS

- ☐ 26. CLAY CARROLL
- ☐ 70. TOMMY HELMS
- ☐ 81. MEL QUEEN
- ☐ 95. JOHNNY BENCH
- ☐ 120. PETE ROSE
- ☐ 142. WOODY WOODWARD
- ☐ 187. LEON WAGNER
- ☐ 213. GERRY ARRIGO
- ☐ 234. DAVE BRISTOL(M)
- ☐ 259. BILL SHORT
- ☐ 280. ALEX JOHNSON
- ☐ 295. TONY PEREZ
- ☐ 318. JACK FISHER
- ☐ 339. STEVE MINGORI(R)
- ☐ 339. JOE PENA(R)
- ☐ 362. JIM MALONEY
- ☐ 382. PAT CORRALES
- ☐ 405. LEE MAY
- ☐ 448. BOB TOLAN
- ☐ 469. CHICO RUIZ
- ☐ 492. TONY CLONINGER
- ☐ 518. FRED WHITFIELD
- ☐ 551. WAYNE GRANGER
- ☐ 581. GARY NOLAN
- ☐ 613. JIM BEAUCHAMP
- ☐ 624. DARREL CHANEY(R)
- ☐ 635. GEORGE CULVER
- ☐ 661. JIM MERRITT

CLEVELAND INDIANS

- ☐ 19. KEN SUAREZ
- ☐ 61. JIMMIE HALL
- ☐ 91. ALVIN DARK(M)
- ☐ 118. STAN WILLIAMS
- ☐ 145. MAX ALVIS
- ☐ 176. JOE AZCUE
- ☐ 201. RUSS SNYDER
- ☐ 220. SAM MCDOWELL
- ☐ 244. RAY FOSSE(R)
- ☐ 244. GEORGE WOODSON(R)
- ☐ 267. VICENTE ROMO
- ☐ 291. VERN FULLER
- ☐ 325. JOSE CARDENAL
- ☐ 348. STEVE HARGAN
- ☐ 367. LOU JOHNSON
- ☐ 414. DUKE SIMS
- ☐ 455. SONNY SIEBERT
- ☐ 479. RICHIE SCHEINBLUM
- ☐ 503. LARRY BROWN
- ☐ 537. MIKE PAUL
- ☐ 560. LUIS TIANT
- ☐ 571. CAP PETERSON
- ☐ 579. DAVE NELSON
- ☐ 595. LEE MAYE
- ☐ 597. LARRY BURCHART(R)

DETROIT TIGERS

- ☐ 13. MICKEY STANLEY
- ☐ 40. MAYO SMITH(M)
- ☐ 80. NORM CASH
- ☐ 101. DARYL PATTERSON
- ☐ 126. DICK TRACEWSKI
- ☐ 150. DENNY MCLAIN
- ☐ 180. WILLIE HORTON
- ☐ 207. ROY FACE
- ☐ 231. PAT DOBSON
- ☐ 256. GATES BROWN
- ☐ 270. MICKEY LOLICH
- ☐ 305. DICK MCAULIFFE
- ☐ 324. LES CAIN(R)
- ☐ 324. DAVE CAMPBELL(R)
- ☐ 344. TOM MATCHICK
- ☐ 373. FRED LASHER
- ☐ 390. BILL FREEHAN
- ☐ 410. AL KALINE
- ☐ 443. DON WERT
- ☐ 472. JIM PRICE
- ☐ 488. JOE SPARMA
- ☐ 525. EARL WILSON
- ☐ 544. MIKE KILKENNEY(R)
- ☐ 544. RON WOODS(R)
- ☐ 580. JIM NORTHRUP
- ☐ 616. DON MCMAHON
- ☐ 642. JOHN HILLER
- ☐ 663. DICK RADATZ

HOUSTON ASTROS

- ☐ 35. JOE MORGAN
- ☐ 58. FRED GLADDING
- ☐ 76. NORM MILLER
- ☐ 96. DENVER LEMASTER
- ☐ 119. DOUG RADER
- ☐ 156. HAL GILSON(R)
- ☐ 156. LEON MCFADDEN(R)
- ☐ 186. JOHN EDWARDS
- ☐ 202. DON WILSON
- ☐ 208. DONN CLENDENON
- ☐ 257. JIM RAY
- ☐ 278. GARY GEIGER
- ☐ 308. WADE BLASINGAME
- ☐ 337. MARTY MARTINEZ
- ☐ 360. JIM WYNN
- ☐ 389. DAN COOMBS
- ☐ 411. LARRY DIERKER
- ☐ 458. CURT BLEFARY
- ☐ 487. DENIS MENKE
- ☐ 499. DON BRYANT(R)
- ☐ 499. STEVE SHEA(R)
- ☐ 526. HECTOR TORRES
- ☐ 562. BOB WATSON
- ☐ 594. DOOLEY WOMACK
- ☐ 614. TOM GRIFFIN(R)
- ☐ 614. SKIP GUINN(R)
- ☐ 633. HARRY WALKER(M)
- ☐ 656. DAN SCHNEIDER

KANSAS CITY ROYALS

- ☐ 29. DAVE MOREHEAD
- ☐ 49. STEVE JONES
- ☐ 49. ELLIE RODRIGUEZ(R)
- ☐ 71. STEVE WHITAKER
- ☐ 93. JOE FOY
- ☐ 116. CHUCK HARRISON
- ☐ 137. WALLY BUNKER
- ☐ 159. JERRY ADAIR
- ☐ 211. GALEN CISCO
- ☐ 239. BOB TAYLOR
- ☐ 258. JACKIE HERNANDEZ
- ☐ 279. ROGER NELSON
- ☐ 298. DAVE NICHOLSON
- ☐ 352. PAUL SCHAAL
- ☐ 376. MIKE FIORE(R)
- ☐ 376. JIM ROOKER(R)
- ☐ 396. JIM CAMPANIS
- ☐ 437. LUIS ALCARAZ
- ☐ 463. DENNIS RIBANT
- ☐ 484. JOE GORDON(M)
- ☐ 508. MOE DRABOWSKY
- ☐ 529. ED KIRKPATRICK

- ☐ 605. DICK ELLSWORTH
- ☐ 629. JACK HAMILTON
- ☐ 644. CHUCK HINTON

☐ 558. TOM BURGMEIER
☐ 569. BILLY HARRIS
☐ 591. MIKE HEDLUND
☐ 603. JOE KEOUGH
☐ 619. BILL BUTLER(R)
☐ 619. H. PAT KELLY(R)
☐ 619. JUAN RIOS(R)
☐ 632. JON WARDEN
☐ 647. DAVE WICKERSHAM
☐ 662. DICK DRAGO(R)
☐ 662. GEORGE SPRIGGS(R)
☐ 662. BOB OLIVER(R)

LOS ANGELES DODGERS

☐ 24. WALTER ALSTON(M)
☐ 47. PAUL POPOVICH
☐ 65. WILLIE DAVIS
☐ 94. HANK AGUIRRE
☐ 122. RON FAIRLY
☐ 139. ANDY KOSCO
☐ 140. JIM LEFEBVRE
☐ 161. JOHN PURDIN
☐ 216. DON SUTTON
☐ 241. JIM BREWER
☐ 266. TOM HUTTON(R)
☐ 266. ALAN FOSTER(R)
☐ 289. BART SHIRLEY
☐ 310. TOM HALLER
☐ 327. WILLIE CRAWFORD
☐ 353. JEFF TORBORG
☐ 379. KEN BOYER
☐ 400. DON DRYSDALE
☐ 444. JOE MOELLER
☐ 471. TED SAVAGE
☐ 493. WES PARKER
☐ 528. CLAUDE OSTEEN
☐ 552. TED SIZEMORE(R)
☐ 552. BILL SUDAKIS(R)
☐ 575. BILL SINGER
☐ 615. LEN GABRIELSON
☐ 641. BOBBY DARWIN(R)
☐ 641. JOHN MILLER(R)

MINNESOTA TWINS

☐ 30. BOB ALLISON
☐ 56. RICH REESE
☐ 77. RON PERRANOSKI
☐ 99. DANNY MORRIS(R)
☐ 99. GRAIG NETTLES(R)
☐ 121. JOE GRZENDA
☐ 146. JIM PERRY
☐ 194. TED UHLAENDER
☐ 218. JOHN ROSEBORO
☐ 242. FRANK KOSTRO
☐ 265. CHICO CARDENAS
☐ 290. JIM KAAT
☐ 317. BRUCE LOOK
☐ 336. JIM ROLAND
☐ 356. FRANK QUILICI
☐ 375. HARMON KILLEBREW
☐ 403. BOB L. MILLER
☐ 459. DAVE BOSWELL
☐ 491. JERRY CRIDER(R)
☐ 491. GEORGE MITTERWALD(R)
☐ 510. ROD CAREW
☐ 530. CESAR TOVAR
☐ 547. BILLY MARTIN(M)
☐ 561. RON CLARK
☐ 600. TONY OLIVA
☐ 620. DEAN CHANCE
☐ 658. TOM HALL(R)

MONTREAL EXPOS

☐ 22. JESUS ALOU
☐ 45. MAURY WILLS
☐ 67. BILL STONEMAN
☐ 92. JACK BILLINGHAM
☐ 117. JIM FAIREY
☐ 138. JOHN BATEMAN
☐ 183. DON SHAW
☐ 230. RUSTY STAUB
☐ 236. MANNY MOTA
☐ 284. JERRY ROBERTSON(R)
☐ 284. MIKE WEGENER(R)
☐ 306. JIM GRANT
☐ 326. GARY SUTHERLAND
☐ 351. CARROLL SEMBERA

☐ 378. JOSE HERRERA
☐ 399. BOB BAILEY
☐ 442. TY CLINE
☐ 466. JOHN BOCCABELLA
☐ 496. LARRY JASTER
☐ 524. JOSE LABOY(R)
☐ 524. FLOYD WICKER(R)
☐ 549. RON BRAND
☐ 578. DON BOSCH
☐ 606. GENE MAUCH(M)
☐ 625. MACK JONES
☐ 646. DAN MCGINN(R)
☐ 646. CARL MORTON(R)
☐ 648. BOBBY WINE

NEW YORK METS

☐ 31. GARY GENTRY(R)
☐ 31. AMOS OTIS(R)
◼ 55. JERRY GROTE
◼ 72. RON TAYLOR
◼ 90. JERRY KOOSMAN
◼ 112. J.C. MARTIN
◼ 127. KEVIN COLLINS
◼ 144. BOB HENDLEY
◼ 193. DON CARDWELL
◼ 221. ART SHAMSKY
◼ 245. ED CHARLES
◼ 269. AL WEIS
◼ 303. CAL KOONCE
☐ 321. JIM MCANDREW
☐ 343. DAN FRISELLA
◼ 364. TOMMIE AGEE
☐ 381. ED KRANEPOOL
☐ 402. KEN BOSWELL
☐ 456. BUD HARRELSON
☐ 480. TOM SEAVER
☐ 512. CLEON JONES
☐ 533. NOLAN RYAN
◼ 564. GIL HODGES(M)
☐ 585. RON SWOBODA
☐ 601. TUG MCGRAW
☐ 624. DUFFY DYER(R)
☐ 649. AL JACKSON

NEW YORK YANKEES

☐ 25. ROY WHITE
☐ 46. FRITZ PETERSON
☐ 69. STEVE HAMILTON
☐ 87. HORACE CLARKE
☐ 114. ALAN CLOSTER(R)
☐ 114. JOHN CUMBERLAND(R)
☐ 191. LINDY MCDANIEL
☐ 212. TOM TRESH
☐ 237. BOBBY COX
☐ 262. MIKE KEKICH
☐ 292. AL DOWNING
☐ 313. BILL ROBINSON
☐ 332. FRED TALBOT
☐ 354. NATE OLIVER
☐ 380. STAN BAHNSEN
☐ 401. JAKE GIBBS
☐ 447. RALPH HOUK(M)
☐ 470. MEL STOTTLEMYRE
☐ 500. MICKEY MANTLE
☐ 519. GERRY KENNEY(R)
☐ 519. LEN BOEHMER(R)
☐ 541. JOE VERBANIC
☐ 557. FRANK FERNANDEZ
☐ 589. JOE PEPITONE
☐ 608. DICK SIMPSON
☐ 626. GENE MICHAEL
☐ 643. BILLY COWAN
☐ 657. BOBBY MURCER
☐ 658. BILL BURBACH(R)

OAKLAND A'S

☐ 23. LEW KRAUSSE
☐ 44. DANNY CATER
☐ 68. DAVE DUNCAN
☐ 105. RICK MONDAY
☐ 124. HANK BAUER(M)
☐ 143. JOE NOSSEK
☐ 195. JOHN ODOM
☐ 217. JOHN DONALDSON
☐ 235. JIM HUNTER
☐ 260. REGGIE JACKSON

☐ 281. TED KUBIAK
☐ 302. JIM PAGLIARONI
☐ 334. PHIL ROOF
☐ 358. GEORGE LAUZERIQUE(R)
☐ 358. ROBERTO RODRIQUEZ(R)
☐ 371. SAL BANDO
☐ 397. CHUCK DOBSON
☐ 449. PAUL LINDBLAD
☐ 467. TOM REYNOLDS
☐ 495. BERT CAMPANERIS
☐ 515. DICK GREEN
☐ 546. JIM NASH
☐ 587. JOE RUDI
☐ 597. ROLLIE FINGERS(R)
☐ 618. RAMON WEBSTER
☐ 638. ED SPRAGUE
☐ 655. MIKE HERSHBERGER

PHILADELPHIA PHILLIES

☐ 28. MIKE RYAN
☐ 51. WOODY FRYMAN
☐ 73. JOHNNY BRIGGS
☐ 108. TONY TAYLOR
☐ 133. JOHNNY CALLISON
☐ 174. GRANT JACKSON
☐ 188. RICK WISE
☐ 206. LARRY HISLE(R)
☐ 206. BARRY LERSCH(R)
☐ 229. DON LOCK
☐ 253. JERRY JOHNSON
☐ 276. GARY WAGNER
☐ 297. DERON JOHNSON
☐ 329. RICK JOSEPH
☐ 350. RICHIE ALLEN
☐ 369. BOB SKINNER
☐ 395. CHRIS SHORT
☐ 454. LARRY COLTON(R)
☐ 454. DON MONEY(R)
☐ 477. JEFF JAMES
☐ 507. COOKIE ROJAS
☐ 531. DICK FARRELL
☐ 576. RON STONE(R)
☐ 576. BILL WILSON(R)
☐ 599. JOHN BOOZER
☐ 624. TERRY HARMON(R)

PITTSBURGH PIRATES

☐ 36. LUKE WALKER
☐ 50. BOB CLEMENTE
☐ 82. RICH HEBNER(R)
☐ 82. AL OLIVER(R)
☐ 104. STEVE BLASS
☐ 131. CHRIS CANNIZZARO
☐ 152. TOMMIE SISK
☐ 175. JIM BUNNING
☐ 192. JOSE PAGAN
☐ 219. FREDDIE PATEK
☐ 243. RON KLINE
☐ 263. JERRY MAY
☐ 286. DOCK ELLIS
☐ 307. GARY KOLB
☐ 335. BILL MAZEROSKI
☐ 357. CARL TAYLOR
☐ 384. LARRY SHEPARD(M)
☐ 409. BOB MOOSE
☐ 436. GENE ALLEY
☐ 468. BRUCE DAL CANTON(R)
☐ 468. BOB ROBERTSON(R)
☐ 490. MATTY ALOU
☐ 509. MANNY SANGUILLEN
☐ 520. BOB VEALE
☐ 545. WILLIE STARGELL
☐ 553. RON DAVIS
☐ 567. ELVIO JIMENEZ(R)
☐ 567. JIM SHELLENBACK(R)
☐ 596. CHUCK HARTENSTEIN

ST. LOUIS CARDINALS

☐ 18. DICK SCHOFIELD
☐ 39. DICK HUGHES
☐ 60. NELSON BRILES
☐ 85. LOU BROCK
☐ 110. MIKE SHANNON
☐ 136. STEVE HUNTZ(R)
☐ 136. MIKE TORREZ(R)
☐ 160. VADA PINSON

☐ 181. MEL NELSON
☐ 200. BOB GIBSON
☐ 232. DAVE RICKETTS
☐ 255. STEVE CARLTON
☐ 273. RON WILLIS
☐ 320. DAL MAXVILL
☐ 341. DAVE ADLESH
☐ 366. BO BELINSKY
☐ 415. RAY WASHBURN
☐ 438. GARY WASLEWSKI
☐ 460. JOE TORRE
☐ 462. RED SCHOENDIENST(M)
☐ 475. TIM MCCARVER
☐ 497. JULIAN JAVIER
☐ 522. JOE HOERNER
☐ 540. CURT FLOOD
☐ 559. JOE HAGUE(R)
☐ 559. JIM HICKS(R)
☐ 588. BILL WHITE
☐ 609. PHIL GAGLIANO

SAN DIEGO PADRES

☐ 14. AL MCBEAN
☐ 38. ZOILO VERSALLES
☐ 74. PRESTON GOMEZ(M)
☐ 98. DAVE GIUSTI
☐ 129. BILL MCCOOL
☐ 149. OLLIE BROWN
☐ 184. ROBERTO PENA
☐ 197. DICK SELMA
☐ 223. TOM DUKES
☐ 249. ED SPIEZIO
☐ 271. LARRY STAHL
☐ 304. BILL DAVIS(R)
☐ 304. CLARENCE GASTON(R)
☐ 333. IVAN MURRELL
☐ 359. DICK KELLEY
☐ 387. BOBBY KLAUS
☐ 408. NATE COLBERT
☐ 452. AL FERRARA
☐ 473. JOSE ARCIA
☐ 501. TONY GONZALEZ
☐ 536. DANNY BREEDEN(R)
☐ 536. DAVE A. ROBERTS(R)
☐ 592. RAFAEL ROBLES(R)
☐ 592. AL SANTORINI(R)
☐ 617. JESSE GONDER
☐ 637. JERRY DAVANON(R)
☐ 637. FRANK REBERGER(R)
☐ 637. CLAY KIRBY(R)
☐ 641. TOMMY DEAN(R)
☐ 659. JOHNNY PODRES

SAN FRANCISCO GIANTS

☐ 16. CESAR GUTIERREZ(R)
☐ 16. RICH ROBERTSON(R)
☐ 41. BOB BARTON
☐ 64. BILL MONBOUQUETTE
☐ 102. JIM DAVENPORT
☐ 125. RAY SADECKI
☐ 158. JOE GIBBON
☐ 190. WILLIE MAYS
☐ 204. JACK HIATT
☐ 227. FRANK JOHNSON
☐ 251. RON HERBEL
☐ 274. CLYDE KING(M)
☐ 293. DICK DIETZ
☐ 316. HAL LANIER
☐ 345. FRANK LINZY
☐ 370. JUAN MARICHAL
☐ 392. BOB BURDA
☐ 440. WILLIE MCCOVEY
☐ 464. DAVE MARSHALL
☐ 485. GAYLOR PERRY
☐ 505. BOBBY BOLIN
☐ 517. MIKE MCCORMICK
☐ 555. JIM HART
☐ 584. DON MASON
☐ 604. BOBBY ETHERIDGE
☐ 630. BOBBY BONDS
☐ 664. RON HUNT

SEATTLE PILOTS

☐ 17. MIKE MARSHALL
☐ 42. TOMMY HARPER
☐ 62. CHICO SALMON
☐ 83. MIKE FERRARO
☐ 111. JOHNNY MORRIS
☐ 135. TOMMY DAVIS
☐ 178. RAY OYLER
☐ 209. LARRY HANEY
☐ 233. STEVE BARBER
☐ 254. JOE SCHULTZ(M)
☐ 285. DON MINCHER
☐ 301. DARRELL BRANDON
☐ 322. JOSE VIDAL
☐ 346. WAYNE COMER
☐ 377. GARY BELL
☐ 394. LOU PINIELLA(R)
☐ 394. MARV STAEHLE(R)
☐ 413. ROLAND SHELDON
☐ 451. RICH ROLLINS
☐ 482. JIM GOSGER
☐ 511. DIEGO SEGUI
☐ 534. JERRY MCNERTNEY
☐ 563. MARTY PATTIN
☐ 577. MIKE HEGAN
☐ 612. JACK AKER
☐ 631. JOHN KENNEDY
☐ 651. GUS GIL

WASHINGTON SENATORS

☐ 27. BERNIE ALLEN
☐ 48. BRANT ALYEA
☐ 84. BOB HUMPHREYS
☐ 106. JIM HANNAN
☐ 132. DAVE BALDWIN
☐ 153. ED BRINKMAN
☐ 170. FRANK HOWARD
☐ 199. JIM FRENCH
☐ 226. BRUCE HOWARD
☐ 246. JOE COLEMAN
☐ 272. ED STROUD
☐ 294. JIM LEMON(M)
☐ 319. KEN MCMULLEN
☐ 338. DEL UNSER
☐ 361. GARY HOLMAN
☐ 383. CASEY COX

☐ 406. PHIL ORTEGA
☐ 441. DENNIS HIGGINS
☐ 461. MIKE EPSTEIN
☐ 486. PAUL CASANOVA
☐ 513. CAMILO PASCUAL
☐ 554. FRANK BERTAINA
☐ 586. TIM CULLEN
☐ 607. DICK BOSMAN
☐ 623. HANK ALLEN
☐ 639. BARRY MOORE
☐ 650. TED WILLIAMS(M)
☐ 658. JIM MILES(R)

1970 TOPPS (720)
2 1/2" X 3 1/2"

ATLANTA BRAVES

☐ 17. HOYT WILHELM
☐ 48. GIL GARRIDO
☐ 86. LUM HARRIS(M)
☐ 105. TONY GONZALEZ
☐ 122. GEORGE STONE
☐ 145. RICO CARTY
☐ 160. PHIL NIEKRO
☐ 171. JIM NASH
☐ 172. GARRY HILL(R)
☐ 172. RALPH GARR(R)
☐ 206. CLETE BOYER
☐ 232. BOB DIDIER
☐ 278. TOMMIE AARON
☐ 295. CECIL UPSHAW
☐ 327. HAL KING
☐ 367. MIKE LUM
☐ 384. GARY NEIBAUER
☐ 413. SONNY JACKSON
☐ 438. PAT JARVIS
☐ 472. TEAM CARD
☐ 500. HANK AARON
☐ 529. BOB ASPROMONTE
☐ 546. RON REED
☐ 555. ORLANDO CEPEDA
☐ 576. MILT PAPPAS
☐ 621. MIKE MCQUEEN(R)
☐ 621. DARRELL EVANS(R)
☐ 621. RICK KESTER(R)
☐ 668. BOB TILLMAN
☐ 687. BOB PRIDDY
☐ 710. FELIX MILLAN

BALTIMORE ORIOLES

☐ 20. DAVE MCNALLY
☐ 45. DAVE A. JOHNSON
☐ 81. DAVE MAY
☐ 101. BOBBY FLOYD
☐ 121. FRED BEENE(R)
☐ 121. TERRY CROWLEY(R)
☐ 148. EARL WEAVER(M)
☐ 182. DICK HALL
☐ 213. ANDY ETCHEBARREN
☐ 230. BROOKS ROBINSON
☐ 261. CURT MOTTON
☐ 285. PAUL BLAIR
☐ 301. CHICO SALMON
☐ 319. CLAYTON DALRYMPLE
☐ 344. MARCELINO LOPEZ

☐ 363. TOMY SHOPAY
☐ 387. TEAM CARD
☐ 410. BOOG POWELL
☐ 428. DON BUFORD
☐ 449. JIM PALMER
☐ 477. AL SEVERINSEN(R)
☐ 477. ROGER FREED(R)
☐ 497. EDDIE WATT
☐ 528. ELROD HENDRICKS
☐ 590. MIKE CUELLAR
☐ 601. PETE RICHERT
☐ 615. MARK BELANGER
☐ 629. MERV RETTENMUND
☐ 638. FRANK BERTAINA
☐ 656. JIM HARDIN
☐ 674. DAVE LEONHARD
☐ 700. FRANK ROBINSON
☐ 717. TOM PHOEBUS

BOSTON RED SOX

☐ 10. CARL YASTRZEMSKI
☐ 39. MIKE NAGY
☐ 78. JOE LAHOUD
☐ 104. GERRY MOSES
☐ 116. SPARKY LYLE
☐ 144. RAY CULP
☐ 163. SYD O'BRIEN
☐ 191. VICENTE ROMO
☐ 215. REGGIE SMITH
☐ 237. RUSS GIBSON
☐ 251. DICK SCHOFIELD
☐ 279. BILL LEE
☐ 317. BILL CONIGLIARO(R)
☐ 317. LUIS ALVARADO(R)
☐ 340. TONY CONIGLIARO
☐ 361. RAY JARVIS
☐ 385. GEORGE SCOTT
☐ 406. MIKE ANDREWS
☐ 447. LEE STANGE
☐ 489. EDDIE KASKO(M)
☐ 504. DON PAVLETICH
☐ 540. GARY PETERS
☐ 563. TEAM CARD
☐ 581. TOM SATRIANO
☐ 597. SONNY SIEBERT
☐ 627. GARY WAGNER
☐ 647. TOM MATCHICK
☐ 665. JIM LONBORG
☐ 680. RICO PETROCELLI
☐ 708. JOSE SANTIAGO

CALIFORNIA ANGELS

☐ 4. TOM EGAN
☐ 29. SANDY ALOMAR
☐ 74. GREG WASHBURN(R)
☐ 74. WALLY WOLF(R)
☐ 132. JIM MCGLOTHLIN
☐ 156. EDDIE FISHER
☐ 173. JIM HICKS
☐ 203. RUDY MAY
☐ 228. AURELIO RODRIGUEZ
☐ 255. JIM SPENCER
☐ 277. PAUL DOYLE
☐ 294. JOSE AZCUE
☐ 326. BILL VOSS
☐ 351. TOM MURPHY
☐ 376. LEFTY PHILLIPS(M)
☐ 397. ROGER REPOZ
☐ 430. ANDY MESSERSMITH
☐ 485. JAY JOHNSTONE
☐ 522. TEAM CARD
☐ 543. CLYDE WRITHT
☐ 570. JIM FREGOSI
☐ 586. RICKEY CLARK
☐ 606. CHICO RUIZ
☐ 642. GREG GARRETT(R)
☐ 642. GORDON LUND(R)
☐ 642. JARVIS TATUM(R)
☐ 658. KEN TATUM
☐ 684. JACK FISHER
☐ 720. RICK REICHARDT

CHICAGO CUBS

☐ 46. KEN RUDOLPH
☐ 80. DON KESSINGER
☐ 117. DON YOUNG
☐ 170. BILLY WILLIAMS

☐ 192. JIM QUALLS
☐ 223. NATE OLIVER
☐ 240. FERGIE JENKINS
☐ 258. PAUL POPOVICH
☐ 265. RANDY HUNDLEY
☐ 291. LEO DUROCHER(M)
☐ 318. WILLIE SMITH
☐ 334. PHIL REGAN
☐ 375. JOHNNY CALLISON
☐ 405. BILL HANDS
☐ 429. RANDY BOBB(R)
☐ 429. JIM COSMAN(R)
☐ 480. GLENN BECKERT
☐ 505. KEN HOLTZMAN
☐ 541. BILL HEATH
☐ 562. TED ABERNATHY
☐ 593. TEAM CARD
☐ 612. JIM HICKMAN
☐ 630. ERNIE BANKS
☐ 649. JIMMIE HALL
☐ 654. BOOTS DAY(R)
☐ 670. RON SANTO
☐ 699. HANK AGUIRRE
☐ 714. AL SPANGLER

CHICAGO WHITE SOX

☐ 18. CARLOS MAY
☐ 35. JOE HORLEN
☐ 51. BOB CHRISTIAN
☐ 91. RICH MORALES
☐ 123. DON GUTTERIDGE(M)
☐ 146. DANNY MURPHY
☐ 180. TOMMY JOHN
☐ 217. RON HANSEN
☐ 239. KEN BERRY
☐ 263. DUANE JOSEPHSON
☐ 274. GERRY ARRIGO
☐ 299. BUDDY BRADFORD
☐ 315. LUIS APARICIO
☐ 342. WILBUR WOOD
☐ 368. ED HERRMANN
☐ 395. WALT WILLIAMS
☐ 414. PAUL EDMONDSON
☐ 444. BILLY FARMER(R)
☐ 444. JOHN MATIAS(R)
☐ 483. GAIL HOPKINS
☐ 501. TEAM CARD
☐ 518. BILL MELTON
☐ 561. TOM MCCRAW
☐ 618. BILLY WYNNE
☐ 669. BART JOHNSON(R)
☐ 669. DAN LAZAR(R)
☐ 669. MICKEY SCOTT(R)
☐ 695. BOBBY KNOOP

CINCINNATI REDS

☐ 3. DARRELL CHANEY
☐ 22. RAY WASHBURN
☐ 36. DANNY BREEDEN(R)
☐ 36. BERNIE CARBO(R)
☐ 73. WAYNE GRANGER
☐ 115. ALEX JOHNSON
☐ 133. CLAY CARROLL
☐ 159. TOMMY HELMS
☐ 181. SPARKY ANDERSON(M)
☐ 225. LEE MAY
☐ 254. CAMILO PASCUAL
☐ 283. ANGEL BRAVO
☐ 296. WOOODY WOODWARD
☐ 320. JIM MALONEY
☐ 358. PEDRO BORBON
☐ 380. TONY PEREZ
☐ 409. BOB TOLAN
☐ 443. AL JACKSON
☐ 484. GARY NOLAN
☐ 507. PAT CORRALES
☐ 544. TEAM CARD
☐ 580. PETE ROSE
☐ 602. TED SAVAGE
☐ 616. JIM MERRITT
☐ 636. JIM STEWART
☐ 660. JOHNNY BENCH
☐ 683. VERN GEISHERT(R)
☐ 683. HAL MCRAE(R)
☐ 683. WAYNE SIMPSON(R)
☐ 705. TONY CLONINGER

CLEVELAND INDIANS

☐ 7. GARY BOYD(R)
☐ 7. RUSS NAGELSON(R)
☐ 27. CHUCK HINTON
☐ 59. DICK ELLSWORTH
☐ 85. MAX ALVIS
☐ 112. DAVE NELSON
☐ 136. STEVE HARGAN
☐ 161. RICHIE SCHEINBLUM
☐ 184. RAY FOSSE
☐ 209. KEN SUAREZ
☐ 247. LOU KLIMCHOCK
☐ 257. DENNIS HIGGINS
☐ 275. DUKE SIMS
☐ 292. EDDIE LEON
☐ 347. RUSS SNYDER
☐ 366. BARRY MOORE
☐ 391. LARRY BROWN
☐ 412. LARRY BURCHART
☐ 445. VADA PINSON
☐ 491. GRAIG NETTLES
☐ 524. ALVIN DARK(M)
☐ 545. KEN HARRELSON
☐ 558. VERN FULLER
☐ 582. MIKE PAUL
☐ 625. DEAN CHANCE
☐ 637. TEAM CARD
☐ 650. SAM MCDOWELL
☐ 673. TED UHLAENDER
☐ 704. FRANK BAKER

DETROIT TIGERS

☐ 12. JOHN HILLER
☐ 33. DON WERT
☐ 95. EARL WILSON
☐ 98. GATES BROWN
☐ 129. JIMMIE PRICE
☐ 152. IKE BROWN
☐ 177. JIM NORTHRUP
☐ 207. NORMAN MCRAE(R)
☐ 207. BOB REED(R)
☐ 269. CESAR GUTIERREZ
☐ 313. MAYO SMITH(M)
☐ 335. BILL FREEHAN
☐ 356. FRED LASHER
☐ 383. MICKEY STANLEY
☐ 400. DENNY MCLAIN
☐ 424. MIKE KILKENNY
☐ 475. DICK MCAULIFFE
☐ 508. JOE NIEKRO
☐ 520. WILLIE HORTON
☐ 554. TOM TIMMERMANN
☐ 579. TEAM CARD
☐ 592. DARYL PATTERSON
☐ 611. NORM CASH
☐ 640. AL KALINE
☐ 661. JERRY ROBERTSON
☐ 682. DALTON JONES
☐ 698. TOM TRESH
☐ 715. MICKEY LOLICH

HOUSTON ASTROS

☐ 15. LARRY DIERKER
☐ 32. HARRY WALKER(M)
☐ 60. JIM WYNN
☐ 113. JIM RAY
☐ 126. MARTY MARTINEZ
☐ 155. DENIS MENKE
☐ 178. DENNY LEMASTER
☐ 208. FRED GLADDING
☐ 227. JOHN MAYBERRY(R)
☐ 227. BOB WATKINS(R)
☐ 248. JESUS ALOU
☐ 272. HECTOR TORRES
☐ 316. SKIP GUINN
☐ 339. JOHNNY EDWARDS
☐ 355. DOUG RADER
☐ 382. JACK DILAURO
☐ 407. BOB WATSON
☐ 448. TEAM CARD
☐ 492. KEITH LAMPARD(R)
☐ 492. SCIPIO SPINKS(R)
☐ 515. DON WILSON
☐ 537. JOE MORGAN
☐ 559. TOMMY DAVIS
☐ 578. TOM GRIFFIN
☐ 598. JOE PEPITONE
☐ 619. NORM MILLER
☐ 672. LEON MCFADDEN
☐ 701. JACK BILLINGHAM

1970 Topps

Paul Schaal 3RD BASE

KANSAS CITY ROYALS

- ☐ 16. CHARLIE METRO(M)
- ☐ 37. DICK DRAGO
- ☐ 57. H. PAT KELLY
- ☐ 89. JUAN RIOS
- ☐ 108. TOM BURGMEIER
- ☐ 165. ED KIRKPATRICK
- ☐ 187. MIKE HEDLUND
- ☐ 222. JIM ROOKER
- ☐ 241. AL FITZMORRIS(R)
- ☐ 241. SCOTT NORTHEY(R)
- ☐ 266. WALLY BUNKER
- ☐ 321. LOU PINIELLA
- ☐ 338. PAUL SCHAAL
- ☐ 354. AMOS OTIS
- ☐ 377. BILL BUTLER
- ☐ 402. ELLIE RODRIGUEZ
- ☐ 422. TEAM CARD
- ☐ 471. CHRIS ZACHARY
- ☐ 495. DAVE MOREHEAD
- ☐ 512. BILLY HARRIS
- ☐ 525. JERRY ADAIR
- ☐ 552. DON O'RILEY(R)
- ☐ 552. DENNIS PAEPKE(R)
- ☐ 552. FRED RICO(R)
- ☐ 567. BOB OLIVER
- ☐ 589. JOE KEOUGH
- ☐ 609. BUCK MARTINEZ
- ☐ 633. ROGER NELSON
- ☐ 653. MOE DRABOWSKY
- ☐ 671. JIM CAMPANIS
- ☐ 686. JACKIE HERNANDEZ
- ☐ 702. BOB D. JOHNSON(R)
- ☐ 709. MIKE FIORE

LOS ANGELES DODGERS

- ☐ 5. WES PARKER
- ☐ 34. WILLIE CRAWFORD
- ☐ 54. JEFF TORBORG
- ☐ 97. JOE MOELLER
- ☐ 131. RAY LAMB(R)
- ☐ 131. BOB STINSON(R)
- ☐ 157. MANNY MOTA
- ☐ 174. TED SIZEMORE
- ☐ 204. LEN GABRIELSON
- ☐ 242. WALTER ALSTON(M)
- ☐ 260. CLAUDE OSTEEN
- ☐ 286. JACK JENKINS(R)
- ☐ 286. BILL BUCKNER(R)
- ☐ 304. BILL RUSSELL
- ☐ 341. BILL SUDAKIS
- ☐ 369. ALAN FOSTER
- ☐ 390. WILLIE DAVIS
- ☐ 411. TEAM CARD
- ☐ 427. FRED NORMAN
- ☐ 446. BILL GRABARKEWITZ
- ☐ 490. BILL SINGER
- ☐ 523. JOSE PENA
- ☐ 535. ANDY KOSCO
- ☐ 553. JIM LEFEBVRE
- ☐ 571. JIM BREWER
- ☐ 595. MAURY WILLS
- ☐ 622. DON SUTTON
- ☐ 641. AL MCBEAN
- ☐ 685. TOM HALLER

MILWAUKEE BREWERS*

- ☐ 2. DIEGO SEGUI
- ☐ 31. MARTY PATTIN
- ☐ 53. JOHN KENNEDY
- ☐ 88. MIGUEL FUENTES(R)
- ☐ 88. DICK BANEY(R)
- ☐ 111. MIKE HEGAN
- ☐ 134. DANNY WALTON
- ☐ 158. JERRY MCNERTNEY
- ☐ 185. DON MINCHER
- ☐ 224. STEVE BARBER
- ☐ 249. BOB LOCKER
- ☐ 271. GREG GOOSSEN
- ☐ 289. GENE BRABENDER
- ☐ 323. WAYNE COMER
- ☐ 359. PHIL ROOF
- ☐ 370. TOMMY HARPER
- ☐ 393. JOHN GELNAR
- ☐ 418. JOHN DONALDSON
- ☐ 441. JOHN O'DONOGHUE
- ☐ 473. DON BRYANT
- ☐ 499. SKIP LOCKWOOD
- ☐ 514. STEVE HOVLEY
- ☐ 533. BUZZ STEPHEN
- ☐ 556. DAVE BRISTOL(M)
- ☐ 574. BOBBY BOLIN
- ☐ 596. MIKE HERSHBERGER
- ☐ 613. DAVE BALDWIN
- ☐ 652. RICH ROLLINS
- ☐ 667. BOB MEYER
- ☐ 688. TED KUBIAK
- ☐ 713. TEAM CARD

MINNESOTA TWINS

- ☐ 25. CESAR TOVAR
- ☐ 47. BOB L. MILLER
- ☐ 75. JIM KAAT
- ☐ 93. RICK RENICK
- ☐ 118. GEORGE MITTERWALD
- ☐ 150. HARMON KILLEBREW
- ☐ 169. TOM HALL
- ☐ 194. CHUCK MANUEL
- ☐ 226. RON PERRANOSKI
- ☐ 231. LUIS TIANT
- ☐ 245. LEO CARDENAS
- ☐ 267. HERMAN HILL(R)
- ☐ 267. PAUL RATLIFF(R)
- ☐ 290. ROD CAREW
- ☐ 325. DAVE BOSWELL
- ☐ 353. STAN WILLIAMS
- ☐ 379. TOM TISCHINSKI
- ☐ 404. RICH REESE
- ☐ 426. BILL RIGNEY(M)
- ☐ 479. DICK WOODSON
- ☐ 510. TONY OLIVA
- ☐ 534. TEAM CARD
- ☐ 572. FRANK QUILICI
- ☐ 620. JIM PERRY
- ☐ 635. BOB ALLISON
- ☐ 702. BILL ZEPP(R)

MONTREAL EXPOS

- ☐ 19. JOHN BOCCABELLA
- ☐ 38. MACK JONES
- ☐ 87. STEVE RENKO
- ☐ 109. GARRY JESTADT(R)
- ☐ 109. CARL MORTON(R)
- ☐ 124. LARRY JASTER
- ☐ 147. ANGEL HERMOSO
- ☐ 164. TY CLINE
- ☐ 193. MIKE WEGENER
- ☐ 221. RON BRAND
- ☐ 238. JOSE LABOY
- ☐ 243. JOE SPARMA
- ☐ 268. CLAUDE RAYMOND
- ☐ 293. BOB BAILEY
- ☐ 332. BOBBY WINE
- ☐ 364. DAN MCGINN
- ☐ 398. BILL STONEMAN
- ☐ 417. JOHN BATEMAN
- ☐ 442. GENE MAUCH(M)
- ☐ 476. DON SHAW
- ☐ 509. TEAM CARD
- ☐ 527. DON BOSCH
- ☐ 548. HOWIE REED
- ☐ 585. RUSTY STAUB
- ☐ 607. GARY WASLEWSKI
- ☐ 632. GARY SUTHERLAND
- ☐ 646. JIM BRITTON
- ☐ 666. ADOLFO PHILLIPS
- ☐ 690. RON FAIRLY
- ☐ 707. KEVIN COLLINS

NEW YORK METS

- ☐ 1. TEAM CARD
- ■ 26. TUG MCGRAW
- ■ 50. TOMMIE AGEE
- ■ 83. DON CARDWELL
- ■ 99. BOBBY PFEIL
- ■ 137. ART SHAMSKY
- ■ 138. JOE FOY
- ■ 153. GARY GENTRY
- ■ 183. JERRY GROTE
- ☐ 214. KEN BOSWELL
- ■ 246. JIM MCANDREW
- ☐ 280. DONN CLENDENON
- ■ 300. TOM SEAVER
- ☐ 348. MIKE JORGENSEN(R)
- ☐ 348. JESSE HUDSON(R)
- ■ 371. ROD GASPAR
- ☐ 394. GIL HODGES(M)
- ☐ 419. RON TAYLOR
- ☐ 431. RON SWOBODA
- ☐ 488. J.C. MARTIN
- ☐ 498. AL WEIS
- ☐ 521. CAL KOONCE
- ☐ 557. ED KRANEPOOL
- ☐ 575. CLEON JONES
- ☐ 610. JERRY KOOSMAN
- ☐ 628. WAYNE GARRETT
- ☐ 634. BUD HARRELSON
- ☐ 679. RAY SADECKI
- ☐ 692. DUFFY DYER
- ☐ 712. NOLAN RYAN

NEW YORK YANKEES

- ☐ 23. BILL ROBINSON
- ☐ 43. JACK AKER
- ☐ 82. FRANK FERNANDEZ
- ☐ 100. MEL STOTTLEMYRE
- ☐ 114. GENE MICHAEL
- ☐ 142. FRITZ PETERSON
- ☐ 167. BILL BURBACH
- ☐ 189. THURMAN MUNSON(R)
- ☐ 189. DAVE MCDONALD(R)
- ☐ 219. JERRY KENNEY
- ☐ 253. RON WOODS
- ☐ 273. RALPH HOUK(M)
- ☐ 297. CURT BLEFARY
- ☐ 333. BOBBY MURCER
- ☐ 349. STEVE HAMILTON
- ☐ 373. ROY WHITE
- ☐ 399. TEAM CARD
- ☐ 416. JOE VERBANIC
- ☐ 437. DANNY CATER
- ☐ 493. LINDY MCDANIEL
- ☐ 516. JOHN ELLIS(R)
- ☐ 516. JIM LYTTLE(R)
- ☐ 536. MIKE KEKICH
- ☐ 568. STAN BAHNSEN
- ☐ 594. JAKE GIBBS
- ☐ 623. HORACE CLARKE
- ☐ 659. PETE WARD
- ☐ 689. FRANK TEPEDINO
- ☐ 702. RON KLIMKOWSKI(R)

Dave Boswell PITCHER

* All cards appear as Seattle Pilots.

OAKLAND A'S

- [ ] 21. VIDA BLUE(R)
- [ ] 21. GENE TENACE(R)
- [ ] 41. GEORGE LAUZERIQUE
- [ ] 55. JOHN ODOM
- [ ] 102. JOE RUDI
- [ ] 120. SAL BANDO
- [ ] 140. REGGIE JACKSON
- [ ] 205. BERT CAMPENERIS
- [ ] 233. LEW KRAUSSE
- [ ] 259. TOMMIE REYNOLDS
- [ ] 287. FRED TALBOT
- [ ] 311. DICK GREEN
- [ ] 331. CHUCK DOBSON
- [ ] 381. BOBBY BROOKS(R)
- [ ] 381. MIKE OLIVO(R)
- [ ] 408. PAUL LINDBLAD
- [ ] 434. FELIPE ALOU
- [ ] 481. JOSE TARTABULL
- [ ] 502. ROLLIE FINGERS
- [ ] 531. RON CLARK
- [ ] 547. RICK MONDAY
- [ ] 565. JIM HUNTER
- [ ] 584. AL DOWNING
- [ ] 603. RAY OYLER
- [ ] 631. TEAM CARD
- [ ] 648. LARRY HANEY
- [ ] 663. TITO FRANCONA
- [ ] 678. DAVE DUNCAN
- [ ] 693. BOB W. JOHNSON
- [ ] 706. JOHN MCNAMARA(M)
- [ ] 719. JIM ROLAND

PHILADELPHIA PHILLIES

- [ ] 6. GRANT JACKSON
- [ ] 24. DICK SELMA
- [ ] 28. BILLY WILSON
- [ ] 56. JOE LIS(R)
- [ ] 56. SCOTT REID(R)
- [ ] 90. TIM MCCARVER
- [ ] 125. DERON JOHNSON
- [ ] 149. BILLY CHAMPION
- [ ] 168. DAVE WATKINS
- [ ] 186. RICK JOSEPH
- [ ] 218. RON STONE
- [ ] 252. LOWELL PALMER
- [ ] 270. CHRIS SHORT
- [ ] 288. LARRY HISLE
- [ ] 302. JEFF JAMES
- [ ] 324. TONY TAYLOR
- [ ] 360. CURT FLOOD
- [ ] 388. BYRON BROWNE
- [ ] 403. JIM BUNNING
- [ ] 436. TEAM CARD
- [ ] 486. TERRY HARMON
- [ ] 511. JOE HOERNER
- [ ] 539. DENNY DOYLE(R)
- [ ] 539. LARRY BOWA(R)
- [ ] 564. JOHNNY BRIGGS
- [ ] 591. MIKE RYAN
- [ ] 605. RICK WISE
- [ ] 645. DON MONEY
- [ ] 654. OSCAR GAMBLE(R)
- [ ] 662. FRANK LUCCHESI(M)
- [ ] 677. WOODIE FRYMAN

PITTSBURGH PIRATES

- [ ] 8. JOSE MARTINEZ
- [ ] 30. MATTY ALOU
- [ ] 52. BRUCE DAL CANTON
- [ ] 94. FRED PATEK
- [ ] 110. BOB MOOSE
- [ ] 141. DAVE CASH(R)
- [ ] 141. JOHNNY JETER(R)
- [ ] 166. AL OLIVER
- [ ] 188. MANNY SANGUILLEN
- [ ] 216. CHUCK HARTENSTEIN
- [ ] 236. BOB VEALE
- [ ] 264. RICH HEBNER
- [ ] 322. LUKE WALKER
- [ ] 350. ROBERTO CLEMENTE
- [ ] 372. DAVE GIUSTI
- [ ] 396. STEVE BLASS
- [ ] 423. JERRY MAY
- [ ] 440. BILL MAZEROSKI
- [ ] 470. WILLIE STARGELL
- [ ] 517. JOE GIBBON

- [ ] 532. DANNY MURTAUGH(M)
- [ ] 551. DOCK ELLIS
- [ ] 566. GENE ALLEY
- [ ] 608. TEAM CARD
- [ ] 626. DAVE RICKETTS
- [ ] 643. JOSE PAGAN
- [ ] 654. ANGEL MANGUAL(R)
- [ ] 664. BOB ROBERTSON
- [ ] 703. LOU MARONE

ST. LOUIS CARDINALS

- [ ] 40. RICH ALLEN
- [ ] 76. CARL TAYLOR
- [ ] 92. GEORGE CULVER
- [ ] 96. LERON LEE(R)
- [ ] 96. JERRY REUSS(R)
- [ ] 119. CHUCK TAYLOR
- [ ] 139. RICH NYE
- [ ] 143. PHIL GAGLIANO
- [ ] 162. JERRY JOHNSON
- [ ] 190. JOE TORRE
- [ ] 220. STEVE CARLTON
- [ ] 256. VIC DAVALILLO
- [ ] 282. STEVE HUNTZ
- [ ] 312. MIKE TORREZ
- [ ] 330. LOU BROCK
- [ ] 346. RED SCHOENDIENST(M)
- [ ] 362. JOE HAGUE
- [ ] 386. BILL DILLMAN
- [ ] 415. JULIAN JAVIER
- [ ] 435. NELSON BRILES
- [ ] 482. TOM HILGENDORF
- [ ] 503. DAL MAXVILL
- [ ] 530. BOB GIBSON
- [ ] 549. TEAM CARD
- [ ] 569. COOKIE ROJAS
- [ ] 614. MIKE SHANNON
- [ ] 675. JOSE CARDENAL
- [ ] 716. SAL CAMPISI(R)
- [ ] 716. REGGIE CLEVELAND(R)
- [ ] 716. SANTIAGO GUZMAN(R)

SAN DIEGO PADRES

- [ ] 11. NATE COLBERT
- [ ] 44. ROBERTO PENA
- [ ] 79. CLAY KIRBY
- [ ] 103. FRANK REBERGER
- [ ] 130. OLLIE BROWN
- [ ] 151. DAVE A. ROBERTS
- [ ] 179. IVAN MURRELL
- [ ] 212. AL SANTORINI
- [ ] 234. TOMMY DEAN
- [ ] 262. JERRY MORALES(R)
- [ ] 262. JIM WILLIAMS(R)
- [ ] 284. JACK BALDSCHUN
- [ ] 314. BILL MCCOOL
- [ ] 329. CHRIS CANNIZZARO
- [ ] 345. AL FERRARA
- [ ] 352. BOB BARTON
- [ ] 374. TOMMIE SISK
- [ ] 392. WALT HRINIAK
- [ ] 421. PAT DOBSON
- [ ] 474. DICK KELLEY
- [ ] 494. LARRY STAHL
- [ ] 513. PRESTON GOMEZ(M)
- [ ] 526. RON HERBEL
- [ ] 573. MIKE CORKINS(R)
- [ ] 573. RAFAEL ROBLES(R)
- [ ] 573. RON SLOCUM(R)
- [ ] 587. JOSE ARCIA
- [ ] 604. CLARENCE GASTON
- [ ] 639. DAVE CAMPBELL
- [ ] 644. GERRY NYMAN
- [ ] 657. TEAM CARD
- [ ] 694. GARY ROSS
- [ ] 718. ED SPIEZIO

SAN FRANCISCO GIANTS

- [ ] 13. JACK HIATT
- [ ] 42. TITO FUENTES
- [ ] 58. DAVE MARSHALL
- [ ] 77. FRANK LINZY
- [ ] 107. BOBBY ETHERIDGE
- [ ] 135. DICK DIETZ
- [ ] 176. JIM HART
- [ ] 210. JUAN MARICHAL
- [ ] 229. RICH ROBERTSON

- [ ] 250. WILLIE MCCOVEY
- [ ] 276. RON HUNT
- [ ] 298. KEN HENDERSON
- [ ] 337. MIKE MCCORMICK
- [ ] 357. BOB BURDA
- [ ] 378. JIM DAVENPORT
- [ ] 401. JOHN HARRELL(R)
- [ ] 401. BERNIE WILLIAMS(R)
- [ ] 425. BOBBY BONDS
- [ ] 433. RON BRYANT
- [ ] 478. BOB HEISE
- [ ] 496. STEVE WHITAKER
- [ ] 519. DON MCMAHON
- [ ] 560. GAYLORD PERRY
- [ ] 583. HAL LANIER
- [ ] 600. WILLIE MAYS
- [ ] 624. CLYDE KING(M)
- [ ] 651. JIM GOSGER
- [ ] 681. BOB GARIBALDI
- [ ] 696. TEAM CARD

WASHINGTON SENATORS

- [ ] 14. HANK ALLEN
- [ ] 49. TIM CULLEN
- [ ] 84. PAUL CASANOVA
- [ ] 106. DAROLD KNOWLES
- [ ] 127. JOE COLEMAN
- [ ] 154. JIM MILES(R)
- [ ] 154. JAN DUKES(R)
- [ ] 175. DICK BOSMAN
- [ ] 211. TED WILLIAMS(M)
- [ ] 235. MIKE EPSTEIN
- [ ] 281. CASEY COX
- [ ] 303. BRANT ALYEA
- [ ] 328. GEORGE BRUNET
- [ ] 336. DEL UNSER
- [ ] 365. ZOILO VERSALLES
- [ ] 389. JIM SHELLENBACK
- [ ] 420. KEN MCMULLEN
- [ ] 439. LEE MAYE
- [ ] 487. CISCO CARLOS
- [ ] 506. ED STROUD
- [ ] 538. BOB HUMPHREYS
- [ ] 550. FRANK HOWARD
- [ ] 577. BERNIE ALLEN
- [ ] 599. DICK STELMASZEK(R)
- [ ] 599. GENE MARTIN(R)
- [ ] 599. DICK SUCH(R)
- [ ] 617. JIM FRENCH
- [ ] 655. JOHN ROSEBORO
- [ ] 676. TEAM CARD
- [ ] 691. JOE GRZENDA
- [ ] 697. JIM HANNAN
- [ ] 711. ED BRINKMAN

1971 TOPPS (752)
2 1/2" X 3 1/2"

ATLANTA BRAVES

- [ ] 8. MIKE MCQUEEN
- [ ] 30. PHIL NIEKRO
- [ ] 52. OSCAR BROWN(R)
- [ ] 52. EARL WILLIAMS(R)
- [ ] 81. FELIX MILLAN
- [ ] 88. HAL KING

☐ 147. BOB PRIDDY
☐ 173. GIL GARRIDO
☐ 194. MIKE LUM
☐ 223. CECIL UPSHAL
☐ 244. BOB TILLMAN
☐ 270. RICO CARTY
☐ 306. JIM NASH
☐ 346. LUM HARRIS(M)
☐ 359. RON REED
☐ 374. CLETE BOYER
☐ 387. RON HERBEL
☐ 400. HANK AARON
☐ 432. BOB DIDIER
☐ 463. TOM KELLEY
☐ 494. RALPH GARR(R)
☐ 494. RICK KESTER(R)
☐ 507. GEORGE STONE
☐ 529. MARTY PEREZ(R)
☐ 587. SONNY JACKSON
☐ 605. ORLANDO CEPEDA
☐ 623. PAT JARVIS
☐ 652. TEAM CARD
☐ 663. MARV STAEHLE
☐ 668. GARY NEIBAUER
☐ 709. DUSTY BAKER(R)
☐ 717. TOMMIE AARON

BALTIMORE ORIOLES

☐   1. TEAM CARD
☐ 29. DON BUFORD
☐ 53. PAUL BLAIR
☐ 99. MARK BELANGER
☐ 122. EDDIE WATT
☐ 137. MARCELINO LOPEZ
☐ 170. MIKE CUELLAR
☐ 193. BOB GRICH
☐ 219. ELROD HENDRICKS
☐ 249. CHICO SALMON
☐ 273. PETE RICHERT
☐ 300. BROOKS ROBINSON
☐ 320. DAVE MCNALLY
☐ 362. MIKE ADAMSON(R)
☐ 362. ROGER FREED(R)
☐ 392. GRANT JACKSON
☐ 393. MERV RETTENMUND
☐ 417. DICK HALL
☐ 453. TERRY CROWLEY
☐ 477. EARL WEAVER(M)
☐ 491. JIM HARDIN
☐ 501. ANDY ETCHEBARREN
☐ 547. PAT DOBSON
☐ 570. JIM PALMER
☐ 595. DAVE A. JOHNSON
☐ 617. CLAY DALRYMPLE
☐ 640. FRANK ROBINSON
☐ 684. CURT MOTTON
☐ 700. BOOG POWELL
☐ 709. DON BAYLOR(R)
☐ 716. DAVE LEONHARD

BOSTON RED SOX

☐   9. GEORGE SCOTT
☐ 31. EDDIE KASKO(M)
☐ 58. BILL LEE
☐ 89. KEN BRETT
☐ 114. BILLY CONIGLIARO
☐ 159. JARVIS TATUM
☐ 176. BOB MONTGOMERY(R)
☐ 176. DOUG GRIFFIN(R)
☐ 191. MIKE ANDREWS
☐ 225. GARY PETERS
☐ 254. CAL KOONCE
☐ 287. MIKE FIORE
☐ 302. PHIL GAGLIANO
☐ 305. REGGIE SMITH
☐ 340. RICO PETROCELLI
☐ 363. MIKE NAGY
☐ 386. TEAM CARD
☐ 409. DON PAVLETICH
☐ 446. BOBBY BOLIN
☐ 473. GARY WAGNER
☐ 498. JOHN KENNEDY
☐ 512. DICK MILLS(R)
☐ 512. MIKE GARMAN(R)
☐ 530. CARL YASTRZEMSKI
☐ 557. TOM SATRIANO
☐ 577. JIM LONBORG
☐ 601. KEN TATUM

☐ 622. JOE LAHOUD
☐ 649. SPARKY LYLE
☐ 660. RAY CULP
☐ 678. GEORGE THOMAS
☐ 692. ROGELIO MORET(R)
☐ 710. SONNY SIEBERT
☐ 740. LUIS APARICIO

CALIFORNIA ANGELS

☐ 15. ANDY MESSERSMITH
☐ 43. STEVE KEALEY
☐ 78. JIM SPENCER
☐ 105. TONY CONIGLIARO
☐ 152. LLOYD ALLEN(R)
☐ 152. WINSTON LLENAS(R)
☐ 174. DAVE LAROCHE
☐ 205. GERRY MOSES
☐ 240. CLYDE WRITHT
☐ 256. TONY GONZALEZ
☐ 279. LEFTY PHILLIPS(M)
☐ 318. RUDY MAY
☐ 360. JIM FREGOSI
☐ 401. TOM MURPHY
☐ 421. JOHN STEPHENSON
☐ 442. TEAM CARD
☐ 466. KEN BERRY
☐ 485. KEN MCMULLEN
☐ 508. ROGER REPOZ
☐ 526. RAY JARVIS
☐ 559. TERRY COX(R)
☐ 561. SYD O'BRIEN
☐ 590. ALEX JOHNSON
☐ 614. BILLY COWAN
☐ 631. EDDIE FISHER
☐ 645. JIM MALONEY
☐ 657. JOSE AZCUE
☐ 664. ARCHIE REYNOLDS(R)
☐ 666. GENE BRABENDER
☐ 676. TOMMIE REYNOLDS
☐ 686. CHICO RUIZ
☐ 697. RICKEY CLARK
☐ 707. FRED LASHER
☐ 718. BILLY WYNNE
☐ 736. MEL QUEEN
☐ 745. SANDY ALOMAR

CHICAGO CUBS

☐ 12. JOHNNY CALLISON
☐ 38. JIM COLBORN
☐ 90. JOE PEPITONE
☐ 98. JOE DECKER
☐ 121. JIM DUNEGAN(R)
☐ 121. ROE SKIDMORE(R)
☐ 151. TOMMY DAVIS
☐ 175. JIM HICKMAN
☐ 203. LARRY GURA
☐ 220. RON SANTO
☐ 248. HOYT WILHELM
☐ 280. FERGIE JENKINS
☐ 350. BILLY WILLIAMS
☐ 390. GLENN BECKERT
☐ 410. KEN HOLTZMAN
☐ 424. ROBERTO RODRIQUEZ
☐ 441. MILT PAPPAS
☐ 455. DON KESSINGER
☐ 472. KEN RUDOLPH
☐ 502. TEAM CARD
☐ 525. ERNIE BANKS
☐ 542. BOB L. MILLER
☐ 558. HECTOR TORRES
☐ 576. ADRIAN GARRETT(R)
☐ 576. BROCK DAVIS(R)
☐ 576. GARRY JESTADT(R)
☐ 592. RANDY HUNDLEY
☐ 609. LEO DUROCHER(M)
☐ 634. PHIL REGAN
☐ 647. JUAN PIZARRO
☐ 670. BILL HANDS
☐ 704. J.C. MARTIN
☐ 726. PAUL POPOVICH

CHICAGO WHITE SOX

☐ 13. CHARLIE BRINKMAN(R)
☐ 13. DICK MOLONEY(R)
☐ 37. RICH MCKINNEY
☐ 56. DUANE JOSEPHSON

☐ 80. BILL MELTON
☐ 113. JERRY CRIDER
☐ 156. BART JOHNSON
☐ 169. ED HERRMAN
☐ 186. BOB SPENCE
☐ 227. FLOYD WEAVER
☐ 243. CARLOS MAY
☐ 267. RICH MORALES
☐ 289. TEAM CARD
☐ 292. JAY JOHNSTONE
☐ 311. LEE STANGE
☐ 345. JOE HORLEN
☐ 373. TOM MCCRAW
☐ 413. H. PAT KELLY
☐ 436. WILBUR WOOD
☐ 458. RON LOLICH(R)
☐ 458. DAVE LEMONDS(R)
☐ 489. LUIS ALVARADO
☐ 506. BOBBY KNOOP
☐ 520. TOMMY JOHN
☐ 537. TOM EGAN
☐ 555. WALT WILLIAMS
☐ 588. TOM BRADLEY
☐ 627. STEVE HAMILTON
☐ 643. RICK REICHARDT
☐ 661. CHUCK TANNER(M)
☐ 679. DON O'RILEY
☐ 723. VICENTE ROMO
☐ 733. LEE MAYE
☐ 748. JOHN PURDIN

CINCINNATI REDS

☐ 14. DAVE CONCEPCION
☐ 40. LEE MAY
☐ 75. GARY NOLAN
☐ 100. PETE ROSE
☐ 124. DON GULLETT
☐ 164. FRANK DUFFY(R)
☐ 164. MILT WILCOX(R)
☐ 177. HAL MCRAE
☐ 190. BOB TOLAN
☐ 218. TONY CLONINGER
☐ 250. JOHNNY BENCH
☐ 272. TOMMY HELMS
☐ 293. PAT CORRALES
☐ 319. TY CLINE
☐ 339. WAYNE SIMPSON
☐ 357. TEAM CARD
☐ 377. GREG GARRETT
☐ 379. WAYNE GRANGER
☐ 394. CLAY CARROLL
☐ 420. JIM MERRITT
☐ 457. WILLIE SMITH
☐ 478. BERNIE CARBO
☐ 496. WOODY WOODWARD
☐ 538. ANGEL BRAVO
☐ 556. JIM MCGLOTHLIN
☐ 580. TONY PEREZ
☐ 613. PEDRO BORBON
☐ 632. DARREL CHANEY
☐ 644. JIM STEWART
☐ 688. SPARKY ANDERSON(M)
☐ 731. JIM QUALLS

CLEVELAND INDIANS

☐ 24. RICH HAND
☐ 41. RICK AUSTIN
☐ 87. JACK HEIDEMANN
☐ 107. ROY FOSTER
☐ 125. RAY FOSSE
☐ 150. SAM MCDOWELL
☐ 172. DUKE SIMS
☐ 211. PHIL HENNIGAN
☐ 231. VINCE COLBERT(R)
☐ 231. JOHN LOWENSTEIN(R)
☐ 252. EDDIE LEON
☐ 275. VADA PINSON
☐ 294. STEVE DUNNING
☐ 324. GRAIG NETTLES
☐ 347. TED UHLAENDER
☐ 375. STEVE HARGAN
☐ 397. ALVIN DARK(M)
☐ 429. CHUCK HINTON
☐ 454. MIKE PAUL
☐ 479. DENNIS HIGGINS
☐ 510. KEN HARRELSON
☐ 539. LARRY BROWN
☐ 552. BUDDY BRADFORD

☐ 584. TEAM CARD
☐ 597. KEN SUAREZ
☐ 612. LOU CAMILLI(R)
☐ 612. TED FORD(R)
☐ 612. STEVE MINGORI(R)
☐ 689. FRANK BAKER
☐ 727. RAY LAMB

DETROIT TIGERS

☐   3. DICK MCAULIFFE
☐ 39. LERRIN LAGROW(R)
☐ 39. GENE LAMONT(R)
☐ 86. MIKE KILKENNY
☐ 101. LES CAIN
☐ 120. WILLIE HORTON
☐ 133. MICKEY LOLICH
☐ 154. CESAR GUTIERREZ
☐ 180. AL KALINE
☐ 208. BILLY MARTIN
☐ 229. JIM HANNAN
☐ 265. JIM NORTHRUP
☐ 296. TOM TIMMERMANN
☐ 316. FRED SCHERMAN
☐ 336. TEAM CARD
☐ 367. DALTON JONES
☐ 389. ED BRINKMAN
☐ 403. JOE COLEMAN
☐ 423. DENNIS SAUNDERS(R)
☐ 423. TIM MARTING(R)
☐ 444. JIMMIE PRICE
☐ 464. AURELIO RODRIGUEZ
☐ 481. DARYL PATTERSON
☐ 503. GATES BROWN
☐ 524. MICKEY STANLEY
☐ 553. KEVIN COLLINS
☐ 575. BILL FREEHAN
☐ 599. NORM CASH
☐ 629. JOHN HILLER
☐ 669. IKE BROWN
☐ 695. JOE NIEKRO
☐ 708. RUSS NAGELSON
☐ 732. BOB REED
☐ 749. KEN SZOTKIEWICZ

HOUSTON ASTROS

☐ 18. NORM MILLER
☐ 44. JOHNNY EDWARDS
☐ 79. WADE BLASINGAME
☐ 102. KEN FORSCH(R)
☐ 102. LARRY HOWARD(R)
☐ 130. DENIS MENKE
☐ 148. JOHN MAYBERRY
☐ 162. JACK BILLINGHAM
☐ 222. BOB WATSON
☐ 237. CESAR CEDENO
☐ 242. JIM RAY
☐ 264. JOE MORGAN
☐ 291. GEORGE CULVER
☐ 312. HARRY WALKER(M)
☐ 337. JESUS ALOU
☐ 371. JACK HIATT
☐ 381. FRED GLADDING
☐ 404. BUDDY HARRIS(R)
☐ 404. ROGER METZGER(R)
☐ 425. DOUG RADER
☐ 447. CESAR GERONIMO
☐ 471. TOM GRIFFIN
☐ 484. DON WILSON
☐ 540. LARRY DIERKER
☐ 565. JIM WYNN
☐ 583. RON COOK
☐ 602. MARTY MARTINEZ
☐ 636. DENNY LEMASTER
☐ 677. JACK DILAURO
☐ 722. TEAM CARD
☐ 728. KEITH LAMPARD(R)
☐ 741. SKIP GUINN
☐ 747. SCIPIO SPINKS(R)

KANSAS CITY ROYALS

☐ 17. BILLY SORRELL
☐ 35. LOU PINIELLA
☐ 91. BOB LEMON(M)
☐ 103. RICH SEVERSON
☐ 118. COOKIE ROJAS
☐ 129. AURELIO MONTEAGUDO
☐ 144. JACKIE HERNANDEZ

☐ 163. BUCK MARTINEZ
☐ 187. TED ABERNATHY
☐ 221. DAVE MOREHEAD
☐ 247. JERRY CRAM(R)
☐ 247. PAUL SPLITTORFF(R)
☐ 269. GAIL HOPKINS
☐ 299. ED KIRKPATRICK
☐ 321. TOM MATCHICK
☐ 344. ELLIE RODRIGUEZ
☐ 411. GEORGE SPRIGGS
☐ 431. TOM BURGMEIER
☐ 451. JOE KEOUGH
☐ 470. BOB OLIVER
☐ 487. PAUL SCHAAL
☐ 504. KEN WRIGHT
☐ 528. WALLY BUNKER
☐ 546. JOHN MATIAS
☐ 564. AL FITZMORRIS
☐ 581. ROGER NELSON
☐ 610. AMOS OTIS
☐ 626. FREEDIE PATEK
☐ 633. SCOTT NORTHEY(R)
☐ 646. BOBBY FLOYD
☐ 662. MIKE HEDLUND
☐ 681. BILL BUTLER
☐ 701. BOB GARIBALDI
☐ 719. JERRY MAY
☐ 730. JIM ROOKER
☐ 742. TEAM CARD
☐ 752. DICK DRAGO

LOS ANGELES DODGERS

☐ 10. CLAUDE OSTEEN
☐ 34. SANDY VANCE
☐ 57. VON JOSHUA
☐ 85. BILLY GRABARKEWITZ
☐ 112. MANNY MOTA
☐ 145. BILL SINGER
☐ 188. BOB VALENTINE(R)
☐ 188. MIKE STRAHLER(R)
☐ 207. ALAN FOSTER
☐ 226. BILL RUSSELL
☐ 253. BILL SUDAKIS
☐ 288. JOE MOELLER
☐ 314. JEFF TORBORG
☐ 341. STEVE GARVEY
☐ 361. DON SUTTON
☐ 385. MAURY WILLS
☐ 402. TEAM CARD
☐ 430. WES PARKER
☐ 459. JIM LEFEBVRE
☐ 488. JERRY STEPHENSON
☐ 519. WILLIE CRAWFORD
☐ 529. BILL BUCKNER(R)
☐ 549. JIM BREWER
☐ 567. WALT ALSTON(M)
☐ 585. WILLIE DAVIS
☐ 639. TOM HALLER
☐ 650. RICH ALLEN
☐ 693. JOSE PENA
☐ 709. TOM PACIOREK(R)

MILWAUKEE BREWERS

☐ 22. PHIL ROOF
☐ 48. DAVE BALDWIN
☐ 76. TED SAVAGE
☐ 97. FLOYD WICKER

☐ 116. KEN SANDERS
☐ 149. MIKE HERSHBERGER
☐ 182. AL DOWNING
☐ 204. BERNIE SMITH(R)
☐ 204. GEORGE KOPACZ(R)
☐ 236. BOB HUMPHREYS
☐ 260. TOMMY HARPER
☐ 281. DANNY WALTON
☐ 309. DICK ELLSWORTH
☐ 334. ROBERTO PENA
☐ 353. CARL TAYLOR
☐ 372. LEW KRAUSSE
☐ 415. MIKE HEGAN
☐ 433. SKIP LOCKWOOD
☐ 456. BOB MEYER
☐ 493. DAVE MAY
☐ 516. TED KUBIAK
☐ 579. MARTY PATTIN
☐ 604. JOHN GELNAR
☐ 633. PETE KOEGEL(R)
☐ 637. DAVE BRISTOL(M)
☐ 653. RUSS SNYDER
☐ 671. BILL VOSS
☐ 692. WAYNE TWITCHELL(R)
☐ 698. TEAM CARD
☐ 721. JOHN MORRIS
☐ 746. ANDY KOSCO

MINNESOTA TWINS

☐   7. JIM HOLT
☐ 26. BERT BLYLEVEN
☐ 74. PETE HAMM(R)
☐ 74. JIM NETTLES(R)
☐ 95. LUIS TIANT
☐ 127. DANNY THOMPSON
☐ 141. FRANK QUILICI
☐ 165. CESAR TOVAR
☐ 189. GEORGE MITTERWALD
☐ 210. ROD CAREW
☐ 245. JIM KATT
☐ 271. BILL ZEPP
☐ 290. TONY OLIVA
☐ 313. TOM HALL
☐ 349. RICH REESE
☐ 391. STEVE BRYE(R)
☐ 391. COTTON NASH(R)
☐ 405. LEO CARDENAS
☐ 449. BRANT ALYEA
☐ 475. RON PERRANOSKI
☐ 500. JIM PERRY
☐ 522. TEAM CARD
☐ 532. BILL RIGNEY(M)
☐ 550. HARMON KILLEBREW
☐ 568. SAL CAMPISI
☐ 586. DICK WOODSON
☐ 607. PAUL RATLIFF
☐ 638. STAN WILLIAMS
☐ 675. DAVE BOSWELL
☐ 692. HAL HAYDEL(R)
☐ 694. RICK RENICK
☐ 724. TOM TISCHINSKI
☐ 744. CHUCK MANUEL

MONTREAL EXPOS

☐ 21. DAN MCGINN
☐ 42. BOOTS DAY
☐ 59. GENE MAUCH(M)
☐ 94. DON HAHN
☐ 132. JOSE LABOY
☐ 142. MACK JONES
☐ 157. BOB BAILEY
☐ 171. BOBBY WINE
☐ 209. STEVE RENKO
☐ 232. JOHN STROHMAYER
☐ 266. BILL STONEMAN
☐ 284. JIM GOSGER
☐ 304. RON BRAND
☐ 315. RON FAIRLY
☐ 376. CLYDE MASHORE(R)
☐ 376. ERNIE MCANALLY(R)
☐ 398. HOWIE REED
☐ 418. ADOLFO PHILLIPS
☐ 434. GARY SUTHERLAND
☐ 452. JOHN BOCCABELLA
☐ 474. JIM FAIREY
☐ 515. CARL MORTON
☐ 536. CLAUDE RAYMOND

☐ 560. RUSTY STAUB
☐ 578. RON HUNT
☐ 608. MIKE WEGENER
☐ 628. JOHN BATEMAN
☐ 664. BOB REYNOLDS(R)
☐ 665. RON SWOBODA
☐ 674. TEAM CARD
☐ 699. JIM BRITTON
☐ 713. MIKE MARSHALL
☐ 743. JOHN O'DONOGHUE
☐ 747. BALOR MOORE(R)

NEW YORK METS

▪ 16. KEN SINGLETON
▪ 36. DEAN CHANCE
☐ 83. TIM FOLI(R)
☐ 83. RANDY BOBB(R)
▪ 104. DAN FRISELLA
▪ 115. DONN CLENDENON
▪ 136. DUFFY DYER
▪ 160. TOM SEAVER
▪ 183. GIL HODGES(M)
☐ 228. WAYNE GARRETT
▪ 259. DAVE MARSHALL
☐ 278. JERRY GROTE
☐ 310. TOMMIE AGEE
☐ 335. JERRY KOOSMAN
☐ 355. BUD HARRELSON
☐ 406. RAY SADECKI
▪ 428. JIM MCANDREW
☐ 445. ART SHAMSKY
▪ 469. BOB ASPROMONTE
▪ 492. KEN BOSWELL
▪ 513. NOLAN RYAN
☐ 527. CLEON JONES
☐ 573. ED KRANEPOOL
▪ 596. MIKE JORGENSEN
☐ 618. TUG MCGRAW
▪ 641. TEAM CARD
☐ 648. RICH FOLKERS(R)
☐ 648. TED MARTINEZ(R)
☐ 648. JON MATLACK(R)
☐ 651. JERRY ROBERTSON
☐ 687. RON TAYLOR
▪ 725. GARY GENTRY
☐ 751. AL WEIS

NEW YORK YANKEES

☐ 5. THURMAN MUNSON
☐ 28. RON KLIMKOWSKI
☐ 51. STEVE KLINE
☐ 111. LOYD COLSON(R)
☐ 111. BOBBY MITCHELL(R)
☐ 131. CURT BLEFARY
☐ 146. RALPH HOUK(M)
☐ 184. STAN BAHNSEN
☐ 213. FRANK W. BAKER
☐ 234. JIM LYTTLE
☐ 263. JOHN ELLIS
☐ 277. GARY WASLEWSKI
☐ 303. LINDY MCDANIEL
☐ 342. FRANK TEPEDINO
☐ 358. DANNY CATER
☐ 382. JAKE GIBBS
☐ 395. ROY WHITE
☐ 419. RON HANSEN
☐ 438. MIKE MCCORMICK
☐ 460. FRITZ PETERSON
☐ 483. GENE MICHAEL
☐ 514. RON WOODS
☐ 543. TEAM CARD
☐ 559. GARY JONES(R)
☐ 572. JERRY KENNEY
☐ 593. JACK AKER
☐ 615. MEL STOTTLEMYRE
☐ 635. BOBBY MURCER
☐ 667. PETE WARD
☐ 683. BILL BURBACH
☐ 703. MIKE KEKICH
☐ 715. HORACE CLARKE
☐ 734. ROB GARDNER

OAKLAND A'S

☐ 20. REGGIE JACKSON
☐ 45. JIM HUNTER
☐ 84. MARCEL LACHEMANN
☐ 109. STEVE HOVLEY

☐ 135. RICK MONDAY
☐ 178. DAVE DUNCAN
☐ 215. DIEGO SEGUI
☐ 238. CHUCK DOBSON
☐ 258. DICK GREEN
☐ 285. SAL BANDO
☐ 317. JIM DRISCOLL(R)
☐ 317. ANGEL MANGUAL(R)
☐ 338. GENE TENACE
☐ 356. BOB LOCKER
☐ 384. ROLLIE FINGERS
☐ 407. JOE RUDI
☐ 440. BERT CAMPANERIS
☐ 468. FRANK FERNANDEZ
☐ 495. FELIPE ALOU
☐ 523. JOHN ODOM
☐ 544. VIDA BLUE
☐ 624. TEAM CARD
☐ 633. BOBBY BROOKS(R)
☐ 642. JIM ROLAND
☐ 658. PAUL LINDBLAD
☐ 680. DON MINCHER
☐ 714. DICK WILLIAMS(M)

PHILADELPHIA PHILLIES

☐ 23. OSCAR GAMBLE
☐ 49. DON MONEY
☐ 77. MIKE COMPTON
☐ 92. FRED WENZ
☐ 119. FRANK LUCCHESI(M)
☐ 138. JOE LIS(R)
☐ 138. WILLIE MONTANEZ(R)
☐ 166. JOE HOERNER
☐ 192. BILLY WILSON
☐ 233. LARRY BOWA
☐ 246. TONY TAYLOR
☐ 268. TEAM CARD
☐ 297. JOHNNY BRIGGS
☐ 323. BILLY CHAMPION
☐ 352. DENNY DOYLE
☐ 366. RON STONE
☐ 414. WOODIE FRYMAN
☐ 439. GREG LUZINSKI(R)
☐ 439. SCOTT REID(R)
☐ 465. TIM MCCARVER
☐ 490. DERON JOHNSON
☐ 511. CHRIS SHORT
☐ 533. MIKE RYAN
☐ 554. LOWELL PALMER
☐ 574. JIM BUNNING
☐ 598. RICK WISE
☐ 616. LARRY HISLE
☐ 659. BYRON BROWNE
☐ 664. KEN REYNOLDS(R)
☐ 682. TERRY HARMON
☐ 705. DICK SELMA
☐ 728. WAYNE REDMOND(R)
☐ 739. BARRY LERSCH

PITTSBURGH PIRATES

☐ 2. DOCK ELLIS
☐ 27. FRED CAMBRIA(R)
☐ 27. GENE CLINES(R)
☐ 47. JOHNNY JETER
☐ 73. GEORGE BRUNET
☐ 110. BILL MAZEROSKI
☐ 143. STEVE BLASS
☐ 168. BRUCE DAL CANTON
☐ 212. RICH HEBNER
☐ 230. WILLIE STARGELL
☐ 255. BOB ROBERTSON
☐ 282. JOSE PAGAN
☐ 298. JIM NELSON
☐ 343. ED ACOSTA(R)
☐ 343. MILT MAY(R)
☐ 365. BOB D. JOHNSON
☐ 368. BOB VEALE
☐ 388. AL OLIVER
☐ 416. GENE ALLEY
☐ 437. DANNY MURTAUGH(M)
☐ 480. MANNY SANGUILLEN
☐ 509. JIM GRANT
☐ 534. LUKE WALKER
☐ 562. DAVE GIUSTI
☐ 582. DAVE CASH
☐ 603. TEAM CARD
☐ 630. ROBERTO CLEMENTE
☐ 690. BOB MOOSE
☐ 712. JOSE MARTINEZ

ST. LOUIS CARDINALS

☐ 4. VIC DAVALILLO
☐ 32. JERRY DAVANON
☐ 55. STEVE CARLTON
☐ 96. JOE HAGUE
☐ 117. TED SIMMONS
☐ 158. JERRY REUSS
☐ 185. JULIAN JAVIER
☐ 216. REGGIE CLEVELAND(R)
☐ 216. LUIS MELENDEZ(R)
☐ 239. RED SCHOENDIENST(M)
☐ 257. NELSON BRILES
☐ 286. JERRY MCNERTNEY
☐ 308. TEAM CARD
☐ 322. JIM BEAUCHAMP
☐ 348. FRED NORMAN
☐ 370. JOE TORRE
☐ 396. DICK SCHOFIELD
☐ 422. FRANK BERTAINA
☐ 435. JOSE CARDENAL
☐ 450. BOB GIBSON
☐ 476. DAL MAXVILL
☐ 521. LERON LEE
☐ 531. MIKE TORREZ
☐ 541. BOB BURDA
☐ 551. FRANK LINZY
☐ 571. TED SIZEMORE
☐ 594. BOB CHLUPSA(R)
☐ 594. BOB STINSON(R)
☐ 594. AL HRABOSKY(R)
☐ 606. CHUCK TAYLOR
☐ 625. LOU BROCK
☐ 654. DON SHAW
☐ 672. ED CROSBY
☐ 685. MOE DRABOWSKY
☐ 702. MILT RAMIREZ
☐ 720. MATTY ALOU
☐ 735. MIKE SHANNON

SAN DIEGO PADRES

☐ 6. ED SPIEZIO
☐ 25. CLARENCE GASTON
☐ 46. DAVE CAMPBELL
☐ 106. TOM DUKES
☐ 126. DANNY COOMBS
☐ 134. JOSE ARCIA
☐ 153. GARY ROSS
☐ 179. MIKE CORKINS
☐ 214. AL FERRARA
☐ 235. NATE COLBERT
☐ 262. JIM WILLIAMS(R)
☐ 262. DAVE ROBINSON(R)
☐ 274. RON SLOCUM
☐ 301. EARL WILSON
☐ 333. CLAY KIRBY
☐ 364. TOMMY DEAN
☐ 383. ROD GASPAR
☐ 408. RAFAEL ROBLES
☐ 426. CHRIS CANNIZZARO
☐ 448. DAVE A. ROBERTS
☐ 467. AL SANTORINI
☐ 482. TEAM CARD
☐ 505. OLLIE BROWN
☐ 529. ENZO HERNANDEZ(R)
☐ 548. DON MASON
☐ 569. IVAN MURRELL
☐ 589. BOB BARTON
☐ 611. TOM PHOEBUS

☐ 656. GERRY NYMAN
☐ 696. JERRY MORALES
☐ 711. LARRY STAHL
☐ 737. PRESTON GOMEZ(M)
☐ 747. AL SEVERINSEN(R)

SAN FRANCISCO GIANTS

☐ 19. SKIP PITLOCK
☐ 50. WILLIE MCCOVEY
☐ 108. JOHN CUMBERLAND
☐ 128. FRANK JOHNSON
☐ 140. GAYLORD PERRY
☐ 155. KEN HENDERSON
☐ 181. HAL LANIER
☐ 224. ALAN GALLAGHER
☐ 251. FRANK REBERGER
☐ 276. MIKE DAVISON(R)
☐ 276. GEORGE FOSTER(R)
☐ 295. BOBBY BONDS
☐ 325. JUAN MARICHAL
☐ 354. DON MCMAHON
☐ 378. TITO FUENTES
☐ 412. JERRY JOHNSON
☐ 443. RICH ROBERTSON
☐ 461. JIM HART
☐ 486. STEVE HUNTZ
☐ 517. CHARLIE FOX(M)
☐ 545. DICK DIETZ
☐ 563. TEAM CARD
☐ 600. WILLIE MAYS
☐ 621. RON BRYANT
☐ 691. BOB HEISE
☐ 728. BERNIE WILLIAMS(R)
☐ 738. RUSS GIBSON

WASHINGTON SENATORS

☐ 11. ELLIOTT MADDOX
☐ 33. DEL UNSER
☐ 60. DICK BOSMAN
☐ 82. CASEY COX
☐ 93. NORM MCRAE(R)
☐ 93. DENNY RIDDLEBERGER(R)
☐ 139. PAUL CASANOVA
☐ 167. TOM GRIEVE
☐ 217. ED STROUD
☐ 241. DAVE NELSON
☐ 261. DAROLD KNOWLES
☐ 283. DICK SUCH
☐ 307. DON WERT
☐ 326. RICHIE SCHEINBLUM
☐ 351. JIM SHELLENBACK
☐ 380. TED WILLIAMS(M)
☐ 399. JIM FRENCH
☐ 427. BERNIE ALLEN
☐ 462. TEAM CARD
☐ 497. HORACIO PINA
☐ 518. JOE GRZENDA
☐ 535. CURT FLOOD
☐ 559. BILL GOGOLEWSKI
☐ 566. TIM CULLEN
☐ 591. JACKIE BROWN
☐ 620. FRANK HOWARD
☐ 655. MIKE EPSTEIN
☐ 673. GERRY JANESKI
☐ 706. JOE FOY
☐ 729. DICK BILLINGS
☐ 750. DENNY MCLAIN

1972 TOPPS (787)
2 1/2" X 3 1/2"

ROD CAREW

ATLANTA BRAVES

☐ 21. TEAM CARD
☐ 74. CECIL UPSHAW
☐ 97. TOM KELLEY
☐ 119. MARTY PEREZ
☐ 149. GARY NEIBAUER
☐ 171. DARRELL EVANS
☐ 195. ORLANDO CEPEDA
☐ 214. MIKE MCQUEEN
☐ 260. RALPH GARR
☐ 299. HANK AARON
☐ 318. SONNY JACKSON
☐ 333. STEVE BARBER
☐ 351. TOM HOUSE(R)
☐ 351. RICK KESTER(R)
☐ 351. JIMMY BRITTON(R)
☐ 380. EARL WILLIAMS
☐ 401. JIM NASH
☐ 451. TONY LARUSSA
☐ 469. RON HERBEL
☐ 484. LUM HARRIS(M)
☐ 516. OSCAR BROWN
☐ 540. FELIX MILLAN
☐ 591. PAUL CASANOVA
☐ 601. GEORGE STONE
☐ 620. PHIL NIEKOR
☐ 641. MIKE LUM
☐ 675. PAT JARVIS
☐ 740. RICO CARTY
☐ 758. GIL GARRIDO
☐ 764. DUSTY BAKER
☐ 787. RON REED

BALTIMORE ORIOLES

☐ 26. ANDY ETCHEBARREN
☐ 70. MIKE CUELLAR
☐ 100. FRANK ROBINSON
☐ 128. EDDIE WATT
☐ 140. PAT DOBSON
☐ 212. GRANT JACKSON
☐ 235. MERV RETTENMUND
☐ 250. BOOG POWELL
☐ 270. JIM PALMER
☐ 323. EARL WEAVER(M)
☐ 338. BOB GRICH
☐ 370. DON BUFORD
☐ 418. TOM SHOPAY
☐ 456. MARK BELANGER
☐ 474. DON BAYLOR(R)
☐ 474. RORIC HARRISON(R)
☐ 474. JOHNNY OATES(R)
☐ 490. DAVE MCNALLY
☐ 508. ELLIE HENDRICKS
☐ 527. DAVE LEONHARD
☐ 550. BROOKS ROBINSON
☐ 579. DOYLE ALEXANDER
☐ 628. TERRY CROWLEY
☐ 646. CHICO SALMON
☐ 660. PAUL BLAIR
☐ 680. DAVE A. JOHNSON
☐ 724. MICKEY SCOTT(R)
☐ 731. TEAM CARD

BOSTON RED SOX

☐ 2. RAY CULP
☐ 30. RICO PETROCELLI
☐ 37. CARL YASTRZEMSKI
☐ 79. MIKE GARMAN(R)
☐ 79. CECIL COOPER(R)
☐ 79. CARLTON FISK(R)
☐ 113. ROGELIO MORET
☐ 144. MARTY PATTIN
☐ 199. MIKE FIORE
☐ 218. EDDIE KASKO(M)
☐ 259. SPARKY LYLE
☐ 266. BOBBY BOLIN
☐ 290. SONNY SIEBERT
☐ 313. LUIS APARICIO
☐ 328. TEAM CARD
☐ 411. BOB MONTGOMERY
☐ 455. TOMMY HARPER
☐ 472. PHIL GAGLIANO
☐ 488. MIKE NAGY
☐ 503. GARY PETERS
☐ 543. DUANE JOSEPHSON
☐ 565. REGGIE SMITH
☐ 592. LEW KRAUSSE
☐ 636. BILL LEE
☐ 674. JOHN KENNEDY
☐ 676. DANNY CATER
☐ 681. BOBBY PFEIL
☐ 703. DOUG GRIFFIN
☐ 724. JOHN CURTIS(R)
☐ 734. BOB BURDA
☐ 741. RICK MILLER(R)
☐ 761. BEN OGLIVIE(R)
☐ 772. KEN TATUM

CALIFORNIA ANGELS

☐ 19. BILLY COWAN
☐ 55. CLYDE WRIGHT
☐ 71. TEAM CARD
☐ 102. LLOYD ALLEN
☐ 115. JIM FREGOSI
☐ 135. VADA PINSON
☐ 160. ANDY MESSERSMITH
☐ 196. MEL QUEEN
☐ 213. BILL PARKER(R)
☐ 213. ART KUSNYER(R)
☐ 213. TOM SILVERIO(R)
☐ 253. SANDY ALOMAR
☐ 272. MICKEY RIVERS
☐ 289. SYD O'BRIEN
☐ 354. TOM MURPHY
☐ 379. KEN BERRY
☐ 404. JEFF TORBORG
☐ 419. JIM SPENCER
☐ 462. RICKEY CLARK
☐ 521. ALAN FOSTER
☐ 541. ROGER REPOZ
☐ 561. LEO CARDENAS
☐ 595. NOLAN RYAN
☐ 629. PAUL DOYLE
☐ 656. RUDY MAY
☐ 672. ARCHIE REYNOLDS
☐ 689. EDDIE FISHER
☐ 718. DEL RICE(M)
☐ 765. KEN MCMULLEN

CHICAGO CUBS

☐ 18. JUAN PIZARRO
☐ 29. BILL BONHAM
☐ 45. GLENN BECKERT
☐ 61. BURT HOOTON(R)
☐ 61. GENE HISER(R)
☐ 61. EARL STEPHENSON(R)
☐ 117. CLEO JAMES
☐ 145. DON KESSINGER
☐ 192. TEAM CARD
☐ 208. MILT PAPPAS
☐ 258. RANDY HUNDLEY
☐ 271. KEN RUDOLPH
☐ 303. JOE PEPITONE
☐ 335. BILL HANDS
☐ 364. JOHNNY CALLISON
☐ 410. FERGIE JENKINS
☐ 439. BILLY WILLIAMS
☐ 485. PHIL REGAN
☐ 512. PAUL POPOVICH

1972 Topps

☐ 534. JIM HICKMAN
☐ 555. RON SANTO
☐ 576. LEO DUROCHER(M)
☐ 612. JOE DECKER
☐ 639. J.C. MARTIN
☐ 666. HECTOR TORRES
☐ 667. RAY NEWMAN
☐ 684. HAL BREEDEN
☐ 730. RICK MONDAY
☐ 766. STEVE HAMILTON

CHICAGO WHITE SOX

☐ 15. WALT WILLIAMS
☐ 73. STEVE HUNTZ
☐ 98. CHUCK TANNER(M)
☐ 126. BART JOHNSON
☐ 146. STEVE KEALEY
☐ 183. BILL MELTON
☐ 207. TOM EGAN
☐ 233. JAY JOHNSTONE
☐ 240. RICH ALLEN
☐ 248. TOM BRADLEY
☐ 326. H. PAT KELLY
☐ 361. MIKE ANDREWS
☐ 381. TEAM CARD
☐ 413. DON EDDY(R)
☐ 413. DAVE LEMONDS(R)
☐ 452. ED HERRMANN
☐ 476. LEE RICHARD
☐ 499. VICENTE ROMO
☐ 525. CARLOS MAY
☐ 539. TERRY FORSTER
☐ 553. WILBUR WOOD
☐ 593. RICH MORALES
☐ 618. RICH ROBERTSON
☐ 648. JIM LYTTLE
☐ 662. STAN BAHNSEN
☐ 685. JOE HORLEN
☐ 746. LOWELL PALMER
☐ 774. LUIS ALVARADO
☐ 786. CHUCK BRINKMAN

CINCINNATI REDS

☐   3. BOB TOLAN
☐ 80. TONY PEREZ
☐ 99. ROSS GRIMSLEY
☐ 121. ED SPRAGUE
☐ 136. DARREL CHANEY
☐ 157. DON GULLETT
☐ 236. JIM MCGLOTHLIN
☐ 256. GEORGE FOSTER
☐ 267. DAVE CONCEPCION
☐ 291. HAL MCRAE
☐ 311. CLAY CARROLL
☐ 358. SPARKY ANDERSON(M)
☐ 382. JOE GIBBON
☐ 417. TOM HALL
☐ 433. JOHNNY BENCH
☐ 463. BERNIE CARBO
☐ 475. GARY NOLAN
☐ 524. ED ARMBRISTER(R)
☐ 524. MEL BEHNEY(R)
☐ 542. JACK BILLINGHAM
☐ 559. PETE ROSE
☐ 586. DENIS MENKE
☐ 614. TED UHLAENDER
☐ 651. TEAM CARD
☐ 659. BOB ASPROMONTE
☐ 705. PAT CORRALES
☐ 719. CESAR GERONIMO
☐ 738. JIM MERRITT
☐ 745. JULIAN JAVIER
☐ 762. WAYNE SIMPSON

CLEVELAND INDIANS

☐ 24. TED FORD
☐ 59. FRED STANLEY
☐ 84. VINCE COLBERT
☐ 116. ED FARMER
☐ 142. CHRIS CHAMBLISS
☐ 193. KURT BEVACQUA
☐ 215. ALEX JOHNSON
☐ 261. STEVE MINGORI
☐ 285. GAYLORD PERRY
☐ 356. GERRY MOSES
☐ 374. JACK HEIDEMANN
☐ 399. MILT WILCOX

☐ 422. RAY LAMB
☐ 470. RAY FOSSE
☐ 486. JOHN LOWENSTEIN
☐ 506. TERRY LEY(R)
☐ 506. JIM MOYER(R)
☐ 506. DICK TIDROW(R)
☐ 547. TEAM CARD
☐ 590. GRAIG NETTLES
☐ 607. FRANK DUFFY
☐ 615. STEVE HARGAN
☐ 642. DENNY RIDDLEBERGER
☐ 658. STEVE DUNNING
☐ 687. DEL UNSER
☐ 721. EDDIE LEON
☐ 748. PHIL HENNIGAN
☐ 784. KEN ASPROMONTE(M)

DETROIT TIGERS

☐   6. FRED SCHERMAN
☐ 33. BILLY MARTIN(M)
☐ 83. DALTON JONES
☐ 120. BILL FREEHAN
☐ 150. NORM CASH
☐ 175. TOM HALLER
☐ 187. GATES BROWN
☐ 216. JOE NIEKRO
☐ 239. TOM TIMMERMANN
☐ 257. JIM FOOR(R)
☐ 257. TIM HOSLEY(R)
☐ 257. PAUL JATA(R)
☐ 284. IKE BROWN
☐ 319. AURELIO RODRIGUEZ
☐ 337. MIKE KILKENNY
☐ 367. RON PERRANOSKI
☐ 385. MICKEY STANLEY
☐ 408. JIM NORTHRUP
☐ 450. MICKEY LOLICH
☐ 487. TEAM CARD
☐ 511. TONY TAYLOR
☐ 535. ED BRINKMAN
☐ 600. AL KALINE
☐ 640. JOE COLEMAN
☐ 725. DICK MCAULIFFE
☐ 750. WILLIE HORTON
☐ 783. LES CAIN

HOUSTON ASTROS

☐ 20. DON WILSON
☐ 56. RICH CHILES
☐ 65. CESAR CEDENO
☐ 101. BILL GREIF(R)
☐ 101. J.R. RICHARD(R)
☐ 101. RAY BUSSE(R)
☐ 132. JOE MORGAN
☐ 155. LARRY DIERKER
☐ 202. SCIPIO SPINKS
☐ 204. TOMMY HELMS
☐ 217. ROGER METZGER
☐ 249. HARRY WALKER(M)
☐ 282. TEAM CARD
☐ 339. RON COOK
☐ 355. BOB WATSON
☐ 360. DAVE A. ROBERTS
☐ 394. KEN FORSCH
☐ 416. JOHNNY EDWARDS
☐ 466. NORM MILLER
☐ 480. LEE MAY
☐ 507. FRED GLADDING
☐ 536. DOUG RADER
☐ 581. WADE BLASINGAME
☐ 603. JIM RAY
☐ 633. JACK HIATT
☐ 679. BOB FENWICK(R)
☐ 679. BOB STINSON(R)
☐ 716. JESUS ALOU
☐ 732. GEORGE CULVER
☐ 747. JIM STEWART
☐ 770. JIM WYNN

KANSAS CITY ROYALS

☐ 10. AMOS OTIS
☐ 57. BOB OLIVER
☐ 68. JIM YORK
☐ 81. MIKE HEDLUND
☐ 109. JERRY MAY
☐ 133. JOE KEOUGH

☐ 177. PAUL SCHAAL
☐ 205. DICK DRAGO
☐ 246. TOM BURGMEIER
☐ 273. BOBBY FLOYD
☐ 315. PAUL SPLITTORFF
☐ 332. BUCK MARTINEZ
☐ 349. AL FITZMORRIS
☐ 372. LANCE CLEMONS(R)
☐ 372. MONTY MONTGOMERY(R)
☐ 373. JOHN MAYBERRY
☐ 415. COOKIE ROJAS
☐ 449. BOB LEMON(M)
☐ 468. RICHIE SCHEINBLUM
☐ 519. TED ABERNATHY
☐ 531. FREDDIE PATEK
☐ 569. ED KIRKPATRICK
☐ 580. LOU PINIELLA
☐ 617. TEAM CARD
☐ 638. KEN WRIGHT
☐ 664. BOBBY KNOOP
☐ 683. STEVE HOVLEY
☐ 717. BRUCE DAL CANTON
☐ 728. GAIL HOPKINS
☐ 742. JIM ROOKER
☐ 763. RON HANSEN

LOS ANGELES DODGERS

☐ 11. BOBBY VALENTINE
☐ 25. BILL SINGER
☐ 63. DUKE SIMS
☐ 114. BILL BUCKNER
☐ 151. JIM BREWER
☐ 198. CHARLIE HOUGH(R)
☐ 198. BOB O'BRIEN(R)
☐ 198. MIKE STRAHLER(R)
☐ 264. TOMMY JOHN
☐ 265. WES PARKER
☐ 297. CLAUDE OSTEEN
☐ 322. JOSE PENA
☐ 369. JIM LEFEBVRE
☐ 390. WILLIE DAVIS
☐ 398. LARRY HISLE
☐ 437. MAURY WILLS
☐ 460. AL DOWNING
☐ 522. TEAM CARD
☐ 530. DON SUTTON
☐ 578. BILLY GRABARKEWITZ
☐ 596. MANNY MOTA
☐ 616. JOE FERGUSON
☐ 649. PETE RICHERT
☐ 669. WILLIE CRAWFORD
☐ 686. STEVE GARVEY
☐ 736. BILL RUSSELL
☐ 749. WALTER ALSTON(M)
☐ 759. CHRIS CANNIZZARO
☐ 761. RON CEY(R)
☐ 777. HOYT WILHELM

MILWAUKEE BREWERS

☐ 12. JOSE CARDENAL
☐ 77. RON THEOBALD
☐ 106. TEAM CARD
☐ 118. SKIP LOCKWOOD
☐ 153. RICK AUERBACK
☐ 161. BROCK DAVIS
☐ 162. JERRY BELL(R)
☐ 162. DARRELL PORTER(R)
☐ 162. BOB REYNOLDS(R)
☐ 197. JOHNNY BRIGGS
☐ 255. JIM LONBORG
☐ 281. BILL PARSONS
☐ 321. JOE LAHOUD
☐ 359. DON PAVLETICH
☐ 376. ANDY KOSCO
☐ 386. JIM COLBORN
☐ 391. KEN SANDERS
☐ 393. CURT MOTTON
☐ 402. BOBBY HEISE
☐ 421. ELLIE RODRIGUEZ
☐ 458. AURELIO MONTEAGUDO
☐ 481. BILLY CONIGLIARO
☐ 517. KEN BRETT
☐ 549. DAVE MAY
☐ 585. GEORGE SCOTT
☐ 602. DAVE BRISTOL(M)
☐ 613. MIKE FERRARO
☐ 652. MARCELINO LOPEZ
☐ 744. JIM SLATON
☐ 776. BILL VOSS

121

MINNESOTA TWINS

- ☐ 28. BOB GEBHARD(R)
- ☐ 28. STEVE BRYE(R)
- ☐ 28. HAL HAYDEL(R)
- ☐ 51. HARMON KILLEBREW
- ☐ 66. RAY CORBIN
- ☐ 131. JIM NETTLES
- ☐ 156. TEAM CARD
- ☐ 201. PHIL ROOF
- ☐ 220. JIM PERRY
- ☐ 244. STEVE BRAUN
- ☐ 275. CESAR TOVAR
- ☐ 301. GEORGE MITTERWALD
- ☐ 352. DAVE LAROCHE
- ☐ 368. DANNY THOMPSON
- ☐ 389. BILL RIGNEY(M)
- ☐ 400. TONY OLIVA
- ☐ 459. RICK RENICK
- ☐ 501. PETE HAMM
- ☐ 515. BERT BLYLEVEN
- ☐ 545. WAYNE GRANGER
- ☐ 588. JIM HOLT
- ☐ 611. RICH REESE
- ☐ 634. DICK WOODSON
- ☐ 678. STEVE LUEBBER
- ☐ 695. ROD CAREW
- ☐ 709. JIM KAAT
- ☐ 778. VIC ALBURY(R)
- ☐ 778. RICK DEMPSEY(R)
- ☐ 778. JIM STRICKLAND(R)

JOHN BOCCABELLA

MONTREAL EXPOS

- ☐ 5. JOHN BATEMAN
- ☐ 58. ERNIE MCANALLY
- ☐ 82. RON WOODS
- ☐ 110. RON HUNT
- ☐ 134. CARL MORTON
- ☐ 159. JOHN BOCCABELLA
- ☐ 211. GARY SUTHERLAND
- ☐ 234. RON TAYLOR
- ☐ 254. BOOTS DAY
- ☐ 276. GENE MAUCH(M)
- ☐ 307. STEVE RENKO
- ☐ 331. STAN SWANSON
- ☐ 371. DENNY LEMASTER
- ☐ 405. RON FAIRLY
- ☐ 473. DAN MCGINN
- ☐ 489. TERRY HUMPHREY(R)
- ☐ 489. KEITH LAMPARD(R)
- ☐ 505. MIKE MARSHALL
- ☐ 526. BOB BAILEY
- ☐ 582. TEAM CARD
- ☐ 610. BILL STONEMAN
- ☐ 631. JOHN STROHMAYER
- ☐ 653. JIM FAIREY
- ☐ 657. BOBBY WINE
- ☐ 727. JOSE LABOY
- ☐ 743. CESAR GUTIERREZ
- ☐ 773. RON BRAND

NEW YORK METS

- ■ 16. MIKE JORGENSEN
- ☐ 31. CLEON JONES
- ■ 53. BUD HARRELSON
- ■ 105. GARY GENTRY
- ■ 127. DUFFY DYER
- ☐ 141. BUZZ CAPRA(R)
- ☐ 141. LEROY STANTON(R)
- ☐ 141. JON MATLACK(R)
- ☐ 163. TUG MCGRAW
- ■ 181. ED KRANEPOOL
- ■ 245. TOMMIE AGEE
- ■ 269. DON HAHN
- ■ 293. DANNY FRISELLA
- ■ 305. KEN BOSWELL
- ■ 362. TEAM CARD
- ■ 388. CHARLIE WILLIAMS
- ■ 407. CHUCK TAYLOR
- ■ 425. KEN SINGLETON
- ■ 445. TOM SEAVER
- ■ 465. GIL HODGES(M)
- ☐ 518. WAYNE GARRETT
- ■ 544. TED MARTINEZ
- ☐ 563. RAY SADECKI
- ■ 594. JIM BEAUCHAMP
- ■ 655. JERRY GROTE
- ☐ 673. DAVE MARSHALL
- ■ 697. JERRY KOOSMAN
- ■ 707. TIM FOLI
- ☐ 722. BILL SUDAKIS
- ☐ 741. JOHN MILNER(R)
- ☐ 781. JIM MCANDREW

NEW YORK YANKEES

- ☐ 8. RON SWOBODA
- ☐ 22. ROB GARDNER
- ☐ 47. JOHN ELLIS
- ☐ 108. GARY WASLEWSKI
- ☐ 124. ALAN CLOSTER(R)
- ☐ 124. RUSTY TORRES(R)
- ☐ 124. ROGER HAMBRIGHT(R)
- ☐ 138. MIKE KEKICH
- ☐ 158. JERRY KENNEY
- ☐ 203. RON BLOMBERG
- ☐ 237. TEAM CARD
- ☐ 263. FELIPE ALOU
- ☐ 287. JIM HARDIN
- ☐ 325. MEL STOTTLEMYRE
- ☐ 340. ROY WHITE
- ☐ 387. HORACE CLARKE
- ☐ 409. FRANK W. BAKER
- ☐ 441. THURMAN MUNSON
- ☐ 467. STEVE KLINE
- ☐ 513. LINDY MCDANIEL
- ☐ 533. RALPH HOUK(M)
- ☐ 573. FRITZ PETERSON
- ☐ 589. HAL LANIER
- ☐ 597. JIM MAGNUSON
- ☐ 619. RICH MCKINNEY
- ☐ 644. BERNIE ALLEN
- ☐ 699. BOBBY MURCER
- ☐ 713. GENE MICHAEL
- ☐ 724. RICH HINTON(R)
- ☐ 769. JACK AKER

OAKLAND A'S

- ☐ 17. DAVE DUNCAN
- ☐ 41. TOMMY DAVIS
- ☐ 62. ANGEL MANGUAL
- ☐ 75. BERT CAMPANERIS
- ☐ 111. JIM GRANT
- ☐ 137. DICK WILLIAMS(M)
- ☐ 169. VIDA BLUE
- ☐ 189. GENE TENACE
- ☐ 209. JOE RUDI
- ☐ 241. ROLLIE FINGERS
- ☐ 268. DWAIN ANDERSON(R)
- ☐ 268. CHRIS FLOETHE(R)
- ☐ 279. LARRY BROWN
- ☐ 330. JIM HUNTER
- ☐ 363. RON KLIMKOWSKI
- ☐ 383. BRANT ALYEA
- ☐ 406. GEORGE HENDRICK
- ☐ 435. REGGIE JACKSON
- ☐ 454. TEAM CARD
- ☐ 464. JIM ROLAND
- ☐ 523. CHUCK DOBSON
- ☐ 537. BOB LOCKER
- ☐ 557. JOHN ODOM
- ☐ 583. DAROLD KNOWLES
- ☐ 632. MIKE HEGAN
- ☐ 650. SAL BANDO
- ☐ 670. KEN HOLTZMAN
- ☐ 691. CURT BLEFARY
- ☐ 715. MIKE EPSTEIN
- ☐ 735. DIEGO SEGUI
- ☐ 780. DICK GREEN

PHILADELPHIA PHILLIES

- ☐ 14. PETE KOEGEL(R)
- ☐ 14. MIKE ANDERSON(R)
- ☐ 14. WAYNE TWITCHELL(R)
- ☐ 43. RICK WISE
- ☐ 69. ROGER FREED
- ☐ 112. GREG LUZINSKI
- ☐ 139. TIM MCCARVER
- ☐ 167. DERON JOHNSON
- ☐ 188. FRANK LUCCHESI(M)
- ☐ 252. KEN REYNOLDS
- ☐ 283. DARRELL BRANDON
- ☐ 324. MIKE RYAN
- ☐ 357. WOODIE FRYMAN
- ☐ 377. TERRY HARMON
- ☐ 397. TEAM CARD
- ☐ 423. OSCAR GAMBLE
- ☐ 453. BARRY LERSCH
- ☐ 482. JOE HOERNER
- ☐ 520. LARRY BOWA
- ☐ 528. RON STONE
- ☐ 587. BILLY WILSON
- ☐ 599. BILLY CHAMPION
- ☐ 635. DON MONEY
- ☐ 665. CHRIS SHORT
- ☐ 690. WILLIE MONTANEZ
- ☐ 726. DICK SELMA
- ☐ 741. TOM HUTTON(R)
- ☐ 768. DENNY DOYLE

PITTSBURGH PIRATES

- ☐ 1. TEAM CARD
- ☐ 27. BOB D. JOHNSON
- ☐ 60. MANNY SANGUILLEN
- ☐ 72. BRUCE KISON
- ☐ 125. DAVE CASH
- ☐ 152. GENE CLINES
- ☐ 179. DOCK ELLIS
- ☐ 190. DAVE GIUSTI
- ☐ 219. RENNIE STENNETT
- ☐ 247. MILT MAY
- ☐ 286. GENE ALLEY
- ☐ 309. ROBERTO CLEMENTE
- ☐ 320. STEVE BLASS
- ☐ 392. FRED CAMBRIA(R)
- ☐ 392. RICHIE ZISK(R)
- ☐ 414. BOB L. MILLER
- ☐ 429. BOB ROBERTSON
- ☐ 447. WILLIE STARGELL
- ☐ 471. LUKE WALKER
- ☐ 502. JACKIE HERNANDEZ
- ☐ 538. CHARLIE SANDS
- ☐ 575. AL OLIVER
- ☐ 605. NELSON BRILES
- ☐ 630. RICH HEBNER
- ☐ 647. BOB MOOSE
- ☐ 661. BILL VIRDON(M)
- ☐ 701. JOSE PAGAN
- ☐ 729. BOB VEALE
- ☐ 760. BILL MAZEROSKI
- ☐ 785. VIC DAVALILLO

ST. LOUIS CARDINALS

- ☐ 9. STAN WILLIAMS
- ☐ 13. JOE GRZENDA
- ☐ 67. RED SCHOENDIENST(M)
- ☐ 107. JOSE CRUZ
- ☐ 130. BOB GIBSON
- ☐ 154. TED SIMMONS
- ☐ 200. LOU BROCK
- ☐ 206. DAL MAXVILL
- ☐ 243. FRANK LINZY
- ☐ 278. DENNIS HIGGINS
- ☐ 316. JIM BIBBY(R)
- ☐ 316. JORGE ROQUE(R)
- ☐ 316. SANTIAGO GUZMAN(R)
- ☐ 336. MARTY MARTINEZ
- ☐ 353. ART SHAMSKY
- ☐ 375. REGGIE CLEVELAND
- ☐ 395. MATTY ALOU
- ☐ 420. STEVE CARLTON
- ☐ 479. DON SHAW
- ☐ 500. JOE TORRE
- ☐ 514. TED SIZEMORE
- ☐ 546. JOE HAGUE
- ☐ 584. JERRY MCNERTNEY
- ☐ 606. LUIS MELENDEZ

☐ 627. MOE DRABOWSKY
☐ 645. JIM MALONEY
☐ 671. DONN CLENDENON
☐ 688. TEAM CARD
☐ 723. AL SANTORINI
☐ 775. JERRY REUSS
☐ 779. TONY CLONINGER

SAN DIEGO PADRES

☐   7. ENZO HERNANDEZ
☐ 39. BOB BARTON
☐ 78. STEVE ARLIN
☐ 123. ED ACOSTA
☐ 143. GARRY JESTADT
☐ 173. CLAY KIRBY
☐ 194. FRED NORMAN
☐ 238. LERON LEE
☐ 262. TEAM CARD
☐ 274. AL SEVERINSEN
☐ 288. JOHNNY JETER
☐ 384. DAVE CAMPBELL
☐ 412. DICK KELLEY
☐ 431. CLARENCE GASTON
☐ 457. DARCY FAST(R)
☐ 457. DERREL THOMAS(R)
☐ 457. MIKE IVIE(R)
☐ 477. TOM PHOEBUS
☐ 504. ED SPIEZIO
☐ 532. FRED KENDALL
☐ 551. OLLIE BROWN
☐ 571. NATE COLBERT
☐ 608. MIKE CORKINS
☐ 637. PRESTON GOMEZ(M)
☐ 677. IVAN MURRELL
☐ 739. DON MASON
☐ 782. LARRY STAHL

SAN FRANCISCO GIANTS

☐ 35. JERRY JOHNSON
☐ 49. WILLIE MAYS
☐ 76. DON CARRITHERS
☐ 129. CHARLIE FOX(M)
☐ 147. DAVE KINGMAN
☐ 165. CHRIS SPEIER
☐ 185. RON BRYANT
☐ 232. CHRIS ARNOLD(R)
☐ 232. JIM BARR(R)
☐ 232. DAVE RADER(R)
☐ 280. WILLIE MCCOVEY
☐ 295. DICK DIETZ
☐ 327. STEVE STONE
☐ 366. JIMMY ROSARIO
☐ 403. JOHN CUMBERLAND
☐ 427. TITO FUENTES
☐ 443. KEN HENDERSON
☐ 509. DON MCMAHON
☐ 548. FRANK REBERGER
☐ 567. JUAN MARICHAL
☐ 643. RUSS GIBSON
☐ 663. FRAN HEALY
☐ 682. MIKE MCCORMICK
☐ 693. ALAN GALLAGHER
☐ 711. BOBBY BONDS
☐ 720. SAM MCDOWELL
☐ 733. JIM HART
☐ 761. BERNIE WILLIAMS(R)
☐ 771. TEAM CARD

TEXAS RANGERS

☐ 23. TED KUBIAK
☐ 64. PETE BROBERG
☐ 104. TOBY HARRAH
☐ 122. LARRY BIITTNER
☐ 148. DICK BILLINGS
☐ 191. JEFF BURROUGHS
☐ 210. DENNY MCLAIN
☐ 231. CASEY COX
☐ 242. DON MINCHER
☐ 277. ELLIOTT MADDOX
☐ 317. RICH HAND
☐ 329. ROY FOSTER
☐ 334. BILL FAHEY(R)
☐ 334. JIM MASON(R)
☐ 334. TOM RAGLAND(R)
☐ 350. FRANK HOWARD
☐ 365. DICK BOSMAN
☐ 396. PAUL LINDBLAD

☐ 424. BILL GOGOLEWSKI
☐ 461. TIM CULLEN
☐ 483. KEN SUAREZ
☐ 510. TED WILLIAMS(M)
☐ 529. DAVE NELSON
☐ 577. MIKE PAUL
☐ 598. HAL KING
☐ 609. TOM GRIEVE
☐ 654. HORACIO PINA
☐ 668. TEAM CARD
☐ 737. LENNY RANDLE
☐ 767. TOM MCCRAW

CASEY COX

1973 TOPPS (660)
2 1/2″ X 3 1/2″

DON SUTTON
PITCHER

ATLANTA BRAVES

☐ 15. RALPH GARR
☐ 33. JIM BREAZEALE
☐ 72. RON REED
☐ 100. HANK AARON
☐ 124. JIM HARDIN
☐ 144. MARTY PEREZ
☐ 169. RON SCHUELER
☐ 192. PAT JARVIS
☐ 215. DUSTY BAKER
☐ 237. MATHEWS(M) & COACHES
☐ 266. MIKE LUM
☐ 288. GARY GENTRY
☐ 312. OSCAR BROWN
☐ 359. CECIL UPSHAW
☐ 374. DARRELL EVANS
☐ 403. SONNY JACKSON
☐ 432. DAN FRISELLA
☐ 452. PAUL CASANOVA
☐ 503. PHIL NIEKRO
☐ 521. TEAM CARD
☐ 550. DAVE A. JOHNSON
☐ 574. BOB DIDIER
☐ 609. LARVELL BLANKS(R)
☐ 610. JIMMY FREEMAN(R)
☐ 630. DENNY MCLAIN
☐ 653. JOE HOERNER

BALTIMORE ORIOLES

☐   9. JOHNNY OATES
☐   34. PAT DOBSON
☐   56. MERV RETTENMUND
☐   90. BROOKS ROBINSON
☐ 109. DOYLE ALEXANDER
☐ 136. WEAVER(M) & COACHES
☐ 160. JIM PALMER
☐ 183. DON BUFORD
☐ 229. RORIC HARRISON
☐ 253. MARK BELANGER
☐ 278. TEAM CARD
☐ 302. TERRY CROWLEY
☐ 325. BOOG POWELL
☐ 362. EDDIE WATT
☐ 384. DON BAYLOR
☐ 396. GRANT JACKSON
☐ 418. BOBBY GRICH
☐ 470. MIKE CUELLAR
☐ 504. EARL WILLIAMS
☐ 528. PAUL BLAIR
☐ 553. MICKEY SCOTT
☐ 600. DAVE MCNALLY
☐ 601. SERGIO ROBLES(R)
☐ 604. JESSE JEFFERSON(R)
☐ 605. ENOS CABELL(R)
☐ 611. RICH COGGINS(R)
☐ 612. BOB REYNOLDS(R)
☐ 614. AL BUMBRY(R)
☐ 618. ANDY ETCHEBARREN
☐ 631. TOM MATCHICK

BOSTON RED SOX

☐ 14. SONNY SIEBERT
☐ 40. REGGIE SMITH
☐ 69. PHIL GAGLIANO
☐ 96. DOUG GRIFFIN
☐ 114. LYNN MCGLOTHEN
☐ 131. KASKO(M) & COACHES
☐ 143. JOHN CURTIS
☐ 165. LUIS APARICIO
☐ 193. CARLTON FISK
☐ 224. BILL LEE
☐ 245. CARL YASTRZEMSKI
☐ 270. LUIS TIANT
☐ 291. ROGELIO MORET
☐ 317. DANNY CATER
☐ 365. RICO PETROCELLI
☐ 388. BEN OGLIVIE
☐ 415. MARTY PATTIN
☐ 437. JOHN KENNEDY
☐ 463. KEN TATUM
☐ 491. BOB MONTGOMERY
☐ 518. BOB VEALE
☐ 541. BOB BOLIN
☐ 566. LEW KRAUSSE
☐ 596. TEAM CARD
☐ 607. MARIO GUERRERO(R)
☐ 614. DWIGHT EVANS(R)
☐ 616. MIKE GARMAN(R)
☐ 620. TOMMY HARPER

CALIFORNIA ANGELS

☐ 18. LEROY STANTON
☐ 36. STEVE BARBER
☐ 75. VADA PINSON
☐ 102. RUDY MAY
☐ 123. SANDY ALOMAR
☐ 154. JEFF TORBORG
☐ 175. FRANK ROBINSON
☐ 178. DON ROSE
☐ 220. NOLAN RYAN
☐ 243. TEAM CARD
☐ 267. LLOYD ALLEN
☐ 279. MIKE STRAHLER
☐ 289. BOB OLIVER
☐ 301. BILLY GRABARKEWITZ
☐ 319. JIM SPENCER
☐ 354. BILLY PARKER
☐ 373. CLYDE WRIGHT
☐ 402. JACK HIATT
☐ 421. WINKLES(M) & COACHES
☐ 445. KEN BERRY
☐ 502. BOBBY VALENTINE
☐ 522. LEO CARDENAS
☐ 543. ALAN FOSTER
☐ 570. BILL SINGER
☐ 597. MICKEY RIVERS
☐ 636. RICK CLARK

CHICAGO CUBS

- ☐ 21. RANDY HUNDLEY
- ☐ 44. RICK MONDAY
- ☐ 70. MILT PAPPAS
- ☐ 81. LOCKMAN(M) & COACHES
- ☐ 115. RON SANTO
- ☐ 139. CARMEN FANZONE
- ☐ 180. FERGIE JENKINS
- ☐ 200. BILLY WILLIAMS
- ☐ 262. JACK AKER
- ☐ 285. DON KESSINGER
- ☐ 309. PAUL POPOVICH
- ☐ 328. BILL BONHAM
- ☐ 367. BURT HOOTON
- ☐ 393. JOSE CARDENAL
- ☐ 414. KEN RUDOLPH
- ☐ 426. DAVE LAROCHE
- ☐ 440. GLENN BECKERT
- ☐ 464. TEAM CARD
- ☐ 482. RICK REUSCHEL
- ☐ 501. LARRY GURA
- ☐ 527. DAN MCGINN
- ☐ 552. J.C. MARTIN
- ☐ 565. JIM HICKMAN
- ☐ 580. JOE PEPITONE
- ☐ 603. TERRY HUGHES(R)
- ☐ 605. PAT BOURQUE(R)
- ☐ 645. BOB LOCKER

CHICAGO WHITE SOX

- ☐ 20. STAN BAHNSEN
- ☐ 42. MIKE ANDREWS
- ☐ 73. ED HERRMANN
- ☐ 105. CARLOS MAY
- ☐ 129. TERRY FORSTER
- ☐ 150. WILBUR WOOD
- ☐ 174. RICH GOSSAGE
- ☐ 194. JORGE ORTA
- ☐ 238. TONY MUSER
- ☐ 261. H. PAT KELLY
- ☐ 287. EDDIE LEON
- ☐ 310. DICK ALLEN
- ☐ 356. TANNER(M) & COACHES
- ☐ 379. CY ACOSTA
- ☐ 404. CHUCK BRINKMAN
- ☐ 423. JOHNNY JETER
- ☐ 439. EDDIE FISHER
- ☐ 455. BILL MELTON
- ☐ 481. TEAM CARD
- ☐ 494. RICH MORALES
- ☐ 506. BART JOHNSON
- ☐ 534. DAVE LEMONDS
- ☐ 561. JIM GEDDES
- ☐ 581. STEVE KEALEY
- ☐ 604. DENNIS O'TOOLE(R)
- ☐ 627. LUIS ALVARADO
- ☐ 648. TOM EGAN

CINCINNATI REDS

- ☐ 8. TOM HALL
- ☐ 28. HAL MCRAE
- ☐ 52. DENIS MENKE
- ☐ 89. JACK BILLINGHAM
- ☐ 130. PETE ROSE
- ☐ 156. CESAR GERONIMO
- ☐ 177. BILL PLUMMER
- ☐ 195. CLAY CARROLL
- ☐ 230. JOE MORGAN
- ☐ 260. GARY NOLAN
- ☐ 275. TONY PEREZ
- ☐ 296. ANDERSON(M) & COACHES
- ☐ 318. JIM MCGLOTHLIN
- ☐ 335. BOB TOLAN
- ☐ 357. ROSS GRIMSLEY
- ☐ 380. JOHNNY BENCH
- ☐ 399. GEORGE FOSTER
- ☐ 447. JOE HAGUE
- ☐ 492. PEDRO BORBON
- ☐ 507. DARREL CHANEY
- ☐ 533. LARRY STAHL
- ☐ 554. DAVE CONCEPCION
- ☐ 595. DON GULLETT
- ☐ 602. MEL BEHNEY(R)
- ☐ 626. BOB BARTON
- ☐ 641. TEAM CARD

CLEVELAND INDIANS

- ☐ 11. CHRIS CHAMBLISS
- ☐ 31. BUDDY BELL
- ☐ 53. STEVE DUNNING
- ☐ 86. TOM MCCRAW
- ☐ 134. MILT WILCOX
- ☐ 157. DENNY RIDDLEBERGER
- ☐ 181. JACK BROHAMER
- ☐ 226. RAY FOSSE
- ☐ 247. DEL UNSER
- ☐ 272. ED FARMER
- ☐ 297. WALT WILLIAMS
- ☐ 327. JOHN LOWENSTEIN
- ☐ 339. DICK TIDROW
- ☐ 372. OSCAR GAMBLE
- ☐ 376. FRANK DUFFY
- ☐ 400. GAYLORD PERRY
- ☐ 425. ALEX JOHNSON
- ☐ 449. ASPROMONTE(M) & CHS.
- ☐ 496. RAY LAMB
- ☐ 514. JERRY KENNEY
- ☐ 532. STEVE MINGORI
- ☐ 551. MIKE KILKENNY
- ☐ 571. RUSTY TORRES
- ☐ 591. MIKE HEDLUND
- ☐ 601. GEORGE PENA(R)
- ☐ 608. DICK COLPAERT(R)
- ☐ 612. BRENT STROM(R)
- ☐ 614. CHARLIE SPIKES(R)
- ☐ 629. TEAM CARD
- ☐ 644. JACK HEIDEMANN
- ☐ 656. JOHN ELLIS

DETROIT TIGERS

- ☐ 5. ED BRINKMAN
- ☐ 29. TONY TAYLOR
- ☐ 51. CHUCK SEELBACH
- ☐ 88. MICKEY STANLEY
- ☐ 120. JOE COLEMAN
- ☐ 146. WOODIE FRYMAN
- ☐ 168. JIM NORTHRUP
- ☐ 191. TEAM CARD
- ☐ 218. AURELIO RODRIGUEZ
- ☐ 256. CHRIS ZACHARY
- ☐ 280. AL KALINE
- ☐ 304. DUKE SIMS
- ☐ 323. MARTIN(M) & COACHES
- ☐ 349. DICK MCAULIFFE
- ☐ 369. LERRIN LAGROW
- ☐ 390. MICKEY LOLICH
- ☐ 413. TOM TIMMERMANN
- ☐ 433. WILLIE HORTON
- ☐ 448. JOHN HILLER
- ☐ 460. BILL FREEHAN
- ☐ 485. NORM CASH
- ☐ 508. GATES BROWN
- ☐ 537. BILL SLAYBACK
- ☐ 560. FRANK HOWARD
- ☐ 585. JOE NIEKRO
- ☐ 604. BOB STRAMPE(R)
- ☐ 633. IKE BROWN
- ☐ 660. FRED SCHERMAN

HOUSTON ASTROS

- ☐ 17. FRED GLADDING
- ☐ 39. DAVE A. ROBERTS
- ☐ 76. DOUG RADER
- ☐ 93. JESUS ALOU
- ☐ 110. BOB WATSON
- ☐ 135. LEE MAY
- ☐ 158. TEAM CARD
- ☐ 185. JIM WYNN
- ☐ 217. DON WILSON
- ☐ 242. GEORGE CULVER
- ☐ 290. CESAR CEDENO
- ☐ 313. JIM RAY
- ☐ 351. JIMMY STEWART
- ☐ 375. LARRY DIERKER
- ☐ 395. ROGER METZGER
- ☐ 420. TOMMIE AGEE
- ☐ 446. JERRY REUSS
- ☐ 468. TOM GRIFFIN
- ☐ 495. TOMMY HELMS
- ☐ 519. JOHN EDWARDS
- ☐ 546. JIM YORK
- ☐ 572. GARY SUTHERLAND
- ☐ 589. KEN FORSCH
- ☐ 613. SKIP JUTZE(R)
- ☐ 624. DUROCHER(M) & COACHES
- ☐ 637. NORM MILLER

KANSAS CITY ROYALS

- ☐ 22. TED ABERNATHY
- ☐ 48. PAUL SPLITTORFF
- ☐ 78. RICHIE SCHEINBLUM
- ☐ 99. CARL TAYLOR
- ☐ 118. JOHN MAYBERRY
- ☐ 140. LOU PINIELLA
- ☐ 164. MONTY MONTGOMERY
- ☐ 188. COOKIE ROJAS
- ☐ 233. ED KIRKPATRICK
- ☐ 251. ROGER NELSON
- ☐ 282. STEVE HOVLEY
- ☐ 306. TOM BURGMEIER
- ☐ 334. FREDDIE PATEK
- ☐ 347. TEAM CARD
- ☐ 392. DICK DRAGO
- ☐ 416. PAUL SCHAAL
- ☐ 428. WAYNE SIMPSON
- ☐ 441. GAIL HOPKINS
- ☐ 466. JOSE ARCIA
- ☐ 487. BRUCE DAL CANTON
- ☐ 510. AMOS OTIS
- ☐ 539. TOM MURPHY
- ☐ 558. JERRY MAY
- ☐ 578. KEN WRIGHT
- ☐ 593. MCKEON(M) & COACHES
- ☐ 608. STEVE BUSBY(R)
- ☐ 611. JIM WOHLFORD(R)
- ☐ 616. NORM ANGELINI(R)
- ☐ 643. AL FITZMORRIS

LOS ANGELES DODGERS

- ☐ 10. DON SUTTON
- ☐ 35. WILLIE DAVIS
- ☐ 59. STEVE YEAGER
- ☐ 91. TEAM CARD
- ☐ 108. BILL RUSSELL
- ☐ 126. JIM BREWER
- ☐ 151. WES PARKER
- ☐ 196. KEN MCMULLEN
- ☐ 213. STEVE GARVEY
- ☐ 239. PETE RICHERT
- ☐ 258. TOMMY JOHN
- ☐ 324. AL DOWNING
- ☐ 368. BILL BUCKNER
- ☐ 391. LEE LACY
- ☐ 412. MANNY MOTA
- ☐ 442. DICK DIETZ
- ☐ 490. CLAUDE OSTEEN
- ☐ 515. ANDY MESSERSMITH
- ☐ 544. VON JOSHUA
- ☐ 569. ALSTON(M) & COACHES
- ☐ 602. DOUG RAU(R)
- ☐ 606. TOM PACIOREK(R)
- ☐ 609. DAVE LOPES(R)
- ☐ 610. CHARLIE HOUGH(R)
- ☐ 615. RON CEY(R)
- ☐ 621. JOE FERGUSON
- ☐ 639. WILLIE CRAWFORD

MILWAUKEE BREWERS

- ☐ 45. ELLIE RODRIGUEZ
- ☐ 71. JOHNNY BRIGGS
- ☐ 74. BILLY CHAMPION
- ☐ 92. JERRY BELL
- ☐ 127. TEAM CARD
- ☐ 152. DAVE MAY
- ☐ 176. CHUCK TAYLOR
- ☐ 212. JOE LAHOUD
- ☐ 231. BILL PARSONS
- ☐ 263. GEORGE SCOTT
- ☐ 286. FRANK LINZY
- ☐ 308. SKIP LOCKWOOD
- ☐ 332. JOHN FELSKE
- ☐ 366. BROCK DAVIS
- ☐ 386. DON MONEY
- ☐ 408. JIM COLBORN
- ☐ 427. RICK AUERBACH
- ☐ 451. JOHN VUKOVICH
- ☐ 526. OLLIE BROWN
- ☐ 547. BOBBY HEISE
- ☐ 568. RAY NEWMAN
- ☐ 582. DARRELL PORTER
- ☐ 609. PEDRO GARCIA(R)
- ☐ 628. JIM SLATON
- ☐ 646. CRANDALL(M) & COACHES

MINNESOTA TWINS

- ☐ 16. STEVE BRAUN
- ☐ 49. QUILICI(M) & COACHES
- ☐ 80. TONY OLIVA
- ☐ 98. DICK WOODSON
- ☐ 122. JIM STRICKLAND
- ☐ 148. DAVE GOLTZ
- ☐ 170. HARMON KILLEBREW
- ☐ 199. BERT BLYLEVEN
- ☐ 228. BOBBY DARWIN
- ☐ 259. JIM HOLT
- ☐ 284. GLENN BORGMANN
- ☐ 311. JOE DECKER
- ☐ 330. ROD CAREW
- ☐ 353. STEVE BRYE
- ☐ 358. JIM NETTLES
- ☐ 385. JIM PERRY
- ☐ 411. RAY CORBIN
- ☐ 443. DANNY THOMPSON
- ☐ 469. DAN MONZON
- ☐ 516. DANNY WALTON
- ☐ 530. JIM KAAT
- ☐ 555. BILL HANDS
- ☐ 577. ERIC SODERHOLM
- ☐ 598. PHIL ROOF
- ☐ 622. LARRY HISLE
- ☐ 638. KEN REYNOLDS
- ☐ 654. TEAM CARD

MONTREAL EXPOS

- ☐ 19. TIM FOLI
- ☐ 41. TOM WALKER
- ☐ 77. MIKE TORREZ
- ☐ 106. TERRY HUMPHREY
- ☐ 125. RON FAIRLY
- ☐ 149. RON HUNT
- ☐ 173. HAL BREEDEN
- ☐ 211. BALOR MOORE
- ☐ 232. KEN SINGLETON
- ☐ 254. BILL STONEMAN
- ☐ 281. MIKE JORGENSEN
- ☐ 307. BOOTS DAY
- ☐ 331. CARL MORTON
- ☐ 355. MIKE MARSHALL
- ☐ 377. MAUCH(M) & COACHES
- ☐ 401. CLYDE MASHORE
- ☐ 429. JIM FAIREY
- ☐ 457. JOHN STROHMAYER
- ☐ 484. ERNIE MCANALLY
- ☐ 505. BOB BAILEY
- ☐ 531. RON WOODS
- ☐ 576. TEAM CARD
- ☐ 592. JOHN BOCCABELLA
- ☐ 606. JORGE ROQUE(R)
- ☐ 607. PEPE FRIAS(R)
- ☐ 623. STEVE RENKO
- ☐ 642. JOSE LABOY

TUG
McGRAW
NEW YORK METS   PITCHER

NEW YORK METS

- ■ 4. JOHN MILNER
- ☐ 30. TUG MCGRAW
- ■ 55. JON MATLACK
- ☐ 87. KEN BOSWELL
- ■ 107. PHIL HENNIGAN
- ■ 113. JERRY GROTE
- ■ 137. JIM BEAUCHAMP

- ☐ 161. TED MARTINEZ
- ■ 184. JERRY KOOSMAN
- ■ 223. BUD HARRELSON
- ☐ 257. BERRA(M) & COACHES
- ■ 283. RAY SADECKI
- ■ 305. WILLIE MAYS
- ☐ 329. ED KRANEPOOL
- ■ 350. TOM SEAVER
- ☐ 389. TEAM CARD
- ■ 407. FELIX MILLAN
- ■ 436. JIM MCANDREW
- ☐ 493. DUFFY DYER
- ☐ 525. JIM FREGOSI
- ■ 540. CLEON JONES
- ☐ 562. WAYNE GARRETT
- ■ 586. BILL SUDAKIS
- ☐ 610. HANK WEBB(R)
- ■ 617. RICH CHILES
- ■ 647. GEORGE STONE

NEW YORK YANKEES

- ☐ 25. ROY WHITE
- ☐ 46. LINDY MCDANIEL
- ☐ 82. FRITZ PETERSON
- ☐ 103. CELERINO SANCHEZ
- ☐ 116. HOUK(M) & COACHES
- ☐ 132. MATTY ALOU
- ☐ 142. THURMAN MUNSON
- ☐ 172. STEVE KLINE
- ☐ 198. HORACE CLARKE
- ☐ 240. BOBBY MURCER
- ☐ 265. GENE MICHAEL
- ☐ 293. BERNIE ALLEN
- ☐ 314. RON SWOBODA
- ☐ 371. MIKE KEKICH
- ☐ 394. SPARKY LYLE
- ☐ 419. CASEY COX
- ☐ 431. GERRY MOSES
- ☐ 462. RON BLOMBERG
- ☐ 479. HAL LANIER
- ☐ 498. GRAIG NETTLES
- ☐ 520. MEL STOTTLEMYRE
- ☐ 535. JOHN CALLISON
- ☐ 556. TEAM CARD
- ☐ 573. FRED BEENE
- ☐ 608. GEORGE MEDICH(R)
- ☐ 616. STEVE BLATERIC(R)
- ☐ 634. ALAN CLOSTER
- ☐ 650. FELIPE ALOU

OAKLAND A'S

- ☐ 13. GEORGE HENDRICK
- ☐ 38. MIKE EPSTEIN
- ☐ 60. KEN HOLTZMAN
- ☐ 84. ROLLIE FINGERS
- ☐ 155. SAL BANDO
- ☐ 179. WILLIAMS(M) & COACHES
- ☐ 214. DAVE HAMILTON
- ☐ 222. ROB GARDNER
- ☐ 234. BILL NORTH
- ☐ 235. JIM HUNTER
- ☐ 255. REGGIE JACKSON
- ☐ 274. DAROLD KNOWLES
- ☐ 295. BERT CAMPANERIS
- ☐ 315. JOHN ODOM
- ☐ 337. DAVE DUNCAN
- ☐ 360. JOE RUDI
- ☐ 382. MIKE HEGAN
- ☐ 406. PAUL LINDBLAD
- ☐ 430. VIDA BLUE
- ☐ 456. DICK GREEN
- ☐ 483. DAL MAXVILL
- ☐ 500. TEAM CARD
- ☐ 524. GENE TENACE
- ☐ 545. ORLANDO CEPEDA
- ☐ 563. LARRY HANEY
- ☐ 587. RICH MCKINNEY
- ☐ 605. GONZALO MARQUEZ(R)
- ☐ 625. ANGEL MANGUAL
- ☐ 652. TED KUBIAK

PHILADELPHIA PHILLIES

- ☐ 3. JIM LONBORG
- ☐ 6. MAC SCARCE
- ☐ 37. BILL ROBINSON
- ☐ 97. WILLIE MONTANEZ
- ☐ 119. LARRY BOWA

- ☐ 147. MIKE ANDERSON
- ☐ 166. TERRY HARMON
- ☐ 189. GREG LUZINSKI
- ☐ 227. WAYNE TWITCHELL
- ☐ 246. KEN SANDERS
- ☐ 271. TOM HUTTON
- ☐ 300. STEVE CARLTON
- ☐ 326. DARRELL BRANDON
- ☐ 405. CESAR TOVAR
- ☐ 424. DENNY DOYLE
- ☐ 444. KEN BRETT
- ☐ 454. TOM HALLER
- ☐ 467. MIKE RYAN
- ☐ 486. OZARK(M) & COACHES
- ☐ 509. JIM NASH
- ☐ 536. TEAM CARD
- ☐ 559. BARRY LERSCH
- ☐ 590. DERON JOHNSON
- ☐ 613. BOB BOONE(R)
- ☐ 615. MIKE SCHMIDT(R)
- ☐ 619. BILLY WILSON
- ☐ 632. DICK SELMA
- ☐ 659. JOSE PAGAN

PITTSBURGH PIRATES

- ☐ 2. RICH HEBNER
- ☐ 26. TEAM CARD
- ☐ 50. ROBERTO CLEMENTE
- ☐ 95. STEVE BLASS
- ☐ 117. RAMON HERNANDEZ
- ☐ 141. BRUCE KISON
- ☐ 163. VIC DAVALILLO
- ☐ 187. LUKE WALKER
- ☐ 225. AL OLIVER
- ☐ 250. MANNY SANGUILLEN
- ☐ 277. BOB L. MILLER
- ☐ 303. NELSON BRILES
- ☐ 333. GENE CLINES
- ☐ 348. RENNIE STENNETT
- ☐ 363. JACKIE HERNANDEZ
- ☐ 370. WILLIE STARGELL
- ☐ 397. DAVE CASH
- ☐ 422. BOB ROBERTSON
- ☐ 465. DAVE GIUSTI
- ☐ 499. BOB MOOSE
- ☐ 517. VIRDON(M) & COACHES
- ☐ 529. MILT MAY
- ☐ 575. DOCK ELLIS
- ☐ 611. RICHIE ZISK(R)
- ☐ 635. GENE ALLEY
- ☐ 657. BOB D. JOHNSON

ST. LOUIS CARDINALS

- ☐ 24. AL SANTORINI
- ☐ 47. LUIS MELENDEZ
- ☐ 85. TED SIMMONS
- ☐ 104. REGGIE CLEVELAND
- ☐ 128. TED SIZEMORE
- ☐ 153. AL HRABOSKY
- ☐ 171. BERNIE CARBO
- ☐ 190. BOB GIBSON
- ☐ 219. TEAM CARD
- ☐ 241. DWAIN ANDERSON
- ☐ 269. TIM MCCARVER
- ☐ 292. JOSE CRUZ
- ☐ 320. LOU BROCK
- ☐ 364. RICK WISE
- ☐ 383. DIEGO SEGUI
- ☐ 417. SCIPIO SPINKS
- ☐ 450. JOE TORRE
- ☐ 497. SCHOENDIENST(M) & CHS.
- ☐ 523. WAYNE GRANGER
- ☐ 548. DON DURHAM
- ☐ 567. BOB FENWICK
- ☐ 599. ED CROSBY
- ☐ 603. KEN REITZ(R)
- ☐ 607. RAY BUSSE(R)
- ☐ 649. RICH FOLKERS

SAN DIEGO PADRES

- ☐ 12. ZIMMER(M) & COACHES
- ☐ 32. FRED NORMAN
- ☐ 57. DERREL THOMAS
- ☐ 83. LERON LEE
- ☐ 112. GARY ROSS
- ☐ 133. DAVE W. ROBERTS
- ☐ 159. CLARENCE GASTON

☐ 182. MIKE CALDWELL
☐ 221. FRED KENDALL
☐ 244. ED ACOSTA
☐ 268. JERRY MORALES
☐ 294. STEVE ARLIN
☐ 316. TEAM CARD
☐ 340. NATE COLBERT
☐ 381. VICENTE ROMO
☐ 409. IVAN MURRELL
☐ 438. ENZO HERNANDEZ
☐ 461. MIKE CORKINS
☐ 488. DAVE CAMPBELL
☐ 513. DAVE MARSHALL
☐ 542. PAT CORRALES
☐ 583. BILL GREIF
☐ 602. RALPH GARCIA(R)
☐ 613. MIKE IVIE(R)
☐ 615. JOHN HILTON(R)
☐ 655. CLAY KIRBY

SAN FRANCISCO GIANTS

☐ 23. DAVE KINGMAN
☐ 43. RANDY MOFFITT
☐ 79. JIM WILLOUGHBY
☐ 101. KEN HENDERSON
☐ 121. DAVE RADER
☐ 145. BOBBY BONDS
☐ 167. STEVE STONE
☐ 197. ED GOODSON
☐ 236. TITO FUENTES
☐ 248. JERRY JOHNSON
☐ 252. FOX(M) & COACHES
☐ 273. CHRIS SPEIER
☐ 298. RON BRYANT
☐ 322. GARRY MADDOX
☐ 336. TOM BRADLEY
☐ 361. FRAN HEALY
☐ 387. JIM BARR
☐ 410. WILLIE MCCOVEY
☐ 434. TEAM CARD
☐ 459. JIMMY HOWARTH
☐ 480. JUAN MARICHAL
☐ 511. SAM MCDOWELL
☐ 538. JIM HART
☐ 557. BERNIE WILLIAMS
☐ 584. CHRIS ARNOLD
☐ 606. GARY MATTHEWS(R)
☐ 651. DON CARRITHERS

JIM
MASON
TEXAS RANGERS   SHORTSTOP

TEXAS RANGERS

☐ 7. TEAM CARD
☐ 27. BILL GOGOLEWSKI
☐ 58. MIKE PAUL
☐ 94. DICK BILLINGS
☐ 111. DAVE NELSON
☐ 138. HORACIO PINA
☐ 162. PETE BROBERG
☐ 186. BILL FAHEY
☐ 216. TOBY HARRAH
☐ 249. LARRY BIITTNER
☐ 276. JOE LOVITTO
☐ 299. TED FORD
☐ 321. RICH HINTON
☐ 352. DON STANHOUSE
☐ 378. LENNY RANDLE
☐ 398. RICH HAND
☐ 435. RICO CARTY

☐ 458. JIM MASON
☐ 489. JEFF BURROUGHS
☐ 512. DALTON JONES
☐ 549. HERZOG(M) & COACHES
☐ 564. MIKE THOMPSON
☐ 579. TOM GRIEVE
☐ 594. VIC HARRIS
☐ 601. RICK STELMASZEK(R)
☐ 603. BILL MCNULTY(R)
☐ 612. STEVE LAWSON(R)
☐ 640. DICK BOSMAN
☐ 658. ELLIOTT MADDOX

1974 TOPPS (660)
2 1/2″ X 3 1/2″

ATLANTA   MANAGER

* COACHES *

Herm   Connie   Jim   Ken
Starrette   Ryan   Busby   Silvestri

EDDIE
MATHEWS   BRAVES

ATLANTA BRAVES

☐ 1. HANK AARON
☐ 29. PHIL NIEKRO
☐ 45. DAVE A. JOHNSON
☐ 71. DANNY FRISELLA
☐ 93. ROD GILBREATH
☐ 140. DARRELL EVANS
☐ 164. TOM HOUSE
☐ 183. JOHNNY OATES
☐ 227. MIKE LUM
☐ 244. CARL MORTON
☐ 272. PAUL CASANOVA
☐ 298. RORIC HARRISON
☐ 320. DUSTY BAKER
☐ 346. RON REED
☐ 374. MARTY PEREZ
☐ 415. GARY GENTRY
☐ 439. NORM MILLER
☐ 457. CHUCK GOGGIN
☐ 483. TEAM CARD
☐ 504. JOE NIEKRO
☐ 526. FRANK TEPEDINO
☐ 544. RON SCHUELER
☐ 570. RALPH GARR
☐ 591. SONNY JACKSON
☐ 607. LEO FOSTER(R)
☐ 614. ADRIAN DEVINE
☐ 634. MATHEWS(M) & COACHES

BALTIMORE ORIOLES

☐ 16. TEAM CARD
☐ 40. JIM PALMER
☐ 68. GRANT JACKSON
☐ 92. PAUL BLAIR
☐ 109. BOB GRICH
☐ 137. AL BUMBRY
☐ 160. BROOKS ROBINSON
☐ 187. DON BAYLOR
☐ 235. DAVE MCNALLY
☐ 259. BOB REYNOLDS
☐ 282. DOYLE ALEXANDER
☐ 306. WEAVER(M) & COACHES
☐ 329. MARK BELANGER
☐ 353. RICH COGGINS
☐ 375. EARL WILLIAMS
☐ 396. TOMMY DAVIS
☐ 411. FRANK W. BAKER
☐ 436. DON HOOD
☐ 460. BOOG POWELL
☐ 488. ANDY ETCHEBARREN

☐ 509. JESSE JEFFERSON
☐ 534. EDDIE WATT
☐ 560. MIKE CUELLAR
☐ 585. MERV RETTENMUND
☐ 596. WAYNE GARLAND(R)
☐ 603. SERGIO ROBLES(R)
☐ 606. JIM FULLER(R)
☐ 648. TERRY CROWLEY

BOSTON RED SOX

☐ 33. DON NEWHAUSER
☐ 61. LUIS APARICIO
☐ 83. ORLANDO CEPEDA
☐ 84. RICK WISE
☐ 105. CARLTON FISK
☐ 113. DICK DRAGO
☐ 118. BILL LEE
☐ 167. LUIS TIANT
☐ 192. MARIO GUERRERO
☐ 219. DOUG GRIFFIN
☐ 247. RICK MILLER
☐ 280. CARL YASTRZEMSKI
☐ 301. BOB MONTGOMERY
☐ 325. TOMMY HARPER
☐ 351. DWIGHT EVANS
☐ 373. JOHN CURTIS
☐ 403. JOHNSON(M) & COACHES
☐ 427. BOBBY BOLIN
☐ 495. DICK MCAULIFFE
☐ 523. CECIL COOPER
☐ 543. DANNY CATER
☐ 567. TEAM CARD
☐ 590. ROGELIO MORET
☐ 596. DICK POLE(R)
☐ 609. RICO PETROCELLI
☐ 621. BERNIE CARBO
☐ 647. JUAN BENIQUEZ

CALIFORNIA ANGELS

☐ 20. NOLAN RYAN
☐ 37. DAVE SELLS
☐ 55. FRANK ROBINSON
☐ 76. MICKEY RIVERS
☐ 101. BOBBY VALENTINE
☐ 114. TEAM CARD
☐ 139. AURELIO MONTEAGUDO
☐ 188. RUDY MEOLI
☐ 210. BILL SINGER
☐ 243. BOB OLIVER
☐ 276. WINKLES(M) & COACHES
☐ 302. RUDY MAY
☐ 323. RICHIE SCHEINBLUM
☐ 347. SANDY ALOMAR
☐ 381. CHARLIE SANDS
☐ 405. ELLIE RODRIGUEZ
☐ 429. DICK LANGE
☐ 449. TOM MCCRAW
☐ 467. WINSTON LLENAS
☐ 490. VADA PINSON
☐ 512. JOE LAHOUD
☐ 532. SKIP LOCKWOOD
☐ 552. DENNY DOYLE
☐ 571. RICH HAND
☐ 594. LEROY STANTON
☐ 597. DAVE CHALK(R)
☐ 605. FRANK TANANA(R)
☐ 611. RICK STELMASZEK
☐ 625. OLLIE BROWN
☐ 650. MIKE EPSTEIN

CHICAGO CUBS

☐ 14. PAUL POPOVICH
☐ 38. DON KESSINGER
☐ 62. BOB LOCKER
☐ 110. BILLY WILLIAMS
☐ 136. RICK REUSCHEL
☐ 157. VIC HARRIS
☐ 161. RAY BURRIS
☐ 185. JOSE CARDENAL
☐ 211. TEAM CARD
☐ 258. JERRY MORALES
☐ 270. RON SANTO
☐ 295. RICK MONDAY
☐ 319. RANDY HUNDLEY
☐ 354. LOCKMAN(M) & COACHES
☐ 378. BURT HOOTON
☐ 399. MIKE PAUL

☐ 422. GONZALO MARQUEZ
☐ 452. GENE HISER
☐ 484. CARMEN FANZONE
☐ 502. DAVE LAROCHE
☐ 528. BILL BONHAM
☐ 562. JACK AKER
☐ 584. KEN RUDOLPH
☐ 598. JIM TYRONE(R)
☐ 600. BILL MADLOCK(R)
☐ 603. TOM LUNDSTEDT(R)
☐ 604. ANDY THORNTON(R)
☐ 607. DAVE ROSELLO(R)
☐ 616. LARRY GURA
☐ 640. MILT PAPPAS
☐ 656. ADRIAN GARRETT

CHICAGO WHITE SOX

☐ 22. CY ACOSTA
☐ 46. H. PAT KELLY
☐ 70. DICK ALLEN
☐ 96. JERRY HAIRSTON
☐ 120. WILBUR WOOD
☐ 147. BART JOHNSON
☐ 170. BILL MELTON
☐ 195. CARLOS MAY
☐ 221. TANNER(M) & COACHES
☐ 254. STAN BAHNSEN
☐ 286. TONY MUSER
☐ 310. TERRY FORSTER
☐ 357. BUDDY BRADFORD
☐ 376. JORGE ORTA
☐ 394. KEN HENDERSON
☐ 416. TEAM CARD
☐ 438. ED HERRMANN
☐ 440. JIM KAAT
☐ 462. LUIS ALVARADO
☐ 486. STEVE STONE
☐ 501. EDDIE LEON
☐ 519. BILL SHARP
☐ 542. RICH GOSSAGE
☐ 557. JIM MCGLOTHLIN
☐ 582. BUCKY DENT
☐ 601. BRIAN DOWNING(R)
☐ 605. KEN FRAILING(R)
☐ 615. JOHNNY JETER
☐ 641. CHUCK BRINKMAN

CINCINNATI REDS

☐ 10. JOHNNY BENCH
☐ 34. ANDY KOSCO
☐ 59. ROSS GRIMSLEY
☐ 85. JOE MORGAN
☐ 111. CLAY CARROLL
☐ 134. DENIS MENKE
☐ 158. JACK BILLINGHAM
☐ 181. CESAR GERONIMO
☐ 230. TONY PEREZ
☐ 248. TOM HALL
☐ 277. GARY NOLAN
☐ 287. CLAY KIRBY
☐ 300. PETE ROSE
☐ 326. ANDERSON(M) & CHS.
☐ 341. DAN DRIESSEN
☐ 362. HAL KING
☐ 385. DON GULLETT
☐ 410. PEDRO BORBON
☐ 435. DAVE CONCEPCION
☐ 459. TEAM CARD
☐ 491. ROGER NELSON
☐ 507. LARRY STAHL
☐ 524. BILL PLUMMER
☐ 559. DARREL CHANEY
☐ 581. FRED NORMAN
☐ 598. KEN GRIFFEY(R)
☐ 601. ED ARMBRISTER(R)
☐ 608. DICK BANEY(R)
☐ 622. PHIL GAGLIANO
☐ 646. GEORGE FOSTER

CLEVELAND INDIANS

☐ 13. TOM HILGENDORF
☐ 35. GAYLORD PERRY
☐ 58. CHARLIE SPIKES
☐ 81. FRANK DUFFY
☐ 128. JOHN ELLIS
☐ 152. OSCAR GAMBLE
☐ 176. JOHN LOWENSTEIN

☐ 199. MIKE KEKICH
☐ 231. DICK TIDROW
☐ 257. BUDDY BELL
☐ 284. DAVE DUNCAN
☐ 303. GEORGE HENDRICK
☐ 327. TOM TIMMERMANN
☐ 359. BRENT STROM
☐ 384. CHRIS CHAMBLISS
☐ 418. WALT WILLIAMS
☐ 441. TOM RAGLAND
☐ 465. DICK BOSMAN
☐ 499. RUSTY TORRES
☐ 521. ASPROMONTE(M) & CHS.
☐ 541. TEAM CARD
☐ 565. MILT WILCOX
☐ 586. JACK BROHAMER
☐ 606. TOMMY SMITH(R)
☐ 617. TED FORD
☐ 638. KEN SANDERS

DETROIT TIGERS

☐ 9. MICKEY LOLICH
☐ 24. JOHN HILLER
☐ 48. DICK SHARON
☐ 72. AURELIO RODRIGUEZ
☐ 94. TEAM CARD
☐ 115. WILLIE HORTON
☐ 138. ED BRINKMAN
☐ 162. BILL FREEHAN
☐ 186. FRED SCHERMAN
☐ 215. AL KALINE
☐ 240. JOE COLEMAN
☐ 256. JIM NORTHRUP
☐ 292. CHUCK SEELBACH
☐ 316. JIM PERRY
☐ 367. NORM CASH
☐ 389. GATES BROWN
☐ 409. IKE BROWN
☐ 433. LERRIN LAGROW
☐ 482. BOB DIDIER
☐ 506. ED FARMER
☐ 530. MICKEY STANLEY
☐ 555. WOODIE FRYMAN
☐ 578. RALPH HOUK(M)
☐ 596. FRED HOLDSWORTH(R)
☐ 597. JOHN GAMBLE(R)
☐ 600. RON CASH(R)
☐ 600. REGGIE SANDERS(R)
☐ 604. JOHN KNOX(R)

BOB WATSON

HOUSTON ASTROS

☐ 21. BOB GALLAGHER
☐ 31. GOMEZ(M) & COACHES
☐ 43. JIM WYNN
☐ 67. TOMMY HELMS
☐ 91. KEN FORSCH
☐ 154. TEAM CARD
☐ 177. DAVE A. ROBERTS
☐ 200. CESAR CEDENO
☐ 224. ROGER METZGER
☐ 256. TOM GRIFFIN
☐ 279. JIM CRAWFORD
☐ 293. MILT MAY
☐ 304. DON WILSON
☐ 328. SKIP JUTZE
☐ 370. BOB WATSON
☐ 395. DOUG RADER

☐ 428. GARY SUTHERLAND
☐ 458. JIM RAY
☐ 500. LEE MAY
☐ 522. J.R. RICHARD
☐ 556. DAVE CAMPBELL
☐ 579. CECIL UPSHAW
☐ 635. JOHN EDWARDS
☐ 660. LARRY DIERKER

KANSAS CITY ROYALS

☐ 17. DOUG BIRD
☐ 41. BOBBY FLOYD
☐ 65. AMOS OTIS
☐ 88. FREDDIE PATEK
☐ 150. JOHN MAYBERRY
☐ 166. MCKEON(M) & COACHES
☐ 191. AL FITZMORRIS
☐ 225. PAUL SPLITTORFF
☐ 238. FRAN HEALY
☐ 262. ED KIRKPATRICK
☐ 278. COOKIE ROJAS
☐ 308. BRUCE DAL CANTON
☐ 343. TEAM CARD
☐ 365. STEVE BUSBY
☐ 390. LOU PINIELLA
☐ 407. JIM WOHLFORD
☐ 431. GENE GARBER
☐ 454. KURT BEVACQUA
☐ 493. JOE HOERNER
☐ 514. PAUL SCHAAL
☐ 537. STEVE MINGORI
☐ 563. HAL MCRAE
☐ 583. MARTY PATTIN
☐ 596. MARK LITTELL(R)
☐ 604. FRANK WHITE(R)
☐ 627. CARL TAYLOR
☐ 652. GAIL HOPKINS

LOS ANGELES DODGERS

☐ 42. CLAUDE OSTEEN
☐ 64. DOUG RAU
☐ 86. JOE FERGUSON
☐ 112. DAVE LOPES
☐ 127. TOM PACIOREK
☐ 144. ALSTON(M) & COACHES
☐ 165. WILLIE DAVIS
☐ 189. JIM BREWER
☐ 220. DON SUTTON
☐ 239. BILL RUSSEL
☐ 267. ANDY MESSERSMITH
☐ 289. RICK AUERBACH
☐ 315. RON CEY
☐ 348. PETE RICHERT
☐ 368. MANNY MOTA
☐ 408. CHARLIE HOUGH
☐ 434. KEN MCMULLEN
☐ 451. TOMMY JOHN
☐ 480. WILLIE CRAWFORD
☐ 505. BILL BUCKNER
☐ 551. VON JOSHUA
☐ 575. STEVE GARVEY
☐ 593. STEVE YEAGER
☐ 599. GREG SHANAHAN(R)
☐ 620. AL DOWNING
☐ 643. TEAM CARD
☐ 658. LEE LACY

MILWAUKEE BREWERS

☐ 12. DAVE MAY
☐ 27. GEORGE SCOTT
☐ 51. BOBBY HEISE
☐ 75. JIM COLBORN
☐ 99. CRANDALL(M) & COACHES
☐ 124. BOB COLUCCIO
☐ 142. PEDRO GARCIA
☐ 163. KEN BERRY
☐ 171. EDUARDO RODRIGUEZ
☐ 194. DARRELL PORTER
☐ 218. JOHNNY BRIGGS
☐ 261. JERRY BELL
☐ 288. GORMAN THOMAS
☐ 314. TEAM CARD
☐ 349. JOHN VUKOVICH
☐ 371. JIM SLATON
☐ 391. BILLY CHAMPION
☐ 413. DON MONEY

☐ 497. BOBBY MITCHELL
☐ 525. CLYDE WRIGHT
☐ 554. TIM JOHNSON
☐ 574. BILL PARSONS
☐ 603. CHARLIE MOORE(R)
☐ 605. KEVIN KOBEL(R)
☐ 606. WILBUR HOWARD(R)
☐ 631. STEVE BARBER

MINNESOTA TWINS

☐   26. BILL CAMPBELL
☐   50. ROD CAREW
☐   74. TEAM CARD
☐   98. BERT BLYLEVEN
☐ 122. JIM HOLT
☐ 143. DICK WOODSON
☐ 168. DANNY THOMPSON
☐ 190. TONY OLIVA
☐ 232. STEVE BRYE
☐ 249. GEORGE MITTERWALD
☐ 271. BILL HANDS
☐ 296. RAY CORBIN
☐ 321. STEVE BRAUN
☐ 366. LARRY HISLE
☐ 388. PHIL ROOF
☐ 400. HARMON KILLEBREW
☐ 421. DAN FIFE
☐ 447. QUILICI(M) & COACHES
☐ 469. JOE DECKER
☐ 481. JERRY TERRELL
☐ 503. ERIC SODERHOLM
☐ 527. BOBBY DARWIN
☐ 547. GLENN BORGMANN
☐ 573. MIKE ADAMS
☐ 592. ED BANE
☐ 602. DAN VOSSLER(R)
☐ 605. VIC ALBURY(R)
☐ 613. DAN MONZON
☐ 636. DAVE GOLTZ
☐ 659. JOE LIS

MONTREAL EXPOS

☐   25. KEN SINGLETON
☐   49. STEVE RENKO
☐   73. MIKE MARSHALL
☐   97. BOB BAILEY
☐ 121. LARRY LINTZ
☐ 146. RON FAIRLY
☐ 169. STEVE ROGERS
☐ 193. TOM WALKER
☐ 217. TIM FOLI
☐ 253. JOHN BOCCABELLA
☐ 275. RON HUNT
☐ 297. HAL BREEDEN
☐ 322. ERNIE MCANALLY
☐ 352. BILL STONEMAN
☐ 377. RON WOODS
☐ 412. CHUCK TAYLOR
☐ 437. JIM LYTTLE
☐ 453. BALOR MOORE
☐ 468. PEPE FRIAS
☐ 485. FELIPE ALOU
☐ 508. TEAM CARD
☐ 531. MAUCH(M) & COACHES
☐ 549. MIKE JORGENSEN
☐ 568. MIKE TORREZ
☐ 589. BOOTS DAY
☐ 600. JIM COX(R)
☐ 603. BARRY FOOTE(R)
☐ 653. BOB STINSON

NEW YORK METS

■   8. GEORGE THEODORE
■   56. TEAM CARD
■   80. TOM SEAVER
■ 106. HARRY PARKER
■ 132. FELIX MILLAN
☐ 153. JON MATLACK
■ 179. BERRA(M) & COACHES
■ 216. RAY SADECKI
☐ 234. JOHN MILNER
■ 245. CLEON JONES
■ 265. TUG MCGRAW
■ 291. DON HAHN
■ 311. JERRY GROTE
☐ 356. JERRY KOOSMAN
■ 380. BUD HARRELSON

■ 397. GEORGE STONE
■ 424. JIM BEAUCHAMP
■ 448. RON HODGES
■ 487. TED MARTINEZ
■ 510. WAYNE GARRETT
■ 536. DUFFY DYER
☐ 561. ED KRANEPOOL
☐ 602. CRAIG SWAN(R)
☐ 608. BOB APODACA(R)
■ 624. BOB L. MILLER
☐ 629. RUSTY STAUB
☐ 645. KEN BOSWELL

NEW YORK YANKEES

☐   19. GERRY MOSES
☐   44. MEL STOTTLEMYRE
☐   66. SPARKY LYLE
☐   90. BOBBY MURCER
☐ 117. RON BLOMBERG
☐ 135. ROY WHITE
☐ 159. JIM HART
☐ 182. LINDY MCDANIEL
☐ 229. FRITZ PETERSON
☐ 251. GRAIG NETTLES
☐ 274. FRED BEENE
☐ 299. GENE MICHAEL
☐ 324. STEVE KLINE
☐ 340. THURMAN MUNSON
☐ 363. TEAM CARD
☐ 398. DUKE SIMS
☐ 423. FRED STANLEY
☐ 445. GEORGE MEDICH
☐ 463. PAT DOBSON
☐ 517. MIKE HEGAN
☐ 529. HORACE CLARKE
☐ 550. SAM MCDOWELL
☐ 569. RICK DEMPSEY
☐ 588. HAL LANIER
☐ 601. RICH BLADT(R)
☐ 606. OTTO VELEZ(R)
☐ 623. CELERINO SANCHEZ
☐ 644. WAYNE GRANGER

OAKLAND A'S

☐   7. JIM HUNTER
☐   57. DAROLD KNOWLES
☐   79. GENE TENACE
☐ 103. SAL BANDO
☐ 130. REGGIE JACKSON
☐ 141. PAT BOURQUE
☐ 155. BERT CAMPANERIS
☐ 180. KEN HOLTZMAN
☐ 212. ROLLIE FINGERS
☐ 228. TED KUBIAK
☐ 246. TEAM CARD
☐ 264. JOE RUDI
☐ 290. VIDA BLUE
☐ 312. DERON JOHNSON
☐ 345. BILL NORTH
☐ 369. PAUL LINDBLAD
☐ 392. DICK GREEN
☐ 420. RAY FOSSE
☐ 444. VIC DAVALILLO
☐ 461. JOHN ODOM
☐ 516. HORACIO PINA
☐ 545. BILLY CONIGLIARO
☐ 597. MANNY TRILLO(R)
☐ 602. GLENN ABBOTT(R)
☐ 633. DAVE HAMILTON
☐ 654. JESUS ALOU

PHIADELPHIA PHILLIES

☐   23. CRAIG ROBINSON
☐   47. DICK RUTHVEN
☐   69. DEL UNSER
☐   95. STEVE CARLTON
☐ 119. OZARK(M) & COACHES
☐ 131. BOB BOONE
☐ 149. MAC SCARCE
☐ 174. BILL ROBINSON
☐ 198. DAVE CASH
☐ 214. BILLY GRABARKEWITZ
☐ 255. LARRY BOWA
☐ 283. MIKE SCHMIDT
☐ 313. BARRY LERSCH
☐ 342. JIM LONBORG
☐ 360. GREG LUZINSKI

☐ 383. TEAM CARD
☐ 419. WAYNE TWITCHELL
☐ 443. TOM HUTTON
☐ 492. MIKE ROGODZINSKI
☐ 515. WILLIE MONTANEZ
☐ 538. CESAR TOVAR
☐ 564. MIKE RYAN
☐ 587. LARRY CHRISTENSON
☐ 599. RON DIORIO(R)
☐ 608. MIKE WALLACE(R)
☐ 619. MIKE ANDERSON
☐ 632. GEORGE CULVER
☐ 642. TERRY HARMON

PITTSBURGH PIRATES

☐   28. MANNY SANGUILLEN
☐   52. AL OLIVER
☐   82. DAVE GIUSTI
☐ 100. WILLIE STARGELL
☐ 116. JERRY REUSS
☐ 123. NELSON BRILES
☐ 145. DOCK ELLIS
☐ 172. GENE CLINES
☐ 222. RAMON HERNANDEZ
☐ 237. KEN BRETT
☐ 252. DAVE PARKER
☐ 269. BOB D. JOHNSON
☐ 317. RICHIE ZISK
☐ 358. DAL MAXVILL
☐ 382. BOB MOOSE
☐ 402. JIM ROOKER
☐ 426. RENNIE STENNETT
☐ 450. RICH HEBNER
☐ 489. MURTAUGH(M) & COACHES
☐ 513. JIM CAMPANIS
☐ 540. BOB ROBERTSON
☐ 566. JACKIE HERNANDEZ
☐ 595. STEVE BLASS
☐ 598. DAVE AUGUSTINE(R)
☐ 607. FRANK TAVERAS(R)
☐ 612. LUKE WALKER
☐ 626. TEAM CARD
☐ 649. FERNANDO GONZALEZ

ST. LOUIS CARDINALS

☐   15. JOE TORRE
☐   36. TEAM CARD
☐   60. LOU BROCK
☐ 108. AL HRABOSKY
☐ 151. DIEGO SEGUI
☐ 175. REGGIE CLEVELAND
☐ 209. TED SIZEMORE
☐ 236. SCHOENDIENST(M) & CHS.
☐ 260. TED SIMMONS
☐ 285. REGGIE SMITH
☐ 307. LUIS MELENDEZ
☐ 350. BOB GIBSON
☐ 372. KEN REITZ
☐ 393. ORLANDO PENA
☐ 417. RICH FOLKERS
☐ 442. ALAN FOSTER
☐ 464. JOSE CRUZ
☐ 496. TOM MURPHY
☐ 520. TIM MCCARVER
☐ 548. SONNY SIEBERT
☐ 576. SCIPIO SPINKS
☐ 601. BAKE MCBRIDE(R)
☐ 604. TERRY HUGHES(R)
☐ 607. TOM HEINTZELMAN(R)
☐ 630. TOMMIE AGEE
☐ 655. MIKE TYSON

SAN DIEGO PADRES

☐   32. JOHN GRUBB*
☐   53. FRED KENDALL*
☐   77. RICH TROEDSON*
☐ 102. BILL GREIF*
☐ 125. NATE COLBERT*
☐ 148. DAVE HILTON*
☐ 173. RANDY JONES*
☐ 197. VICENTE ROMO*
☐ 226. TEAM CARD*
☐ 241. GLENN BECKERT*
☐ 250. WILLIE MCCOVEY*
☐ 309. DAVE W. ROBERTS*
☐ 364. CLARENCE GASTON*
☐ 387. RICH MORALES*

* Cards appear with both San Diego Padres and Washington National League Iden- tifications.

☐ 406. STEVE ARLIN
☐ 430. MATTY ALOU
☐ 456. DAVE WINFIELD
☐ 498. PAT CORRALES
☐ 518. DERREL THOMAS
☐ 535. BOB TOLAN
☐ 546. MIKE CORKINS
☐ 572. ENZO HERNANDEZ
☐ 599. DAVE FREISLEBEN(R)*
☐ 628. IVAN MURRELL
☐ 651. LERON LEE

SAN FRANCISCO GIANTS

☐ 18. GARY THOMASSON
☐ 30. BOBBY BONDS
☐ 54. ELIAS SOSA
☐ 78. FOX(M) & COACHES
☐ 104. RON BRYANT
☐ 129. CHRIS SPEIER
☐ 156. RANDY MOFFITT
☐ 178. GARRY MADDOX
☐ 213. DAVE RADER
☐ 233. JIM BARR
☐ 281. TEAM CARD
☐ 305. TITO FUENTES
☐ 330. JUAN MARICHAL
☐ 344. MIKE CALDWELL
☐ 361. DON CARRITHERS
☐ 386. GARY MATTHEWS
☐ 404. JIM HOWARTH
☐ 432. CHRIS ARNOLD
☐ 455. TOM BRADLEY
☐ 494. ED GOODSON
☐ 533. MIKE PHILLIPS
☐ 553. JIM WILLOUGHBY
☐ 577. MIKE SADEK
☐ 598. STEVE ONTIVEROS(R)
☐ 599. FRANK RICELLI(R)
☐ 608. JOHN D'ACQUISTO(R)
☐ 610. DAVE KINGMAN

TOBY HARRAH

TEXAS RANGERS

☐ 11. JIM BIBBY
☐ 39. KEN SUAREZ
☐ 63. BILL SUDAKIS
☐ 87. FERGIE JENKINS
☐ 89. JACKIE BROWN
☐ 107. ALEX JOHNSON
☐ 133. DAVID CLYDE
☐ 184. TEAM CARD
☐ 196. JIM FREGOSI
☐ 223. JEFF BURROUGHS
☐ 242. BILL GOGOLEWSKI
☐ 268. TOM GRIEVE
☐ 294. STEVE FOUCAULT
☐ 318. JIM MERRITT
☐ 355. DAVE NELSON
☐ 379. MARTIN(M) & COACHES
☐ 401. ELLIOTT MADDOX
☐ 425. PETE BROBERG
☐ 446. LEN RANDLE
☐ 466. DICK BILLINGS
☐ 511. TOBY HARRAH
☐ 539. LLOYD ALLEN
☐ 558. BILL FAHEY
☐ 580. JIM SPENCER

☐ 597. PETE MACKANIN(R)
☐ 602. RICK HENNINGER(R)
☐ 618. JIM MASON
☐ 639. JOE LOVITTO
☐ 657. JIM SHELLENBACK

1974 TOPPS TRADED (44)
2 1/2" X 3 1/2"

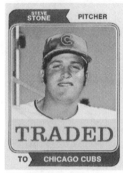

STEVE STONE — PITCHER — TRADED TO CHICAGO CUBS

ATLANTA BRAVES

☐ 23T. CRAIG ROBINSON
☐ 313T. BARRY LERSCH

BALTIMORE ORIOLES

☐ 59T. ROSS GRIMSLEY

BOSTON RED SOX

☐ 151T. DIEGO SEGUI
☐ 175T. REGGIE CLEVELAND
☐ 330T. JUAN MARICHAL

CALIFORNIA ANGELS

NO CARDS ISSUED

CHICAGO CUBS

☐ 249T. GEORGE MITTERWALD
☐ 486T. STEVE STONE
☐ 516T. HORACIO PINA

CHICAGO WHITE SOX

☐ 270T. RON SANTO

CINCINNATI REDS

☐ 585T. MERV RETTENMUND

CLEVELAND INDIANS

☐ 269T. BOB JOHNSON
☐ 579T. CECIL UPSHAW

DETROIT TIGERS

☐ 428T. GARY SUTHERLAND
☐ 458T. JIM RAY
☐ 612T. LUKE WALKER

HOUSTON ASTROS

☐ 42T. CLAUDE OSTEEN
☐ 186T. FRED SCHERMAN

KANSAS CITY ROYALS

☐ 123T. NELSON BRILES
☐ 182T. LINDY MCDANIEL
☐ 649T. FERNANDO GONZALEZ

MIKE MARSHALL — PITCHER — TRADED TO LOS ANGELES DODGERS

LOS ANGELES DODGERS

☐ 43T. JIM WYNN
☐ 73T. MIKE MARSHALL
☐ 630T. TOMMIE AGEE

MILWAUKEE BREWERS

☐ 485T. FELIPE ALOU
☐ 496T. TOM MURPHY

MINNESOTA TWINS

☐ 319T. RANDY HUNDLEY

MONTREAL EXPOS

☐ 165T. WILLIE DAVIS

NEW YORK METS

NO CARDS ISSUED

NEW YORK YANKEES

☐ 63T. BILL SUDAKIS
☐ 390T. LOU PINIELLA
☐ 618T. JIM MASON

OAKLAND A'S

☐ 62T. BOB LOCKER

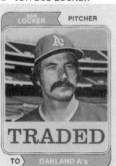

BOB LOCKER — PITCHER — TRADED TO OAKLAND A's

PHILADELPHIA PHILLIES

☐ 139T. AURELIO MONTEAGUDO
☐ 534T. EDDIE WATT
☐ 544T. RON SCHUELER

PITTSBURGH PIRATES

☐ 262T. ED KIRKPATRICK
☐ 454T. KURT BEVACQUA

ST. LOUIS CARDINALS

☐ 51T. BOBBY HEISE
☐ 348T. PETE RICHERT
☐ 373T. JOHN CURTIS

SAN DIEGO PADRES

NO CARDS ISSUED

SAN FRANCISCO GIANTS

NO CARDS ISSUED

TEXAS RANGERS

☐ 538T. CESAR TOVAR
☐ 616T. LARRY GURA
☐ 648T. TERRY CROWLEY

1975 TOPPS (660)
2 1/2″ X 3 1/2″

1975 TOPPS
MINIS (660)
2 1/4″ X 3 1/8″

ROBIN YOUNT

ATLANTA BRAVES

☐ 9. FRANK TEPEDINO
☐ 33. DUSTY BAKER
☐ 57. DAVE A. JOHNSON
☐ 81. RON REED
☐ 105. BUZZ CAPRA
☐ 130. PHIL NIEKRO
☐ 154. MIKE LUM
☐ 177. VIC CORRELL
☐ 237. CARL MORTON
☐ 262. ROWLAND OFFICE
☐ 287. RORIC HARRISON
☐ 319. JOHNNY OATES
☐ 367. CRAIG ROBINSON
☐ 393. GARY GENTRY
☐ 394. LARVELL BLANKS
☐ 418. LEO FOSTER
☐ 427. CLARENCE GASTON
☐ 431. ROD GILBREATH
☐ 442. MAXIMINO LEON
☐ 475. DARRELL EVANS
☐ 499. MARTY PEREZ
☐ 525. TOM HOUSE
☐ 550. RALPH GARR
☐ 589. TEAM & KING(M)
☐ 595. JOE NIEKRO
☐ 603. LEW KRAUSSE
☐ 618. JAMIE EASTERLY(R)
☐ 633. PAUL CASANOVA
☐ 650. DAVE MAY

BALTIMORE ORIOLES

☐ 26. DAVE MCNALLY
☐ 50. BROOKS ROBINSON
☐ 74. MARK BELANGER
☐ 97. EARL WILLIAMS
☐ 117. TEAM & WEAVER(M)
☐ 142. BOB REYNOLDS
☐ 167. RICH COGGINS
☐ 225. BOB GRICH

☐ 247. ENOS CABELL
☐ 275. PAUL BLAIR
☐ 303. GRANT JACKSON
☐ 335. JIM PALMER
☐ 358. AL BUMBRY
☐ 382. DON BAYLOR
☐ 410. MIKE CUELLER
☐ 458. ROSS GRIMSLEY
☐ 491. DOYLE ALEXANDER
☐ 516. DON HOOD
☐ 539. JESSE JERRERSON
☐ 564. TOMMY DAVIS
☐ 583. ANDY ETCHEBARREN
☐ 594. JIM FULLER
☐ 609. ELLIE HENDRICKS
☐ 614. DYAR MILLER(R)
☐ 617. DOUG DECINCES(R)
☐ 625. BOOG POWELL
☐ 641. JIM NORTHRUP
☐ 657. BOB OLIVER

BOSTON RED SOX

☐ 8. ROGELIO MORET
☐ 32. REGGIE CLEVELAND
☐ 56. RICK WISE
☐ 80. CARLTON FISK
☐ 103. RICK MILLER
☐ 128. BILL LEE
☐ 152. MARIO GUERRERO
☐ 172. TEAM & JOHNSON(M)
☐ 232. DIEGO SEGUI
☐ 255. DWIGHT EVANS
☐ 280. CARL YASTRZEMSKI
☐ 302. RICK BURLESON
☐ 333. DICK DRAGO
☐ 356. RICO PETROCELLI
☐ 379. BERNIE CARBO
☐ 430. LUIS TIANT
☐ 454. DOUG GRIFFIN
☐ 489. CECIL COOPER
☐ 513. DICK POLE
☐ 537. TOMMY HARPER
☐ 559. BOB MONTGOMERY
☐ 586. TIM MCCARVER
☐ 601. JUAN BENIQUEZ
☐ 612. TERRY HUGHES
☐ 616. JIM RICE(R)
☐ 622. FRED LYNN(R)
☐ 645. DANNY CATER

CALIFORNIA ANGELS

☐ 16. FRANK TANANA
☐ 40. BILL SINGER
☐ 64. DAVE CHALK
☐ 88. TOM EGAN
☐ 114. DICK LANGE
☐ 139. HORACIO PINA
☐ 164. MICKEY RIVERS
☐ 187. DENNY DOYLE
☐ 215. BOBBY VALENTINE
☐ 236. TEAM & WILLIAMS(M)
☐ 261. ANDY HASSLER
☐ 285. ELLIE RODRIGUEZ
☐ 317. JOE LAHOUD
☐ 342. LEROY STANTON
☐ 366. KEN SANDERS
☐ 392. BRUCE BOCHTE
☐ 417. SKIP LOCKWOOD
☐ 441. BOBBY HEISE
☐ 476. ED FIGUEROA
☐ 500. NOLAN RYAN
☐ 524. JOHN DOHERTY
☐ 533. RUDY MEOLI
☐ 548. CHARLIE SANDS
☐ 573. ORLANDO PENA
☐ 597. WINSTON LLENAS
☐ 632. MORRIS NETTLES
☐ 635. CHUCK DOBSON

CHICAGO CUBS

☐ 15. JOSE CARDENAL
☐ 39. ANDY THRONTON
☐ 63. STEVE SWISHER
☐ 85. BILL BONHAM
☐ 104. BILL MADLOCK
☐ 129. RICK MONDAY

☐ 153. RICK REUSCHEL
☐ 176. BURT HOOTON
☐ 233. BILLY GRABARKEWITZ
☐ 258. DAVE LAROCHE
☐ 282. JERRY MORALES
☐ 315. DON KESSINGER
☐ 338. RICK STELMASZEK
☐ 352. DAROLD KNOWLES
☐ 363. CARMEN FANZONE
☐ 388. STEVE STONE
☐ 411. GEORGE MITTERWALD
☐ 434. BOB LOCKER
☐ 436. KEN FRAILING
☐ 469. TOM DETTORE
☐ 494. PETE LACOCK
☐ 519. JIM TOOD
☐ 566. RAY BURRIS
☐ 587. CHRIS WARD
☐ 604. OSCAR ZAMORA
☐ 617. MANNY TRILLO(R)
☐ 638. TEAM & MARSHALL(M)
☐ 658. VIC HARRIS

CHICAGO WHITE SOX

☐ 11. BILL MELTON
☐ 35. RON SANTO
☐ 59. KEN HENDERSON
☐ 82. H. PAT KELLY
☐ 110. WILBUR WOOD
☐ 137. TERRY FORSTER
☐ 161. STAN BAHNSEN
☐ 184. JORGE ORTA
☐ 219. ED HERRMANN
☐ 243. JIM KAAT
☐ 276. TEAM & TANNER(M)
☐ 299. BUCKY DENT
☐ 327. JERRY HAIRSTON
☐ 348. TONY MUSER
☐ 373. BILL SHARP
☐ 400. DICK ALLEN
☐ 422. BRIAN DOWNING
☐ 446. BART JOHNSON
☐ 480. CARLOS MAY
☐ 504. BUDDY BRADFORD
☐ 528. EDDIE LEON
☐ 554. RICH GOSSAGE
☐ 572. ROGER NELSON
☐ 579. SKIP PITLOCK
☐ 614. JACK KUCEK(R)
☐ 619. NYLS NYMAN(R)
☐ 624. JIM OTTEN(R)
☐ 634. CY ACOSTA
☐ 653. LEE RICHARD

CINCINNATI REDS

☐ 17. DAVE CONCEPCION
☐ 41. CESAR GERONIMO
☐ 65. DON GULLETT
☐ 87. GEORGE FOSTER
☐ 108. TOM HALL
☐ 133. DAN DRIESSEN
☐ 157. PEDRO BORBON
☐ 180. JOE MORGAN
☐ 235. JACK BILLINGHAM
☐ 260. JOHNNY BENCH
☐ 284. KEN GRIFFEY
☐ 320. PETE ROSE
☐ 345. CLAY CARROLL
☐ 369. MERV RETTENMUND
☐ 396. FRED NORMAN
☐ 423. CLAY KIRBY
☐ 447. TERRY CROWLEY
☐ 481. WILL MCENANEY
☐ 507. TOM CARROLL
☐ 531. TEAM & ANDERSON(M)
☐ 560. TONY PEREZ
☐ 562. GARY NOLAN
☐ 581. DARREL CHANEY
☐ 602. JOHN VUKOVICH
☐ 615. PAT DARCY(R)
☐ 621. RAWLY EASTWICK(R)
☐ 622. ED ARMBRISTER(R)
☐ 656. BILL PLUMMER

CLEVELAND INDIANS

☐ 14. MILT WILCOX
☐ 38. BUDDY BELL
☐ 62. FRITZ PETERSON

1975 Topps

☐ 86. JOE LIS
☐ 109. GEORGE HENDRICK
☐ 135. CHARLIE SPIKES
☐ 159. STEVE ARLIN
☐ 181. FRED BEENE
☐ 213. OSCAR GAMBLE
☐ 238. DAVE DUNCAN
☐ 263. JIM PERRY
☐ 288. BRUCE ELLINGSEN
☐ 331. TEAM & ROBINSON(M)
☐ 354. DICK BOSMAN
☐ 377. TOM HILGENDORF
☐ 403. TOM BUSKEY
☐ 424. JOHN LOWENSTEIN
☐ 448. FRANK DUFFY
☐ 482. TOM MCCRAW
☐ 506. LERON LEE
☐ 530. GAYLORD PERRY
☐ 552. JACK BROHAMER
☐ 580. FRANK ROBINSON
☐ 605. JOHN ELLIS
☐ 619. TOMMY SMITH(R)
☐ 621. JIM KERN(R)
☐ 639. STEVE KLINE
☐ 655. RICO CARTY

DETROIT TIGERS

☐ 18. TEAM & HOUK(M)
☐ 42. JOE COLEMAN
☐ 66. WILLIE HORTON
☐ 89. JIM RAY
☐ 116. LERRIN LAGROW
☐ 141. MICKEY STANLEY
☐ 166. WOODIE FRYMAN
☐ 221. AURELIO RODRIGUEZ
☐ 245. MICKEY LOLICH
☐ 271. JERRY MOSES
☐ 293. DICK SHARON
☐ 323. FRED HOLDSWORTH
☐ 344. BEN OGLIVIE
☐ 371. GATES BROWN
☐ 397. BILL FREEHAN
☐ 415. JOHN HILLER
☐ 439. ED BRINKMAN
☐ 474. LUKE WALDER
☐ 497. JIM NETTLES
☐ 522. GARY SUTHERLAND
☐ 546. JOHN KNOX
☐ 571. DAVE LEMANCZYK
☐ 593. GENE LAMONT
☐ 599. NATE COLBERT
☐ 614. VERN RUHLE(R)
☐ 617. REGGIE SANDERS(R)
☐ 620. DANNY MEYER(R)
☐ 620. LEON ROBERTS(R)
☐ 623. TOM VERYZER(R)
☐ 628. RON LEFLORE

HOUSTON ASTROS

☐ 25. LEE MAY
☐ 49. LARRY DIERKER
☐ 73. J.R. RICHARD
☐ 96. MIKE COSGROVE
☐ 119. TOMMY HELMS
☐ 143. CLIFF JOHNSON
☐ 165. DOUG RADER
☐ 188. TOM GRIFFIN
☐ 218. JERRY JOHNSON
☐ 227. BOB WATSON
☐ 252. FRED SCHERMAN
☐ 279. MILT MAY
☐ 301. DAVE A. ROBERTS
☐ 334. GREG GROSS
☐ 357. KEN FORSCH
☐ 383. JIM YORK
☐ 455. DON WILSON
☐ 479. KEN BOSWELL
☐ 487. TEAM & GOMEZ(M)
☐ 512. LARRY MILBOURNE
☐ 514. JOSE CRUZ
☐ 541. ROGER METZGER
☐ 563. WILBUR HOWARD
☐ 590. CESAR CEDENO
☐ 614. PAUL SIEBERT(R)
☐ 624. DOUG KONIECZNY(R)

GEORGE BRETT 3rd Base

KANSAS CITY ROYALS

☐ 24. AL FITZMORRIS
☐ 48. FREDDIE PATEK
☐ 72. TEAM & MCKEON(M)
☐ 95. JOHN MAYBERRY
☐ 120. STEVE BUSBY
☐ 144. JIM WOHLFORD
☐ 169. COOKIE ROJAS
☐ 228. GEORGE BRETT
☐ 251. FRAN HEALY
☐ 268. HAL MCRAE
☐ 295. VADA PINSON
☐ 314. BUCK MARTINEZ
☐ 340. PAUL SPLITTORFF
☐ 364. DOUG BIRD
☐ 389. TONY SOLAITA
☐ 413. MARTY PATTIN
☐ 437. AL COWENS
☐ 472. BRUCE DAL CANTON
☐ 495. NELSON BRILES
☐ 520. AMOS OTIS
☐ 544. STEVE MINGORI
☐ 569. FRANK WHITE
☐ 615. DENNIS LEONARD(R)
☐ 622. TOM POQUETTE(R)
☐ 629. JOE HOERNER
☐ 652. LINDY MCDANIEL

LOS ANGELES DODGERS

☐ 23. BILL RUSSELL
☐ 47. TOMMY JOHN
☐ 71. CHARLIE HOUGH
☐ 93. DAVE LOPES
☐ 115. JOE FERGUSON
☐ 140. STEVE GARVEY
☐ 163. JIM BREWER
☐ 186. WILLIE CRAWFORD
☐ 220. DON SUTTON
☐ 244. BILL BUCKNER
☐ 269. DOUG RAU
☐ 294. GEOFF ZAHN
☐ 330. MIKE MARSHALL
☐ 361. TEAM ALSTON(M)
☐ 376. STEVE YEAGER
☐ 390. RON CEY
☐ 414. MANNY MOTA
☐ 440. ANDY MESSERSMITH
☐ 473. KEN MCMULLEN
☐ 498. AL DOWNING
☐ 523. TOM PACIOREK
☐ 547. VON JOSHUA
☐ 570. JIM WYNN
☐ 588. RICK AUERBACH
☐ 618. RICK RHODEN(R)
☐ 624. EDDIE SOLOMON(R)
☐ 631. LEE LACY

MILWAUKEE BREWERS

☐ 28. TOM MURPHY
☐ 52. DARRELL PORTER
☐ 76. ED SPRAGUE
☐ 99. MIKE HEGAN
☐ 123. JOHNNY BRIGGS
☐ 147. PEDRO GARCIA
☐ 175. DON MONEY

☐ 223. ROBIN YOUNT
☐ 256. BILLY CHAMPION
☐ 281. JIM SLATON
☐ 305. JIM COLBORN
☐ 337. KEVIN KOBEL
☐ 360. GEORGE SCOTT
☐ 384. TEAM & CRANDALL(M)
☐ 408. CLYDE WRIGHT
☐ 432. KEN BERRY
☐ 456. BOB COLUCCIO
☐ 468. BOBBY MITCHELL
☐ 488. BILL TRAVERS
☐ 508. BOB HANSEN
☐ 532. GORMAN THOMAS
☐ 556. TIM JOHNSON
☐ 582. EDUARDO RODRIGUEZ
☐ 623. BOB SHELDON(R)
☐ 636. CHARLIE MOORE
☐ 660. HANK AARON

MINNESOTA TWINS

☐ 30. BERT BLYLEVEN
☐ 54. ERIC SODERHOLM
☐ 78. RAY CORBIN
☐ 102. JOE DECKER
☐ 127. GLENN BORGMANN
☐ 151. STEVE BRYE
☐ 226. BILL CAMPBELL
☐ 249. DANNY THOMPSON
☐ 273. STEVE BRAUN
☐ 297. CRAIG KUSICK
☐ 325. TONY OLIVA
☐ 346. BOBBY DARWIN
☐ 368. VIC ALBURY
☐ 419. DAVE GOLTZ
☐ 443. TEAM & QUILICI(M)
☐ 478. TOM BURGMEIER
☐ 526. LARRY HISLE
☐ 549. BILL BUTLER
☐ 576. PHIL ROOF
☐ 600. ROD CAREW
☐ 618. TOM JOHNSON(R)
☐ 621. JUAN VEINTIDOS(R)
☐ 640. HARMON KILLEBREW
☐ 654. JERRY TERRELL

WILLIE DAVIS Outfield

MONTREAL EXPOS

☐ 10. WILLIE DAVIS
☐ 34. STEVE RENKO
☐ 58. CHUCK TAYLOR
☐ 101. TEAM & MAUCH(M)
☐ 125. KEN SINGLETON
☐ 149. TIM FOLI
☐ 173. STEVE ROGERS
☐ 229. BARRY FOOTE
☐ 254. MIKE TORREZ
☐ 270. RON FAIRLY
☐ 286. MIKE JORGENSON
☐ 318. ERNIE MCANALLY
☐ 341. HAL BREEDEN
☐ 365. BOB BAILEY
☐ 391. DON DEMOLA
☐ 405. JOHN MONTAGUE
☐ 416. LARRY LINTZ
☐ 438. DON CARRITHERS
☐ 471. BOB STINSON
☐ 496. PEPE FRIAS
☐ 521. DENNIS BLAIR

- 543. LARRY BIITTNER
- 568. DALE MURRAY
- 592. BALOR MOORE
- 616. PEPE MANGUAL(R)
- 620. GARY CARTER(R)
- 627. TOM WALKER

NEW YORK METS

- ■ 19. JERRY KOOSMAN
- 43. CLEON JONES
- 67. TUG MCGRAW
- 90. RUSTY STAUB
- ■ 111. WAYNE GARETT
- ■ 134. RON HODGES
- ■ 158. JERRY GROTE
- ■ 182. DON HAHN
- ■ 214. HARRY PARKER
- ■ 239. GEORGE STONE
- ■ 264. JOHN MILNER
- ■ 290. JON MATLACK
- 324. ED KRANEPOOL
- 370. TOM SEAVER
- ■ 395. BUD HARRELSON
- ■ 406. BOB GALLAGHER
- 421. TEAM & BERRA(M)
- ■ 445. FELIX MILLAN
- ■ 565. JOE TORRE
- ■ 575. GENE CLINES
- 615. HANK WEBB(R)
- 619. BENNY AYALA(R)
- ■ 637. TED MARTINEZ
- 659. BOB APODACA

NEW YORK YANKEES

- 20. THURMAN MUNSON
- 44. PAT DOBSON
- 55. BOBBY BONDS
- 68. RON BLOMBERG
- 92. CECIL UPSHAW
- 113. ELLIOTT MADDOX
- 136. JIM MASON
- 160. GRAIG NETTLES
- 183. MEL STOTTLEMYRE
- 217. LOU PINIELLA
- 241. DICK TIDROW
- 266. SANDY ALOMAR
- 291. BILL SUDAKIS
- 321. RUDY MAY
- 375. ROY WHITE
- 401. MIKE WALLACE
- 426. GEORGE MEDICH
- 451. RICK DEMPSEY
- 485. SPARKY LYLE
- 503. FRED STANLEY
- 534. ALEX JOHNSON
- 557. LARRY GURA
- 585. CHRIS CHAMBLISS
- 608. GENE MICHAEL
- 611. TEAM & VIRDON(M)
- 618. SCOTT MCGREGOR(R)
- 622. TERRY WHITFIELD(R)
- 648. DAVE PAGAN

OAKLAND A'S

- 21. ROLLIE FINGERS
- 45. JOE RUDI
- 69. JOHNNY ODOM
- 91. DICK GREEN
- 121. BILL NORTH
- 145. KEN HOLTZMAN
- 170. BERT CAMPANERIS
- 230. JIM HUNTER
- 253. JESUS ALOU
- 278. PAUL LINDBLAD
- 300. REGGIE JACKSON
- 329. TED KUBIAK
- 380. SAL BANDO
- 407. HERB WASHINGTON
- 428. DAVE HAMILTON
- 452. ANGEL MANGUAL
- 486. RAY FOSSE
- 502. PAT BOURQUE
- 510. VIDA BLUE
- 535. GENE TENACE
- 545. BILLY WILLIAMS
- 561. TEAM & DARK(M)
- 591. GLENN ABBOTT

- 607. JIM HOLT
- 613. BILL PARSONS
- 623. PHIL GARNER(R)
- 626. LARRY HANEY
- 647. CLAUDELL WASHINGTON

PHILADELPHIA PHILLIES

- 22. DAVE CASH
- 46. TEAM & OZARK(M)
- 70. MIKE SCHMIDT
- 94. JIM LONBORG
- 118. MIKE ANDERSON
- 138. DEL UNSER
- 162. WILLIE MONTANEZ
- 185. STEVE CARLTON
- 242. JAY JOHNSTONE
- 267. DICK RUTHVEN
- 292. RON SCHUELER
- 326. WAYNE TWITCHELL
- 351. BOB BOONE
- 374. EDDIE WATT
- 399. TERRY HARMON
- 420. LARRY BOWA
- 444. GENE GARBER
- 477. TOM HUTTON
- 501. BILL ROBINSON
- 527. MAC SCARCE
- 551. LARRY CHRISTENSON
- 574. TONY TAYLOR
- 596. OLLIE BROWN
- 615. TOM UNDERWOOD(R)
- 630. GREG LUZINSKI

PITTSBURGH PIRATES

- 29. DAVE PARKER
- 53. DAVE GIUSTI
- 77. RICHIE ZISK
- 100. WILLIE STARGELL
- 124. JERRY REUSS
- 148. JIM ROOKER
- 171. ED KIRKPATRICK
- 224. RAMON HERNANDEZ
- 250. KEN BRETT
- 277. FRANK TAVERAS
- 304. TEAM & MURTAUGH(M)
- 336. RENNIE STENNETT
- 359. PAUL POPOVICH
- 385. DOCK ELLIS
- 409. BOB ROBERTSON
- 433. LARRY DEMEREY
- 457. MARIO MENDOZA
- 492. RICH HEBNER
- 515. MANNY SANGUILLEN
- 536. BOB MOOSE
- 538. DUFFY DYER
- 555. AL OLIVER
- 598. BRUCE KISON
- 616. DAVE AUGUSTINE(R)
- 651. JOHN MORLAN

ST. LOUIS CARDINALS

- 27. KEN REITZ
- 51. BOB FORSCH
- 75. TED SIMMONS
- 98. RICH FOLKERS
- 122. AL HRABOSKY
- 150. BOB GIBSON
- 174. BAKE MCBRIDE
- 231. MIKE TYSON
- 246. TEAM & SCHOENDIENST(M)
- 272. LYNN MCGLOTHEN
- 289. KEN RUDOLPH
- 296. ALAN FOSTER
- 328. SONNY SIEBERT
- 349. RAY SADECKI
- 353. LUIS MELENDEZ
- 381. JOHN CURTIS
- 398. ELIAS SOSA
- 404. TED SIZEMORE
- 429. JIM DWYER
- 453. CLAUDE OSTEEN
- 490. REGGIE SMITH
- 540. LOU BROCK
- 584. MIKE GARMAN
- 610. RON HUNT
- 621. JOHN DENNY(R)
- 623. KEITH HERNANDEZ(R)
- 649. JACK HEIDEMANN

SAN DIEGO PADRES

- 13. GENE LOCKLEAR
- 37. DAVE FREISLEBEN
- 61. DAVE WINFIELD
- 84. ENZO HERNANDEZ
- 112. LARRY HARDY
- 146. TEAM & MCNAMARA(M)
- 168. BILL GREIF
- 222. DAN SPILLNER
- 248. RANDY JONES
- 274. VICENTE ROMO
- 298. JOHNNY GRUBB
- 332. FRED KENDALL
- 343. DANNY FRIESELLA
- 355. CHRIS CANNIZZARO
- 378. DERREL THOMAS
- 402. BOB TOLAN
- 450. WILLIE MCCOVEY
- 484. GLENN BECKERT
- 509. DAVE HILTON
- 558. DAVE W. ROBERTS
- 578. DAVE TOMLIN
- 616. JOHN SCOTT(R)
- 619. JERRY TURNER(R)
- 643. BRENT STROM

SAN FRANCISCO GIANTS

- 31. DAVE RADER
- 79. GARY MATTHEWS
- 107. JIM BARR
- 132. RANDY MOFFITT
- 156. DAVE KINGMAN
- 179. TOM BRADLEY
- 216. TEAM & WESTRUM(M)
- 240. GARRY MADDOX
- 265. RON BRYANT
- 322. ED GOODSON
- 347. MIKE CALDWELL
- 350. BOBBY MURCER
- 372. JOHN D'ACQUISTO
- 425. TITO FUENTES
- 449. CHARLIE WILLIAMS
- 467. ED HALICKI
- 483. STEVE ONTIVEROS
- 505. CHRIS SPEIER
- 529. GARY THOMASSON
- 553. JOHN BOCCABELLA
- 577. JOHN MORRIS
- 606. BRUCE MILLER
- 620. MARC HILL(R)
- 624. GARY LAVELLE(R)
- 642. MIKE PHILLIPS

TEXAS RANGERS

- 12. DAVID CLYDE
- 36. JOE LOVITTO
- 60. FERGIE JENKINS
- 83. JIM MERRITT
- 106. MIKE HARGROVE
- 131. TOBY HARRAH
- 155. JIM BIBBY
- 178. CESAR TOVAR
- 234. TOM GRIEVE
- 259. LEN RANDLE
- 283. STEVE FOUCAULT
- 316. JACKIE BROWN
- 339. JIM FREGOSI
- 362. STEVE HARGAN
- 387. JIM SPENCER
- 412. BILL HANDS
- 435. DAVE NELSON
- 470. JEFF BURROUGHS
- 493. DON STANHOUSE
- 511. TEAM & MARTIN(M)
- 518. LEO CARDENAS
- 542. PETE BROBERG
- 567. JIM SUNDBERG
- 617. MIKE CUBBAGE(R)
- 644. BILL FAHEY

1976 TOPPS (660)
2 1/2" X 3 1/2"

GEORGE SCOTT
FIRST BASE BREWERS

ATLANTA BRAVES

- ☐ 28. DUSTY BAKER
- ☐ 53. MIKE BEARD
- ☐ 81. DARRELL EVANS
- ☐ 103. BIFF POCOROBA
- ☐ 127. LARVELL BLANKS
- ☐ 153. BUZZ CAPRA
- ☐ 177. MARTY PEREZ
- ☐ 208. MIKE LUM
- ☐ 231. TOM HOUSE
- ☐ 256. ROWLAND OFFICE
- ☐ 281. DAVE MAY
- ☐ 306. ROD GILBREATH
- ☐ 328. CARL MORTON
- ☐ 364. ELIAS SOSA
- ☐ 395. JIM WYNN
- ☐ 410. RALPH GARR
- ☐ 435. PHIL NIEKRO
- ☐ 458. EARL WILLIAMS
- ☐ 486. BRUCE DAL CANTON
- ☐ 511. JAMIE EASTERLY
- ☐ 536. MIKE THOMPSON
- ☐ 558. CLARENCE GASTON
- ☐ 576. MAXIMINO LEON
- ☐ 589. PABLO TORREALBA(R)
- ☐ 592. JERRY ROYSTER(R)
- ☐ 597. FRANK LACORTE(R)
- ☐ 608. VIC CORRELL
- ☐ 631. TEAM & BRISTOL(M)
- ☐ 641. TOM PACIOREK
- ☐ 651. JOHN ODOM

BALTIMORE ORIOLES

- ☐ 25. MIKE TORREZ
- ☐ 49. DAVE DUNCAN
- ☐ 73. TEAM & WEAVER(M)
- ☐ 95. BROOKS ROBINSON
- ☐ 125. DON BAYLOR
- ☐ 149. TOMMY DAVIS
- ☐ 175. KEN SINGLETON
- ☐ 210. LEE MAY
- ☐ 233. GRANT JACKSON
- ☐ 252. TIM NORDBROOK
- ☐ 257. ROSS GRIMSLEY
- ☐ 285. MIKE CUELLAR
- ☐ 307. AL BUMBRY
- ☐ 335. BOB GRICH
- ☐ 371. ELLIE HENDRICKS
- ☐ 393. PAUL MITCHELL
- ☐ 414. WAYNE GARLAND
- ☐ 438. DOUG DECINCES
- ☐ 450. JIM PALMER
- ☐ 473. PAUL BLAIR
- ☐ 505. MARK BELANGER
- ☐ 537. TONY MUSER
- ☐ 555. DYAR MILLER
- ☐ 589. MIKE FLANAGAN(R)
- ☐ 594. ROYLE STILLMAN(R)
- ☐ 638. DOYLE ALEXANDER

BOSTON RED SOX

- ☐ 29. RICK BURLESON
- ☐ 50. FRED LYNN
- ☐ 78. CECIL COOPER
- ☐ 102. JIM WILLOUGHBY
- ☐ 118. TEAM & JOHNSON(M)
- ☐ 130. LUIS TIANT
- ☐ 142. DICK DRAGO
- ☐ 170. RICK WISE
- ☐ 230. CARL YASTRZEMSKI
- ☐ 278. BERNIE CARBO
- ☐ 302. RICK MILLER
- ☐ 326. DICK POLE
- ☐ 340. JIM RICE
- ☐ 365. CARLTON FISK
- ☐ 381. DENNY DOYLE
- ☐ 396. BILL LEE
- ☐ 419. REGGIE CLEVELAND
- ☐ 445. RICO PETROCELLI
- ☐ 471. JIM BURTON
- ☐ 523. BOB MONTGOMERY
- ☐ 529. DERON JOHNSON
- ☐ 575. DWIGHT EVANS
- ☐ 594. ANDY MERCHANT(R)
- ☐ 597. DON AASE(R)
- ☐ 632. ROGELIO MORET
- ☐ 654. DOUG GRIFFIN

CALIFORNIA ANGELS

- ☐ 27. ED FIGUEROA
- ☐ 52. DAVE CHALK
- ☐ 85. MICKEY RIVERS
- ☐ 108. DON KIRKWOOD
- ☐ 129. ANDY ETCHEBARREN
- ☐ 152. LEROY STANTON
- ☐ 176. DICK LANGE
- ☐ 207. ANDY HASSLER
- ☐ 229. JERRY REMY
- ☐ 254. RUDY MEOLI(F)
- ☐ 276. MICKEY SCOTT
- ☐ 304. TEAM & WILLIAMS(M)
- ☐ 330. NOLAN RYAN
- ☐ 363. DAVE COLLINS
- ☐ 387. MIKE MILEY
- ☐ 411. BILL SINGER
- ☐ 434. MORRIS NETTLES
- ☐ 459. JIM BREWER
- ☐ 490. FRANK TANANA
- ☐ 512. ELLIE RODRIGUEZ
- ☐ 539. JOHN BALEZ
- ☐ 562. ADRIAN GARRETT
- ☐ 589. JOE PACTWA(R)
- ☐ 595. SID MONGE(R)
- ☐ 612. JOE LAHOUD
- ☐ 623. BOB ALLIETTA
- ☐ 637. BRUCE BOCHTE

CHICAGO CUBS

- ☐ 26. ANDY THORNTON
- ☐ 34. MIKE GARMAN
- ☐ 51. RAY BURRIS
- ☐ 79. JERRY MORALES
- ☐ 101. PETE LACOCK
- ☐ 126. TOM DETTORE
- ☐ 151. BILL BONHAM
- ☐ 173. STEVE SWISHER
- ☐ 206. MANNY TRILLO
- ☐ 227. OSCAR ZAMORA
- ☐ 251. RICK MONDAY
- ☐ 277. TEAM & MARSHALL(M)
- ☐ 299. CHAMP SUMMERS
- ☐ 323. BOB SPERRING
- ☐ 359. RICK REUSCHEL
- ☐ 378. STEVE STONE
- ☐ 403. GEOFF ZAHN
- ☐ 430. JOSE CARDENAL
- ☐ 482. TIM HOSLEY
- ☐ 506. GEORGE MITTERWALD
- ☐ 546. DAVE ROSELLO
- ☐ 593. KEN CROSBY(R)
- ☐ 598. JOE WALLIS(R)
- ☐ 617. DAROLD KNOWLES
- ☐ 640. BILL MADLOCK

CHICAGO WHITE SOX

- ☐ 23. BRIAN DOWNING
- ☐ 47. JESSE JEFFERSON
- ☐ 80. JIM KAAT
- ☐ 110. CARLOS MAY
- ☐ 131. BILL STEIN
- ☐ 154. BUCKY DENT
- ☐ 180. RICH GOSSAGE
- ☐ 212. H. PAT KELLY
- ☐ 237. DAVE HAMILTON
- ☐ 258. NYLS NYMAN
- ☐ 282. DAN OSBORN
- ☐ 309. BILL MELTON
- ☐ 333. BOB COLUCCIO
- ☐ 368. WILBUR WOOD
- ☐ 391. JERRY HAIRSTON
- ☐ 413. PETE VARNEY
- ☐ 437. TERRY FORSTER
- ☐ 464. KEN HENDERSON
- ☐ 488. CLAUDE OSTEEN
- ☐ 513. BART JOHNSON
- ☐ 533. LEE RICHARD
- ☐ 560. JORGE ORTA
- ☐ 590. CHET LEMON(R)
- ☐ 596. LAMAR JOHNSON(R)
- ☐ 597. JACK KUCEK(R)
- ☐ 607. RICH HINTON
- ☐ 656. TEAM & TANNER(M)

CINCINNATI REDS

- ☐ 24. CESAR GERONIMO
- ☐ 48. DAVE CONCEPCION
- ☐ 77. PEDRO BORBON
- ☐ 104. TEAM & ANDERSON(M)
- ☐ 128. KEN GRIFFEY
- ☐ 155. JACK BILLINGHAM
- ☐ 179. GEORGE FOSTER
- ☐ 211. CLAY CARROLL
- ☐ 240. PETE ROSE
- ☐ 259. DARRELL CHANEY
- ☐ 283. MERV RETTENMUND
- ☐ 300. JOHNNY BENCH
- ☐ 325. TONY PEREZ
- ☐ 362. WILL MCENANEY
- ☐ 390. DON GULLETT
- ☐ 420. JOE MORGAN
- ☐ 444. GARY NOLAN
- ☐ 469. RAWLY EASTWICK
- ☐ 491. TERRY CROWLEY
- ☐ 514. DAN DRIESSEN
- ☐ 518. DOUG FLYNN
- ☐ 538. PAT DARCY
- ☐ 561. TOM CARROLL
- ☐ 579. CLAY KIRBY
- ☐ 589. SANTO ALCALA(R)
- ☐ 599. PAT ZACHRY(R)
- ☐ 609. FRED NORMAN
- ☐ 627. BILL PLUMMER
- ☐ 652. ED ARMBRISTER

CLEVELAND INDIANS

- ☐ 21. DAVE LAROCHE
- ☐ 45. BOOG POWELL
- ☐ 74. OSCAR GAMBLE
- ☐ 98. DENNIS ECKERSLEY
- ☐ 132. DON HOOD
- ☐ 156. RICO CARTY
- ☐ 178. TOM BUSKEY
- ☐ 209. ALAN ASHBY
- ☐ 232. FRANK DUFFY
- ☐ 255. FRITZ PETERSON
- ☐ 275. RICK MANNING
- ☐ 301. JACKIE BROWN
- ☐ 324. JIM BIBBY
- ☐ 358. BUDDY BELL
- ☐ 383. JOHN ELLIS
- ☐ 408. CHARLIE SPIKES
- ☐ 433. RICK WAITS
- ☐ 457. ED CROSBY
- ☐ 477. TEAM & ROBINSON(M)
- ☐ 484. ERIC RAICH
- ☐ 508. DUANE KUIPER
- ☐ 547. RORIC HARRISON
- ☐ 570. GEORGE HENDRICK
- ☐ 618. JACK BROHAMER
- ☐ 646. JOHN LOWENSTEIN

1976 Topps

DETROIT TIGERS

- ☐ 13. JOHNNY WOCKENFUSS
- ☐ 37. JOHN HILLER
- ☐ 61. RON LEFLORE
- ☐ 89. VERN RUHLE
- ☐ 113. GARY SUTHERLAND
- ☐ 138. LERRIN LAGROW
- ☐ 162. JACK PIERCE
- ☐ 186. TOM WALKER
- ☐ 218. JOHN KNOX
- ☐ 242. DAN MEYER
- ☐ 267. AURELIO RODRIGUEZ
- ☐ 292. LEON ROBERTS
- ☐ 320. WILLIE HORTON
- ☐ 361. TEAM & HOUK(M)
- ☐ 385. MICKEY LOLICH
- ☐ 409. DAVE LEMANCZYK
- ☐ 432. TOM VERYZER
- ☐ 456. JOE COLEMAN
- ☐ 483. MICKEY STANLEY
- ☐ 507. RAY BARE
- ☐ 540. BILL FREEHAN
- ☐ 552. TERRY HUMPHREY
- ☐ 591. STEVE GRILLI(R)
- ☐ 596. JERRY MANUEL(R)
- ☐ 614. FERNANDO ARROYO
- ☐ 659. BEN OGLIVIE

HOUSTON ASTROS

- ☐ 20. BOB WATSON
- ☐ 44. DOUG RADER
- ☐ 75. LARRY DIERKER
- ☐ 97. WILBUR HOWARD
- ☐ 122. MIKE COSGROVE
- ☐ 147. TEAM & VIRDON(M)
- ☐ 171. GREG GROSS
- ☐ 224. JIM YORK
- ☐ 249. CLIFF JOHNSON
- ☐ 273. JOE NIEKRO
- ☐ 297. ROGER METZGER
- ☐ 321. JOSE CRUZ
- ☐ 357. KEN FORSCH
- ☐ 379. KEN BOSWELL
- ☐ 404. ENOS CABELL
- ☐ 428. JIM CRAWFORD
- ☐ 454. TOM GRIFFIN
- ☐ 460. CESAR CEDENO
- ☐ 489. SKIP JUTZE
- ☐ 516. WAYNE GRANGER
- ☐ 532. MILT MAY
- ☐ 551. JERRY DAVANON
- ☐ 568. ROB ANDREWS
- ☐ 583. TOMMY HELMS
- ☐ 591. JOSE SOSA(R)
- ☐ 602. DOUG KONIECZNY
- ☐ 625. J.R. RICHARD
- ☐ 649. DAVE A. ROBERTS

KANSAS CITY ROYALS

- ☐ 19. GEORGE BRETT
- ☐ 43. PAUL SPLITTORFF
- ☐ 72. HAL MCRAE
- ☐ 96. DOUG BIRD
- ☐ 121. TONY SOLAITA
- ☐ 144. AL FITZMORRIS
- ☐ 167. FREDDIE PATEK
- ☐ 236. TEAM & HERZOG(M)
- ☐ 260. STEVE BUSBY
- ☐ 286. JIM WOHLFORD
- ☐ 311. COOKIE ROJAS
- ☐ 334. DENNIS LEONARD
- ☐ 369. FRANK WHITE
- ☐ 394. FRAN HEALY
- ☐ 415. VADA PINSON
- ☐ 440. JOHN MAYBERRY
- ☐ 466. BOB STINSON
- ☐ 492. MARTY PATTIN
- ☐ 510. AMOS OTIS
- ☐ 535. DAVE NELSON
- ☐ 541. STEVE MINGORI
- ☐ 591. GEORGE THROOP(R)
- ☐ 593. MARK LITTELL(R)
- ☐ 598. JAMIE QUIRK(R)
- ☐ 599. BOB MCCLURE(R)
- ☐ 616. BUCK MARTINEZ
- ☐ 648. AL COWENS

LOS ANGELES DODGERS

- ☐ 22. BILL RUSSELL
- ☐ 46. TEAM & ALSTON(M)
- ☐ 76. WILLIE CRAWFORD
- ☐ 99. LEE LACY
- ☐ 124. DOUG RAU
- ☐ 150. STEVE GARVEY
- ☐ 174. CHARLIE HOUGH
- ☐ 228. JOHN HALE
- ☐ 253. BILL BUCKNER
- ☐ 280. BURT HOOTON
- ☐ 305. ANDY MESSERSMITH
- ☐ 329. JOE FERGUSON
- ☐ 370. RON CEY
- ☐ 386. ED GOODSON
- ☐ 416. TOMMY JOHN
- ☐ 439. RICK RHODEN
- ☐ 465. MIKE MARSHALL
- ☐ 487. LERON LEE
- ☐ 515. STEVE YEAGER
- ☐ 530. DON SUTTON
- ☐ 548. MANNY MOTA
- ☐ 566. KEN MCMULLEN
- ☐ 584. STAN WALL
- ☐ 590. HENRY CRUZ(R)
- ☐ 605. AL DOWNING
- ☐ 622. RICK AUERBACH
- ☐ 660. DAVE LOPES

MILWAUKEE BREWERS

- ☐ 15. GEORGE SCOTT
- ☐ 39. PETE BROBERG
- ☐ 63. BOBBY DARWIN
- ☐ 92. EDUARDO RODRIGUEZ
- ☐ 116. CHARLIE MOORE
- ☐ 139. GORMAN THOMAS
- ☐ 163. JIM SLATON
- ☐ 187. PEDRO GARCIA
- ☐ 219. TOM MURPHY
- ☐ 244. BILL SHARP
- ☐ 269. RICK AUSTIN
- ☐ 293. BILL CASTRO
- ☐ 316. ROBIN YOUNT
- ☐ 353. SIXTO LEZCANO
- ☐ 377. MIKE HEGAN
- ☐ 402. DON MONEY
- ☐ 427. KURT BEVACQUA
- ☐ 452. TOM HAUSMAN
- ☐ 479. ROBBY MITCHELL
- ☐ 501. BILLY CHAMPION
- ☐ 521. JIM COLBORN
- ☐ 550. HANK AARON
- ☐ 573. BILL TRAVERS
- ☐ 588. KEVIN KOBEL
- ☐ 593. LARRY ANDERSON(R)
- ☐ 606. TEAM & GRAMMAS(M)
- ☐ 613. TIM JOHNSON
- ☐ 626. BOB SHELDON
- ☐ 645. DARRELL PORTER

MINNESOTA TWINS

- ☐ 11. JIM HUGHES
- ☐ 35. TONY OLIVA
- ☐ 59. LARRY HISLE
- ☐ 87. TOM BURGMEIER
- ☐ 111. DANNY THOMPSON
- ☐ 136. DAVE GOLTZ
- ☐ 159. JERRY TERRELL
- ☐ 183. STEVE BRAUN
- ☐ 214. ERIC SODERHOLM
- ☐ 235. BERT BLYLEVEN
- ☐ 263. LYMAN BOSTOCK
- ☐ 288. BILL CAMPBELL
- ☐ 313. DAN FORD
- ☐ 336. VIC ALBURY
- ☐ 373. JOHNNY BRIGGS
- ☐ 400. ROD CAREW
- ☐ 424. PHIL ROOF
- ☐ 448. TOM JOHNSON
- ☐ 474. RAY CORBIN
- ☐ 498. GLENN BORGMANN
- ☐ 519. STEVE BRYE
- ☐ 556. TEAM & MAUCH(M)
- ☐ 592. DAVE MCKAY(R)
- ☐ 597. MIKE PAZIK(R)
- ☐ 619. BILL BUTLER
- ☐ 636. JOE DECKER

MONTREAL EXPOS

- ☐ 18. DALE MURRAY
- ☐ 42. BARRY FOOTE
- ☐ 71. STEVE ROGERS
- ☐ 94. JIM DWYER
- ☐ 117. MIKE JORGENSEN
- ☐ 141. LARRY PARRISH
- ☐ 164. PEPE MANGUAL
- ☐ 188. FRED SCHERMAN
- ☐ 216. TEAM & KUEHL(M)
- ☐ 238. LARRY BIITTNER
- ☐ 264. STEVE RENKO
- ☐ 287. PETE MACKANIN
- ☐ 312. DON CARRITHERS
- ☐ 338. BOB BAILEY
- ☐ 374. DAN WARTHEN
- ☐ 397. TIM FOLI
- ☐ 418. JOSE MORALES
- ☐ 441. GARY CARTER
- ☐ 467. WOODIE FRYMAN
- ☐ 495. NATE COLBERT
- ☐ 544. PEPE FRIAS
- ☐ 571. DON DEMOLA
- ☐ 590. ELLIS VALENTINE(R)
- ☐ 594. JERRY WHITE(R)
- ☐ 642. DENNIS BLAIR

NEW YORK METS

- ■ 16. BOB APODACA
- ☐ 40. DAVE KINGMAN
- ■ 64. JERRY KOOSMAN
- ■ 93. MIKE PHILLIPS
- ■ 120. RUSTY STAUB
- ■ 143. JERRY GROTE
- ■ 166. SKIP LOCKWOOD
- ■ 190. JON MATLACK
- ■ 222. WAYNE GARRETT
- ■ 245. FELIX MILLAN
- ■ 268. DEL UNSER
- ■ 291. KEN SANDERS
- ■ 314. ED KRANEPOOL
- ■ 337. BUD HARRELSON
- ■ 372. RICK BALDWIN
- ■ 417. GENE CLINES
- ■ 442. HANK WEBB
- ■ 468. JESUS ALOU
- ■ 494. CRAIG SWAN
- ■ 517. JOHN MILNER
- ■ 531. TEAM & FRAZIER(M)
- ■ 549. RANDY TATE
- ■ 567. GEORGE STONE
- ■ 585. JOE TORRE
- ☐ 592. ROY STAIGER(R)
- ■ 600. TOM SEAVER
- ■ 621. TOM HALL
- ■ 633. JOHN STEARNS
- ■ 655. MIKE VAIL

NEW YORK YANKEES

- ☐ 17. TEAM & MARTIN(M)
- ☐ 41. TIPPY MARTINEZ
- ☐ 65. CHRIS CHAMBLISS
- ☐ 100. JIM HUNTER
- ☐ 123. WALT WILLIAMS
- ☐ 146. GEORGE MEDICH
- ☐ 169. GRAIG NETTLES
- ☐ 225. ROY WHITE
- ☐ 248. DICK TIDROW
- ☐ 272. RICK DEMPSEY
- ☐ 296. PAT DOBSON
- ☐ 319. LARRY GURA
- ☐ 354. RON BLOMBERG
- ☐ 380. BOBBY BONDS
- ☐ 406. ED HERRMANN
- ☐ 429. FRED STANLEY
- ☐ 453. LOU PINIELLA
- ☐ 481. RUDY MAY
- ☐ 503. ELLIOTT MADDOX
- ☐ 545. SPARKY LYLE
- ☐ 572. RICH COGGINS
- ☐ 590. TERRY WHITFIELD(R)
- ☐ 599. RON GUIDRY(R)
- ☐ 629. SANDY ALOMAR
- ☐ 650. THURMAN MUNSON

MIKE NORRIS
PITCHER A'S

OAKLAND A'S

- ☐ 9. PAUL LINDBLAD
- ☐ 33. BILL NORTH
- ☐ 57. PHIL GARNER
- ☐ 90. SAL BANDO
- ☐ 109. LARRY LINTZ
- ☐ 115. KEN HOLTZMAN
- ☐ 140. VIDA BLUE
- ☐ 165. GENE TENACE
- ☐ 189. CLAUDELL WASHINGTON
- ☐ 221. JIM TODD
- ☐ 246. CESAR TOVAR
- ☐ 274. TOMMY HARPER
- ☐ 298. DICK BOSMAN
- ☐ 322. GLENN ABBOTT
- ☐ 356. TED MARTINEZ
- ☐ 382. MATT ALEXANDER
- ☐ 405. ROLLIE FINGERS
- ☐ 421. TEAM CARD
- ☐ 446. LARRY HANEY
- ☐ 475. JOE RUDI
- ☐ 500. REGGIE JACKSON
- ☐ 525. BILLY WILLIAMS
- ☐ 534. STAN BAHNSEN
- ☐ 554. RAY FOSSE
- ☐ 580. BERT CAMPANERIS
- ☐ 591. CRAIG MITCHELL(R)
- ☐ 603. JIM HOLT
- ☐ 653. MIKE NORRIS

PHIALDELPHIA PHILLIES

- ☐ 14. GENE GARBER
- ☐ 38. GARRY MADDOX
- ☐ 62. JOHNNY OATES
- ☐ 91. TOM HUTTON
- ☐ 114. JAY JOHNSTONE
- ☐ 145. LARRY BOWA
- ☐ 168. TOM HILGENDORF
- ☐ 223. OLLIE BROWN
- ☐ 247. TERRY HARMON
- ☐ 271. JIM LONBORG
- ☐ 295. DAVE CASH
- ☐ 318. BOB BOONE
- ☐ 355. STEVE CARLTON
- ☐ 384. TEAM & OZARK(M)
- ☐ 407. TOM UNDERWOOD
- ☐ 431. DICK RUTHVEN
- ☐ 455. DICK ALLEN
- ☐ 480. MIKE SCHMIDT
- ☐ 502. TIM MCCARVER
- ☐ 527. MIKE ANDERSON
- ☐ 543. WAYNE TWITCHELL
- ☐ 565. TUG MCGRAW
- ☐ 586. RON SCHUELER
- ☐ 595. RANDY LERCH(R)
- ☐ 610. GREG LUZINSKI
- ☐ 624. TONY TAYLOR
- ☐ 634. LARRY CHRISTENSON

PITTSBURGH PIRATES

- ☐ 12. RICHIE ZISK
- ☐ 36. FRANK TAVERAS
- ☐ 60. JERRY REUSS
- ☐ 88. DUFFY DYER
- ☐ 112. KENT TEKULVE

- ☐ 137. BILL ROBINSON
- ☐ 161. BRUCE KISON
- ☐ 185. DAVE PARKER
- ☐ 220. MANNY SANGUILLEN
- ☐ 243. JIM ROOKER
- ☐ 270. WILLIE STARGELL
- ☐ 294. ED KIRKPATRICK
- ☐ 317. JOHN CANDELARIA
- ☐ 352. DAVE GIUSTI
- ☐ 376. RICH HEBNER
- ☐ 401. KEN BRETT
- ☐ 425. RENNIE STENNETT
- ☐ 449. BOB ROBERTSON
- ☐ 476. BOB MOOSE
- ☐ 504. TEAM & MURTAUGH(M)
- ☐ 528. DOCK ELLIS
- ☐ 563. LARRY DEMERY
- ☐ 592. WILLIE RANDOLPH(R)
- ☐ 594. ED OTT(R)
- ☐ 596. CRAIG REYNOLDS(R)
- ☐ 620. AL OLIVER
- ☐ 647. RAMON HERNANDEZ

ST. LOUIS CARDINALS

- ☐ 10. LOU BROCK
- ☐ 58. RON REED
- ☐ 86. MIKE TYSON
- ☐ 135. BAKE MCBRIDE
- ☐ 158. KEN REITZ
- ☐ 182. ERIC RASMUSSEN
- ☐ 215. REGGIE SMITH
- ☐ 239. JOHN CURTIS
- ☐ 290. TED SIMMONS
- ☐ 315. AL HRABOSKY
- ☐ 339. JOHN DENNY
- ☐ 375. RON FAIRLY
- ☐ 399. LUIS MELENDEZ
- ☐ 426. BOB FORSCH
- ☐ 451. BUDDY BRADFORD
- ☐ 478. LYNN MCGLOTHEN
- ☐ 499. MARIO GUERRERO
- ☐ 522. TED SIZEMORE
- ☐ 542. KEITH HERNANDEZ
- ☐ 574. DON KESSINGER
- ☐ 581. TEAM & SCHOENDIENST(M)
- ☐ 598. HECTOR CRUZ(R)
- ☐ 601. KEN RUDOLPH

BOBBY VALENTINE
OUTFIELD PADRES

SAN DIEGO PADRES

- ☐ 8. TITO FUENTES
- ☐ 32. DANNY FRISELLA
- ☐ 56. BOB TOLAN
- ☐ 84. BRENT STROM
- ☐ 107. DAVE W. ROBERTS
- ☐ 134. MIKE IVIE
- ☐ 160. DAVE WINFIELD
- ☐ 184. BILL GREIF
- ☐ 217. DAVE FREISLEBEN
- ☐ 241. HECTOR TORRES
- ☐ 254. RUDY MEOLI(B)
- ☐ 265. WILLIE DAVIS
- ☐ 266. ALAN FOSTER
- ☐ 289. ENZO HERNANDEZ
- ☐ 310. RANDY JONES
- ☐ 331. TEAM & MCNAMARA(M)
- ☐ 351. RANDY HUNDLEY
- ☐ 366. BOBBY VALENTINE

- ☐ 398. DAVE TOMLIN
- ☐ 422. JOHNNY GRUBB
- ☐ 447. GENE LOCKLEAR
- ☐ 472. BOB DAVIS
- ☐ 497. JOE MCINTOSH
- ☐ 520. WILLIE MCCOVEY
- ☐ 557. DAN SPILLNER
- ☐ 578. TED KUBIAK
- ☐ 593. BUTCH METZGER(R)
- ☐ 598. JERRY TURNER(R)
- ☐ 611. RICH FOLKERS
- ☐ 639. FRED KENDALL
- ☐ 658. JERRY JOHNSON

SAN FRANCISCO GIANTS

- ☐ 30. JOHN MONTEFUSCO
- ☐ 54. DAVE RADER
- ☐ 82. VON JOSHUA
- ☐ 105. GARY LAVELLE
- ☐ 133. GARY MATTHEWS
- ☐ 157. MIKE CALDWELL
- ☐ 181. WILLIE MONTANEZ
- ☐ 213. DAVE HEAVERLO
- ☐ 234. MIKE SADEK
- ☐ 261. GARY THOMASSON
- ☐ 283. STEVE ONTIVEROS
- ☐ 308. JIM BARR
- ☐ 332. CHARLIE WILLIAMS
- ☐ 367. BRUCE MILLER
- ☐ 389. GLENN ADAMS
- ☐ 423. ED HALICKI
- ☐ 443. TEAM CARD
- ☐ 470. BOBBY MURCER
- ☐ 493. DERREL THOMAS
- ☐ 524. PETE FALCONE
- ☐ 553. RANDY MOFFITT
- ☐ 577. MARC HILL
- ☐ 596. JOHNNIE LEMASTER(R)
- ☐ 599. ROB DRESSLER(R)
- ☐ 628. JOHN D'ACQUISTO
- ☐ 630. CHRIS SPEIER
- ☐ 644. TOM BRADLEY

TEXAS RANGERS

- ☐ 7. JIM UMBARGER
- ☐ 31. LEN RANDLE
- ☐ 55. GAYLORD PERRY
- ☐ 83. JIM SPENCER
- ☐ 106. TOM GRIEVE
- ☐ 148. STAN THOMAS
- ☐ 172. TEAM & LUCCHESI(M)
- ☐ 226. JIM SUNDBERG
- ☐ 250. FERGIE JENKINS
- ☐ 279. ROY HOWELL
- ☐ 303. STEVE FOUCAULT
- ☐ 327. DAVE MOATES
- ☐ 360. JEFF BURROUGHS
- ☐ 388. STAN PERZANOWSKI
- ☐ 412. TOBY HARRAH
- ☐ 436. BILL FAHEY
- ☐ 463. STEVE HARGAN
- ☐ 485. MIKE HARGROVE
- ☐ 496. JUAN BENIQUEZ
- ☐ 509. BILL HANDS
- ☐ 559. CLYDE WRIGHT
- ☐ 569. NELSON BRILES
- ☐ 582. MIKE KEKICH
- ☐ 587. LEO CARDENAS
- ☐ 595. ART DEFILIPPIS(R)
- ☐ 595. STEVE BARR(R)
- ☐ 604. JOE LOVITTO
- ☐ 615. MIKE CUBBAGE
- ☐ 635. JIM FREGOSI
- ☐ 657. ROY SMALLEY

1976 TOPPS
TRADED (44)
2 1/2" X 3 1/2"

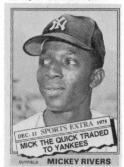

ATLANTA BRAVES

- [ ] 99T. LEE LACY
- [ ] 259T. DARREL CHANEY
- [ ] 464T. KEN HENDERSON
- [ ] 632T. ROGELIO MORET

BALTIMORE ORIOLES

NO CARDS ISSUED

BOSTON RED SOX

- [ ] 231T. TOM HOUSE
- [ ] 250T. FERGIE JENKINS

CALIFORNIA ANGELS

- [ ] 309T. BILL MELTON
- [ ] 380T. BOBBY BONDS

CHICAGO CUBS

NO CARDS ISSUED

CHICAGO WHITE SOX

- [ ] 83T. JIM SPENCER
- [ ] 211T. CLAY CARROLL
- [ ] 410T. RALPH GARR
- [ ] 434T. MORRIS NETTLES
- [ ] 618T. JACK BROHAMER

CINCINNATI REDS

- [ ] 208T. MIKE LUM
- [ ] 338T. BOB BAILEY

CLEVELAND INDIANS

- [ ] 127T. LARVELL BLANKS
- [ ] 296T. PAT DOBSON
- [ ] 554T. RAY FOSSE

DETROIT TIGERS

- [ ] 120T. RUSTY STAUB
- [ ] 428T. JIM CRAWFORD
- [ ] 532T. MILT MAY
- [ ] 649T. DAVE A. ROBERTS

HOUSTON ASTROS

- [ ] 292T. LEON ROBERTS
- [ ] 497T. JOE MCINTOSH

KANSAS CITY ROYALS

NO CARDS ISSUED

LOS ANGELES DODGERS

- [ ] 28T. DUSTY BAKER

MILWAUKEE BREWERS

NO CARDS ISSUED

MINNESOTA TWINS

NO CARDS ISSUED

MONTREAL TWINS

NO CARDS ISSUED

MONTREAL EXPOS

- [ ] 579T. CLAY KIRBY

NEW YORK METS

- [ ] 358T. MICKEY LOLICH

NEW YORK YANKEES

- [ ] 27T. ED FIGUEROA
- [ ] 74T. OSCAR GAMBLE
- [ ] 85T. MICKEY RIVERS
- [ ] 401T. KEN BRETT
- [ ] 528T. DOCK ELLIS
- [ ] 592T. WILLIE RANDOLPH

OAKLAND A'S

NO CARDS ISSUED

PHILADELPHIA PHILLIES

- [ ] 58T. RON REED
- [ ] 80T. JIM KAAT

PITTSBURGH PIRATES

- [ ] 146T. GEORGE MEDICH
- [ ] 583T. TOMMY HELMS

ST. LOUIS CARDINALS

- [ ] 524T. PETE FALCONE
- [ ] 527T. MIKE ANDERSON

SAN DIEGO PADRES

- [ ] 44T. DOUG RADER

SAN FRANCISCO GIANTS

- [ ] 158T. KEN REITZ

TEXAS RANGERS

- [ ] 383T. JOHN ELLIS
- [ ] 411T. BILL SINGER

1977 TOPPS (660)
2 1/2" X 3 1/2"

ATLANTA BRAVES

- [ ] 24. CARL MORTON
- [ ] 48. TOM PACIOREK
- [ ] 80. ANDY MESSERSMITH
- [ ] 114. BRUCE DAL CANTON
- [ ] 126. ROD GILBREATH
- [ ] 165. JIM WYNN
- [ ] 192. CLARENCE GASTON
- [ ] 194. GARY MATTHEWS
- [ ] 213. MAXIMINO LEON
- [ ] 242. KEN HENDERSON
- [ ] 263. MIKE MARSHALL
- [ ] 292. ROGELIO MORET
- [ ] 312. ROB BELLOIR
- [ ] 339. ADRIAN DEVINE
- [ ] 364. VIC CORRELL
- [ ] 384. DARREL CHANEY
- [ ] 410. WILLIE MONTANEZ
- [ ] 432. BUZZ CAPRA
- [ ] 442. TEAM & BRISTOL(M)
- [ ] 475. RICK CAMP(R)
- [ ] 476. DALE MURPHY(R)
- [ ] 479. BRIAN ASSELSTINE(R)
- [ ] 499. PABLO TORREALBA
- [ ] 524. ROWLAND OFFICE
- [ ] 549. JERRY ROYSTER
- [ ] 575. DICK RUTHVEN
- [ ] 594. BIFF POCOROBA
- [ ] 615. PHIL NIEKRO

BALTIMORE ORIOLES

- [ ] 56. RUDY MAY
- [ ] 77. DYAR MILLER
- [ ] 106. MIKE FLANAGAN
- [ ] 135. MARK BELANGER
- [ ] 162. MIKE CUELLAR
- [ ] 189. RICK DEMPSEY
- [ ] 216. DOUG DECINCES
- [ ] 238. TIPPY MARTINEZ
- [ ] 251. TONY MUSER
- [ ] 285. BROOKS ROBINSON
- [ ] 313. PAUL BLAIR
- [ ] 380. LEE MAY
- [ ] 414. TOMMY HARPER
- [ ] 445. KEN SINGLETON
- [ ] 466. FRED HOLDSWORTH
- [ ] 469. H. PAT KELLY
- [ ] 474. KIKO GARCIA(R)
- [ ] 475. SCOTT MCGREGOR(R)
- [ ] 477. RICH DAUER(R)
- [ ] 491. DENNY MARTINEZ(R)

☐ 546. TEAM & WEAVER(M)
☐ 572. ROSS GRIMSLEY
☐ 600. JIM PALMER
☐ 626. AL BUMBRY
☐ 646. ANDRES MORA

BOSTON RED SOX

☐ 25. DWIGHT EVANS
☐ 60. JIM RICE
☐ 89. BUTCH HOBSON
☐ 111. RICO PETROCELLI
☐ 142. STEVE DILLARD
☐ 166. BILL CAMPBELL
☐ 191. DOUG GRIFFIN
☐ 210. FRED LYNN
☐ 235. CECIL COOPER
☐ 258. LUIS TIANT
☐ 288. BOB MONTGOMERY
☐ 309. TEAM & ZIMMER(M)
☐ 336. DENNY DOYLE
☐ 358. TOM HOUSE
☐ 396. TOM MURPHY
☐ 430. FERGIE JENKINS
☐ 455. RICK WISE
☐ 472. DON AASE(R)
☐ 480. CARL YASTRZEMSKI
☐ 503. BILL LEE
☐ 532. JIM WILLOUGHBY
☐ 566. RICK MILLER
☐ 585. RICK BURLESON
☐ 613. REGGIE CLEVELAND
☐ 617. BOBBY DARWIN
☐ 640. CARLTON FISK

CALIFORNIA ANGELS

☐ 16. BOB JONES
☐ 34. TEAM & SHERRY(M)
☐ 68. BRUCE BOCHTE
☐ 91. JOHN VERHOEVEN
☐ 107. BILL MELTON
☐ 131. ORLANDO RAMIREZ
☐ 153. RON JACKSON
☐ 155. JOE RUDI
☐ 179. PAUL HARTZELL
☐ 200. FRANK TANANA
☐ 224. RUSTY TORRES
☐ 257. MIKE MILEY
☐ 282. SID MONGE
☐ 315. DAVE CHALK
☐ 342. JERRY REMY
☐ 369. TERRY HUMPHREY
☐ 401. MICKEY SCOTT
☐ 426. DICK DRAGO
☐ 454. ANDY ETCHEBARREN
☐ 462. DON BAYLOR
☐ 482. TONY SOLAITA
☐ 489. MIKE OVERY(R)
☐ 519. DON KIRKWOOD
☐ 521. BOB GRICH
☐ 544. GARY ROSS
☐ 570. BOBBY BONDS
☐ 592. DAN BRIGGS
☐ 628. MARIO GUERRERO
☐ 650. NOLAN RYAN

CHICAGO CUBS

☐ 64. LARRY BIITTNER
☐ 92. DAVE ROSELLO
☐ 124. GEORGE MITTERWALD
☐ 144. BRUCE SUTTER
☐ 169. DAROLD KNOWLES
☐ 190. RAY BURRIS
☐ 219. JOE COLEMAN
☐ 250. BILL MADLOCK
☐ 279. JOE WALLIS
☐ 302. MIKE GARMAN
☐ 333. PAUL REUSCHEL
☐ 360. RICK MONDAY
☐ 395. MANNY TRILLO
☐ 419. STEVE SWISHER
☐ 446. BILL BONHAM
☐ 468. RAMON HERNANDEZ
☐ 493. MIKE KRUKOW(R)
☐ 502. RANDY HUNDLEY
☐ 518. TEAM & FRANKS(M)
☐ 530. RICK REUSCHEL

☐ 561. PETE LACOCK
☐ 586. STEVE RENKO
☐ 610. JOSE CARDENAL
☐ 639. JERRY MORALES
☐ 657. MICK KELLEHER

CHICAGO WHITE SOX

☐ 17. STEVE STONE
☐ 29. BUCKY DENT
☐ 58. CHET LEMON
☐ 83. KEVIN BELL
☐ 109. JORGE ORTA
☐ 133. RALPH GARR
☐ 157. KEN BRETT
☐ 177. BART JOHNSON
☐ 198. WILBUR WOOD
☐ 222. FRANCISCO BARRIOS
☐ 247. CHRIS KNAPP
☐ 271. TERRY FORSTER
☐ 273. ERIC SODERHOLM
☐ 293. JACK BROHAMER
☐ 319. RICH GOSSAGE
☐ 338. DAVE DUNCAN
☐ 344. BRIAN DOWNING
☐ 367. DAVE HAMILTON
☐ 389. KEN KRAVEC
☐ 418. TEAM & LEMON(M)
☐ 443. LAMAR JOHNSON
☐ 487. GREG TERLECKY(R)
☐ 493. JIM OTTEN(R)
☐ 497. CLAY CARROLL
☐ 529. JIM ESSIAN
☐ 559. ALAN BANNISTER
☐ 623. JACK KUCEK
☐ 648. JIM SPENCER

CINCINNATI REDS

☐ 23. DAN DRIESSEN
☐ 45. RAWLY EASTWICK
☐ 70. JOHNNY BENCH
☐ 86. PAT ZACHRY
☐ 100. JOE MORGAN
☐ 121. GARY NOLAN
☐ 139. FRED NORMAN
☐ 160. WILL MCENANEY
☐ 186. DOUG FLYNN
☐ 203. ED ARMBRISTER
☐ 221. BOB BAILEY
☐ 239. BILL PLUMMER
☐ 287. TEAM & ANDERSON(M)
☐ 320. KEN GRIFFEY
☐ 347. GEORGE FOSTER
☐ 450. PETE ROSE
☐ 475. MANNY SARMIENTO(R)
☐ 487. JOE HENDERSON(R)
☐ 512. JACK BILLINGHAM
☐ 535. CESAR GERONIMO
☐ 548. JOEL YOUNGBLOOD
☐ 560. DAVE CONCEPCION
☐ 581. PEDRO BORBON
☐ 601. MIKE LUM
☐ 636. SANTO ALCALA
☐ 655. TONY PEREZ

CLEVELAND INDIANS

☐ 18. TEAM & ROBINSON(M)
☐ 33. WAYNE GARLAND
☐ 41. JIM KERN
☐ 62. ERIC RAICH
☐ 85. DUANE KUIPER
☐ 115. RICK MANNING
☐ 147. JACKIE BROWN
☐ 168. CHARLIE SPIKES
☐ 206. BOOG POWELL
☐ 236. TOM BUSKEY
☐ 267. RAY FOSSE
☐ 296. DON HOOD
☐ 306. RICK WAITS
☐ 330. GEORGE HENDRICK
☐ 385. DAVE LAROCHE
☐ 393. JOHN LOWENSTEIN
☐ 441. LARVELL BLANKS
☐ 449. AL FITZMORRIS
☐ 476. RICK CERONE(R)
☐ 477. ORLANDO GONZALEZ(R)
☐ 501. JIM BIBBY
☐ 525. DENNIS ECKERSLEY

☐ 542. FRANK DUFFY
☐ 590. BUDDY BELL
☐ 618. PAT DOBSON
☐ 654. RON PRUITT

DETROIT TIGERS

☐ 22. BILL FREEHAN
☐ 43. RAY BARE
☐ 69. JIM CRAWFORD
☐ 98. MILT MAY
☐ 122. BEN OGLIVIE
☐ 145. TOM VERYZER
☐ 173. CHUCK SCRIVENER
☐ 240. RON LEFLORE
☐ 265. MARK FIDRYCH
☐ 291. JASON THOMPSON
☐ 311. VERN RUHLE
☐ 363. DAVE A. ROBERTS
☐ 420. RUSTY STAUB
☐ 453. PEDRO GARCIA
☐ 477. PHIL MANKOWSKI(R)
☐ 487. ED GLYNN(R)
☐ 490. MARK WAGNER(R)
☐ 491. BOB SYKES(R)
☐ 492. STEVE KEMP(R)
☐ 506. STEVE GRILLI
☐ 533. MICKEY STANLEY
☐ 554. BRUCE KIMM
☐ 574. AURELIO RODRIGUEZ
☐ 595. JOHN HILLER
☐ 621. TEAM & HOUK(M)
☐ 637. ALEX JOHNSON
☐ 660. WILLIE HORTON

HOUSTON ASTROS

☐ 21. KEN FORSCH
☐ 42. JOSE CRUZ
☐ 67. JOAQUIN ANDUJAR
☐ 90. CESAR CEDENO
☐ 116. JOE NIEKRO
☐ 143. ED HERRMANN
☐ 184. BO MCLAUGHLIN
☐ 209. ROB ANDREWS
☐ 227. JOE SAMBITO
☐ 248. WILBUR HOWARD
☐ 260. J.R. RICHARD
☐ 283. JERRY DAVANON
☐ 308. GENE PENTZ
☐ 327. TEAM & VIRDON(M)
☐ 350. LARRY DIERKER
☐ 429. KEN BOSWELL
☐ 456. LEON ROBERTS
☐ 474. ALEX TAVERAS(R)
☐ 478. MARK LEMONGELLO(R)
☐ 481. ROGER METZGER
☐ 514. CLIFF JOHNSON
☐ 540. BOB WATSON
Ⓔ 567. ENOS CABELL
☐ 589. MIKE COSGROVE
☐ 614. GREG GROSS
☐ 641. DAN LARSON

KANSAS CITY ROYALS

☐ 46. BUCK MARTINEZ
☐ 75. DENNIS LEONARD
☐ 93. TOM POQUETTE

☐ 117. FRANK WHITE
☐ 141. MARK LITTELL
☐ 171. KEN SANDERS
☐ 193. LARRY GURA
☐ 218. JOHN WATHAN
☐ 244. JOHN MAYBERRY
☐ 262. AL COWENS
☐ 290. AMOS OTIS
☐ 314. STEVE MINGORI
☐ 340. HAL MCRAE
☐ 362. TOMMY DAVIS
☐ 371. TEAM & HERZOG(M)
☐ 422. FREDDIE PATEK
☐ 463. JAMIE QUIRK
☐ 472. BOB MCCLURE(R)
☐ 509. COOKIE ROJAS
☐ 534. PAUL SPLITTORFF
☐ 556. DOUG BIRD
☐ 580. GEORGE BRETT
☐ 602. ANDY HASSLER
☐ 622. JIM WOHLFORD
☐ 658. MARTY PATTIN

LOS ANGELES DODGERS

☐ 27. BILL BUCKNER
☐ 50. RON CEY
☐ 88. STAN WALL
☐ 105. STEVE YEAGER
☐ 128. TOMMY JOHN
☐ 146. DUSTY BAKER
☐ 180. DAVE LOPES
☐ 245. RICK RHODEN
☐ 253. JOHN HALE
☐ 272. LEE LACY
☐ 298. CHARLIE HOUGH
☐ 322. BILL RUSSELL
☐ 345. REGGIE SMITH
☐ 366. TED SIZEMORE
☐ 386. MANNY MOTA
☐ 400. STEVE GARVEY
☐ 421. DOUG RAU
☐ 448. ELLIE RODRIGUEZ
☐ 476. KEVIN PASLEY(R)
☐ 484. BURT HOOTON
☐ 504. TEAM & LASORDA(M)
☐ 558. ELIAS SOSA
☐ 584. ED GOODSON
☐ 620. DON SUTTON

MILWAUKEE BREWERS

☐ 26. RAY SADECKI
☐ 51. TEAM & GRAMMAS(M)
☐ 79. DON MONEY
☐ 99. TOM HAUSMAN
☐ 125. BILL TRAVERS
☐ 159. BERNIE CARBO
☐ 185. SIXTO LEZCANO
☐ 214. DARRELL PORTER
☐ 255. GEORGE SCOTT
☐ 278. DANNY FRISELLA
☐ 307. GARY SUTHERLAND
☐ 331. JIM COLBORN
☐ 361. EDUARDO RODRIGUEZ
☐ 382. CHARLIE MOORE
☐ 406. TIM JOHNSON
☐ 439. GORMAN THOMAS
☐ 488. DAN THOMAS(R)
☐ 494. JIM GANTNER(R)
☐ 498. SAL BANDO
☐ 507. MIKE HEGAN
☐ 528. BILL CASTRO
☐ 553. JACK HEIDEMANN
☐ 577. JERRY AUGUSTINE
☐ 604. JIM SLATON
☐ 635. ROBIN YOUNT
☐ 651. VON JOSHUA

MINNESOTA TWINS

☐ 13. LUIS GOMEZ
☐ 38. CRAIG KUSICK
☐ 66. ROY SMALLEY
☐ 87. GLENN BORGMANN
☐ 120. ROD CAREW
☐ 149. MIKE CUBBAGE
☐ 175. BUTCH WYNEGAR
☐ 202. TOM JOHNSON
☐ 228. TEAM & MAUCH(M)

☐ 249. PETE REDFERN
☐ 304. JIM HUGHES
☐ 321. DAVE GOLTZ
☐ 375. LARRY HISLE
☐ 398. TOM BURGMEIER
☐ 424. STEVE BRYE
☐ 457. STEVE LUEBBER
☐ 478. JIM GIDEON(R)
☐ 486. ED BANE
☐ 513. JERRY TERRELL
☐ 531. LYMAN BOSTOCK
☐ 536. VIC ALBURY
☐ 555. DAN FORD
☐ 578. BOB RANDALL
☐ 643. MIKE PAZIK

MONTREAL EXPOS

☐ 28. WOODIE FRYMAN
☐ 52. ELLIS VALENTINE
☐ 76. TIM FOLI
☐ 102. JOSE MORALES
☐ 112. BILL GREIF
☐ 132. CHIP LANG
☐ 156. PETE MACKANIN
☐ 178. BOMBO RIVERA
☐ 199. PEPE FRIAS
☐ 223. EARL WILLIAMS
☐ 252. DALE MURRAY
☐ 274. DON STANHOUSE
☐ 295. GARY CARTER
☐ 316. STEVE ROGERS
☐ 341. JOE KERRIGAN
☐ 368. MIKE JORGENSEN
☐ 391. DAN WARTHEN
☐ 417. WAYNE GARRETT
☐ 471. DEL UNSER
☐ 473. ANDRE DAWSON(R)
☐ 479. SAM MEJIAS(R)
☐ 526. LARRY PARRISH
☐ 557. JERRY WHITE
☐ 579. DON CARRITHERS
☐ 593. DENNIS BLAIR
☐ 612. BARRY FOOTE
☐ 647. TEAM & WILLIAMS(M)
☐ 649. DAVE CASH

NEW YORK METS

☐ 44. BUD HARRELSON
☐ 65. SKIP LOCKWOOD
☐ 94. CRAIG SWAN
☐ 119. JOHN STEARNS
☐ 150. TOM SEAVER
☐ 172. JOHN MILNER
☐ 201. ED KRANEPOOL
☐ 225. BOB APODACA
☐ 246. MIKE VAIL
☐ 259. TEAM & FRAZIER(M)
☐ 281. ROY STAIGER
☐ 300. JERRY KOOSMAN
☐ 329. RON HODGES
☐ 352. MIKE PHILLIPS
☐ 376. NINO ESPINOSA
☐ 399. BRUCE BOISCLAIR
☐ 425. JOE TORRE
☐ 440. JON MATLACK
☐ 458. LEO FOSTER
☐ 488. LEE MAZZILLI(R)
☐ 500. DAVE KINGMAN
☐ 552. PEPE MANGUAL
☐ 565. MICKEY LOLICH
☐ 587. RICK BALDWIN
☐ 605. FELIX MILLAN
☐ 627. BOB MYRICK

NEW YORK YANKEES

☐ 10. REGGIE JACKSON
☐ 15. DON GULLETT
☐ 20. GRAIG NETTLES
☐ 54. SANDY ALOMAR
☐ 71. DOCK ELLIS
☐ 96. LOU PINIELLA
☐ 123. FRED STANLEY
☐ 148. FRAN HEALY
☐ 170. THURMAN MUNSON
☐ 195. ED FIGUEROA
☐ 220. CHRIS CHAMBLISS

☐ 280. JIM HUNTER
☐ 305. MICKEY RIVERS
☐ 332. ELLIOTT MADDOX
☐ 359. WILLIE RANDOLPH
☐ 387. TEAM & MARTIN(M)
☐ 408. CESAR TOVAR
☐ 461. DICK TIDROW
☐ 472. GIL PATTERSON(R)
☐ 485. ROY WHITE
☐ 490. MICKEY KLUTTS(R)
☐ 505. OSCAR GAMBLE
☐ 543. RON BLOMBERG
☐ 568. CARLOS MAY
☐ 598. SPARKY LYLE
☐ 625. KEN HOLTZMAN
☐ 656. RON GUIDRY

OAKLAND A'S

☐ 12. LARRY HANEY
☐ 31. JIM TODD
☐ 53. PAUL MITCHELL
☐ 61. MANNY SANGUILLEN
☐ 74. TEAM & MCKEON(M)
☐ 101. DICK BOSMAN
☐ 127. RON FAIRLY
☐ 181. KEN MCMULLEN
☐ 204. JEFF NEWMAN
☐ 230. VIDA BLUE
☐ 261. PHIL GARNER
☐ 284. MIKE NORRIS
☐ 323. LARRY LINTZ
☐ 349. JIM HOLT
☐ 365. MIKE TORREZ
☐ 383. STAN BAHNSEN
☐ 402. TOMMY HELMS
☐ 405. CLAUDELL WASHINGTON
☐ 473. DENNY WALLING(R)
☐ 475. CHRIS BATTON(R)
☐ 479. WAYNE GROSS(R)
☐ 491. CRAIG MITCHELL(R)
☐ 551. BILL NORTH
☐ 583. PAUL LINDBLAD
☐ 616. TOMMY SANDT
☐ 644. MATT ALEXANDER

PHILADELPHIA PHILLIES

☐ 30. GREG LUZINSKI
☐ 59. LARRY CHRISTENSON
☐ 84. OLLIE BROWN
☐ 110. STEVE CARLTON
☐ 140. MIKE SCHMIDT
☐ 164. TUG MCGRAW
☐ 188. BOB TOLAN
☐ 217. TOM UNDERWOOD
☐ 243. RON REED
☐ 264. TOM HUTTON
☐ 289. GENE GARBER
☐ 310. LARRY BOWA
☐ 337. RON SCHUELER
☐ 357. TIM MCCARVER
☐ 388. TERRY HARMON
☐ 415. JAY JOHNSTONE
☐ 444. WAYNE TWITCHELL
☐ 467. TEAM & OZARK(M)
☐ 489. RANDY LERCH(R)
☐ 520. GARRY MADDOX
☐ 545. BOB BOONE

☐ 569. JIM LONBORG
☐ 596. JERRY MARTIN
☐ 619. JOHNNY OATES
☐ 638. JIM KAAT

PITTSBURGH PIRATES

☐ 35. RENNIE STENNETT
☐ 82. JIM ROOKER
☐ 104. OMAR MORENO
☐ 130. AL OLIVER
☐ 154. DAVE GIUSTI
☐ 167. RICH HEBNER
☐ 176. BOB ROBERTSON
☐ 197. ED OTT
☐ 270. DAVE PARKER
☐ 294. DOC MEDICH
☐ 318. DUFFY DYER
☐ 335. BILL ROBINSON
☐ 354. TEAM & TANNER(M)
☐ 374. KENT TEKULVE
☐ 460. WILLIE STARGELL
☐ 474. CRAIG REYNOLDS(R)
☐ 483. RICHIE ZISK
☐ 492. TONY ARMAS(R)
☐ 510. JOHN CANDELARIA
☐ 538. FRANK TAVERAS
☐ 563. BRUCE KISON
☐ 582. ED KIRKPATRICK
☐ 607. LARRY DEMERY
☐ 645. JERRY REUSS

ST. LOUIS CARDINALS

☐ 19. JOHN D'ACQUISTO
☐ 47. LYNN MCGLOTHEN
☐ 72. MIKE ANDERSON
☐ 95. KEITH HERNANDEZ
☐ 136. JERRY MUMPHREY
☐ 161. GARRY TEMPLETON
☐ 183. TEAM & RAPP(M)
☐ 205. PETE FALCONE
☐ 229. DON KESSINGER
☐ 355. LOU BROCK
☐ 381. BOB FORSCH
☐ 404. ERIC RASMUSSEN
☐ 427. DAVE RADER
☐ 452. MIKE CALDWELL
☐ 470. TED SIMMONS
☐ 495. AL HRABOSKY
☐ 516. BAKE MCBRIDE
☐ 541. JOHN DENNY
☐ 573. JOE FERGUSON
☐ 599. MIKE TYSON
☐ 624. HECTOR CRUZ
☐ 652. TOM WALKER

SAN DIEGO PADRES

☐ 9. DOUG RADER
☐ 39. TOM GRIFFIN
☐ 63. TITO FUENTES
☐ 78. BOB DAVIS
☐ 108. ALAN FOSTER
☐ 134. TEAM & MCNAMARA(M)
☐ 158. TED KUBIAK
☐ 182. DAN SPILLNER
☐ 215. BUTCH METZGER
☐ 241. DAVE TOMLIN
☐ 268. RICK SAWYER
☐ 286. JOHNNY GRUBB
☐ 303. GENE TENACE
☐ 325. MIKE IVIE
☐ 348. BRENT STROM
☐ 372. RICH FOLKERS
☐ 390. DAVE WINFIELD
☐ 407. DAVE FREISLEBEN
☐ 447. JERRY TURNER
☐ 472. DAVE WEHRMEISTER(R)
☐ 473. GENE RICHARDS(R)
☐ 490. BILLY ALMON(R)
☐ 491. MIKE DUPREE(R)
☐ 494. MIKE CHAMPION(R)
☐ 522. ENZO HERNANDEZ
☐ 523. ROLLIE FINGERS
☐ 550. RANDY JONES
☐ 576. FRED KENDALL
☐ 603. WILLIE DAVIS
☐ 629. BOBBY VALENTINE
☐ 659. MERV TETTENMUND

SAN FRANCISCO GIANTS

☐ 11. ROB DRESSLER
☐ 40. BOBBY MURCER
☐ 57. MARC HILL
☐ 73. CHARLIE WILLIAMS
☐ 97. DAVE HEAVERLO
☐ 129. MIKE SADEK
☐ 151. JOHNNIE LEMASTER
☐ 211. TEAM & ALTOBELLI(M)
☐ 266. DERRELL THOMAS
☐ 297. KEN REITZ
☐ 324. JOHN CURTIS
☐ 343. ED HALICKI
☐ 370. JOHN MONTEFUSCO
☐ 397. LARRY HERNDON
☐ 423. GARY LAVELLE
☐ 438. MARTY PEREZ
☐ 464. RANDY MOFFITT
☐ 476. GARY ALEXANDER(R)
☐ 488. JACK CLARK(R)
☐ 489. GREG MINTON(R)
☐ 496. GARY THOMASSON
☐ 515. CHRIS SPEIER
☐ 547. WILLIE MCCOVEY
☐ 571. DARRELL EVANS
☐ 591. CHRIS ARNOLD
☐ 609. JIM BARR
☐ 642. WILLIE CRAWFORD

SEATTLE MARINERS

☐ 14. TOMMY SMITH
☐ 49. GRANT JACKSON
☐ 118. RICK JONES
☐ 138. BOB STINSON
☐ 187. DICK POLE
☐ 207. GLENN ABBOTT
☐ 226. LEROY STANTON
☐ 269. JOE LIS
☐ 317. KURT BEVACQUA
☐ 334. BILL STEIN
☐ 353. STAN THOMAS
☐ 379. LARRY COX
☐ 394. BILL LAXTON
☐ 409. PETE BROBERG
☐ 431. DAVE COLLINS
☐ 478. DAVE C. JOHNSON(R)
☐ 488. RUPPERT JONES(R)
☐ 490. TOMMY MCMILLAN(R)
☐ 492. CARLOS LOPEZ(R)
☐ 493. GARY WHEELOCK(R)
☐ 494. JUAN BERNHARDT(R)
☐ 508. DAVE PAGAN
☐ 527. DAN MEYER
☐ 597. JOHNSON(M) & COACHS
☐ 606. STEVE BRAUN
☐ 653. DIEGO SEGUI

TEXAS RANGERS

☐ 36. JOHN ELLIS
☐ 55. JEFF BURROUGHS
☐ 81. JUAN BENIQUEZ
☐ 103. MIKE BACSIK
☐ 137. JEFF TERPKO
☐ 152. GAYLORD PERRY
☐ 174. NELSON BRILES
☐ 196. LEN RANDLE
☐ 237. GENE CLINES
☐ 254. DOYLE ALEXANDER
☐ 256. JOE HOERNER
☐ 275. MIKE HARGROVE
☐ 301. TOBY HARRAH
☐ 328. TOMMY BOGGS
☐ 351. JIM SUNDBERG
☐ 373. BERT CAMPANERIS
☐ 378. JIM UMBARGER
☐ 403. TOM GRIEVE
☐ 428. TEAM & LUCCHESI(M)
☐ 459. STEVE FOUCAULT
☐ 489. LEN BARKER(R)
☐ 494. BUMP WILLS(R)
☐ 511. BILL FAHEY
☐ 539. MIKE WALLACE
☐ 588. DAVE MOATES
☐ 608. ROY HOWELL
☐ 630. BERT BLYLEVEN

TORONTO BLUE JAYS

☐ 37. STEVE HARGAN
☐ 113. HARTSFIELD(M) & CHS.
☐ 163. DAVE HILTON
☐ 212. JIM MASON
☐ 299. OTTO VELEZ
☐ 326. JESSE JEFFERSON
☐ 346. BILL SINGER
☐ 377. DAVE MCKAY
☐ 392. PHIL ROOF
☐ 416. CHUCK HARTENSTEIN
☐ 465. RICO CARTY
☐ 473. JOHN SCOTT(R)
☐ 474. BOB BAILOR(R)
☐ 477. DOUG AULT(R)
☐ 478. LEON HOOTEN(R)
☐ 479. ALVIS WOODS(R)
☐ 487. LARRY ANDERSON(R)
☐ 492. GARY WOODS(R)
☐ 493. MIKE WILLIS(R)
☐ 517. PETE VUCKOVICH
☐ 537. DAVE W. ROBERTS
☐ 564. ALAN ASHBY
☐ 611. DAVE LEMANCZYK

1978 TOPPS (726)
2 1/2" X 3 1/2"

JORGE ORTA

ATLANTA BRAVES

☐ 10. PHIL NIEKRO
☐ 38. WILLIE MONTANEZ
☐ 75. DICK RUTHVEN
☐ 93. BOBBY COX(M)
☐ 130. JEFF BURROUGHS
☐ 156. ANDY MESSERSMITH
☐ 187. JERRY ROYSTER
☐ 217. ROD GILBREATH
☐ 242. BARRY BONNELL
☐ 264. JAMIE EASTERLY
☐ 296. BIFF POCOROBA
☐ 322. TOM PACIOREK
☐ 349. RICK CAMP
☐ 372. BRIAN ASSELSTINE
☐ 402. DAVE CAMPBELL
☐ 443. DARREL CHANEY
☐ 475. GARY MATTHEWS
☐ 502. PAT ROCKETT
☐ 527. VIC CORRELL
☐ 551. TEAM CARD
☐ 578. BUZZ CAPRA
☐ 598. EDDIE SOLOMON
☐ 617. JOE NOLAN
☐ 632. ROWLAND OFFICE
☐ 681. ROB BELLOIR
☐ 703. MICKEY MAHLER(R)
☐ 708. DALE MURPHY(M)
☐ 716. CLARENCE GASTON

BALTIMORE ORIOLES

☐ 9. DOUG DECINCES
☐ 36. EDDIE MURRAY
☐ 65. KEN SINGLETON
☐ 96. TEAM CARD
☐ 119. DENNY MARTINEZ
☐ 160. JIM PALMER

1978 Topps

□ 188. AL BUMBRY
□ 211. EARL WEAVER(M)
□ 237. RICH DAUER
□ 262. RUDY MAY
□ 287. KIKO GARCIA
□ 315. MARK BELANGER
□ 341. MIKE FLANAGAN
□ 367. RICK DEMPSEY
□ 393. TIPPY MARTINEZ
□ 418. TONY MUSER
□ 466. DENNIS BLAIR
□ 491. SCOTT MCGREGOR
□ 517. ANDRES MORA
□ 543. LARRY HARLOW
□ 593. DAVE SKAGGS
□ 616. H. PAT KELLY
□ 640. LEE MAY
□ 666. BILLY SMITH
□ 691. ROSS GRIMSLEY
□ 717. NELSON BRILES

BOSTON RED SOX

□ 12. DON AASE
□ 40. CARL YASTRZEMSKI
□ 63. DON ZIMMER(M)
□ 83. BOB MONTGOMERY
□ 105. REGGIE CLEVELAND
□ 125. GEORGE SCOTT
□ 155. BUTCH HOBSON
□ 186. BOB STANLEY
□ 216. MIKE PAXTON
□ 245. RICK BURLESON
□ 270. CARLTON FISK
□ 295. BILL LEE
□ 320. FRED LYNN
□ 345. LUIS TIANT
□ 373. JIM WILLOUGHBY
□ 416. JACK BROHAMER
□ 424. TEAM CARD
□ 457. BOB BAILEY
□ 482. RICK MILLER
□ 524. BERNIE CARBO
□ 545. BILL CAMPBELL
□ 567. DICK DRAGO
□ 572. RICK WISE
□ 597. STEVE DILLARD
□ 618. TOMMY HELMS
□ 642. DENNY DOYLE
□ 645. MIKE TORREZ
□ 670. JIM RICE
□ 695. DWIGHT EVANS
□ 706. TED COX(R)
□ 708. BO DIAZ(R)
□ 720. FERGIE JENKINS

CALIFORNIA ANGELS

□ 18. BOB GRICH
□ 48. DON BAYLOR
□ 71. TERRY HUMPHREY
□ 115. GARY NOLAN
□ 150. BOBBY BONDS
□ 178. DAVE CHALK
□ 214. TEAM CARD
□ 239. DYAR MILLER
□ 268. GIL FLORES
□ 291. GARY ROSS
□ 313. ANDY ETCHEBARREN
□ 339. MARIO GUERRERO
□ 368. BALOR MOORE
□ 400. NOLAN RYAN
□ 429. MIKE BARLOW
□ 454. DAVE LAROCHE
□ 478. JERRY REMY
□ 503. IKE HAMPTON
□ 529. PAUL HARTZELL
□ 557. TONY SOLAITA
□ 579. RANCE MULLINIKS
□ 600. FRANK TANANA
□ 619. THAD BOSLEY
□ 635. JOE RUDI
□ 655. LYMAN BOSTOCK
□ 656. DAVE GARCIA(M)
□ 682. KEN BRETT
□ 718. RON JACKSON

CHICAGO CUBS

□ 17. MIKE KRUKOW
□ 50. RICK REUSCHEL
□ 76. STEVE ONTIVEROS
□ 99. WILLIE HERNANDEZ
□ 123. MANNY TRILLO
□ 152. IVAN DEJESUS
□ 175. JERRY MORALES
□ 234. HERMAN FRANKS(M)
□ 252. STEVE SWISHER
□ 302. TEAM CARD
□ 325. BRUCE SUTTER
□ 346. LARRY BIITTNER
□ 371. RAY BURRIS
□ 397. GREG GROSS
□ 423. DAVE ROSELLO
□ 473. BILL BUCKNER
□ 489. RUDY MEOLI
□ 501. DAVE A. ROBERTS
□ 523. DONNIE MOORE
□ 541. LARRY COX
□ 564. MICK KELLEHER
□ 570. DAVE KINGMAN
□ 585. WOODIE FRYMAN
□ 590. BOBBY MURCER
□ 614. JOE WALLIS
□ 639. GENE CLINES
□ 663. PAUL REUSCHEL
□ 688. GEORGE MITTERWALD
□ 711. DENNIS LAMP(R)
□ 722. PETE BROBERG

CHICAGO WHITE SOX

□ 14. LERRIN LAGROW
□ 42. JORGE ORTA
□ 66. TEAM CARD
□ 98. JIM ESSIAN
□ 127. CHET LEMON
□ 153. STEVE STONE
□ 182. JIM SPENCER
□ 213. ALAN BANNISTER
□ 231. WAYNE NORDHAGEN
□ 251. DON KIRKWOOD
□ 272. ROYLE STILLMAN
□ 288. DAVE HAMILTON
□ 316. HENRY CRUZ
□ 329. JOHN VERHOEVEN
□ 361. CHRIS KNAPP
□ 395. JIM HUGHES
□ 409. RON SCHUELER
□ 421. JUNIOR MOORE
□ 439. KEN KRAVEC
□ 463. KEVIN BELL
□ 493. STEVE RENKO
□ 506. RON BLOMBERG
□ 519. BRIAN DOWNING
□ 552. FRANCISCO BARRIOS
□ 574. BOB LEMON(M)
□ 602. ERIC SODERHOLM
□ 615. CLAY CARROLL
□ 628. RALPH GARR
□ 672. DON KESSINGER
□ 693. LAMAR JOHNSON
□ 702. BILL NAHORODNY(R)
□ 726. WILBUR WOOD

CINCINNATI REDS

□ 20. PETE ROSE
□ 47. JACK BILLINGHAM
□ 80. KEN GRIFFEY
□ 106. BILL PLUMMER
□ 126. PAUL MOSKAU
□ 149. DALE MURRAY
□ 180. DAVE CONCEPCION
□ 220. PEDRO BORBON
□ 246. DAN DRIESSEN
□ 273. FRED NORMAN
□ 276. BILL BONHAM
□ 300. JOE MORGAN
□ 326. MIKE LUM
□ 354. CESAR GERONIMO
□ 377. MANNY SARMIENTO
□ 401. SPARKY ANDERSON(M)
□ 427. MARIO SOTO
□ 450. TOM SEAVER
□ 477. DOUG CAPILLA
□ 500. GEORGE FOSTER

□ 526. TEAM CARD
□ 556. ED ARMBRISTER
□ 622. CHAMP SUMMERS
□ 646. RICK AUERBACH
□ 674. RAY KNIGHT
□ 700. JOHNNY BENCH
□ 701. TOM HUME(R)
□ 702. DON WERNER(R)
□ 706. DAVE REVERING(R)

CLEVELAND INDIANS

□ 11. RICK MANNING
□ 37. RICK WAITS
□ 61. LARVELL BLANKS
□ 87. JOHN LOWENSTEIN
□ 101. SID MONGE
□ 122. DENNIS ECKERSLEY
□ 148. ANDRE THORNTON
□ 174. WAYNE GARLAND
□ 198. RON PRUITT
□ 227. AL FITZMORRIS
□ 253. JIM KERN
□ 280. BUDDY BELL
□ 305. RICO CARTY
□ 332. DUANE KUIPER
□ 351. JEFF TORBORG(M)
□ 398. DON HOOD
□ 426. FRED KENDALL
□ 459. CHARLIE SPIKES
□ 484. JIM NORRIS
□ 511. FRANK DUFFY
□ 537. BRUCE BOCHTE
□ 575. PAT DOBSON
□ 608. JOHNNY GRUBB
□ 636. JIM BIBBY
□ 662. PAUL DADE
□ 689. TEAM CARD
□ 703. LARRY ANDERSEN(R)
□ 704. DAVE OLIVER(R)
□ 706. WAYNE CAGE(R)
□ 711. CARDELL CAMPER(R)

DETROIT TIGERS

□ 21. STEVE KEMP
□ 45. MARK FIDRYCH
□ 68. STEVE FOUCAULT
□ 94. CHUCK SCRIVENER
□ 124. DAVE ROZEMA
□ 151. MILT WILCOX
□ 176. MILT MAY
□ 232. MICKEY STANLEY
□ 258. JOHN HILLER
□ 286. BEN OGLIVIE
□ 342. AURELIO RODRIGUEZ
□ 370. RUSTY STAUB
□ 385. TITO FUENTES
□ 404. TEAM CARD
□ 456. VERN RUHLE
□ 480. RON LEFLORE
□ 515. TIM CORCORAN
□ 536. RORIC HARRISON
□ 559. PHIL MANKOWSKI
□ 607. FERNANDO ARROYO
□ 633. TOM VERYZER
□ 660. JASON THOMPSON
□ 684. RALPH HOUK(M)
□ 701. BRUCE TAYLOR(R)
□ 703. JACK MORRIS(R)
□ 704. LOU WHITAKER(R)
□ 707. ALAN TRAMMELL(R)
□ 708. LANCE PARRISH(R)
□ 723. JOHN WOCKENFUSS

HOUSTON ASTROS

□ 13. ART HOWE
□ 39. FLOYD BANNISTER
□ 64. GENE PENTZ
□ 91. OSCAR ZAMORA
□ 112. TEAM CARD
□ 132. ENOS CABELL
□ 158. JOAQUIN ANDUJAR
□ 181. KEN FORSCH
□ 226. JOE FERGUSON
□ 263. DANNY WALTON
□ 279. BILL VIRDON(M)
□ 306. JOE NIEKRO
□ 330. BOB WATSON

☐ 358. MARK LEMONGELLO
☐ 389. JULIO GONZALEZ
☐ 437. BO MCLAUGHLIN
☐ 470. J.R. RICHARD
☐ 498. JOE SAMBITO
☐ 514. ROB SPERRING
☐ 534. WILBUR HOWARD
☐ 553. TERRY PUHL
☐ 625. JOSE CRUZ
☐ 650. CESAR CEDENO
☐ 677. ED HERRMANN
☐ 697. ROGER METZGER
☐ 705. DAVE BERGMAN(R)
☐ 711. ROY THOMAS(R)

KANSAS CITY ROYALS

☐ 19. DARRELL PORTER
☐ 46. AL COWENS
☐ 73. ANDY HASSLER
☐ 100. GEORGE BRETT
☐ 129. JIM COLBORN
☐ 157. PETE LACOCK
☐ 183. DOUG BIRD
☐ 218. MARTY PATTIN
☐ 248. FRANK WHITE
☐ 274. FRED PATEK
☐ 299. WHITEY HERZOG(M)
☐ 331. MARK LITTELL
☐ 336. STEVE BUSBY
☐ 343. JOHN WATHAN
☐ 357. TOM POQUETTE
☐ 382. JOE LAHOUD
☐ 408. JOE ZDEB
☐ 441. LARRY GURA
☐ 465. HAL MCRAE
☐ 490. AMOS OTIS
☐ 525. JERRY TERRELL
☐ 550. JOHN MAYBERRY
☐ 571. BUCK MARTINEZ
☐ 638. PAUL SPLITTORFF
☐ 665. DENNIS LEONARD
☐ 696. STEVE MINGORI
☐ 705. CLINT HURDLE(R)
☐ 707. U.L. WASHINGTON(R)
☐ 724. TEAM CARD

LOS ANGELES DODGERS

☐ 22. CHARLIE HOUGH
☐ 41. BURT HOOTON
☐ 104. LEE LACY
☐ 128. BILL RUSSELL
☐ 145. RICK MONDAY
☐ 168. REGGIE SMITH
☐ 189. TOM LASORDA(M)
☐ 228. MANNY MOTA
☐ 259. TEAM CARD
☐ 285. STEVE YEAGER
☐ 310. DON SUTTON
☐ 347. TERRY FORSTER
☐ 350. STEVE GARVEY
☐ 375. TOMMY JOHN
☐ 417. MIKE GARMAN
☐ 440. DAVE LOPES
☐ 464. JERRY GROTE
☐ 508. JOHNNY OATES
☐ 539. VIC DAVALILLO
☐ 546. TED MARTINEZ
☐ 562. GLENN BURKE
☐ 586. ED GOODSON
☐ 605. RICK RHODEN
☐ 630. RON CEY
☐ 641. DOUG RAU
☐ 668. DUSTY BAKER
☐ 694. ELIAS SOSA
☐ 709. LANCE RAUTZHAN(R)

MILWAUKEE BREWERS

☐ 24. DON MONEY
☐ 51. CHARLIE MOORE
☐ 77. ED KIRKPATRICK
☐ 95. JAMIE QUIRK
☐ 108. VON JOSHUA
☐ 133. JERRY AUGUSTINE
☐ 154. CECIL COOPER
☐ 173. ROBIN YOUNT
☐ 212. MIKE CALDWELL
☐ 243. BOB MCCLURE

☐ 265. SAL BANDO
☐ 303. SAM HINDS
☐ 328. TEAM CARD
☐ 355. BILL TRAVERS
☐ 376. JIM WOHLFORD
☐ 391. LARRY HANEY
☐ 415. RAY FOSSE
☐ 448. BILL CASTRO
☐ 474. JIM SLATON
☐ 516. GARY BEARE
☐ 520. LARRY HISLE
☐ 542. TIM JOHNSON
☐ 569. LARY SORENSEN
☐ 595. SIXTO LEZCANO
☐ 623. EDUARDO RODRIGUEZ
☐ 649. MOOSE HAAS
☐ 673. STEVE BRYE
☐ 707. PAUL MOLITOR(R)

DAN FORD

MINNESOTA TWINS

☐ 27. GEOFF ZAHN
☐ 54. TOM JOHNSON
☐ 81. PETE REDFERN
☐ 113. DON CARRITHERS
☐ 137. CRAIG KUSICK
☐ 162. PAUL THORMODSGARD
☐ 193. RICH CHILES
☐ 219. MIKE CUBBAGE
☐ 249. DAVE GOLTZ
☐ 275. DAN FORD
☐ 307. GLENN BORGMANN
☐ 363. BOB RANDALL
☐ 386. BOB GORINSKI
☐ 432. TERRY BULLING
☐ 451. TEAM CARD
☐ 471. ROY SMALLEY
☐ 497. GLENN ADAMS
☐ 555. BUTCH WYNEGAR
☐ 580. ROD CAREW
☐ 601. GENE MAUCH(M)
☐ 627. DAVE C. JOHNSON
☐ 657. BOMBO RIVERA
☐ 678. TOM BURGMEIER
☐ 704. SAM PERLOZZO(R)
☐ 705. WILLIE NORWOOD(R)

MONTREAL EXPOS

☐ 15. TONY PEREZ
☐ 43. BILL ATKINSON
☐ 72. ANDRE DAWSON
☐ 97. STAN BAHNSEN
☐ 120. GARY CARTER
☐ 185. ELLIS VALENTINE
☐ 221. CHRIS SPEIER
☐ 244. TEAM CARD
☐ 269. WAYNE TWITCHELL
☐ 294. LARRY PARRISH
☐ 321. SANTO ALCALA
☐ 348. DEL UNSER
☐ 374. JOSE MORALES
☐ 399. PETE MACKANIN
☐ 414. DAROLD KNOWLES
☐ 425. STEVE ROGERS
☐ 449. TIM BLACKWELL
☐ 468. WARREN CROMARTIE
☐ 495. DAVE CASH
☐ 522. DICK WILLIAMS(M)

☐ 549. JOE KERRIGAN
☐ 576. SAM MEJIAS
☐ 603. WILL MCENANEY
☐ 629. DON STANHOUSE
☐ 654. PEPE FRIAS
☐ 679. WAYNE GARRETT
☐ 699. JACKIE BROWN
☐ 701. LARRY LANDRETH(R)
☐ 709. DAN SCHATZEDER(R)

NEW YORK METS

☐ 25. JON MATLACK
☐ 49. ED KRANEPOOL
☐ 69. MIKE VAIL
☐ 109. JOE TORRE
☐ 134. STEVE HENDERSON
☐ 147. LEE MAZZILLI
☐ 171. PAT ZACHRY
☐ 197. NINO ESPINOSA
☐ 229. LEO FOSTER
☐ 277. BRUCE BOISCLAIR
☐ 304. JOHN MILNER
☐ 334. JOHN STEARNS
☐ 356. TEAM CARD
☐ 379. SKIP LOCKWOOD
☐ 403. BUD HARRELSON
☐ 428. JOEL YOUNGBLOOD
☐ 442. ELLIOTT MADDOX
☐ 453. DOUG FLYNN
☐ 481. JACKSON TODD
☐ 505. FELIX MILLAN
☐ 544. LEN RANDLE
☐ 565. JERRY KOOSMAN
☐ 592. BOB APODACA
☐ 621. CRAIG SWAN
☐ 653. RON HODGES
☐ 676. BOB MYRICK
☐ 712. BOBBY VALENTINE

NEW YORK YANKEES

☐ 16. ROY WHITE
☐ 35. SPARKY LYLE
☐ 60. THURMAN MUNSON
☐ 70. RICH GOSSAGE
☐ 89. KEN CLAY
☐ 114. PAUL BLAIR
☐ 135. RON GUIDRY
☐ 159. LOU PINIELLA
☐ 179. DICK TIDROW
☐ 200. REGGIE JACKSON
☐ 225. DON GULLETT
☐ 250. GRAIG NETTLES
☐ 282. TEAM CARD
☐ 309. CLIFF JOHNSON
☐ 335. BUCKY DENT
☐ 365. ED FIGUEROA
☐ 387. KEN HOLTZMAN
☐ 460. JIM HUNTER
☐ 485. CHRIS CHAMBLISS
☐ 582. FRAN HEALY
☐ 591. GEORGE ZEBER
☐ 620. WILLIE RANDOLPH
☐ 664. FRED STANLEY
☐ 690. MICKEY RIVERS
☐ 707. MICKEY KLUTTS(R)
☐ 710. DELL ALSTON(R)
☐ 721. BILLY MARTIN(M)

OAKLAND A'S

☐ 29. BOB LACEY
☐ 55. MITCHELL PAGE
☐ 78. PABLO TORREALBA
☐ 102. MATT ALEXANDER
☐ 139. WAYNE GROSS
☐ 163. BILL NORTH
☐ 191. RODNEY SCOTT
☐ 224. JERRY TABB
☐ 261. TIM HOSLEY
☐ 298. TONY ARMAS
☐ 327. RICK LANGFORD
☐ 353. DOUG BAIR
☐ 378. BOBBY WINKLES(M)
☐ 406. MIKE JORGENSEN
☐ 434. MIKE NORRIS
☐ 458. JEFF NEWMAN
☐ 487. JIM TYRONE
☐ 507. WILLIE CRAWFORD

☐ 528. ROB PICCIOLO
☐ 554. JOE COLEMAN
☐ 577. TEAM CARD
☐ 604. EARL WILLIAMS
☐ 613. MARTY PEREZ
☐ 647. STEVE DUNNING
☐ 658. MANNY SANGUILLEN
☐ 680. VIDA BLUE
☐ 701. STEVE MCCATTY(R)
☐ 709. MATT KEOUGH(R)
☐ 711. CRAIG MITCHELL(R)

PHILADELPHIA PHILLIES

☐ 26. RICH HEBNER
☐ 52. JIM LONBORG
☐ 90. LARRY BOWA
☐ 118. TERRY HARMON
☐ 136. TED SIZEMORE
☐ 161. BOB BOONE
☐ 177. GENE GARBER
☐ 210. JOSE CARDENAL
☐ 222. JERRY MARTIN
☐ 235. TIM MCCARVER
☐ 247. LARRY CHRISTENSON
☐ 271. RANDY LERCH
☐ 297. WARREN BRUSSTAR
☐ 317. DAVE A. JOHNSON
☐ 340. BAKE MCBRIDE
☐ 360. MIKE SCHMIDT
☐ 381. TEAM CARD
☐ 420. GREG LUZINSKI
☐ 446. TUG MCGRAW
☐ 472. RON REED
☐ 513. BARRY FOOTE
☐ 540. STEVE CARLTON
☐ 568. TOM HUTTON
☐ 610. GARRY MADDOX
☐ 631. DANNY OZARK(M)
☐ 675. JAY JOHNSTONE
☐ 715. JIM KAAT

PITTSBURGH PIRATES

☐ 28. ED OTT
☐ 53. PHIL GARNER
☐ 84. KENT TEKULVE
☐ 138. LARRY DEMERY
☐ 165. RENNIE STENNETT
☐ 190. JOHN CANDELARIA
☐ 223. BRUCE KISON
☐ 255. JERRY REUSS
☐ 283. OMAR MORENO
☐ 308. JIM ROOKER
☐ 323. JIM FREGOSI
☐ 383. MARIO MENDOZA
☐ 407. ODELL JONES
☐ 430. AL OLIVER
☐ 433. FERNANDO GONZALEZ
☐ 455. BILL ROBINSON
☐ 483. KEN MACHA
☐ 494. CHUCK TANNER(M)
☐ 510. WILLIE STARGELL
☐ 560. DAVE PARKER
☐ 606. TEAM CARD
☐ 637. DUFFY DYER
☐ 661. GRANT JACKSON
☐ 685. FRANK TAVERAS
☐ 703. TIM JONES(R)
☐ 705. MIGUEL DILONE(R)
☐ 710. MIKE EASLER(R)

ST. LOUIS CARDINALS

☐ 32. GARRY TEMPLETON
☐ 58. BOB FORSCH
☐ 88. MIKE PHILLIPS
☐ 111. MIKE TYSON
☐ 143. KEITH HERNANDEZ
☐ 170. LOU BROCK
☐ 195. LARRY DIERKER
☐ 230. AL HRABOSKY
☐ 257. HECTOR CRUZ
☐ 281. ERIC RASMUSSEN
☐ 301. BUDDY SCHULTZ
☐ 324. VERN RAPP(M)
☐ 352. TONY SCOTT
☐ 380. TED SIMMONS
☐ 405. RAWLY EASTWICK

☐ 431. BUTCH METZGER
☐ 452. JERRY MUMPHREY
☐ 479. TEAM CARD
☐ 504. ROGER FREED
☐ 531. TOM UNDERWOOD
☐ 563. DAVE RADER
☐ 587. JOHN URREA
☐ 609. JOHN DENNY
☐ 644. JIM DWYER
☐ 669. PETE FALCONE
☐ 692. KEN REITZ
☐ 710. RICK BOSETTI(R)
☐ 714. MIKE ANDERSON

ROLLIE FINGERS

SAN DIEGO PADRES

☐ 30. GEORGE HENDRICK
☐ 56. RANDY JONES
☐ 86. DAVE TOMLIN
☐ 116. TUCKER ASHFORD
☐ 140. ROLLIE FINGERS
☐ 164. BOB OWCHINKO
☐ 192. TEAM CARD
☐ 240. GENE TENACE
☐ 266. BOB SHIRLEY
☐ 292. GENE RICHARDS
☐ 318. TOM GRIFFIN
☐ 364. JERRY TURNER
☐ 390. OSCAR GAMBLE
☐ 392. BILLY ALMON
☐ 445. MIKE IVIE
☐ 467. ALVIN DARK(M)
☐ 488. DAN SPILLNER
☐ 509. BRENT STROM
☐ 530. DAVE WINFIELD
☐ 566. MERV RETTENMUND
☐ 594. DAVE FREISLEBEN
☐ 611. PAT SCANLON
☐ 683. MIKE CHAMPION
☐ 702. RICK SWEET(R)
☐ 713. BOB DAVIS

SAN FRANCISCO GIANTS

☐ 8. MIKE SADEK
☐ 34. WILLIE MCCOVEY
☐ 62. JIM BARR
☐ 82. TEAM CARD
☐ 107. ED HALICKI
☐ 142. JOHN MONTEFUSCO
☐ 167. TIM FOLI
☐ 194. DERREL THOMAS
☐ 215. DARRELL EVANS
☐ 236. TERRY WHITFIELD
☐ 256. JOE ALTOBELLI(M)
☐ 284. RANDY MOFFITT
☐ 312. GREG MINTON
☐ 338. DAVE HEAVERLO
☐ 359. MARC HILL
☐ 384. JACK CLARK
☐ 410. BILL MADLOCK
☐ 436. VIC HARRIS
☐ 461. ROB ANDREWS
☐ 486. JOHN CURTIS
☐ 512. LARRY HERNDON
☐ 538. JOHNNIE LEMASTER
☐ 561. CHARLIE WILLIAMS
☐ 581. LYNN MCGLOTHEN

☐ 589. BOB KNEPPER
☐ 624. GARY ALEXANDER
☐ 648. GARY THOMASSON
☐ 671. GARY LAVELLE
☐ 719. RANDY ELLIOTT

SEATTLE MARINERS

☐ 31. GLENN ABBOTT
☐ 57. DAN MEYER
☐ 79. DARRELL JOHNSON(M)
☐ 117. JOHN MONTAGUE
☐ 141. RUPPERT JONES
☐ 166. CARLOS LOPEZ
☐ 199. CRAIG REYNOLDS
☐ 233. DICK POLE
☐ 254. DAVE COLLINS
☐ 278. ENRIQUE ROMO
☐ 311. JOSE BAEZ
☐ 333. JIM TODD
☐ 366. LARRY MILBOURNE
☐ 396. BOB STINSON
☐ 422. STEVE BRAUN
☐ 447. LEROY STANTON
☐ 476. BILL STEIN
☐ 499. TEAM CARD
☐ 532. SKIP JUTZE
☐ 558. PAUL MITCHELL
☐ 584. JOHN HALE
☐ 596. GARY WHEELOCK
☐ 643. TOM HOUSE
☐ 687. JULIO CRUZ
☐ 698. JUAN BERNHARDT
☐ 702. KEVIN PASLEY(R)
☐ 709. STEVE BURKE(R)

TEXAS RANGERS

☐ 23. BUMP WILLS
☐ 44. TOBY HARRAH
☐ 67. CLAUDELL WASHINGTON
☐ 92. ADRIAN DEVINE
☐ 110. RICHIE ZISK
☐ 131. BERT BLYLEVEN
☐ 146. DOYLE ALEXANDER
☐ 172. MIKE HARGROVE
☐ 209. DOCK ELLIS
☐ 238. JUAN BENIQUEZ
☐ 260. BERT CAMPANERIS
☐ 290. WILLIE HORTON
☐ 314. PAUL LINDBLAD
☐ 337. TOM GRIEVE
☐ 362. DAVE MAY
☐ 388. BILL FAHEY
☐ 438. JOHN ELLIS
☐ 462. ROGELIO MORET
☐ 492. JIM SUNDBERG
☐ 518. TOMMY BOGGS
☐ 533. SANDY ALOMAR
☐ 548. BILLY HUNTER(M)
☐ 583. DOC MEDICH
☐ 588. JIM MASON
☐ 612. KEN HENDERSON
☐ 634. LEN BARKER
☐ 659. TEAM CARD
☐ 686. GAYLORD PERRY
☐ 706. PAT PUTNAM(R)
☐ 710. KEITH SMITH(R)
☐ 725. KURT BEVACQUA

TORONTO BLUE JAYS

☐ 33. DAVE LEMANCZYK
☐ 59. OTTO VELEZ
☐ 85. RON FAIRLY
☐ 103. TOM MURPHY
☐ 121. ALVIS WOODS
☐ 144. JESSE JEFFERSON
☐ 169. JERRY JOHNSON
☐ 196. BOB BAILOR
☐ 241. PETE VUCKOVICH
☐ 267. DOUG AULT
☐ 293. MIKE WILLIS
☐ 319. ALAN ASHBY
☐ 344. SAM EWING
☐ 369. TIM NORDBROOK
☐ 394. ROY HOWELL
☐ 419. JERRY GARVIN
☐ 444. ROY HARTSFIELD(M)
☐ 469. RICK CERONE

□ 496. JIM CLANCY
□ 521. STEVE STAGGS
□ 547. JOHN SCOTT
□ 573. LUIS GOMEZ
□ 599. GARY WOODS
□ 626. TEAM CARD
□ 651. DOUG RADER
□ 667. JEFF BYRD
□ 704. GARTH IORG(R)
□ 708. ERNIE WHITT(R)

1979 TOPPS (726)
2 1/2" X 3 1/2"

PAUL MOLITOR SS
BREWERS

ATLANTA BRAVES

□   9. DAVE CAMPBELL
□ 39. DALE MURPHY
□ 85. GARY MATTHEWS
□ 105. RICK CAMP
□ 132. ROWLAND OFFICE
□ 156. BUDDY SOLOMON
□ 184. DARREL CHANEY
□ 222. BOB BEALL
□ 245. JEFF BURROUGHS
□ 257. ADRIAN DEVINE
□ 296. PRESTON HANNA
□ 302. TEAM & COX(M)
□ 331. MICKEY MAHLER
□ 344. JERRY ROYSTER
□ 363. CRAIG SKOK
□ 384. TOMMY BOGGS
□ 464. JOE NOLAN
□ 496. BARRY BONNELL
□ 504. LARRY MCWILLIAMS
□ 529. BRIAN ASSELSTINE
□ 555. BIFF POCOROBA
□ 572. ROD GILBREATH
□ 586. BOB HORNER
□ 595. PHIL NIEKRO
□ 629. GENE GARBER
□ 684. JAMIE EASTERLY
□ 715. BRUCE BENEDICT(P)
□ 715. GLENN HUBBARD(P)
□ 715. LARRY WHISENTON(P)

BALTIMORE ORIOLES

□ 10. LEE MAY
□ 37. JOE KERRIGAN
□ 65. MARK BELANGER
□ 91. TERRY CROWLEY
□ 102. MIKE ANDERSON
□ 119. DON STANHOUSE
□ 160. MIKE FLANAGAN
□ 188. H. PAT KELLY
□ 211. DENNY MARTINEZ
□ 237. BILLY SMITH
□ 262. NELSON BRILES
□ 287. ANDRES MORA
□ 314. LARRY HARLOW
□ 340. JIM PALMER
□ 367. DAVE SKAGGS
□ 393. SCOTT MCGREGOR
□ 421. DOUG DECINCES
□ 491. TIPPY MARTINEZ
□ 517. AL BUMBRY
□ 543. KIKO GARCIA

□ 568. CARLOS LOPEZ
□ 593. RICK DEMPSEY
□ 615. KEN SINGLETON
□ 640. EDDIE MURRAY
□ 666. RICH DAUER
□ 689. TEAM & WEAVER(M)
□ 701. MARK COREY(P)
□ 701. JOHN FLINN(P)
□ 701. SAMMY STEWART(P)

BOSTON RED SOX

□ 12. DICK DRAGO
□ 40. DENNIS ECKERSLEY
□ 63. JACK BROHAMER
□ 83. FRED KENDALL
□ 106. FRANK DUFFY
□ 125. RICK BURLESON
□ 155. DWIGHT EVANS
□ 185. MIKE TORREZ
□ 214. TEAM & ZIMMER(M)
□ 270. BUTCH HOBSON
□ 320. CARL YASTRZEMSKI
□ 349. JIM C. WRIGHT
□ 375. BILL CAMPBELL
□ 400. JIM RICE
□ 423. BOB MONTGOMERY
□ 455. BILL LEE
□ 480. FRED LYNN
□ 524. TOM BURGMEIER
□ 549. BOB BAILEY
□ 575. LUIS TIANT
□ 597. BOB STANLEY
□ 618. JERRY REMY
□ 645. GEORGE SCOTT
□ 680. CARLTON FISK
□ 696. ANDY HASSLER
□ 702. JOEL FINCH(P)
□ 702. GARRY HANCOCK(P)
□ 702. ALLEN RIPLEY(P)

CALIFORNIA ANGELS

□ 18. TONY SOLAITA
□ 48. MERV RETTENMUND
□ 71. BRIAN DOWNING
□ 115. NOLAN RYAN
□ 212. CARNEY LANSFORD
□ 267. JOE RUDI
□ 291. TOM GRIFFIN
□ 313. DYAR MILLER
□ 322. DANNY GOODWIN
□ 339. RON JACKSON
□ 368. DON AASE
□ 402. PAUL HARTZELL
□ 424. TEAM & FREGOSI(M)
□ 453. CHRIS KNAPP
□ 477. BOB GRICH
□ 503. TERRY HUMPHREY
□ 530. FRANK TANANA
□ 557. KEN BRETT
□ 580. RON FAIRLY
□ 601. DAVE LAROCHE
□ 619. KEN LANDREAUX
□ 635. DON BAYLOR
□ 638. AL FITZMORRIS
□ 654. RICK MILLER
□ 682. DAVE CHALK
□ 703. JIM ANDERSON(P)
□ 703. DAVE FROST(P)
□ 703. BOB SLATER(P)

CHICAGO CUBS

□ 17. DONNIE MOORE
□ 53. MICK KELLEHER
□ 86. RODNEY SCOTT
□ 98. RAY BURRIS
□ 135. BOBBY MURCER
□ 153. DENNIS LAMP
□ 171. GENE CLINES
□ 240. RICK REUSCHEL
□ 299. STEVE ONTIVEROS
□ 323. LYNN MCGLOTHEN
□ 346. BILL BUCKNER
□ 370. DAVE KINGMAN
□ 398. IVAN DEJESUS
□ 433. LARRY BIITTNER
□ 457. BRUCE SUTTER

□ 473. DAVE A. ROBERTS
□ 489. LARRY COX
□ 494. JERRY WHITE
□ 513. DAVE A. JOHNSON
□ 522. KEN HOLTZMAN
□ 551. TEAM & FRANKS(M)
□ 579. GREG GROSS
□ 592. MIKE KRUKOW
□ 614. WILLIE HERNANDEZ
□ 639. MANNY TRILLO
□ 663. MIKE VAIL
□ 693. DAVE RADER
□ 716. DAVE GEISEL(P)
□ 716. KARL PAGEL(P)
□ 716. SCOT THOMPSON(P)

CHICAGO WHITE SOX

□ 42. RON BLOMBERG
□ 88. BOB MOLINARO
□ 127. THAD BOSLEY
□ 134. ALAN BANNISTER
□ 169. BILL NAHORODNY
□ 186. ERIC SODERHOLM
□ 216. WILBUR WOOD
□ 227. STEVE STONE
□ 242. PABLO TORREALBA
□ 266. JIM WILLOUGHBY
□ 275. JUNIOR MOORE
□ 283. KEN KRAVEC
□ 309. RALPH GARR
□ 333. CHET LEMON
□ 351. WAYNE NORDHAGEN
□ 372. LAMAR JOHNSON
□ 386. FRANCISCO BARRIOS
□ 404. TEAM & KESSINGER(M)
□ 467. DON KESSINGER
□ 514. MIKE PROLY
□ 527. LERRIN LAGROW
□ 559. GREG PRYOR
□ 574. CLAUDELL WASHINGTON
□ 631. JORGE ORTA
□ 662. KEVIN BELL
□ 686. RON SCHUELER
□ 704. ROSS BAUMGARTEN(P)
□ 704. MIKE COLBERN(P)
□ 704. MIKE SQUIRES(P)

CINCINNATI REDS

□ 20. JOE MORGAN
□ 47. FRED NORMAN
□ 73. KEN HENDERSON
□ 100. TOM SEAVER
□ 126. DOUG BAIR
□ 149. MANNY SARMIENTO
□ 174. RICK AUERBACH
□ 200. JOHNNY BENCH
□ 220. CESAR GERONIMO
□ 259. TEAM & ANDERSON(M)
□ 281. VIC CORRELL
□ 301. TOM HUME
□ 326. PEDRO BORBON
□ 354. BILL BONHAM
□ 377. PAUL MOSKAU
□ 401. RAY KNIGHT
□ 420. KEN GRIFFEY
□ 450. DAVE CONCEPCION
□ 475. DAN DRIESSEN
□ 501. JUNIOR KENNEDY
□ 516. CHAMP SUMMERS
□ 556. MIKE LUM
□ 600. GEORGE FOSTER
□ 622. DAVE COLLINS
□ 650. PETE ROSE
□ 674. DAVE TOMLIN
□ 717. MIKE LACOSS(P)
□ 717. RON OESTER(P)
□ 717. HARRY SPILMAN(P)

CLEVELAND INDIANS

□ 13. PAUL DADE
□ 38. BERNIE CARBO
□ 61. BO DIAZ
□ 77. DAN BRIGGS
□ 79. TED COX
□ 96. TEAM & TORBORG(M)
□ 122. MIKE PAXTON
□ 146. DUANE KUIPER

☐ 150. WAYNE CAGE
☐ 168. DAVE FREISLEBEN
☐ 226. RON PRUITT
☐ 253. RICK WISE
☐ 280. ANDRE THORNTON
☐ 307. LARVELL BLANKS
☐ 332. GARY ALEXANDER
☐ 359. DAN SPILLNER
☐ 399. DAVID CLYDE
☐ 425. RICK MANNING
☐ 438. HORACE SPEED
☐ 459. SID MONGE
☐ 484. RICK WAITS
☐ 511. PAUL REUSCHEL
☐ 537. TOM VERYZER
☐ 573. JIM KERN
☐ 611. JIM NORRIS
☐ 636. WAYNE GARLAND
☐ 667. DON HOOD
☐ 690. BUDDY BELL
☐ 705. ALFREDO GRIFFIN(P)
☐ 705. TIM NORRID(P)
☐ 705. DAVE OLIVER(P)

DETROIT TIGERS

☐ 33. DAVE ROZEMA
☐ 66. TEAM & MOSS(M)
☐ 80. JASON THOMPSON
☐ 93. PHIL MANKOWSKI
☐ 123. LOU WHITAKER
☐ 151. JOHN HILLER
☐ 176. AURELIO RODRIGUEZ
☐ 196. STEVE KEMP
☐ 217. STEVE DILLARD
☐ 231. JOHNNY WOCKENFUSS
☐ 251. JACK MORRIS
☐ 272. TIM CORCORAN
☐ 288. MILT WILCOX
☐ 316. MILT MAY
☐ 343. ED GLYNN
☐ 358. ALAN TRAMMELL
☐ 388. JACK BILLINGHAM
☐ 440. RUSTY STAUB
☐ 469. LANCE PARRISH
☐ 541. JIM SLATON
☐ 569. BOB SYKES
☐ 598. MARK WAGNER
☐ 625. MARK FIDRYCH
☐ 660. RON LEFLORE
☐ 692. MICKEY STANLEY
☐ 706. DAVE STEGMAN(P)
☐ 706. DAVE TOBIK(P)
☐ 706. KIP YOUNG(P)

HOUSTON ASTROS

☐ 14. RAFAEL LANDESTORY
☐ 49. VERN RUHLE
☐ 68. JOE NIEKRO
☐ 107. JESUS ALOU
☐ 130. BOB WATSON
☐ 139. LUIS PUJOLS
☐ 158. JOE SAMBITO
☐ 187. MARK LEMONGELLO
☐ 232. JIMMY SEXTON
☐ 268. JULIO GONZALEZ
☐ 289. JOSE CRUZ
☐ 306. FLOYD BANNISTER
☐ 327. ART HOWE
☐ 361. TOM DIXON
☐ 381. TEAM & VIRDON(M)
☐ 437. RICK WILLIAMS
☐ 471. JOAQUIN ANDUJAR
☐ 515. ENOS CABELL
☐ 534. KEN FORSCH
☐ 553. DENNY WALLING
☐ 570. CESAR CEDENO
☐ 590. J.R. RICHARD
☐ 617. TERRY PUHL
☐ 642. WILBUR HOWARD
☐ 697. DAVE BERGMAN
☐ 718. BRUCE BOCHY(P)
☐ 718. MIKE FISCHLIN(P)
☐ 718. DON PISKER(P)

KANSAS CITY ROYALS

☐ 19. LARRY GURA
☐ 26. JAMIE QUIRK
☐ 45. AL HRABOSKY

☐ 72. STEVE MINGORI
☐ 99. JOHN WATHAN
☐ 129. MARTY PATTIN
☐ 157. U.L. WASHINGTON
☐ 183. PAUL SPLITTORFF
☐ 218. DENNIS LEONARD
☐ 248. PETE LACOCK
☐ 273. JERRY TERRELL
☐ 298. RICH GALE
☐ 330. GEORGE BRETT
☐ 360. AMOS OTIS
☐ 389. JOE ZDEB
☐ 409. WILLIE WILSON
☐ 439. FRANK WHITE
☐ 451. TEAM & HERZOG(M)
☐ 476. TOM POQUETTE
☐ 490. AL COWENS
☐ 502. STEVE BRAUN
☐ 525. FREDDIE PATEK
☐ 547. CLINT HURDLE
☐ 571. DARRELL PORTER
☐ 585. HAL MCRAE
☐ 664. DOUG BIRD
☐ 707. RANDY BASS(P)
☐ 707. JIM GAUDET(P)
☐ 707. RANDY MCGILBERRY(P)

LOS ANGELES DODGERS

☐ 23. TERRY FORSTER
☐ 50. STEVE GARVEY
☐ 75. STEVE YEAGER
☐ 104. JOHNNY OATES
☐ 128. TED MARTINEZ
☐ 145. RICK RHODEN
☐ 170. DON SUTTON
☐ 190. RON CEY
☐ 228. VIC DAVALILLO
☐ 255. TOMMY JOHN
☐ 279. JERRY GROTE
☐ 290. DAVE LOPES
☐ 318. BOB WELCH
☐ 347. DOUG RAU
☐ 373. LANCE RAUTZHAN
☐ 441. LEE LACY
☐ 465. REGGIE SMITH
☐ 508. CHARLIE HOUGH
☐ 526. TEAM & LASORDA(M)
☐ 546. BILL RUSSELL
☐ 562. DUSTY BAKER
☐ 605. RICK MONDAY
☐ 641. BOBBY CASTILLO
☐ 644. MANNY MOTA
☐ 668. BILL NORTH
☐ 671. JOE FERGUSON
☐ 694. BURT HOOTON
☐ 719. PEDRO GUERRERO(P)
☐ 719. RUDY LAW(P)
☐ 719. JOE SIMPSON(P)

MILWAUKEE BREWERS

☐ 24. PAUL MOLITOR
☐ 51. RAY FOSSE
☐ 95. ROBIN YOUNT
☐ 108. EDUARDO RODRIGUEZ
☐ 133. BILL CASTRO
☐ 154. JIM GANTNER
☐ 180. LARRY HISLE
☐ 213. BILL TRAVERS
☐ 243. BUCK MARTINEZ
☐ 265. DON MONEY

☐ 303. LARY SORENSEN
☐ 325. CECIL COOPER
☐ 357. JERRY AUGUSTINE
☐ 376. GORMAN THOMAS
☐ 394. RANDY STEIN
☐ 408. CHARLIE MOORE
☐ 427. ANDY REPLOGLE
☐ 448. MOOSE HAAS
☐ 474. DICK DAVIS
☐ 519. BEN OGLIVIE
☐ 550. SAL BANDO
☐ 577. TEAM & BAMBERGER(M)
☐ 596. JIM WOHLFORD
☐ 623. BOB MCCLURE
☐ 651. MIKE CALDWELL
☐ 685. SIXTO LEZCANO
☐ 708. KEVIN BASS(P)
☐ 708. EDDIE ROMERO(P)
☐ 708. NED YOST(P)

MINNESOTA TWINS

☐ 27. DAVE GOLTZ
☐ 41. TEAM & MAUCH(M)
☐ 58. BOB RANDALL
☐ 81. ROGER ERICKSON
☐ 113. PETE REDFERN
☐ 137. LARRY WOLFE
☐ 162. TOM JOHNSON
☐ 193. GLENN ADAMS
☐ 219. ROY SMALLEY
☐ 246. DARRELL JACKSON
☐ 249. PAUL THORMODSGARD
☐ 274. WILLIE NORWOOD
☐ 300. ROD CAREW
☐ 362. MIKE CUBBAGE
☐ 371. JEFF HOLLY
☐ 385. DAN FORD
☐ 405. BUTCH WYNEGAR
☐ 431. GLENN BORGMANN
☐ 449. BOMBO RIVERA
☐ 472. CRAIG KUSICK
☐ 498. RICH CHILES
☐ 552. JOSE MORALES
☐ 627. GARY SERUM
☐ 633. ROB WILFONG
☐ 656. HOSKEN POWELL
☐ 676. JOHNNY SUTTON
☐ 678. GEOFF ZAHN
☐ 709. SAM PERLOZZO(P)
☐ 709. RICK SOFIELD(P)
☐ 709. KEVIN STANFIELD(P)

MONTREAL EXPOS

☐ 15. ROSS GRIMSLEY
☐ 43. WAYNE TWITCHELL
☐ 76. WARREN CROMARTIE
☐ 97. SAM MEJIAS
☐ 124. DAN SCHATZEDER
☐ 181. MIKE GARMAN
☐ 235. STEVE ROGERS
☐ 269. WOODIE FRYMAN
☐ 294. PEPE FRIAS
☐ 348. ANDRE DAWSON
☐ 374. ED HERRMANN
☐ 395. DAVE CASH
☐ 426. CHRIS SPEIER
☐ 468. STAN BAHNSEN
☐ 495. TONY PEREZ
☐ 520. GARY CARTER
☐ 535. ELLIS VALENTINE
☐ 581. DAROLD KNOWLES
☐ 603. RUDY MAY
☐ 606. TEAM & WILLIAMS(M)
☐ 628. DEL UNSER
☐ 652. STAN PAPI
☐ 673. TOM HUTTON
☐ 677. LARRY PARRISH
☐ 699. HAL DUES
☐ 720. JERRY FRY(P)
☐ 720. JERRY PIRTLE(P)
☐ 720. SCOTT SANDERSON(P)

NEW YORK METS

☐ 21. KEVIN KOBEL
☐ 46. RON HODGES
☐ 69. ELLIOTT MADDOX
☐ 82. TEAM & TORRE(M)
☐ 109. JOEL YOUNGBLOOD
☐ 148. BRUCE BOISCLAIR
☐ 172. MIKE BRUHERT
☐ 197. BOB APODACA
☐ 229. DOUG FLYNN
☐ 277. TOM GRIEVE

☐ 305. WILLIE MONTANEZ
☐ 334. CRAIG SWAN
☐ 355. LEE MAZZILLI
☐ 379. DALE MURRAY
☐ 397. SERGIO FERRER
☐ 403. TIM FOLI
☐ 428. BOBBY VALENTINE
☐ 445. STEVE HENDERSON
☐ 454. LEN RANDLE
☐ 481. SKIP LOCKWOOD
☐ 505. ED KRANEPOOL
☐ 545. JOHN STEARNS
☐ 566. NINO ESPINOSA
☐ 621. PAT ZACHRY
☐ 643. TOM HAUSMAN
☐ 655. JERRY KOOSMAN
☐ 721. JUAN BERENGUER(P)
☐ 721. DWIGHT BERNARD(P)
☐ 721. DAN NORMAN(P)

NEW YORK YANKEES

☐ 16. FRED STANLEY
☐ 35. ED FIGUEROA
☐ 60. MICKEY RIVERS
☐ 89. DICK TIDROW
☐ 114. CLIFF JOHNSON
☐ 140. DON GULLETT
☐ 159. ROY WHITE
☐ 179. JIM BEATTIE
☐ 225. RICH GOSSAGE
☐ 250. WILLIE RANDOLPH
☐ 278. ANDY MESSERSMITH
☐ 310. THURMAN MUNSON
☐ 335. CHRIS CHAMBLISS
☐ 365. SPARKY LYLE
☐ 387. GARY THOMASSON
☐ 434. KEN CLAY
☐ 460. GRAIG NETTLES
☐ 485. BUCKY DENT
☐ 500. RON GUIDRY
☐ 558. JAY JOHNSTONE
☐ 582. PAUL BLAIR
☐ 599. JIM SPENCER
☐ 626. TEAM & LEMON(M)
☐ 634. PAUL LINDBLAD
☐ 648. LOU PINIELLA
☐ 670. JIM HUNTER
☐ 700. REGGIE JACKSON
☐ 710. BRIAN DOYLE(P)
☐ 710. MIKE HEATH(P)
☐ 710. DAVE RAJSICH(P)

OAKLAND A'S

☐ 29. RICK LANGFORD
☐ 54. DELL ALSTON
☐ 78. ELIAS SOSA
☐ 163. GLENN BURKE
☐ 191. MIKE NORRIS
☐ 224. DAVE REVERING
☐ 261. MARIO GUERRERO
☐ 295. MITCHELL PAGE
☐ 328. TEAM & MCKEON(M)
☐ 352. STEVE RENKO
☐ 378. ROB PICCIOLO
☐ 406. JOE WALLIS
☐ 432. DAVE HEAVERLO
☐ 458. JIM ESSIAN
☐ 487. MIGUEL DILONE
☐ 507. TONY ARMAS
☐ 528. WAYNE GROSS
☐ 554. MATT KEOUGH
☐ 565. RICO CARTY
☐ 578. PETE BROBERG
☐ 604. JEFF NEWMAN
☐ 613. MIKE EDWARDS
☐ 647. BOB LACEY
☐ 658. TAYLOR DUNCAN
☐ 681. JOHN HENRY JOHNSON
☐ 711. DWAYNE MURPHY(P)
☐ 711. BRUCE ROBINSON(P)
☐ 711. ALAN WIRTH(P)

PHILADELPHIA PHILLIES

☐ 25. STEVE CARLTON
☐ 52. RANDY LERCH
☐ 90. BOB BOONE
☐ 112. TEAM & OZARK(M)

☐ 118. BUD HARRELSON
☐ 136. JIM KAAT
☐ 161. BARRY FOOTE
☐ 177. RON REED
☐ 210. LARRY BOWA
☐ 271. RAWLY EASTWICK
☐ 297. TED SIZEMORE
☐ 317. JOSE CARDENAL
☐ 345. TUG MCGRAW
☐ 382. JERRY MARTIN
☐ 419. DICK RUTHVEN
☐ 446. JIM LONBORG
☐ 470. GARRY MADDOX
☐ 493. LARRY CHRISTENSON
☐ 540. GREG LUZINSKI
☐ 567. RICH HEBNER
☐ 610. MIKE SCHMIDT
☐ 630. BAKE MCBRIDE
☐ 653. WARREN BRUSSTAR
☐ 675. TIM MCCARVER
☐ 722. JIM MORRISON(P)
☐ 722. LONNIE SMITH(P)
☐ 722. JIM L. WRIGHT(P)

PITTSBURGH PIRATES

☐ 28. STEVE BRYE
☐ 55. WILLIE STARGELL
☐ 70. JOHN CANDELARIA
☐ 92. JIM BIBBY
☐ 117. GRANT JACKSON
☐ 147. DAVE HAMILTON
☐ 165. FRANK TAVERAS
☐ 189. EDDIE WHITSON
☐ 208. CLARENCE GASTON
☐ 223. KENT TEKULVE
☐ 244. TEAM & TANNER(M)
☐ 264. DON ROBINSON
☐ 286. DUFFY DYER
☐ 308. BERT BLYLEVEN
☐ 383. PHIL GARNER
☐ 430. DAVE PARKER
☐ 447. MANNY SANGUILLEN
☐ 509. MARIO MENDOZA
☐ 523. JOHN MILNER
☐ 536. JERRY REUSS
☐ 561. ED OTT
☐ 584. JIM ROOKER
☐ 607. OMAR MORENO
☐ 637. BILL ROBINSON
☐ 661. BRUCE KISON
☐ 687. RENNIE STENNETT
☐ 723. DALE BERRA(P)
☐ 723. EUGENIO COTES(P)
☐ 723. BEN WILTBANK(P)

ST. LOUIS CARDINALS

☐ 32. JERRY MUMPHREY
☐ 59. JOHN DENNY
☐ 87. PETE FALCONE
☐ 111. ROGER FREED
☐ 143. TONY SCOTT
☐ 175. GEORGE HENDRICK
☐ 192. TEAM & BOYER(M)
☐ 230. BOB FORSCH
☐ 258. MIKE PHILLIPS
☐ 304. STEVE SWISHER
☐ 319. WAYNE GARRETT
☐ 324. MIKE TYSON
☐ 350. GARRY TEMPLETON
☐ 407. PETE VUCKOVICH
☐ 429. JOHN URREA
☐ 444. AURELIO LOPEZ
☐ 452. JERRY MORALES
☐ 466. MARK LITTELL
☐ 510. TED SIMMONS
☐ 532. BUDDY SCHULTZ
☐ 563. ROY THOMAS
☐ 587. KEN REITZ
☐ 609. SILVIO MARTINEZ
☐ 665. LOU BROCK
☐ 695. KEITH HERNANDEZ
☐ 724. TOM BRUNO(P)
☐ 724. GEORGE FRAZIER(P)
☐ 724. TERRY KENNEDY(P)

SAN DIEGO PADRES

☐ 30. DAVE WINFIELD
☐ 57. ERIC RASMUSSEN
☐ 116. OZZIE SMITH

☐ 138. MARK LEE
☐ 164. MICKEY LOLICH
☐ 194. RANDY JONES
☐ 247. TUCKER ASHFORD
☐ 263. OSCAR GAMBLE
☐ 292. DON REYNOLDS
☐ 321. GAYLORD PERRY
☐ 342. DAVE W. ROBERTS
☐ 364. GENE RICHARDS
☐ 390. ROLLIE FINGERS
☐ 435. GENE TENACE
☐ 456. CHUCK BAKER
☐ 479. TEAM & CRAIG(M)
☐ 488. BOB OWCHINKO
☐ 506. JOHN D'ACQUISTO
☐ 531. FERNANDO GONZALEZ
☐ 564. JERRY TURNER
☐ 594. BOB SHIRLEY
☐ 616. BILLY ALMON
☐ 646. RICK SWEET
☐ 679. DERREL THOMAS
☐ 725. JIM BESWICK(P)
☐ 725. STEVE MURA(P)
☐ 725. BRODERICK PERKINS(P)

SAN FRANCISCO GIANTS

☐ 11. MARC HILL
☐ 34. ROB ANDREWS
☐ 62. RANDY MOFFITT
☐ 84. GREG MINTON
☐ 110. VIDA BLUE
☐ 142. CHARLIE WILLIAMS
☐ 167. ROGER METZGER
☐ 195. BILL MADLOCK
☐ 215. WILLIE MCCOVEY
☐ 236. JIM DWYER
☐ 256. MIKE SADEK
☐ 284. JOHNNIE LEMASTER
☐ 311. GARY LAVELLE
☐ 338. VIC HARRIS
☐ 356. TEAM & ALTOBELLI(M)
☐ 410. DARRELL EVANS
☐ 436. HECTOR CRUZ
☐ 461. JIM BARR
☐ 486. BOB KNEPPER
☐ 512. JACK CLARK
☐ 538. MIKE IVIE
☐ 560. JOHN MONTEFUSCO
☐ 589. TERRY WHITFIELD
☐ 624. LARRY HERNDON
☐ 649. JOHN CURTIS
☐ 672. ED HALICKI
☐ 726. GREG JOHNSTON(P)
☐ 726. JOE STRAIN(P)
☐ 726. JOHN TAMARGO(P)

SEATTLE MARINERS

☐ 31. TOM HOUSE
☐ 56. JOHN HALE
☐ 74. SHANE RAWLEY
☐ 103. JIM TODD
☐ 141. TOM PACIOREK
☐ 166. LEON ROBERTS
☐ 199. LARRY MILBOURNE
☐ 233. PAUL MITCHELL
☐ 252. BOB STINSON
☐ 276. JIM COLBORN ·
☐ 312. BOB ROBERTSON
☐ 337. JOHN MONTAGUE
☐ 366. JUAN BERNHARDT
☐ 396. BILL PLUMMER
☐ 422. RUPPERT JONES
☐ 443. BRUCE BOCHTE
☐ 482. CRAIG REYNOLDS
☐ 497. GLENN ABBOTT
☐ 533. LEROY STANTON
☐ 548. ENRIQUE ROMO
☐ 576. MIKE PARROTT
☐ 583. JULIO CRUZ
☐ 612. RICK HONEYCUTT
☐ 659. TEAM & JOHNSON(M)
☐ 683. DAN MEYER
☐ 698. BILL STEIN
☐ 712. BUD ANDERSON(P)
☐ 712. GREG BIERCEVICZ(P)
☐ 712. BYRON MCLAUGHLIN(P)

RANGERS

TEXAS RANGERS

- [ ] 22. MIKE JORGENSEN
- [ ] 44. KURT BEVACQUA
- [ ] 67. JIM MASON
- [ ] 94. LEN BARKER
- [ ] 120. JIM SUNDBERG
- [ ] 144. SANDY ALOMAR
- [ ] 173. JOHN LOWENSTEIN
- [ ] 198. JOHNNY GRUBB
- [ ] 209. REGGIE CLEVELAND
- [ ] 234. TOBY HARRAH
- [ ] 260. RICHIE ZISK
- [ ] 285. BOBBY BONDS
- [ ] 315. JON MATLACK
- [ ] 336. BOBBY THOMPSON
- [ ] 369. BUMP WILLS
- [ ] 391. AL OLIVER
- [ ] 442. DOYLE ALEXANDER
- [ ] 463. STEVE COMER
- [ ] 478. JUAN BENIQUEZ
- [ ] 499. TEAM & CORRALES(M)
- [ ] 518. JIM UMBARGER
- [ ] 539. JOHN ELLIS
- [ ] 544. FERGIE JENKINS
- [ ] 591. MIKE HARGROVE
- [ ] 620. BERT CAMPANERIS
- [ ] 657. GEORGE MEDICH
- [ ] 691. DOCK ELLIS
- [ ] 713. DANNY DARWIN(P)
- [ ] 713. PAT PUTNAM(P)
- [ ] 713. BILLY SAMPLE(P)

TORONTO BLUE JAYS

- [ ] 36. ALAN ASHBY
- [ ] 64. TOM UNDERWOOD
- [ ] 101. ROY HOWELL
- [ ] 131. JIM CLANCY
- [ ] 152. RICK CERONE
- [ ] 178. ALVIS WOODS
- [ ] 182. TIM JOHNSON
- [ ] 207. DAVE LEMANCZYK
- [ ] 221. JESSE JEFFERSON
- [ ] 238. BALOR MOORE
- [ ] 239. WILLIE HORTON
- [ ] 254. LUIS GOMEZ
- [ ] 282. TEAM & HARTSFIELD(M)
- [ ] 293. JERRY GARVIN
- [ ] 329. JOE COLEMAN
- [ ] 341. WILLIE UPSHAW
- [ ] 380. JOHN MAYBERRY
- [ ] 392. DOUG AULT
- [ ] 462. OTTO VELEZ
- [ ] 492. BOB BAILOR
- [ ] 521. SAM EWING
- [ ] 542. RICK BOSETTI
- [ ] 588. TOM MURPHY
- [ ] 608. DAVE MCKAY
- [ ] 632. DON KIRKWOOD
- [ ] 688. MIKE WILLIS
- [ ] 714. VICTOR CRUZ(P)
- [ ] 714. D. PAT KELLY(P)
- [ ] 714. ERNIE WHITT(P)

1980 TOPPS (726) 2 1/2" X 3 1/2"

OUTFIELD RICK MONDAY

DODGERS

ATLANTA BRAVES

- [ ] 7. MIKE LUM
- [ ] 39. ROWLAND OFFICE
- [ ] 64. JOE NOLAN
- [ ] 87. PEPE FRIAS
- [ ] 108. BOB HORNER
- [ ] 132. BIFF POCOROBA
- [ ] 156. TONY BRIZZOLARA
- [ ] 192. TEAM & COX(M)
- [ ] 245. PHIL NIEKRO
- [ ] 274. DALE MURPHY
- [ ] 294. CHARLIE SPIKES
- [ ] 309. LARRY MCWILLIAMS
- [ ] 326. BO MCLAUGHLIN
- [ ] 346. BUDDY SOLOMON
- [ ] 355. GARY MATTHEWS
- [ ] 384. JOEY MCLAUGHLIN
- [ ] 463. JERRY ROYSTER
- [ ] 489. PRESTON HANNA
- [ ] 504. GENE GARBER
- [ ] 528. ADRIAN DEVINE
- [ ] 545. JEFF BURROUGHS
- [ ] 596. RICK MATULA
- [ ] 632. BARRY BONNELL
- [ ] 675. BRUCE BENEDICT(FS)
- [ ] 675. LARRY BRADFORD(FS)
- [ ] 675. EDDIE MILLER(FS)

BALTIMORE ORIOLES

- [ ] 10. DENNY MARTINEZ
- [ ] 37. KIKO GARCIA
- [ ] 65. AL BUMBRY
- [ ] 91. RICK DEMPSEY
- [ ] 102. RICH DAUER
- [ ] 119. SAMMY STEWART
- [ ] 160. EDDIE MURRAY
- [ ] 188. TERRY CROWLEY
- [ ] 211. DAVE SKAGGS
- [ ] 237. SCOTT MCGREGOR
- [ ] 262. BENNY AYALA
- [ ] 287. JOHN LOWENSTEIN
- [ ] 314. TIM STODDARD
- [ ] 340. KEN SINGLETON
- [ ] 367. BILLY SMITH
- [ ] 404. TEAM & WEAVER(M)
- [ ] 425. MARK BELANGER
- [ ] 490. LEE MAY
- [ ] 517. DON STANHOUSE
- [ ] 543. H. PAT KELLY
- [ ] 568. GARY ROENICKE
- [ ] 590. JIM PALMER
- [ ] 615. DOUG DECINCES
- [ ] 640. MIKE FLANAGAN
- [ ] 661. MARK COREY(FS)
- [ ] 661. DAVE FORD(FS)
- [ ] 661. WAYNE KRENCHICKI(FS)
- [ ] 688. STEVE STONE
- [ ] 706. TIPPY MARTINEZ

BOSTON RED SOX

- [ ] 15. BILL CAMPBELL
- [ ] 40. CARLTON FISK
- [ ] 63. BOB STANLEY

- [ ] 81. TED SIZEMORE
- [ ] 110. FRED LYNN
- [ ] 128. TOM BURGMEIER
- [ ] 155. JERRY REMY
- [ ] 184. STEVE RENKO
- [ ] 200. JIM RICE
- [ ] 271. DICK DRAGO
- [ ] 320. DENNIS ECKERSLEY
- [ ] 349. JACK BROHAMER
- [ ] 376. GARY ALLENSON
- [ ] 405. DWIGHT EVANS
- [ ] 413. ALLEN RIPLEY
- [ ] 420. BUTCH HOBSON
- [ ] 455. MIKE TORREZ
- [ ] 480. BOB WATSON
- [ ] 524. JIM C. WRIGHT
- [ ] 549. LARRY WOLFE
- [ ] 576. JIM DWYER
- [ ] 597. TOM POQUETTE
- [ ] 618. BOB MONTGOMERY
- [ ] 645. RICK BURLESON
- [ ] 662. JOEL FINCH(FS)
- [ ] 662. MIKE O'BERRY(FS)
- [ ] 662. CHUCK RAINEY(FS)
- [ ] 689. TEAM & ZIMMER(M)
- [ ] 720. CARL YASTRZEMSKI

CALIFORNIA ANGELS

- [ ] 20. DAN FORD
- [ ] 48. RICK MILLER
- [ ] 68. LARRY HARLOW
- [ ] 105. FRANK TANANA
- [ ] 183. JIM ANDERSON
- [ ] 214. TEAM & FREGOSI(M)
- [ ] 239. DON AASE
- [ ] 253. JOHN MONTAGUE
- [ ] 263. DAVE LAROCHE
- [ ] 285. DON BAYLOR
- [ ] 312. MIKE BARLOW
- [ ] 337. CARNEY LANSFORD
- [ ] 368. WILLIE AIKENS
- [ ] 402. MERV RETTENMUND
- [ ] 423. DAVE FROST
- [ ] 454. TOM DONOHUE
- [ ] 505. BERT CAMPANERIS
- [ ] 529. JIM BARR
- [ ] 556. JOE RUDI
- [ ] 580. NOLAN RYAN
- [ ] 602. BRIAN DOWNING
- [ ] 621. BOB GRICH
- [ ] 638. MARK CLEAR
- [ ] 658. CHRIS KNAPP
- [ ] 663. RALPH BOTTING(FS)
- [ ] 663. BOB CLARK(FS)
- [ ] 663. DICKIE THON(FS)
- [ ] 700. ROD CAREW

CHICAGO CUBS

- [ ] 17. BRUCE SUTTER
- [ ] 54. DENNIS LAMP
- [ ] 103. BILL CAUDILL
- [ ] 135. BILL BUCKNER
- [ ] 153. TIM BLACKWELL
- [ ] 175. RICK REUSCHEL
- [ ] 240. DAVE KINGMAN
- [ ] 298. KEN HOLTZMAN
- [ ] 232. MICK KELLEHER
- [ ] 343. MIKE VAIL
- [ ] 381. TEAM & GOMEZ(M)
- [ ] 398. BARRY FOOTE
- [ ] 431. MIKE KRUKOW
- [ ] 452. STEVE DILLARD
- [ ] 472. WILLIE HERNANDEZ
- [ ] 493. JERRY MARTIN
- [ ] 514. STEVE ONTIVEROS
- [ ] 523. KEN HENDERSON
- [ ] 541. MIGUEL DILONE
- [ ] 574. SCOT THOMPSON
- [ ] 594. DICK TIDROW
- [ ] 628. DOUG CAPILLA
- [ ] 639. LARRY BIITTNER
- [ ] 676. DAVE GEISEL(FS)
- [ ] 676. STEVE MACKO(FS)
- [ ] 676. KARL PAGEL(FS)
- [ ] 691. IVAN DEJESUS
- [ ] 716. LYNN MCGLOTHEN

1980 Topps

CHICAGO WHITE SOX

- ☐ 36. RUSTY TORRES
- ☐ 72. FRED HOWARD
- ☐ 83. STEVE TROUT
- ☐ 107. FRANCISCO BARRIOS
- ☐ 112. TEAM & LARUSSA(M)
- ☐ 138. ROSS BAUMGARTEN
- ☐ 164. GREG PRYOR
- ☐ 186. JUNIOR MOORE
- ☐ 242. LAMAR JOHNSON
- ☐ 272. RALPH GARR
- ☐ 291. RANDY SCARBERY
- ☐ 322. CLAUDELL WASHINGTON
- ☐ 347. HARRY CHAPPAS
- ☐ 379. KEVIN BELL
- ☐ 399. MIKE PROLY
- ☐ 412. THAD BOSLEY
- ☐ 442. JORGE ORTA
- ☐ 466. MIKE SQUIRES
- ☐ 487. WAYNE NORDHAGEN
- ☐ 502. RICH WORTHAM
- ☐ 522. JIM MORRISON
- ☐ 552. BILL NAHORODNY
- ☐ 575. KEN KRAVEC
- ☐ 589. CHET LEMON
- ☐ 608. ALAN BANNISTER
- ☐ 647. MILT MAY
- ☐ 664. MIKE COLBERN(FS)
- ☐ 664. GUY HOFFMAN(FS)
- ☐ 664. DEWEY ROBINSON(FS)
- ☐ 702. ED FARMER

CINCINNATI REDS

- ☐ 21. MANNY SARMIENTO
- ☐ 47. BILL BONHAM
- ☐ 73. DAVE COLLINS
- ☐ 100. JOHNNY BENCH
- ☐ 126. DAVE TOMLIN
- ☐ 149. TOM HUME
- ☐ 174. RAY KNIGHT
- ☐ 199. MIKE LACOSS
- ☐ 220. DAVE CONCEPCION
- ☐ 258. PAUL MOSKAU
- ☐ 281. PAUL BLAIR
- ☐ 325. DAN DRIESSEN
- ☐ 354. RICK AUERBACH
- ☐ 377. JUNIOR KENNEDY
- ☐ 400. GEORGE FOSTER
- ☐ 419. VIC CORRELL
- ☐ 449. DOUG BAIR
- ☐ 475. CESAR GERONIMO
- ☐ 500. TOM SEAVER
- ☐ 516. HECTOR CRUZ
- ☐ 550. KEN GRIFFEY
- ☐ 606. TEAM & MCNAMARA(M)
- ☐ 622. MARIO SOTO
- ☐ 650. JOE MORGAN
- ☐ 677. ART DEFREITES(FS)
- ☐ 677. FRANK PASTORE(FS)
- ☐ 677. HARRY SPILMAN(FS)
- ☐ 714. FRED NORMAN

CLEVELAND INDIANS

- ☐ 13. RON PRUITT
- ☐ 38. DAN SPILLNER
- ☐ 74. SID MONGE
- ☐ 99. VICTOR CRUZ
- ☐ 122. DAVE ROSELLO
- ☐ 141. GARY ALEXANDER
- ☐ 168. RICK WAITS
- ☐ 198. DELL ALSTON
- ☐ 208. WAYNE CAGE
- ☐ 222. RON HASSEY
- ☐ 227. LEN BARKER
- ☐ 252. TED COX
- ☐ 276. TOM VERYZER
- ☐ 308. MIKE HARGROVE
- ☐ 333. JIM NORRIS
- ☐ 361. WAYNE GARLAND
- ☐ 388. MIKE PAXTON
- ☐ 410. BOBBY BONDS
- ☐ 429. DUANE KUIPER
- ☐ 451. TEAM & GARCIA(M)
- ☐ 483. BO DIAZ
- ☐ 511. ERIC WILKINS
- ☐ 534. ANDRE THORNTON
- ☐ 564. RICK MANNING
- ☐ 612. CLIFF JOHNSON

- ☐ 636. TOBY HARRAH
- ☐ 665. LARRY ANDERSEN(FS)
- ☐ 665. BOBBY CUELLAR(FS)
- ☐ 665. SANDY WIHTOL(FS)
- ☐ 697. DAVID CLYDE
- ☐ 725. RICK WISE

DETROIT TIGERS

- ☐ 29. MARK WAGNER
- ☐ 59. EDDY PUTMAN
- ☐ 80. RON LEFLORE
- ☐ 101. AURELIO LOPEZ
- ☐ 123. LYNN JONES
- ☐ 150. JASON THOMPSON
- ☐ 176. CHAMP SUMMER
- ☐ 196. LANCE PARRISH
- ☐ 216. PHIL MANKOWSKI
- ☐ 232. ALAN TRAMMELL
- ☐ 251. KIP YOUNG
- ☐ 269. DAVE TOBIK
- ☐ 288. DAVE ROZEMA
- ☐ 315. STEVE KEMP
- ☐ 338. JOHNNY WOCKENFUSS
- ☐ 358. LOU WHITAKER
- ☐ 371. JACK MORRIS
- ☐ 373. DAN PETRY
- ☐ 392. MILT WILCOX
- ☐ 416. TOM BROOKENS
- ☐ 445. MARK FIDRYCH
- ☐ 468. AURELIO RODRIGUEZ
- ☐ 572. JERRY MORALES
- ☐ 603. JACK BILLINGHAM
- ☐ 614. JOHN HILLER
- ☐ 626. TEAM & ANDERSON(M)
- ☐ 666. MIKE CHRIS(FS)
- ☐ 666. AL GREENE(FS)
- ☐ 666. BRUCE ROBBINS(FS)
- ☐ 709. PAT UNDERWOOD

HOUSTON ASTROS

- ☐ 11. JIMMY SEXTON
- ☐ 50. J.R. RICHARD
- ☐ 69. RICK WILLIAMS
- ☐ 82. TEAM & VIRDON(M)
- ☐ 106. JEFF LEONARD
- ☐ 129. CRAIG REYNOLDS
- ☐ 147. TERRY PUHL
- ☐ 187. ALAN ASHBY
- ☐ 234. VERN RUHLE
- ☐ 247. FRANK RICCELLI
- ☐ 268. RAFAEL LANDESTOY
- ☐ 289. BRUCE BOCHY
- ☐ 306. DENNY WALLING
- ☐ 329. BERT ROBERGE
- ☐ 370. CESAR CEDENO
- ☐ 385. ENOS CABELL
- ☐ 411. FRANK LACORTE
- ☐ 437. JOE NIEKRO
- ☐ 469. RANDY NIEMANN
- ☐ 513. TOM DIXON
- ☐ 554. ART HOWE
- ☐ 571. JOE SAMBITO
- ☐ 593. JESUS ALOU
- ☐ 617. JOAQUIN ANDUJAR
- ☐ 642. KEN FORSCH
- ☐ 678. REGGIE BALDWIN(FS)
- ☐ 678. ALAN KNICELY(FS)
- ☐ 678. PETE LADD(FS)
- ☐ 696. JULIO GONZALEZ
- ☐ 722. JOSE CRUZ

KANSAS CITY ROYALS

- ☐ 9. STEVE BRAUN
- ☐ 26. MARTY PATTIN
- ☐ 45. FRANK WHITE
- ☐ 66. TEAM CARD
- ☐ 98. JERRY TERRELL
- ☐ 130. AMOS OTIS
- ☐ 157. WILLIE WILSON
- ☐ 185. HAL MCRAE
- ☐ 219. STEVE MINGORI
- ☐ 248. JAMIE QUIRK
- ☐ 273. EDUARDO RODRIGUEZ
- ☐ 295. LARRY GURA
- ☐ 330. AL COWENS
- ☐ 360. DARRELL PORTER
- ☐ 389. PETE LACOCK
- ☐ 409. PAUL SPLITTORFF

- ☐ 417. CRAIG CHAMBERLAIN
- ☐ 433. RICH GALE
- ☐ 450. GEORGE BRETT
- ☐ 474. STEVE BUSBY
- ☐ 492. TODD CRUZ
- ☐ 508. U.L. WASHINGTON
- ☐ 525. CLINT HURDLE
- ☐ 547. JOHN WATHAN
- ☐ 565. DENNIS LEONARD
- ☐ 585. AL HRABOSKY
- ☐ 667. RENIE MARTIN(FS)
- ☐ 667. BILL PASCHALL(FS)
- ☐ 667. DAN QUISENBERRY(FS)
- ☐ 705. FREDDIE PATEK

LOS ANGELES DODGERS

- ☐ 23. DERREL THOMAS
- ☐ 51. JOE FERGUSON
- ☐ 75. BILL RUSSELL
- ☐ 104. MANNY MOTA
- ☐ 127. GARY THOMASSON
- ☐ 146. BOB WELCH
- ☐ 170. BURT HOOTON
- ☐ 191. TED MARTINEZ
- ☐ 209. VON JOSHUA
- ☐ 228. JOHNNY OATES
- ☐ 255. DUSTY BAKER
- ☐ 290. STEVE GARVEY
- ☐ 302. TEAM & LASORDA(M)
- ☐ 318. JERRY REUSS
- ☐ 440. DON SUTTON
- ☐ 465. RICK MONDAY
- ☐ 510. RON CEY
- ☐ 521. KEN BRETT
- ☐ 527. DOUG RAU
- ☐ 544. RICK SUTCLIFFE
- ☐ 560. DAVE LOPES
- ☐ 605. TERRY FORSTER
- ☐ 624. LERRIN LAGROW
- ☐ 644. CHARLIE HOUGH
- ☐ 679. JOE BECKWITH(FS)
- ☐ 679. MICKEY HATCHER(FS)
- ☐ 679. DAVE PATTERSON(FS)
- ☐ 695. REGGIE SMITH
- ☐ 726. STEVE YEAGER

MILWAUKEE BREWERS

- ☐ 24. JIM SLATON
- ☐ 53. BEN OGLIVIE
- ☐ 95. CECIL COOPER
- ☐ 109. BILL TRAVERS
- ☐ 131. PAUL MITCHELL
- ☐ 154. LARY SORENSEN
- ☐ 181. MOOSE HAAS
- ☐ 215. SIXTO LEZCANO
- ☐ 243. JERRY AUGUSTINE
- ☐ 265. ROBIN YOUNT
- ☐ 303. BILL CASTRO
- ☐ 327. RAY FOSSE
- ☐ 357. BOB MCCLURE
- ☐ 374. JIM GANTNER
- ☐ 394. REGGIE CLEVELAND
- ☐ 406. PAUL MOLITOR
- ☐ 430. LARRY HISLE
- ☐ 448. JIM WOHLFORD
- ☐ 477. BUCK MARTINEZ
- ☐ 515. MIKE CALDWELL
- ☐ 553. DICK DAVIS
- ☐ 579. CHARLIE MOORE
- ☐ 595. DON MONEY
- ☐ 623. GORMAN THOMAS
- ☐ 659. TEAM & BAMBERGER(M)
- ☐ 668. DANNY BOITANO(FS)
- ☐ 668. WILLIE MUELLER(FS)
- ☐ 668. LENN SAKATA(FS)
- ☐ 711. BOB GALASSO
- ☐ 715. SAL BANDO

MINNESOTA TWINS

- ☐ 18. RON JACKSON
- ☐ 43. BOMBO RIVERA
- ☐ 61. GARY SERUM
- ☐ 88. KEN LANDREAUX
- ☐ 113. GEOFF ZAHN
- ☐ 137. JOHN CASTINO
- ☐ 162. BOB RANDALL
- ☐ 193. DAVE GOLTZ

☐ 218. JOSE MORALES
☐ 238. ROB WILFONG
☐ 256. ROGER ERICKSON
☐ 275. JERRY KOOSMAN
☐ 304. BUTCH WYNEGAR
☐ 328. TEAM & MAUCH(M)
☐ 362. DANNY GOODWIN
☐ 386. DARRELL JACKSON
☐ 403. PETE REDFERN
☐ 432. WILLIE NORWOOD
☐ 453. MIKE BACSIK
☐ 471. HOSKEN POWELL
☐ 503. MIKE CUBBAGE
☐ 570. ROY SMALLEY
☐ 604. GLENN ADAMS
☐ 634. GLENN BORGMANN
☐ 657. DAVE EDWARDS
☐ 669. DAN GRAHAM(FS)
☐ 669. RICK SOFIELD(FS)
☐ 669. GARY WARD(FS)
☐ 721. PAUL HARTZELL

MONTREAL EXPOS

☐ 14. DAVE CASH
☐ 42. DAVE PALMER
☐ 70. GARY CARTER
☐ 97. BILL LEE
☐ 125. TONY PEREZ
☐ 180. WARREN CROMARTIE
☐ 235. ANDRE DAWSON
☐ 267. DAN SCHATZEDER
☐ 293. ELIAS SOSA
☐ 319. CHRIS SPEIER
☐ 345. LARRY PARRISH
☐ 375. ROSS GRIMSLEY
☐ 395. ELLIS VALENTINE
☐ 415. BILL ATKINSON
☐ 427. TOM HUTTON
☐ 446. DUFFY DYER
☐ 479. TEAM & WILLIAMS(M)
☐ 497. JIM MASON
☐ 520. STEVE ROGERS
☐ 539. RUDY MAY
☐ 559. DALE MURRAY
☐ 578. SCOTT SANDERSON
☐ 607. WOODIE FRYMAN
☐ 653. STAN BAHNSEN
☐ 660. RUSTY STAUB
☐ 680. TONY BERNAZARD(FS)
☐ 680. RANDY MILLER(FS)
☐ 680. JOHN TAMARGO(FS)
☐ 712. RODNEY SCOTT
☐ 724. JERRY WHITE

NEW YORK METS

☐ 8. CRAIG SWAN
☐ 25. LEE MAZZILLI
☐ 58. DOUG FLYNN
☐ 76. JOHN STEARNS
☐ 94. NEIL ALLEN
☐ 117. DOCK ELLIS
☐ 151. TOM HAUSMAN
☐ 172. RON HODGES
☐ 189. KEVIN KOBEL
☐ 259. TEAM & TORRE(M)
☐ 299. STEVE HENDERSON
☐ 331. RICH HEBNER
☐ 353. ANDY HASSLER
☐ 364. RAY BURRIS

☐ 372. JOEL YOUNGBLOOD
☐ 401. PETE FALCONE
☐ 428. PAT ZACHRY
☐ 456. FRANK TAVERAS
☐ 478. GIL FLORES
☐ 509. ED GLYNN
☐ 512. JOSE CARDENAL
☐ 537. ALEX TREVINO
☐ 567. SKIP LOCKWOOD
☐ 619. SERGIO FERRER
☐ 633. BOB APODACA
☐ 641. ED KRANEPOOL
☐ 654. BRUCE BOISCLAIR
☐ 681. DAN NORMAN(FS)
☐ 681. JESSE OROSCO(FS)
☐ 681. MIKE SCOTT(FS)
☐ 707. ELLIOTT MADDOX

NEW YORK YANKEES

☐ 16. JERRY NARRON
☐ 35. LUIS TIANT
☐ 60. BUCKY DENT
☐ 89. DON HOOD
☐ 114. JUAN BENIQUEZ
☐ 140. RICH GOSSAGE
☐ 159. KEN CLAY
☐ 179. RON DAVIS
☐ 225. LOU PINIELLA
☐ 250. JIM KAAT
☐ 278. JIM SPENCER
☐ 300. RON GUIDRY
☐ 334. JIM BEATTIE
☐ 365. BOBBY MURCER
☐ 387. FRED STANLEY
☐ 414. GEORGE SCOTT
☐ 424. TEAM & HOWSER(M)
☐ 435. DON GULLETT
☐ 460. WILLIE RANDOLPH
☐ 555. ED FIGUEROA
☐ 582. BRAIN DOYLE
☐ 600. REGGIE JACKSON
☐ 625. CHRIS CHAMBLISS
☐ 648. ROY WHITE
☐ 670. BOBBY BROWN(FS)
☐ 670. BRAD GULDEN(FS)
☐ 670. DARRYL JONES(FS)
☐ 690. TOMMY JOHN
☐ 698. OSCAR GAMBLE
☐ 710. GRAIG NETTLES

OAKLAND A'S

☐ 34. JEFF NEWMAN
☐ 49. MARIO GUERRERO
☐ 86. DAVE HAMILTON
☐ 96. TEAM & MARSHALL(M)
☐ 134. MATT KEOUGH
☐ 158. ROB PICCIOLO
☐ 177. DAVE HEAVERLO
☐ 231. STEVE MCCATTY
☐ 261. DAVE CHALK
☐ 284. LARRY MURRAY
☐ 301. MIKE EDWARDS
☐ 316. BOB LACEY
☐ 341. JIM ESSIAN
☐ 363. WAYNE GROSS
☐ 391. TONY ARMAS
☐ 438. DAVE REVERING
☐ 461. DWAYNE MURPHY
☐ 482. RICKEY HENDERSON
☐ 494. CRAIG MINETTO
☐ 546. RICK LANGFORD
☐ 562. JOE WALLIS
☐ 586. MITCHELL PAGE
☐ 599. MIKE NORRIS
☐ 629. JIM TODD
☐ 671. DEREK BRYANT(FS)
☐ 671. BRIAN KINGMAN(FS)
☐ 671. MIKE MORGAN(FS)
☐ 687. MIKE HEATH
☐ 717. MICKEY KLUTTS

PHILADELPHIA PHILLIES

☐ 27. DEL UNSER
☐ 52. WARREN BRUSSTAR
☐ 90. MANNY TRILLO
☐ 120. GREG LUZINSKI
☐ 136. DICK RUTHVEN
☐ 161. LARRY CHRISTENSON

☐ 178. TIM MCCARVER
☐ 210. STEVE CARLTON
☐ 270. MIKE SCHMIDT
☐ 296. DAVE RADER
☐ 317. MIKE ANDERSON
☐ 344. RANDY LERCH
☐ 380. GARRY MADDOX
☐ 421. DOUG BIRD
☐ 447. NINO ESPINOSA
☐ 470. BOB BOONE
☐ 495. BAKE MCBRIDE
☐ 526. TEAM & GREEN(M)
☐ 540. PETE ROSE
☐ 566. BUD HARRELSON
☐ 609. RON REED
☐ 630. LARRY BOWA
☐ 655. TUG MCGRAW
☐ 682. RAMON AVILES(FS)
☐ 682. DICKIE NOLES(FS)
☐ 682. KEVIN SAUCIER(FS)
☐ 692. RAWLY EASTWICK
☐ 718. GREG GROSS

PITTSBURGH PIRATES

☐ 28. BRUCE KISON
☐ 55. BILL MADLOCK
☐ 71. JOHN MILNER
☐ 92. RICK RHODEN
☐ 118. PHIL GARNER
☐ 148. MANNY SANGUILLEN
☐ 165. OMAR MORENO
☐ 194. MIKE EASLER
☐ 212. DAVE A. ROBERTS
☐ 229. JIM BIBBY
☐ 246. TIM FOLI
☐ 264. BILL ROBINSON
☐ 292. DALE BERRA
☐ 310. DAVE PARKER
☐ 332. ENRIQUE ROMO
☐ 383. ED OTT
☐ 426. GRANT JACKSON
☐ 457. BERT BLYLEVEN
☐ 501. RENNIE STENNETT
☐ 519. STEVE NICOSIA
☐ 536. LEE LACY
☐ 542. JOE COLEMAN
☐ 551. TEAM & TANNER(M)
☐ 573. KENT TEKULVE
☐ 610. WILLIE STARGELL
☐ 635. JOHN CANDELARIA
☐ 683. DORIAN BOYLAND(FS)
☐ 683. ALBERTO LOIS(FS)
☐ 683. HERRY SAFERIGHT(FS)
☐ 694. JIM ROOKER
☐ 719. DON ROBINSON

ST. LOUIS CARDINALS

☐ 33. TONY SCOTT
☐ 57. PETE VUCKOVICH
☐ 85. TED SIMMONS
☐ 139. DANE IORG
☐ 152. JOHN FULGHAM
☐ 163. STEVE SWISHER
☐ 182. KEN REITZ
☐ 223. BOB SYKES
☐ 244. TEAM & BOYER(M)
☐ 266. BERNIE CARBO
☐ 286. DAROLD KNOWLES
☐ 321. KEITH HERNANDEZ
☐ 350. GEORGE HENDRICK
☐ 378. JERRY MUMPHREY
☐ 397. ROY THOMAS
☐ 418. ROGER FREED
☐ 439. MIKE PHILLIPS
☐ 464. JOHN DENNY
☐ 486. MIKE TYSON
☐ 496. SILVIO MARTINEZ
☐ 535. BOB FORSCH
☐ 563. WILL MCEANEY
☐ 569. TERRY KENNEDY
☐ 587. GARRY TEMPLETON
☐ 601. BUDDY SCHULTZ
☐ 631. MARK LITTELL
☐ 684. GEORGE FRAZIER(FS)
☐ 684. TOM HERR(FS)
☐ 684. DAN O'BRIEN(FS)
☐ 701. KEN OBERKFELL

SAN DIEGO PADRES

- ☐ 31. JAY JOHNSTONE
- ☐ 44. BILL FAHEY
- ☐ 79. BOB OWCHINKO
- ☐ 133. JERRY TURNER
- ☐ 171. FERNANDO GONZALEZ
- ☐ 230. DAVE WINFIELD
- ☐ 254. PAUL DADE
- ☐ 280. GAYLORD PERRY
- ☐ 305. RANDY JONES
- ☐ 339. JOHN D'ACQUISTO
- ☐ 352. DAN BRIGGS
- ☐ 356. TEAM & COLEMAN(M)
- ☐ 393. OZZIE SMITH
- ☐ 436. BILLY ALMON
- ☐ 459. MICKEY LOLICH
- ☐ 476. BOB SHIRLEY
- ☐ 491. STEVE MURA
- ☐ 531. ERIC RASMUSSEN
- ☐ 557. MARK LEE
- ☐ 584. KURT BEVACQUA
- ☐ 598. FRED KENDALL
- ☐ 616. GENE RICHARDS
- ☐ 651. ROLLIE FINGERS
- ☐ 685. TIM FLANNERY(FS)
- ☐ 685. BRIAN GREER(FS)
- ☐ 685. JIM WILHELM(FS)
- ☐ 704. GENE TENACE
- ☐ 708. BOB TOLAN

SAN FRANCISCO GIANTS

- ☐ 12. JOHN CURTIS
- ☐ 30. VIDA BLUE
- ☐ 62. MIKE IVIE
- ☐ 84. GARY LAVELLE
- ☐ 111. BOB KNEPPER
- ☐ 145. DARRELL EVANS
- ☐ 167. JACK CLARK
- ☐ 195. JOHN MONTEFUSCO
- ☐ 217. ED HALICKI
- ☐ 236. MARC HILL
- ☐ 257. LARRY HERNDON
- ☐ 279. ROB ANDREWS
- ☐ 311. ROGER METZGER
- ☐ 335. WILLIE MCCOVEY
- ☐ 359. RANDY MOFFITT
- ☐ 408. BILL NORTH
- ☐ 434. JOHNNIE LEMASTER
- ☐ 462. MIKE SADEK
- ☐ 499. TEAM & BRISTOL(M)
- ☐ 538. JOE STRAIN
- ☐ 561. EDDIE WHITSON
- ☐ 588. GREG MINTON
- ☐ 627. PEDRO BORBON
- ☐ 649. TOM GRIFFIN
- ☐ 686. GREG JOHNSTON(FS)
- ☐ 686. DENNIS LITTLEJOHN(FS)
- ☐ 686. PHIL NASTU(FS)
- ☐ 713. TERRY WHITFIELD

SEATTLE MARINERS

- ☐ 32. JULIO CRUZ
- ☐ 56. BOBBY VALENTINE
- ☐ 78. RUPPERT JONES
- ☐ 116. LARRY COX
- ☐ 143. BRUCE BOCHTE

- ☐ 166. GLENN ABBOTT
- ☐ 197. BYRON MCLAUGHLIN
- ☐ 226. BILL STEIN
- ☐ 282. TEAM & JOHNSON(M)
- ☐ 307. RICK HONEYCUTT
- ☐ 342. ODELL JONES
- ☐ 366. ROB DRESSLER
- ☐ 396. DAN MEYER
- ☐ 422. LARRY MILBOURNE
- ☐ 443. MIKE PARROTT
- ☐ 481. TOM PACIOREK
- ☐ 507. LEON ROBERTS
- ☐ 532. WILLIE HORTON
- ☐ 583. BOB STINSON
- ☐ 613. RANDY STEIN
- ☐ 637. JOE SIMPSON
- ☐ 652. MARIO MENDOZA
- ☐ 672. CHARLIE BEAMON(FS)
- ☐ 672. RODNEY CRAIG(FS)
- ☐ 672. RAFAEL VASQUEZ(FS)
- ☐ 699. FLOYD BANNISTER
- ☐ 723. SHANE RAWLEY

TEXAS RANGERS

- ☐ 22. PAT PUTNAM
- ☐ 41. TEAM & CORRALES(M)
- ☐ 67. DOYLE ALEXANDER
- ☐ 93. DAVE W. ROBERTS
- ☐ 115. SPARKY LYLE
- ☐ 144. STEVE COMER
- ☐ 173. JOHN HENRY JOHNSON
- ☐ 190. BUDDY BELL
- ☐ 213. MIKE JORGENSEN
- ☐ 224. WILLIE MONTANEZ
- ☐ 233. LARUE WASHINGTON
- ☐ 260. AL OLIVER
- ☐ 283. JOHN ELLIS
- ☐ 313. JOHNNY GRUBB
- ☐ 336. GEORGE MEDICH
- ☐ 369. JIM KERN
- ☐ 390. FERGIE JENKINS
- ☐ 441. ERIC SODERHOLM
- ☐ 458. BILLY SAMPLE
- ☐ 473. BUMP WILLS
- ☐ 485. MICKEY RIVERS
- ☐ 498. DANNY DARWIN
- ☐ 518. NELSON NORMAN
- ☐ 530. JIM SUNDBERG
- ☐ 548. DAVE RAJSICH
- ☐ 592. JON MATLACK
- ☐ 620. RICHIE ZISK
- ☐ 656. LARVELL BLANKS
- ☐ 673. BRIAN ALLARD(FS)
- ☐ 673. JERRY DON GLEATON(FS)
- ☐ 673. GREG MAHLBERG(FS)

TORONTO BLUE JAYS

- ☐ 19. BALOR MOORE
- ☐ 46. RICO CARTY
- ☐ 77. DAVE STIEB
- ☐ 124. DAVE LEMANCZYK
- ☐ 142. PHIL HUFFMAN
- ☐ 169. LUIS GOMEZ
- ☐ 221. JOE CANNON
- ☐ 249. JIM CLANCY
- ☐ 277. RICK BOSETTI
- ☐ 297. TIM JOHNSON
- ☐ 324. TOM UNDERWOOD
- ☐ 351. BOB DAVIS
- ☐ 382. DAVE FREISLEBEN
- ☐ 407. TONY SOLAITA
- ☐ 444. ALVIS WOODS
- ☐ 467. JESSE JEFFERSON
- ☐ 488. ROY HOWELL
- ☐ 506. TOM BUSKEY
- ☐ 558. ALFREDO GRIFFIN
- ☐ 577. TEAM CARD
- ☐ 581. BOB BAILOR
- ☐ 591. RICK CERONE
- ☐ 611. JERRY GARVIN
- ☐ 643. JOHN MAYBERRY
- ☐ 674. BUTCH EDGE(FS)
- ☐ 674. D. PAT KELLY(FS)
- ☐ 674. TED WILBORN(FS)
- ☐ 693. CRAIG KUSICK
- ☐ 703. OTTO VELEZ

1981 TOPPS (726)
2 1/2" X 3 1/2"

ATLANTA BRAVES

- ☐ 20. JEFF BURROUGHS
- ☐ 44. LARRY MCWILLIAMS
- ☐ 64. BRIAN ASSELSTINE
- ☐ 87. RICK CAMP
- ☐ 108. BRUCE BENEDICT
- ☐ 132. TOMMY BOGGS
- ☐ 155. CHRIS CHAMBLISS
- ☐ 192. TERRY HARPER(FS)
- ☐ 192. ED MILLER(FS)
- ☐ 192. RAFAEL RAMIREZ(FS)
- ☐ 247. GLENN HUBBARD
- ☐ 268. JERRY ROYSTER
- ☐ 296. BILL NAHORODNY
- ☐ 307. GENE GARBER
- ☐ 326. BIFF POCOROBA
- ☐ 355. BOB HORNER
- ☐ 387. PHIL NIEKRO
- ☐ 457. MIKE LUM
- ☐ 477. LUIS GOMEZ
- ☐ 504. DALE MURPHY
- ☐ 528. GARY MATTHEWS
- ☐ 542. LARRY BRADFORD
- ☐ 594. PRESTON HANNA
- ☐ 611. RICK MATULA
- ☐ 636. AL HRABOSKY
- ☐ 675. TEAM & COX(M)
- ☐ 708. DOYLE ALEXANDER

BALTIMORE ORIOLES

- ☐ 10. MIKE FLANAGAN
- ☐ 37. GARY ROENICKE
- ☐ 65. SCOTT MCGREGOR
- ☐ 91. TIM STODDARD
- ☐ 101. BENNY AYALA
- ☐ 119. TIPPY MARTINEZ
- ☐ 161. DAN GRAHAM
- ☐ 188. DOUG DECINCES
- ☐ 210. JIM PALMER
- ☐ 262. SAMMY STEWART
- ☐ 287. LENN SAKATA
- ☐ 314. RICH DAUER
- ☐ 367. DENNY MARTINEZ
- ☐ 399. MIKE BODDICKER(FS)
- ☐ 399. MARK COREY(FS)
- ☐ 399. FLOYD RAYFORD(FS)
- ☐ 425. AL BUMBRY
- ☐ 490. EDDIE MURRAY
- ☐ 520. STEVE STONE
- ☐ 543. TERRY CROWLEY
- ☐ 570. KEN SINGLETON
- ☐ 591. JOHN LOWENSTEIN
- ☐ 615. RICK DEMPSEY
- ☐ 641. MARK BELANGER
- ☐ 661. TEAM & WEAVER(M)
- ☐ 688. KIKO GARCIA
- ☐ 706. DAVE FORD

BOSTON RED SOX

- ☐ 14. JOHN TUDOR
- ☐ 38. WIN REMMERSWAAL
- ☐ 63. STEVE RENKO
- ☐ 81. DAVE STAPLETON

☐ 110. CARL YASTRZEMSKI
☐ 128. GARY ALLENSON
☐ 153. TOM POQUETTE
☐ 184. JIM DWYER
☐ 199. CHUCK RAINEY
☐ 233. SKIP LOCKWOOD
☐ 275. DWIGHT EVANS
☐ 320. TOM BURGMEIER
☐ 349. GLENN HOFFMAN
☐ 378. DAVE RADER
☐ 396. BILL CAMPBELL
☐ 421. BOB STANLEY
☐ 455. RICK BURLESON
☐ 480. CARLTON FISK
☐ 500. JIM RICE
☐ 525. MIKE TORREZ
☐ 549. JERRY REMY
☐ 575. TONY PEREZ
☐ 595. BUTCH HOBSON
☐ 620. DENNIS ECKERSLEY
☐ 647. DICK DRAGO
☐ 662. TEAM & HOUK(M)
☐ 689. BRUCE HURST(FS)
☐ 689. KEITH MACWHORTER(FS)
☐ 689. REID NICHOLS(FS)
☐ 720. FRED LYNN

CALIFORNIA ANGELS

☐ 12. MARK CLEAR
☐ 48. DAVE SKAGGS
☐ 69. ED HALICKI
☐ 100. ROD CAREW
☐ 121. LARRY HARLOW
☐ 182. BOB GRICH
☐ 209. DICKIE THON
☐ 214. RALPH BOTTING(FS)
☐ 214. JIM DORSEY(FS)
☐ 214. JOHN HARRIS(FS)
☐ 227. FRED MARTINEZ
☐ 239. RICK MILLER
☐ 263. BRIAN DOWNING
☐ 286. DAVE FROST
☐ 288. BOB CLARK
☐ 311. FREDDIE PATEK
☐ 340. BRUCE KISON
☐ 369. FRANK TANANA
☐ 391. DAVE LEMANCZYK
☐ 410. BERT CAMPANERIS
☐ 422. DAN FORD
☐ 454. ANDY HASSLER
☐ 505. JASON THOMPSON
☐ 529. DAVE LAROCHE
☐ 557. CHRIS KNAPP
☐ 580. DON BAYLOR
☐ 601. DON AASE
☐ 621. TOM DONOHUE
☐ 639. CARNEY LANSFORD
☐ 652. JOHN MONTAGUE
☐ 663. TEAM & FREGOSI(M)
☐ 701. JOE RUDI
☐ 717. JIM BARR

CHICAGO CUBS

☐ 17. CLIFF JOHNSON
☐ 54. IVAN DEJESUS
☐ 78. STEVE DILLARD
☐ 103. JERRY MARTIN
☐ 136. DOUG CAPILLA
☐ 176. MIKE KRUKOW

☐ 238. WILLIE HERNANDEZ
☐ 294. MIKE TYSON
☐ 331. DENNIS LAMP
☐ 352. DICK TIDROW
☐ 381. CARLOS LEZCANO(FS)
☐ 381. STEVE MACKO(FS)
☐ 381. RANDY MARTZ(FS)
☐ 395. SCOT THOMPSON
☐ 429. MICK KELLEHER
☐ 450. DAVE KINGMAN
☐ 471. MIKE VAIL
☐ 492. BARRY FOOTE
☐ 514. GEORGE RILEY
☐ 533. JESUS FIGUEROA
☐ 553. TIM BLACKWELL
☐ 574. BILL CAUDILL
☐ 590. BRUCE SUTTER
☐ 609. LYNN MCGLOTHEN
☐ 625. BILL BUCKNER
☐ 645. RICK REUSCHEL
☐ 676. TEAM & AMALFITANO(M)
☐ 692. LENNY RANDLE
☐ 718. LARRY BIITTNER

CHICAGO WHITE SOX

☐ 36. ED FARMER
☐ 67. KEN KRAVEC
☐ 83. MIKE PROLY
☐ 107. RICH WORTHAM
☐ 112. RUSTY KUNTZ(FS)
☐ 112. FRAN MULLINS(FS)
☐ 112. LEO SUTHERLAND(FS)
☐ 138. RICH DOTSON
☐ 164. LAMARR HOYT
☐ 186. WAYNE NORDHAGEN
☐ 242. CHET LEMON
☐ 272. BRUCE KIMM
☐ 292. MIKE SQUIRES
☐ 323. JIM MORRISON
☐ 347. HAROLD BAINES
☐ 398. ROSS BAUMGARTEN
☐ 412. BRITT BURNS
☐ 442. RON PRUITT
☐ 466. BOB MOLINARO
☐ 487. DEWEY ROBINSON
☐ 522. MIKE COLBERN
☐ 552. STEVE TROUT
☐ 571. TODD CRUZ
☐ 589. LAMAR JOHNSON
☐ 608. GREG PRYOR
☐ 646. MARVIS FOLEY
☐ 664. TEAM & LARUSSA(M)
☐ 716. GLENN BORGMANN

CINCINNATI REDS

☐ 21. RON OESTER
☐ 52. HECTOR CRUZ
☐ 73. DOUG BAIR
☐ 94. HARRY SPILMAN
☐ 126. CHARLIE LEIBRANDT
☐ 149. JOE NOLAN
☐ 175. DAVE COLLINS
☐ 200. GEORGE FOSTER
☐ 220. TOM SEAVER
☐ 258. JOE PRICE
☐ 280. KEN GRIFFEY
☐ 325. RAY KNIGHT
☐ 354. MARIO SOTO
☐ 375. DAVE CONCEPCION
☐ 390. CESAR GERONIMO
☐ 419. TOM HUME
☐ 447. JUNIOR KENNEDY
☐ 474. MIKE LACOSS
☐ 499. FRANK PASTORE
☐ 521. SAM MEJIAS
☐ 546. PAUL MOSKAU
☐ 600. JOHNNY BENCH
☐ 606. BRUCE BERENYI(FS)
☐ 606. GEOFF COMBE(FS)
☐ 606. PAUL HOUSEHOLDER(FS)
☐ 628. VIC CORRELL
☐ 655. DAN DRIESSEN
☐ 677. TEAM & MCNAMARA(M)
☐ 712. BILL BONHAM

CLEVELAND INDIANS

☐ 13. JOE CHARBONEAU
☐ 39. TOM VERYZER
☐ 74. MIKE HARGROVE

☐ 99. ERIC WILKINS
☐ 122. JOHN DENNY
☐ 141. MIGUEL DILONE
☐ 170. ROSS GRIMSLEY
☐ 198. JERRY DYBZINSKI
☐ 222. JORGE ORTA
☐ 252. VICTOR CRUZ
☐ 276. DAN SPILLNER
☐ 308. RICK MANNING
☐ 333. SID MONGE
☐ 362. BO DIAZ
☐ 388. ANDRE THORNTON
☐ 416. GARY ALEXANDER
☐ 432. LEN BARKER
☐ 451. CHRIS BANDO(FS)
☐ 451. TOM BRENNAN(FS)
☐ 451. SANDY WIHTOL(FS)
☐ 462. JACK BROHAMER
☐ 511. WAYNE GARLAND
☐ 536. BOB OWCHINKO
☐ 564. RON HASSEY
☐ 612. DUANE KUIPER
☐ 632. ALAN BANNISTER
☐ 665. TEAM & GARCIA(M)
☐ 697. RICK WAITS
☐ 721. TOBY HARRAH

DETROIT TIGERS

☐ 27. CHAMP SUMMERS
☐ 59. DAN PETRY
☐ 79. BRUCE ROBBINS
☐ 102. DAVE TOBIK
☐ 123. AL COWENS
☐ 150. MARK FIDRYCH
☐ 177. RICK PETERS
☐ 196. DUFFY DYER
☐ 217. RICH HEBNER
☐ 234. LOU WHITAKER
☐ 251. TOM BROOKENS
☐ 273. STAN PAPI
☐ 291. AURELIO LOPEZ
☐ 315. KIRK GIBSON
☐ 337. LYNN JONES
☐ 358. MARK WAGNER
☐ 373. PAT UNDERWOOD
☐ 392. LANCE PARRISH
☐ 417. DAN SCHATZEDER
☐ 448. TIM CORCORAN
☐ 468. JOHNNY WOCKENFUSS
☐ 572. JACK MORRIS
☐ 593. STEVE KEMP
☐ 614. DAVE ROZEMA
☐ 626. DAVE STEFFEN(FS)
☐ 626. JERRY UJDUR(FS)
☐ 626. ROGER WEAVER(FS)
☐ 658. MILT WILCOX
☐ 666. TEAM & ANDERSON(M)
☐ 709. ALAN TRAMMELL

HOUSTON ASTROS

☐ 45. ENOS CABELL
☐ 82. DANNY HEEP(FS)
☐ 82. ALAN KNICELY(FS)
☐ 82. BOBBY SPROWL(FS)
☐ 105. JOSE CRUZ
☐ 129. ART HOWE
☐ 148. RANDY NIEMANN
☐ 172. GARY WOODS
☐ 190. CESAR CEDENO
☐ 240. NOLAN RYAN
☐ 253. DAVE BERGMAN
☐ 269. KEN FORSCH
☐ 313. LUIS PUJOLS
☐ 329. JOAQUIN ANDUJAR
☐ 350. J.R. RICHARD
☐ 385. JOE SAMBITO
☐ 411. TERRY PUHL
☐ 439. DENNY WALLING
☐ 469. JEFF LEONARD
☐ 491. GORDY PLADSON
☐ 513. FRANK LACORTE
☐ 534. DAVE SMITH
☐ 560. JOE MORGAN
☐ 597. RAFAEL LANDESTOY
☐ 617. CRAIG REYNOLDS
☐ 642. VERN RUHLE
☐ 678. TEAM & VIRDON(M)
☐ 696. ALAN ASHBY
☐ 722. JOE NIEKRO

KANSAS CITY ROYALS

- [ ] 9. PETE LACOCK
- [ ] 26. U.L. WASHINGTON
- [ ] 47. KEN BRETT
- [ ] 66. MANNY CASTILLO(FS)
- [ ] 66. TIM IRELAND(FS)
- [ ] 66. MIKE JONES(FS)
- [ ] 98. CLINT HURDLE
- [ ] 130. LARRY GURA
- [ ] 157. JOHN WATHAN
- [ ] 185. DENNIS LEONARD
- [ ] 218. PAUL SPLITTORFF
- [ ] 274. CRAIG CHAMBERLAIN
- [ ] 295. HAL MCRAE
- [ ] 330. FRANK WHITE
- [ ] 360. WILLIE WILSON
- [ ] 389. MARTY PATTIN
- [ ] 433. RANCE MULLINIKS
- [ ] 452. RENIE MARTIN
- [ ] 473. JOSE CARDENAL
- [ ] 493. DAN QUISENBERRY
- [ ] 507. JAMIE QUIRK
- [ ] 524. WILLIE AIKENS
- [ ] 544. RICH GALE
- [ ] 585. AMOS OTIS
- [ ] 610. DARRELL PORTER
- [ ] 667. TEAM & FREY(M)
- [ ] 700. GEORGE BRETT

LOS ANGELES DODGERS

- [ ] 24. DON STANHOUSE
- [ ] 50. DAVE LOPES
- [ ] 75. REGGIE SMITH
- [ ] 104. TERRY FORSTER
- [ ] 127. RUDY LAW
- [ ] 146. BOBBY CASTILLO
- [ ] 174. DOUG RAU
- [ ] 191. RICK SUTCLIFFE
- [ ] 211. DERREL THOMAS
- [ ] 231. JOE BECKWITH
- [ ] 260. RON CEY
- [ ] 289. MICKEY HATCHER
- [ ] 302. JACK PERCONTE(FS)
- [ ] 302. MIKE SCIOSCIA(FS)
- [ ] 302. FERNANDO VALENZUELA(FS)
- [ ] 318. STEVE YEAGER
- [ ] 372. JAY JOHNSTONE
- [ ] 440. JERRY REUSS
- [ ] 465. BILL RUSSELL
- [ ] 495. DUSTY BAKER
- [ ] 512. GARY THOMASSON
- [ ] 530. STEVE GARVEY
- [ ] 548. DAVE GOLTZ
- [ ] 565. BURT HOOTON
- [ ] 605. DON SUTTON
- [ ] 624. BOB WELCH
- [ ] 651. PEDRO GUERRERO
- [ ] 679. TEAM & LA SORDA(M)
- [ ] 693. STEVE HOWE
- [ ] 711. JOE FERGUSON
- [ ] 726. RICK MONDAY

MILWAUKEE BREWERS

- [ ] 25. SIXTO LEZCANO
- [ ] 56. BUCK MARTINEZ
- [ ] 85. MIKE CALDWELL
- [ ] 106. DON MONEY
- [ ] 135. GORMAN THOMAS
- [ ] 156. BOB MCCLURE
- [ ] 183. DICK DAVIS
- [ ] 215. LARRY HISLE
- [ ] 237. CHARLIE MOORE
- [ ] 271. BILL CASTRO
- [ ] 300. PAUL MOLITOR
- [ ] 327. MOOSE HAAS
- [ ] 357. JIM SLATON
- [ ] 379. LARY SORENSEN
- [ ] 415. BEN OGLIVIE
- [ ] 449. PAUL MITCHELL
- [ ] 482. JIM GANTNER
- [ ] 515. ROBIN YOUNT
- [ ] 555. CECIL COOPER
- [ ] 576. REGGIE CLEVELAND
- [ ] 596. JERRY AUGUSTINE
- [ ] 623. SAL BANDO
- [ ] 659. JOHN FLINN(FS)
- [ ] 659. ED ROMERO(FS)

MINNESOTA TWINS

- [ ] 18. GLENN ADAMS
- [ ] 43. JOSE MORALES
- [ ] 61. BUTCH WYNEGAR
- [ ] 89. DARRELL JACKSON
- [ ] 115. ROY SMALLEY
- [ ] 137. HOSKEN POWELL
- [ ] 162. DOUG CORBETT
- [ ] 219. KEN LANDREAUX
- [ ] 243. SAL BUTERA
- [ ] 256. BOMBO RIVERA
- [ ] 278. RICK SOFIELD
- [ ] 304. JOHN CASTINO
- [ ] 328. DAVE ENGLE(FS)
- [ ] 328. GREG JOHNSTON(FS)
- [ ] 328. GARY WARD(FS)
- [ ] 363. GEOFF ZAHN
- [ ] 386. DAVE EDWARDS
- [ ] 408. FERNANDO ARROYO
- [ ] 434. ROGER ERICKSON
- [ ] 453. ROB WILFONG
- [ ] 476. JERRY KOOSMAN
- [ ] 509. PETE MACKANIN
- [ ] 527. DANNY GOODWIN
- [ ] 569. AL WILLIAMS
- [ ] 603. JOHN VERHOEVEN
- [ ] 631. RON JACKSON
- [ ] 657. MIKE CUBBAGE
- [ ] 669. TEAM & GORYL(M)
- [ ] 714. PETE REDFERN

MONTREAL EXPOS

- [ ] 15. LARRY PARRISH
- [ ] 42. JERRY WHITE
- [ ] 71. HAL DUES
- [ ] 97. CHRIS SPEIER
- [ ] 125. ANDRE DAWSON
- [ ] 181. ELIAS SOSA
- [ ] 235. SCOTT SANDERSON
- [ ] 267. STAN BAHNSEN
- [ ] 293. CHARLIE LEA
- [ ] 319. ROWLAND OFFICE
- [ ] 345. WARREN CROMARTIE
- [ ] 374. TOM HUTTON
- [ ] 394. WOODIE FRYMAN
- [ ] 413. TONY BERNAZARD
- [ ] 427. JOHN D'ACQUISTO
- [ ] 445. ELLIS VALENTINE
- [ ] 479. BOBBY PATE(FS)
- [ ] 479. TIM RAINES(FS)
- [ ] 479. ROBERTO RAMOS(FS)
- [ ] 497. FRED NORMAN
- [ ] 519. JOHN TAMARGO
- [ ] 539. RODNEY SCOTT
- [ ] 559. WILLIE MONTANEZ
- [ ] 578. BILL GULLICKSON
- [ ] 607. DAVE PALMER
- [ ] 633. BILL LEE
- [ ] 660. GARY CARTER
- [ ] 680. TEAM & WILLIAMS(M)
- [ ] 710. RON LEFLORE
- [ ] 725. STEVE ROGERS

NEW YORK METS

- [ ] 23. ALEX TREVINO
- [ ] 58. JOEL YOUNGBLOOD
- [ ] 93. ED GLYNN
- [ ] 109. MIKE SCOTT
- [ ] 117. PETE FALCONE
- [ ] 151. CLAUDELL WASHINGTON
- [ ] 163. BILLY ALMON
- [ ] 189. CRAIG SWAN
- [ ] 223. ROY LEE JACKSON
- [ ] 224. PAT ZACHRY
- [ ] 259. JUAN BERENGUER(FS)
- [ ] 259. HUBIE BROOKS(FS)
- [ ] 259. MOOKIE WILSON(FS)
- [ ] 299. ELLIOTT MADDOX
- [ ] 322. NEIL ALLEN
- [ ] 343. FRANK TAVERAS
- [ ] 359. TOM HAUSMAN
- [ ] 377. JERRY MORALES
- [ ] 414. JOHN PACELLA
- [ ] 428. JOHN STEARNS

MINNESOTA TWINS

- [ ] 456. JEFF REARDON
- [ ] 472. DYAR MILLER
- [ ] 510. LEE MAZZILLI
- [ ] 537. ROD HODGES
- [ ] 567. MARK BOMBACK
- [ ] 619. STEVE HENDERSON
- [ ] 634. DOUG FLYNN
- [ ] 654. RAY BURRIS
- [ ] 681. TEAM & TORRE(M)
- [ ] 698. MIKE JORGENSEN

NEW YORK YANKEES

- [ ] 16. RON DAVIS
- [ ] 34. AURELIO RODRIGUEZ
- [ ] 60. WILLIE RANDOLPH
- [ ] 88. JOE LEFEBVRE
- [ ] 114. TOM UNDERWOOD
- [ ] 139. OSCAR GAMBLE
- [ ] 159. BRIAN DOYLE
- [ ] 179. RUDY MAY
- [ ] 225. RUPPERT JONES
- [ ] 250. RON GUIDRY
- [ ] 281. FRED STANLEY
- [ ] 303. JOHNNY OATES
- [ ] 335. RICK CERONE
- [ ] 365. GRAIG NETTLES
- [ ] 383. ERIC SODERHOLM
- [ ] 400. REGGIE JACKSON
- [ ] 418. BOBBY BROWN
- [ ] 424. TIM LOLLAR(FS)
- [ ] 424. BRUCE ROBINSON(FS)
- [ ] 424. DENNIS WERTH(FS)
- [ ] 435. JIM SPENCER
- [ ] 460. RICH GOSSAGE
- [ ] 483. MIKE GRIFFIN
- [ ] 516. DOUG BIRD
- [ ] 550. TOMMY JOHN
- [ ] 582. GAYLORD PERRY
- [ ] 602. BOBBY MURCER
- [ ] 627. LUIS TIANT
- [ ] 650. BUCKY DENT
- [ ] 670. TEAM & MICHAEL(M)
- [ ] 690. BOB WATSON
- [ ] 724. LOU PINIELLA

OAKLAND A'S

- [ ] 35. MITCHELL PAGE
- [ ] 55. MIKE NORRIS
- [ ] 86. WAYNE GROSS
- [ ] 96. DAVE BEARD(FS)
- [ ] 96. ERNIE CAMACHO(FS)
- [ ] 96. PAT DEMPSEY(FS)
- [ ] 133. JEFF COX
- [ ] 154. RICK LANGFORD
- [ ] 178. JIM ESSIAN
- [ ] 232. MICKEY KLUTTS
- [ ] 261. RICKEY HENDERSON
- [ ] 284. BRIAN KINGMAN
- [ ] 301. MATT KEOUGH
- [ ] 316. CRAIG MINETTO
- [ ] 341. DWAYNE MURPHY
- [ ] 364. MIKE DAVIS
- [ ] 437. MIKE HEATH
- [ ] 461. DAVE MCKAY
- [ ] 481. BOB LACEY
- [ ] 503. STEVE MCCATTY
- [ ] 547. MARIO GUERRERO
- [ ] 568. DAVE REVERING
- [ ] 587. JEFF NEWMAN
- [ ] 604. ROB PICCIOLO
- [ ] 629. TONY ARMAS
- [ ] 671. TEAM & MARTIN(M)
- [ ] 687. JEFF JONES

PHILADELPHIA PHILLIES

- [ ] 40. TUG MCGRAW
- [ ] 53. KEVIN SAUCIER
- [ ] 90. BAKE MCBRIDE
- [ ] 120. LARRY BOWA
- [ ] 131. KEITH MORELAND
- [ ] 160. GARRY MADDOX
- [ ] 180. PETE ROSE
- [ ] 270. GREG LUZINSKI
- [ ] 290. BOB BOONE
- [ ] 317. LONNIE SMITH
- [ ] 346. LARRY CHRISTENSON
- [ ] 376. RON REED

☐ 405. NINO ESPINOSA
☐ 406. DICKIE NOLES
☐ 426. WARREN BRUSSTAR
☐ 459. GREG GROSS
☐ 470. MANNY TRILLO
☐ 494. BOB WALK
☐ 526. MARTY BYSTROM(FS)
☐ 526. JAY LOVIGLIO(FS)
☐ 526. JIM L. WRGHT(FS)
☐ 540. MIKE SCHMIDT
☐ 566. DEL UNSER
☐ 584. RANDY LERCH
☐ 598. GEORGE VUKOVICH
☐ 630. STEVE CARLTON
☐ 644. RAMON AVILES
☐ 682. TEAM & GREEN(M)
☐ 691. DICK RUGHVEN
☐ 719. SPARKY LYLE

PITTSBURGH PIRATES

☐ 28. ENRIQUE ROMO
☐ 51. BILL ROBINSON
☐ 68. MATT ALEXANDER
☐ 92. MIKE EASLER
☐ 118. KURT BEVACQUA
☐ 147. DALE BERRA
☐ 168. DON ROBINSON
☐ 194. ROD SCURRY
☐ 212. STEVE NICOSIA
☐ 226. MANNY SANGUILLEN
☐ 246. ED OTT
☐ 265. JOHN CANDELARIA
☐ 298. BUDDY SOLOMON
☐ 312. RICK RHODEN
☐ 332. LEE LACY
☐ 380. WILLIE STARGELL
☐ 430. JIM BIBBY
☐ 501. TIM FOLI
☐ 518. GRANT JACKSON
☐ 535. OMAR MORENO
☐ 551. VANCE LAW(FS)
☐ 551. TONY PENA(FS)
☐ 551. PASCUAL PEREZ(FS)
☐ 554. BERT BLYLEVEN
☐ 573. PHIL GARNER
☐ 618. JOHN MILNER
☐ 640. DAVE PARKER
☐ 683. TEAM & TANNER(M)
☐ 695. KENT TEKULVE
☐ 715. BILL MADLOCK

ST. LOUIS CARDINALS

☐ 32. KEN OBERKFELL
☐ 113. MIKE PHILLIPS
☐ 140. BOB FORSCH
☐ 152. JOHN URREA
☐ 165. TONY SCOTT
☐ 193. PETE VUCKOVICH
☐ 230. GEORGE HENDRICK
☐ 244. TITO LANDRUM(FS)
☐ 244. AL OLMSTED(FS)
☐ 244. ANDY RINCON(FS)
☐ 255. MARK LITTELL
☐ 266. TOM HERR
☐ 321. LEON DURHAM
☐ 334. DANE IORG
☐ 348. BOB SYKES
☐ 353. TERRY KENNEDY
☐ 366. MIKE RAMSEY
☐ 420. KEITH HERNANDEZ
☐ 441. KEN REITZ
☐ 485. GARRY TEMPLETON
☐ 489. JOHN LITTLEFIELD
☐ 523. JOHN FULGHAM
☐ 541. STEVE SWISHER
☐ 563. JIM KAAT
☐ 586. SILVIO MARTINEZ
☐ 635. BOBBY BONDS
☐ 684. TEAM & HERZOG(M)
☐ 705. TED SIMMONS

SAN DIEGO PADRES

☐ 29. GENE TENACE
☐ 49. BOB SHIRLEY
☐ 72. BARRY EVANS
☐ 134. STEVE MURA
☐ 171. GENE RICHARDS
☐ 229. ROLLIE FINGERS

☐ 254. OZZIE SMITH
☐ 285. JERRY TURNER
☐ 309. LUIS SALAZAR
☐ 342. ERIC RASMUSSEN
☐ 356. GEORGE STABLEIN(FS)
☐ 356. CRAIG STIMAC(FS)
☐ 356. TOM TELLMAN(FS)
☐ 370. DAVE WINFIELD
☐ 393. BRODERICK PERKINS
☐ 436. GARY LUCAS
☐ 458. RANDY JONES
☐ 478. JUAN EICHELBERGER
☐ 496. PAUL DADE
☐ 531. JOHN CURTIS
☐ 556. JERRY MUMPHREY
☐ 579. TIM FLANNERY
☐ 579. DENNIS KINNEY
☐ 616. RICK WISE
☐ 653. BILL FAHEY
☐ 685. TEAM & HOWARD(M)
☐ 707. DAVE CASH

SAN FRANCISCO GIANTS

☐ 11. JIM WOHLFORD
☐ 30. JACK CLARK
☐ 62. JOE PETTINI
☐ 84. JOHNNIE LEMASTER
☐ 111. GREG MINTON
☐ 144. ALLEN RIPLEY
☐ 167. TERRY WHITFIELD
☐ 195. RICH MURRAY
☐ 213. AL HOLLAND
☐ 236. MIKE IVIE
☐ 257. RENNIE STENNETT
☐ 279. BOB KNEPPER
☐ 310. VIDA BLUE
☐ 336. EDDIE WHITSON
☐ 361. JOE STRAIN
☐ 384. MIKE SADEK
☐ 409. LARRY HERNDON
☐ 438. JOHN MONTEFUSCO
☐ 463. MILT MAY
☐ 484. MAX VENABLE
☐ 502. CHRIS BOURJOS(FS)
☐ 502. AL HARGESHEIMER(FS)
☐ 502. MIKE ROWLAND(FS)
☐ 538. TOM GRIFFIN
☐ 561. DENNIS LITTLEJOHN
☐ 588. GARY LAVELLE
☐ 622. RANDY MOFFITT
☐ 648. DARRELL EVANS
☐ 686. TEAM & BRISTOL(M)
☐ 713. BILL NORTH

SEATTLE MARINERS

☐ 33. RICK HONEYCUTT
☐ 57. DAVE A. ROBERTS
☐ 76. MARIO MENDOZA
☐ 116. JOE SIMPSON
☐ 143. DAN MEYER
☐ 166. FLOYD BANNISTER
☐ 187. MIKE PARROTT
☐ 228. TOM PACIOREK
☐ 249. LARRY COX
☐ 282. RICK ANDERSON(FS)
☐ 282. GREG BIERCEVICZ(FS)
☐ 282. RODNEY CRAIG(FS)
☐ 306. JUAN BENIQUEZ
☐ 344. BYRON MCLAUGHLIN

☐ 368. LEON ROBERTS
☐ 397. JULIO CRUZ
☐ 423. SHANE RAWLEY
☐ 443. JIM BEATTIE
☐ 486. MARC HILL
☐ 508. ROB DRESSLER
☐ 532. BILL STEIN
☐ 583. LARRY MILBOURNE
☐ 613. JIM ANDERSON
☐ 637. JERRY NARRON
☐ 649. MANNY SARMIENTO
☐ 672. TEAM & WILLS(M)
☐ 699. GLENN ABBOTT
☐ 723. BRUCE BOCHTE

TEXAS RANGERS

☐ 22. DANNY DARWIN
☐ 41. BOB BABCOCK(FS)
☐ 41. JOHN BUTCHER(FS)
☐ 41. JERRY DON GLEATON(FS)
☐ 70. AL OLIVER
☐ 80. RUSTY STAUB
☐ 95. JIM SUNDBERG
☐ 145. MICKEY RIVERS
☐ 158. FERGIE JENKINS
☐ 173. BUMP WILLS
☐ 197. JIM KERN
☐ 216. JOHN HENRY JOHNSON
☐ 245. ED FIGUEROA
☐ 264. JIM NORRIS
☐ 283. BILLY SAMPLE
☐ 305. KEN CLAY
☐ 339. JOHN ELLIS
☐ 371. CHARLIE HOUGH
☐ 431. DAVE W. ROBERTS
☐ 464. ADRIAN DEVINE
☐ 475. BUDDY BELL
☐ 498. PAT PUTNAM
☐ 517. RICHIE ZISK
☐ 545. JOHNNY GRUBB
☐ 592. STEVE COMER
☐ 656. JON MATLACK
☐ 673. TEAM & ZIMMER(M)
☐ 694. BUD HARRELSON
☐ 702. GEORGE MEDICH

TORONTO BLUE JAYS

☐ 19. JIM CLANCY
☐ 46. RICK BOSETTI
☐ 77. MIKE BARLOW
☐ 124. JERRY GARVIN
☐ 142. JACKSON TODD
☐ 169. JOHN MAYBERRY
☐ 221. BOB DAVIS
☐ 248. JOEY MCLAUGHLIN
☐ 277. ALFREDO GRIFFIN
☐ 297. BOB BAILOR
☐ 324. MIKE WILLIS
☐ 351. OTTO VELEZ
☐ 382. PAUL MIRABELLA
☐ 407. ERNIE WHITT
☐ 444. GARTH IORG
☐ 467. DAVE STIEB
☐ 488. DAMASO GARCIA
☐ 506. PHIL HUFFMAN
☐ 558. BARRY BONNELL
☐ 577. LUIS LEAL(FS)
☐ 577. BRIAN MILNER(FS)
☐ 577. KEN SCHROM(FS)
☐ 581. ROY HOWELL
☐ 643. LLOYD MOSEBY
☐ 674. TEAM & MATTICK(M)
☐ 703. ALVIS WOODS

1981 TOPPS
TRADED (132)
2 1/2" X 3 1/2"

ATLANTA BRAVES

☐ 804. JOHN MONTEFUSCO
☐ 812. GAYLORD PERRY
☐ 853. BOB WALK
☐ 854. CLAUDELL WASHINGTON

BALTIMORE ORIOLES

☐ 757. JIM DWYER
☐ 806. JOSE MORALES

BOSTON RED SOX

☐ 748. MARK CLEAR
☐ 788. CARNEY LANSFORD
☐ 803. RICK MILLER
☐ 826. JOE RUDI
☐ 841. FRANK TANANA

CALIFORNIA ANGELS

☐ 733. JUAN BENIQUEZ
☐ 743. RICK BURLESON
☐ 764. KEN FORSCH
☐ 771. BUTCH HOBSON
☐ 797. FRED LYNN
☐ 810. ED OTT
☐ 818. DOUG RAU
☐ 821. STEVE RENKO
☐ 845. BILL TRAVERS
☐ 856. GEOFF ZAHN

CHICAGO CUBS

☐ 737. DOUG BIRD
☐ 740. BOBBY BONDS
☐ 750. HECTOR CRUZ
☐ 756. LEON DURHAM
☐ 769. STEVE HENDERSON
☐ 783. KEN KRAVEC
☐ 795. MIKE LUM
☐ 805. JERRY MORALES
☐ 820. KEN REITZ
☐ 837. JOE STRAIN

CHICAGO WHITE SOX

☐ 730. BILLY ALMON
☐ 735. TONY BERNAZARD
☐ 759. JOM ESSIAN
☐ 762. CARLTON FISK
☐ 770. MARC HILL
☐ 785. DENNIS LAMP
☐ 791. RON LEFLORE
☐ 796. GREG LUZINSKI

CINCINNATI REDS

☐ 736. LARRY BIITTNER
☐ 786. RAFAEL LANDESTOY
☐ 848. MIKE VAIL

CLEVELAND INDIANS

☐ 738. BERT BLYLEVEN
☐ 784. BOB LACEY

DETROIT TIGERS

☐ 760. BILL FAHEY
☐ 779. MICK KELLEHER
☐ 827. KEVIN SAUCIER

HOUSTON ASTROS

☐ 765. KIKO GARCIA
☐ 774. MIKE IVIE
☐ 782. BOB KNEPPER
☐ 824. DAVE W. ROBERTS
☐ 828. TONY SCOTT
☐ 833. HARRY SPILMAN
☐ 839. DON SUTTON
☐ 844. DICKIE THON

KANSAS CITY ROYALS

☐ 766. CESAR GERONIMO

LOS ANGELES DODGERS

☐ 787. KEN LANDREAUX
☐ 850. FERNANDO VALENZUELA

MILWAUKEE BREWERS

☐ 761. ROLLIE FINGERS
☐ 773. ROY HOWELL
☐ 792. RANDY LERCH
☐ 830. TED SIMMONS
☐ 851. PETE VUCKOVICH

MINNESOTA TWINS

☐ 768. MICKEY HATCHER

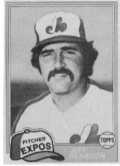

MONTREAL EXPOS

☐ 744. RAY BURRIS
☐ 813. MIKE PHILLIPS
☐ 816. TIM RAINES
☐ 819. JEFF REARDON

NEW YORK METS

☐ 732. BOB BAILOR
☐ 742. HUBIE BROOKS
☐ 752. MIKE CUBBAGE
☐ 777. RANDY JONES
☐ 781. DAVE KINGMAN
☐ 835. RUSTY STAUB
☐ 849. ELLIS VALENTINE

NEW YORK YANKEES

☐ 763. BARRY FOOTE
☐ 789. DAVE LAROCHE
☐ 802. LARRY MILBOURNE
☐ 808. JERRY MUMPHREY
☐ 809. GENE NELSON
☐ 822. RICK REUSCHEL
☐ 823. DAVE REVERING
☐ 855. DAVE WINFIELD

OAKLAND A'S

☐ 741. RICK BOSETTI
☐ 754. BRIAN DOYLE
☐ 776. CLIFF JOHNSON
☐ 811. BOB OWCHINKO
☐ 832. JIM SPENCER
☐ 834. FRED STANLEY
☐ 846. TOM UNDERWOOD

PHILADELPHIA PHILLIES

☐ 753. DICK DAVIS
☐ 800. GARY MATTHEWS
☐ 815. MIKE PROLY

PITTSBURGH PIRATES

☐ 729. GARY ALEXANDER
☐ 751. VICTOR CRUZ
☐ 843. JASON THOMPSON

ST. LOUIS CARDINALS

☐ 731. JOAQUIN ANDUJAR
☐ 793. SIXTO LEZCANO
☐ 814. DARRELL PORTER
☐ 829. BOB SHIRLEY
☐ 831. LARY SORENSEN
☐ 838. BRUCE SUTTER
☐ 842. GENE TENACE

SAN DIEGO PADRES

☐ 758. DAVE EDWARDS
☐ 778. RUPPERT JONES
☐ 780. TERRY KENNEDY
☐ 790. JOE LEFEVRE
☐ 794. JOHN LITTLEFIELD
☐ 840. STEVE SWISHER
☐ 847. JOHN URREA

SAN FRANCISCO GIANTS

☐ 728. DOYLE ALEXANDER
☐ 734. DAVE BERGMAN
☐ 746. ENOS CABELL
☐ 798. JERRY MARTIN
☐ 807. JOE MORGAN

SEATTLE MARINERS

☐ 745. JEFF BURROUGHS
☐ 747. KEN CLAY
☐ 755. DICK DRAGO
☐ 767. GARY GRAY
☐ 817. LENNY RANDLE
☐ 857. RICHIE ZISK

TEXAS RANGERS

☐ 749. LARRY COX
☐ 772. RICK HONEYCUTT
☐ 801. MARIO MENDOZA
☐ 825. LEON ROBERTS
☐ 836. BILL STEIN
☐ 852. MARK WAGNER

TORONTO BLUE JAYS

☐ 727. DANNY AINGE
☐ 739. MARK BOMBACK
☐ 775. ROY LEE JACKSON
☐ 799. BUCK MARTINEZ

1982 TOPPS (792)
2 1/2" X 3 1/2"

ANGELS
ROD CAREW

ATLANTA BRAVES

- ☐ 32. GENE GARBER
- ☐ 61. TOMMY BOGGS
- ☐ 88. BIFF POCOROBA
- ☐ 115. GAYLORD PERRY
- ☐ 126. TEAM LEADER CARD
- ☐ 145. BOB HORNER
- ☐ 185. PHIL NIEKRO
- ☐ 214. BRIAN ASSELSTINE
- ☐ 244. RUFINO LINARES
- ☐ 271. LARRY BRADFORD
- ☐ 296. BOB WALK
- ☐ 320. CHRIS CHAMBLISS
- ☐ 372. LUIS GOMEZ
- ☐ 393. AL HRABOSKY
- ☐ 424. BRUCE BENEDICT
- ☐ 451. ED MILLIER
- ☐ 482. GLENN HUBBARD
- ☐ 502. STEVE BEDROSIAN(FS)
- ☐ 502. BRETT BUTLER(FS)
- ☐ 502. LARRY OWEN(FS)
- ☐ 507. TERRY HARPER
- ☐ 536. RAFAEL RAMIREZ
- ☐ 579. RICK MAHLER
- ☐ 608. JERRY ROYSTER
- ☐ 637. RICK CAMP
- ☐ 668. DALE MURPHY
- ☐ 697. JOHN MONTEFUSCO
- ☐ 733. LARRY MCWILLIAMS
- ☐ 758. CLAUDELL WASHINGTON

BALTIMORE ORIOLES

- ☐ 8. RICH DAUER
- ☐ 21. BOB BONNER(FS)
- ☐ 21. CAL RIPKEN(FS)
- ☐ 21. JEFF SCHNEIDER(FS)
- ☐ 37. DAN GRAHAM
- ☐ 80. JIM PALMER
- ☐ 107. WAYNE KRENCHICKI
- ☐ 136. LENN SAKATA
- ☐ 174. DAVE FORD
- ☐ 204. GARY ROENICKE
- ☐ 232. TERRY CROWLEY
- ☐ 265. AL BUMBRY
- ☐ 290. KEN SINGLETON
- ☐ 331. BENNY AYALA
- ☐ 359. JIM DWYER
- ☐ 390. EDDIE MURRAY
- ☐ 419. STEVE STONE
- ☐ 426. TEAM LEADER CARD
- ☐ 457. TIM STODDARD
- ☐ 489. RICK DEMPSEY
- ☐ 520. MIKE FLANAGAN
- ☐ 564. DOUG DECINCES
- ☐ 583. TIPPY MARTINEZ
- ☐ 617. SCOTT MCGREGOR
- ☐ 648. JOSE MORALES
- ☐ 679. SAMMY STEWART
- ☐ 712. DENNY MARTINEZ
- ☐ 747. JOHN LOWENSTEIN
- ☐ 776. MARK BELANGER

BOSTON RED SOX

- ☐ 25. JERRY REMY
- ☐ 59. RICH GEDMAN
- ☐ 91. CARNEY LANSFORD
- ☐ 124. REID NICHOLS
- ☐ 157. STEVE CRAWFORD
- ☐ 189. GLENN HOFFMAN
- ☐ 225. MIKE TORREZ
- ☐ 255. TONY PEREZ
- ☐ 274. BOB OJEDA
- ☐ 289. BOB STANLEY
- ☐ 322. GARRY HANCOCK
- ☐ 355. DWIGHT EVANS
- ☐ 381. BRUCE HURST(FS)
- ☐ 381. DAVE F. SCHMIDT(FS)
- ☐ 381. JULIO VALDEZ(FS)
- ☐ 388. JOE RUDI
- ☐ 421. MARK CLEAR
- ☐ 455. TOM BURGMEIER
- ☐ 490. DENNIS ECKERSLEY
- ☐ 522. CHUCK RAINEY
- ☐ 558. JOHN TUDOR
- ☐ 589. DAVE STAPLETON
- ☐ 619. BILL CAMPBELL
- ☐ 650. CARL YASTRZEMSKI
- ☐ 686. GARY ALLENSON
- ☐ 717. RICK MILLER
- ☐ 750. JIM RICE
- ☐ 786. TEAM LEADER CARD
- ☐ 792. FRANK TANANA

CALIFORNIA ANGELS

- ☐ 24. DAVE FROST
- ☐ 55. RICK BURLESON
- ☐ 58. JOHN D'ACQUISTO
- ☐ 74. BOB CLARK
- ☐ 94. ANDY HASSLER
- ☐ 134. DAN FORD
- ☐ 158. BRIAN DOWNING
- ☐ 199. DON AASE
- ☐ 229. GEOFF ZAHN
- ☐ 251. FRED LYNN
- ☐ 257. LARRY HARLOW
- ☐ 276. TEAM LEADER CARD
- ☐ 284. BOB GRICH
- ☐ 313. JOHN HARRIS
- ☐ 357. BUTCH HOBSON
- ☐ 385. KEN FORSCH
- ☐ 415. DON BAYLOR
- ☐ 442. BRUCE KISON
- ☐ 469. ED OTT
- ☐ 500. ROD CAREW
- ☐ 514. JOE FERGUSON
- ☐ 572. JUAN BENIQUEZ
- ☐ 602. FREDDIE PATEK
- ☐ 628. BILL TRAVERS
- ☐ 653. TOM BRUNANSKY(FS)
- ☐ 653. LUIS SANCHEZ(FS)
- ☐ 653. DARYL SCONIERS(FS)
- ☐ 659. FRED MARTINEZ
- ☐ 682. JESSE JEFFERSON
- ☐ 702. STEVE RENKO
- ☐ 744. MIKE WITT
- ☐ 772. BERT CAMPANERIS

CHICAGO CUBS

- ☐ 23. WILLIE HERNANDEZ
- ☐ 33. JERRY MORALES
- ☐ 51. JAY HOWELL(FS)
- ☐ 51. CARLOS LEZCANO(FS)
- ☐ 51. TY WALLER(FS)
- ☐ 62. MIKE TYSON
- ☐ 89. STEVE HENDERSON
- ☐ 117. RAWLY EASTWICK
- ☐ 146. MIKE GRIFFIN
- ☐ 188. RANDY MARTZ
- ☐ 215. MIKE KRUKOW
- ☐ 245. KEN REITZ
- ☐ 273. DOUG GIRD
- ☐ 303. BILL CAUDILL
- ☐ 324. STEVE DILLARD
- ☐ 374. TIM BLACKWELL
- ☐ 403. JIM TRACY
- ☐ 436. JOE STRAIN
- ☐ 452. LEE SMITH
- ☐ 456. TEAM LEADER CARD
- ☐ 484. IVAN DEJESUS
- ☐ 508. JODY DAVIS

CHICAGO WHITE SOX

- ☐ 13. LAMAR JOHNSON
- ☐ 44. BRITT BURNS
- ☐ 76. GREG PRYOR
- ☐ 85. LYNN MCGLOTHEN
- ☐ 110. CARLTON FISK
- ☐ 140. RON LEFLORE
- ☐ 176. DEWEY ROBINSON
- ☐ 206. TONY BERNAZARD
- ☐ 216. TEAM LEADER CARD
- ☐ 237. RUSTY KUNTZ
- ☐ 269. JIM ESSIAN
- ☐ 299. STEVE TROUT
- ☐ 328. ED FARMER
- ☐ 363. BOB MOLINARO
- ☐ 398. MIKE SQUIRES
- ☐ 428. LAMARR HOYT
- ☐ 461. RICH DOTSON
- ☐ 493. CHET LEMON
- ☐ 521. BILLY ALMON
- ☐ 563. ROSS BAUMGARTEN
- ☐ 597. WAYNE NORDHAGEN
- ☐ 599. JAY LOVIGLIO(FS)
- ☐ 599. REGGIE PATTERSON(FS)
- ☐ 599. LEO SUTHERLAND(FS)
- ☐ 622. DENNIS LAMP
- ☐ 654. JIM MORRISON
- ☐ 684. HAROLD BAINES
- ☐ 714. JERRY KOOSMAN
- ☐ 720. GREG LUZINSKI
- ☐ 736. JERRY TURNER
- ☐ 748. MARC HILL
- ☐ 778. KEVIN HICKEY

CINCINNATI REDS

- ☐ 30. TOM SEAVER
- ☐ 63. MARIO SOTO
- ☐ 97. PAUL MOSKAU
- ☐ 128. FRANK PASTORE
- ☐ 159. LARRY BIITTNER
- ☐ 169. CHARLIE LEIBRANDT
- ☐ 194. MIKE VAIL
- ☐ 228. SAM MEJIAS
- ☐ 294. MIKE LACOSS
- ☐ 327. JOE NOLAN
- ☐ 351. SCOTT BROWN(FS)
- ☐ 351. GEOFF COMBE(FS)
- ☐ 351. PAUL HOUSEHOLDER(FS)
- ☐ 361. RAFAEL LANDESTOY
- ☐ 400. JOHNNY BENCH
- ☐ 427. RON OESTER
- ☐ 459. BRUCE BERENYI
- ☐ 492. JOE PRICE
- ☐ 525. RAY KNIGHT
- ☐ 562. MIKE O'BERRY
- ☐ 595. DAVE COLLINS
- ☐ 620. KEN GRIFFEY
- ☐ 660. DAVE CONCEPCION
- ☐ 700. GEORGE FOSTER
- ☐ 723. JUNIOR KENNEDY
- ☐ 756. TEAM LEADER CARD
- ☐ 763. TOM HUME
- ☐ 785. DAN DRIESSEN

CLEVELAND INDIANS

- ☐ 26. JORGE ORTA
- ☐ 54. RON HASSEY
- ☐ 77. MIGUEL DILONE
- ☐ 141. CHRIS BANDO(FS)
- ☐ 141. TOM BRENNAN(FS)
- ☐ 141. VON HAYES(FS)
- ☐ 202. RICK MANNING
- ☐ 233. DUANE KUIPER
- ☐ 258. BO DIAZ
- ☐ 287. ALAN BANNISTER
- ☐ 310. MIKE HARGROVE
- ☐ 356. DENNY LEWALLYN
- ☐ 360. LEN BARKER
- ☐ 387. TOM VERYZER

CHICAGO WHITE SOX

- ☐ 537. DOUG CAPILLA
- ☐ 580. BOBBY BONDS
- ☐ 607. LEON DURHAM
- ☐ 639. KEN DRAVEC
- ☐ 663. HECTOR CRUZ
- ☐ 699. DICK TIDROW
- ☐ 732. MIKE LUM
- ☐ 760. BILL BUCKNER

☐ 417. H. PAT KELLY
☐ 446. WAYNE GARLAND
☐ 473. MIKE STANTON
☐ 512. JERRY DYBZINSKI
☐ 532. TOBY HARRAH
☐ 559. TEAM LEADER CARD
☐ 573. RICK WAITS
☐ 601. SID MONGE
☐ 630. JOE CHARBONEAU
☐ 664. DAN SPILLNER
☐ 685. BERT BLYLEVEN
☐ 724. DAVE ROSELLO
☐ 746. ANDRE THORNTON
☐ 773. JOHN DENNY

DETROIT TIGERS

☐ 39. LOU WHITAKER
☐ 64. LYNN JONES
☐ 105. KIRK GIBSON
☐ 133. PAT UNDERWOOD
☐ 137. GEORGE CAPPUZZELLO
☐ 184. MICK KELLEHER
☐ 211. DAN PETRY
☐ 238. KEVIN SAUCIER
☐ 261. HOWARD BAILEY(FS)
☐ 261. MARTY CASTILLO(FS)
☐ 261. DAVE RUCKER(FS)
☐ 266. RICK LEACH
☐ 286. BILL FAHEY
☐ 319. DAVE ROZEMA
☐ 369. CHAMP SUMMERS
☐ 391. DAVE TOBIK
☐ 423. STAN PAPI
☐ 450. JACK MORRIS
☐ 475. ALAN TRAMMELL
☐ 488. RON JACKSON
☐ 504. RICK PETERS
☐ 535. LANCE PARRISH
☐ 575. AL COWENS
☐ 603. RICH HEBNER
☐ 629. JOHNNY WOCKENFUSS
☐ 666. TEAM LEADER CARD
☐ 670. STEVE KEMP
☐ 691. DAN SCHATZEDER
☐ 728. AURELIO LOPEZ
☐ 753. TOM BROOKENS
☐ 784. MILT WILCOX

ASTROS
PITCHER DON SUTTON

HOUSTON ASTROS

☐ 34. JOE SAMBITO
☐ 57. CRAIG REYNOLDS
☐ 66. TEAM LEADER CARD
☐ 90. NOLAN RYAN
☐ 119. JOE PITTMAN
☐ 147. DANNY WALLING
☐ 190. J. R. RICHARD
☐ 218. DAVE W. ROBERTS
☐ 248. FRANK LACORTE
☐ 277. TERRY PUHL
☐ 305. DON SUTTON
☐ 325. JOSE CRUZ
☐ 377. KIKO GARCIA
☐ 404. DICKIE THON
☐ 433. ALAN ASHBY
☐ 441. DANNY HEEP(FS)
☐ 441. BILLY L. SMITH(FS)
☐ 441. BOBBY SPROWL(FS)
☐ 453. ART HOWE

☐ 483. GARY WOODS
☐ 509. HARRY SPILMAN
☐ 539. VERN RUHLE
☐ 582. LUIS PUJOLS
☐ 611. JOE NIEKRO
☐ 640. CESAR CEDENO
☐ 672. BOB KNEPPER
☐ 683. PHIL GARNER
☐ 698. TONY SCOTT
☐ 734. MIKE IVIE
☐ 761. DAVE SMITH

KANSAS CITY ROYALS

☐ 35. WILLIE AIKENS
☐ 67. RICH GALE
☐ 96. TEAM LEADER CARD
☐ 104. RANCE MULLINIKS
☐ 132. LEE MAY
☐ 173. JAMIE QUIRK
☐ 200. GEORGE BRETT
☐ 230. WILLIE WILSON
☐ 264. DAN QUISENBERRY
☐ 297. CLINT HURDLE
☐ 329. U.L. WASHINGTON
☐ 362. JIM L. WRIGHT
☐ 397. KEN BRETT
☐ 429. JOHN WATHAN
☐ 462. DAVE CHALK
☐ 471. ATLEE HAMMAKER(FS)
☐ 471. MIKE JONES(FS)
☐ 471. DARRYL MOTLEY(FS)
☐ 495. DENNIS LEONARD
☐ 594. RENIE MARTIN
☐ 625. HAL MCRAE
☐ 645. FRANK WHITE
☐ 693. CESAR GERONIMO
☐ 725. AMOS OTIS
☐ 759. PAUL SPLITTORFF
☐ 790. LARRY GURA

LOS ANGELES DODGERS

☐ 14. STEVE HOWE
☐ 48. BOBBY CASTILLO
☐ 82. BOB WELCH
☐ 114. KEN LANDREAUX
☐ 179. STEVE GARVEY
☐ 213. DAVE STEWART
☐ 247. PEDRO GUERRERO
☐ 279. BILL RUSSELL
☐ 311. TEAM LEADER CARD
☐ 315. BURT HOOTON
☐ 348. DERREL THOMAS
☐ 375. DUSTY BAKER
☐ 410. RON CEY
☐ 444. TERRY FORSTER
☐ 477. STEVE YEAGER
☐ 510. FERNANDO VALENZUELA
☐ 545. REGGIE SMITH
☐ 577. RICK MONDAY
☐ 609. RICK SUTCLIFFE
☐ 642. MIKE SCIOSCIA
☐ 674. DAVE GOLTZ
☐ 681. MIKE A. MARSHALL(FS)
☐ 681. RON ROENICKE(FS)
☐ 681. STEVE SAX(FS)
☐ 710. JERRY REUSS
☐ 740. DAVE LOPES
☐ 774. JAY JOHNSTONE

MILWAUKEE BREWERS

☐ 12. MOOSE HAAS
☐ 46. JERRY AUGUSTINE
☐ 68. ROY HOWELL
☐ 93. LARRY HISLE
☐ 122. JAMIE EASTERLY
☐ 150. TED SIMMONS
☐ 195. PAUL MOLITOR
☐ 221. JIM SLATON
☐ 268. RICKEY KEETON
☐ 280. BEN OGLIVIE
☐ 308. CHARLIE MOORE
☐ 333. FRANK DIPINO(FS)
☐ 333. MARSHALL EDWARDS(FS)
☐ 333. CHUCK PORTER(FS)
☐ 350. THAD BOSLEY
☐ 378. MIKE CALDWELL
☐ 408. ED ROMERO

☐ 435. ROBIN YOUNT
☐ 466. RANDY LERCH
☐ 487. BOB MCCLURE
☐ 517. MARK BROUHARD
☐ 542. NED YOST
☐ 585. ROLLIE FINGERS
☐ 613. JIM GANTNER
☐ 643. PETE VUCKOVICH
☐ 675. CECIL COOPER
☐ 703. TEAM LEADER CARD
☐ 709. DON MONEY
☐ 737. REGGIE CLEVELAND
☐ 765. GORMAN THOMAS

MINNESOTA TWINS

☐ 18. FERNANDO ARROYO
☐ 42. RICK SOFIELD
☐ 69. AL WILLIAMS
☐ 92. BRAD HAVENS
☐ 123. DANNY GOODWIN
☐ 153. ROGER ERICKSON
☐ 193. DARRELL JACKSON
☐ 222. BUTCH WYNEGAR
☐ 253. CHUCK BAKER
☐ 281. JOHN VERHOEVEN
☐ 309. PETE REDFERN
☐ 353. JACK O'CONNOR
☐ 379. ROB WILFONG
☐ 396. TEAM LEADER CARD
☐ 409. DON COOPER
☐ 438. PETE MACKANIN
☐ 467. MICKEY HATCHER
☐ 519. GLENN ADAMS
☐ 560. DOUG CORBETT
☐ 584. HOSKEN POWELL
☐ 612. GARY WARD
☐ 644. JOHN CASTINO
☐ 676. SAL BUTERA
☐ 738. DAVE ENGLE
☐ 766. LENNY FAEDO(FS)
☐ 766. KENT HRBEK(FS)
☐ 766. TIM LAUDNER(FS)
☐ 767. ROY SMALLEY

EXPOS
OUTFIELD TIM RAINES

MONTREAL EXPOS

☐ 7. SCOTT SANDERSON
☐ 38. CHARLIE LEA
☐ 70. TIM RAINES
☐ 102. DAN BRIGGS
☐ 118. TERRY FRANCONA(FS)
☐ 118. BRAD MILLS(FS)
☐ 118. BRYN SMITH(FS)
☐ 131. STAN BAHNSEN
☐ 172. BILL GULLICKSON
☐ 191. TIM WALLACH
☐ 198. CHRIS SPEIER
☐ 227. RAY BURRIS
☐ 259. RODNEY SCOTT
☐ 292. DAVE PALMER
☐ 323. BILL LEE
☐ 354. ROBERTO RAMOS
☐ 386. JERRY WHITE
☐ 414. ELIAS SOSA
☐ 445. LARRY PARRISH
☐ 479. ROWLAND OFFICE
☐ 526. TEAM LEADER CARD
☐ 540. ANDRE DAWSON
☐ 605. STEVE ROGERS
☐ 638. JOHN MILNER

☐ 667. JEFF REARDON
☐ 695. WARREN CROMARTIE
☐ 730. GARY CARTER
☐ 762. MIKE PHILLIPS
☐ 779. GRANT JACKSON
☐ 788. WOODIE FRYMAN

NEW YORK METS

☐ 15. ELLIS VALENTINE
☐ 43. MIKE CUBBAGE
☐ 79. BOB BAILOR
☐ 121. ED LYNCH
☐ 143. MOOKIE WILSON
☐ 178. DYAR MILLER
☐ 205. NEIL ALLEN
☐ 234. RON HODGES
☐ 246. TEAM LEADER CARD
☐ 270. RUSTY STAUB
☐ 302. DOUG FLYNN
☐ 326. PETE FALCONE
☐ 368. ALEX TREVINO
☐ 399. PAT ZACHRY
☐ 432. MIKE SCOTT
☐ 465. LEE MAZZILLI
☐ 478. RAY SEARAGE
☐ 494. HUBIE BROOKS
☐ 524. TOM HAUSMAN
☐ 566. MIKE JORGENSEN
☐ 592. CRAIG SWAN
☐ 623. RON GARDENHIRE(FS)
☐ 623. TERRY LEACH(FS)
☐ 623. TIM LEARY(FS)
☐ 626. RANDY JONES
☐ 655. JOEL YOUNGBLOOD
☐ 690. DAVE KINGMAN
☐ 743. JOHN STEARNS
☐ 782. FRANK TAVERAS
☐ 783. GREG HARRIS

NEW YORK YANKEES

☐   9. RON GUIDRY
☐ 45. RICK CERONE
☐ 75. TOMMY JOHN
☐ 83. STEVE BALBONI(FS)
☐ 83. ANDY MCGAFFIGAN(FS)
☐ 83. ANDRE ROBERTSON(FS)
☐ 109. DAVE REVERING
☐ 142. DAVE LAROCHE
☐ 154. DENNIS WERTH
☐ 175. JERRY MUMPHREY
☐ 208. BOBBY MURCER
☐ 240. BUCKY DENT
☐ 275. BOB WATSON
☐ 300. REGGIE JACKSON
☐ 334. AURELIO RODRIGUEZ
☐ 349. GEORGE FRAZIER
☐ 373. GENE NELSON
☐ 405. RICK REUSCHEL
☐ 439. DAVE RIGHETTI
☐ 472. OSCAR GAMBLE
☐ 486. TEAM LEADER CARD
☐ 505. GRAIG NETTLES
☐ 538. LOU PINIELLA
☐ 569. WILLIE RANDOLPH
☐ 600. DAVE WINFIELD
☐ 635. RON DAVIS
☐ 669. LARRY MILBOURNE
☐ 694. DAVE WEHRMEISTER
☐ 706. BARRY FOOTE
☐ 735. RUDY MAY
☐ 770. RICH GOSSAGE
☐ 791. BOBBY BROWN

OAKLAND A'S

☐ 29. DWAYNE MURPHY
☐ 60. TONY ARMAS
☐ 87. MATT KEOUGH
☐ 113. STEVE MCCATTY
☐ 139. JEFF JONES
☐ 148. MICKEY KLUTTS
☐ 156. TEAM LEADER CARD
☐ 187. JEFF NEWMAN
☐ 217. BO MCLAUGHLIN
☐ 243. BOB OWCHINKO
☐ 293. ROB PICCIOLO
☐ 318. MIKE HEATH
☐ 370. MIKE NORRIS
☐ 392. RICK BOSETTI
☐ 422. CLIFF JOHNSON

☐ 454. RICK LANGFORD
☐ 476. BRIAN KINGMAN
☐ 531. RICH BORDI(FS)
☐ 531. MARK BUDASKA(FS)
☐ 531. KELVIN MOORE(FS)
☐ 534. DAVE MCKAY
☐ 578. SHOOTY BABITT
☐ 610. RICKEY HENDERSON
☐ 633. MITCHELL PAGE
☐ 671. MIKE DAVIS
☐ 673. KEITH DRUMRIGHT
☐ 692. WAYNE GROSS
☐ 729. JIM SPENCER
☐ 757. TOM UNDERWOOD
☐ 787. FRED STANLEY

PHILADELPHIA PHILLIES

☐ 20. GARRY MADDOX
☐ 53. GREG GROSS
☐ 100. MIKE SCHMIDT
☐ 127. LONNIE SMITH
☐ 152. RAMON AVILES
☐ 183. MIKE PROLY
☐ 220. MANNY TRILLO
☐ 231. MARK DAVIS(FS)
☐ 231. BOB DERNIER(FS)
☐ 231. OZZIE VIRGIL(FS)
☐ 250. TUG MCGRAW
☐ 285. SPARKY LYLE
☐ 317. DICK RUTHVEN
☐ 352. DICK DAVIS
☐ 384. KEITH MORELAND
☐ 389. GEORGE VUKOVICH
☐ 416. MARTY BYSTROM
☐ 449. LUIS AGUAYO
☐ 480. STEVE CARLTON
☐ 515. LARRY BOWA
☐ 530. DICKIE NOLES
☐ 544. LARRY CHRISTENSON
☐ 581. RON REED
☐ 615. BOB BOONE
☐ 636. TEAM LEADER CARD
☐ 647. WARREN BRUSSTAR
☐ 680. GARY MATTHEWS
☐ 713. DEL UNSER
☐ 745. BAKE MCBRIDE
☐ 780. PETE ROSE

PITTSBURGH PIRATES

☐ 11. GARY ALEXANDER
☐ 40. DAVE PARKER
☐ 73. BUDDY SOLOMON
☐ 106. ENRIQUE ROMO
☐ 138. TONY PENA
☐ 160. LUIS TIANT
☐ 170. JIM BIBBY
☐ 207. ROD SCURRY
☐ 235. MIKE EASLER
☐ 263. VICTOR CRUZ
☐ 267. KURT BEVACQUA
☐ 291. VANCE LAW(FS)
☐ 291. BOB LONG(FS)
☐ 291. JOHNNY RAY(FS)
☐ 295. JASON THOMPSON
☐ 332. DON ROBINSON
☐ 365. BILL MADLOCK
☐ 383. PASCUAL PEREZ
☐ 395. OMAR MORENO
☐ 425. JOHN CANDELARIA
☐ 458. WILLIE MONTANEZ
☐ 485. KENT TEKULVE
☐ 513. RICK RHODEN
☐ 528. MATT ALEXANDER
☐ 543. BILL ROBINSON
☐ 588. DALE BERRA
☐ 618. TIM FOLI
☐ 652. STEVE NICOSIA
☐ 696. TEAM LEADER CARD
☐ 715. WILLIE STARGELL
☐ 752. LEE LACY

ST. LOUIS CARDINALS

☐ 27. TOM HERR
☐ 56. MARK LITTELL
☐ 86. DANE IORG
☐ 108. BOB SYKES
☐ 135. ANDY RINCON
☐ 181. SILVIO MARTINEZ

☐ 186. TEAM LEADER CARD
☐ 210. KEITH HERNANDEZ
☐ 236. JOHN MARTIN
☐ 260. BRUCE SUTTER
☐ 262. DOUG BAIR
☐ 288. GARRY TEMPLETON
☐ 316. STEVE BRAUN
☐ 367. JIM KAAT
☐ 420. GEORGE HENDRICK
☐ 447. DARRELL PORTER
☐ 474. KEN OBERKFELL
☐ 503. JULIO GONZALEZ
☐ 533. JOAQUIN ANDUJAR
☐ 561. GLENN BRUMMER(FS)
☐ 561. LUIS DELEON(FS)
☐ 561. GENE ROOF(FS)
☐ 574. MIKE RAMSEY
☐ 604. ORLANDO SANCHEZ
☐ 631. GENE TENACE
☐ 658. TITO LANDRUM
☐ 689. LARY SORENSEN
☐ 727. SIXTO LEZCANO
☐ 749. BOB SHIRLEY
☐ 775. BOB FORSCH

SAN DIEGO PADRES

☐ 28. JOHN URREA
☐ 65. TERRY KENNEDY
☐ 95. OZZIE SMITH
☐ 120. GARY LUCAS
☐ 151. DAVE EDWARDS
☐ 192. BRODERICK PERKINS
☐ 219. JOHN CURTIS
☐ 249. TIM FLANNERY
☐ 278. JOHN LITTLEFIELD
☐ 307. RANDY BASS
☐ 330. RICK WISE
☐ 366. TEAM LEADER CARD
☐ 376. CHRIS WELSH
☐ 407. DANNY BOONE
☐ 434. JOE LEFEBVRE
☐ 464. JUAN BONILLA
☐ 511. RUPPERT JONES
☐ 541. BARRY EVANS
☐ 587. TIM LOLLAR
☐ 614. JUAN EICHELBERGER
☐ 641. STEVE MURA
☐ 662. LUIS SALAZAR
☐ 708. GENE RICHARDS
☐ 731. MIKE ARMSTRONG(FS)
☐ 731. DOUG GWOSDZ(FS)
☐ 731. FRED KUHAULUA(FS)
☐ 764. STEVE SWISHER

SAN FRANCISCO GIANTS

☐ 17. DARRELL EVANS
☐ 47. JEFF LEONARD
☐ 84. RENNIE STENNETT
☐ 116. JIM WOHLFORD
☐ 144. FRED BREINING
☐ 171. BOB BRENLY(FS)
☐ 171. CHILI DAVIS(FS)
☐ 171. BOB TUFTS(FS)
☐ 182. LARRY HERNDON
☐ 209. GARY LAVELLE
☐ 242. MILT MAY
☐ 304. JOHNNIE LEMASTER
☐ 364. DOYLE ALEXANDER
☐ 406. AL HOLLAND
☐ 430. VIDA BLUE
☐ 460. JACK CLARK
☐ 498. DAVE BERGMAN
☐ 529. ALLEN RIPLEY
☐ 568. JOE PETTINI
☐ 576. TEAM LEADER CARD
☐ 593. BILLY E. SMITH
☐ 627. ENOS CABELL
☐ 656. EDDIE WHITSON
☐ 687. GREG MINTON
☐ 722. JERRY MARTIN
☐ 754. JOE MORGAN
☐ 777. TOM GRIFFIN

SEATTLE MARINERS

☐ 22. JIM BEATTIE
☐ 52. LARRY ANDERSON
☐ 72. RICK AUERBACH
☐ 98. TERRY BULLING

☐ 130. JULIO CRUZ
☐ 197. SHANE RAWLEY
☐ 224. BRUCE BOCHTE
☐ 283. BRIAN ALLARD
☐ 312. LENNY RANDLE
☐ 336. TEAM LEADER CARD
☐ 358. MIKE PARROTT
☐ 371. JERRY DON GLEATON
☐ 382. JOE SIMPSON
☐ 413. DAN MEYER
☐ 440. JEFF BURROUGHS
☐ 468. FLOYD BANNISTER
☐ 497. JIM ANDERSON
☐ 523. GARY GRAY
☐ 571. GLENN ABBOTT
☐ 598. BOB GALASSO
☐ 632. BRYAN CLARK
☐ 649. KEN CLAY
☐ 678. TOM PACIOREK
☐ 711. DAVE EDLER(FS)
☐ 711. DAVE HENDERSON(FS)
☐ 711. REGGIE WALTON(FS)
☐ 719. JERRY NARRON
☐ 742. DICK DRAGO
☐ 769. RICHIE ZISK

TEXAS RANGERS

☐ 16. STEVE COMER
☐ 36. TEAM LEADER CARD
☐ 50. BUDDY BELL
☐ 78. GEORGE MEDICH
☐ 103. BOB LACEY
☐ 112. BILLY SAMPLE
☐ 149. PAT PUTNAM
☐ 177. JOHN ELLIS
☐ 212. MARIO MENDOZA
☐ 239. JON MATLACK
☐ 272. BUMP WILLS
☐ 298. DANNY DARWIN
☐ 335. JIM SUNDBERG
☐ 402. BILL STEIN
☐ 418. JOHN BUTCHER(FS)
☐ 418. BOBBY JOHNSON(FS)
☐ 418. DAVE J. SCHMIDT(FS)
☐ 443. MARK WAGNER
☐ 463. JIM KERN
☐ 496. JOHNNY GRUBB
☐ 527. JOHN HERNY JOHNSON
☐ 567. BOB BABCOCK
☐ 590. AL OLIVER
☐ 624. FERGIE JENKINS
☐ 657. TOM POQUETTE
☐ 688. LEON ROBERTS
☐ 704. MICKEY RIVERS
☐ 718. CHARLIE HOUGH
☐ 751. RICK HONEYCUTT

TORONTO BLUE JAYS

☐ 19. ERNIE WHITT
☐ 49. ALVIS WOODS
☐ 71. ROY LEE JACKSON
☐ 99. BARRY BONNELL
☐ 125. DANNY AINGE
☐ 155. OTTO VELEZ
☐ 196. WILLIE UPSHAW
☐ 203. JESSE BARFIELD(FS)
☐ 203. BRIAN MILNER(FS)
☐ 203. BOOMER WELLS(FS)
☐ 223. LLOYD MOSEBY
☐ 254. JORGE BELL
☐ 282. KEN MACHA
☐ 314. BUCK MARTINEZ
☐ 380. DAVE STIEB
☐ 412. LUIS LEAL
☐ 437. JUAN BERENGUER
☐ 470. JOHN MAYBERRY
☐ 499. PAUL MIRABELLA
☐ 518. GARTH IORG
☐ 565. JACKSON TODD
☐ 596. DAMASO GARCIA
☐ 606. TEAM LEADER CARD
☐ 665. JIM CLANCY
☐ 677. ALFREDO GRIFFIN
☐ 707. MARK BOMBACK
☐ 739. JOEY MCLAUGHLIN
☐ 768. JERRY GARVIN

1982 TOPPS TRADED (132) 2 1/2" X 3 1/2"

ORIOLES
CAL RIPKEN

ATLANTA BRAVES

☐ 4T. STEVE BEDROSIAN
☐ 125T. BOB WATSON

BALTIMORE ORIOLES

☐ 35T. DAN FORD
☐ 81T. JOE NOLAN
☐ 98T. CAL RIPKEN

BOSTON RED SOX

NO CARDS ISSUED

CALIFORNIA ANGELS

☐ 9T. BOB BOONE
☐ 21T. DOUG CORBETT
☐ 26T. DOUG DECINCES
☐ 34T. TIM FOLI
☐ 47T. REGGIE JACKSON
☐ 48T. RON JACKSON
☐ 53T. MICK KELLEHER
☐ 128T. ROB WILFONG

CHICAGO CUBS

☐ 10T. LARRY BOWA
☐ 11T. DAN BRIGGS
☐ 16T. BILL CAMPBELL
☐ 49T. FERGIE JENKINS
☐ 52T. JAY JOHNSTONE
☐ 55T. JUNIOR KENNEDY
☐ 76T. KEITH MORELAND
☐ 82T. DICKIE NOLES
☐ 92T. MIKE PROLY
☐ 99T. ALLEN RIPLEY
☐ 129T. BUMP WILLS
☐ 130T. GARY WOODS

CHICAGO WHITE SOX

☐ 54T. STEVE KEMP
☐ 85T. TOM PACIOREK
☐ 101T. AURELIO RODRIGUEZ

CINCINNATI REDS

☐ 19T. CESAR CEDENO
☐ 41T. GREG HARRIS
☐ 56T. JIM KERN
☐ 58T. WAYNE KRENCHICKI
☐ 72T. EDDIE MILNER
☐ 105T. BOB SHIRLEY
☐ 120T. ALEX TREVINO

CLEVELAND INDIANS

☐ 42T. VON HAYES
☐ 69T. BAKE MCBRIDE
☐ 71T. LARRY MILBOURNE
☐ 87T. JACK PERCONTE
☐ 111T. LARY SORENSEN
☐ 116T. RICK SUTCLIFFE
☐ 127T. EDDIE WHITSON

DETROIT TIGERS

☐ 15T. ENOS CABELL
☐ 43T. LARRY HERNDON
☐ 45T. MIKE IVIE
☐ 62T. CHET LEMON
☐ 112T. ELIAS SOSA
☐ 121T. JERRY TURNER

HOUSTON ASTROS

☐ 57T. RAY KNIGHT
☐ 61T. MIKE LACOSS

KANSAS CITY ROYALS

☐ 8T. VIDA BLUE
☐ 37T. DAVE FROST
☐ 46T. GRANT JACKSON
☐ 65T. JERRY MARTIN
☐ 93T. GREG PRYOR
☐ 126T. DENNIS WERTH

LOS ANGELES DODGERS

☐ 5T. MARK BELANGER
☐ 75T. JOSE MORALES
☐ 84T. JORGE ORTA
☐ 103T. STEVE SAX

MILWAUKEE BREWERS

☐ 89T. ROB PICIOLO

TWINS
KENT HRBEK

MINNESOTA TWINS

☐ 13T. TOM BRUNANSKY
☐ 17T. BOBBY CASTILLO
☐ 25T. RON DAVIS
☐ 44T. KENT HRBEK
☐ 51T. RANDY JOHNSON
☐ 124T. RON WASHINGTON

MONTREAL EXPOS

☐ 7T. TIM BLACKWELL
☐ 83T. AL OLIVER
☐ 104T. DAN SCHATZEDER
☐ 118T. FRANK TAVERAS

NEW YORK METS

☐ 36T. GEORGE FOSTER
☐ 39T. RON GARDENHIRE
☐ 94T. CHARLIE PULEO
☐ 123T. TOM VERYZER

NEW YORK YANKEES

☐ 1T. DOYLE ALEXANDER
☐ 20T. DAVE COLLINS
☐ 30T. ROGER ERICKSON
☐ 40T. KEN GRIFFEY
☐ 67T. JOHN MAYBERRY
☐ 95T. SHANE RAWLEY
☐ 107T. ROY SMALLEY
☐ 131T. BUTCH WYNEGAR

OAKLAND A'S

- ☐ 14T. JEFF BURROUGHS
- ☐ 64T. DAVE LOPES
- ☐ 70T. DAN MEYER
- ☐ 102T. JOE RUDI

PHILADELPHIA PHILLIES

- ☐ 27T. IVAN DEJESUS
- ☐ 28T. BOB DERNIER
- ☐ 29T. BO DIAZ
- ☐ 32T. ED FARMER
- ☐ 59T. MIKE KRUKOW
- ☐ 73T. SID MONGE
- ☐ 100T. BILL ROBINSON

PITTSBURGH PIRATES

- ☐ 3T. ROSS BAUGARTEN
- ☐ 24T. DICK DAVIS
- ☐ 77T. JIM MORRISON
- ☐ 96T. JOHNNY RAY

ST. LOUIS CARDINALS

- ☐ 79T. STEVE MURA
- ☐ 108T. LONNIE SMITH
- ☐ 109T. OZZIE SMITH

SAN DIEGO PADRES

- ☐ 6T. KURT BEVACQUA
- ☐ 63T. SIXTO LEZCANO
- ☐ 74T. JOHN MONTEFUSCO
- ☐ 90T. JOE PITTMAN
- ☐ 106T. ERIC SHOW
- ☐ 119T. GARRY TEMPLETON

SAN FRANCISCO GIANTS

- ☐ 23T. CHILI DAVIS
- ☐ 38T. RICH GALE
- ☐ 60T. DUANE KUIPER
- ☐ 66T. RENIE MARTIN
- ☐ 110T. REGGIE SMITH
- ☐ 115T. CHAMP SUMMERS

SEATTLE MARINERS

- ☐ 12T. BOBBY BROWN
- ☐ 18T. BILL CAUDILL
- ☐ 22T. AL COWENS
- ☐ 31T. JIM ESSIAN
- ☐ 80T. GENE NELSON
- ☐ 88T. GAYLORD PERRY
- ☐ 113T. MIKE STANTON
- ☐ 114T. STEVE STROUGHTER
- ☐ 122T. ED VANDEBERG

TEXAS RANGERS

- ☐ 33T. DOUG FLYNN
- ☐ 50T. LAMAR JOHNSON
- ☐ 68T. LEE MAZZILLI
- ☐ 86T. LARRY PARRISH
- ☐ 117T. FRANK TANANA

TORONTO BLUE JAYS

- ☐ 2T. JESSE BARFIELD
- ☐ 78T. RANCE MULLINIKS
- ☐ 91T. HOSKEN POWELL
- ☐ 97T. DAVE REVERING

1983 TOPPS (792)
2 1/2" X 3 1/2"

ATLANTA BRAVES

- ☐ 26. JERRY ROYSTER
- ☐ 50. BOB HORNER
- ☐ 76. RICK MAHLER
- ☐ 104. BOB WALK
- ☐ 126. JOE TORRE(M)
- ☐ 157. STEVE BEDROSIAN
- ☐ 207. RICK CAMP
- ☐ 235. CLAUDELL WASHINGTON
- ☐ 255. GENE GARBER
- ☐ 288. JOE COWLEY
- ☐ 314. KEN DAYLEY
- ☐ 339. TERRY HARPER
- ☐ 364. BRETT BUTLER
- ☐ 410. PHIL NIEKRO
- ☐ 417. TOM HAUSMAN
- ☐ 439. RAFAEL RAMIREZ
- ☐ 467. RUFINO LINARES
- ☐ 502. TEAM LEADER CARD
- ☐ 521. BRUCE BENEDICT
- ☐ 544. LARRY WHISENTON
- ☐ 572. BOB WATSON
- ☐ 596. RANDY JOHNSON
- ☐ 624. GLENN HUBBARD
- ☐ 649. TOMMY BOGGS
- ☐ 676. BIFF POCOROBA
- ☐ 760. DALE MURPHY
- ☐ 792. CHRIS CHAMBLISS

BALTIMORE ORIOLES

- ☐ 21. TEAM LEADER CARD
- ☐ 59. BENNY AYALA
- ☐ 85. KEN SINGLETON
- ☐ 138. RICK DEMPSEY
- ☐ 163. CAL RIPKEN
- ☐ 192. FLOYD RAYFORD
- ☐ 217. TIM STODDARD
- ☐ 242. JOE NOLAN
- ☐ 268. STORM DAVIS
- ☐ 293. GLENN GULLIVER
- ☐ 319. LENN SAKATA
- ☐ 347. SAMMY STEWART
- ☐ 372. TERRY CROWLEY
- ☐ 426. EARL WEAVER(M)
- ☐ 445. MIKE FLANAGAN
- ☐ 473. JOHN LOWENSTEIN
- ☐ 490. JIM PALMER
- ☐ 530. EDDIE MURRAY
- ☐ 553. DENNY MARTINEZ
- ☐ 579. RICH DAUER
- ☐ 605. GARY ROENICKE
- ☐ 631. TIPPY MARTINEZ
- ☐ 655. AL BUMBRY
- ☐ 683. DAN FORD
- ☐ 718. JIM DWYER
- ☐ 745. SCOTT MCGREGOR

BOSTON RED SOX

- ☐ 30. JIM RICE
- ☐ 56. CHUCK RAINEY
- ☐ 82. BRUCE HURST
- ☐ 108. GLENN HOFFMAN
- ☐ 135. DWIGHT EVANS

- ☐ 162. MARK CLEAR
- ☐ 188. RICK MILLER
- ☐ 213. TOM BURGMEIER
- ☐ 239. DAVE STAPLETON
- ☐ 270. DENNIS ECKERSLEY
- ☐ 295. JERRY REMY
- ☐ 318. JOHN TUDOR
- ☐ 344. ROGER LAFRANCOIS
- ☐ 381. TEAM LEADER CARD
- ☐ 419. STEVE CRAWFORD
- ☐ 446. REID NICHOLS
- ☐ 472. GARY ALLENSON
- ☐ 498. WADE BOGGS
- ☐ 523. CARNEY LANSFORD
- ☐ 550. CARL YASTRZEMSKI
- ☐ 577. LUIS APONTE
- ☐ 602. RICH GEDMAN
- ☐ 628. JULIO VALDEZ
- ☐ 654. BOB OJEDA
- ☐ 682. BOB STANLEY
- ☐ 715. TONY PEREZ
- ☐ 743. MIKE TORREZ
- ☐ 786. RALPH HOUK(M)

CALIFORNIA ANGELS

- ☐ 27. DOUG CORBETT
- ☐ 53. MIKE WITT
- ☐ 79. MICK KELLEHER
- ☐ 105. DON BAYLOR
- ☐ 131. ED OTT
- ☐ 158. ROB WILFONG
- ☐ 178. LUIS TIANT
- ☐ 184. BOB CLARK
- ☐ 200. ROD CAREW
- ☐ 236. STEVE RENKO
- ☐ 262. RON JACKSON
- ☐ 276. GENE MAUCH(M)
- ☐ 315. RICK BURLESON
- ☐ 341. DOUG DECINCES
- ☐ 416. JOE FERGUSON
- ☐ 442. BRIAN DOWNING
- ☐ 468. DAVE GOLTZ
- ☐ 500. REGGIE JACKSON
- ☐ 520. FRED LYNN
- ☐ 547. GEOFF ZAHN
- ☐ 573. ANDY HASSLER
- ☐ 599. DON AASE
- ☐ 623. LUIS SANCHEZ
- ☐ 625. KEN FORSCH
- ☐ 651. TEAM LEADER CARD
- ☐ 678. JUAN BENIQUEZ
- ☐ 712. BRUCE KISON
- ☐ 735. TOMMY JOHN
- ☐ 738. TIM FOLI
- ☐ 765. BOB BOONE
- ☐ 777. JOHN CURTIS
- ☐ 790. BOB GRICH

CHICAGO CUBS

- ☐ 22. RANDY MARTZ
- ☐ 51. TEAM LEADER CARD
- ☐ 73. ALLEN RIPLEY
- ☐ 83. RYNE SANDBERG
- ☐ 99. DICKIE NOLES
- ☐ 125. LEON DURHAM
- ☐ 152. JAY JOHNSTONE
- ☐ 204. JUNIOR KENNEDY
- ☐ 230. FERGIE JENKINS
- ☐ 250. BILL BUCKNER
- ☐ 305. LARRY BOWA
- ☐ 335. STEVE HENDERSON
- ☐ 356. GARY WOODS
- ☐ 436. BILL CAMPBELL
- ☐ 456. LEE ELIA(M)
- ☐ 481. SCOT THOMPSON
- ☐ 508. TOM FILER
- ☐ 542. JODY DAVIS
- ☐ 568. WILLIE HERNANDEZ
- ☐ 597. MIKE PROLY
- ☐ 619. KEITH MORELAND
- ☐ 643. BUMP WILLS
- ☐ 699. LEE SMITH
- ☐ 729. JERRY MORALES
- ☐ 759. DOUG BIRD
- ☐ 787. DICK TIDROW

CHICAGO WHITE SOX

- ☐ 20. CARLTON FISK
- ☐ 46. RICHARD DOTSON
- ☐ 72. TOM PACIOREK

- ☐ 98. VANCE LAW
- ☐ 124. MARC HILL
- ☐ 153. JERRY KOOSMAN
- ☐ 177. HAROLD BAINES
- ☐ 216. TONY LARUSSA(M)
- ☐ 260. STEVE KEMP
- ☐ 278. KEVIN HICKEY
- ☐ 310. GREG LUZINSKI
- ☐ 362. BILL ALMON
- ☐ 409. MARVIS FOLEY
- ☐ 434. DENNIS LAMP
- ☐ 461. STEVE TROUT
- ☐ 487. JERRY HAIRSTON
- ☐ 514. RUDY LAW
- ☐ 541. BRITT BURNS
- ☐ 560. RON LEFLORE
- ☐ 591. TEAM LEADER CARD
- ☐ 618. LAMARR LOYT
- ☐ 669. MIKE SQUIRES
- ☐ 693. SPARKY LYLE
- ☐ 698. TONY BERNAZARD
- ☐ 758. AURELIO RODRIGUEZ
- ☐ 772. JIM KERN

CINCINNATI REDS

- ☐ 34. PAUL HOUSEHOLDER
- ☐ 60. JOHNNY BENCH
- ☐ 86. TOM HUME
- ☐ 112. BOB SHIRLEY
- ☐ 139. BRUCE BERENYI
- ☐ 165. DAN DRIESSEN
- ☐ 191. JOE PRICE
- ☐ 215. MARIO SOTO
- ☐ 243. DUANE WALKER
- ☐ 269. RON OESTER
- ☐ 296. GREG HARRIS
- ☐ 322. DAVE VAN GORDER
- ☐ 351. TEAM LEADER CARD
- ☐ 374. WAYNE KRENCHICKI
- ☐ 423. TOM LAWLESS
- ☐ 449. EDDIE MILNER
- ☐ 475. CESAR CEDENO
- ☐ 527. LARRY BIITTNER
- ☐ 554. MIKE VAIL
- ☐ 580. TOM SEAVER
- ☐ 607. CHARLIE LEIBRANDT
- ☐ 632. ALEX TREVINO
- ☐ 658. FRANK PASTORE
- ☐ 684. RAFAEL LANDESTOY
- ☐ 720. DAVE CONCEPION
- ☐ 756. RUSS NIXON(M)

CLEVELAND INDIANS

- ☐ 48. LARY SORENSEN
- ☐ 91. LARRY MILBOURNE
- ☐ 120. LEN BARKER
- ☐ 141. TEAM LEADER CARD
- ☐ 182. MIKE FISCHLIN
- ☐ 227. CHRIS BANDO
- ☐ 248. BAKE MCBRIDE
- ☐ 280. BERT BLYLEVEN
- ☐ 289. JERRY DYBZINSKI
- ☐ 303. MIGUEL DILONE
- ☐ 325. VON HAYES
- ☐ 348. ALAN BANNISTER
- ☐ 367. BUD ANDERSON
- ☐ 429. EDDIE WHITSON
- ☐ 480. TOBY HARRAH
- ☐ 497. RICK SUTCLIFFE
- ☐ 524. TOM BRENNAN
- ☐ 546. DAVE GARCIA(M)
- ☐ 569. JACK PERCONTE
- ☐ 614. ED GLYNN
- ☐ 616. BILL NAHORODNY
- ☐ 640. ANDRE THORNTON
- ☐ 660. MIKE HARGROVE
- ☐ 689. RON HASSEY
- ☐ 725. DAN SPILLNER
- ☐ 757. RICK MANNING
- ☐ 779. RICK WAITS

DETROIT TIGERS

- ☐ 13. LARRY HERNDON
- ☐ 41. JERRY TURNER
- ☐ 65. JACK MORRIS
- ☐ 95. ALAN TRAMMELL
- ☐ 119. TOM BROOKENS

- ☐ 147. RICK LEACH
- ☐ 174. JERRY UJDUR
- ☐ 196. BILL FAHEY
- ☐ 225. ENOS CABELL
- ☐ 261. TEAM LEADER CARD
- ☐ 285. LANCE PARRISH
- ☐ 304. DAVE RUCKER
- ☐ 332. GLENN WILSON
- ☐ 373. KEVIN SAUCIER
- ☐ 430. KIRK GIBSON
- ☐ 457. MILT WILCOX
- ☐ 483. LYNN JONES
- ☐ 509. LOU WHITAKER
- ☐ 536. JOHNNY WOCKENFUSS
- ☐ 562. DAVE ROZEMA
- ☐ 588. PAT UNDERWOOD
- ☐ 613. MIKE IVIE
- ☐ 638. DAN PETRY
- ☐ 666. SPARKY ANDERSON(M)
- ☐ 691. DAVE TOBIK
- ☐ 727. CHET LEMON
- ☐ 753. ELIAS SOSA

HOUSTON ASTROS

- ☐ 14. FRANK LACORTE
- ☐ 39. TERRY PUHL
- ☐ 66. BOB LILLIS(M)
- ☐ 92. MIKE LACOSS
- ☐ 117. ALAN KNICELY
- ☐ 172. VERN RUHLE
- ☐ 193. HARRY SPILMAN
- ☐ 198. KIKO GARCIA
- ☐ 221. JOE NIEKRO
- ☐ 247. DAVE SMITH
- ☐ 275. RAY KNIGHT
- ☐ 328. CRAIG REYNOLDS
- ☐ 360. NOLAN RYAN
- ☐ 382. BOB KNEPPER
- ☐ 422. GEORGE CAPPUZZELLO
- ☐ 441. TEAM LEADER CARD
- ☐ 478. PHIL GARNER
- ☐ 507. TONY SCOTT
- ☐ 538. DANNY HEEP
- ☐ 558. DICKIE THON
- ☐ 585. JOSE CRUZ
- ☐ 611. BERT ROBERGE
- ☐ 639. ART HOWE
- ☐ 662. JOE SAMBITO
- ☐ 692. DENNY WALLING
- ☐ 723. RANDY MOFFITT
- ☐ 774. ALAN ASHBY
- ☐ 752. LUIS PUJOLS

KANSAS CITY ROYALS

- ☐ 25. HAL MCRAE
- ☐ 52. ONIX CONCEPION
- ☐ 75. AMOS OTIS
- ☐ 96. DICK HOWSER (M)
- ☐ 136. WILLIE AIKENS
- ☐ 155. DAN QUISENBERRY
- ☐ 194. CESAR GERONIMO
- ☐ 219. MIKE ARMSTRONG
- ☐ 238. BUD BLACK
- ☐ 264. JAMIE QUIRK
- ☐ 316. PAUL SPLITTORFF
- ☐ 340. LARRY GURA
- ☐ 377. LEE MAY
- ☐ 418. GREG PRYOR
- ☐ 443. DON HOOD
- ☐ 471. TEAM LEADER CARD
- ☐ 525. FRANK WHITE
- ☐ 570. VIDA BLUE
- ☐ 600. GEORGE BRETT
- ☐ 626. JERRY MARTIN
- ☐ 656. DAVE FROST
- ☐ 687. U. L. WASHINGTON
- ☐ 710. WILLIE WILSON
- ☐ 746. JOHN WATHAN
- ☐ 785. DENNIS LEONARD

LOS ANGELES DODGERS

- ☐ 15. RON CEY
- ☐ 40. FERNANDO VALENZUELA
- ☐ 63. RICK MONDAY
- ☐ 90. JERRY REUSS
- ☐ 113. RON ROENICKE
- ☐ 170. STEVE HOWE
- ☐ 220. DUSTY BAKER

- ☐ 245. STEVE SAX
- ☐ 273. MARK BELANGER
- ☐ 306. TOM LASORDA(M)
- ☐ 324. MIKE MARSHALL
- ☐ 352. MIKE SCIOSCIA
- ☐ 376. KEN LANDREAUX
- ☐ 425. PEDRO GUERRERO
- ☐ 454. BOB WELCH
- ☐ 477. TOM NIEDENFUER
- ☐ 532. DAVE STEWART
- ☐ 555. STEVE YEAGER
- ☐ 583. TERRY FORSTER
- ☐ 610. STEVE GARVEY
- ☐ 633. VICENTE ROMO
- ☐ 661. BILL RUSSELL
- ☐ 681. TEAM LEADER CARD
- ☐ 722. JORGE ORTA
- ☐ 748. DERREL THOMAS
- ☐ 775. BURT HOOTON

MILWAUKEE BREWERS

- ☐ 10. GORMAN THOMAS
- ☐ 35. ROLLIE FINGERS
- ☐ 62. BOB MCCLURE
- ☐ 88. JIM GANTNER
- ☐ 114. JIM SLATON
- ☐ 142. MIKE CALDWELL
- ☐ 145. DON SUTTON
- ☐ 167. MARK BROUHARD
- ☐ 190. CECIL COOPER
- ☐ 218. ROY HOWELL
- ☐ 244. DWIGHT BERNARD
- ☐ 271. ED ROMERO
- ☐ 297. NED YOST
- ☐ 321. TEAM LEADER CARD
- ☐ 350. ROBIN YOUNT
- ☐ 375. PETE VUCKOVICH
- ☐ 424. JERRY AUGUSTINE
- ☐ 450. TED SIMMONS
- ☐ 476. ROB PICCIOLO
- ☐ 503. MOOSE HAAS
- ☐ 528. JAMIE EASTERLY
- ☐ 582. MARSHALL EDWARDS
- ☐ 608. DON MONEY
- ☐ 630. PAUL MOLITOR
- ☐ 659. CHARLIE MOORE
- ☐ 726. HARVEY KUENN(M)
- ☐ 750. BEN OGLIVIE
- ☐ 773. LARRY HISLE

MINNESOTA TWINS

- ☐ 11. BILLY GARDNER(M)
- ☐ 33. JACK O'CONNOR
- ☐ 67. SAL BUTERA
- ☐ 93. JOHN CASTINO
- ☐ 121. MICKEY HATCHER
- ☐ 166. JOHN PACELLA
- ☐ 181. TERRY FELTON
- ☐ 197. JIM EISENREICH
- ☐ 232. TOM BRUNANSKY
- ☐ 266. PAUL BORIS
- ☐ 294. DAVE ENGLE
- ☐ 308. JESUS VEGA
- ☐ 327. BOBBY CASTILLO
- ☐ 354. RANDY JOHNSON
- ☐ 380. RON DAVIS
- ☐ 431. GARY GAETTI
- ☐ 458. RON WASHINGTON
- ☐ 499. JEFF LITTLE
- ☐ 517. GARY WARD
- ☐ 529. TIM LAUDNER
- ☐ 559. PETE REDFERN
- ☐ 586. FRANK VIOLA
- ☐ 647. BOBBY MITCHELL
- ☐ 671. LENNY FAEDO
- ☐ 690. KENT HRBEK
- ☐ 731. AL WILLIAMS
- ☐ 751. BRAD HAVENS
- ☐ 771. TEAM LEADER CARD

MONTREAL EXPOS

- ☐ 31. BILL GULLICKSON
- ☐ 57. TIM BLACKWELL
- ☐ 111. TEAM LEADER CARD
- ☐ 137. WOODIE FRYMAN
- ☐ 164. DAVE PALMER
- ☐ 169. DOUG FLYNN

☐ 189. DAN SCHATZEDER
☐ 214. JERRY WHITE
☐ 237. DAN NORMAN
☐ 265. JOEL YOUNGBLOOD
☐ 267. TERRY FRANCONA
☐ 290. JEFF REARDON
☐ 320. STEVE ROGERS
☐ 370. GARY CARTER
☐ 420. AL OLIVER
☐ 447. BRYN SMITH
☐ 474. RAY BURRIS
☐ 495. WARREN CROMARTIE
☐ 516. BILL VIRDON(M)
☐ 552. TIM WALLACH
☐ 595. TIM RAINES
☐ 629. CHARLIE LEA
☐ 657. MIKE GATES
☐ 680. ANDRE DAWSON
☐ 686. RANDY LERCH
☐ 717. SCOTT SANDERSON
☐ 744. BRAD MILLS
☐ 768. CHRIS SPEIER

NEW YORK METS

☐ 29. RANDY JONES
☐ 55. MOOKIE WILSON
☐ 80. GEROGE FOSTER
☐ 107. MIKE JORGENSEN
☐ 134. HUBIE BROOKS
☐ 160. DAVE KINGMAN
☐ 187. TERRY LEACH
☐ 212. JOHN STEARNS
☐ 246. GEORGE BAMBERGER(M)
☐ 292. CRAIG SWAN
☐ 317. GARY RAJSICH
☐ 343. BOB BAILOR
☐ 369. JESSE OROSCO
☐ 444. WALLY BACKMAN
☐ 469. RON GARDENHIRE
☐ 496. TOM VERYZER
☐ 522. PAT ZACHRY
☐ 548. BRIAN GILES
☐ 549. CHARLIE PULEO
☐ 575. NEIL ALLEN
☐ 601. ED LYNCH
☐ 621. TEAM LEADER CARD
☐ 653. ELLIS VALENTINE
☐ 679. MIKE SCOTT
☐ 713. RON HODGES
☐ 739. RICK OWNBEY
☐ 740. RUSTY STAUB
☐ 764. PETE FALCONE

MOOKIE
WILSON
OUTFIELD
METS

NEW YORK YANKEES

☐   8. STEVE BALBONI
☐ 19. OSCAR GAMBLE
☐ 45. JOHN MAYBERRY
☐ 81. TEAM LEADER CARD
☐ 110. KEN GRIFFEY
☐ 123. GEORGE FRAZIER
☐ 140. WILLIE RANDOLPH
☐ 176. DAVE RIGHETTI
☐ 203. MIKE MORGAN
☐ 240. RICH GOSSAGE
☐ 254. RICK CERONE
☐ 281. ANDRE ROBERTSON
☐ 307. LOU PINIELLA
☐ 333. DAVE LAROCHE

☐ 359. DAVE COLLINS
☐ 408. RUDY MAY
☐ 440. RON GUIDRY
☐ 460. ROY SMALLEY
☐ 486. CLYDE KING(M)
☐ 512. DOYLE ALEXANDER
☐ 539. ROGER ERICKSON
☐ 592. SHANE RAWLEY
☐ 617. BUTCH WYNEGAR
☐ 635. GRAIG NETTLES
☐ 652. BUTCH HOBSON
☐ 670. JERRY MUMPHREY
☐ 685. LEE MAZZILLI
☐ 697. BARRY FOOTE
☐ 770. DAVE WINFIELD
☐ 782. BOBBY MURCER

OAKLAND A'S

☐ 23. MIKE HEATH
☐ 47. DAVE MCKAY
☐ 87. JOE RUDI
☐ 102. DAVE BEARD
☐ 127. PRESTON HANNA
☐ 156. BILLY MARTIN(M)
☐ 180. RICKEY HENDERSON
☐ 208. DAN MEYER
☐ 233. WAYNE GROSS
☐ 259. JEFF JONES
☐ 286. RICK LANDFORD
☐ 312. BRIAN KINGMAN
☐ 338. BOB OWCHINKO
☐ 365. DAVE LOPES
☐ 413. MATT KEOUGH
☐ 435. TONY ARMAS
☐ 466. TOM UNDERWOOD
☐ 493. STEVE MCCATTY
☐ 513. FRED STANLEY
☐ 531. TEAM LEADER CARD
☐ 571. MICKEY KLUTTS
☐ 598. DWAYNE MURPHY
☐ 620. MIKE NORRIS
☐ 648. JEFF BURROUGHS
☐ 709. JIMMY SEXTON
☐ 737. MITCHELL PAGE
☐ 762. CLIFF JOHNSON
☐ 784. JEFF NEWMAN

PHILADELPHIA PHILLIES

☐ 16. GEORGE VUKOVICH
☐ 43. BOB DERNIER
☐ 70. STEVE CARLTON
☐ 100. PETE ROSE
☐ 148. DAVE W. ROBERTS
☐ 175. BO DIAZ
☐ 199. MARTY BYSTROM
☐ 211. JOHN DENNY
☐ 229. TEAM LEADER CARD
☐ 252. LUIS AGUAYO
☐ 279. GREG GROSS
☐ 300. MIKE SCHMIDT
☐ 331. MIKE KRUKOW
☐ 357. LEN MATUSZEK
☐ 383. OZZIE VIRGIL
☐ 432. PORFIRIO ALTAMIRANO
☐ 459. ED FARMER
☐ 484. DICK RUTHVEN
☐ 510. TUG MCGRAW
☐ 535. MANNY TRILLO
☐ 564. SID MONGE
☐ 587. IVAN DEJESUS
☐ 615. GARRY MADDOX
☐ 637. PAT CORRALES(M)
☐ 664. BOB MOLINARO
☐ 668. LARRY CHRISTENSON
☐ 728. RON REED
☐ 754. BILL ROBINSON
☐ 780. GARY MATTHEWS

PITTSBURGH PIRATES

☐ 17. KENT TEKULVE
☐ 44. DON ROBINSON
☐ 69. LEE LACY
☐ 97. ROSS BAUMGARTEN
☐ 122. JIMMY SMITH
☐ 149. JOHNNY RAY
☐ 173. JIM MORRISON
☐ 205. DAVE PARKER

☐ 226. ENRIQUE ROMO
☐ 253. LARRY MCWILLIAMS
☐ 291. TEAM LEADER CARD
☐ 329. RANDY NIEMANN
☐ 355. JIM BIBBY
☐ 385. MIKE EASLER
☐ 433. DALE BERRA
☐ 462. STEVE NICOSIA
☐ 485. OMAR MORENO
☐ 537. ROD SCURRY
☐ 566. MANNY SARMIENTO
☐ 590. TONY PENA
☐ 645. BILL MADLOCK
☐ 667. DICK DAVIS
☐ 696. CHUCK TANNER(M)
☐ 730. JASON THOMPSON
☐ 755. JOHN CANDELARIA
☐ 778. RICH HEBNER
☐ 781. RICK RHODEN

ST. LOUIS CARDINALS

☐ 24. STEVE MURA
☐ 49. WILLIE MCGEE
☐ 74. JULIO GONZALEZ
☐ 103. DARRELL PORTER
☐ 128. MIKE RAMSEY
☐ 150. BRUCE SUTTER
☐ 186. WHITEY HERZOG(M)
☐ 206. KEN OBERKFELL
☐ 228. JOAQUIN ANDUJAR
☐ 284. JEFF LAHTI
☐ 311. GLENN BRUMMER
☐ 337. TITO LANDRUM
☐ 363. JOHN STUPER
☐ 415. BOB FORSCH
☐ 438. DAVE LAPOINT
☐ 465. LONNIE SMITH
☐ 489. TOM HERR
☐ 515. GENE TENACE
☐ 540. OZZIE SMITH
☐ 561. TEAM LEADER CARD
☐ 578. DAVID GREEN
☐ 594. ERIC RASMUSSEN
☐ 627. DOUG BAIR
☐ 650. GEORGE HENDRICK
☐ 672. JIM KAAT
☐ 700. KEITH HERNANDEZ
☐ 721. JOHN MARTIN
☐ 734. STEVE BRAUN
☐ 788. DANE IORG

SAN DIEGO PADRES

☐   7. GENE RICHARDS
☐ 38. TIM FLANNERY
☐ 68. ERIC SHOW
☐ 94. DAVE EDWARDS
☐ 118. CHRIS WELSH
☐ 168. JUAN EICHELBERGER
☐ 185. TIM LOLLAR
☐ 223. JOHN MONTEFUSCO
☐ 251. ALAN WIGGINS
☐ 274. TERRY KENNEDY
☐ 298. FLOYD CHIFFER
☐ 323. LUIS DELEON
☐ 346. JOE PITTMAN
☐ 366. DICK WILLIAMS(M)
☐ 384. DAVE DRAVECKY
☐ 455. SIXTO LEZCANO
☐ 482. TONY GWYNN
☐ 505. GARRY TEMPLETON
☐ 533. LUIS SALAZAR
☐ 563. JUAN BONILLA
☐ 593. BRODERICK PERKINS
☐ 612. STEVE SWISHER
☐ 644. JOE LEFEBVRE
☐ 674. KURT BEVACQUA
☐ 695. RUPPERT JONES
☐ 742. TEAM LEADER CARD
☐ 761. GARY LUCAS

SAN FRANCISCO GIANTS

☐ 32. DAVE BERGMAN
☐ 58. AL HOLLAND
☐ 84. MILT MAY
☐ 115. CHILI DAVIS
☐ 133. JIM BARR
☐ 143. JOE PETTINI

1983 Topps

☐ 154. JOHNNIE LEMASTER
☐ 171. TEAM LEADER CARD
☐ 210. JACK CLARK
☐ 263. RENIE MARTIN
☐ 282. REGGIE SMITH
☐ 309. JEFF LEONARD
☐ 342. ATLEE HAMMAKER
☐ 379. GUY SULARZ
☐ 428. CHAMP SUMMERS
☐ 448. DARRELL EVANS
☐ 470. GREG MINTON
☐ 494. BOB BRENLY
☐ 518. BILL LASKEY
☐ 543. ALAN FOWLKES
☐ 576. FRANK ROBINSON(M)
☐ 603. JOE MORGAN
☐ 634. MAX VENABLE
☐ 663. TOM O'MALLEY
☐ 688. JIM WOHLFORD
☐ 719. RICH GALE
☐ 747. FRED BREINING
☐ 767. DUANE KUIPER
☐ 791. GARY LAVELLE

SEATTLE MARINERS

☐ 28. BRUCE BOCHTE
☐ 54. JIM MALER
☐ 78. BILL CAUDILL
☐ 106. GENE NELSON
☐ 132. TODD CRUZ
☐ 159. MIKE STANTON
☐ 183. ED VANDE BERG
☐ 195. BOB STODDARD
☐ 209. MIKE MOORE
☐ 234. LARRY ANDERSEN
☐ 258. MANNY CASTILLO
☐ 287. BOBBY BROWN
☐ 313. GARY GRAY
☐ 336. RENE LACHEMANN(M)
☐ 368. RICHIE ZISK
☐ 414. JULIO CRUZ
☐ 437. RICK SWEET
☐ 463. GAYLORD PERRY
☐ 492. PAUL SERNA
☐ 519. TERRY BULLING
☐ 545. FLOYD BANNISTER
☐ 567. JOE SIMPSON
☐ 622. DAVE EDLER
☐ 646. JIM ESSIAN
☐ 675. JIM BEATTIE
☐ 677. DAVE REVERING
☐ 711. TEAM LEADER CARD
☐ 732. DAVE HENDERSON
☐ 763. AL COWENS
☐ 789. BRYAN CLARK

TEXAS RANGERS

☐ 12. PAUL MIRABELLA
☐ 37. DARRELL JOHNSON(M)
☐ 64. BILL STEIN
☐ 116. DAVE J. SCHMIDT
☐ 144. MARK WAGNER
☐ 224. MICKEY RIVERS
☐ 272. FRANK TANANA
☐ 299. GEORGE WRIGHT
☐ 330. BUDDY BELL
☐ 353. STEVE COMER
☐ 371. MIKE RICHARDT

☐ 4'12. TEAM LEADER CARD
☐ 453. LAMAR JOHNSON
☐ 479. CHARLIE HOUGH
☐ 504. DON WERNER
☐ 534. JOHN BUTCHER
☐ 557. RICK HONEYCUTT
☐ 565. BUCKY DENT
☐ 584. DAVE HOSTETLER
☐ 609. DANNY DARWIN
☐ 641. BILLY SAMPLE
☐ 665. JIM SUNDBERG
☐ 724. JOHNNY GRUBB
☐ 749. JON MATLACK
☐ 776. LARRY PARRISH

TORONTO BLUE JAYS

☐   9. JOE MCLAUGHLIN
☐ 42. DALE MURRAY
☐ 77. HOSKEN POWELL
☐ 89. LEON ROBERTS
☐ 109. LUIS LEAL
☐ 130. DAVE STIEB
☐ 202. TEAM LEADER CARD
☐ 222. DAMASO GARCIA
☐ 257. JESSE BARFIELD
☐ 277. RANCE MULLINIKS
☐ 302. ERNIE WHITT
☐ 326. GARTH IORG
☐ 345. JIM CLANCY
☐ 358. JERRY GARVIN
☐ 427. ROY LEE JACKSON
☐ 452. LLOYD MOSEBY
☐ 488. ALFREDO GRIFFIN
☐ 506. JIM GOTT
☐ 556. WILLIE UPSHAW
☐ 574. GLENN ADAMS
☐ 589. ALVIS WOODS
☐ 606. BOBBY COX(M)
☐ 714. WAYNE NORDHAGEN
☐ 733. BUCK MARTINEZ
☐ 766. BARRY BONNELL

1983 TOPPS TRADED (132)
2 1/2" X 3 1/2"

ATLANTA BRAVES

☐ 31T. PETE FALCONE
☐ 33T. TERRY FORSTER
☐ 51T. MIKE JORGENSEN
☐ 69T. CRAIG MCMURTRY
☐ 84T. PASCUAL PEREZ

BALTIMORE ORIOLES

☐   3T. JOE ALTOBELLI(M)
☐ 44T. LEO HERNANDEZ
☐ 97T. AURELIO RODRIGUEZ
☐ 102T. JOHN SHELBY

BOSTON RED SOX

☐   4T. TONY ARMAS
☐ 12T. DOUB BIRD
☐ 15T. MIKE BROWN
☐ 80T. JEFF NEWMAN

CALIFORNIA ANGELS

☐ 70T. JOHN MCNAMARA(M)
☐ 99T. DARYL SCONIERS
☐ 120T. ELLIS VALENTINE

CHICAGO CUBS

☐ 19T. RON CEY
☐ 39T. MEL HALL
☐ 92T. CHUCK RAINEY
☐ 98T. DICK RUTHVEN
☐ 117T. STEVE TROUT
☐ 121T. TOM VERYZER

CHICAGO WHITE SOX

☐   7T. FLOYD BANNISTER
☐ 23T. JULIO CRUZ
☐ 27T. JERRY DYBZINSKI
☐ 55T. RON KITTLE
☐ 112T. DICK TIDROW
☐ 124T. GREG WALKER

CINCINNATI REDS

☐ 11T. DANN BILARDELLO
☐ 35T. RICH GALE
☐ 57T. ALAN KNICELY
☐ 88T. CHARLIE PULEO
☐ 84T. GARY REDUS

CLEVELAND INDIANS

☐ 28T. JAMIE EASTERLY
☐ 29T. JUAN EICHELBERGER
☐ 30T. JIM ESSIAN
☐ 32T. MIKE FERRARO(M)
☐ 34T. JULIO FRANCO
☐ 86T. BRODERICK PERKINS
☐ 111T. GORMAN THOMAS
☐ 116T. MANNY TRILLO
☐ 122T. GEORGE VUKOVICH

DETROIT TIGERS

☐   5T. DOUG BAIR
☐ 38T. JOHNNY GRUBB
☐ 63T. AURELIO LOPEZ

HOUSTON ASTROS

☐ 25T. FRANK DIPINO
☐ 26T. BILL DORAN
☐ 64T. MIKE MADDEN
☐ 76T. OMAR MORENO
☐ 100T. MIKE SCOTT

KANSAS CITY ROYALS

☐ 95T. STEVE RENKO
☐ 96T. LEON ROBERTS
☐ 104T. JOE SIMPSON

LOS ANGELES DODGERS

☐ 14T. GREG BROCK
☐ 59T. RAFAEL LANDESTOY
☐ 75T. JOSE MORALES
☐ 83T. ALEJANDRO PENA
☐ 131T. PAT ZACHRY

MILWAUKEE BREWERS

- ☐ 65T. RICK MANNING
- ☐ 109T. TOM TELLMANN
- ☐ 123T. RICK WAITS

MINNESOTA TWINS

- ☐ 17T. RANDY BUSH
- ☐ 126T. LEN WHITEHOUSE

MONTREAL EXPOS

- ☐ 22T. TERRY CROWLEY
- ☐ 62T. BRYAN LITTLE
- ☐ 93T. BOBBY RAMOS
- ☐ 119T. MIKE VAIL
- ☐ 125T. CHRIS WELSH
- ☐ 128T. JIM WOHLFORD

NEW YORK METS

- ☐ 41T. DANNY HEEP
- ☐ 43T. KEITH HERNANDEZ
- ☐ 47T. FRANK HOWARD(M)
- ☐ 101T. TOM SEAVER
- ☐ 105T. DOUG SISK
- ☐ 108T. DARRYL STRAWBERRY
- ☐ 115T. MIKE TORREZ

TOM SEAVER
PITCHER
METS

NEW YORK YANKEES

- ☐ 8T. DON BAYLOR
- ☐ 18T. BERT CAMPANERIS
- ☐ 53T. STEVE KEMP
- ☐ 54T. MATT KEOUGH
- ☐ 66T. BILLY MARTIN(M)
- ☐ 79T. DALE MURRAY
- ☐ 103T. BOB SHIRLEY

OAKLAND A'S

- ☐ 2T. BILL ALMON
- ☐ 6T. STEVE BAKER
- ☐ 13T. STEVE BOROS(M)
- ☐ 16T. TOM BURGMEIER
- ☐ 20T. CHRIS CODIROLI
- ☐ 24T. MIKE DAVIS
- ☐ 52T. BOB KEARNEY
- ☐ 60T. CARNEY LANSFORD
- ☐ 87T. TONY PHILLIPS

PHILADELPHIA PHILLIES

- ☐ 36T. KIKO GARCIA
- ☐ 40T. VON HAYES
- ☐ 45T. WILLIE HERNANDEZ
- ☐ 46T. AL HOLLAND
- ☐ 61T. JOE LEFEBVRE
- ☐ 72T. LARRY MILBOURNE
- ☐ 77T. JOE MORGAN
- ☐ 85T. TONY PEREZ

PITTSBURGH PIRATES

- ☐ 67T. LEE MAZZILLI
- ☐ 110T. GENE TENACE
- ☐ 118T. LEE TUNNELL

ST. LOUIS CARDINALS

- ☐ 1T. NEIL ALLEN
- ☐ 90T. JAMIE QUIRK

SAN DIEGO PADRES

- ☐ 37T. STEVE GARVEY
- ☐ 74T. SID MONGE
- ☐ 107T. ELIAS SOSA
- ☐ 127T. ED WHITSON

SAN FRANCISCO GIANTS

- ☐ 58T. MIKE KRUKOW
- ☐ 68T. ANDY MCGAFFIGAN
- ☐ 130T. JOEL YOUNGBLOOD

SEATTLE MARINERS

- ☐ 9T. TONY BERNAZARD
- ☐ 42T. STEVE HENDERSON
- ☐ 71T. ORLANDO MERCADO
- ☐ 89T. PAT PUTNAM
- ☐ 129T. MATT YOUNG

TEXAS RANGERS

- ☐ 10T. LARRY BITTNER
- ☐ 48T. BOBBY JOHNSON
- ☐ 50T. ODELL JONES
- ☐ 81T. PETE O'BRIEN
- ☐ 91T. DOUG RADER(M)
- ☐ 106T. MIKE SMITHSON
- ☐ 113T. DAVE TOBIK
- ☐ 114T. WAYNE TOLLESON

TORONTO BLUE JAYS

- ☐ 21T. DAVE COLLINS
- ☐ 49T. CLIFF JOHNSON
- ☐ 56T. MICKEY KLUTTS
- ☐ 73T. RANDY MOFFITT
- ☐ 78T. MIKE MORGAN
- ☐ 82T. JORGE ORTA

1984 TOPPS (792)
2 1/2" X 3 1/2"

ORIOLES
JIM DWYER OF

ATLANTA BRAVES

- ☐ 25. GLENN HUBBARD
- ☐ 50. CHRIS CHAMBLISS
- ☐ 77. BRETT BUTLER
- ☐ 104. KEN DAYLEY
- ☐ 126. TEAM LEADER CARD
- ☐ 150. DALE MURPHY
- ☐ 207. DONNIE MOORE
- ☐ 234. RAFAEL RAMIREZ
- ☐ 255. BRUCE BENEDICT
- ☐ 289. RANDY JOHNSON
- ☐ 313. MIKE JORGENSEN
- ☐ 365. STEVE BEDROSIAN
- ☐ 410. CLAUDELL WASHINGTON
- ☐ 438. BIFF POCORBA
- ☐ 466. GENE GARBER
- ☐ 502. JOE TORRE(M)
- ☐ 521. PETE FALCONE

BALTIMORE ORIOLES

- ☐ 543. CRAIG MCMURTRY
- ☐ 572. JERRY ROYSTER
- ☐ 597. RICK CAMP
- ☐ 614. LEN BARKER
- ☐ 624. TERRY HARPER
- ☐ 650. PHIL NIEKRO
- ☐ 675. PASCUAL PEREZ
- ☐ 739. BOB WATSON
- ☐ 760. BOB HORNER
- ☐ 791. TERRY FORSTER

BALTIMORE ORIOLES

- ☐ 21. JOE ALTOBELLI(M)
- ☐ 59. SAMMY STEWART
- ☐ 71. LEO HERNANDEZ
- ☐ 86. JOHN SHELBY
- ☐ 106. TIM STODDARD
- ☐ 140. STORM DAVIS
- ☐ 165. KEN SINGLETON
- ☐ 191. MIKE BODDICKER
- ☐ 215. TIPPY MARTINEZ
- ☐ 240. EDDIE MURRAY
- ☐ 260. SCOTT MCGREGOR
- ☐ 272. RICK DEMPSEY
- ☐ 295. MIKE FLANAGAN
- ☐ 319. AL BUMBRY
- ☐ 347. ALLAN RAMIREZ
- ☐ 372. GARY ROENICKE
- ☐ 426. TEAM CARD LEADER
- ☐ 443. BENNY AYALA
- ☐ 473. JIM DWYER
- ☐ 490. CAL RIPKEN
- ☐ 530. DAN FORD
- ☐ 553. JOE NOLAN
- ☐ 578. LENN SAKATA
- ☐ 604. JOHN LOWENSTEIN
- ☐ 631. DENNY MARTINEZ
- ☐ 682. DAN MOROGIELLO
- ☐ 723. RICH DAUER
- ☐ 750. JIM PALMER
- ☐ 773. TODD CRUZ

BOSTON RED SOX

- ☐ 30. WADE BOGGS
- ☐ 56. GARY ALLENSON
- ☐ 82. DOUG BIRD
- ☐ 105. TONY ARMAS
- ☐ 162. BOB OJEDA
- ☐ 187. LUIS APONTE
- ☐ 213. BRUCE HURST
- ☐ 238. REID NICHOLS
- ☐ 296. JEFF NEWMAN
- ☐ 320. BOB STANLEY
- ☐ 344. RICK MILLER
- ☐ 381. RALPH HOUK(M)
- ☐ 419. JOHN HENRY JOHNSON
- ☐ 445. JERRY REMY
- ☐ 472. MIKE BROWN
- ☐ 498. RICH GEDMAN
- ☐ 523. GLENN HOFFMAN
- ☐ 550. JIM RICE
- ☐ 577. MARK CLEAR
- ☐ 601. JOHN TUDOR
- ☐ 628. ED JURAK
- ☐ 653. DAVE STAPLETON
- ☐ 683. MARTY BARRETT
- ☐ 720. DWIGHT EVANS
- ☐ 745. DENNIS ECKERSLEY
- ☐ 786. TEAM LEADER CARD

CALIFORNIA ANGELS

- ☐ 27. DARYL SCONIERS
- ☐ 53. JUAN BENIQUEZ
- ☐ 79. ROB WILFONG
- ☐ 100. REGGIE JACKSON
- ☐ 158. JOHN CURTIS
- ☐ 184. MIKE O'BERRY
- ☐ 201. BRUCE KISON
- ☐ 236. ELLIS VALENTINE
- ☐ 258. LUIS SANCHEZ
- ☐ 266. STEVE LUBRATICH
- ☐ 276. TEAM LEADER CARD
- ☐ 315. BOB GRICH
- ☐ 342. TIM FOLI
- ☐ 414. TOMMY JOHN
- ☐ 442. BYRON MCLAUGHLIN
- ☐ 468. GEOFF ZAHN

LARRY FRITSCH CARDS

735 OLD WAUSAU RD.
P.O. BOX 863, DEPT 579
STEVENS POINT, WI 54481
(715) 344-8687

Largest, over 34 Million cards in stock.

First, FULL-TIME since 1970. 40th year in cards.

Caring, we care about our customers and the hobby.

DARYL
BOSTON
APPLETON FOXES

Get the **REAL** Rookie cards of Jose Canseco, Kirby Puckett, Billy Joe Robidoux, Edwin Correa, Jose Guzman, Dwayne Henry, Kal Daniels and many many more!!!

1982 & 1983 Official Minor League Card Sets
Printed and Distributed Exclusively
By Fritsch Cards

All Sets in Beautiful Full-Color.
Complete Statistics on Back.

DANNY
COX
SPRINGFIELD CARDINALS

These 23 team sets were the official team sets that the clubs sold at their ball parks. The Midwest League has supplied more current Major Leaguers than any other minor league. All team sets feature a special team logo card with a list of the cards issued for that team on reverse. Names listed after the team are the more prominent players.

1982 Teams	# in set		
Appleton Foxes (White Sox)	(31)	**Boston,** Jones, Rowdon	$3.50
Beloit Brewers	(27)	**Wegman,** Clutterbuck	3.50
Burlington Rangers...........	(30)	**Henry,** Wilkerson, Cook	3.50
Clinton Giants	(32)	Grant, Ouellette.............................	2.50
Danville Suns (Angels)	(28)	Lugo, Schofield.............................	3.25
Madison Muskies (A's)	(34)	Kiefer, Romano	2.50
Springfield Cardinals	(24)	**Cox,** Hunt, Lyons	3.50
Waterloo Indians	(28)	Noboa, Roman	2.50
Wausau Timbers (Mariners) ...	(31)	Calderon, Nixon	3.25
Wisconsin Rapids Twins	(27)	Espinoza, Portugal	2.50
All 10 1982 Teams..			$23.75

DWAYNE
HENRY
BURLINGTON RANGERS

1983 Teams	# in set		
Appleton Foxes (White Sox)	(30)	**Correa,** Cangelosi, Trujillo, Jones.................	$3.50
Beloit Brewers	(30)	**Robidoux,** Williams, Bosio	4.50
Burlington Rangers...........	(30)	**Guzman,** Gonzalez, Buckley, Cook	3.50
Cedar Rapids Reds...........	(26)	**Daniels,** Kimm..............................	5.50
Clinton Giants	(30)	DeMerritt, Lachemann	2.25
Madison Muskies (A's)........	(32)	**Canseco,** Dawson	9.50
Peoria Suns (Angels)	(30)	Lugo, McLemore, Kipper......................	3.00
Springfield Cardinals	(26)	Ford, Young	3.00
Waterloo Indians	(29)	Noboa, Roman	2.25
Wausau Timbers (Mariners)	(31)	Dixon, Parent..............................	2.25
Wisconsin Rapids Twins	(28)	Cardenas, Manuel	2.25
Visalia Oaks (Twins-Cal.)	(25)	**Puckett,** Espinoza, Portugal, Eufemia	7.50
San Jose Bees (Co-op Cal) .	(26)	Featuring five Japanese players...........	3.00
All 13 1983 Teams			$38.50

BILL
WEGMAN
BELOIT BREWERS

1982 & 1983 Midwest League Checklist. Check which Midwest League players of 1982 & 1983 are now in the Big Leagues, includes Danny Cox, Billy Joe Robidoux, Jose Canseco, Daryl Boston, Dick Schofield, and many more. Complete checklists of the 1982 & 1983 Midwest league cards are now available for 50¢ and a SASE (self-addressed stamped envelope).

PUCKETT
Visalia Oaks

JOSE
CANSECO
MADISON MUSKIES

CORREA

DANIELS

BILLY JOE
ROBIDOUX
BELOIT BREWERS

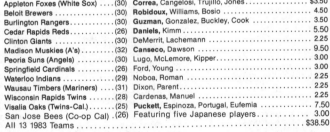

☐ 487. RICKY ADAMS
☐ 499. MIKE WITT
☐ 520. BOB BOONE
☐ 548. RON JACKSON
☐ 574. BRIAN DOWNING
☐ 600. ROD CAREW
☐ 626. BOB CLARK
☐ 643. MIKE BROWN
☐ 651. JOHN MCNAMARA(M)
☐ 680. FRED LYNN
☐ 719. ANDY HASSLER
☐ 735. RICK BURLESON
☐ 765. KEN FORSCH
☐ 790. DOUG DECINCES

CHICAGO CUBS

☐ 23. KEITH MORELAND
☐ 51. JIM FREY(M)
☐ 73. JODY DAVIS
☐ 99. CRAIG LEFFERTS
☐ 117. TOM VERYZER
☐ 151. STEVE TROUT
☐ 176. LEE SMITH
☐ 231. GARY WOODS
☐ 249. JAY JOHNSTONE
☐ 267. CARMELO MARTINEZ
☐ 304. WARREN BRUSSTAR
☐ 334. CHUCK RAINEY
☐ 357. RON CEY
☐ 437. MIKE PROLY
☐ 456. TEAM LEADER CARD
☐ 483. FERGIE JENKINS
☐ 508. MEL HALL
☐ 545. BILL BUCKNER
☐ 565. LEON DURHAM
☐ 596. RYNE SANDBERG
☐ 618. DICKIE NOLES
☐ 657. THAD BOSLEY
☐ 691. STEVE LAKE
☐ 736. DICK RUTHVEN
☐ 757. LARRY BOWA
☐ 787. BILL CAMPBELL

CHICAGO WHITE SOX

☐ 20. GREG LUZINSKI
☐ 47. RUDY LAW
☐ 72. MIKE SQUIRES
☐ 97. LAMARR HOYT
☐ 125. BRITT BURNS
☐ 153. DICK TIDROW
☐ 163. LORENZO GRAY
☐ 177. JERRY HAIRSTON
☐ 216. TEAM LEADER CARD
☐ 257. JULIO CRUZ
☐ 269. AURELIO RODRIGUEZ
☐ 280. FLOYD BANNISTER
☐ 311. JERRY KOOSMAN
☐ 364. SCOTT FLETCHER
☐ 382. CHRIS NYMAN
☐ 409. JUAN AGOSTO
☐ 434. HAROLD BAINES
☐ 459. KEVIN HICKEY
☐ 480. RON KITTLE
☐ 518. GREG WALKER
☐ 541. DENNIS LAMP
☐ 560. CARLTON FISK
☐ 591. TONY LARUSSA(M)
☐ 619. JERRY DYBZINSKI
☐ 664. DAVE STEGMAN
☐ 667. VANCE LAW
☐ 698. MARC HILL
☐ 759. RICHARD DOTSON
☐ 777. TOM PACIOREK

CINCINNATI REDS

☐ 34. EDDIE MILNER
☐ 55. DAVE CONCEPCION
☐ 87. FRANK PASTORE
☐ 113. KELLY PARIS
☐ 142. RICH GALE
☐ 160. MARIO SOTO
☐ 192. NICK ESASKY
☐ 214. PAUL HOUSEHOLDER
☐ 242. ALEX TREVINO
☐ 270. JEFF RUSSELL
☐ 273. CHARLIE PULEO
☐ 297. BRUCE BERENYI
☐ 323. ALAN KNICELY

☐ 351. RUSS NIXON(M)
☐ 373. BILL SCHERRER
☐ 424. DANN BILARDELLO
☐ 448. BEN HAYES
☐ 475. GARY REDUS
☐ 526. RON OESTER
☐ 554. TED POWER
☐ 585. DAN DRIESSEN
☐ 607. TOM HUME
☐ 632. TOM FOLEY
☐ 659. DUANE WALKER
☐ 686. JOE PRICE
☐ 725. CESAR CEDENO
☐ 756. TEAM LEADER CARD

CLEVELAND INDIANS

☐ 48. JULIO FRANCO
☐ 91. DAN SPILLNER
☐ 115. ANDRE THORNTON
☐ 141. PAT CORRALES(M)
☐ 212. BRODERICK PERKINS
☐ 226. JUAN EICHELBERGER
☐ 245. RICK SUTCLIFFE
☐ 286. LARY SORENSEN
☐ 308. RON HASSEY
☐ 329. PAT TABLER
☐ 348. TOBY HARRAH
☐ 367. JAMIE EASTERLY
☐ 431. CHRIS BANDO
☐ 478. ALAN BANNISTER
☐ 497. BUD ANDERSON
☐ 515. GORMAN THOMAS
☐ 546. TEAM LEADER CARD
☐ 569. BAKE MCBRIDE
☐ 638. GEORGE VUKOVICH
☐ 662. TOM BRENNAN
☐ 689. MIKE FISCHLIN
☐ 737. JIM ESSIAN
☐ 764. MIKE HARGROVE
☐ 789. BERT BLYLEVEN

DETROIT TIGERS

☐ 14. TOM BROOKENS
☐ 24. JOHN MARTIN
☐ 42. JOHNNY GRUBB
☐ 65. KIRK GIBSON
☐ 95. AURELIO LOPEZ
☐ 119. JOHNNY WOCKENFUSS
☐ 147. DAN PETRY
☐ 174. JUAN BERENGUER
☐ 195. JACK MORRIS
☐ 223. WAYNE KRENCHICKI
☐ 259. SPARKY ANDERSON(M)
☐ 284. HOWARD BAILEY
☐ 303. MARTY CASTILLO
☐ 333. LARRY HERDON
☐ 356. GLENN ABBOTT
☐ 371. DAVE GUMPERT
☐ 427. RICK LEACH
☐ 457. DAVE ROZEMA
☐ 482. ENOS CABELL
☐ 510. ALAN TRAMMELL
☐ 536. DOUG BAIR
☐ 563. GLENN WILSON
☐ 588. MILT WILCOX
☐ 611. CHET LEMON
☐ 640. LANCE PARRISH
☐ 666. TEAM LEADER CARD
☐ 695. LOU WHITKER
☐ 731. LYNN JONES

HOUSTON ASTROS

☐ 36. DENNY WALLING
☐ 45. JERRY MUMPHREY
☐ 66. TEAM LEADER CARD
☐ 93. BOB KNEPPER
☐ 116. GEORGE BJORKMAN
☐ 127. MIKE MADDEN
☐ 172. FRANK DIPINO
☐ 198. BILL DORAN
☐ 217. ALAN ASHBY
☐ 248. BILL DAWLEY
☐ 292. TONY SCOTT
☐ 301. FRANK LACORTE
☐ 328. VERN RUHLE
☐ 361. DAVE SMITH
☐ 383. TERRY PUHL

☐ 422. JOSE CRUZ
☐ 441. BOB LILLIS(M)
☐ 446. LUIS PUJOLS
☐ 470. NOLAN RYAN
☐ 507. MIKE LACOSS
☐ 438. KEVIN BASS
☐ 559. MIKE SCOTT
☐ 586. JOE NIEKRO
☐ 612. HARRY SPILMAN
☐ 660. RAY KNIGHT
☐ 679. ART HOWE
☐ 692. DICKIE THON
☐ 752. PHIL GARNER
☐ 776. CRAIG REYNOLDS

MIKE SCOTT P

KANSAS CITY ROYALS

☐ 26. BUD BLACK
☐ 52. PAUL SPLITTORFF
☐ 74. JERRY MARTIN
☐ 96. TEAM LEADER CARD
☐ 121. PAT SHERIDAN
☐ 155. FRANK WHITE
☐ 196. DON SLAUGHT
☐ 219. JOE SIMPSON
☐ 247. ONIX CONCEPCION
☐ 294. U.L. WASHINGTON
☐ 317. GREG PRYOR
☐ 340. HAL MCRAE
☐ 375. DENNIS LEONARD
☐ 417. MIKE ARMSTRONG
☐ 444. STEVE RENKO
☐ 471. DICK HOWSER(M)
☐ 500. GEORGE BRETT
☐ 525. WILLIE WILSON
☐ 544. CESAR GERONIMO
☐ 570. DAN QUISENBERRY
☐ 602. JOHN WATHAN
☐ 625. LARRY GURA
☐ 655. AMOS OTIS
☐ 685. WILLIE AIKENS
☐ 724. ERIC RASMUSSEN
☐ 743. DON HOOD
☐ 784. LEON ROBERTS

LOS ANGELES DODGERS

☐ 15. BURT HOOTON
☐ 40. DUSTY BAKER
☐ 64. MIKE SCIOSCIA
☐ 90. PEDRO GUERRERO
☐ 112. TOM NIEDENFUER
☐ 142. JOSE MORALES
☐ 170. JERRY REUSS
☐ 220. FERANDO VALENZUELA
☐ 222. RICK HONEYCUTT
☐ 244. CANDY MALDONADO
☐ 263. JACK FIMPLE
☐ 274. RICK MONDAY
☐ 306. TEAM LEADER CARD
☐ 324. ALEJANDRO PENA
☐ 376. DAVE ANDERSON
☐ 425. STEVE HOWE
☐ 454. JOE BECKWITH
☐ 477. RAFAEL LANDESTOY
☐ 533. KEN LANDREAUX
☐ 555. GREG BROCK
☐ 583. DERREL THOMAS
☐ 610. STEVE SAX

☐ 634. MIKE MARSHALL
☐ 661. STEVE YEAGER
☐ 681. TOM LASORDA(M)
☐ 722. BOB WELCH
☐ 747. PAT ZACHRY
☐ 792. BILL RUSSELL

MILWAUKEE BREWERS

☐ 10. ROBIN YOUNT
☐ 35. DON SUTTON
☐ 60. PAUL MOLITOR
☐ 88. ROB PICCIOLO
☐ 107. NED YOST
☐ 128. RICK MANNING
☐ 146. ED ROMERO
☐ 167. MARSHALL EDWARDS
☐ 190. BEN OGLIVIE
☐ 218. RICK WAITS
☐ 243. PETE LADD
☐ 262. TOM CANDIOTTI
☐ 271. MOOSE HAAS
☐ 298. JIM GANTNER
☐ 321. HARVEY KUENN(M)
☐ 349. BOB GIBSON
☐ 374. DON MONEY
☐ 420. CECIL COOPER
☐ 452. CHUCK PORTER
☐ 476. TOM TELLMANN
☐ 495. ROLLIE FINGERS
☐ 505. PETE VUCKOVICH
☐ 528. MARK BROUHARD
☐ 582. BOB MCCLURE
☐ 605. MIKE CALDWELL
☐ 630. TED SIMMONS
☐ 658. JERRY AUGUSTINE
☐ 687. ROY HOWELL
☐ 726. TEAM LEADER CARD
☐ 738. BILL SCHROEDER
☐ 751. CHARLIE MOORE
☐ 772. JIM SLATON

MINNESOTA TWINS

☐ 11. TEAM CARD LEADER CARD
☐ 28. FRANK VIOLA
☐ 46. RAY SMITH
☐ 67. GARY WARD
☐ 84. LENNY FAEDO
☐ 157. GARY GAETTI
☐ 183. AL WILLIAMS
☐ 193. DARRELL BROWN
☐ 237. JOHN CASTINO
☐ 268. JACK O'CONNOR
☐ 307. BOBBY MITCHELL
☐ 322. KEN SCHROM
☐ 345. KENT HRBEK
☐ 363. TIM LAUDNER
☐ 411. HOUSTON JIMENEZ
☐ 429. RANDY BUSH
☐ 447. TOM BRUNANSKY
☐ 463. DAVE ENGLE
☐ 491. BOBBY CASTILLO
☐ 509. BRAD HAVENS
☐ 519. RON DAVIS
☐ 551. SCOTT ULLGER
☐ 568. PETE FILSON
☐ 598. RUSTY KUNTZ
☐ 623. RON WASHINGTON
☐ 639. RICK LYSANDER
☐ 648. LEN WHITEHOUSE
☐ 673. MIKE WALTERS
☐ 746. MICKEY HATCHER
☐ 771. BILLY GARDNER(M)

MONTREAL EXPOS

☐ 32. BOBBY RAMOS
☐ 57. DAN SCHATZEDER
☐ 80. STEVE ROGERS
☐ 111. BILL VIRDON(M)
☐ 164. SCOTT SANDERSON
☐ 180. MANNY TRILLO
☐ 188. BRYAN LITTLE
☐ 200. ANDRE DAWSON
☐ 232. TIM WALLACH
☐ 253. JIM WOHLFORD
☐ 287. WARREN CROMARTIE
☐ 318. BILL GULLICKSON
☐ 370. TIM RAINES
☐ 421. CHARLIE LEA

☐ 450. GARY CARTER
☐ 474. GREG BARGAR
☐ 496. TERRY FRANCONA
☐ 516. TEAM LEADER CARD
☐ 552. RAY BURRIS
☐ 579. BOB JAMES
☐ 595. JEFF REARDON
☐ 620. AL OLIVER
☐ 656. BRYN SMITH
☐ 678. CHRIS SPEIER
☐ 732. TERRY CROWLEY
☐ 749. DOUG FLYNN
☐ 766. MIKE VAIL

NEW YORK METS

☐ 13. SCOTT HOLMAN
☐ 29. DANNY HEEP
☐ 54. JESSE OROSCO
☐ 78. MIKE TORREZ
☐ 120. KEITH HERNANDEZ
☐ 161. JUNIOR ORTIZ
☐ 182. DARRYL STRAWBERRY
☐ 208. JOSE OQUENDO
☐ 246. TEAM LEADER CARD
☐ 293. ED LYNCH
☐ 316. MARK BARDLEY
☐ 350. GEORGE FOSTER
☐ 368. HUBIE BROOKS
☐ 418. RON HODGES
☐ 430. RUSTY STAUB
☐ 465. MOOKIE WILSON
☐ 492. TUCKER ASHFORD
☐ 524. CARLOS DIAZ
☐ 549. WALT TERRELL
☐ 573. DAVE KINGMAN
☐ 599. DOUG SISK
☐ 621. FRANK HOWARD(M)
☐ 654. BOB BAILOR
☐ 676. BRIAN GILES
☐ 740. TOM SEAVER
☐ 763. CRAIG SWAN
☐ 774. TOM GORMAN

NEW YORK YANKEES

☐ 8. DON MATTINGLY
☐ 16. OMAR MORENO
☐ 19. RAY FONTENOT
☐ 81. BILLY MARTIN(M)
☐ 110. RON GUIDRY
☐ 123. BUTCH WYNEGAR
☐ 139. BERT CAMPANERIS
☐ 175. GRAIG NETTLES
☐ 203. MATT KEOUGH
☐ 204. BOBBY MEACHAM
☐ 239. JAY HOWELL
☐ 254. SHANE RAWLEY
☐ 281. LARRY MILBOURNE
☐ 305. ROY SMALLEY
☐ 335. DON BAYLOR
☐ 360. WILLIE RANDOLPH
☐ 408. LOU PINIELLA
☐ 440. STEVE KEMP
☐ 460. DAVE WINFIELD
☐ 486. TEAM LEADER CARD
☐ 512. OSCAR GAMBLE
☐ 539. GEORGE FRAZIER
☐ 592. ANDRE ROBERTSON
☐ 617. RICK CERONE
☐ 635. DAVE RIGHETTI
☐ 652. RUDY MAY
☐ 670. RICH GOSSAGE
☐ 684. BOB SHIRLEY
☐ 697. DALE MURRAY
☐ 761. JOHN MONTEFUSCO
☐ 770. KEN GRIFFEY
☐ 782. STEVE BALBONI

OAKLAND A'S

☐ 33. TOM BURGMEIER
☐ 61. CHRIS CODIROLI
☐ 103. DWAYNE MURPHY
☐ 156. TEAM LEADER CARD
☐ 159. DARRYL CIAS
☐ 178. BILL KRUEGER
☐ 189. TIM CONROY
☐ 197. GARRY HANCOCK
☐ 230. RICKEY HENDERSON

☐ 241. BILL ALMON
☐ 265. DONNIE HILL
☐ 309. TONY PHILLIPS
☐ 326. BOB KEARNEY
☐ 338. MIKE WARREN
☐ 354. JEFF BURROUGHS
☐ 369. STEVE MCCATTY
☐ 414. MITCHELL PAGE
☐ 436. RICK PETERS
☐ 464. JEFF JONES
☐ 493. MIKE NORRIS
☐ 513. DAVE BEARD
☐ 529. KEITH ATHERTON
☐ 521. STEVE BOROS(M)
☐ 558. MIKE DAVIS
☐ 567. MIKE HEATH
☐ 609. DAN MEYER
☐ 629. RICK LANGFORD
☐ 642. TOM UNDERWOOD
☐ 669. DAVE LOPES
☐ 741. WAYNE GROSS
☐ 767. CARNEY LANSFORD

PHILADELPHIA PHILLIES

☐ 17. JOHN DENNY
☐ 43. RON REED
☐ 70. GARY MATTHEWS
☐ 101. PORFIRIO ALTAMIRANO
☐ 158. JOE LEFEBVRE
☐ 185. SIXTO LEZCANO
☐ 199. WILLIE HERNANDEZ
☐ 210. JOE MORGAN
☐ 229. PAUL OWENS(M)
☐ 252. LARRY CHRISTENSON
☐ 275. LEN MATUSZEK
☐ 279. IVAN DEJESUS
☐ 300. PETE ROSE
☐ 332. KEVIN GROSS
☐ 358. BOB DERNIER
☐ 385. TONY PEREZ
☐ 432. CHARLIE HUDSON
☐ 458. KIKO GARCIA
☐ 484. OZZIE VIRGIL
☐ 511. MARTY BYSTROM
☐ 535. BO DIAZ
☐ 564. AL HOLLAND
☐ 587. VON HAYES
☐ 613. GREG GROSS
☐ 637. TEAM LEADER CARD
☐ 700. MIKE SCHMIDT
☐ 728. TUG MCGRAW
☐ 755. GARRY MADDOX
☐ 780. STEVE CARLTON

PITTSBURGH PIRATES

☐ 18. DALE BERRA
☐ 44. JIM MORRISON
☐ 69. ROD SCURRY
☐ 122. CECILIO GUANTE
☐ 144. BRIAN HARPER
☐ 173. MARVELL WYNNE
☐ 209. MANNY SARMIENTO
☐ 225. LEE MAZZILLI
☐ 250. BILL MADLOCK
☐ 264. DOUG FROBEL
☐ 291. CHUCK TANNER(M)
☐ 330. JOHN CANDELARIA
☐ 355. JASON THOMPSON
☐ 384. LEE TUNNELL
☐ 433. RICH HEBNER
☐ 462. LEE LACY
☐ 485. RICK RHODEN
☐ 537. JOHNNY RAY
☐ 566. JIM BIBBY
☐ 581. JOSE DELEON
☐ 589. MIKE EASLER
☐ 616. DON ROBINSON
☐ 645. TONY PENA
☐ 668. LARRY MCWILLIAMS
☐ 696. TEAM LEADER CARD
☐ 729. GENE TENACE
☐ 754. KENT TEKULVE
☐ 775. DAVE PARKER
☐ 788. MILT MAY

ST. LOUIS CARDINALS

- ☐ 49. JOHN STUPER
- ☐ 75. BOB FORSCH
- ☐ 102. KEN OBERKFELL
- ☐ 130. OZZIE SMITH
- ☐ 152. GLENN BRUMMER
- ☐ 186. TEAM LEADER CARD
- ☐ 206. ANDY VAN SLYKE
- ☐ 227. STEVE BRAUN
- ☐ 285. DARRELL PORTER
- ☐ 310. WILLIE MCGEE
- ☐ 337. KEVIN HAGEN
- ☐ 362. DAVID GREEN
- ☐ 416. DANE IORG
- ☐ 435. NEIL ALLEN
- ☐ 467. MIKE RAMSEY
- ☐ 489. DAVE VON OHLEN
- ☐ 514. FLOYD RAYFORD
- ☐ 540. GEORGE HENDRICK
- ☐ 561. WHITEY HERZOG(M)
- ☐ 580. LONNIE SMITH
- ☐ 593. JEFF LAHTI
- ☐ 627. DAVE LAPOINT
- ☐ 649. TOM HERR
- ☐ 671. JAMIE QUIRK
- ☐ 699. DAVE RUCKER
- ☐ 730. BRUCE SUTTER
- ☐ 785. JOAQUIN ANDUJAR

SAN DIEGO PADRES

- ☐ 7. GARY LUCAS
- ☐ 38. LUIS DELEON
- ☐ 68. LUIS SALAZAR
- ☐ 94. MARIO RAMIREZ
- ☐ 168. JUAN BONILLA
- ☐ 224. SID MONGE
- ☐ 251. TONY GWYNN
- ☐ 261. BOBBY BROWN
- ☐ 277. EDDIE WHITSON
- ☐ 290. DAVE DRAVECKY
- ☐ 327. RUPPERT JONES
- ☐ 346. KURT BEVACQUA
- ☐ 366. TEAM LEADER CARD
- ☐ 380. STEVE GARVEY
- ☐ 455. TERRY KENNEDY
- ☐ 481. MARK THURMOND
- ☐ 503. ELIAS SOSA
- ☐ 532. ERIC SHOW
- ☐ 571. BRUCE BOCHY
- ☐ 594. GENE RICHARDS
- ☐ 615. GARRY TEMPLETON
- ☐ 644. TIM LOLLAR
- ☐ 674. TIM FLANNERY
- ☐ 693. ALAN WIGGINS
- ☐ 742. DICK WILLIAMS(M)
- ☐ 753. DOUG GWOSDZ
- ☐ 778. ANDY HAWKINS

SAN FRANCISCO GIANTS

- ☐ 31. ANDY MCGAFFIGAN
- ☐ 58. MAX VENABLE
- ☐ 85. ATLEE HAMMAKER
- ☐ 98. STEVE NICOSIA
- ☐ 109. BRAD WELLMAN
- ☐ 129. BILL LASKEY
- ☐ 145. GARY LAVELLE
- ☐ 171. FRANK ROBINSON(M)
- ☐ 205. GREG MINTON
- ☐ 228. JOHN RABB
- ☐ 282. JIM BARR
- ☐ 325. DARRELL EVANS
- ☐ 343. MARK DAVIS
- ☐ 378. BOB BRENLY
- ☐ 428. FRED BREINING
- ☐ 449. JOE PETTINI
- ☐ 469. TOM O'MALLEY
- ☐ 494. CHILI DAVIS
- ☐ 522. DAVE BERGMAN
- ☐ 542. DUANE KUIPER
- ☐ 576. TEAM LEADER CARD
- ☐ 603. RENIE MARTIN
- ☐ 633. MIKE KRUKOW
- ☐ 663. JOHNNIE LEMASTER
- ☐ 690. JACK CLARK
- ☐ 727. JOEL YOUNGBLOOD
- ☐ 748. JEFF LEONARD
- ☐ 768. CHAMP SUMMERS

SEATTLE MARINERS

- ☐ 22. BRYAN CLARK
- ☐ 41. TONY BERNAZARD
- ☐ 63. ED VANDE BERG
- ☐ 83. RICHIE ZISK
- ☐ 154. DAVE HENDERSON
- ☐ 166. JAMIE NELSON
- ☐ 181. ROY THOMAS
- ☐ 194. DOMINGO RAMOS
- ☐ 211. RICK SWEET
- ☐ 235. MATT YOUNG
- ☐ 288. JIM BEATTIE
- ☐ 314. ORLANDO MERCADO
- ☐ 336. TEAM LEADER CARD
- ☐ 413. SPIKE OWEN
- ☐ 439. BOB STODDARD
- ☐ 461. JIM MALER
- ☐ 501. STEVE HENDERSON
- ☐ 517. JOHN MOSES
- ☐ 547. MIKE MOORE
- ☐ 562. MANNY CASTILLO
- ☐ 622. AL COWENS
- ☐ 636. PAT PUTNAM
- ☐ 647. RON ROENICKE
- ☐ 672. RICKY NELSON
- ☐ 694. MIKE STANTON
- ☐ 721. DEL CRANDALL(M)
- ☐ 744. JAMIE ALLEN
- ☐ 769. BILL CAUDILL

TEXAS RANGERS

- ☐ 12. BILLY SAMPLE
- ☐ 37. TEAM LEADER CARD
- ☐ 62. DAVE HOSTETLER
- ☐ 89. MIKE SMITHSON
- ☐ 118. CHARLIE HOUGH
- ☐ 149. JON MATLACK
- ☐ 169. LARRY PARRISH
- ☐ 283. LARRY BITTNER
- ☐ 299. JOHN BUTCHER
- ☐ 331. BUCKY DENT
- ☐ 341. DAVE TOBIK
- ☐ 352. DAVE STEWART
- ☐ 353. JIM ANDERSON
- ☐ 377. DANNY DARWIN
- ☐ 412. DOUG RADER(M)
- ☐ 451. BOB JONES
- ☐ 479. FRANK TANANA
- ☐ 504. MICKEY RIVERS
- ☐ 534. PETE O'BRIEN
- ☐ 557. WAYNE TOLLESON
- ☐ 584. DAVE SCHMIDT
- ☐ 608. BOBBY JOHNSON
- ☐ 641. MIKE RICHARDT
- ☐ 665. BUDDY BELL
- ☐ 688. GEORGE WRIGHT
- ☐ 734. ODELL JONES
- ☐ 758. BILL STEIN
- ☐ 779. JIM SUNDBERG

TORONTO BLUE JAYS

- ☐ 9. JIM GOTT
- ☐ 39. GARTH IORG
- ☐ 76. ALFREDO GRIFFIN
- ☐ 92. LLOYD MOSEBY
- ☐ 108. RANDY MOFFITT
- ☐ 124. DAMASO GARCIA
- ☐ 179. BUCK MARTINEZ
- ☐ 202. BOBBY COX(M)
- ☐ 221. CLIFF JOHNSON
- ☐ 256. DAVE GEISEL
- ☐ 278. JORGE BELL
- ☐ 302. BARRY BONNELL
- ☐ 312. JORGE ORTA
- ☐ 339. ROY LEE JACKSON
- ☐ 359. JIM ACKER
- ☐ 423. MIKE MORGAN
- ☐ 453. WILLIE UPSHAW
- ☐ 488. JESSE BARFIELD
- ☐ 506. ERNIE WHITT
- ☐ 556. JOEY MCLAUGHLIN
- ☐ 575. JIM CLANCY
- ☐ 590. DAVE STIEB
- ☐ 606. TEAM LEADER CARD
- ☐ 677. DOYLE ALEXANDER
- ☐ 733. DAVE COLLINS
- ☐ 762. RANCE MULLINKS
- ☐ 783. LUIS LEAL

1984 TOPPS TRADED (132) 2 1/2" X 3 1/2"

ATLANTA BRAVES

- ☐ 30T. JEFF DEDMON
- ☐ 85T. KEN OBERKFELL
- ☐ 92T. GERALD PERRY
- ☐ 120T. ALEX TREVINO

BALTIMORE ORIOLES

- ☐ 44T. WAYNE GROSS
- ☐ 96T. FLOYD RAYFORD
- ☐ 123T. TOM UNDERWOOD

BOSTON RED SOX

- ☐ 17T. BILL BUCKNER
- ☐ 33T. MIKE EASLER
- ☐ 40T. RICH GALE
- ☐ 46T. JACKIE GUTIERREZ

CALIFORNIA ANGELS

- ☐ 68T. FRANK LACORTE
- ☐ 93T. GARY PETTIS
- ☐ 94T. ROB PICCIOLO
- ☐ 102T. RON ROMANICK
- ☐ 107T. DICK SCHOFIELD
- ☐ 109T. JIM SLATON
- ☐ 116T. CRAIG SWAN

CHICAGO CUBS

- ☐ 31T. BOB DERNIER
- ☐ 34T. DENNIS ECKERSLEY
- ☐ 39T. GEORGE FRAZIER
- ☐ 49T. RON HASSEY
- ☐ 50T. RICH HEBNER
- ☐ 77T. GARY MATTHEWS
- ☐ 106T. SCOTT SANDERSON
- ☐ 112T. TIM STODDARD
- ☐ 115T. RICK SUTCLIFFE

1984 Topps Traded

CHICAGO WHITE SOX

- 98T. RON REED
- 108T. TOM SEAVER

CINCINNATI REDS

- 65T. WAYNE KRENCHICKI
- 90T. DAVE PARKER
- 91T. TONY PEREZ
- 95T. VERN RAPP(M)

CLEVELAND INDIANS

- 2T. LUIS APONTE
- 12T. TONY BERNAZARD
- 20T. BRETT BUTLER
- 47T. MEL HALL
- 55T. BROOK JACOBY
- 56T. MIKE JEFFCOAT
- 125T. TOM WADDELL

DETROIT TIGERS

- 11T. DAVE BERGMAN
- 36T. DARRELL EVANS
- 41T. BARBARO GARBEY
- 51T. WILLIE HERNANDEZ
- 59T. RUPPERT JONES
- 66T. RUSTY KUNTZ
- 80T. SID MONGE

HOUSTON ASTROS

- 21T. ENOS CABELL

KANSAS CITY ROYALS

- 6T. STEVE BALBONI
- 9T. JOE BECKWITH
- 45T. MARK GUBICZA
- 54T. DANE IORG
- 57T. LYNN JONES
- 88T. JORGE ORTA
- 104T. BRET SABERHAGEN

LOS ANGELES DODGERS

- 4T. BOB BAILOR
- 32T. CARLOS DIAZ
- 124T. MIKE VAIL

MILWAUKEE BREWERS

- 24T. BOB CLARK
- 26T. JAIME COCANOWER
- 67T. RENE LACHEMANN(M)
- 97T. RANDY READY
- 114T. JIM SUNDBERG

MINNESOTA TWINS

- 19T. JOHN BUTCHER
- 110T. MIKE SMITHSON
- 117T. TIM TEUFEL

MONTREAL EXPOS

- 16T. FRED BREINING
- 73T. GARY LUCAS
- 78T. ANDY MCGAFFIGAN
- 103T. PETE ROSE
- 118T. DERREL THOMAS

NEW YORK METS

- 10T. BRUCE BERENYI
- 27T. RON DARLING
- 37T. MIKE FITZGERALD
- 42T. DWIGHT GOODEN
- 57T. DAVE JOHNSON(M)
- 74T. JERRY MARTIN

NEW YORK YANKEES

- 3T. MIKE ARMSTRONG
- 13T. YOGI BERRA(M)
- 38T. TIM FOLI
- 48T. TOBY HARRAH
- 84T. PHIL NIEKRO
- 86T. MIKE O'BERRY
- 100T. JOSE RIJO

OAKLAND A'S

- 18T. RAY BURRIS
- 23T. BILL CAUDILL
- 35T. JIM ESSIAN
- 63T. DAVE KINGMAN
- 81T. JACKIE MOORE(M)
- 82T. JOE MORGAN
- 111T. LARY SORENSEN

PHIADELPHIA PHILLIES

- 22T. BILL CAMPBELL
- 64T. JERRY KOOSMAN
- 105T. JUAN SAMUEL
- 129T. GLENN WILSON
- 130T. JOHNNY WOCKENFUSS

PITTSBURGH PIRATES

- 89T. AMOS OTIS
- 122T. JOHN TUDOR

ST. LOUIS CARDINALS

- 29T. KEN DAYLEY
- 52T. RICKY HORTON
- 53T. ART HOWE
- 60T. MIKE JORGENSEN

SAN DIEGO PADRES

- 43T. RICH GOSSAGE
- 72T. CRAIG LEFFERTS
- 75T. CARMELO MARTINEZ
- 83T. GRAIG NETTLES
- 113T. CHAMP SUMMERS

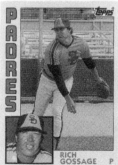

RICH GOSSAGE P

SAN FRANCISCO GIANTS

- 5T. DUSTY BAKER
- 87T. AL OLIVER
- 99T. GENE RICHARDS
- 101T. JEFF ROBINSON
- 121T. MANNY TRILLO
- 128T. FRANK WILLIAMS

SEATTLE MARINERS

- 8T. DAVE BEARD
- 14T. BARRY BONNELL
- 15T. PHIL BRADLEY
- 28T. ALVIN DAVIS
- 61T. BOB KEARNEY
- 70T. MARK LANGSTON
- 79T. LARRY MILBOURNE
- 119T. GORMAN THOMAS

TEXAS RANGERS

- 7T. ALAN BANNISTER
- 76T. MIKE MASON
- 126T. GARY WARD
- 127T. CURT WILDERSON
- 131. NED YOST

TORONTO BLUE JAYS

- 1T. WILLIE AIKENS
- 25T. BRYAN CLARK
- 62T. JIMMY KEY
- 69T. DENNIS LAMP
- 71T. RICK LEACH

1985 TOPPS (792)
2 1/2" X 3 1/2"

CAL RIPKEN SHORTSTOP ALL STAR

ATLANTA BRAVES

- 25. STEVE BEDROSIAN
- 51. BOB WATSON
- 79. RICK MAHLER
- 106. PASCUAL PEREZ
- 129. GENE GARBER
- 167. RUFINO LINARES
- 195. GLENN HUBBARD
- 219. GERALD PERRY
- 248. TERRY FORSTER
- 292. BRAD KOMMINSK
- 320. DALE MURPHY
- 335. BRUCE BENEDICT
- 362. CRAIG MCMURTRY
- 410. BOB HORNER
- 438. JOE TORRE(M)
- 458. RANDY JOHNSON
- 491. RICK CAMP
- 518. CHRIS CHAMBLISS
- 540. CLAUDELL WASHINGTON
- 557. LEN BARKER
- 569. KEN OBERKFELL
- 602. JEFF DEDMON
- 618. PETE FALCONE
- 647. RAFAEL RAMIREZ
- 676. ALBERT HALL
- 699. DONNIE MOORE
- 747. ALEX TREVINO
- 776. JERRY ROYSTER

BALTIMORE ORIOLES

- ☐ 30. CAL RIPKEN
- ☐ 56. JIM DWYER
- ☐ 81. LENN SAKATA
- ☐ 109. GARY ROENICKE
- ☐ 147. BILL SWAGGERTY
- ☐ 173. MIKE YOUNG
- ☐ 199. DENNY MARTINEZ
- ☐ 225. MIKE BODDICKER
- ☐ 252. DAN FORD
- ☐ 289. TOM UNDERWOOD
- ☐ 316. JOHN LOWENSTEIN
- ☐ 341. FLOYD RAYFORD
- ☐ 366. TODD CRUZ
- ☐ 416. WAYNE GROSS
- ☐ 445. TIPPY MARTINEZ
- ☐ 469. SAMMY STEWART
- ☐ 494. RICH DAUER
- ☐ 508. JOHN SHELBY
- ☐ 521. RICK DEMPSEY
- ☐ 550. SCOTT MCGREGOR
- ☐ 574. JOE ALTOBELLI(M)
- ☐ 599. STORM DAVIS
- ☐ 624. BENNY AYALA
- ☐ 652. JOE NOLAN
- ☐ 700. EDDIE MURRAY
- ☐ 726. AL BUMBRY
- ☐ 755. KEN SINGLETON
- ☐ 780. MIKE FLANAGAN

BOSTON RED SOX

- ☐ 11. RALPH HOUK(M)
- ☐ 37. REID NICHOLS
- ☐ 65. BILL BUCKNER
- ☐ 89. JACKIE GUTIERREZ
- ☐ 116. DENNIS BOYD
- ☐ 150. JIM RICE
- ☐ 181. ROGER CLEMENS
- ☐ 207. MARK CLEAR
- ☐ 233. ED JURAK
- ☐ 259. GARY ALLENSON
- ☐ 298. MARTY BARRETT
- ☐ 322. DAVE STAPLETON
- ☐ 350. WADE BOGGS
- ☐ 376. JEFF NEWMAN
- ☐ 424. AL NIPPER
- ☐ 451. BRUCE HURST
- ☐ 477. BOB OJEDA
- ☐ 502. RICK MILLER
- ☐ 529. RICH GEDMAN
- ☐ 555. BOB STANLEY
- ☐ 580. DWIGHT EVANS
- ☐ 606. RICH GALE
- ☐ 633. GLENN HOFFMAN
- ☐ 661. STEVE CRAWFORD
- ☐ 686. MIKE EASLER
- ☐ 734. JOHN HENRY JOHNSON
- ☐ 761. JERRY REMY
- ☐ 785. TONY ARMAS

CALIFORNIA ANGELS

- ☐ 42. LUIS SANCHEZ
- ☐ 61. CURT KAUFMAN
- ☐ 86. DON AASE
- ☐ 111. DOUG DECINCES
- ☐ 153. FRANK LACORTE
- ☐ 179. TOMMY JOHN
- ☐ 200. REGGIE JACKSON
- ☐ 220. FRED LYNN
- ☐ 226. JUAN BENIQUEZ
- ☐ 234. JERRY NARRON
- ☐ 258. MIKE BROWN
- ☐ 300. ROD CAREW
- ☐ 309. MIKE WITT
- ☐ 348. BOB BOONE
- ☐ 374. BRIAN DOWNING
- ☐ 442. KEN FORSCH
- ☐ 465. BOB GRICH
- ☐ 497. GARY PETTIS
- ☐ 524. ROB WILFONG
- ☐ 544. BRUCE KISON
- ☐ 579. RON ROMANICK
- ☐ 604. DARYL SCONIERS
- ☐ 629. DICK SCHOFIELD
- ☐ 657. JIM SLATON
- ☐ 682. DOUG CORBETT

- ☐ 732. JOHN MCNAMARA(M)
- ☐ 756. ROB PICCIOLO
- ☐ 771. GEOFF ZAHN

CINCINNATI REDS

- ☐ 28. DANN BILARDELLO
- ☐ 54. CESAR CEDENO
- ☐ 82. JOE PRICE
- ☐ 107. TOM FOLEY
- ☐ 146. GARY REDUS
- ☐ 175. DAVE PARKER
- ☐ 198. EDDIE MILNER
- ☐ 223. TOM HUME
- ☐ 251. BRAD GULDEN
- ☐ 314. RON OESTER
- ☐ 323. ANDY MCGAFFIGAN
- ☐ 342. TED POWER
- ☐ 367. KEEFE CATO
- ☐ 417. JOHN FRANCO
- ☐ 441. DUANE WALKER
- ☐ 468. WAYNE KRENCHICKI
- ☐ 495. MARIO SOTO
- ☐ 515. DAVE CONCEPCION
- ☐ 547. PETE ROSE(M)
- ☐ 573. JAY TIBBS
- ☐ 597. BRAD LESLEY
- ☐ 600. PETE ROSE
- ☐ 627. ERIC DAVIS
- ☐ 651. JEFF RUSSELL
- ☐ 675. TONY PEREZ
- ☐ 727. FRANK PASTORE
- ☐ 752. BOB OWCHINKO
- ☐ 779. NICK ESASKY

CLEVELAND INDIANS

- ☐ 14. CHRIS BANDO
- ☐ 41. MIKE FISCHLIN
- ☐ 93. DON SCHULZE
- ☐ 119. PAT CORRALES(M)
- ☐ 158. PAT TABLER
- ☐ 184. CARMEN CASTILLO
- ☐ 212. GEORGE VUKOVICH
- ☐ 237. JULIO FRANCO
- ☐ 263. MEL HALL
- ☐ 303. MIKE JEFFCOAT
- ☐ 327. BROOK JACOBY
- ☐ 355. BERT BLYLEVEN
- ☐ 381. ROY SMITH
- ☐ 425. MIKE HARGROVE
- ☐ 453. TOM WADDELL
- ☐ 475. ANDRE THORNTON
- ☐ 504. JERRY WILLARD
- ☐ 533. TONY BERNAZARD
- ☐ 609. BRODERICK PERKINS
- ☐ 637. BRETT BUTLER
- ☐ 664. STEVE FARR
- ☐ 694. JOE CARTER
- ☐ 739. ERNIE CAMACHO
- ☐ 764. JAMIE EASTERLY
- ☐ 788. STEVE COMER

JODY DAVIS

CHICAGO CUBS

- ☐ 19. GEORGE FRAZIER
- ☐ 46. GARY WOODS
- ☐ 72. RICK SUTCLIFFE
- ☐ 98. STEVE LAKE
- ☐ 124. RICH HEBNER
- ☐ 163. DENNIS ECKERSLEY

- ☐ 189. WARREN BRUSSTAR
- ☐ 210. GARY MATTHEWS
- ☐ 241. JIM FREY(M)
- ☐ 267. HENRY COTTO
- ☐ 306. RICK REUSCHEL
- ☐ 330. LEON DURHAM
- ☐ 357. RICH BORDI
- ☐ 384. JODY DAVIS
- ☐ 405. TOM VERYZER
- ☐ 432. THAD BOSLEY
- ☐ 460. RYNE SANDBERG
- ☐ 484. LARRY BOWA
- ☐ 511. LEE SMITH
- ☐ 538. KEITH MORELAND
- ☐ 563. DICK RUTHVEN
- ☐ 589. BOB DERNIER
- ☐ 616. SCOTT SANDERSON
- ☐ 642. DAVE OWEN
- ☐ 668. STEVE TROUT
- ☐ 693. TIM STODDARD
- ☐ 742. RON HASSEY
- ☐ 768. RON CEY

CHICAGO WHITE SOX

- ☐ 26. ROY SMALLEY
- ☐ 52. JERRY DYBZINSKI
- ☐ 78. SCOTT FLETCHER
- ☐ 105. RON KITTLE
- ☐ 169. DAN SPILLNER
- ☐ 194. DAVE STEGMAN
- ☐ 216. JERRY DON GLEATON
- ☐ 221. RON REED
- ☐ 249. HAROLD BAINES
- ☐ 286. RUDY LAW
- ☐ 312. MARC HILL
- ☐ 338. BRITT BURNS
- ☐ 351. JUAN AGOSTO
- ☐ 364. RICHARD DOTSON
- ☐ 388. BERT ROBERGE
- ☐ 413. VANCE LAW
- ☐ 437. AL JONES
- ☐ 466. TONY LARUSSA(M)
- ☐ 488. JOEL SKINNER
- ☐ 520. LAMARR HOYT
- ☐ 543. MIKE SQUIRES
- ☐ 572. TOM PACIOREK
- ☐ 596. JERRY HAIRSTON
- ☐ 623. GREG WALKER
- ☐ 650. GREG LUZINSKI
- ☐ 670. TOM SEAVER
- ☐ 725. FLOYD BANNISTER
- ☐ 749. JULIO CRUZ
- ☐ 770. CARLTON FISK

DETROIT TIGERS

- ☐ 20. CHET LEMON
- ☐ 47. DAVE ROZEMA
- ☐ 73. RUSTY KUNTZ
- ☐ 99. MILT WILCOX
- ☐ 126. RUPPERT JONES
- ☐ 160. LANCE PARRISH
- ☐ 192. HOWARD JOHNSON
- ☐ 243. BARBARO GARBEY
- ☐ 269. DOUG BAKER
- ☐ 307. SPARKY ANDERSON(M)
- ☐ 333. WILLIE HERNANDEZ
- ☐ 368. DAVE BERGMAN
- ☐ 408. SID MONGE
- ☐ 435. DAN PETRY
- ☐ 461. MARTY CASTILLO
- ☐ 480. LOU WHITAKER
- ☐ 512. TOM BROOKENS
- ☐ 539. AURELIO LOPEZ
- ☐ 565. KIRK GIBSON
- ☐ 586. BILL SCHERRER
- ☐ 591. LARRY HERNDON
- ☐ 610. JACK MORRIS
- ☐ 643. JOHNNY GRUBB
- ☐ 672. JUAN BERENGUER
- ☐ 690. ALAN TRAMMELL
- ☐ 744. DOUG BAIR
- ☐ 792. DARRELL EVANS

HOUSTON ASTROS

- ☐ 17. MIKE SCOTT
- ☐ 44. DICKIE THON
- ☐ 64. MARK BAILEY
- ☐ 95. JOSE CRUZ

☐ 123. DAVE SMITH
☐ 156. CRAIG REYNOLDS
☐ 186. BOB LILLIS(M)
☐ 206. PHIL GARNER
☐ 264. JOE SAMBITO
☐ 295. JOE NIEKRO
☐ 326. KEVIN BASS
☐ 353. JULIO SOLANO
☐ 382. DENNY WALLING
☐ 426. VERN RUHLE
☐ 455. BOB KNEPPER
☐ 479. MIKE MADDEN
☐ 482. HARRY SPILMAN
☐ 532. FRANK DIPINO
☐ 564. ALAN ASHBY
☐ 613. TERRY PUHL
☐ 634. BILL DAWLEY
☐ 666. MIKE LACOSS
☐ 684. BILL DORAN
☐ 736. JERRY MUMPHREY
☐ 760. NOLAN RYAN
☐ 786. ENOS CABELL

ASTROS
P
NOLAN RYAN

KANSAS CITY ROYALS

☐ 23. BRET SABERHAGEN
☐ 49. BUTCH DAVIS
☐ 77. JOE BECKWITH
☐ 100. GEORGE BRETT
☐ 127. MARK GUBICZA
☐ 164. JORGE ORTA
☐ 188. GREG PRYOR
☐ 217. LEON ROBERTS
☐ 244. MIKE JONES
☐ 270. DAN QUISENBERRY
☐ 308. JOHN WATHAN
☐ 334. DICK HOWSER(M)
☐ 359. PAT SHERIDAN
☐ 387. BUDDY BIANCALANA
☐ 412. BUD BLACK
☐ 431. U.L. WASHINGTON
☐ 459. CHARLIE LEIBRANDT
☐ 486. STEVE BALBONI
☐ 513. LYNN JONES
☐ 542. DON SLAUGHT
☐ 561. DARRYL MOTLEY
☐ 595. LARRY GURA
☐ 617. WILLIE WILSON
☐ 644. MARK HUISMANN
☐ 671. DANE IORG
☐ 697. ONIX CONCEPCION
☐ 743. FRANK WHITE
☐ 773. HAL MCRAE

LOS ANGELES DODGERS

☐ 31. TERRY WHITFIELD
☐ 57. PAT ZACHRY
☐ 85. MIKE MARSHALL
☐ 110. ALEJANDRO PENA
☐ 148. STEVE YEAGER
☐ 159. CARLOS DIAZ
☐ 174. RICK HONEYCUTT
☐ 201. BURT HOOTON
☐ 253. SID BREAM
☐ 291. BOB WELCH
☐ 343. BILL RUSSELL
☐ 369. R.J. REYNOLDS
☐ 418. KEN LANDREAUX
☐ 440. FERNANDO VALENZUELA

☐ 470. STEVE SAX
☐ 493. OREL HERSHISER
☐ 506. FRANKLIN STUBBS
☐ 523. CANDY MALDONADO
☐ 549. MIKE SCIOSCIA
☐ 575. PEDRO GUERRERO
☐ 601. TOM LASORDA(M)
☐ 626. GERMAN RIVERA
☐ 654. DAVE ANDERSON
☐ 680. JERRY REUSS
☐ 728. BOB BAILOR
☐ 753. GREG BROCK
☐ 782. TOM NIEDENFUER

MILWAUKEE BREWERS

☐ 32. CHUCK PORTER
☐ 59. RICK WAITS
☐ 83. CHARLIE MOORE
☐ 112. TOM TELLMANN
☐ 151. MOOSE HAAS
☐ 176. BILL SCHROEDER
☐ 203. BOB MCCLURE
☐ 228. DION JAMES
☐ 254. PETE VUCKOVICH
☐ 290. CECIL COOPER
☐ 317. JACK LAZORKO
☐ 318. TED SIMMONS
☐ 340. ROBIN YOUNT
☐ 372. ROY HOWELL
☐ 419. MIKE CALDWELL
☐ 446. JIM SUNDBERG
☐ 471. PETE LADD
☐ 498. ED ROMERO
☐ 522. PAUL MOLITOR
☐ 553. BOB CLARK
☐ 576. JAIME COCANOWER
☐ 603. RICK MANNING
☐ 628. RENE LACHEMANN(M)
☐ 653. MARK BROUHARD
☐ 681. BEN OGLIVIE
☐ 729. DON SUTTON
☐ 750. ROLLIE FINGERS
☐ 781. JIM GANTNER

MINNESOTA TWINS

☐ 18. MICKEY HATCHER
☐ 43. ANDRE DAVID
☐ 71. TIM LAUDNER
☐ 97. PETE FILSON
☐ 122. TOM BRUNANSKY
☐ 161. KEN SCHROM
☐ 187. MIKE WALTERS
☐ 213. BILLY GARDNER(M)
☐ 239. TIM TEUFEL
☐ 266. FRANK VIOLA
☐ 304. GARY GAETTI
☐ 329. RON WASHINGTON
☐ 356. DAVE MEIER
☐ 383. RICK LYSANDER
☐ 406. LEN WHITEHOUSE
☐ 430. RON DAVIS
☐ 452. JOHN CASTINO
☐ 483. MIKE SMITHSON
☐ 510. KENT HRBEK
☐ 535. PAT PUTNAM
☐ 536. KIRBY PUCKETT
☐ 562. HOUSTON JIMENEZ
☐ 577. CHRIS SPEIER
☐ 588. BOBBY CASTILLO
☐ 614. AL WILLIAMS
☐ 639. ED HODGE
☐ 667. DAVE ENGLE
☐ 692. RANDY BUSH
☐ 741. JOHN BUTCHER
☐ 767. DARRELL BROWN

MONTREAL EXPOS

☐ 36. FRED BREINING
☐ 62. MIKE RAMSEY
☐ 88. BRYN SMITH
☐ 114. BOB JAMES
☐ 154. ARGENIS SALAZAR
☐ 178. MIGUEL DILONE
☐ 205. STEVE ROGERS
☐ 230. GARY CARTER
☐ 257. BRYAN LITTLE
☐ 285. DAN DRIESSEN

☐ 297. GARY LUCAS
☐ 345. CHARLIE LEA
☐ 375. JEFF REARDON
☐ 407. BOBBY RAMOS
☐ 420. ANDRE DAWSON
☐ 448. DERREL THOMAS
☐ 473. TIM WALLACH
☐ 501. DAN SCHATZEDER
☐ 526. DAVE PALMER
☐ 554. DOUG FLYNN
☐ 578. TERRY FRANCONA
☐ 630. TIM RAINES
☐ 658. MIKE STENHOUSE
☐ 687. BILL GULLICKSON
☐ 733. TONY SCOTT
☐ 759. JIM FANNING(M)
☐ 787. JIM WOHLFORD

NEW YORK METS

☐ 27. BRUCE BERENYI
☐ 53. TOM GORMAN
☐ 67. RAFAEL SANTANA
☐ 80. KEITH HERNANDEZ
☐ 104. MIKE FITZGERALD
☐ 144. RON GARDENHIRE
☐ 170. GEORGE FOSTER
☐ 190. RUSTY STAUB
☐ 222. HUBIE BROOKS
☐ 250. JESSE OROSCO
☐ 287. WALT TERRELL
☐ 315. DOUG SISK
☐ 339. DANNY HEEP
☐ 363. RON HODGES
☐ 415. RON DARLING
☐ 439. JUNIOR ORTIZ
☐ 467. ED LYNCH
☐ 492. DAVE JOHNSON(M)
☐ 517. JERRY MARTIN
☐ 546. BRENT GAFF
☐ 570. DARRYL STRAWBERRY
☐ 590. RAY KNIGHT
☐ 598. JOSE EQUENDO
☐ 620. DWIGHT GOODEN
☐ 649. SID FERNANDEZ
☐ 677. WALLY BACKMAN
☐ 751. KELVIN CHAPMAN
☐ 775. MOOKIE WILSON

NEW YORK YANKEES

☐ 16. BOBBY MEACHAM
☐ 40. PHIL NIEKRO
☐ 70. DON BAYLOR
☐ 94. TOBY HARRAH
☐ 120. STEVE KEMP
☐ 155. YOGI BERRA(M)
☐ 180. DAVE WINFIELD
☐ 211. CLAY CHRISTIANSEN
☐ 238. JOSE RIJO
☐ 260. DAVE RIGHETTI
☐ 284. MARTY BYSTROM
☐ 301. JOHN MONTEFUSCO
☐ 328. BOB SHIRLEY
☐ 354. ANDRE ROBERTSON
☐ 380. KEN GRIFFEY
☐ 429. RICK CERONE
☐ 456. TIM FOLI
☐ 481. DALE MURRAY
☐ 507. RAY FONTENOT
☐ 534. BRIAN DAYETT
☐ 559. JAY HOWELL
☐ 585. BUTCH WYNEGAR
☐ 612. MIKE ARMSTRONG
☐ 638. MIKE PAGLIARULO
☐ 665. DON MITTINGLY
☐ 691. DENNIS RASMUSSEN
☐ 724. OSCAR GAMBLE
☐ 738. OMAR MORENO
☐ 765. WILLIE RANDOLPH
☐ 769. JOE COWLEY
☐ 790. RON GUIDRY

OAKLAND A'S

☐ 12. DAVE LOPES
☐ 38. JACKIE MOORE(M)
☐ 63. STEVE MCCATTY
☐ 91. JEFF BURROUGHS
☐ 115. RICKEY HENDERSON

□ 166. KEITH ATHERON
□ 197. MIKE WARREN
□ 231. DWAYNE MURPHY
□ 246. MIKE NORRIS
□ 293. CURT YOUNG
□ 319. JEFF JONES
□ 347. RICK LANGFORD
□ 352. JOE MORGAN
□ 422. CARNEY LANSFORD
□ 444. TONY PHILLIPS
□ 472. JIM ESSIAN
□ 503. TIM CONROY
□ 528. BILL KRUEGER
□ 552. CHRIS CODIROLI
□ 581. MARK WAGNER
□ 607. BILL ALMON
□ 632. BRUCE BOCHTE
□ 662. MIKE HEATH
□ 685. BILL CAUDILL
□ 730. DAVE KINGMAN
□ 758. RAY BURRIS
□ 778. MIKE DAVIS

PHILADEPHIA PHILLIES

□ 15. JERRY KOOSMAN
□ 39. JOHNNY WOCKENFUSS
□ 68. VON HAYES
□ 92. PAUL OWENS(M)
□ 117. GREG GROSS
□ 130. AL OLVIER
□ 157. TUG MCGRAW
□ 185. AL HOLLAND
□ 209. BILL CAMPBELL
□ 235. GARRY MADDOX
□ 265. JUAN SAMUEL
□ 302. TIM CORCORAN
□ 325. JOHN DENNY
□ 360. STEVE CARLTON
□ 379. CHARLES HUDSON
□ 428. LARRY ANDERSEN
□ 454. GLENN WILSON
□ 476. JEFF STONE
□ 500. MIKE SCHMIDT
□ 531. JOE LEFEBVRE
□ 556. SIXTON LEZCANO
□ 584. KEVIN GROSS
□ 611. OZZIE VIRGIL
□ 636. SHANE RAWLEY
□ 663. LUIS AGUAYO
□ 688. LEN MATUSZEK
□ 737. BO DIAZ
□ 763. KIKO GARCIA
□ 791. IVAN DEJESUS

PITTSBURGH PIRATES

□ 21. LEE TUNNELL
□ 50. JOHN CANDELARIA
□ 69. JIM WINN
□ 96. JOHNNY RAY
□ 125. KENT TEKULVE
□ 162. BENNY DISTEFANO
□ 183. LARRY MCWILLIAMS
□ 214. JOHN TUDOR
□ 268. CHUCK TANNER(M)
□ 305. DALE BERRA
□ 332. BRIAN HARPER
□ 358. TONY PENA
□ 385. JOSE DELEON
□ 433. JIM MORRISON
□ 457. CECILIO GUANTE
□ 490. JASON THOMPSON
□ 509. MILT MAY
□ 537. DON ROBINSON
□ 560. BILL MADLOCK
□ 587. DOUG FROBEL
□ 615. MARVELL WYNNE
□ 641. ROD SCURRY
□ 669. LEE LACY
□ 695. RICK RHODEN
□ 748. LEE MAZZILLI

ST. LOUIS CARDINALS

□ 33. TITO LANDRUM
□ 60. GEORGE HENDRICK
□ 87. DAVID GREEN
□ 113. TOM HERR
□ 152. STEVE BRAUN

□ 177. DAVE VON OHLEN
□ 204. ART HOWE
□ 229. DAVE LAPOINT
□ 255. LONNIE SMITH
□ 294. TOM JIETO
□ 321. RICKY HORTON
□ 346. TERRY PENDLETON
□ 370. BRUCE SUTTER
□ 421. DAVE RUCKER
□ 447. JEFF LAHTI
□ 474. KURT KEPSHIRE
□ 499. DANNY COX
□ 525. DARRELL PORTER
□ 551. ANDY VAN SLYKE
□ 605. OZZIE SMITH
□ 631. BOB FORSCH
□ 655. JOAQUIN ANDUJAR
□ 683. WHITE HERZOG(M)
□ 731. NEIL ALLEN
□ 757. WILLIE MCGEE
□ 783. MIKE JORGENSEN

SAN DIEGO PADRES

□ 13. TIM LOLLAR
□ 35. GRAIG NETTLES
□ 66. DICK WILLIAMS(M)
□ 90. RICH GOSSAGE
□ 118. ERIC SHOW
□ 182. TIM FLANNERY
□ 208. CHAMP SUMMERS
□ 236. MARK THURMOND
□ 242. GREG HARRIS
□ 262. GREG BOOKER
□ 299. ANDY HAWKINS
□ 324. BRUCE BOCHY
□ 378. ALAN WIGGINS
□ 427. MARIO RAMIREZ
□ 450. STEVE GARVEY
□ 478. KURT BEVACQUA
□ 530. DAVE DRAVECKY
□ 558. CARMELO MARTINEZ
□ 583. BOBBY BROWN
□ 608. CRAIG LEFFERTS
□ 635. TERRY KENNEDY
□ 660. TONY GWYNN
□ 689. LUIS DELEON
□ 735. GARRY TEMPLETON
□ 762. EDDIE WHITSON
□ 789. LUIS SALAZAR

SAN FRANCISCO GIANTS

□ 22. DUANE KUIPER
□ 45. GREG MINTON
□ 74. MIKE KRUKOW
□ 103. RANDY LERCH
□ 165. DUSTY BAKER
□ 191. STEVE NICOSIA
□ 215. BOB BRENLY
□ 245. CHILI DAVIS
□ 283. FRAN MULLINS
□ 310. MANNY TRILLO
□ 331. BILL LASKEY
□ 365. DANNY OZARK(M)
□ 386. DAN GLADDEN
□ 409. BRAD WELLMAN
□ 434. GENE RICHARDS
□ 462. GARY LAVELLE
□ 487. FRANK WILLIAMS
□ 514. JEFF CORNELL
□ 541. MARK DAVIS
□ 567. JOEL YOUNGBLOOD
□ 592. JEFF ROBINSON
□ 619. JEFF LEONARD
□ 646. SCOT THOMPSON
□ 674. ATLEE HAMMAKER
□ 696. JOHN RABB
□ 740. JACK CLARK
□ 772. JOHNNIE LEMASTER

SEATTLE MARINERS

□ 34. ED NUNEZ
□ 58. ORLANDO MERCADO
□ 84. SPIKE OWEN
□ 108. DARNELL COLES
□ 145. ALVIN DAVIS
□ 172. JACK PERCONTE
□ 202. GORMAN THOMAS
□ 224. AL COWENS

□ 232. DAVE BEARD
□ 256. MIKE STANTON
□ 296. RICKY NELSON
□ 344. DAVE HENDERSON
□ 349. DOMINGO RAMOS
□ 373. MIKE MOORE
□ 423. BARRY BONNELL
□ 449. PHIL BRADLEY
□ 485. MATT YOUNG
□ 505. JIM BEATTIE
□ 566. ED VAND BERG
□ 582. KEN PHELPS
□ 625. MARK LANGSTON
□ 640. STEVE HENDERSON
□ 656. CHUCK COTTIER(M)
□ 679. BOB KEARNEY
□ 754. LARRY MILBOURNE
□ 766. PAUL MIRABRELLA

TEXAS RANGERS

□ 29. ODELL JONES
□ 55. FRANK TANANA
□ 76. ALAN BANNISTER
□ 102. TOMMY DUNBAR
□ 149. DICKIE NOLES
□ 171. BILL STEIN
□ 196. PETE O'BRIEN
□ 227. DANNY DARWIN
□ 247. WAYNE TOLLESON
□ 288. JEFF KUNKEL
□ 313. DAVE SCHMIDT
□ 337. BILLY SAMPLE
□ 371. MICKEY RIVERS
□ 414. GARY WARD
□ 443. GEORGE WRIGHT
□ 464. MIKE MASON
□ 496. DONNIE SCOTT
□ 519. DOUG RADER(M)
□ 548. LARRY PARRISH
□ 571. CHARLIE HOUGH
□ 594. CURT WILKERSON
□ 621. MARVIS FOLEY
□ 648. BOB JONES
□ 678. JOEY MCLAUGHLIN
□ 723. DAVE STEWART
□ 745. BUDDY BELL
□ 777. NED YOST

TORONTO BLUE JAYS

□ 24. JESSE BARFIELD
□ 48. TONY FERNANDEZ
□ 75. WILLIE UPSHAW
□ 101. JIM ACKER
□ 128. ERNIE WHITT
□ 168. GARTH IORG
□ 193. JIMMY KEY
□ 218. DOYLE ALEXANDER
□ 240. DAVE STIEB
□ 311. JIM GOTT
□ 336. RANCE MULLINIKS
□ 361. ALFREDO GRIFFIN
□ 411. BOBBY COX(M)
□ 436. WILLIE AIKENS
□ 463. DAVE COLLINS
□ 489. BRYAN CLARK
□ 516. ROY LEE JACKSON
□ 545. LLOYD MOSEBY
□ 568. CLIFF JOHNSON
□ 593. RICK LEACH
□ 622. LUIS LEAD
□ 645. DAMASCO GARCIA
□ 673. BUCK MARTINEZ
□ 698. JORGE BELL
□ 746. JIM CLANCY
□ 774. DENNIS LAMP

1985 TOPPS
TRADED (132)
2 1/2 X 3 1/2

DON SUTTON

ATLANTA BRAVES

- ☐ 20T. RICK CERONE
- ☐ 44T. EDDIE HAAS(M)
- ☐ 45T. TERRY HARPER
- ☐ 100T. PAUL RUNGE
- ☐ 115T. BRUCE SUTTER

BALTIMORE ORIOLES

- ☐ 1T. DON AASE
- ☐ 31T. KEN DIXON
- ☐ 70T. LEE LACY
- ☐ 77T. FRED LYNN
- ☐ 106T. LARRY SHEETS
- ☐ 110T. NATE SNELL
- ☐ 129T. EARL WEAVER(M)

BOSTON RED SOX

- ☐ 67T. BRUCE KISON
- ☐ 84T. JOHN MCNAMARA(M)

CALIFORNIA ANGELS

- ☐ 23T. PAT CLEMENTS
- ☐ 65T. RUPPERT JONES
- ☐ 81T. GENE MAUCH(M)
- ☐ 85T. DONNIE MOORE

CHICAGO CUBS

- ☐ 29T. BRIAN DAYETT
- ☐ 35T. RAY FONTENOT
- ☐ 111T. CHRIS SPEIER

CHICAGO WHITE SOX

- ☐ 8T. DARYL BOSTON
- ☐ 37T. OSCAR GAMBLE
- ☐ 43T. OZZIE GUILLEN
- ☐ 60T. TIM HULETT
- ☐ 61T. BOB JAMES
- ☐ 76T. TIM LOLLAR
- ☐ 86T. GENE NELSON
- ☐ 102T. LUIS SALAZAR

CINCINNATI REDS

- ☐ 11T. TOM BROWNING
- ☐ 68T. ALAN KNICELY

CLEVELAND INDIANS

- ☐ 3T. BENNY AYALA
- ☐ 21T. BRYAN CLARK
- ☐ 99T. VERN RUHLE
- ☐ 122T. RICH THOMPSON
- ☐ 127T. DAVE VON OHLEN

DETROIT TIGERS

- ☐ 91T. CHRIS PITTARO
- ☐ 119T. WALT TERRELL

HOUSTON ASTROS

- ☐ 79T. RON MATHIS

KANSAS CITY ROYALS

- ☐ 69T. MIKE LACOSS
- ☐ 109T. LONNIE SMITH
- ☐ 114T. JIM SUNDBERG

LOS ANGELES DODGERS

- ☐ 18T. BOBBY CASTILLO
- ☐ 32T. MARIANO DUNCAN
- ☐ 58T. KEN HOWELL
- ☐ 88T. AL OLIVER

MILWAUKEE BREWERS

- ☐ 5T. GEORGE BAMBERGER(M)
- ☐ 13T. RAY BURRIS
- ☐ 26T. DANNY DARWIN
- ☐ 39T. BOB GIBSON
- ☐ 53T. TEDDY HIGUERA

MINNESOTA TWINS

- ☐ 36T. GREG GAGNE
- ☐ 101T. MARK SALAS
- ☐ 108T. ROY SMALLEY
- ☐ 112T. MIKE STENHOUSE

MONTREAL EXPOS

- ☐ 9T. HUBIE BROOKS
- ☐ 34T. MIKE FITZGERALD
- ☐ 52T. JOE HESKETH
- ☐ 73T. VANCE LAW
- ☐ 87T. STEVE NICOSIA
- ☐ 94T. BERT ROBERGE
- ☐ 95T. BOB RODGERS(M)
- ☐ 128T. U.L. WASHINGTON
- ☐ 131T. HERM WINNINGHAM

NEW YORK METS

- ☐ 17T. GARY CARTER
- ☐ 64T. HOWARD JOHNSON
- ☐ 83T. ROGER MCDOWELL
- ☐ 103T. JOE SAMBITO

NEW YORK YANKEES

- ☐ 6T. DALE BERRA
- ☐ 7T. RICH BORDI
- ☐ 48T. RON HASSEY
- ☐ 49T. RICKEY HENDERSON
- ☐ 78T. BILLY MARTIN(M)
- ☐ 130T. EDDIE WHITSON

YANKEES OF
RICKEY HENDERSON

OAKLAND A'S

- ☐ 4T. DUSTY BAKER
- ☐ 25T. DAVE COLLINS
- ☐ 42T. ALFREDO GRIFFIN
- ☐ 50T. STEVE HENDERSON
- ☐ 54T. DONNIE HILL
- ☐ 57T. JAY HOWELL
- ☐ 90T. ROB PICCIOLO
- ☐ 116T. DON SUTTON
- ☐ 118T. TOM TELLMANN
- ☐ 120T. MICKEY TETTLETON

PHILADELPHIA PHILLIES

- ☐ 16T. DON CARMAN
- ☐ 33T. JOHN FELSKE(M)
- ☐ 62T. STEVE JELTZ
- ☐ 98T. DAVE RUCKER
- ☐ 104T. RICK SCHU
- ☐ 117T. KENT TEKULVE
- ☐ 121T. DERREL THOMAS

PITTSBURGH PIRATES

- ☐ 2T. BILL ALMON
- ☐ 51T. GEORGE HENDRICK
- ☐ 55T. AL HOLLAND
- ☐ 66T. STEVE KEMP
- ☐ 74T. JOHNNIE LEMASTER
- ☐ 75T. SIXTO LEZCANO
- ☐ 89T. JOE ORSULAK
- ☐ 93T. RICK REUSCHEL

CARDINALS OF
VINCE COLEMAN

ST. LOUIS CARDINALS

- ☐ 15T. BILL CAMPBELL
- ☐ 22T. JACK CLARK
- ☐ 24T. VINCE COLEMAN
- ☐ 30T. IVAN DEJESUS
- ☐ 124T. JOHN TUDOR

SAN DIEGO PADRES

- ☐ 12T. AL BUMBRY
- ☐ 28T. JERRY DAVIS
- ☐ 59T. LAMARR HOYT
- ☐ 96T. JERRY ROYSTER
- ☐ 113T. TIM STODDARD

SAN FRANCISCO GIANTS

- ☐ 10T. CHRIS BROWN
- ☐ 27T. JIM DAVENPORT(M)
- ☐ 38T. SCOTT GARRELTS
- ☐ 40T. JIM GOTT
- ☐ 41T. DAVID GREEN
- ☐ 71T. DAVE LAPOINT
- ☐ 123T. ALEX TREVINO
- ☐ 125T. JOSE URIBE

SEATTLE MARINERS

- ☐ 92T. JIM PRESLEY
- ☐ 105T. DONNIE SCOTT

TEXAS RANGERS

- ☐ 46T. TOBY HARRAH
- ☐ 47T. GREG HARRIS
- ☐ 56T. BURT HOOTON
- ☐ 63T. CLIFF JOHNSON
- ☐ 82T. ODDIBE MCDOWELL
- ☐ 97T. DAVE ROZEMA
- ☐ 107T. DON SLAUGHT
- ☐ 126T. BOBBY VALENTINE(M)

TORONTO BLUE JAYS

- ☐ 14T. JEFF BURROUGHS
- ☐ 19T. BILL CAUDILL
- ☐ 72T. GARY LAVELLE
- ☐ 80T. LEN MATUSZEK

1986 TOPPS (792)
2 1/2 X 3 1/2

EDDIE MURRAY

ATLANTA BRAVES

- [ ] 24. LEN BARKER
- [ ] 57. BOBBY WINE(M)
- [ ] 78. BRUCE BENEDICT
- [ ] 107. RAFAEL RAMIREZ
- [ ] 129. JEFF DEDMON
- [ ] 167. ZANE SMITH
- [ ] 194. CRAIG MCMURTRY
- [ ] 220. BOB HORNER
- [ ] 247. TERRY HARPER
- [ ] 293. CHRIS CHAMBLISS
- [ ] 319. RICK CAMP
- [ ] 334. KEN OBERKFELL
- [ ] 363. TERRY FORSTER
- [ ] 409. PAUL RUNGE
- [ ] 437. RICK MAHLER
- [ ] 456. TEAM LEADER CARD
- [ ] 491. PASCUAL PEREZ
- [ ] 517. MILT THOMPSON
- [ ] 539. GLENN HUBBARD
- [ ] 557. GERALD PERRY
- [ ] 572. PAUL ZUVELLA
- [ ] 600. DALE MURPHY
- [ ] 620. BRUCE SUTTER
- [ ] 648. STEVE BEDROSIAN
- [ ] 675. CLAUDELL WASHINGTON
- [ ] 698. BRAD KOMMINSK
- [ ] 747. RICK CERONE
- [ ] 776. GENE GARBER

BALTIMORE ORIOLES

- [ ] 30. EDDIE MURRARY
- [ ] 55. FRED LYNN
- [ ] 82. TIPPY MARTINEZ
- [ ] 110. SCOTT MCGREGOR
- [ ] 147. LARRY SHEETS
- [ ] 173. WAYNE GROSS
- [ ] 198. KEN DIXON
- [ ] 226. LEE LACY
- [ ] 251. RICH DAUER
- [ ] 279. AL PARDO
- [ ] 288. DON AASE
- [ ] 309. JOHN SHELBY
- [ ] 321. EARL WEAVER(M)
- [ ] 340. CAL RIPKEN
- [ ] 358. RICK DEMPSEY
- [ ] 365. MIKE FLANAGAN
- [ ] 416. DENNY MARTINEZ
- [ ] 446. LENN SAKATA
- [ ] 469. STORM DAVIS
- [ ] 494. GARY ROENICKE
- [ ] 508. ALAN WIGGINS
- [ ] 521. NATE SNELL
- [ ] 548. MIKE YOUNG
- [ ] 575. MIKE BODDICKER
- [ ] 597. SAMMY STEWART
- [ ] 623. FLOYD RAYFORD
- [ ] 653. JIM DWYER
- [ ] 726. TEAM LEADER CARD
- [ ] 753. DAN FORD
- [ ] 781. JOE NOLAN

BOSTON RED SOX

- [ ] 11. BOB OJEDA
- [ ] 38. GLENN HOFFMAN
- [ ] 60. DWIGHT EVANS
- [ ] 91. STEVE CRAWFORD
- [ ] 117. BRUCE KISON
- [ ] 151. DAVE STAPLETON
- [ ] 181. AL NIPPER
- [ ] 233. STEVE LYONS
- [ ] 255. TONY ARMAS
- [ ] 297. TIM LOLLAR
- [ ] 307. DAVE SAX
- [ ] 320. JIM RICE
- [ ] 349. MARK CLEAR
- [ ] 375. RICH GEDMAN
- [ ] 396. TEAM LEADER CARD
- [ ] 424. RICK MILLER
- [ ] 443. BILL BUCKNER
- [ ] 477. MIKE EASLER
- [ ] 510. WADE BOGGS
- [ ] 529. MARC SULLIVAN
- [ ] 581. BRUCE HURST
- [ ] 605. DENNIS BOYD
- [ ] 633. JACKIE GUTIERREZ
- [ ] 661. ROGER CLEMENS
- [ ] 687. MIKE TRUJILLO
- [ ] 734. MARTY BARRETT
- [ ] 749. ED JURAK
- [ ] 771. JOHN MCNAMARA(M)
- [ ] 785. BOB STANLEY

CALIFORNIA ANGELS

- [ ] 42. GEOFF ZAHN
- [ ] 62. BOB BOONE
- [ ] 81. GENE MAUCH(M)
- [ ] 124. LUIS SANCHEZ
- [ ] 127. JACK HOWELL
- [ ] 140. JOHN CANDELARIA
- [ ] 155. BOB GRICH
- [ ] 179. STU CLIBURN
- [ ] 190. GEORGE HENDRICK
- [ ] 193. DARYL SCONIERS
- [ ] 222. CRAIG GERBER
- [ ] 234. DOUG CORBETT
- [ ] 257. DOUG DECINCES
- [ ] 311. DICK SCHOFIELD
- [ ] 325. JUAN BENIQUEZ
- [ ] 335. DON SUTTON
- [ ] 345. DONNIE MOORE
- [ ] 369. AL HOLLAND
- [ ] 373. URBANO LUGO
- [ ] 400. ROD CAREW
- [ ] 464. RUPPERT JONES
- [ ] 486. TEAM LEADER CARD
- [ ] 524. DARRELL MILLER
- [ ] 543. JERRY NARRON
- [ ] 579. JIM SLATON
- [ ] 604. GARY PETTIS
- [ ] 628. KIRK MCCASKILL
- [ ] 658. ROB WILFONG
- [ ] 700. REGGIE JACKSON
- [ ] 733. RON ROMANICK
- [ ] 772. BRIAN DOWNING

CHICAGO CUBS

- [ ] 19. RICH HEBNER
- [ ] 46. BILLY HATCHER
- [ ] 72. SHAWON DUNSTON
- [ ] 98. DICK RUTHVEN
- [ ] 125. DAVE LOPES
- [ ] 188. BOB DERNIER
- [ ] 212. CHRIS SPEIER
- [ ] 231. JIM FREY(M)
- [ ] 266. KEITH MORELAND
- [ ] 284. BRIAN DAYETT
- [ ] 308. RAY FONTENOT
- [ ] 330. RICK SUTCLIFFE
- [ ] 355. LEE SMITH
- [ ] 384. STEVE TROUT
- [ ] 406. SCOTT SANDERSON
- [ ] 431. GOERGE FRAZIER
- [ ] 460. LEON DURHAM
- [ ] 485. GARY MATTHEWS
- [ ] 512. THAD BOSLEY
- [ ] 538. DENNIS ECKERSLEY
- [ ] 564. WARREN BRUSSTAR
- [ ] 588. STEVE LAKE
- [ ] 611. GARY WOODS

- [ ] 636. TEAM LEADER CARD
- [ ] 669. RON CEY
- [ ] 690. RYNE SANDBERG
- [ ] 744. LARY SORENSEN
- [ ] 767. JODY DAVIS

CHICAGO WHITE SOX

- [ ] 14. JULIO CRUZ
- [ ] 64. FLOYD BANNISTER
- [ ] 103. LUIS SALAZAR
- [ ] 123. GREG WALKER
- [ ] 139. DARYL BOSTON
- [ ] 156. TEAM LEADER CARD
- [ ] 187. SCOTT FLETCHER
- [ ] 227. AL JONES
- [ ] 239. JOEL SKINNER
- [ ] 254. OZZIE GUILLEN
- [ ] 290. CARLTON FISK
- [ ] 313. JOE DESA
- [ ] 346. BRYAN LITTLE
- [ ] 364. REID NICHOLS
- [ ] 390. TOM SEAVER
- [ ] 423. DAN SPILLNER
- [ ] 447. JERRY DON GLEATON
- [ ] 467. BOB JAMES
- [ ] 493. GENE NELSON
- [ ] 531. TONY LARUSSA(M)
- [ ] 552. MARC HILL
- [ ] 574. RON KITTLE
- [ ] 612. RICHARD DOTSON
- [ ] 637. RUDY LAW
- [ ] 657. JUAN AGOSTO
- [ ] 679. BRITT BURNS
- [ ] 724. TIM HULETT
- [ ] 755. HAROLD BAINES
- [ ] 778. JERRY HAIRSTON

CINCINNATI REDS

- [ ] 1. PETE ROSE
- [ ] 28. ERIC DAVIS
- [ ] 54. JOHN FRANCO
- [ ] 85. TONY PEREZ
- [ ] 108. TED POWER
- [ ] 133. ANDY MCGAFFIGAN
- [ ] 143. DAVE VAN GORDER
- [ ] 176. JAY TIBBS
- [ ] 195. DAVE CONCEPCION
- [ ] 253. DANN BILARDELLO
- [ ] 285. BUDDY BELL
- [ ] 314. FRANK PASTORE
- [ ] 342. GARY REDUS
- [ ] 366. TEAM LEADER CARD
- [ ] 428. MAX VENABLE
- [ ] 442. RON ROBINSON
- [ ] 497. JOHN STUPER
- [ ] 523. JOE PRICE
- [ ] 544. EDDIE MILNER
- [ ] 573. TOM HUME
- [ ] 595. DAVE PARKER
- [ ] 627. RON OESTER
- [ ] 639. BO DIAZ
- [ ] 652. TOM BROWNING
- [ ] 677. NICK ESASKY
- [ ] 725. MARIO SOTO
- [ ] 741. PETE ROSE(M)
- [ ] 777. WAYNE KRENCHICKI

CLEVELAND INDIANS

- [ ] 9. ROY SMITH
- [ ] 31. JAMIE EASTERLY
- [ ] 59. ANDRE THORNTON
- [ ] 86. TOM WADDELL
- [ ] 116. BROOK JACOBY
- [ ] 136. MIKE HARGROVE
- [ ] 149. BRETT BUTLER
- [ ] 172. JERRY REED
- [ ] 208. RAMON ROMERO
- [ ] 242. RICH THOMPSON
- [ ] 273. JERRY WILLARD
- [ ] 283. MIKE FISCHLIN
- [ ] 303. CURT WARDLE
- [ ] 336. TEAM LEADER CARD
- [ ] 354. TONY BERNAZARD
- [ ] 377. JOE CARTER
- [ ] 391. JULIO FRANCO
- [ ] 483. GEORGE VUKOVICH
- [ ] 509. ERNIE CAMACHO
- [ ] 542. DON SCHULZE

☐ 567. JEFF BARKLEY
☐ 594. CHRIS BANDO
☐ 632. DAVE VON OHLEN
☐ 647. MEL HALL
☐ 674. PAT TABLER
☐ 699. PAT CORRALES(M)
☐ 768. VERN RUHLE

DETROIT TIGERS

☐ 20. LOU WHITAKER
☐ 36. TEAM LEADER CARD
☐ 47. JUAN BERENGUER
☐ 73. RANDY O'NEAL
☐ 101. DAVE BERGMAN
☐ 121. NELSON SIMMONS
☐ 130. ALAN TRAMMELL
☐ 160. CHET LEMON
☐ 192. MILT WILCOX
☐ 217. BILL SCHERRER
☐ 243. JOHNNY GRUBB
☐ 270. JACK MORRIS
☐ 295. KIRK GIVSON
☐ 367. AURELIO LOPEZ
☐ 393. CHRIS PITTARO
☐ 411. SPARKY ANDERSON(M)
☐ 436. DOUG FLYNN
☐ 461. WALT TERRELL
☐ 479. BOB MELVIN
☐ 515. DARRELL EVANS
☐ 540. DAN PETRY
☐ 563. ALEJANDRO SANCHEZ
☐ 592. FRANK TANANA
☐ 609. BARBARO GARBEY
☐ 643. TOM BROOKENS
☐ 670. WILLIE HERNANDEZ
☐ 688. LARRY HERNDON
☐ 740. LANCE PARRISH
☐ 788. MARTY CASTILLO

HOUSTON ASTROS

☐ 26. FRANK DIPINO
☐ 57. BILL DORAN
☐ 83. PHIL GARNER
☐ 100. NOLAN RYAN
☐ 166. DICKIE THON
☐ 186. TEAM LEADER CARD
☐ 268. MIKE SCOTT
☐ 272. TIM TOLMAN
☐ 282. JERRY MUMPHREY
☐ 298. CRAIG REYNOLDS
☐ 331. ALAN ASHBY
☐ 352. HARRY SPILMAN
☐ 376. BILL DAWLEY
☐ 389. GLENN DAVIS
☐ 408. DAVE SMITH
☐ 432. MARK BAILEY
☐ 458. KEVIN BASS
☐ 476. RON MATHIS
☐ 504. DENNY WALLING
☐ 534. JEFF CALHOUN
☐ 561. BOB LILLIS(M)
☐ 590. BOB KNEPPER
☐ 618. JIM PANKOVITS
☐ 640. JOSE CRUZ
☐ 691. MIKE MADDEN
☐ 763. TERRY PUHL

KANSAS CITY ROYALS

☐ 25. WILLIE WILSON
☐ 50. DAN QUISENBERRY
☐ 77. CHARLIE LEIBRANDT
☐ 99. BUDDY BIANCALANA
☐ 128. JOHN WATHAN
☐ 164. STEVE BALBONI
☐ 199. DICK HOWSER(M)
☐ 215. FRANK WHITE
☐ 245. JIM SUNDBERG
☐ 269. DANE IORG
☐ 300. GEORGE BRETT
☐ 332. DARRYL MOTLEY
☐ 359. MIKE LACOSS
☐ 415. HAL MCRAE
☐ 487. BRET SABERHAGEN
☐ 514. MIKE JONES
☐ 541. JORGE ORTA
☐ 562. JOE BECKWITH
☐ 596. ONIX CONCEPCION
☐ 606. TEAM LEADER CARD

☐ 617. LONNIE SMITH
☐ 644. MARK GUBICZA
☐ 671. LYNN JONES
☐ 697. BUD BLACK
☐ 743. PAT SHERIDAN
☐ 773. GREG PRYOR

LOS ANGELES DODGERS

☐ 32. STEVE YEAGER
☐ 56. TOM NIEDENFUER
☐ 87. CANDY MALDONADO
☐ 109. LEN MATUSZEK
☐ 145. PEDRO GUERRERO
☐ 159. OREL HERSHISER
☐ 175. STEVE SAX
☐ 197. ENOS CABELL
☐ 252. BOBBY CASTILLO
☐ 291. TOM LASORDA(M)
☐ 318. TERRY WHITFIELD
☐ 343. CARLOS DIAZ
☐ 368. GREG BROCK
☐ 439. RICK HONEYCUTT
☐ 468. MIKE SCIOSCIA
☐ 470. BILL MADLOCK
☐ 496. JAY JOHNSTONE
☐ 506. BILL RUSSELL
☐ 522. BOB BAILOR
☐ 549. BOB WELCH
☐ 577. JERRY REUSS
☐ 602. MARIANO DUNCAN
☐ 630. FERNANDO VALENZUELA
☐ 654. KEN HOWELL
☐ 665. ALEJANDRO PENA
☐ 696. TEAM LEADER CARD
☐ 728. MIKE MARSHALL
☐ 758. DAVE ANDERSON
☐ 782. KEN LANDREAUX

MILWAUKEE BREWERS

☐ 21. GEORGE BAMBERGER(M)
☐ 49. RICK MANNING
☐ 76. DION JAMES
☐ 106. RAY BURRIS
☐ 137. CHARLIE MOORE
☐ 163. PETE LADD
☐ 185. ROLLIE FINGERS
☐ 209. RANDY READY
☐ 237. TED SIMMONS
☐ 267. PAUL MOLITOR
☐ 277. JAIME COCANOWER
☐ 292. CHUCK PORTER
☐ 317. ED ROMERO
☐ 347. TEDDY HIGUERA
☐ 372. BEN OGLIVIE
☐ 385. CECIL COOPER
☐ 398. EARNIE RILES
☐ 426. TEAM LEADER CARD
☐ 452. BOB CLARK
☐ 473. MARK BROUHARD
☐ 499. BOB GIBSON
☐ 519. DANNY DARWIN
☐ 554. PAUL HOUSEHOLDER
☐ 582. JIM GANTNER
☐ 614. RICK WAITS
☐ 642. RAY SEARAGE
☐ 662. BILL SCHROEDER
☐ 684. BOB MCCLURE
☐ 737. PETE VUCKOVICH
☐ 759. MOOSE HAAS
☐ 780. ROBIN YOUNT

MINNESOTA TWINS

☐ 17. MIKE STENHOUSE
☐ 43. DAVE ENGLE
☐ 71. KEN SCHROM
☐ 97. GARY GAETTI
☐ 122. PETE FILSON
☐ 162. GREG GAGNE
☐ 184. TIM LAUDNER
☐ 214. RANDY BUSH
☐ 236. FRANK EUFEMIA
☐ 265. RON DAVIS
☐ 329. KIRBY PUCKETT
☐ 356. MICKEY HATCHER
☐ 381. RAY MILLER(M)
☐ 430. KENT HRBEK
☐ 445. BERT BLYLEVEN

☐ 451. MARK BROWN
☐ 482. RICK LYSANDER
☐ 513. RON WASHINGTON
☐ 537. MARK SALAS
☐ 565. TOM BRUNANSKY
☐ 613. ROY SMALLEY
☐ 638. JOHN BUTCHER
☐ 667. TIM TEUFEL
☐ 695. MIKE SMITHSON
☐ 742. FRANK VIOLA
☐ 786. TEAM LEADER CARD

MONTREAL EXPOS

☐ 35. JEFF REARDON
☐ 89. RANDY ST. CLAIRE
☐ 93. SCOT THOMPSON
☐ 113. U.L. WASHINGTON
☐ 132. RAZOR SHINES
☐ 154. BERT ROBERGE
☐ 141. BOB RODGERS(M)
☐ 229. BILL GULLICKSON
☐ 258. TIM BURKE
☐ 280. TIM RAINES
☐ 299. BRYN SMITH
☐ 324. DAN SCHATZEDER
☐ 344. JIM WOHLFORD
☐ 374. TERRY FRANCONA
☐ 407. SAL BUTERA
☐ 421. DAVE PALMER
☐ 448. HERM WINNINGHAM
☐ 472. JOE HESKETH
☐ 503. MIKE FITZGERALD
☐ 526. CHARLIE LEA
☐ 555. HUBIE BROOKS
☐ 576. TEAM LEADER CARD
☐ 601. GARY LUCAS
☐ 603. BILL LASKEY
☐ 629. MITCH WEBSTER
☐ 685. TIM WALLACH
☐ 732. FLOYD YOUMANS
☐ 760. ANDRE DAWSON
☐ 787. VANCE LAW

LEN DYKSTRA

NEW YORK METS

☐ 18. BRENT GAFF
☐ 27. RAY KNIGHT
☐ 53. LEN DYKSTRA
☐ 68. ED LYNCH
☐ 80. DARRYL STRAWBERRY
☐ 104. SID FERNANDEZ
☐ 126. TEAM LEADER CARD
☐ 144. DOUG SISK
☐ 170. GARY CARTER
☐ 191. WALLY BACKMAN
☐ 210. CALVIN SCHIRALDI
☐ 225. RON DARLING
☐ 250. DWIGHT GOODEN
☐ 274. RON GARDENHIRE
☐ 287. JOHN CHRISTENSEN
☐ 315. MOOKIE WILSON
☐ 339. BRUCE BERENYI
☐ 362. TOM PACIOREK
☐ 414. TOM GORMAN
☐ 438. CLINT HURDLE
☐ 465. JESSE OROSCO
☐ 492. KELVIN CHAPMAN
☐ 501. DAVE JOHNSON(M)
☐ 520. KEITH HERNANDEZ
☐ 547. ROGER MCDOWELL

1986 Topps

☐ 570. RUSTY STAUB
☐ 587. RAFAEL SANTANA
☐ 599. RICK AGUILERA
☐ 619. DANNY HEEP
☐ 649. RONN REYNOLDS
☐ 680. GEORGE FOSTER
☐ 751. HOWARD JOHNSON
☐ 774. TERRY LEACH

NEW YORK YANKEES

☐ 15. EDDIE WHITSON
☐ 40. KEN GRIFFEY
☐ 70. DAVE WINFIELD
☐ 94. RICH BORDI
☐ 135. JOE NIEKRO
☐ 157. RON HASSEY
☐ 180. DON MATTINGLY
☐ 213. BOB SHIRLEY
☐ 235. BUTCH WYNEGAR
☐ 259. DAN PASQUA
☐ 276. TEAM LEADER CARD
☐ 301. DENNIS RASMUSSEN
☐ 327. MIKE PAGLIARULO
☐ 379. BOBBY MEACHAM
☐ 427. JOE COWLEY
☐ 449. ROD SCURRY
☐ 455. WILLIE RANDOLPH
☐ 481. SCOTT BRADLEY
☐ 500. RICKEY HENDERSON
☐ 533. BILLY SAMPLE
☐ 560. DAVE RIGHETTI
☐ 584. BRIAN FISHER
☐ 610. RON GUIDRY
☐ 651. BILLY MARTIN(M)
☐ 663. NEIL ALLEN
☐ 692. DALE BERRA
☐ 723. MARTY BYSTROM
☐ 738. ANDRE ROBERTSON
☐ 765. DON BAYLOR
☐ 790. PHIL NIEKRO

OAKLAND A'S

☐ 8. DWAYNE MURPHY
☐ 29. TONY PHILLIPS
☐ 58. BILL KRUEGER
☐ 84. CURT YOUNG
☐ 115. JAY HOWELL
☐ 134. CARNEY LANSFORD
☐ 148. MIKE HEATH
☐ 165. MIKE DAVIS
☐ 216. TEAM LEADER CARD
☐ 240. TOMMY JOHN
☐ 271. DAVE COLLINS
☐ 281. STEVE MURA
☐ 304. MIKE GALLEGO
☐ 353. KEITH ATHERTON
☐ 378. BRUCE BOCHTE
☐ 410. DAVE KINGMAN
☐ 433. CHRIS CODIROLI
☐ 457. MICKEY TETTLETON
☐ 484. DONNIE HILL
☐ 507. STEVE ONTIVEROS
☐ 536. JOE RIJO
☐ 566. ALFREDO GRIFFIN
☐ 591. JACKIE MOORE
☐ 624. STEVE MCCATTY
☐ 645. DUSTY BAKER
☐ 672. ROB PICCIOLO
☐ 693. TOM TELLMAN
☐ 748. STEVE HENDERSON
☐ 766. RICK LANGFORD

PHILADELPHIA PHILLIES

☐ 16. RICK SCHU
☐ 39. DAVE RUCKER
☐ 69. LUIS AGUAYO
☐ 95. OZZIE VIRGIL
☐ 120. STEVE CARLTON
☐ 158. DERREL THOMAS
☐ 183. LARRY ANDERSEN
☐ 200. MIKE SCHMIDT
☐ 246. TEAM LEADER CARD
☐ 264. DARREN DAULTON
☐ 302. GREG GROSS
☐ 326. KENT TEKULVE
☐ 361. SHANE RAWLEY
☐ 392. JOHN RUSSELL
☐ 418. ALAN KNICELY

☐ 420. VON HAYES
☐ 453. STEVE JELTZ
☐ 466. TOM FOLEY
☐ 475. JUAN SAMUEL
☐ 505. JERRY KOOSMAN
☐ 532. DON CARMAN
☐ 556. JOHN DENNY
☐ 585. GARRY MADDOX
☐ 621. JOHN FELSKE(M)
☐ 664. TIM CORCORAN
☐ 686. JEFF STONE
☐ 689. DAVE STEWART
☐ 736. GLENN WILSON
☐ 764. KEVIN GROSS
☐ 792. CHARLES HUDSON

PITTSBURGH PIRATES

☐ 48. BILL ALMON
☐ 75. JOSE DELEON
☐ 102. JOE ORSULAK
☐ 114. MIKE BROWN
☐ 161. LEE TUNNELL
☐ 232. RICK RHODEN
☐ 260. TONY PENA
☐ 278. SIXTO LEZCANO
☐ 289. JOHNNIE LEMASTER
☐ 316. SAMMY KHALIFA
☐ 351. CHUCK TANNER(M)
☐ 387. STEVE KEMP
☐ 417. R.J. REYNOLDS
☐ 425. LARRY MCWILLIAMS
☐ 489. JIM WINN
☐ 525. MARVELL WYNNE
☐ 553. JIM MORRISON
☐ 578. LEE MAZZILLI
☐ 589. SID BREAM
☐ 615. JOHNNY RAY
☐ 635. JASON THOMPSON
☐ 668. CECILIO GUANTE
☐ 682. JUNIOR ORTIZ
☐ 731. DON ROBINSON
☐ 746. DENNY GONZALEZ
☐ 754. PAT CLEMENTS
☐ 756. TEAM LEADER CARD
☐ 779. RICK REUSCHEL

ST. LOUIS CARDINALS

☐ 33. JEFF LAHTI
☐ 66. TEAM LEADER CARD
☐ 88. TOM NIETO
☐ 112. BILL CAMPBELL
☐ 150. JOAQUIN ANDUJAR
☐ 178. IVAN DEJESUS
☐ 218. RANDY HUNT
☐ 224. CESAR CEDENO
☐ 228. TOM LAWLESS
☐ 256. KURT KEPSHIRE
☐ 294. DANNY COX
☐ 322. BOB FORSCH
☐ 350. JACK CLARK
☐ 370. VINCE COLEMAN
☐ 422. MIKE JORGENSEN
☐ 441. WHITEY HERZOG(M)
☐ 474. JOHN TUDOR
☐ 498. TITO LANDRUM
☐ 528. TERRY PENDLETON
☐ 550. TOM HERR
☐ 580. WILLIE MCGEE
☐ 607. KEN DAYLEY
☐ 631. STEVE BRAUN
☐ 656. BRIAN HARPER
☐ 683. ANDY VAN SLYKE
☐ 730. OZZIE SMITH
☐ 757. DARRELL PORTER
☐ 783. RICKY HORTON

SAN DIEGO PADRES

☐ 10. TONY GWYNN
☐ 37. MARK THURMOND
☐ 44. LANCE MCCULLERS
☐ 67. CARMELO MARTINEZ
☐ 90. GARRY TEMPLETON
☐ 118. JERRY ROYSTER
☐ 182. BOBBY BROWN
☐ 211. ED WOJNA
☐ 230. TERRY KENNEDY
☐ 244. CRAIG LEFFERTS
☐ 262. MARIO RAMIREZ

☐ 286. LUIS DELEON
☐ 306. TEAM LEADER CARD
☐ 323. JERRY DAVIS
☐ 380. LAMARR HOYT
☐ 413. TIM FLANNERY
☐ 429. GREG BOOKER
☐ 450. GRAIG NETTLES
☐ 478. ANDY HAWKINS
☐ 530. RICH GOSSAGE
☐ 558. TIM STODDARD
☐ 583. AL BUMBRY
☐ 608. BRUCE BOCHY
☐ 634. ROY LEE JACKSON
☐ 660. STEVE GARVEY
☐ 681. DICK WILLIAMS(M)
☐ 735. DAVE DRAVECKY
☐ 762. ERIC SHOW
☐ 789. KURT BEVACQUA

SAN FRANCISCO GIANTS

☐ 12. JOSE URIBE
☐ 41. BRAD WELLMAN
☐ 63. RON ROENICKE
☐ 65. DAN DRIESSEN
☐ 111. ROGER CRAIG(M)
☐ 138. MARK DAVIS
☐ 153. RICKY ADAMS
☐ 177. JOEL YOUNGBLOOD
☐ 223. ATLEE HAMMAKER
☐ 249. ROB DEER
☐ 310. GREG MINTON
☐ 341. FRANK WILLIAMS
☐ 383. CHRIS BROWN
☐ 395. SCOTT GARRELTS
☐ 444. ALEX TREVINO
☐ 463. JIM GOTT
☐ 490. JEFF LEONARD
☐ 516. TEAM LEADER CARD
☐ 551. DAVE LAPOINT
☐ 571. MIKE JEFFCOAT
☐ 625. BOB BRENLY
☐ 655. MANNY TRILLO
☐ 678. DAN GLADDEN
☐ 727. DAVID GREEN
☐ 752. MIKE KRUKOW
☐ 770. VIDA BLUE

SEATTLE MARINERS

☐ 13. BOB KEARNEY
☐ 34. KEN PHELPS
☐ 61. KARL BEST
☐ 92. AL COWENS
☐ 119. BARRY BONNELL
☐ 141. CHUCK COTTIER(M)
☐ 146. JACK PERCONTE
☐ 152. MIKE MORGAN
☐ 174. BRIAN SNYDER
☐ 221. DAVE HENDERSON
☐ 248. SPIKE OWEN
☐ 305. PHIL BRADLEY
☐ 337. DARNELL COLES
☐ 357. ED VANDEBERG
☐ 382. IVAN CALDERON
☐ 399. BILL SWIFT
☐ 419. FRANK WILLS
☐ 440. ALVIN DAVIS
☐ 462. DOMINGO RAMOS
☐ 495. MARK LANGSTON

☐ 511. ED NUNEZ
☐ 546. TEAM LEADER CARD
☐ 568. DONNIE SCOTT
☐ 598. JIM PRESLEY
☐ 626. ROY THOMAS
☐ 646. MIKE MOORE
☐ 676. MATT YOUNG
☐ 729. JIM BEATTIE
☐ 750. GORMAN THOMAS
☐ 769. HAROLD REYNOLDS

TEXAS RANGERS

☐ 22. DUANE WALKER
☐ 52. CHRIS WELSH
☐ 79. DAVE SCHMIDT
☐ 105. GARY WARD
☐ 142. BOB JONES
☐ 169. GEORGE WRIGHT
☐ 189. MIKE MASON
☐ 238. LARRY PARRISH
☐ 261. BOBBY VALENTINE(M)
☐ 275. CHARLIE HOUGH
☐ 296. GENO PETRALLI
☐ 328. PETE O'BRIAN
☐ 371. BILL STEIN
☐ 388. DICKIE NOLES
☐ 397. STEVE BUECHELE
☐ 434. CURT WILKERSON
☐ 454. BURT HOOTON
☐ 480. ODDIBE MCDOWELL
☐ 502. GLEN COOK
☐ 535. TOBY HARRAH
☐ 559. TOMMY DUNBAR
☐ 586. GREG HARRIS
☐ 616. GLENN BRUMMER
☐ 641. WAYNE TOLLESON
☐ 666. TEAM LEADER CARD
☐ 739. DAVE ROZEMA
☐ 761. DON SLAUGHT
☐ 784. ALAN BANNISTER

TORONTO BLUE JAYS

☐ 23. MANNY LEE
☐ 45. DAMASO GARCIA
☐ 74. RANCE MULLINIKS
☐ 96. TEAM LEADER CARD
☐ 168. JEFF BURROUGHS
☐ 196. DOYLE ALEXANDER
☐ 219. DENNIS LAMP
☐ 241. TONY FERNANDEZ
☐ 312. TOM FILER
☐ 333. TOM HENKE
☐ 338. JORGE BELL
☐ 348. CLIFF JOHNSON
☐ 360. LLOYD MOSEBY
☐ 386. CECIL FIELDER
☐ 412. JIM CLANCY
☐ 435. BILL CAUDILL
☐ 459. LUIS LEAL
☐ 471. BOBBY COX(M)
☐ 488. LOU THORNTON
☐ 518. BUCK MARTINEZ
☐ 545. JIMMY KEY
☐ 569. JIM ACKER
☐ 593. JESSE BARFIELD
☐ 622. GARY LAVELLE
☐ 650. DAVE STIEB
☐ 673. ERNIE WHITT
☐ 694. GARTH IORG
☐ 745. WILLIE UPSHAW
☐ 775. AL OLIVER

1986 TOPPS
TRADED (132)
2 1/2 X 3 1/2

PETE INCAVIGLIA

ATLANTA BRAVES

☐ 4T. PAUL ASSENMACHER
☐ 41T. KEN GRIFFEY
☐ 75T. OMAR MORENO
☐ 84T. DAVE PALMER
☐ 98T. BILLY SAMPLE
☐ 102T. TED SIMMONS
☐ 107T. CHUCK TANNER(M)
☐ 111T. ANDRES THOMAS
☐ 119T. OZZIE VIRGIL

BALTIMORE ORIOLES

☐ 8T. JUAN BENIQUEZ
☐ 13T. JUAN BONILLA
☐ 14T. RICH BORDI

BOSTON RED SOX

☐ 6T. DON BAYLOR
☐ 89T. REY QUINONES
☐ 95T. ED ROMERO
☐ 97T. JOE SAMBITO
☐ 101T. TOM SEAVER
☐ 103T. SAMMY STEWART

CALIFORNIA ANGELS

☐ 16T. RICK BURLESON
☐ 37T. TERRY FORSTER
☐ 51T. WALLY JOYNER

CHICAGO CUBS

☐ 38T. TERRY FRANCONA
☐ 73T. GENE MICHAEL(M)
☐ 76T. JERRY MUMPHREY
☐ 117T. MANNY TRILLO

CHICAGO WHITE SOX

☐ 2T. NEIL ALLEN
☐ 12T. BOBBY BONILLA
☐ 19T. JOHN CANGELOSI
☐ 29T. JOE COWLEY
☐ 30T. JOEL DAVIS
☐ 39T. JIM FREGOSI(M)
☐ 67T. STEVE LYONS
☐ 99T. DAVE SCHMIDT
☐ 115T. WAYNE TOLLESON

CINCINNATI REDS

☐ 32T. JOHN DENNY
☐ 42T. BILL GULLICKSON
☐ 104T. KURT STILLWELL

CLEVELAND INDIANS

☐ 1T. ANDY ALLANSON
☐ 5T. SCOTT BAILES
☐ 18T. TOM CANDIOTTI
☐ 21T. CARMEN CASTILLO

☐ 77T. PHIL NIEKRO
☐ 80T. OTIS NIXON
☐ 100T. KEN SCHROM

DETROIT TIGERS

☐ 17T. BILL CAMBELL
☐ 26T. DARNELL COLES
☐ 27T. DAVE COLLINS
☐ 53T. ERIC KING
☐ 59T. MIKE LAGA
☐ 61T. DAVE LAPOINT

HOUSTON ASTROS

☐ 45T. BILLY HATCHER
☐ 52T. CHARLIE KERFELD
☐ 60T. HAL LANIER(M)

KANSAS CITY ROYALS

☐ 35T. STEVE FARR
☐ 50T. BO JACKSON
☐ 62T. RUDY LAW
☐ 65T. DENNIS LEONARD
☐ 96T. ARGENIS SALAZAR

LOS ANGELES DODGERS

☐ 105T. FRANKLIN STUBBS
☐ 116T. ALEX TREVINO
☐ 118T. ED VANDEBERG

MILWAUKEE BREWERS

☐ 22T. RICK CERONE
☐ 25T. MARK CLEAR
☐ 31T. ROB DEER
☐ 64T. TIM LEARY
☐ 79T. JUAN NIEVES
☐ 87T. DAN PLESAC
☐ 92T. BILL JO ROBIDOUX
☐ 106T. DALE SVEUM
☐ 123T. BILL WEGMAN

MINNESOTA TWINS

☐ 85T. FRANK PASTORE

MONTREAL EXPOS

☐ 40T. ANDRES GALARRAGA
☐ 55T. WAYNE KRENCHICKI
☐ 71T. BOB MCCLURE
☐ 72T. ANDY MCGAFFIGAN
☐ 114T. JAY TIBBS
☐ 128T. GEORGE WRIGHT

NEW YORK METS

☐ 74T. KEVIN MITCHELL
☐ 78T. RANDY NIEMANN
☐ 81T. BOB OJEDA
☐ 109T. TIM TEUFEL

NEW YORK YANKEES

☐ 33T. MIKE EASLER
☐ 86T. LOU PINIELLA
☐ 94T. GARY ROENICKE
☐ 110T. BOB TEWKSBURY
☐ 131T. PAUL ZUVELLA
☐ 122T. CLAUDELL WASHINGTON

JOSE CANSECO

OAKLAND A'S

- ☐ 3T. JOAQUIN ANDUJAR
- ☐ 20T. JOSE CANSECO
- ☐ 44T. MOOSE HAAS

PHILADELPHIA PHILLIES

- ☐ 7T. STEVE BEDROSIAN
- ☐ 47T. TOM HUME
- ☐ 90T. GARY REDUS
- ☐ 112T. MILT THOMPSON

PITTSBURGH PIRATES

- ☐ 10T. MIKE BIELECKI
- ☐ 11T. BARRY BONDS
- ☐ 54T. BOB KNIPPER
- ☐ 66T. JIM LEYLAND(M)
- ☐ 120T. BOB WALK

ST. LOUIS CARDINALS

- ☐ 28T. TIM CONROY
- ☐ 46T. MIKE HEATH
- ☐ 82T. JOSE OQUENDO
- ☐ 127T. TODD WORRELL

SAN DIEGO PADRES

- ☐ 15T. STEVE BOROS(M)
- ☐ 49T. DANE IORG
- ☐ 56T. JOHN KRUK
- ☐ 91T. BIP ROBERTS
- ☐ 121T. GENE WALTERS

WILL CLARK

SAN FRANCISCO GIANTS

- ☐ 9T. JUAN BERENGUER
- ☐ 24T. WILL CLARK
- ☐ 57T. MIKE LACOSS
- ☐ 69T. CANDY MALDONADO
- ☐ 70T. ROGER MASON
- ☐ 93T. JEFF ROBINSON
- ☐ 113T. ROBBY THOMPSON

SEATTLE MARINERS

- ☐ 58T. PETE LADD
- ☐ 108T. DANNY TARTABULL
- ☐ 124T. DICK WILLIAMS(M)
- ☐ 130T. STEVE YEAGER

TEXAS RANGERS

- ☐ 36T. SCOTT FLETCHER
- ☐ 43T. JOSE GUZMAN
- ☐ 48T. PETE INCAVIGLIA
- ☐ 68T. MICKEY MAHLER
- ☐ 83T. TOM PACIOREK
- ☐ 88T. DARRELL PORTER
- ☐ 125T. MITCH WILLIAMS
- ☐ 126T. BOBBY WITT
- ☐ 129T. RICKY WRIGHT

TORONTO BLUE JAYS

- ☐ 23T. JOHN CERUTTI
- ☐ 34T. MARK EICHHORN
- ☐ 63T. RICK LEACH

1987 TOPPS (792)
2 1/2 X 3 1/2

LEE SMITH

ATLANTA BRAVES

- ☐ 31. TEAM LEADER CARD
- ☐ 49. TERRY HARPER
- ☐ 76. RAFAEL RAMIREZ
- ☐ 104. BILLY SAMPLE
- ☐ 132. PAUL ASSENMACHER
- ☐ 159. ED OLWINE
- ☐ 186. BRUCE BENEDICT
- ☐ 214. OMAR MORENO
- ☐ 242. RICH MAHLER
- ☐ 269. CLIFF SPECK
- ☐ 296. ANDRES THOMAS
- ☐ 324. DAVE PALMER
- ☐ 351. GENE GARBER
- ☐ 373. JEFF DEDMON
- ☐ 407. JIM ACKER
- ☐ 435. BRUCE SUTTER
- ☐ 461. CRAIG MCMURTRY
- ☐ 490. DALE MURPHY
- ☐ 516. TED SIMMONS
- ☐ 544. ZANE SMITH
- ☐ 571. OZZIE VIRGIL
- ☐ 593. CHUCK TANNER(M)
- ☐ 627. KEN OBERKFELL
- ☐ 639. GERALD PERRY
- ☐ 660. BOB HORNER
- ☐ 686. DOYLE ALEXANDER
- ☐ 711. KEN GRIFFEY
- ☐ 745. GLENN HUBBARD
- ☐ 777. CHRIS CHAMBLISS

BALTIMORE ORIOLES

- ☐ 28. RICK DEMPSEY
- ☐ 86. NATE SNELL
- ☐ 120. EDDIE MURRAY
- ☐ 154. TOM O'MALLEY
- ☐ 182. LEE LACY
- ☐ 208. JOHN SHELBY
- ☐ 246. JIM DWYER
- ☐ 276. JACKIE GUTIERREZ
- ☐ 309. MIKE YOUNG
- ☐ 349. STORM DAVIS
- ☐ 370. FRED LYNN
- ☐ 398. BRAD HAVENS
- ☐ 426. FLOYD RAYFORD
- ☐ 455. MIKE BODDICKER
- ☐ 484. JIM TRABER
- ☐ 506. TEAM LEADER CARD
- ☐ 528. KEN DIXON
- ☐ 552. LARRY SHEETS
- ☐ 563. JOHN STEFERO
- ☐ 568. EARL WEAVER(M)
- ☐ 638. RICH BORDI
- ☐ 668. JUAN BONILLA
- ☐ 688. JUAN BENIQUEZ
- ☐ 708. SCOTT MCGREGOR
- ☐ 728. TIPPY MARTINEZ
- ☐ 748. MIKE FLANAGAN
- ☐ 766. DON AASE
- ☐ 784. CAL RIPKEN

BOSTON RED SOX

- ☐ 12. JEFF SELLERS
- ☐ 39. MARTY BARRETT
- ☐ 66. MARC SULLIVAN
- ☐ 94. CALVIN SCHIRALDI
- ☐ 121. KEVIN ROMINE
- ☐ 150. WADE BOGGS
- ☐ 175. BOB STANLEY
- ☐ 204. SAMMY STEWART
- ☐ 230. DON BAYLOR
- ☐ 259. MIKE GREENWELL
- ☐ 285. DENNIS BOYD
- ☐ 306. TEAM LEADER CARD
- ☐ 340. ROGER CLEMENS
- ☐ 368. JOHN MCNAMARA(M)
- ☐ 374. GLENN HOFFMAN
- ☐ 396. TIM LOLLAR
- ☐ 425. TOM SEAVER
- ☐ 449. PAT DODSON
- ☐ 451. JOE SAMBITO
- ☐ 452. DAVE HENDERSON
- ☐ 480. JIM RICE
- ☐ 507. DAVE STAPLETON
- ☐ 535. TONY ARMAS
- ☐ 589. STEVE CRAWFORD
- ☐ 591. SPIKE OWEN
- ☐ 617. AL NIPPER
- ☐ 632. ROB WOODWARD
- ☐ 645. DWIGHT EVANS
- ☐ 675. ED ROMERO
- ☐ 705. BRUCE HURST
- ☐ 740. RICH GEDMAN
- ☐ 764. BILL BUCKNER

BRUCE HURST

CALIFORNIA ANGELS

- ☐ 22. DOUG DECINCES
- ☐ 53. RUPPERT JONES
- ☐ 80. WALLY JOYNER
- ☐ 92. URBANO LUGO
- ☐ 115. DONNIE MOORE
- ☐ 136. RON ROMANICK
- ☐ 139. DEVON WHITE
- ☐ 166. BOB BOONE
- ☐ 194. KIRK MCCASKILL
- ☐ 221. VERN RUHLE
- ☐ 251. ROB WILFONG
- ☐ 278. GARY PETTIS
- ☐ 300. REGGIE JACKSON
- ☐ 337. DARRELL MILLER
- ☐ 359. DOUG CORBETT
- ☐ 387. T.R. BRYDEN
- ☐ 422. JACK HOWELL
- ☐ 446. CHUCK FINLEY
- ☐ 474. JERRY NARRON
- ☐ 502. DICK SCHOFIELD
- ☐ 518. GENE MAUCH(M)
- ☐ 556. TEAM LEADER CARD
- ☐ 579. RICK BURLESON
- ☐ 630. JOHN CANDELARIA
- ☐ 652. TERRY FORSTER
- ☐ 673. DON SUTTON
- ☐ 677. BOB GRICH
- ☐ 696. GARY LUCAS
- ☐ 725. GEORGE HENDRICK
- ☐ 760. MIKE WITT
- ☐ 782. BRIAN DOWNING

CHICAGO CUBS

- [ ] 23. LEE SMITH
- [ ] 43. GENE MICHAEL(M)
- [ ] 58. THAD BOSLEY
- [ ] 142. RICK SUTCLIFFE
- [ ] 177. KEITH MORELAND
- [ ] 227. JAMIE MOYER
- [ ] 270. JODY DAVIS
- [ ] 290. LEON DURHAM
- [ ] 346. SHAWON DUNSTON
- [ ] 369. BRIAN DAYETT
- [ ] 372. JERRY MUMPHREY
- [ ] 383. RON DAVIS
- [ ] 390. GARY MATTHEWS
- [ ] 424. CHRIS SPEIER
- [ ] 459. DENNIS ECKERSLEY
- [ ] 487. DAVE GUMPERT
- [ ] 534. SCOTT SANDERSON
- [ ] 581. TEAM LEADER CARD
- [ ] 634. RAFAEL PALMEIRO
- [ ] 662. FRANK DIPINO
- [ ] 680. RYNE SANDBERG
- [ ] 695. CHICO WALKER
- [ ] 697. ED LYNCH
- [ ] 715. BOB DERNIER
- [ ] 732. MANNY TRILLO
- [ ] 750. STEVE TROUT
- [ ] 767. RON CEY
- [ ] 785. TERRY FRANCONA

CHICAGO WHITE SOX

- [ ] 27. JOE COWLEY
- [ ] 54. BILL DAWLEY
- [ ] 61. BOBBY THIGPEN
- [ ] 89. OZZIE GUILLEN
- [ ] 113. NEIL ALLEN
- [ ] 149. RAY SEARAGE
- [ ] 201. JOHN CANGELOSI
- [ ] 233. RUSS MORMAN
- [ ] 273. GENE NELSON
- [ ] 299. JOEL DAVIS
- [ ] 318. JIM FREGOSI(M)
- [ ] 342. BOB JAMES
- [ ] 356. TEAM LEADER CARD
- [ ] 397. GREG WALKER
- [ ] 421. JOSE DELEON
- [ ] 454. LUIS SALAZAR
- [ ] 482. DARYL BOSTON
- [ ] 491. RON KARKOVICE
- [ ] 511. STEVE LYONS
- [ ] 539. REID NICHOLS
- [ ] 566. TIM HULETT
- [ ] 667. RON HASSEY
- [ ] 685. JERRY HAIRSTON
- [ ] 703. DAVE SCHMIDT
- [ ] 718. STEVE CARLTON
- [ ] 720. RICHARD DOTSON
- [ ] 737. FLOYD BANNISTER
- [ ] 756. CARLTON FISK
- [ ] 772. HAROLD BAINES
- [ ] 790. JULIO CRUZ

CINCINNATI REDS

- [ ] 13. NICK ESASKY
- [ ] 41. BO DIAZ
- [ ] 65. TOM BROWNING
- [ ] 82. ROB MURPHY
- [ ] 101. CARL WILLIS
- [ ] 119. RON ROBINSON
- [ ] 146. TRACY JONES
- [ ] 172. RON OESTER
- [ ] 200. PETE ROSE
- [ ] 226. MAX VENABLE
- [ ] 253. EDDIE MILNER
- [ ] 281. TEAM LEADER CARD
- [ ] 305. JOHN FRANCO
- [ ] 332. JOE PRICE
- [ ] 358. SAL BUTERA
- [ ] 393. PETE ROSE(M)
- [ ] 412. ERIC DAVIS
- [ ] 437. TED POWER
- [ ] 453. SCOTT TERRY
- [ ] 466. KAL DANIELS
- [ ] 489. BILL GULLICKSON
- [ ] 517. MARIO SOTO
- [ ] 545. BUDDY BELL
- [ ] 569. WADE ROWDON
- [ ] 592. CHRIS WELSH

- [ ] 623. KURT STILLWELL
- [ ] 644. JOHN DENNY
- [ ] 648. BARRY LARKIN
- [ ] 691. DAVE PARKER
- [ ] 731. DAVE CONCEPCION

CLEVELAND INDIANS

- [ ] 11. TEAM LEADER CARD
- [ ] 51. MEL HALL
- [ ] 77. BRYAN OELKERS
- [ ] 107. JOHN BUTCHER
- [ ] 134. RICH YETT
- [ ] 160. JULIO FRANCO
- [ ] 192. CORY SNYDER
- [ ] 220. JOE CARTER
- [ ] 244. DICKIE NOLES
- [ ] 268. PAT CORRALES(M)
- [ ] 297. DON SCHULZE
- [ ] 319. GREG SWINDELL
- [ ] 322. CHRIS BANDO
- [ ] 353. ERNIE CAMACHO
- [ ] 405. BROOK JACOBY
- [ ] 436. ANDY ALLANSON
- [ ] 463. TOM CANDIOTTI
- [ ] 486. OTIS NIXON
- [ ] 513. CARMEN CASTILLO
- [ ] 551. FRANK WILLS
- [ ] 575. PAT TABLER
- [ ] 585. SCOTT BAILES
- [ ] 635. KEN SCHROM
- [ ] 657. TOM WADDELL
- [ ] 694. PHIL NIEKRO
- [ ] 723. BRETT BUTLER
- [ ] 758. TONY BERNAZARD
- [ ] 780. ANDRE THORNTON

DETROIT TIGERS

- [ ] 36. ERIC KING
- [ ] 72. WALT TERRELL
- [ ] 98. BILL SCHERRER
- [ ] 148. DAVE COLLINS
- [ ] 171. CHUCK CARY
- [ ] 196. RANDY O'NEAL
- [ ] 218. SPARKY ANDERSON(M)
- [ ] 234. PAT SHERIDAN
- [ ] 265. DARRELL EVANS
- [ ] 298. LARRY HERNDON
- [ ] 361. MARK THURMOND
- [ ] 384. JOHNNY GRUBB
- [ ] 411. DARNELL COLES
- [ ] 432. JIM SLATON
- [ ] 483. DWIGHT LOWRY
- [ ] 492. MIKE HEATH
- [ ] 515. WILLIE HERNANDEZ
- [ ] 631. TEAM LEADER CARD
- [ ] 661. LOU WHITAKER
- [ ] 674. BILL CAMPBELL
- [ ] 687. ALAN TRAMMELL
- [ ] 700. DAVE BERGMAN
- [ ] 713. TOM BROOKENS
- [ ] 726. FRANK TANANA
- [ ] 739. CHET LEMON
- [ ] 752. DAN PETRY
- [ ] 765. KIRK GIBSON
- [ ] 778. JACK MORRIS
- [ ] 791. LANCE PARRISH

HOUSTON ASTROS

- [ ] 24. TONY WALKER
- [ ] 50. DAVE SMITH
- [ ] 85. KEVIN BASS
- [ ] 112. ALAN ASHBY
- [ ] 145. CHARLIE KERFELD
- [ ] 157. DANNY DARWIN
- [ ] 167. JIM DESHAIES
- [ ] 197. MARK BAILEY
- [ ] 222. DENNY WALLING
- [ ] 249. JIM PANKOVITS
- [ ] 282. JEFF CALHOUN
- [ ] 304. PHIL GARNER
- [ ] 330. MIKE SCOTT
- [ ] 343. HAL LANIER(M)
- [ ] 386. DICKIE THON
- [ ] 408. JOHN MIZEROCK
- [ ] 445. DAVE LOPES
- [ ] 472. BILL DORAN
- [ ] 503. LARRY ANDERSON
- [ ] 531. TEAM LEADER CARD
- [ ] 560. GLENN DAVIS
- [ ] 578. BILLY HATCHER
- [ ] 659. AURELIO LOPEZ
- [ ] 670. JOSE CRUZ
- [ ] 693. TERRY PUHL
- [ ] 722. BOB KNEPPER
- [ ] 757. NOLAN RYAN
- [ ] 779. CRAIG REYNOLDS

KANSAS CITY ROYALS

- [ ] 18. DICK HOWSER(M)
- [ ] 38. DENNIS LEONARD
- [ ] 69. LONNIE SMITH
- [ ] 99. DARRYL MOTLEY
- [ ] 140. BRET SABERHAGEN
- [ ] 170. BO JACKSON
- [ ] 190. JIM SUNDBERG
- [ ] 203. MIKE KINGERY
- [ ] 223. CHARLIE LEIBRANDT
- [ ] 240. STEVE BALBONI
- [ ] 256. TEAM LEADER CARD
- [ ] 326. MARK GUBICZA
- [ ] 354. JAMIE QUIRK
- [ ] 382. RUDY LAW
- [ ] 400. GEORGE BRETT
- [ ] 473. STEVE FARR
- [ ] 508. SCOTT BANKHEAD
- [ ] 533. ARGENIS SALAZAR
- [ ] 554. BUDDY BIANCALANA
- [ ] 573. HAL MCRAE
- [ ] 669. BUD BLACK
- [ ] 692. FRANK WHITE
- [ ] 714. DAN QUISENBERRY
- [ ] 738. JORGE ORTA
- [ ] 761. GREG PRYOR
- [ ] 783. WILLIE WILSON

LOS ANGELES DODGERS

- [ ] 26. GREG BROCK
- [ ] 47. DENNIS POWELL
- [ ] 73. DAVE ANDERSON
- [ ] 116. BIL RUSSELL
- [ ] 144. MIKE SCIOSCIA
- [ ] 173. ALEX TREVINO
- [ ] 199. MARIANO DUNCAN
- [ ] 232. REGGIE WILLIAMS
- [ ] 266. JEFF HAMILTON
- [ ] 292. FRANKLIN STUBBS
- [ ] 328. BOB WELCH
- [ ] 360. PEDRO GUERRERO
- [ ] 385. OREL HERSHISER
- [ ] 410. FERNANDO VALENZUELA
- [ ] 431. TEAM LEADER CARD
- [ ] 457. LEN MATUSZEK
- [ ] 477. KEN HOWELL
- [ ] 493. TOM LASORDA(M)
- [ ] 509. ENOS CABELL
- [ ] 538. TOM NIEDENFUER
- [ ] 664. MIKE MARSHALL
- [ ] 682. JERRY REUSS
- [ ] 699. KEN LANDREAUX
- [ ] 717. ED VANDEBERG
- [ ] 734. BILL MADLOCK
- [ ] 753. RICK HONEYCUTT
- [ ] 769. STEVE SAX
- [ ] 787. ALEJANDRO PENA

MILWAUKEE BREWERS

- ☐ 10. CECIL COOPER
- ☐ 32. TIM LEARY
- ☐ 56. TEAM LEADER CARD
- ☐ 79. JUAN NIEVES
- ☐ 108. JIM GANTNER
- ☐ 129. RICK CERONE
- ☐ 179. BILL WEGMAN
- ☐ 216. B.J. SURHOFF
- ☐ 229. MIKE BIRKBECK
- ☐ 250. TEDDY HIGUERA
- ☐ 279. DAN PLASAC
- ☐ 302. BILL SCHROEDER
- ☐ 327. DALE SVEUM
- ☐ 352. MIKE FELDER
- ☐ 377. JOHN HENRY JOHNSON
- ☐ 401. BILL JO ROBIDOUX
- ☐ 423. JAIME COCANOWER
- ☐ 448. CHRIS BOSIO
- ☐ 468. GEORGE BAMBERGER(M)
- ☐ 495. GORMAN THOMAS
- ☐ 523. EARNIE RILES
- ☐ 547. ROB DEER
- ☐ 562. BRYAN CLUTTERBUCK
- ☐ 586. BEN OGLIVIE
- ☐ 622. GLENN BRAGGS
- ☐ 640. MARK CLEAR
- ☐ 676. CHARLIE MOORE
- ☐ 706. RICK MANNING
- ☐ 741. PAUL MOLITOR
- ☐ 773. ROBIN YOUNT

MINNESOTA TWINS

- ☐ 25. BERT BLYLEVEN
- ☐ 52. KEITH ATHERTON
- ☐ 87. MARK SALAS
- ☐ 114. BILLY BEANE
- ☐ 124. RAY FONTENOT
- ☐ 138. ROY LEE JACKSON
- ☐ 169. RON WASHINGTON
- ☐ 206. TEAM LEADER CARD
- ☐ 207. GEORGE FRAZIER
- ☐ 225. MIKE SMITHSON
- ☐ 247. JEFF REED
- ☐ 277. JUAN AGOSTO
- ☐ 310. FRANK VIOLA
- ☐ 336. ALLAN ANDERSON
- ☐ 364. RANDY BUSH
- ☐ 419. MARK PORTUGAL
- ☐ 450. KIRBY PUCKETT
- ☐ 478. TIM LAUDNER
- ☐ 504. MICKEY HATCHER
- ☐ 529. ALVARO ESPINOZA
- ☐ 558. GREG GAGNE
- ☐ 576. FRANK PASTORE
- ☐ 618. TOM KELLY(M)
- ☐ 679. KENT HRBEK
- ☐ 710. GARY GAETTI
- ☐ 744. ROY SMALLEY
- ☐ 776. TOM BRUNANSKY

MONTREAL EXPOS

- ☐ 9. JAY TIBBS
- ☐ 30. TIM RAINES
- ☐ 55. TIM WALLACH
- ☐ 78. TIM FOLEY
- ☐ 105. FLOYD YOUMANS
- ☐ 127. VANCE LAW
- ☐ 141. HERM WINNINGHAM
- ☐ 165. JEFF REARDON
- ☐ 189. JOE HESKETH
- ☐ 212. MIKE FITZGERALD
- ☐ 252. DENNY MARTINEZ
- ☐ 272. ANDRES GALARRAGA
- ☐ 293. BOB RODGERS(M)
- ☐ 323. AL NEWMAN
- ☐ 345. ANDRE DAWSON
- ☐ 381. TEAM LEADER CARD
- ☐ 416. TOM NIETO
- ☐ 442. MITCH WEBSTER
- ☐ 467. RANDY ST. CLAIRE
- ☐ 479. BOB SEBRA
- ☐ 505. BRYN SMITH
- ☐ 527. JIM WOHLFORD
- ☐ 577. DANN BILARDELLO
- ☐ 588. WALLACE JOHNSON
- ☐ 624. TIM BURKE
- ☐ 650. HUBIE BROOKS
- ☐ 707. BOB MCCLURE
- ☐ 742. ANDY MCGAFFIGAN
- ☐ 774. WAYNE KRENCHICKI

NEW YORK METS

- ☐ 20. GARY CARTER
- ☐ 48. WALLY BACKMAN
- ☐ 75. RON DARLING
- ☐ 103. RICK AGUILERA
- ☐ 130. DWIGHT GOODEN
- ☐ 147. RANDY NIEMANN
- ☐ 158. TIM TEUFEL
- ☐ 185. ROGER MCDOWELL
- ☐ 198. LEE MAZZILLI
- ☐ 213. RANDY MYERS
- ☐ 241. DANNY HEEP
- ☐ 267. HOWARD JOHNSON
- ☐ 295. LEN DYKSTRA
- ☐ 331. TEAM LEADER CARD
- ☐ 350. KEITH HERNANDEZ
- ☐ 378. RAFAEL SANTANA
- ☐ 404. DOUG SISK
- ☐ 433. ED HEARN
- ☐ 460. DARRYL STRAWBERRY
- ☐ 488. RAY KNIGHT
- ☐ 512. DAVE MAGADAN
- ☐ 543. DAVE JOHNSON(M)
- ☐ 570. SID FERNANDEZ
- ☐ 582. BRUCE BERENYI
- ☐ 594. RICK ANDERSON
- ☐ 625. MOOKIE WILSON
- ☐ 653. KEVIN MITCHELL
- ☐ 704. JESSE OROSCO
- ☐ 746. BOB OJEDA

NEW YORK YANKEES

- ☐ 15. CLAUDELL WASHINGTON
- ☐ 40. DAVE RIGHETTI
- ☐ 57. SCOTT NIELSEN
- ☐ 62. BOBBY MEACHAM
- ☐ 74. DAN PASQUA
- ☐ 102. PAUL ZUVELLA
- ☐ 135. MIKE EASLER
- ☐ 168. LOU PINIELLA(M)
- ☐ 174. HENRY COTTO
- ☐ 195. MIKE PAGLIARULO
- ☐ 224. WAYNE TOLLESON
- ☐ 236. TOMMY JOHN
- ☐ 239. JUAN ESPINO
- ☐ 254. BOB TEWKSBURY
- ☐ 283. DOUG DRABEK
- ☐ 316. BRIAN FISHER
- ☐ 344. JOE NIEKRO
- ☐ 375. RON GUIDRY
- ☐ 406. TEAM LEADER CARD
- ☐ 434. MIKE FISCHLIN
- ☐ 464. BUTCH WYNEGAR
- ☐ 500. DON MATTINGLY
- ☐ 524. BOB SHIRLEY
- ☐ 555. DENNIS RASMUSSEN
- ☐ 584. RON KITTLE
- ☐ 626. JOEL SKINNER
- ☐ 642. AL PULIDO
- ☐ 665. ROD SCURRY
- ☐ 683. GARY ROENICKE
- ☐ 701. WILLIE RANDOLPH
- ☐ 735. RICKEY HENDERSON
- ☐ 770. DAVE WINFIELD
- ☐ 788. TIM STODDARD

OAKLAND A'S

- ☐ 14. DAVE STEWART
- ☐ 34. JOSE RIJO
- ☐ 68. TONY LARUSSA(M)
- ☐ 83. MIKE DAVIS
- ☐ 111. ALFREDO GRIFFIN
- ☐ 137. JERRY WILLARD
- ☐ 161. STEVE ONTIVEROS
- ☐ 188. TONY PHILLIPS
- ☐ 217. CHRIS CODIROLI
- ☐ 238. BILL KRUEGER
- ☐ 263. STAN JAVIER
- ☐ 287. DAVE VON OHLEN
- ☐ 339. DONNIE HILL
- ☐ 366. MARK MCGWIRE
- ☐ 391. JAY HOWELL
- ☐ 413. MOOSE HAAS
- ☐ 441. DAVE LEIPER

- ☐ 456. TEAM LEADER CARD
- ☐ 496. BRUCE BOCHTE
- ☐ 519. CURT YOUNG
- ☐ 548. BILL MOONEYHAM
- ☐ 565. DUSTY BAKER
- ☐ 587. ERIC PLUNK
- ☐ 620. JOSE CANSECO
- ☐ 649. MICKEY TETTLETON
- ☐ 678. CARNEY LANSFORD
- ☐ 709. DAVE KINGMAN
- ☐ 743. DWAYNE MURPHY
- ☐ 775. JOAQUIN ANDUJAR

PHILADELPHIA PHILLIES

- ☐ 42. GARY REDUS
- ☐ 63. FRED TOLIVER
- ☐ 97. GLENN WILSON
- ☐ 163. KEVIN GROSS
- ☐ 191. CHARLES HUDSON
- ☐ 209. RICK SCHU
- ☐ 255. JUAN SAMUEL
- ☐ 294. STEVE JELTZ
- ☐ 329. RON ROENICKE
- ☐ 355. DON CARMAN
- ☐ 379. JOHN RUSSELL
- ☐ 409. MILT THOMPSON
- ☐ 430. MIKE SCHMIDT
- ☐ 443. JOHN FELSKE(M)
- ☐ 471. RONN REYNOLDS
- ☐ 481. TEAM LEADER CARD
- ☐ 499. BRUCE RUFFIN
- ☐ 532. JEFF STONE
- ☐ 553. MIKE MADDUX
- ☐ 636. DARREN DAULTON
- ☐ 666. VON HAYES
- ☐ 684. KENT TEKULVE
- ☐ 702. GREG GROSS
- ☐ 719. TOM HUME
- ☐ 736. STEVE BEDROSIAN
- ☐ 755. LUIS AGUAYO
- ☐ 771. SHANE RAWLEY
- ☐ 789. DAN SCHATZEDER

PITTSBURGH PIRATES

- ☐ 16. PAT CLEMENTS
- ☐ 35. SID BREAM
- ☐ 60. TONY PENA
- ☐ 93. JIM LEYLAND(M)
- ☐ 109. R.J. REYNOLDS
- ☐ 131. TEAM LEADER CARD
- ☐ 164. SAMMY KHALIFA
- ☐ 184. BOBBY BONILLA
- ☐ 219. CECILIO GUANTE
- ☐ 237. JIM MORRISON
- ☐ 262. JIM WINN
- ☐ 289. BOB KIPPER
- ☐ 320. BARRY BONDS
- ☐ 341. MIKE BROWN
- ☐ 365. RICK RHODEN
- ☐ 394. MIKE BIELECKI
- ☐ 414. JOE ORSULAK
- ☐ 447. BILL ALMON
- ☐ 469. MIKE DIAZ
- ☐ 494. BARY JONES
- ☐ 521. RICK REUSCHEL
- ☐ 541. RAFAEL BELLIARD
- ☐ 564. LARRY MCWILLIAMS
- ☐ 583. JUNIOR ORTIZ
- ☐ 628. BOB WALK
- ☐ 651. BENNY DISTEFANO
- ☐ 712. DON ROBINSON
- ☐ 747. JOHNNY RAY

ST. LOUIS CARDINALS

- ☐ 8. TERRY PENDLETON
- ☐ 33. ANDY VAN SLYKE
- ☐ 59. KEN DAYLEY
- ☐ 84. STEVE LAKE
- ☐ 110. JOHN TUDOR
- ☐ 133. JOSE OQUENDO
- ☐ 162. MIKE LAVALLIERE
- ☐ 181. TEAM LEADER CARD
- ☐ 211. JOHN MORRIS
- ☐ 243. WHITEY HERZOG(M)
- ☐ 257. BOB FORSCH
- ☐ 288. TITO LANDRUM
- ☐ 317. CLINT HURDLE

☐ 321. MIKE LAGA
☐ 338. TIM CONROY
☐ 367. JEFF LAHTI
☐ 399. CURT FORD
☐ 417. PAT PERRY
☐ 440. WILLIE MCGEE
☐ 465. TODD WORRELL
☐ 520. JACK CLARK
☐ 542. RICKY HORTON
☐ 567. GREG MATHEWS
☐ 590. VINCE COLEMAN
☐ 621. DANNY COX
☐ 647. TOM LAWLESS
☐ 671. RAY SOFF
☐ 721. TOM HERR
☐ 749. OZZIE SMITH

SAN DIEGO PADRES

☐ 37. MARVELL WYNNE
☐ 81. TEAM LEADER CARD
☐ 88. ED WOJNA
☐ 100. STEVE GARVEY
☐ 123. JOHN KRUK
☐ 143. STEVE BOROS(M)
☐ 155. EDDIE WHITSON
☐ 183. ANDY HAWKINS
☐ 205. GRAIG NETTLES
☐ 248. GENE WALTER
☐ 275. LAMARR HOYT
☐ 325. GARRY TEMPLETON
☐ 348. CARMELO MARTINEZ
☐ 380. RICH GOSSAGE
☐ 403. JERRY ROYSTER
☐ 428. BRUCE BOCHY
☐ 429. TIM PYZNARSKI
☐ 470. DAVE DRAVECKY
☐ 501. CRAIG LEFFERTS
☐ 530. TONY GWYNN
☐ 540. TERRY KENNEDY
☐ 559. LANCE MCCULLERS
☐ 637. BIP ROBERTS
☐ 690. DANE IORG
☐ 730. ERIC SHOW
☐ 754. DAVE LAPOINT
☐ 763. TIM FLANNERY

SAN FRANCISCO GIANTS

☐ 21. MARK DAVIS
☐ 46. DANNY GLADDEN
☐ 64. HARRY SPILMAN
☐ 71. MIKE ALDRETE
☐ 96. FRANK WILLIAMS
☐ 125. BOB BRENLY
☐ 151. MIKE LACOSS
☐ 180. CHRIS BROWN
☐ 193. ROGER CRAIG(M)
☐ 231. TEAM LEADER CARD
☐ 260. VIDA BLUE
☐ 280. JEFFREY LEONARD
☐ 286. MIKE WOODARD
☐ 303. JUAN BERENGUER
☐ 335. CANDY MALDONADO
☐ 362. LUIS QUINONES
☐ 389. JEFF ROBINSON
☐ 420. WILL CLARK
☐ 438. KELLY DOWNS
☐ 475. SCOTT GARRELTS
☐ 526. ROGER MASON
☐ 536. TERRY MULHOLLAND
☐ 549. BOB MELVIN
☐ 580. MIKE KRUKOW
☐ 633. JOSE URIBE
☐ 658. ROBBY THOMPSON
☐ 672. CHILI DAVIS
☐ 724. GREG MINTON
☐ 759. JOEL YOUNGBLOOD
☐ 781. ATLEE HAMMAKER

SEATTLE MARINERS

☐ 19. MATT YOUNG
☐ 45. JIM PRESLEY
☐ 67. BILL SWIFT
☐ 91. HAROLD REYNOLDS
☐ 117. JIM BEATTIE
☐ 156. TEAM LEADER CARD
☐ 187. MARK HUISMANN
☐ 215. MARK LANGSTON

☐ 235. ALVIN DAVIS
☐ 258. STEVE YEAGER
☐ 271. MIKE BROWN
☐ 284. JOHN MOSES
☐ 307. LEE GUETTERMAN
☐ 333. KEN PHELPS
☐ 347. MICKEY BRANTLEY
☐ 357. STEVE FIREOVID
☐ 376. SCOTT BRADLEY
☐ 402. MIKE TRUJILLO
☐ 418. DICK WILLIAMS(M)
☐ 427. ED NUNEZ
☐ 439. KARL BEST
☐ 476. DANNY TARTABULL
☐ 498. BOB KEARNEY
☐ 525. PHIL BRADLEY
☐ 546. MIKE MORGAN
☐ 561. REY QUINONES
☐ 572. PETE LADD
☐ 619. JERRY REED
☐ 641. DOMINGO RAMOS
☐ 727. MIKE MOORE

TEXAS RANGERS

☐ 17. PETE O'BRIEN
☐ 44. GREG HARRIS
☐ 70. CHARLIE HOUGH
☐ 95. ODDIBE MCDOWELL
☐ 118. BOBBY VALENTINE(M)
☐ 126. MIKE LOYND
☐ 152. TOBY HARRAH
☐ 176. STEVE BUECHELE
☐ 202. RICKY WRIGHT
☐ 228. CURT WILKERSON
☐ 261. RUBEN SIERRA
☐ 291. MITCH WILLIAMS
☐ 308. DON SLAUGHT
☐ 334. ED CORREA
☐ 363. JOSE GUZMAN
☐ 388. GENO PETRALLI
☐ 415. BOBBY WITT
☐ 444. JEFF RUSSELL
☐ 462. SCOTT FLETCHER
☐ 497. DALE MOHORCIC
☐ 514. ORLANDO MERCADO
☐ 550. PETE INCAVIGLIA
☐ 629. LARRY PARRISH
☐ 646. MIKE MASON
☐ 656. TEAM LEADER CARD
☐ 689. DARRELL PORTER
☐ 729. TOM PACIOREK
☐ 762. GARY WARD

TORONTO BLUE JAYS

☐ 29. JIMMY KEY
☐ 90. DAVE STIEB
☐ 106. TEAM LEADER CARD
☐ 122. JIM CLANCY
☐ 153. DUANE WARD
☐ 178. CECIL FIELDER
☐ 210. LLOYD MOSEBY
☐ 245. WILLIE UPSHAW
☐ 274. JEFF HEARRON
☐ 301. LUIS AQUINO
☐ 371. MARK EICHHORN
☐ 395. DAMASO GARCIA
☐ 458. KELLY GRUBER
☐ 485. TONY FERNANDEZ
☐ 510. TOM HENKE
☐ 537. RANCE MULLINIKS
☐ 557. JOHN CERUTTI
☐ 574. MANNY LEE
☐ 643. RON SHEPHERD
☐ 655. JESSE BARFIELD
☐ 663. CLIFF JOHNSON
☐ 681. GEORGE BELL
☐ 698. ERNIE WHITT
☐ 716. RICK LEACH
☐ 733. BILL CAUDILL
☐ 751. GARTH IORG
☐ 768. DENNIS LAMP
☐ 786. JIMY WILLIAMS(M)

T205 (208)
1 1/2" X 2 5/8"

BOSTON RED SOX

- WILLIAM CARRIGAN
- EDWARD V. CICOTTE
- CLYDE ENGLE
- EDWARD KARGER
- JOHN KLEINOW
- TRIS SPEAKER
- JACOB G. STAHL
- CHARLES WAGNER

BOSTON RUSTLERS

- EDW'D J. ABBATICCHIO
- FREDERICK T. BECK
- G.C. FERGUSON
- WILBUR GOOD
- GEORGE F. GRAHAM
- CHARLES L. HERZOG
- A.A. MATTERN
- BAYARD H. SHARPE
- DAVID SHEAN (BOSTON)

BROOKLYN SUPERBAS

- EDWARD B. BARGER
  (FULL B)
- EDWARD B. BARGER
  (PART B)
- GEORGE G. BELL
- WILLIAM BERGEN
- WILLIAM DAHLEN
- JACOB DAUBERT
- JOHN E. HUMMEL
- EDGAR LENNOX
- PRYOR MCELVEEN
- G.N. RUCKER
- W.D. SCANLAN
- TONY SMITH
- ZACH D. WHEAT
- IRVIN K. WILHELM

CHICAGO CUBS

- JAMES P. ARCHER
- MORDECAI BROWN
- FRANK L. CHANCE
- JOHN J. EVERS
- WILLIAM A. FOXEN
- GEORGE F. GRAHAM
- JOHN KLING
- FLOYD M. KROH
- HARRY MCINTIRE
- THOMAS J. NEEDHAM
- ORVAL OVERALL
- JOHN A. PFIESTER
- EDWARD M. REULBACH
- LEWIS RICHIE
- FRANK M. SCHULTE
- DAVID SHEAN (CUBS)
- JAMES T. SHECKARD
- HARRY STEINFELDT
- JOSEPH B. TINKER

CHICAGO WHITE SOX

- RUSSEL BLACKBURNE
- J. DONOHUE
- PAT'K H. DOUGHERTY
  (WHITE STOCKING)
- PAT'K H. DOUGHERTY
  (RED STOCKING)
- HUGH DUFFY
- FRANK LANG
- HARRY D. LORD
- AMBROSE MCCONNELL
- MATTHEW MCINTYRE
- FREDERICK OLMSTEAD
- F. PARENT
- FRED PAYNE
- JAMES SCOTT
- LEE FORD TANNEHILL
- EDWARD WALSH
- G.H. WHITE

CINCINNATI REDS

- ROBERT H. BESCHER
- THOMAS W. DOWNEY
- RICHARD J. EGAN
- ARTHUR FROMME
- HARRY L. GASPAR
- EDWARD L. GRANT
- CLARK GRIFFITH
- RICHARD HOBLITZELL
- JOHN B. MCLEAN
- MICHAEL MITCHELL
- GEORGE SUGGS

CLEVELAND NAPS

- NEAL BALL
- JOSEPH BIRMINGHAM
- A. JOSS
- GEORGE T. STOVALL
- TERENCE TURNER
- DENTON T. YOUNG

DETROIT TIGERS

- TYRUS RAYMOND COBB
- JAMES DELAHANTY
- HUGH JENNINGS
- DAVID JONES
- THOMAS JONES
- EDWARD KILLIAN
- GEORGE MORIARITY
- GEORGE J. MULLIN
- CHARLES O'LEARY
- CHARLES SCHMIDT
- GEORGE SIMMONS
- OSCAR STANAGE
- EDGAR SUMMERS
- EDGAR WILLETT

NEW YORK GIANTS

- LEON AMES
- BEALS BECKER
- ALBERT BRIDWELL
- OTIS CRANDALL
- ARTHUR DEVLIN
- JOSHUA DEVORE
- W.R. DICKSON
- LAWRENCE DOYLE
- ARTHUR FLETCHER
- W.A. LATHAM
- RICHARD MARQUARD
- CHRISTY MATHEWSON
- JOHN J. MCGRAW
- FRED MERKLE
- JOHN T. MEYERS
- JOHN J. MURRAY
- ARTHUR L. RAYMOND
- GEOREG H. SCHLEI

- FRED C. SNODGRASS
- GEORGE WILTSE
  (BOTH EARS)
- GEORGE WILTSE
  (RIGHT EAR ONLY)

NEW YORK YANKEES

- JAMES AUSTIN
- HAROLD W. CHASE
  (CHASE ONLY)
- HAROLD W. CHASE
  (HAL CHASE)
- LOUIS CRIGER
- RAY FISHER
- RUSSELL FORD
  (DARK CAP)
- RUSSELL FORD
  (LIGHT CAP)
- EARL GARDNER
- CHARLES HEMPHILL
- JACK KNIGHT
- JOHN QUINN
- EDWARD SWEENEY
- JAMES VAUGHN
- HARRY WOLTER

PHILADELPHIA ATHLETICS

- FRANK BAKER
- JOHN J. BARRY
- CHARLES A. BENDER
- EDWARD T. COLLINS
  (MOUTH CLOSED)
- EDWARD T. COLLINS
  (MOUTH OPEN)
- JAMES H. DYGERT
- FREDERICK T. HARTSEL
- HARRY KRAUSE
- PAT'K J. LIVINGSTON
- BRISCOE LORD
- DANIEL MURPHY
- RUEBEN N. OLDRING
- IRA THOMAS

PHILADELPHIA PHILLIES

- JOHN W. BATES
- WM. E. BRANSFIELD
- CHARLES S. DOOIN
- MICHAEL DOOLAN
- ROBERT EWING
- FRED JACKLITSCH
- JOHN LOBERT
- SHERWOOD R. MAGEE
- PATRICK J. MORAN
- GEORGE PASKERT
- JOHN A. ROWAN
- JOHN TITUS

PITTSBURGH PIRATES

- ROBERT BYRNE
- HOWARD CAMNITZ
- FRED CLARKE
- JOHN FLYNN
- GEORGE GIBSON
- THOMAS W. LEACH
- SAM LEEVER
- ALBERT P. LEIFIELD
- NICHOLAS MADDOX
- JOHN D. MILLER
- CHARLES PHILLIPPE
- KIRB WHITE
- J. OWEN WILSON

ST. LOUIS BROWNS

- WILLIAM BAILEY
- DANIEL J. HOFFMAN
- FRANK LAPORTE
- B. PELTY
- GEORGE STONE
- RODERICK J. WALLACE
  (WITH CAP)
- RODERICK J. WALLACE
  (WITHOUT CAP)

ST. LOUIS CARDINALS

- ☐ ROGER BRESNAHAN (MOUTH CLOSED)
- ☐ ROGER BRESNAHAN (MOUTH OPEN)
- ☐ FRANK J. CORRIDON
- ☐ LOUIS EVANS
- ☐ ROBERT HARMON (BOTH EARS)
- ☐ ROBERT HARMON (LEFT EAR ONLY)
- ☐ ARNOLD J. HAUSER
- ☐ MILLER HUGGINS
- ☐ EDWARD KONETCHY
- ☐ JOHN LUSH
- ☐ "REBEL" OAKES
- ☐ EDWARD PHELPS

WASHINGTON SENATORS

- ☐ NORMAN ELBERFELD
- ☐ GRAY
- ☐ ROBERT GROOM
- ☐ WALTER JOHNSON
- ☐ GEORGE F. MCBRIDE
- ☐ J. CLYDE MILAN
- ☐ HERMAN SCHAEFER
- ☐ CHARLES E. STREET

BALTIMORE

- ☐ DR. MERLE T. ADKINS
- ☐ JOHN DUNN

BUFFALO

- ☐ GEORGE MERRITT

JERSEY CITY

- ☐ CHARLES HANFORD

NEWARK

- ☐ FORREST D. CADY
- ☐ JAMES FRICK
- ☐ WYATT LEE
- ☐ LEWIS MCALLISTER
- ☐ JOHN NEE

PROVIDENCE

- ☐ JAMES COLLINS
- ☐ JAMES PHELAN

ROCHESTER

- ☐ HENRY BATCH

T206 (523)
1 1/2" X 2 5/8"

BOSTON RED SOX

- ☐ ARRELANES
- ☐ CARRIGAN
- ☐ CICOTTE
- ☐ KLEINOW
- ☐ LORD
- ☐ NILES
- ☐ SPEAKER
- ☐ SPENCER
- ☐ STAHL (PORTRAIT)
- ☐ STAHL (FIELDING)
- ☐ WAGNER (BATTING/WAIST)
- ☐ WAGNER (BATTING/HIPS)

BOSTON RUSTLERS

- ☐ BATES
- ☐ BEAUMONT
- ☐ BECK
- ☐ BECKER
- ☐ BOWERMAN
- ☐ DAHLEN
- ☐ FERGUSON
- ☐ GRAHAM
- ☐ HERZOG
- ☐ LINDAMAN
- ☐ MATTERN
- ☐ RITCHEY
- ☐ STARR
- ☐ SWEENEY

BROOKLYN SUPERBAS

- ☐ ALPERMAN
- ☐ BELL (PITCHING/HIPS)
- ☐ BELL (PITCHING/WAIST)
- ☐ BERGEN (BATTING)
- ☐ BERGEN (CATCHING)
- ☐ BURCH (BATTING)
- ☐ BURCH (FIELDING)
- ☐ DAHLEN
- ☐ DUNN
- ☐ HUMMEL
- ☐ HUNTER
- ☐ JORDAN (PORTRAIT)
- ☐ JORDAN (BATTING)
- ☐ LENNOX
- ☐ LUMLEY
- ☐ MARSHALL
- ☐ MCELVEEN
- ☐ MCINTYRE
- ☐ MCINTRYE (BROOKLYN & CHICAGO)
- ☐ PASTORIUS
- ☐ PATTEE
- ☐ RUCKER (PORTRAIT)
- ☐ RUCKER (PITCHING)
- ☐ H. SMITH
- ☐ WHEAT
- ☐ WILHELM (BATTING)
- ☐ WILHELM (PORTRAIT)

CHICAGO CUBS

- ☐ G. BROWN
- ☐ M. BROWN (PORTRAIT)
- ☐ M. BROWN (BLACK COLLAR)
- ☐ M. BROWN (BLUE COLLAR)
- ☐ CHANCE (BATTING)

- ☐ CHANCE (PORTRAIT/RED)
- ☐ CHANCE (PORTRAIT/YELLOW)
- ☐ EVERS (PORTRAIT)
- ☐ EVERS (BATTING/BLUE BACKGROUND)
- ☐ EVERS (BATTING/YELLOW BACKGROUND)
- ☐ HOFMAN
- ☐ HOWARD
- ☐ KLING
- ☐ KROH
- ☐ LUNDGREN
- ☐ MORAN
- ☐ NEEDHAM
- ☐ OVERALL (PORTRAIT)
- ☐ OVERALL (PITCHING/ARMS SIDE)
- ☐ OVERALL (PITCHING/ARMS UP)
- ☐ PFEFFER
- ☐ PFEISTER (PORTRAIT)
- ☐ PFEISTER (PITCHING)
- ☐ REULBACH (PORTRAIT)
- ☐ REULBACH (PITCHING)
- ☐ SCHULTE (BATTING/FRONT)
- ☐ SCHULTE (BATTING/BACK)
- ☐ SHECKARD (THROWING)
- ☐ SHECKARD (PORTRAIT)
- ☐ STEINFELDT (PORTRAIT)
- ☐ STEINFELDT (BATTING)
- ☐ TINKER (PORTRAIT)
- ☐ TINKER (HANDS ON KNEES)
- ☐ TINKER (BAT ON SHOULDER)
- ☐ TINKER (BAT OFF SHOULDER)
- ☐ ZIMMERMAN

CHICAGO WHITE SOX

- ☐ ATZ
- ☐ BURNS
- ☐ G. DAVIS
- ☐ DONOHUE
- ☐ DOUGHERTY (PORTRAIT)
- ☐ DOUGHERTY (FIELDING)
- ☐ DUFFY
- ☐ FIENE (PORTRAIT)
- ☐ FIENE (FIELDING)
- ☐ GANDIL
- ☐ HAHN
- ☐ ISBELL
- ☐ F. JONES (PORTRAIT/HIPS)
- ☐ F. JONES (PORTRAIT)
- ☐ OWEN
- ☐ PARENT
- ☐ PAYNE
- ☐ PURTELL
- ☐ SCOTT
- ☐ F. SMITH
- ☐ SMITH
- ☐ SMITH (CHICAGO & BOSTON)
- ☐ SULLIVAN
- ☐ L. TANNEHILL
- ☐ TANNEHILL
- ☐ WALSH
- ☐ WHITE (PORTRAIT)
- ☐ WHITE (PITCHING/WAIST)

CINCINNATI REDS

- ☐ BESCHER (PORTRAIT)
- ☐ BESCHER (FIELDING)
- ☐ CAMPBELL
- ☐ DOWNEY (BATTING)
- ☐ DOWNEY (FIELDING)
- ☐ DUBUC
- ☐ EGAN
- ☐ EWING
- ☐ FROMME
- ☐ GASPAR
- ☐ GRIFFITH (PORTRAIT)
- ☐ GRIFFITH (BATTING)
- ☐ HOBLITZELL
- ☐ HUGGINS (PORTRAIT)
- ☐ HUGGINS (PORTRAIT/HITTING)
- ☐ KARGER
- ☐ LOBERT
- ☐ MCLEAN
- ☐ MITCHELL
- ☐ MOWREY
- ☐ OAKES
- ☐ PASKERT
- ☐ SPADE

CLEVELAND NAPS

- ☐ BALL
- ☐ BERGER
- ☐ BIRMINGHAM
- ☐ BRADLEY (PORTRAIT)
- ☐ BRADLEY (BATTING)
- ☐ J. J. CLARKE
- ☐ EASTERLY
- ☐ FLICK
- ☐ GOODE
- ☐ HINCHMAN
- ☐ JOSS (PORTRAIT)
- ☐ JOSS (PITCHING)
- ☐ LAJOIE (PORTRAIT)
- ☐ LAJOIE (BATTING)
- ☐ LAJOIE (THROWING)
- ☐ LIEBHARDT
- ☐ PERRING
- ☐ RHOADES (PITCHING/WAIST)
- ☐ RHOADES (PITCHING/HIPS)
- ☐ STOVALL (PORTRAIT)
- ☐ STOVALL (BATTING)
- ☐ TURNER
- ☐ YOUNG (PORTRAIT)
- ☐ YOUNG (PITCHING/SIDE)
- ☐ YOUNG (PITCHING/FRONT)

DETROIT TIGERS

- ☐ BUSH
- ☐ COBB (PORTRAIT/RED)
- ☐ COBB (PORTRAIT/GREEN)
- ☐ COBB (BATTING/BLACK CAP)
- ☐ COBB (BATTING/GRAY CAP)
- ☐ CRAWFORD (BATTING)
- ☐ CRAWFORD (THROWING)
- ☐ DONOVAN (PORTRAIT)
- ☐ DONOVAN (PITCHING)
- ☐ JENNINGS (PORTRAIT)
- ☐ JENNINGS (PORTRAIT/WAIST)
- ☐ JENNINGS (PORTRAIT/HIPS)
- ☐ JONES
- ☐ KILLIAN (PORTRAIT)
- ☐ KILLIAN (PITCHING)
- ☐ MCINTYRE
- ☐ MORIARTY
- ☐ MULLEN
- ☐ MULLIN (BATTING)
- ☐ MULLIN (FIELDING/
  HORIZONTAL)
- ☐ O'LEARY (PORTRAIT)
- ☐ O'LEARY (HANDS ON KNEES)
- ☐ ROSSMAN
- ☐ SCHAEFER
- ☐ SCHMIDT (PORTRAIT)
- ☐ SCHMIDT (THROWING)
- ☐ STANAGE
- ☐ SUMMERS
- ☐ WILLETT
- ☐ WILLETTS

NEW YORK GIANTS

- ☐ AMES (PORTRAIT)
- ☐ AMES (PITCHING/WAIST)
- ☐ AMES (PITCHING/HIPS)
- ☐ BRIDWELL (PORTRAIT)
- ☐ BRIDWELL (PORTRAIT/
  SWEATER)
- ☐ CRANDALL(PORTRAIT)
- ☐ CRANDALL (PORTRAIT/
  SWEATER)
- ☐ DEVLIN
- ☐ DEVORE
- ☐ DONLIN (PORTRAIT/KNEES)
- ☐ DONLIN (PORTRAIT/HANDS ON
  KNEES)
- ☐ DONLIN (BATTING)
- ☐ DOYLE (PORTRAIT/SWEATER)
- ☐ DOYLE (BATTING)
- ☐ DOYLE (THROWING)
- ☐ DURHAM
- ☐ FLETCHER
- ☐ HERZOG
- ☐ LATHAM
- ☐ MARQUARD (PORTRAIT)
- ☐ MARQUARD (PORTRAIT/HIPS)
- ☐ MARQUARD (PITCHING)
- ☐ MATHEWSON (PORTRAIT)

- ☐ MATHEWSON (PITCHING/WHITE
  CAP)
- ☐ MATHEWSON (PITCHING/BLACK
  CAP)
- ☐ MCCORMICK
- ☐ MCGRAW (PORTRAIT)
- ☐ MCGRAW (PORTRAIT/SWEATER)
- ☐ MCGRAW (PORTRAIT/HIPS)
- ☐ MCGRAW (PORTRAIT/KNEES)
- ☐ MERKLE (PORTRAIT)
- ☐ MERKLE (THROWING)
- ☐ MEYERS
- ☐ MURRAY (PORTRAIT)
- ☐ MURRAY (BATTING)
- ☐ MYERS (CATCHING)
- ☐ MYERS (BATTING)
- ☐ O'HARA
- ☐ RAYMOND
- ☐ SCHLEI (PORTRAIT/SWEATER)
- ☐ SCHLEI (BATTING)
- ☐ SCHLEI (CATCHING)
- ☐ SEYMOUR (PORTRAIT)
- ☐ SEYMOUR (BATTING)
- ☐ SEYMOUR (THROWING)
- ☐ SNODGRASS (BATTING)
- ☐ SNODGRASS (CATCHING)
- ☐ TENNEY
- ☐ WEIMER
- ☐ WILTSE (PORTRAIT)
- ☐ WILTSE (PORTRAIT/SWEATER)
- ☐ WILTSE (PITCHING)

NEW YORK YANKEES

- ☐ BALL
- ☐ CHASE (WITH CUP)
- ☐ CHASE (PORTRAIT/PINK)
- ☐ CHASE (PORTRAIT/BLUE)
- ☐ CHASE (THROWING/BLACK CAP)
- ☐ CHASE (THROWING/WHITE CAP)
- ☐ CHESBRO
- ☐ CREE
- ☐ DEMMITT
- ☐ DOYLE
- ☐ ELBERFELD
- ☐ ENGLE
- ☐ FORD
- ☐ FRILL
- ☐ HEMPHILL
- ☐ KEELER (PORTRAIT)
- ☐ KEELER (BATTING)
- ☐ KLEINOW (CATCHING)
- ☐ KLEINOW (BATTING)
- ☐ KNIGHT (PORTRAIT)
- ☐ KNIGHT (BATTING)
- ☐ LAKE
- ☐ LAPORTE
- ☐ MANNING (BATTING)
- ☐ MANNING (PITCHING)
- ☐ QUINN
- ☐ SWEENEY
- ☐ WARHOP

PHILADELPHIA ATHLETICS

- ☐ BAKER
- ☐ BARRY
- ☐ BENDER (PORTRAIT)
- ☐ BENDER (PITCHING/WITH
  TREES)
- ☐ BENDER (PITCHING/NO TREES)
- ☐ COLLINS
- ☐ DAVIS
- ☐ H. DAVIS
- ☐ DYGERT
- ☐ HARTSELL
- ☐ KRAUSE (PORTRAIT)
- ☐ KRAUSE (PITCHING)
- ☐ LIVINGSTONE
- ☐ MURPHY (BATTING)
- ☐ MURPHY (THROWING)
- ☐ NICHOLLS
- ☐ NICHOLS
- ☐ OLDRING (BATTING)
- ☐ OLDRING (FIELDING)
- ☐ PLANK
- ☐ POWERS
- ☐ THOMAS

PHILADELPHIA PHILLIES

- ☐ BRANSFIELD
- ☐ COVALESKI
- ☐ DOOIN
- ☐ DOOLAN (BATTING)
- ☐ DOOLAN (FIELDING)
- ☐ DOOLIN
- ☐ JACKLITSCH
- ☐ KNABE
- ☐ MAGEE (PORTRAIT)
- ☐ MAGIE (NAME MISSPELLED)
- ☐ MAGEE (BATTING)
- ☐ MCQUILLAN (BATTING)
- ☐ MCQUILLAN (PITCHING)
- ☐ TITUS

PITTSBURGH PIRATES

- ☐ ABBATICCHIO (BATTING/HIPS)
- ☐ ABBATICCHIO (BATTING/KNEES)
- ☐ ABSTEIN
- ☐ CAMNITZ (PORTRAIT)
- ☐ CAMNITZ (PITCHING/FRONT)
- ☐ CAMNITZ (PITCHING/SIDE)
- ☐ CLARKE
- ☐ F. CLARKE
- ☐ GIBSON
- ☐ LEACH (PORTRAIT)
- ☐ LEACH (FIELDING)
- ☐ LEIFIELD (PITCHING)
- ☐ LEIFIELD (BATTING)
- ☐ MADDOX
- ☐ MILLER
- ☐ PHILLIPPE
- ☐ WAGNER
- ☐ WILLIS
- ☐ WILSON

ST. LOUIS BROWNS

- ☐ CRIGER
- ☐ CRISS
- ☐ DEMMITT
- ☐ DINEEN
- ☐ FERRIS
- ☐ GRAHAM
- ☐ HOFFMAN
- ☐ HOWELL (PORTRAIT)
- ☐ HOWELL (PORTRAIT/HIPS)
- ☐ JONES
- ☐ LAKE (PITCHING)
- ☐ LAKE (HANDS ABOVE HEAD)
- ☐ MCALEESE
- ☐ PELTY (PITCHING)
- ☐ PELTY (HORIZONTAL)
- ☐ POWELL
- ☐ STEPHENS
- ☐ STONE
- ☐ WADDELL (PORTRAIT)
- ☐ WADDELL (PITCHING)
- ☐ WALLACE
- ☐ WILLIAMS

ST. LOUIS CARDINALS

- ☐ BARBEAU
- ☐ BLISS
- ☐ BRESNAHAN (PORTRAIT)
- ☐ BRESNAHAN (BATTING)
- ☐ BYRNE
- ☐ CHARLES
- ☐ EVANS
- ☐ GEYER
- ☐ GILBERT

☐ HULSWITT
☐ KONETCHY (FIELDING/HIGH BALL)
☐ KONETCHY (FIELDING/LOW BALL)
☐ O'HARA
☐ PHELPS
☐ RHODES
☐ SHAW
☐ WILLIS (BATTING)
☐ WILLIS (FIELDING)

WASHINGTON SENATORS

☐ G. BROWN
☐ CONROY (BATTING)
☐ CONROY (FIELDING)
☐ DELEHANTY
☐ ELBERFELD (PORTRAIT)
☐ ELBERFELD (FIELDING)
☐ GANLEY
☐ GRAY
☐ GROOM
☐ JOHNSON (PORTRAIT)
☐ JOHNSON (PITCHING)
☐ MCBRIDE
☐ MILAN
☐ SCHAEFER
☐ SHIPKE
☐ STREET (PORTRAIT)
☐ STREET (CATCHING)
☐ TANNEHILL
☐ UNGLAUB

AMERICAN ASSOCIATION

COLUMBUS

☐ CLARK
☐ CLYMER
☐ CONGALTON
☐ KRUGER
☐ SCHRECK

INDIANAPOLIS

☐ BURKE
☐ CARR
☐ CROSS
☐ DAVIDSON
☐ HAYDEN

KANSAS CITY

☐ BECKLEY
☐ BRASHEAR
☐ DORNER
☐ HALLMAN
☐ LUNGREN
☐ RITTER
☐ SHANNON

LOUISVILLE

☐ DELAHANTY
☐ PUTTMAN
☐ THIELMAN

MILWAUKEE

☐ BARRY
☐ MCGANN
☐ MCGLYNN
☐ RANDALL

MINNEAPOLIS

☐ COLLINS
☐ CRAVATH
☐ DOWNS
☐ OBERLIN
☐ O'NEIL
☐ PICKERING
☐ QUILLEN
☐ YOUNG

ST. PAUL

☐ ARMBRUSTER
☐ O'BRIEN

TOLEDO

☐ ABBOTT
☐ FREEMAN
☐ HINCHMAN
☐ LATTIMORE
☐ WRIGHT

EASTERN LEAGUE

BALTIMORE

☐ ADKINS
☐ CASSIDY
☐ DESSAU
☐ DUNN
☐ HALL
☐ JACKSON
☐ POLAND
☐ SLAGLE
☐ STRANG

BUFFALO

☐ BRAIN
☐ BURCHELL
☐ CLANCY
☐ FLANAGAN
☐ KISINGER
☐ MALARKEY
☐ NATTRESS
☐ SCHIRM
☐ SMITH
☐ TAYLOR
☐ WHITE

JERSEY CITY

☐ HANNIFAN
☐ MERRITT
☐ MILLIGAN
☐ MOELLER

MONTREAL

☐ CASEY

NEWARK

☐ MCGINNITY
☐ SCHLAFLY
☐ SHARPE

PROVIDENCE

☐ ANDERSON
☐ ARNDT
☐ BLACKBURNE
☐ HOFFMAN
☐ LAVENDER
☐ MORAN
☐ PHELAN
☐ SHAW

ROCHESTER

☐ BARGER
☐ BATCH
☐ BUTLER
☐ CHAPPELLE
☐ GANZEL
☐ MALONEY

TORONTO

☐ GRINSHAW
☐ KELLEY
☐ MCGINLEY
☐ MITCHELL
☐ RUDOLPH

SOUTH ATLANTIC LEAGUE

AUGUSTA

☐ COLES

CHARLESTON

☐ FOSTER
☐ PAIGE

COLUMBIA

☐ KIERNAN
☐ MANION

COLUMBUS

☐ HELM

JACKSONVILLE

☐ MULLANEY
☐ VIOLAT

MACON

☐ LAFITTE

SAVANNAH

☐ HOWARD

SOUTHERN LEAGUE

ATLANTA

☐ JORDAN
☐ SMITH

BIRMINGHAM

☐ MOLESWORTH

LITTLE ROCK

☐ HART
☐ LENTZ

MEMPHIS

☐ CAREY
☐ CRANSTON

MOBILE

☐ HICKMAN
☐ THORNTON

MONTGOMERY

☐ GREMINGER
☐ HART
☐ PERSONS
☐ ROCKENFELD

NASHVILLE

☐ BAY
☐ BERNHARD
☐ ELLAM
☐ PERDUE

NEW ORLEANS

☐ BREITENSTEIN
☐ FRITZ
☐ REGAN

TEXAS LEAGUE

DALLAS

☐ MILLER

HOUSTON

☐ WHITE

SAN ANTONIO

☐ BASTIAN
☐ STARK

SHREVEPORT

☐ SMITH
☐ THEBO

VIRGINIA LEAGUE

DANVILLE

☐ KING
☐ WESTLAKE

LYNCHBURG

☐ HOOKER
☐ ORTH

NORFOLK

☐ OTEY
☐ SEITZ

PORTSMOUTH

☐ GUIHEEN
☐ MCCAULEY

RICHMOND

☐ LIPE
☐ REVELLE

ROANOKE

☐ RYAN
☐ SHAUGHNESSY

T207 (207)
BROWN BACKGROUND
1 1/2″ X 2 5/8″

BOSTON RED SOX

☐ BRADLEY
☐ BUSHELMAN
☐ CARRIGAN/CORRECT BACK
☐ CARRIGAN/ WAGNER BACK
☐ CICOTTTE
☐ ENGLE
☐ GARDNER
☐ HAGEMAN
☐ HALL
☐ HENRIKSEN
☐ HOOPER
☐ LEWIS
☐ NUNAMAKER
☐ O'BRIEN

☐ SPEAKER
☐ THOMAS
☐ WAGNER/CORRECT BACK
☐ WAGNER/CARRIGAN BACK
☐ WOOD
☐ YERKES

BOSTON RUSTLERS

☐ DEVLIN
☐ DONNELLY
☐ GOWDY
☐ HOUSER
☐ KIRKE
☐ KLING
☐ LEWIS
☐ MCDONALD
☐ MILLER
☐ PERDUE
☐ SPRATT
☐ SWEENEY
☐ TYLER

BROOKLYN SUPERBAS

☐ BARGER
☐ COULSON
☐ DAUBERT
☐ ERWIN
☐ KNETZER
☐ MILLER
☐ NORTHEN
☐ RAGAN
☐ RUCKER
☐ SCHARDT
☐ STACK
☐ TOOLEY
☐ WHEAT

CHICAGO CUBS

☐ CHANCE
☐ COLE
☐ LENNOX
☐ MCINTIRE
☐ MILLER
☐ NEEDHAM
☐ REULBACH
☐ SAIER
☐ SCHULTE
☐ TINKER

CHICAGO WHITE SOX

☐ BENZ
☐ BLACKBURNE
☐ BLOCK
☐ BODIE
☐ CALLAHAN
☐ COLLINS
☐ FOURNIER
☐ KUHN
☐ LANGE
☐ LORD
☐ MCINTYRE
☐ MOGRIDGE
☐ PETERS
☐ RATH
☐ SCOTT
☐ SULLIVAN
☐ TANNEHILL
☐ WEAVER
☐ WHITE
☐ ZEIDER

CINCINNATI REDS

☐ ALMEIDA
☐ BESCHER
☐ CLARKE
☐ FROMME
☐ MARSANS
☐ MCLEAN
☐ MITCHELL
☐ PHELAN
☐ SEVEROLD
☐ SMITH

CLEVELAND NAPS

☐ ADAMS
☐ BALL
☐ BIRMINGHAM
☐ BLANDING
☐ BUTCHER
☐ DAVIS
☐ EASTERLY
☐ GEORGE
☐ GRANEY
☐ GREGG
☐ KALER
☐ LIVINGSTON/"A" SHIRT
☐ LIVINGSTON/"C" SHIRT
☐ LIVINGSTON/SMALL "C" SHIRT
☐ MITCHELL
☐ OLSON
☐ RYAN
☐ TURNER

DETROIT TIGERS

☐ BAUMAN
☐ COVINGTON
☐ DELAHANTY
☐ DRAKE
☐ GAINOR
☐ LIVELY
☐ MORIARITY
☐ MULLINS
  WITH "D" ON CAP
☐ MULLINS
  WITHOUT "D" ON CAP
☐ STANAGE
☐ WORKS

NEW YORK GIANTS

☐ BECKER
☐ CRANDALL
☐ DEVORE
☐ DOYLE
☐ FLETCHER
☐ HARTLEY
☐ HERZOG
☐ HIGGINS
☐ LATHAM
☐ MARQUARD
☐ MCGRAW
☐ SNODGRASS
☐ WILSON
☐ WILTSE

NEW YORK YANKEES

☐ DANIELS
☐ FISHER
  WITH WHITE LETTERS ON CAP
☐ FISHER
  WITH BLUE LETTERS ON CAP
☐ HOFF
☐ QUINN
☐ STREET
☐ VAUGHN
☐ WARHOP
☐ WILLIAMS
☐ WOLVERTON

PHILADELPHIA ATHLETICS

☐ BARRY
☐ BENDER
☐ DANFORTH
☐ DERRICK
☐ KRAUSE
☐ LAPP

☐ LORD
☐ MORGAN
☐ OLDRING
☐ STRUNK

PHILADELPHIA PHILLIES

☐ CHALMERS
☐ DOOIN
☐ DOWNEY
☐ GRAHAM
☐ KNABE
☐ MOORE
☐ MORAN
☐ PASKART
☐ RASMUSSEN
☐ SCANLON

BYRNE-PITTSBURG-NAT.

PITTSBURGH PIRATES

☐ BYRNE
☐ CAMNITZ
☐ CAREY
☐ DONLIN
☐ FERRY
☐ HYATT
☐ KELLY
☐ LEACH
☐ LEIFIELD
☐ MCCARTHY
☐ MCKECHNIE
☐ MILLER
☐ O'TOOLE
☐ SIMON
☐ WILSON

ST. LOUIS BROWNS

☐ AUSTIN
  WITH STL ON SHIRT
☐ AUSTIN
  WITHOUT STL ON SHIRT
☐ HALLINAN
☐ E. HAMILTON
☐ HOGAN
☐ KUTINA
☐ NELSON
☐ PELTY
☐ STOVALL
☐ WALLACE

ST. LOUIS CARDINALS

☐ BRESNAHAN
☐ ELLIS
☐ EVANS
☐ GOLDEN
☐ HARMON
☐ KONETCHY
☐ LOUDERMILK
☐ OAKES
☐ SMITH
☐ STEELE
☐ STEINFELDT
☐ WILIE
☐ WINGO
☐ WOODBURN

WASHINGTON SENATORS

☐ AINSMITH
☐ CUNNINGHAM
☐ HENRY
☐ JOHNSON
☐ MCBRIDE
☐ MILAN
☐ MORGAN
☐ SCHAEFER
☐ WALKER

SINGLE TEAM AND REGIONAL CARD SETS

The primary text of this book lists, by team, baseball cards from nationally issued card sets. This section lists, by team, non-nationally-issued card sets in which players from one team comprise all or a significant portion of the cards in the set. While not exhaustive, this lists includes all of this type of card set that has appeared in any of the first nine issues of the Sport Americana Baseball Card Price Guide and the first issue of the Sport Americana Baseball Collectibles Price Guide. The number in parenthes( ) indicates the number of cards of that team in the set. The asterisk* indicates that there is more than one team in the set. Major League teams only are included.

ATLANTA BRAVES

☐ 1966 KAHN'S WEINERS (9)*
☐ 1967 KAHN'S WEINERS (8)*
☐ 1968 KAHN'S WEINERS (5)*
☐ 1969 KAHN'S WEINERS (1)*
☐ 1981 POLICE (27)
☐ 1982 BURGER KING (27)
☐ 1982 POLICE (30)
☐ 1983 POLICE (30)
☐ 1984 POLICE (30)
☐ 1985 HOSTESS (22)
☐ 1985 POLICE (30)
☐ 1986 POLICE (30)

BALTIMORE ORIOLES

☐ 1954 ESSKAY MEATS (36)
☐ 1955 ESSKAY MEATS (27)

BOSTON BRAVES

☐ 1947 TIP TOP BREAD (15)

BOSTON RED SOX

☐ 1910 E91 AMERICAN
  CARAMELS (11)*
☐ 1947 TIP TOP BREAD (15)
☐ 1967 TOPPS STICKERS (33)
☐ 1981 COCA-COLA (12)
☐ 1981 TOPPS 5X7 (12)
☐ 1982 COCA-COLA (23)

BROOKLYN DODGERS

☐ 1947 TIP TOP BREAD (14)
☐ 1953-54 BRIGGS (4)*
☐ 1953 STAHL-MEYER (3)*

☐ 1954 N.Y. JOURNAL-
  AMERICAN (19)*
☐ 1954 STAHL-MEYER (4)*
☐ 1955 STAHL-MEYER (4)*

CALIFORNIA ANGELS

☐ 1981 TOPPS 5X7 (6)
☐ 1983 7-11 COINS (6)*
☐ 1984 SMOKEY THE BEAR (30)
☐ 1985 SMOKEY THE BEAR (24)
☐ 1986 SMOKEY THE BEAR (24)

CHICAGO CUBS

☐ 1908 E91 AMERICAN
  CARAMELS (11)*
☐ 1910 E90-3 AMERICAN
  CARAMELS (11)*
☐ 1910 E91 AMERICAN
  CARAMELS (11)*
☐ 1947 TIP TOP BREAD (15)
☐ 1960 KAHN'S WEINERS (1)*
☐ 1968 KAHN'S WEINERS (3)*
☐ 1969 KAHN'S WEINERS (2)*
☐ 1981 COCA-COLA (12)
☐ 1981 TOPPS 5X7 (9)
☐ 1982 RED LOBSTER (28)
☐ 1970 DUNKIN DONUTS
  STICKERS (6)
☐ 1983 THORN APPLE VALLEY (28)
☐ 1985 SEVEN UP (28)
☐ 1986 GATORADE (28)

CHICAGO WHITE SOX

☐ 1910 E90-3 AMERICAN
  CARAMELS (9)*
☐ 1947 TIP TOP BREAD (15)

☐ 1960 KAHN'S WEINERS (1)*
☐ 1968 KAHN'S WEINERS (2)*
☐ 1968 KAHN'S WEINERS (2)*
☐ 1981 COCA-COLA (12)
☐ 1981 TOPPS 5X7 (9)
☐ 1985 COKE (30)
☐ 1986 COKE (30)

CINCINNATI REDS

☐ 1938-39 W711-1 (32)
☐ 1941 W711-2 (32)
☐ 1955 KAHN'S WEINERS (6)
☐ 1956 KAHN'S WEINERS (15)
☐ 1957 KAHN'S WEINERS (19)*
☐ 1958 KAHN'S WEINERS (15)*
☐ 1959 KAHN'S WEINERS (10)*
☐ 1960 KAHN'S WEINERS (17)*
☐ 1961 KAHN'S WEINERS (15)*
☐ 1962 KAHN'S WEINERS (17)*
☐ 1963 FRENCH BAUER CAPS (25)
☐ 1963 KAHN'S WEINERS (14)*
☐ 1964 KAHN'S WEINERS (11)*
☐ 1965 KAHN'S WEINERS (15)*
☐ 1966 KAHN'S WEINERS (11)*
☐ 1967 KAHN'S WEINERS (14)*
☐ 1968 KAHN'S WEINERS (11)*
☐ 1969 KAHN'S WEINERS (8)*
☐ 1976 ICEE LIDS (12)
☐ 1981 COCA-COLA (12)
☐ 1981 TOPPS 5X7 (12)
☐ 1982 COCA-COLA (23)
☐ 1984 BORDEN'S STICKERS (8)

CLEVELAND INDIANS

☐ 1952 NUM-NUM POTATO
  CHIPS (20)
☐ 1959 KAHN'S WEINERS (14)*

□ 1960 KAHN'S WEINERS (10)*
□ 1961 KAHN'S WEINERS (12)*
□ 1962 KAHN'S WEINERS (13)*
□ 1962 SUGARDALE MEATS (22)
□ 1963 SUGARDALE MEATS (31)
□ 1964 KAHN'S WEINERS (10)*
□ 1965 KAHN'S WEINERS (11)*
□ 1966 KAHN'S WEINERS (6)*
□ 1967 KAHN'S WEINERS (6)*
□ 1968 KAHN'S WEINERS (7)*
□ 1969 KAHN'S WEINERS (4)*
□ 1982 BURGER KING (12)
□ 1982 WHEATIES (30)
□ 1983 WHEATIES (32)
□ 1984 WHEATIES (29)

DETROIT TIGERS

□ 1947 TIP TOP BREAD (15)
□ 1954 GLENDALE MEATS (28)
□ 1968 KAHN'S WEINERS (4)*
□ 1978 BURGER KING (23)
□ 1981 COCA-COLA (12)
□ 1985 WENDY'S (22)
□ 1985 CAIN'S DISCS (20)

HOUSTON ASTROS

□ 1978 BURGER KING (23)
□ 1981 COCA-COLA (12)
□ 1981 TOPPS 5X7 (6)
□ 1984 MOTHER'S COOKIES (28)
□ 1985 MOTHER'S COOKIES (28)
□ 1986 MOTHER'S COOKIES (28)
□ 1986 POLICE (26)

HOUSTON COLT .45'S

□ 1963 PEPSI-COLA (16)

KANSAS CITY ATHLETICS

□ 1955 RODEO MEATS (47)
□ 1956 RODEO MEATS (13)

KANSAS CITY ROYALS

□ 1981 COCA-COLA (12)
□ 1981 POLICE (10)
□ 1983 POLICE (10)
□ 1986 NATIONAL PHOTO (24)
□ 1986 KITTY CLOVER DISCS (20)

LOS ANGELES DODGERS

□ 1958 BELL BRAND (10)
□ 1959 MORRELL MEATS (12)
□ 1960 BELL BRAND (20)
□ 1960 MORRELL MEATS (12)
□ 1961 BELL BRAND (20)
□ 1961 MORRELL MEATS (6)
□ 1962 BELL BRAND (20)
□ 1980 POLICE (30)
□ 1981 POLICE (32)
□ 1981 TOPPS 5X7 (12)
□ 1982 POLICE (30)
□ 1983 POLICE (30)
□ 1983 7-11 COINS (6)*
□ 1984 POLICE (30)
□ 1986 POLICE (30)

MILWAUKEE BRAVES

□ 1953 JOHNSTON'S COOKIES (25)
□ 1954 JOHNSTON'S COOKIES (35)
□ 1955 JOHNSTON'S COOKIES (35)
□ 1960 LAKE TO LAKE DAIRY (28)
□ 1965 KAHN'S WEINERS (9)*

MILWAUKEE BREWERS

□ 1982 POLICE (30)
□ 1983 GARDNER'S BREAD (22)
□ 1983 POLICE (30)
□ 1984 GARDNER'S BREAD (22)
□ 1984 POLICE (30)
□ 1985 GARDNER'S BREAD (22)
□ 1985 POLICE (30)
□ 1986 POLICE (32)

MINNESOTA TWINS

□ 1961 PETER'S MEATS (26)
□ 1962 KAHN'S WEINERS (1)*

MONTREAL EXPOS

□ 1974 WESTON (10)
□ 1982 HYGRADE MEATS (24)
□ 1982 ZELLER DEPARTMENT STORE (20)
□ 1982 O-PEE-CHEE POSTERS (12)*
□ 1983 STUART (30)
□ 1984 STUART (40)
□ 1985 O-PEE-CHEE POSTERS (12)*
□ 1986 PROVIGO (28)

NEW YORK GIANTS

□ 1908 E91 AMERICAN CARAMELS (11)*
□ 1910 E91 AMERICAN CARAMELS (11)*
□ 1947 TIP TOP BREAD (15)
□ 1953-54 BRIGGS (4)*
□ 1955 STAHL-MEYER (3)*
□ 1954 N.Y. JOURNAL-AMERICAN (20)
□ 1954 STAHL-MEYER (4)*
□ 1955 STAHL-MEYER (4)*

NEW YORK METS

□ 1967 KAHN'S WEINERS (6)*
□ 1968 KAHN'S WEINERS (2)*
□ 1970 TRANSOGRAM (15)
□ 1981 COCA-COLA (12)
□ 1981 TOPPS 5X7 (6)

NEW YORK YANKEES

□ 1947 TIP TOP BREAD (15)
□ 1953-54 BRIGGS (4)*
□ 1953 STAHL-MEYER (3)*
□ 1954 N.Y. JOURNAL-AMERICAN (20)*
□ 1954 STAHL-MEYER (4)*
□ 1955 STAHL-MEYER (4)*
□ 1963 KAHN'S WEINERS (6)*
□ 1977 BURGER KING (24)
□ 1978 BURGER KING (23)
□ 1979 BURGER KING (23)
□ 1981 TOPPS 5X7 (12)

OAKLAND A'S

□ 1981 GRANNY GOOSE (15)
□ 1982 GRANNY GOOSE (15)
□ 1983 GRANNY GOOSE (15)
□ 1984 MOTHER'S COOKIES (28)
□ 1985 MOTHER'S COOKIES (28)
□ 1986 MOTHER'S COOKIES (28)

PHILADELPHIA ATHLETICS

□ 1908 E91 AMERICAN CARAMELS (11)*
□ 1910 E91 AMERICAN CARAMELS (11)*

PHILADELPHIA PHILLIES

□ 1949 LUMMIS PEANUT BUTTER (12)
□ 1949 SEALTEST DAIRY (12)
□ 1958 KAHN'S WEINERS (1)*
□ 1979 BURGER KING (23)
□ 1980 BURGER KING (23)
□ 1981 COCA-COLA (12)
□ 1981 TOPPS 5X7 (12)
□ 1985 CIGNA (16)
□ 1986 CIGNA (16)

PITTSBURGH PIRATES

□ 1910 E90-2 AMERICAN CARAMELS (11)
□ 1910 E91 AMERICAN CARAMELS (11)*

1947 TIP TOP BREAD (14)

□ 1947 TIP TOP BREAD (14)
□ 1957 KAHN'S WEINERS (10)*
□ 1958 KAHN'S WEINERS (13)*
□ 1959 KAHN'S WEINERS (14)*
□ 1960 KAHN'S WEINERS (12)*
□ 1961 KAHN'S WEINERS (16)*
□ 1962 KAHN'S WEINERS (10)*
□ 1963 KAHN'S WEINERS (9)*
□ 1964 KAHN'S WEINERS (10)*
□ 1965 KAHN'S WEINERS (10)*
□ 1966 EAST HILLS SHOPPING CENTER (25)
□ 1966 KAHN'S WEINERS (6)*
□ 1967 KAHN'S WEINERS (7)*
□ 1967 TOPPS STICKERS (33)
□ 1968 KAHN'S WEINERS (4)*
□ 1969 KAHN'S WEINERS (4)*
□ 1981 COCA-COLA (12)

ST. LOUIS BROWNS

□ 1941 W753 (29)
□ 1947 TIP TOP BREAD (15)

ST. LOUIS CARDINALS

□ 1941 W754 (29)
□ 1947 TIP TOP BREAD (15)
□ 1953 HUNTER'S WEINERS (26)
□ 1954 HUNTER'S WEINERS (30)
□ 1955 HUNTER'S WEINERS (30)
□ 1960 KAHN'S WEINERS (1)*
□ 1963 KAHN'S WEINERS (1)*
□ 1969 KAHN'S WEINERS (1)*
□ 1981 COCA-COLA (12)
□ 1986 KAS DISCS (20)

SAN DIEGO PADRES

□ 1984 MOTHER'S COOKIES (28)
□ 1984 SMOKEY THE BEAR (29)
□ 1985 MOTHER'S COOKIES (28)

SAN FRANCISCO GIANTS

□ 1958 SAN FRANCISCO CALL-BULLETIN (25)
□ 1979 POLICE (30)
□ 1980 POLICE (31)
□ 1983 MOTHER'S COOKIES (20)
□ 1984 MOTHER'S COOKIES (28)
□ 1985 MOTHER'S COOKIES (28)
□ 1986 MOTHER'S COOKIES (28)

SEATTLE MARINERS

□ 1981 POLICE (16)
□ 1983 NALLEY'S POTATO CHIPS (6)
□ 1984 MOTHER'S COOKIES (28)
□ 1985 MOTHER'S COOKIES (28)
□ 1986 MOTHER'S COOKIES (28)

TEXAS RANGERS

□ 1978 BURGER KING (23)
□ 1981 TOPPS 5X7 (6)
□ 1983 AFFILIATED FOOD STORES (28)
□ 1984 JARVIS PRESS (30)
□ 1985 PERFORMANCE PRINTING (28)
□ 1986 PERFORMANCE PRINTING (28)

TORONTO BLUE JAYS

□ 1982 O-PEE-CHEE POSTERS (12)*
□ 1984 FIRE SAFETY (36)
□ 1985 O-PEE-CHEE POSTERS (12)*
□ 1985 FIRE SAFETY (36)
□ 1986 FIRE SAFETY (36)

WASHINGTON SENATORS

□ 1910 E91 AMERICAN CARAMELS (11)*
□ 1953-54 BRIGGS (25)*

Now! Get
BECKETT BASEBALL CARD MONTHLY

for up to
½ OFF
the cover price!

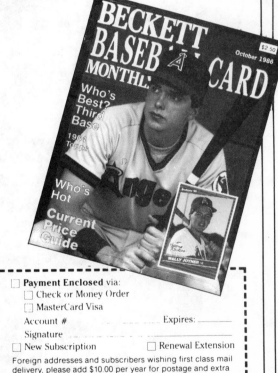